A TREASURY OF

AFRICAN
FOLKLORE

A TREASURY OF

AFRICAN FOLKLORE

THE ORAL LITERATURE, TRADITIONS,
MYTHS, LEGENDS, EPICS, TALES,
RECOLLECTIONS, WISDOM, SAYINGS,
AND HUMOR OF AFRICA

BY

HAROLD COURLANDER

CROWN PUBLISHERS, INC., NEW YORK

Library of Congress Catalog Card Number: 74–80306
Printed in the United States of America
Published simultaneously in Canada by Gen

Designed by Kendra McKenzie

DEDICATED TO THE MEMORY
OF TWO FRIENDS

GEORGE WISLOCKI
and
WILLIAM MENAKER

CONTENTS

ACKNOWLEDGMENTS AND APPRECIATIONS

The assembling of the contents of this book was not only made possible but made enjoyable as well because of the generous cooperation, assistance and suggestions given by numerous individuals, to whom I express my thanks. In particular I am indebted to the following persons:

Dr. Hugh Tracey of Roodepoort, Transvaal, for his help in my search for traditional South African stories, and for his kindness in allowing me to use some Zulu song poetry from his personal collection.

The Reverend Jeroom Callebaut of Teralfene, Belgium, whose extensive and intimate knowledge of the peoples of eastern Zaire greatly facilitated my search for songs and stories from that region. I am also indebted to him for translations of Luba songs and for explanations of Bantu religious concepts.

The Reverend Leo Verwilghen of Kigali, Rwanda, for his generous assistance in the procuring of traditional materials of the Tutsi, and for his translations.

Mr. Daniel A. Osei-Cobbina of Dormaa, Ghana, for his help over the years in the gathering of traditional materials of the Ashanti and other Akan peoples.

Mr. S. E. Adu, now at Hwidiem, Ghana, for his continuing aid to my search for Ashanti tales, legends and lore.

Mr. Albert Kofi Prempeh, now deceased, with whom I worked on an earlier collection of Ashanti stories, some of which are reprinted in this volume.

Dr. Daniel P. P. Marolen of Daveyton, South Africa, for his unstinted efforts in the gathering and translating of some of the Bantu stories that appear in this anthology, especially the tales and traditions of the Shangaan people.

His Excellency M. Boubou Hama, President of the National Assembly of Niger, for his generous permission to use the Fulbe story, "The Valiant Goroo-Bâ-Dicko," an English version of his own original translation in French.

Dr. David W. Ames of San Francisco State College for his kindness in allowing me to use a previously unpublished Wolof epic, "The Lion of Manding," which he set down in the course of a field trip to Gambia.

Dr. Peter Becker of Johannesburg, who helped me locate informants in South Africa.

Dr. James W. Fernandez of Dartmouth College and Professor Pierre H. Alexandre of Paris for information relating to traditions of the Fang.

Mr. Ezekiel Aderogba Adetunji of Lagos, who worked with me on earlier collections of Yoruba tales and legends, some of which are reprinted herein.

Dr. Alan P. Merriam of Indiana University for his suggestions on the subject of African epics, and for his permission to include some of his work in this book.

Mr. Kingsley Kwarteng of Bekwai-Ashanti, Ghana, for providing me with a number of Ashanti stories, one of which appears in this collection.

Dr. George Eaton Simpson of Oberlin, for his many helpful suggestions and comments related to African source materials.

Professor Dan Ben-Amos, University of Pennsylvania, for his kindness in allowing me to include two previously published Bini stories.

Mr. Clyde P. Peters, executive vice president of Stackpole Books, for his generosity in making available a number of Sudanic stories originally gathered by Leo Frobenius.

Dr. Philip M. Peek for permission to use three Isoko poems from materials he gathered in collaboration with Mr. N. E. Owheibor.

My friend and associate, Mr. Moses Asch, for making accessible to me the recorded and printed resources of Folkways Records, the Ethnic Folkways Library, Asch Records and Disc Records.

Professor J. H. Nketia, Director of the Institute of African Studies, University of Ghana, for his permission to reprint some of his previously published writings.

My son, Michael Courlander, for his dedicated assistance in researching some long-out-of-print publications on which this anthology has drawn; and my daughter Susan for her typing assistance.

Dr. A. A. Y. Kyerematen, Ghana, on whose studies of Akan culture I have drawn.

Dr. Gilbert Schneider of Ohio University for permission to include some extracts from his *Cameroons Creole Dictionary*.

Mr. Edmund Demaitre and Mr. Fernando Galvan for their much valued help with translations.

Mr. David McDowell, my editor, whose unflagging interest, constructive suggestions and patience contributed greatly to the making of this book.

And to others whose names inadvertently may have been omitted from this list, but to whom thanks are due.

I also extend my appreciation to the following foundations, professional societies and other organizations for their generous cooperation and assistance:

The Society for Applied Anthropology
The American Folklore Society
The Wenner-Gren Foundation for Anthropological Research
The American Musicological Society
The International Library of African Music
Institute of African Studies (Ghana)
Institute for Cross Cultural Research
African Arts Quarterly
International African Institute
United Nations Office of Public Information

UNESCO
Ghana Information Services
Folkways Records and Service Corporation
And I am of course grateful for the permissions given by many publishing houses to use materials from their books. Acknowledgments for specific items are given on the pages where the reprinted materials appear, but I wish to express my thanks here to Stackpole Books; The Clarendon Press; Oxford University Press, London; Oxford University Press, Eastern Africa; University of California Press; Harcourt Brace Jovanovich; Holt, Rinehart and Winston; C. H. Beck; Crown Publishers; Northwestern University Press; Routledge and Kegan Paul; Frank Cass and Company; *The New York Times;* and, for permission to use copyrighted materials which it administers, the office of The Estates Bursar, University College, Oxford.

"The head of a man is a secret storage place."
—Chagga saying

"The heart of a man is like an intricately woven net."
—Tswana saying

*"The fool would say, 'This world is a virgin girl.' The wise man
knows the world is old."*
—from a Hausa poem

INTRODUCTION

MAN IN AFRICA, AND HIS LITERATURE

The myths, legends, epics, tales, historical poems and countless other traditional oral literary forms of African peoples have been woven out of the substance of human experience: struggles with the land and the elements, movements and migrations, wars between kingdoms, conflicts over pastures and waterholes, and wrestlings with the mysteries of existence, life and death. They are products of long reflections about the relations among humans, between man and woman, between humankind and the animal world; responses to the challenges of the unknown, and to the universal need to create order and reason out of chaos and accident. Man in Africa, as elsewhere, has sought to relate his past to his present, and to tentatively explore the future so that he might not stand lonely and isolated in the great sweep of time, or intimidated by the formidable earth and the vast stretch of surrounding seas. In his myths and legends he bridges back to the very dream morning of creation, while in his systems of divination he projects himself into time not yet come; in his epics he asserts the courage and worth of the human species; in his tales he ponders on what is just or unjust, upon what is feeble or courageous, what is sensible or ridiculous, on what moves the spirit to grief or to exultation; in his proverbs and sayings he capsulates the learnings of centuries about the human character and about the intricate balance between people and the world around them. What we, standing on the periphery, see as lore and tradition is the accumulation of experience that has made mankind in Africa capable and confident in the endless effort not only to survive, but to survive with meaning.

We have gone beyond that age in which, warmed by our own particular accomplishments, we readily divided the world into the "civilized" and the "primitive." We understand now what we were not ready to comprehend a century or so ago—that the diverse social structures and processes of Africa, as elsewhere, are products of the civilizing movements of mankind, other faces of the human response to the challenges of living. When we say "Africans" it is merely a convenient manner of saying "mankind in Africa"—peoples, villages and tribes that through millennia of contest with one another, with the land and with ideas have provided particular answers to questions of organization, survival and the meaning of life. Their religious attitudes, their social establishments, their standards of behavior and their symbols for abstract ideas are the alternatives they have chosen from among those that have been available to men everywhere. Anthropological studies of African life have unwittingly, perhaps, tended to stress differences from our own ways, but those studies have little importance if they are not seen as an examination of ourselves and our own, sometimes irrational, choices.

The oral literature and traditions of African peoples communicate to us the scope and nature of our common identity. We discover there, if we have not already surmised it, how much we share—our views about good and evil; about what is pompous or vain and what is moderate or immodest; and our standards defining the mutual responsibilities of the group and the individual. We discern common desires, aspirations, strengths and foibles, and a familiar vision of man as a special creation of deity or nature. With recognition comes the insight that non-Africans are no less exotic in their customs and beliefs than anyone else, and that, in the end, the similarities of outwardly contrasting societies are more impressive than the differences.

Africa is an enormous continent, and such terms as "the African," "African society" and "the African experience" must be used with caution. The ways of life, the challenges and responses, and the institutions that have been shaped often vary greatly from one region to another, often from one tribe to a neighboring tribe. "The African" may be an urban Yoruba or a Bushman living in the desert; a Spartan-wayed Ituri Forest Pygmy, his life hanging on the perpetual pursuit of game; a grasslands Shilluk whose life centers on cattle, or a desert-roaming Danakil. Some African peoples have old traditions of woodcarving, brass casting, glassmaking or iron forging, while others have turned more to nonmaterial creations.

There are many cultural developments and concepts that over centuries and millennia have permeated most of the continent. Migrations in historic and prehistoric times have taken people, along with their cultural creations, from one edge of Africa to another. Since ancient times traders have journeyed back and forth between inner Africa and the ocean shores. River highways and camel caravans have carried not only men and goods, but information, traditions, tales and beliefs. Today a story told among the Ivory Coast Baoule also may be heard among the Amazulu far to the south. The trickster hare of Zaire performs the same clever mischief as the spider trickster in Ghana and Togo. Many of the musical instruments of West Africa are equally known in the east and south. And while the music of Central Africa may have local characteristics, it nevertheless belongs to a general musical system on which diverse peoples such as the Ashanti of Ghana, the Shangaan of South Africa and the Kamba of Kenya also draw for their music making. Even where Islamic or European influence has intruded and hybridized the sound, the overall African character can be readily recognized. So, too, with dancing, the arts of orating and storytelling, and games played by adults and children. There is no part of the continent that does not know some variant of the counting game played with beans or stones on carved playing boards, and known under the names wari, munkala, adi and many others. Though religious systems vary, there is a generalized African view regarding the forces of nature. Throughout much of West, Central, East and Southern Africa there prevails (except where vitiated by European influence) the concept of a total world made up of the seen and the unseen, of forces that for all their invisibility are none the less real and which must be coped with through rituals and magico-religious means. The goodwill of the ancestors is vital to the well-being of the living, and the dead are therefore supplicated and placated by an unending series of individual acts and prescribed rituals. While contacts with Islam and Christianity have moderated such concepts, the African view of a partly seen, partly unseen universe remains strong. The invocation of a Christian saint is not regarded as greatly different from appeals to one's ancestors; nor, to many, is the Christian God, remote and invisible, incompatible with the supreme sky deities who live in the traditions of the Yoruba, the Ashanti, the Bantu cultures of Central Africa, and others. Intruding non-African religious systems have themselves vouched for the existence of a physical world surrounded by spiritual forces, reinforcing what earlier generations of Africans saw as the real nature of the universe.

Thus the oral literature of Africa reflects ideas, themes, suppositions and truths that are widely shared, at the same time that it reveals creations unique to, and particularized by, a tribe, village or region. A tribe may be united with a mainstream of African traditions and yet have legends of its own heroes, kings and demigods, its own conflicts and migrations, and its unique ancient origins. A village may reshape, to its own liking, a widespread tale. A narrator may embellish, recast and refine stories known elsewhere and give them the mark of his own creative genius, or compose new narratives out of the experience of day-to-day living. The process of creating literature goes on side by side with the process of preserving what is generalized and old. Nowhere in the world is there a richer fare of what for the sake of convenience we call folklore, but what in reality is nothing less than an enormous residue of human experience and a treasury of social values and literary creations.

The range of African oral literary forms is seemingly endless. It includes creation myths, myth-legends, half-legendary chronicles and historical narratives either in song or prose; tales that explain natural phenomena, tribal practices and taboos, and cultural or political institutions; stories and fables that reflect on the nature of man and his strengths and weaknesses; tales of adventure, courage, disaster and love; epics with legendary heroes or fictitious heroes, and tales of confrontation with the supernatural and unseen forces of nature; moralizing stories and stories that define man's place and role in the universe; riddles that amuse and teach, and proverbs that stress social values; and a virtually inexhaustible reservoir of animal tales, many of which, at bottom, are morality plays, while others are pure humor.

What part the expansion and decline of empires played in the development and spread of literature and literary forms we cannot know for certain. But it is possible to speculate that conquerors and conquered borrowed liberally from one another, and that some of the creations of a millennium or more ago continue to survive among descendants of the rulers and the ruled. Some of the epics or heroic tales gathered by Leo Frobenius (see pp. 3–33), for example, date from the period of the great Sudanic states, which began, roughly, about the fourth century A.D. The earliest of these states, justifiably called empires, was Ghana, created by the Soninke people. At its height it controlled most of the territory between the upper reaches of the Niger and Senegal rivers and extended into the Sahara. Ghana's power and influence were built on trade, particularly trade in gold, which was produced in regions to the south and much sought after by the Berber Moslems of the north. Berber attacks in the eleventh century and revolts by subject peoples began the period of Ghana's decline. By the mid-thirteenth century, after a life of about a thousand years, the empire of Ghana came to an end. Its successor was a small and inconsequential kingdom to the south, the Mandingo state of Kangaba. Soon known by the name Mali, Kangaba absorbed all of ancient Ghana, spreading north into the desert region, eastward beyond the northern bend of the Niger, and westward to the sea. In the period of its maximum power, Mali was far larger than its predecessor, Ghana. As in the case of Ghana, attacks from the north and revolts of subject peoples caused Mali's decline, and by the middle of the sixteenth century the empire was no longer a force in the Sudan. But earlier, even while Ghana's power was eroding, the empire of Songhay was taking shape farther east. It began as the city state of Gao, which in time came briefly under the power of Ghana's successor, Mali, but by the early sixteenth century it controlled a large part of what had previously been the Mali Empire and still other territories in the west. Songhay's demise began with a defeat by a Moroccan army in the closing years of the same century. Farther east in the region of Lake Chad a fourth Sudanic empire, Kanem-Bornu, had arisen between the ninth and twelfth centuries. It spread and flourished well into the period of European intrusion into the African continent. Including the earliest, unknown years when Ghana was slowly shaping itself, these four Sudanic empires bridged more than fifteen centuries.

But the Sudanic empires were by no means the only centers of political development in West Africa. A group of Hausa states grew up east of the Niger between the territories controlled by Kanem-Bornu and Songhay, beginning about the ninth or tenth century. Kano is perhaps the best-known name among them, but there were seven "original" Hausa states, according to early chronicles, to which more were added in time. They were centers of marketing and trade, for long periods at peace, but not infrequently at war with one another and the aspiring states around them. South of the Niger, in the southwest of the modern state of Nigeria, Yoruba city states and kingdoms were taking shape about the same time. The cities of Ife, Oyo and Benin are believed to have existed as early as the tenth century, and there is reason to believe that they, and Yoruba culture in general, emerged out of an iron-working civilization that flourished somewhat to the north as early as 300 B.C. The kingdom of Benin, whose language was Edo rather than Yoruba, undoubtedly owed its power and influence to its strategic location in the Niger Delta, where it was accessible to overland trade from the north while at the same time having a river outlet to the sea. At its height it was perhaps the most influential state in this region of Africa. West Africa also had the Mossi states, the Akan states, the Wolof states and others almost too numerous to mention.

Central Africa, too, had its kingdoms and empires, such as Luba, Lunda and Malawi. They emerged as great centers of political and commercial influence somewhat later than did the West African states, but they played a similar role in that they facilitated contacts between distant peoples. The Ovimbundu federation, centered in the highlands of what is now called Angola, exerted a force felt across the entire breadth of Africa. Ovimbundu people were farmers, hunters and cattle raisers, but they were also long-distance traders and raiders. Their trails extended eastward into the depths of Central Africa as far as Lakes Nyassa and Tanganyika, and the Ovimbundu became greatly feared when they added slave trading to their trade in the more usual commodities of life. Ovimbundu slave caravans brought enormous numbers of slaves from the interior and sold them to Europeans on the coast. With the end of the slave trade, the prosperity and energy of the Ovimbundu states waned. Two highly developed kingdoms, Congo and Loango, existed along the lower reaches of the Congo (Zaire) River in the fifteenth century, their influence felt well beyond their borders. And, of course, there were states and city states about which we know very little—Zimbabwe, in Rhodesia, for example, for which we have nothing but archeological evidence. Some of its remarkable stone buildings still stand to awe the passing traveller. But what was Zimbabwe to the peoples who inhabited the region between the tenth and fifteenth centuries? We can only speculate.

In the country bordering on the Upper Nile and the Blue Nile there were kingdoms that strongly reflected influences of the Middle East. The Kingdom of Kush, sometimes called by the name of one of its capital cities, Meroe, began to emerge about 350 B.C., and by A.D. 100 it had become master of its region. The Kushites are generally considered to have been a nonblack people. Their history intertwined over a period of many centuries with that of Egypt to the north. And there was Axum, the forerunner of modern Ethiopia, which took shape, or emerged out of obscurity, in the third or fourth century A.D.

The enumeration of these states, kingdoms and empires tells us something about the political and economic dynamics of the African continent before it was intruded upon by explorers and military forces from Europe and Asia. It can also tell us something about the interplay of cultures and traditions. But we should not confuse states or empires with culture, for they are not necessarily synonymous. There were many peoples in Africa who had neither kings nor great chiefs; whose social and political structures were based on kinship or ties between villages; whose relationships and community obligations were traditional, defined in common law and moral precepts, and without an autocratic or theocratic enforcement mechanism. These people nevertheless had their mythology, their oral literature, their music, their religious beliefs, their concept of good and evil, and their life values. What we speak of as the oral traditions of Africa were the creations not only of the poets and bards of kings, but also of simple men and women living in rustic villages scattered across the continent.

Indeed, one of the most powerful cultural influences in all of Africa—

measured by the territory across which it extended and the number of people it eventually affected—was exerted not by a great state or empire in its prime, but by groups of fishermen, farmers and herdsmen moving through the African hinterlands in a series of migrations that covered a time period of more than two millennia. These people were the Bantu, so called because they spoke dialects of the Bantu language. Their great migrations are believed to have begun in the region of southern Nigeria. The reasons for their emigration from this area are not clear. But once in motion their movement did not cease until they had reached and settled in lands now known as Kenya and Tanzania in the east, and lands to the south in what are presently called Rhodesia, Botswana and South Africa. Bantu settlements extended from the Atlantic through the great forests of the interior to the Indian Ocean. It was not a single great wave but rather a series of washes and eddies upriver and downriver, into forest country and again out of forest country, with later migrations following earlier ones. In the course of two thousand years the Bantu speakers, calling themselves by various names, took over a major portion of the subcontinent, spreading their traditions among earlier inhabitants, absorbing some technology previously unknown to them, and adapting to new environments. Today some of the Bantu dialects are sufficiently distinct from one another to be regarded as separate languages, but the common cultural heritage is evident in many of their traditions and beliefs and, certainly, in their oral literature.

African cultures possess much that is innovative, creative and frequently unique. Nevertheless, there were influences from outside black Africa that affected its traditions and literature. Contacts with the Mediterranean and the Indian Ocean go far back in time. There was commerce with peoples of the Arabic Middle East, even with South Asia, in commodities and slaves. (Today there is in Hyderabad a community of descendants of African slaves brought there centuries ago.) And in the debris of the mysterious Zimbabwe ruins were found numerous fragments of Chinese porcelain. We are aware of the influx of European and Christian ideas over the past five hundred years (in the special case of Ethiopia, Christianity arrived fifteen centuries ago), and of the considerable influence of Islam in the Sudan and East Africa over a much longer period. We need not doubt that Africans have been receptive to myths, legends, epics, tales and music emanating from other places. Few peoples anywhere have totally rejected such innovations. And the African has been adept at receiving ideas, taking their most attractive and compatible features and remolding them into something truly African in character, just as one tribe has borrowed from another without any sense of indignity but rather with a sense of enrichment. So there are tales told in the interior of the continent that may recall the Panchatantra; stories in Somalia whose themes are undoubtedly familiar to Bedouins of the Arabian Desert; heroic poems and epics in the Sudan in a style reminiscent of Arabic literature; and music in the north and east of black Africa that would be readily understood throughout much of Islam. Yet even where outside influence is perceptible, the core of the literature is essentially African, reflecting an African point of view and an African sense of values.

The pages that follow are an exploration of African oral literature. They contain the contributions of peoples whose names are relatively familiar to us, such as the Yoruba, the Hausa, the Akan and the Amhara. They also contain literary possessions of lesser-known peoples, such as the Mensa, the Shangaan, the Nuer, the Shilluk, the Nyanga and numerous others. Much of the substance comes from a variety of publications, some of them recent, others long out of print. A considerable amount comes directly from persons active in the recording of African traditions and lore, and some from Africans eager to contribute so that the literature of their cultures would be represented. The anthology seeks to demonstrate both the affinities that are evident among various African traditions and the particularized, sometimes unique, forms and themes of specific tribes; in short, to project diversity as well as the more widely shared inheritance. Above all, the accent is on what is interesting; what reveals the life and the point of view of the cultures from which the oral traditions come; and—taking into account the inadequacies of translation—what is excellent in a literary sense. We still have much to learn about Africa and its many peoples. And there is hardly a better way to know them than through the oral literature they have created and preserved.

Finally, a brief note about the structuring of this book. One must begin somewhere and then follow a trail to the next point of interest, but there is no altogether satisfactory sequence. And whatever sequence is chosen, no special significance should be attached to it. We begin with the Sudanic peoples as a matter of convenience, and also with the thought that the stage has been set for them by reference in this introduction to the Sudanic empires. And from there we move from one general culture area to another, as defined by the anthropologist Melville J. Herskovits in his book *The Human Factor in Changing Africa:* to the Guinea Coast which lies to the south; then into Central Africa, which Herskovits terms the Congo region, but which includes areas north and south of Zaire, primarily Bantu; and from this area we continue east and south into the East African Cattle Area, south into Khoisan (a territory encompassing South West Africa or Namibia plus regions to its north and east), and north into the East Horn, taking in contemporary Ethiopia, Somalia and adjacent lands. In short, we are surveying Africa south of the Sahara, which we might also call black Africa except that the Amhara of Ethiopia consider themselves to be a blended race, which for the most part they are. The Mediterranean fringe of Africa in the north and Egypt, which also fronts on the Red Sea, are not included for readily apparent reasons. Some tribal groups are better represented in this collection than others, and a good many are not represented at all. The objective is to get the larger view, with pauses on occasion to look at the oral literature and traditions of particular peoples in somewhat greater (though far from complete) detail.

And now, to begin, we turn to the Soninke and Fulbe epics.

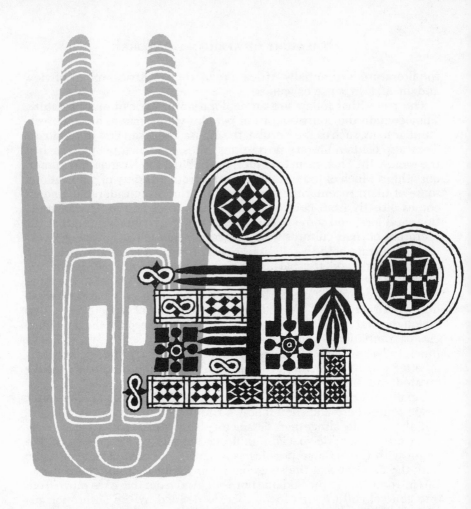

THE ANCIENT SONINKE AND FULBE EPICS

The Soninke (also called Sarakole) and the
Fulbe (also known as Bororo, Fula, Fulani and
Peuhl) have histories going back more than two
thousand years. Fragments of their ancient tra-
ditions survive in the Soninke Dausi and the
Fulbe Baudi, compositions of unknown bards.
Five of these old epics, from a collection of Leo
Frobenius, appear in the pages that follow, in-
troduced by comments of Douglas C. Fox.

*This introduction and the first five epics—"Gassire's Lute," "The Rediscovery
of Wagadu," "The Fight with the Bida Dragon," "Samba Gana" and "The Blue
Blood"—are from* African Genesis, *by Leo Frobenius and Douglas C. Fox.
Reprinted by permission of Stackpole Books.*

Between the Sahara in the north and the treed steppes of the Sudan to the south of it, between the Senegal in the west and the Nile in the east, there lies a strip of grassland which would provide scant fare for pampered European stock, but which is considered a fine grazing ground by the Arabs. They call it the Sahel and prefer it to any other part of Africa. In the western part of this region, between the Upper Niger and its tributary the Bani, lies the fertile land of Faraka which is watered—when not flooded—by both of these streams, a watered island in the dry reaches of the Sahel. This, where now the Soninke live, was once a land of the troubadours, a land in which, in the few centuries before and after the beginning of our era, North African chivalry came to flower. In Faraka lived the aristocratic Fasa who had come from the sea and who fought constantly with the Borojogo and the Burdama (the Fulbe and the Tuareg of today).

In the third century A.D. the Fulbe were finally subdued. This, however, is not the subject of the songs of the fourth to the twelfth centuries which deal rather with the heroic period of a much earlier era, apparently that of the *Garamantenkultur* which Herodotus encountered in the Fezzan and which must have had its high point at around 500 B.C. The epic story of this culture or period is contained in what remains of the Soninke Dausi.

Unfortunately, the culturally destructive influence of Islam and the increasing tendency to think more of agriculture than of fighting have made it difficult for the ethnologist to find more than a scrap or two of the original Dausi. And the scrap given here, "Gassire's Lute," is the best part of the epic which has been preserved. In it we hear repeatedly the four names of Wagadu, the legendary city of the Fasa (men of Fezzan?): Dierra, Agada, Ganna, Silla. Dierra is thought to refer to the place near Mursuk where the ruins of Djerma lie, Agada to Agadez, north of the Haussa states, while Ganna and Silla are believed to have been located on the Upper Niger.

With regard to the fighting which takes place in the story, I would like to remark that single combat could occur only between equals, with spear and sword, and if a hero or any one of the upper castes had to fight with men of lower standing (in our case the Boroma) he showed his contempt for them by using only his saddle girth or a whip. Fighting, like jousting in the Middle Ages, was a very serious sport. If, as the result of it, one won a lady of noble birth and a fine mud castle to go with her, then that was as it might be. But the main thing was that one acquitted oneself with honor.

"The Rediscovery of Wagadu," which follows, has not the epic quality of "Gassire's Lute," but rather a Semitic flavor reminding us very forcibly of the story of Jacob and Esau. The stage properties are the same and the derivation of much of it is obvious but the more kindly African turn of the story gives the situation a fitness and a dignity which are lacking in the unvarnished swindle of which we read in Genesis.

"The Fight with the Bida Dragon" in a somewhat higher key again, gives us human nature at its strongest and weakest. Mamadi Sefe Dekote is willing to wreck a city for Sia Jatta Bari but at the same time Wagana Sako will not challenge his wife's secret lover, for he has heard the man's admission of fear, the Soninke regarding it as unchivalrous to challenge a man who has admitted that he is afraid.

In "Samba Gana" we have the highest type of chivalry, something which Europeans and Americans are prone to think is characteristic only of the Euramerican cultures instead of something which, like the men of Faraka, we received, in adulterated form, from the Beduin in the first millennium of our era. Chivalry is one of the earmarks of the proud Hamitic hunting cultures and it still exists today in a very high form among the pure Beduin of the Arabian Desert. Meanwhile it may be of interest to the reader that gigantic tombs of the type built by Annallja Tu Bari for the hero Samba Gana are still to be found, in varying degrees of preservation, on the Upper Niger today.

In "The Blue Blood" there is chivalry of a sort which we may or may not admire, as well as nationalism of an order not unknown in Europe today. "The Blue Blood" is a Fulbe tale.

The Fulbe, whom Barth identified with the Lucaethiopen, were, at the beginning of our era, probably a subject people of the Garamantae or Fasa in Central North Africa (the Fezzan). We know from the Silimi-Fulbe in Mossi territory that their ancestors suffered under Fasa rule, while the Bororo-Fulbe in Adamaua speak of their enslavement by the Gara-Fasa of the north and relate how they fled southwards to escape it.

The Gassire legend refers to the "doglike Boro-ma," the Soninke bards relate how the Boro-jogo could never look a Fasa in the eye and the people of the northern Sahara speak today of the Kel-boro, a subject race which used cattle instead of camels as beasts of burden. These are all references to the ancestors of the Bororo, the present-day non-Moslem Fulbe herders of the Central Sudan.

Around the year one, then, the Fulbe were a subject people, primitive and despised. After their migration southwards they fared better and the more adventurous of them lived by the sword just as did the European robber barons in the Dark Ages. In the course of time these emigrants developed an aristocracy and an intense national pride which are well reflected in "The Blue Blood." And, perhaps without knowing that they did so, they adopted the myths and legends of their former rulers as their own, sometimes altering names and minor incidents to suit their purpose, sometimes not even troubling to do that. We need not sneer at them. The legends of Europe are few which have not come, in the very beginning, from Asia; and few "good families" in America or Europe can trace their lineage five hundred years, fewer still a thousand.

And so we have the Mabo, the Fulbe bards, singing the Baudi (not to be confused with the Soninke Dausi), the epic of the Fulbe heroes, heroes who were sung on the Mediterranean Coast, among the Garamantae (Fasa) in Fezzan and among the peoples of the Sahel and the

Sudan long before they were adopted by the suddenly racially and nationally conscious Fulbe.

The Fulbe of today, now in no sense of the word a nation, partly mixed with peasant stock but still largely nomads, are to be found in the Sudan from the headwaters of the Senegal to Kano and then southeastwards as far as the northern reaches of the Cameroons.

Gassire's Lute

Four times Wagadu stood there in all her splendor. Four times Wagadu disappeared and was lost to human sight: once through vanity, once through falsehood, once through greed and once through dissension. Four times Wagadu changed her name. First she was called Dierra, then Agada, then Ganna, then Silla. Four times she turned her face. Once to the north, once to the west, once to the east and once to the south. For Wagadu, whenever men have seen her, has always had four gates: one to the north, one to the west, one to the east and one to the south. Those are the directions whence the strength of Wagadu comes, the strength in which she endures no matter whether she be built of stone, wood and earth or lives but as a shadow in the mind and longing of her children. For really, Wagadu is not of stone, not of wood, not of earth. Wagadu is the strength which lives in the hearts of men and is sometimes visible because eyes see her and ears hear the clash of swords and ring of shields, and is sometimes invisible because the indomitability of men has overtired her, so that she sleeps. Sleep came to Wagadu for the first time through vanity, for the second time through falsehood, for the third time through greed and for the fourth time through dissension. Should Wagadu ever be found for the fourth time, then she will live so forcefully in the minds of men that she will never be lost again, so forcefully that vanity, falsehood, greed and dissension will never be able to harm her.

Hoooh! Dierra, Agada, Ganna, Silla! Hoooh! Fasa!

Every time that the guilt of man caused Wagadu to disappear she won a new beauty which made the splendor of her next appearance still more glorious. Vanity brought the song of the bards which all peoples (of the Sudan) imitate and value today. Falsehood brought a rain of gold and pearls. Greed brought writing as the Burdama still practice it today and which in Wagadu was the business of the women. Dissension will enable the fifth Wagadu to be as enduring as the rain of the south and as the rocks of the Sahara, for every man will then have Wagadu in his heart and every woman a Wagadu in her womb.

Hoooh! Dierra, Agada, Ganna, Silla! Hoooh! Fasa!

Wagadu was lost for the first time through vanity. At that time Wagadu faced north and was called Dierra. Her last king was called Nganamba Fasa. The Fasa were strong. But the Fasa were growing old.

Daily they fought against the Burdama and the Boroma. They fought every day and every month. Never was there an end to the fighting. And out of the fighting the strength of the Fasa grew. All Nganamba's men were heroes, all the women were lovely and proud of the strength and the heroism of the men of Wagadu.

All the Fasa who had not fallen in single combat with the Burdama were growing old. Nganamba was very old. Nganamba had a son, Gassire, and he was old enough, for he already had eight grown sons with children of their own. They were all living and Nganamba ruled in his family and reigned as a king over the Fasa and the doglike Boroma. Nganamba grew so old that Wagadu was lost because of him and the Boroma became slaves again to the Burdama who seized power with the sword. Had Nganamba died earlier would Wagadu then have disappeared for the first time?

Hoooh! Dierra, Agada, Ganna, Silla! Hoooh! Fasa!

Nganamba did not die. A jackal gnawed at Gassire's heart. Daily Gassire asked his heart: "When will Nganamba die? When will Gassire be king?" Every day Gassire watched for the death of his father as a lover watches for the evening star to rise. By day, when Gassire fought as a hero against the Burdama and drove the false Boroma before him with a leather girth, he thought only of the fighting, of his sword, of his shield, of his horse. By night, when he rode with the evening into the city and sat in the circle of men and his sons, Gassire heard how the heroes praised his deeds. But his heart was not in the talking; his heart listened for the strains of Nganamba's breathing; his heart was full of misery and longing.

Gassire's heart was full of longing for the shield of his father, the shield which he could carry only when his father was dead, and also for the sword which he might draw only when he was king. Day by day Gassire's rage and longing grew. Sleep passed him by. Gassire lay, and a jackal gnawed at his heart. Gassire felt the misery climbing into his throat. One night Gassire sprang out of bed, left the house and went to an old wise man, a man who knew more than other people. He entered the wise man's house and asked: "Kiekorro! When will my father, Nganamba, die and leave me his sword and shield?" The old man said: "Ah, Gassire, Nganamba will die; but he will not leave you his sword and shield! You will carry a lute. Shield and sword shall others inherit. But your lute shall cause the loss of Wagadu! Ah, Gassire!" Gassire said: "Kiekorro, you lie! I see that you are not wise. How can Wagadu be lost when her heroes triumph daily? Kiekorro, you are a fool!" The old wise man said: "Ah, Gassire, you cannot believe me. But your path will lead you to the partridges in the fields and you will understand what they say and that will be your way and the way of Wagadu."

Hoooh! Dierra, Agada, Ganna, Silla! Hoooh! Fasa!

The next morning Gassire went with the heroes again to do battle against the Burdama. Gassire was angry. Gassire called to the heroes:

"Stay here behind. Today I will battle with the Burdama alone." The heroes stayed behind and Gassire went on alone to do battle with the Burdama. Gassire hurled his spear. Gassire charged the Burdama. Gassire swung his sword. He struck home to the right, he struck home to the left. Gassire's sword was as a sickle in the wheat. The Burdama were afraid. Shocked, they cried, "That is no Fasa, that is no hero, that is a Damo (a being unknown to the singer himself)." The Burdama turned their horses. The Burdama threw away their spears, each man his two spears, and fled. Gassire called the knights. Gassire said, "Gather the spears." The knights gathered the spears. The knights sang: "The Fasa are heroes. Gassire has always been the Fasa's greatest hero. Gassire has always done great deeds. But today Gassire was greater than Gassire!" Gassire rode into the city and the heroes rode behind him. The heroes sang, "Never before has Wagadu won so many spears as today."

Gassire let the women bathe him. The men gathered. But Gassire did not seat himself in their circle. Gassire went into the fields. Gassire heard the partridges. Gassire went close to them. A partridge sat under a bush and sang: "Hear the Dausi! Hear my deeds!" The partridge sang of its battle with the snake. The partridge sang: "All creatures must die, be buried and rot. Kings and heroes die, are buried and rot. I, too, shall die, shall be buried and rot. But the Dausi, the song of my battles, shall not die. It shall be sung again and again and shall outlive all kings and heroes. Hoooh, that I might do such deeds! Hoooh, that I may sing the Dausi! Wagadu will be lost. But the Dausi shall endure and shall live!"

Hoooh! Dierra, Agada, Ganna, Silla! Hoooh! Fasa!

Gassire went to the old wise man. Gassire said: "Kiekorro! I was in the fields. I understood the partridges. The partridge boasted that the song of its deeds would live longer than Wagadu. The partridge sang the Dausi. Tell me whether men also know the Dausi and whether the Dausi can outlive life and death?" The old wise man said: "Gassire, you are hastening to your end. No one can stop you. And since you cannot be a king you shall be a bard. Ah! Gassire. When the kings of the Fasa lived by the sea they were also great heroes and they fought with men who had lutes and sang the Dausi. Oft struck the enemy Dausi fear into the hearts of the Fasa, who were themselves heroes. But they never sang the Dausi because they were of the first rank, of the Horro, and because the Dausi was only sung by those of the second rank, of the Diare. The Diare fought not so much as heroes for the sport of the day but as drinkers for the fame of the evening. But you, Gassire, now that you can no longer be the second of the first (i.e., King), shall be the first of the second. And Wagadu will be lost because of it." Gassire said: "Wagadu can go to blazes!"

Hoooh! Dierra, Agada, Ganna, Silla! Hoooh! Fasa!

Gassire went to a smith. Gassire said, "Make me a lute." The smith said, "I will, but the lute will not sing." Gassire said: "Smith, do your work. The rest is my affair." The smith made the lute. The smith brought the lute to Gassire. Gassire struck on the lute. The lute did not sing. Gassire said, "Look here, the lute does not sing." The smith said, "That's what I told you in the first place." Gassire said, "Well, make it sing." The smith said: "I cannot do anything more about it. The rest is your affair." Gassire said, "What can I do, then?" The smith said: "This is a piece of wood. It cannot sing if it has no heart. You must give it a heart. Carry this piece of wood on your back when you go into battle. The wood must ring with the stroke of your sword. The wood must absorb down-dripping blood, blood of your blood, breath of your breath. Your pain must be its pain, your fame its fame. The wood may no longer be like the wood of a tree, but must be penetrated by and be a part of your people. Therefore it must live not only with you but with your sons. Then will the tone that comes from your heart echo in the ear of your son and live on in the people, and your son's life's blood, oozing out of his heart, will run down your body and live on in this piece of wood. But Wagadu will be lost because of it." Gassire said, "Wagadu can go to blazes!"

Hoooh! Dierra, Agada, Ganna, Silla! Hoooh! Fasa!

Gassire called his eight sons. Gassire said: "My sons, today we go to battle. But the strokes of our swords shall echo no longer in the Sahel alone, but shall retain their ring for the ages. You and I, my sons, will that we live on and endure before all other heroes in the Dausi. My oldest son, today we two, thou and I, will be the first in battle!"

Gassire and his eldest son went into the battle ahead of the heroes. Gassire had thrown the lute over his shoulder. The Burdama came closer. Gassire and his eldest son charged. Gassire and his eldest son fought as the first. Gassire and his eldest son left the other heroes far behind them. Gassire fought not like a human being, but rather like a Damo. His eldest son fought not like a human being, but like a Damo. Gassire came into a tussle with eight Burdama. The eight Burdama pressed him hard. His son came to help him and struck four of them down. But one of the Burdama thrust a spear through his heart. Gassire's eldest son fell dead from his horse. Gassire was angry. And shouted. The Burdama fled. Gassire dismounted and took the body of his eldest son upon his back. Then he mounted and rode slowly back to the other heroes. The eldest son's heart's blood dropped on the lute which was also hanging on Gassire's back. And so Gassire, at the head of his heroes, rode into Dierra.

Hoooh! Dierra, Agada, Ganna, Silla! Hoooh! Fasa!

Gassire's eldest son was buried. Dierra mourned. The urn in which the body crouched was red with blood. That night Gassire took his lute and struck against the wood. The lute did not sing. Gassire was angry. He called his sons. Gassire said to his sons, "Tomorrow we ride against the Burdama."

For seven days Gassire rode with the heroes to battle. Every day one of his sons accompanied him to be the first in the fighting. And on every one of these days Gassire carried the body of one of his sons, over his shoulder and over the lute, back into the city. And thus, on every evening, the blood of one of his sons dripped onto the lute. After the seven days of fighting there was a great mourning in Dierra. All the heroes and all the women wore red and white clothes. The blood of the Boroma (apparently in sacrifice) flowed everywhere. All the women wailed. All the men were angry. Before the eighth day of the fighting all the heroes and the men of Dierra gathered and spoke to Gassire: "Gassire, this shall have an end. We are willing to fight when it is necessary. But you, in your rage, go on fighting without sense or limit. Now go forth from Dierra! A few will join you and accompany you. Take your Boroma and your cattle. The rest of us incline more to life than fame. And while we do not wish to die fameless we have no wish to die for fame alone."

The old wise man said: "Ah, Gassire! Thus will Wagadu be lost today for the first time."

Hoooh! Dierra, Agada, Ganna, Silla! Hoooh! Fasa!

Gassire and his last, his youngest, son, his wives, his friends and his Boroma rode out into the desert. They rode through the Sahel. Many heroes rode with Gassire through the gates of the city. Many turned. A few accompanied Gassire and his youngest son into the Sahara.

They rode far: day and night. They came into the wilderness and in the loneliness they rested. All the heroes and all the women and all the Boroma slept. Gassire's youngest son slept. Gassire was restive. He sat by the fire. He sat there long. Presently he slept. Suddenly he jumped up. Gassire listened. Close beside him Gassire heard a voice. It rang as though it came from himself. Gassire began to tremble. He heard the lute singing. The lute sang the Dausi.

When the lute had sung the Dausi for the first time, King Nganamba died in the city Dierra; when the lute had sung the Dausi for the first time, Gassire's rage melted; Gassire wept. When the lute had sung the Dausi for the first time, Wagadu disappeared—for the first time.

Hoooh! Dierra, Agada, Ganna, Silla! Hoooh! Fasa!

Four times Wagadu stood there in all her splendor. Four times Wagadu disappeared and was lost to human sight: once through vanity, once through falsehood, once through greed and once through dissension. Four times Wagadu changed her name. First she was called Dierra, then Agada, then Ganna, then Silla. Four times she turned her face. Once to the north, once to the west, once to the east and once to the south. For Wagadu, whenever men have seen her, has always had four gates: one to the north, one to the west, one to the east and one to the south. Those are the directions whence the strength of Wagadu comes, the strength in which she endures no matter whether she be built of stone, wood or earth or lives but as a shadow in the mind and longing of her children. For, really, Wagadu is not of stone, not of wood, not of earth. Wagadu is the strength which lives in the hearts of men

and is sometimes visible because eyes see her and ears hear the clash
of swords and ring of shields, and is sometimes invisible because the
indomitability of men has overtired her, so that she sleeps. Sleep came
to Wagadu for the first time through vanity, for the second time through
falsehood, for the third time through greed and for the fourth time
through dissension. Should Wagadu ever be found for the fourth time,
then she will live so forcefully in the minds of men that she will never
be lost again, so forcefully that vanity, falsehood, greed and dissension
will never be able to harm her.

Hoooh! Dierra, Agada, Ganna, Silla! Hoooh! Fasa!

Every time that the guilt of man caused Wagadu to disappear she
won a new beauty which made the splendor of her next appearance still
more glorious. Vanity brought the song of the bards which all peoples
imitate and value today. Falsehood brought a rain of gold and pearls.
Greed brought writing as the Burdama still practice it today and which
in Wagadu was the business of the women. Dissension will enable the
fifth Wagadu to be as enduring as the rain of the south and as the rocks
of the Sahara, for every man will then have Wagadu in his heart and
every woman a Wagadu in her womb.

Hoooh! Dierra, Agada, Ganna, Silla! Hoooh! Fasa!

The Rediscovery of Wagadu

Wagadu disappeared for seven years. No one knew where she was.
Then she was found again. And then she was lost again and did not
reappear for seven hundred and forty years. There was an old King
called Mama Dinga. Mama Dinga said, "If the great war drum, Tabele,
is beaten, Wagadu will be found again." But Tabele had been stolen by
the djinns, the devils, who had tied it fast to the sky.

Mama Dinga had an old bondsman with whom he had been raised.
Mama Dinga had seven sons. The six oldest sons treated the bondsman
badly. This the father, blind with age, did not see. When the bondsman
called the eldest son to a meal with his father the young man gave the
servant a kick as he came into the room and so did the next five sons.
Only the youngest son said "Good day" to the old bondsman. When
they left the room again the eldest son filled his mouth with water
which he spewed over the old man. The second son sprinkled the
bondsman with the water with which he had washed his hands, and it
was only the youngest son who gave the old man a good handful of food.
Mama Dinga saw none of these things.

Mama Dinga was blind. He recognized his eldest son by his arm
which was hairy and decorated with an iron arm ring. Mama Dinga
would stroke the arm experimentally and then sniff his son's gown. Thus
he identified his eldest son. As he was going to bed one evening Mama
Dinga felt that the time was near for him to die. So he called his
bondsman, his old true servant, to him and said: "Summon my eldest

son, for I feel that I shall die soon and I wish to tell him that which it is fitting he should know. Tell him to come after midnight." The bondsman went to seek the eldest son. As he entered the eldest son's house and sought to speak with him the young man gave the old servant a kick. That always happened when the old man had anything to do with the six eldest sons. Only the youngest son had always given him food.

Thereupon the old man went to Lagarre, the youngest son, and said, "Couldn't you borrow your eldest brother's gown and arm ring?" Lagarre said, "Yes, I could do that." The old man continued: "Your father is blind. He can no longer see. He identifies your eldest brother by stroking his arm and arm ring and sniffing his gown. Your father will die soon. He sent me to summon his eldest son. But your older brothers have always treated me badly. And so I will bring you to him instead." Thereupon Lagarre slew a goat and skinned it and drew the hide over his arm so that the arm felt as rough and as hairy as his brother's. Then he went to his eldest brother and said: "Lend me your gown and your arm ring. I am going to see a man who owes me something." The eldest brother replied: "If you cannot collect your debts without my gown and ring—then take them. Go to my wife in that house over there and let her give them to you." Lagarre went there, received the ring and the gown and put them on. At midnight he met the old bondsman.

The old bondsman led Lagarre to Mama Dinga, the king, and said, "Here is your eldest son." The old king's fingers slid over the young man's arm. They felt that the arm was rough and hairy. They felt the ring. The old man took hold of the young man's gown and brought it to his nose. He smelt that it was the gown of his eldest son. Mama Dinga smiled and said, "It is true." And Mama Dinga said further: "On the left bank of the stream stand four great djalla trees. At the foot of these four trees lie nine jars. If you wash yourself in these nine jars and roll yourself in the dirt of the river bank you will always have plenty of followers. Wash yourself first in the first eight jars. And then in the ninth. Let the ninth go at first. But when you have washed yourself finally in this ninth jar, then you will be able to understand the language of the djinns. Then you will know the language of all animals and also of the birds and will be able to speak with them. And then you can speak with the djinns and ask them where the great Tabele, the great war drum, is. The oldest djinn will tell you, and when you have the great Tabele, then you will be able to find Wagadu again." Lagarre left. He went at once to the river. He found the four djalla trees. He found the nine jars. He bathed himself in the jars. And then he understood the speech of the djinns, of the animals and birds.

Meanwhile, the next day the other sons of Mama Dinga joined their father for the morning meal. As the eldest came Mama Dinga asked him, "Have you done what I told you?" The eldest son asked, "What did you tell me, and when?" Mama Dinga said, "Last night I let you come to me and I told you something." The eldest son said, "But I never spoke with you last night." Then said the old true bondservant to the king: "Last night you spoke not with your eldest son but rather with your youngest. You sent me to summon your eldest son, but instead of calling him I called the youngest one. For your six first sons always treat me badly. They are worthless, and if your eldest son found Wagadu he would quickly destroy it. So now if you must slay, slay me—for the blame is mine." Thereupon Mama Dinga said to his eldest son: "My eldest, you will not be king for I have just given all that I had to your youngest brother. So become a wizard and learn how to ask god for rain. When you can make it rain the people will come to you and you will have influence."

Meanwhile the djinns sent the oldest djinn to Lagarre. The old djinn said to Lagarre, "In the bush there is someone seven years older even than I." Lagarre asked, "Who is that?" The djinn said, "That is Kuto."[1] Lagarre said, "In which forest is Kuto?" The djinn showed him the forest.

Lagarre went to the forest. He met Kuto. He could speak with Kuto for he now understood the language of all the animals and even of the birds. He said to Kuto, "Show me my father's Tabele." Kuto asked, "To which people do you belong?" Lagarre said, "I am the son of Dinga." Kuto asked, "What is the name of your father's father?" Lagarre said, "I do not know." Kuto said: "I don't know you, but I know Dinga—I don't know Dinga but I know Kiridjo, Dinga's father. But there is still someone who is seventeen years older even than I." Lagarre said, "Who is that?" Kuto said, "That is Turume, the jackal, who is so old that he has no more teeth." Lagarre asked, "Where is he?" Kuto showed him the forest where Turume was.

Lagarre went with his soldiers to the forest. He met Turume. Turume asked him, "Who are you?" Lagarre said, "I am the son of Dinga." Turume asked, "What is the name of your father's father?" Lagarre said, "I do not know." Turume said: "I do not know you but I know Dinga. I do not know Kiridjo but I do know Kiridjotamani, Kiridjo's father. I am very old but there is still someone who is twenty-seven years older even than I." Lagarre asked, "Who is that?" Turume said, "That is Koliko, the buzzard." Lagarre asked, "Where does Koliko live?" Turume showed him.

Lagarre went with his men to see Koliko. He asked, "Show me the Tabele of my father." Koliko asked, "Who are you?" Lagarre said, "I am the son of Dinga." Koliko said: "I do not know you but I do know Dinga. I do not know Dinga, but I do know Kiridjo. I do not know Kiridjo, but I do know Kiridjotamani. I know where the Tabele is but I am too weak and too old either to show it to you or to fetch it. As you can see, my feathers have fallen out from age and I cannot even fly away from this branch where I sit." Lagarre asked, "What is to be done?" Koliko said: "You must see to it that I grow strong again. You must bring me a great deal. Stay here with me for seven days. Let a young horse and a young donkey be slain every morning and give me the heart and the liver of

---

1. A white varanus or large lizard which is considered especially holy even today. During Ramadan the Marabuts try to catch it to make a magic concoction from its flesh.

both of them. At night and morning you must feed them to me. If you live up to these conditions for seven days I'll have strength again and feathers and will be able to bring you your grandfather's Tabele." Lagarre stayed there for seven days. Every morning he had a young horse and a young donkey killed and he handed the liver and heart of each to Koliko. Morning and night he fed Koliko. The buzzard's strength and feathers grew. He could fly again. He flew to where the djinns had tied the Tabele to the sky. But he did not have enough strength to break the thongs with which it was tied. He flew back and said to Lagarre: "Three days longer must you slay a horse and a donkey a day and hand me the heart and liver of each, for I am still not strong enough to break the thongs with which the Tabele is tied to the sky. At the end of three days I will be strong enough." For three days more Lagarre slaughtered a horse and donkey every day. On the third day Koliko was strong enough. He flew to the sky and wrenched off the Tabele. He brought it to Lagarre.

Koliko said to Lagarre: "Return. For two days you may not touch the Tabele, but on the third day you must beat it. Then you will find Wagadu." Lagarre left. For two days he wandered homewards. Then he beat the Tabele and saw Wagadu before his eyes. The djinns had kept it hidden all that time.

The Fight with the Bida Dragon

Koliko had also said to Lagarre: "When you come to Wagadu you will see the great snake, Bida. Bida used to receive ten young maidens every year from your grandfather. And for these ten young maidens he let it rain three times a year. It rained gold." Lagarre asked, "Must I sacrifice ten maidens, too?" Koliko said: "Bida will make a deal with you. He will demand ten young maidens. This you will refuse. Say you will give one maiden; then keep to your word."

Lagarre came to Wagadu. Before the gates of the city lay Bida in seven great coils. Lagarre asked, "Where are you going?" Bida said, "Who is your father?" Lagarre said, "My father is Dinga." Bida said, "Who is your father's father?" Lagarre said, "I do not know him." Bida said: "I do not know you but I know Dinga. I do not know Dinga but I know Kiridjo. I do not know Kiridjo but I know Kiridjotamani. I do not know Kiridjotamani but I know Wagana Sako. Your grandfather gave me ten maidens every year. And for them I let it rain gold three times a year. Will you do as he did?" Lagarre said, "No." Bida asked, "Will you give me nine maidens every year?" Lagarre said, "No." Bida asked, "Will you give me eight maidens every year?" Lagarre said, "No." Bida asked, "Will you give me seven maidens every year?" Lagarre said, "No." Bida asked, "Will you give me six maidens every year?" Lagarre said, "No." Bida asked, "Will you give me five maidens every year?" Lagarre said, "No." Bida asked, "Will you give me four maidens every year?" Lagarre said, "No." Bida asked, "Will you give me three maidens every year?" Lagarre said, "No." Bida asked, "Will you give me two maidens every year?" Lagarre said, "No." Bida asked, "Will you give me one maiden every year?" Lagarre said, "Yes, I will give you one maiden a year if you will let it rain gold three times a year."

Bida said: "Then I will be satisfied with that and will let golden rain fall three times a year over Wagadu."

There were four respected men in Wagadu: Wagana Sako, Dajabe Sise, Damangile (the founder of the Djaora house from which the aristocratic Soninke families trace their descent) and Mamadi Sefe Dekote (Sefe Dekote means "he speaks seldom").

Wagana Sako was unusually jealous. And for this reason he surrounded his court with a mighty wall in which there was not a single door. The only way to enter the court was to jump over the wall with the horse, Samba Ngarranja. Samba Ngarranja was the only horse which was able to jump over the wall and Wagana Sako guarded the horse as jealously as he guarded his wife. He never permitted Samba Ngarranja to cover a mare for he was afraid that the foal would be as good a jumper as Samba Ngarranja and that somebody else would be able to jump over the wall.

Mamadi Sefe Dekote bought himself a mare. He let Wagana Sako see him shut her up very carefully in his house. Mamadi Sefe Dekote, who was Wagana Sako's uncle, one day stole the stallion, Samba Ngarranja, let him cover his new mare and then secretly returned him to his stall. Mamadi Sefe Dekote's mare threw a foal that promised to be just as good a jumper as Samba Ngarranja and with which Mamadi Sefe Dekote was certain he could leap over the wall. When the foal was three years old it was strong enough for the jump.

Then Wagadu went to war. But in the night Mamadi Sefe Dekote returned secretly to Wagadu on his three-year-old stallion. With a mighty leap he cleared the great wall, tied up his horse in the courtyard and went to Wagana Sako's wife. He spoke with her, lay down beside her and laid his head in her lap.

In the same night Wagana Sako also left the lines and rode home to visit his wife. He put Samba Ngarranja at the wall and was much surprised to find another horse tied up in his courtyard. He tied up Samba Ngarranja and then took a good look at the strange horse. Then he heard his wife talking in the house. He placed his weapons against the wall and listened. But Mamadi Sefe Dekote and Wagana Sako's wife spoke but little. A mouse ran along a beam above them. Below it was a cat. The mouse saw the cat and was so terrified that it fell. The cat pounced on the mouse. Mamadi Sefe Dekote seized Wagana Sako's wife by the arm and said: "Look at that! Just look at that!" The woman said, "Yes, I see." Mamadi Sefe Dekote said, "Just as the mouse fears the cat, so do we fear your husband." Wagana Sako, listening outside, heard what was said. And when he heard it he had to go, for the unknown man had said he was afraid of him. Wagana Sako retrieved his weapons, mounted his horse, jumped over the wall and returned to the lines. Later Mamadi Sefe Dekote also left the court and joined his companions in the grey of the morning.

Wagana Sako did not know who had visited his wife that night, and Mamadi Sefe Dekote had no idea that Wagana Sako had returned to Wagadu and overheard him. Therefore neither could accuse the other and the day passed without a quarrel. In the evening a singer picked up his lute and sang. Later Wagana Sako reached over to the player, plucked at the strings and sang, "Last night I heard a word and had I not heard it Wagadu would have been destroyed." (Meant is the word "fear".) Mamadi Sefe Dekote also plucked at the strings of the lute and sang: "Had anyone heard what was said last night Wagadu would have been destroyed. But no one heard."

Thereupon the people of Wagadu said: "Let us return to Wagadu. For if, at the beginning of a campaign, people begin to quarrel then the matter can come to no good end." So they all went back to Wagadu.

The people of Wagadu said, "The next firstborn female in Wagadu shall be given to Bida." The next firstborn female was Sia Jatta Bari. Sia Jatta Bari was wondrously lovely. She was the most beautiful maiden in Soninkeland. She was so beautiful that even today when the Soninke and other peoples want to give a girl their highest praise they say, "She is as beautiful as Sia Jatta Bari."

Sia Jatta Bari had a lover and the lover was Mamadi Sefe Dekote. Everyone in Wagadu said, "We do not know if Wagadu will ever again have a maiden so lovely as Sia Jatta Bari." And therefore Mamadi Sefe Dekote was very proud of his beloved. One night Sia Jatta Bari came to sleep with her lover (without, however, permitting him to touch her). Sia Jatta Bari said, "Every friendship in this world must come to an end." Mamadi Sefe Dekote said, "Why do you say that?" Sia Jatta Bari said, "There is no friendship that can last forever, and I am the one who is to be given to the snake, Bida." Mamadi Sefe Dekote said, "If that happens then Wagadu may rot, for I shall not stand for it." Sia Jatta Bari said: "Do not make a fuss about it. It is so destined and is an old custom to which we must conform. I am destined to be Bida's bride and there is nothing to be done about it."

The next morning Mamadi Sefe Dekote sharpened his sword. He made it as sharp as possible. He laid a grain of barley on the earth and split it with one blow to test the edge of his weapon. Then he returned the sword to its sheath. The people dressed Sia Jatta Bari as if for her wedding, dressed her in jewelry and fine raiment and formed in a long procession to accompany her to the snake. Bida lived in a great deep well to one side of the town. And there the procession took its way. Mamadi Sefe Dekote girded on his sword, mounted his horse and rode with the procession.

Bida was accustomed, when receiving a sacrifice, to stick his head three times out of the well before seizing his victim. As the procession halted at the place of sacrifice, Mamadi Sefe Dekote took his place close to the rim of the well. Thereupon Bida reared his head. The people of Wagadu said to Sia Jatta Bari and Mamadi Sefe Dekote: "It is time to take farewell. Take farewell!" Bida reared his head a second time. The people of Wagadu cried: "Take farewell, part quickly! It is time!" For the third time Bida reared his head over the rim of the well. Whereupon Mamadi Sefe Dekote drew his sword and with one blow cut off the serpent's head. The head flew far and wide through the air and before it came to earth it spoke: "For seven years, seven months and seven days may Wagadu remain without its golden rain." The head fell to the ground far, far to the south and from it comes the gold which is to be found there.

The people of Wagadu heard Bida's curse. They screamed at Mamadi and closed in on him. But Mamadi leapt to his horse, pulled Sia up behind him and spurred off towards Sama-Markala, a town to the north of Segu on the Niger, where his mother lived. Mamadi Sefe Dekote had a good horse, sired by Samba Ngarranja. The only horse which could overtake it was Samba Ngarranja himself. Whereupon the people of Wagadu demanded that Wagana Sako give chase, that he overtake Mamadi and kill him. Wagana Sako leapt to his horse and pursued his uncle, Mamadi Sefe Dekote.

Wagana Sako quickly caught up with his uncle whose horse was carrying a double load. He took his spear and rammed it fast into the ground. Then he said to Mamadi: "Flee as fast as you can, my uncle, for if the people of Wagadu overtake you they will surely kill you. I will not kill you for I am your nephew. Flee to your mother in Sama." Then he dismounted and pulled at his spear. After a time the other people of Wagadu arrived. He said to them: "Help me to pull my spear out of the ground. I hurled it at Mamadi Sefe Dekote but missed and then it went so far into the ground that I cannot pull it out alone." The people helped him to pull out the spear and sent him off again after Mamadi Sefe Dekote. Wagana soon caught up with his uncle again and once more rammed his spear into the ground and called, "Flee to your mother in Sama!" Again he waited for the people of Wagadu to help him withdraw the spear and then for a third time he repeated the performance with his uncle. By the time the people of Wagadu had caught up with him again Mamadi Sefe Dekote had arrived in Sama.

Mamadi's mother came out of the town to meet the riders from Wagadu. She called to Wagana Sako, "Turn back and let my son come to me in peace." Wagana Sako said, "Ask your son if I did not save him so that he could come to you and if he has not me to thank that he is still alive." Mamadi Sefe Dekote said: "I killed Bida to save this maiden whom I will marry. I cut off the snake's head. Ere it fell to earth Bida's head said, 'For seven years, seven months and seven days may Wagadu remain without its golden rain.' And thereupon the people of Wagadu grew angry and sent Wagana Sako on Samba Ngarranja to pursue and kill me. But he protected me. And so I came here with Sia Jatta Bari."

In Wagadu Mamadi Sefe Dekote had been accustomed to give Sia Jatta Bari mutukalle tamu (about one thousand francs) in gold when she left him in the mornings. For three months long she had received mukutalle tamu every morning. But in spite of this she had not given herself to Mamadi Sefe Dekote. But in Sama, where there was no golden snake to make the land rich, these presents stopped. Sia had no more use for Mamadi. Therefore she said to him one morning: "I have a headache. There is only one way to remedy it: cut off one of your little toes and I will wash my forehead with the blood." Mamadi loved Sia very much indeed. He cut off one of his little toes. After a time Sia said: "I still don't feel any better. The headache will not stop. So cut off your little finger. If I wash my forehead with its blood then surely that will help." Mamadi was very much in love with Sia. So he cut off his finger. Thereupon Sia sent him a message saying: "I love only people with ten fingers and ten toes. I do not love people with nine fingers and nine toes." Mamadi received the message.

When Mamadi heard this he became very angry, so angry that he fell ill and almost died. He summoned an old woman. The old woman came and asked, "What is the matter with you, Mamadi Sefe Dekote?" Mamadi said: "I am sick with rage, rage at the way in which Sia Jatta Bari has treated me. For Sia I killed the snake Bida. For Sia I brought a curse on Wagadu. For Sia I fled from Wagadu. For Sia I have given out great quantities of gold. For Sia I cut off my small toe. For Sia I cut off my little finger. And now Sia sends me a messenger to say: 'I love only people with ten fingers and ten toes. I do not love people with nine fingers and nine toes.' And that has made me ill with rage." The old woman said: "Your case is not so difficult. Give me your snuffbox." Mamadi thought the old woman wanted to snuff a pinch of tobacco. He handed her the snuffbox. The old woman took it and said: "So that you may see it is not difficult, look into the box. A moment ago there was tobacco in it. And now that I have taken it into my hand the tobacco has turned to gold. And your case is not even as hard as that. For it is easier to fill Sia with love than your snuffbox with gold. Tell me, if I give you a karté cake (that is, butter from the butter tree) can you get Sia to smear the butter on her head?" Mamadi Sefe Dekote said, "Yes, I can do that." Thereupon the old woman prepared a karté cake with Borri (a magic preparation) and gave the completed charm to Mamadi.

In Sama there was a woman who was an excellent hairdresser. This woman was called Kumbadamba. Mamadi summoned her and said: "I will give you mutukalle tamu in gold if you can use this karté in dressing Sia Jatta Bari's hair. Can you do it?" Kumbadamba said: "That's not so hard. Certainly I'll do it." Mamadi gave her the magic karté and left the rest of the affair to her.

One day Sia summoned Kumbadamba and said to her, "Dress my hair." She called to her servant and said, "Go into the house and fetch karté." (This so-called tree butter is in general use for hairdressing.) Kumbadamba said, "That is not necessary as I happen to have plenty of karté with me." Thereupon she set to work. As soon as she had ordered one side of Sia's head and had rubbed in the butter Sia sprang up and said, "Mamadi is calling me." She ran to Mamadi and said, "Did you call me, my big brother?" (Expression of the most tender affection.) Mamadi had not called; it was merely the Borri which was beginning to work. Mamadi said, "No, I did not call you, for I have but nine fingers and nine toes and I know that you love only people with ten fingers and ten toes." Sia returned and let Kumbadamba go on with her hairdressing. When she had ordered the other side of her head and had rubbed in the butter Sia suddenly sprang up and said: "Let me go. Mamadi is calling me." She ran quickly to Mamadi Sefe Dekote and said, "Did you call me, my big brother?" Mamadi had not called; it was merely the Borri which was beginning to work on the other side of her head. Mamadi said, "No, I did not call you, for I have only nine fingers and nine toes and I know that you love only people with ten fingers and ten toes." Sia returned to the hairdresser and let Kumbadamba finish her work. Kumbadamba smoothed her hair, and made good use of the Borrikarté so that Sia jumped up impatiently and said: "Now at last you can let me go. Mamadi is calling me." She ran to Mamadi and asked, "Did you call me, my big brother." Mamadi said: "Yes, I called you. I wanted to tell you to come to me tonight." Sia said, "Tonight I will come to our marriage." Till now Mamadi Sefe Dekote's attempts to possess Sia Jatta Bari had not met with success.

Mamadi went to his courtyard and commanded that his house and bed be put in order. He had a young slave called Blali in whom he had confidence and whom he had entrusted with the care of his good horse. He called Blali and said: "Give me your old gown to put on. But first wash and clean it thoroughly. Then wash yourself and lay yourself in my house and upon my bed. At midnight a woman, Sia, will come to you. Don't speak a word to her. She shall think that I am at her side and she is accustomed that I say little. Hence my name, Sefe Dekote. Don't speak with her, but make love to her—properly. You must make love to her. If you haven't done so by morning I will simply have you killed. Have you understood?" Blali said, "I'll do it."

In the night came Sia. Mamadi had left his shoes standing by the bed so that she should see them, recognize them and assume that it was he who lay on the bed. She came, recognized the shoes and lay down beside the slave. She said, "Kassunka" (good night). Blali merely mumbled an answer so as not to give himself away. She said, "My big brother, I know that you speak seldom, but speak with me now. I beg you, answer me now." Blali took Sia in his arms.

The next morning Mamadi Sefe Dekote entered the hut in Blali's clothes and called, "Blali!" Blali answered, "Master!" Mamadi said, "Why haven't you groomed my horse this morning instead of sleeping with this disreputable Sia?" Blali said, "If I haven't done my work this morning isn't it sufficient excuse that I was able to sleep with Sia of whom all Wagadu says she is the most beautiful maiden in the land?" Sia, lying there on the bed, heard his words. Her whole body began to tremble. Trembling she said, "My big brother, you pay back well." Sia, for shame, stayed in the house the whole day long. She did not dare to venture outside. But in the night she crept out and slunk through the shadows to her own house. And there her shame was so great that she died.

That was Mamadi Sefe Dekote's revenge on Sia Jatta Bari.

Samba Gana

Annallja Tu Bari was the daughter of a prince who lived near Wagana and everyone thought of her as very beautiful and very wise. Many knights came to seek her hand, but she demanded of each of them something which he was unwilling to undertake. Annallja Tu Bari's father had owned not only the town where she lived but many farm villages as well. One day he quarrelled with a neighboring ruler about the possession of one of these villages. Annallja's father lost the duel which followed and, in consequence, lost the village, too. And this was such a blow to his pride that he died of it. Annallja inherited the town and the land around it, but she demanded of every suitor not only that he win back the lost village but also that he conquer eighty other towns and villages as well. Years passed. No one cared to venture on so warlike an undertaking. Years passed. Annallja remained unmarried but grew lovelier with every year. But she lost all joy in life. Every year she became more lovely and more melancholy. And, following her example, all the knights, bards, smiths and bondsmen of Annallja's land lost their capacity for laughter.

In Faraka there lived a prince called Gana who had a son called Samba Gana. When Samba Gana grew to manhood he followed the custom of his people and, taking two bards and two servants, left the house of his father and set out to seek and fight for land of his own. Samba Gana was young. His tutor was the bard Tararafe, who accompanied him. Samba Gana was happy and as he set out on his journey he laughed with joy. Samba Gana came to a town and challenged the prince who ruled it. They fought. The townsfolk watched. Samba Gana won. The conquered prince asked for his life and offered Samba Gana his town. Samba Gana said: "Your town means nothing to me. You may keep it." Samba Gana went on his way. He fought with one prince after another and always he returned the towns which he won. Always he said: "Keep your town. It is nothing to me." Finally Samba Gana had conquered all the princes of Faraka and still he had no town or land of his own for he always gave back what he won and continued, laughing, on his way.

One day he was encamped on the Niger. The bard Tararafe sang of Annallja Tu Bari; he sang of Annallja Tu Bari's beauty and melancholy and loneliness. Tararafe sang, "Only he who conquers eighty towns can win Annallja Tu Bari and make her laugh." Samba Gana listened. Samba Gana sprang to his feet. Samba Gana cried: "Up! Saddle the horses! We ride to the land of Annallja Tu Bari!" Samba Gana rode off with his servants and his bards. They rode day and night. They rode for many days. Finally they came to Annallja Tu Bari's town. Samba Gana

saw Annallja Tu Bari. He saw that she was beautiful and that she did
not laugh. Samba Gana said, "Annallja Tu Bari, show me the eighty
towns." Samba Gana set off once more on conquest. He said to Tararafe,
"Stay with Annallja Tu Bari, sing to her, while away the time for her
and make her laugh." Tararafe remained with Annallja Tu Bari. He
sang every day of the heroes of Faraka, of the cities of Faraka and of
the great serpent of the Issa Beer which made the river rise so that one
year the people had a surplus of rice and the next year went hungry.
Annallja Tu Bari listened to everything he sang. Meanwhile Samba
journeyed about the country. He fought with one prince after the other.
He conquered every one of the eighty princes. He said to every conquered prince, "Go to Annallja Tu Bari and tell her that your town is
hers." All the eighty princes and many knights more came to Annallja
Tu Bari and stayed in her town. And so her town grew and grew and
presently Annallja Tu Bari ruled over all the princes and knights of the
land.

Samba Gana returned to Annallja Tu Bari. He said, "Annallja Tu Bari,
all that you wished for is now yours." Annallja Tu Bari said: "You have
done your work well. Now take me." Samba Gana said: "Why don't you
laugh? I will not marry you until you laugh." Annallja Tu Bari said: "At
first I could not laugh because of the pain of my father's shame. Now
I cannot laugh because I am hungry." Samba Gana said, "How can I still
your hunger?" Annallja Tu Bari said, "Conquer the serpent of the Issa
Beer which causes plenty in one year and need in the next." Samba
Gana said, "No one has ever dared to attack the serpent, but I will see
the matter through." Samba Gana set out to look for the serpent.

Samba Gana rode to Faraka and sought the serpent of the Issa Beer.
He went farther and farther. He came to Koriume, found no serpent
and continued upstream. He came to Bamba, found no serpent and
continued farther upstream. Then Samba Gana found the serpent.
They fought. Sometimes Samba Gana won the upper hand, sometimes
the serpent. The Niger flowed first to one side and then to the other.
The mountains collapsed and the earth opened in yawning chasms.
Eight years long Samba Gana struggled with the serpent. And at the
end of eight years victory was finally his. In the course of the fighting
he had splintered eight hundred lances and broken eighty swords. All
he had left was one bloody sword and one bloody lance. He gave the
bloodstained lance to Tararafe and said, "Go to Annallja Tu Bari, give
her the lance, tell her the serpent is conquered and . . . see if she laughs
now."

Tararafe went to Annallja Tu Bari. He said to her what he had been
told to say. Annallja Tu Bari said: "Return to Samba Gana and tell him
to bring the conquered serpent here so that, as my slave, it may lead
the river into my country. Only when Annallja Tu Bari sees Samba
Gana with the serpent, only then will Annallja Tu Bari laugh."

Tararafe returned to Faraka with his message. He gave the message
to Samba Gana. Samba Gana heard Annallja Tu Bari's words. Samba
Gana said, "She asks too much." Samba Gana took up the bloody sword,

plunged it into his breast, laughed once more and died. Tararafe drew out the bloody sword, mounted his horse and rode back to Annallja Tu Bari. Tararafe said: "Here is the sword of Samba Gana. It is red with the blood of the serpent and that of Samba Gana. Samba Gana has laughed for the last time."

Annallja Tu Bari summoned all the princes and all the knights who were gathered in her town. She mounted her horse. The knights and the princes mounted their horses and Annallja Tu Bari rode eastward with her people. They rode till they came to Faraka. Annallja Tu Bari came to Samba Gana's body. Annallja Tu Bari said: "This hero was greater than all before him. Build him a tomb to tower over that of every hero and of every king." The work began. Eight times eight hundred people excavated the shaft. Eight times eight hundred people built the underground burial chamber. Eight times eight hundred people built the sacrificial chamber at ground level. Eight times eight hundred people brought earth from afar, piled it on the building, beat it and burned it to make it hard. The mountain (the tumuluslike pyramid) rose higher and higher.

Every evening Annallja Tu Bari, accompanied by her princes and knights and bards, climbed to the top of the mountain and every evening the bards sang songs of the hero. Every evening Tararafe sang the song of Samba Gana. Every morning Annallja Tu Bari rose and said: "The mountain is not yet high enough. Build on until I can see Wagana." Eight times eight hundred people carried earth and piled it on the mountain and stamped it hard and burned it. Eight years long the mountain rose higher and higher. At the end of eight years, at sunrise, Tararafe looked about him and cried, "Annallja Tu Bari, today I can see Wagana." Annallja peered towards the west. Annallja Tu Bari said: "I see Wagana! Samba Gana's tomb is at last as great as his name deserves."

Annallja Tu Bari laughed.

Annallja Tu Bari laughed and said: "Now leave me, all of you, knights and princes. Go, spread over the world and become heroes like Samba Gana!" Annallja Tu Bari laughed once more and died. She was placed beside Samba Gana in the burial chamber of the mountainous tomb.

The eight times eight hundred princes and horro [nobles] rode away, each in a different direction, fought and became great heroes.

The Blue Blood

Goroba-Dike was of the blood of the Fulbe house of Ardo which had ruled over Massina for five hundred years. But Goroba-Dike was a younger son and had no landed inheritance. So he wandered around in the Bammana country taking no pains to hide either his dissatisfaction with his fate or the bitterness with which it filled him. If he dismounted at a Bammana village for the night he would order a small child to be slaughtered and ground small, the mincemeat to be mixed with water and the resulting mash to be fed to his horse. If he met a smith he would force the poor man to make him knives and lances without permitting him to use a forge. And when he met a leatherworker he would order him to sew up a hippopotamus skull. So, what with one thing and another, the Bammana tribes were thoroughly afraid of Goroba-Dike and of what he might do next.

In their perplexity and their fear the Bammana turned to the Mabo bard Ulal, a wise singer in Goroba-Dike's service. They came with a pot full of gold and said: "You are the only one who can influence Goroba-Dike. We give you this gold that you may tell him that his wildness is only doing the country harm and that neither he nor we have anything to gain by it. Try, if you can, to turn him to something else." The Mabo Ulal said, "Good, I'll see what I can do." He took the gold and a few days later he said to Goroba-Dike: "Hear, the Bammana have not injured you in any way. In your place I'd turn my attention to the Pulu, your own people, the people who owe you a kingdom." Goroba-Dike said: "You are right. Where shall we go to first?" The Mabo Ulal said: "How would it be if we were to journey to Sariam where Hamadi Ardo rules?" Goroba-Dike said: "Good. Let us ride."

The two journeyed towards Sariam and dismounted at a peasant's farm not far from the town. Goroba-Dike said to his bard: "You stay here for awhile. I want to take a look at the city by myself." He took off his good clothes, borrowed the peasant's oldest rags and, looking like a beggar, set off towards the town. At a smithy he halted and said: "I am a Pulu and down on my luck. If you give me something to eat I'll be glad to help you with your work." The smith said, "The only thing I can use you for is to work the bellows." Goroba-Dike said, "Gladly." Goroba-Dike went to work with a will.

As he was working Goroba-Dike asked, "To whom does the town really belong?" The smith said, "It belongs to the Hamadi, a twig of the Ardo tree." Goroba-Dike said: "So, to the Hamadi Ardo! Has he horses, then?" The smith said: "Of course. He has many, many horses. He is a very rich man. The town and he are rich, very rich—he has everything he needs. He also has three daughters and two of them have fine brave Fulbe husbands." Goroba-Dike said: "And the third daughter? She is still a child?" The smith said: "No, she is not a child. She could even have borne many children by now. But she, Kode Ardo, is the proudest Fulbe maiden in all Massina. On her little finger she wears a silver ring and will marry only him whose little finger this ring fits. For she says that a true Fulbe must have delicate bones and tender fingers. Otherwise he can be no true Fulbe."

The next morning, as on every morning, all the well-bred young Fulbe warriors met in front of Hamadi Ardo's house. They sat or stood and chatted among themselves. Then Kode Ardo, the small proud daughter of the king, came out of the house and among them, drew off her silver ring and sought to find among those present a man whose little finger the ring would fit. One man couldn't even get it over his fingertip, with another it reached the first joint, a third, sweating and straining, brought it as far as the second joint, but no one could slip it properly on his finger. Each would have done so if he could, for all wished to marry Kode. For to possess her [would be] a sign of racial purity. She was the king's daughter. To marry her would bring her husband great esteem.

The following morning the same thing occurred. Again there was no one among all the Fulbe, from far and near, who could slip the ring on his finger. But by this time Hamadi Ardo's patience was at an end and he told his daughter, "Now you must marry the best man at hand." The smith who had given Goroba-Dike employment was among those present and overheard the king's words. He said: "I have a man working for me. His clothes are not exactly clean and he comes from the country. He says that he is a Pulu and one can see he is a Fulbe." Hamadi Ardo said: "Bring me the man. He, too, shall try to slip my daughter's ring on his finger." The smith and a few others ran to the smithy and said to Goroba-Dike: "Come quickly. The king will speak with you." Goroba-Dike said: "What? The king will speak with me? But I cannot go, not in torn and dirty clothes like these." The smith said, "Come, the king commands."

Goroba-Dike went to the big square where the king, where Kode Ardo and all the well-born young men were standing. He went in his ragged clothes. The smith said, "Here he is!" Hamadi Ardo asked him, "Are you a Fulbe?" Goroba-Dike said, "Yes, I am a Fulbe." Hamadi Ardo said, "How are you named?" Goroba-Dike said, "That I will not say." Hamadi Ardo took his daughter's ring and said, "Try to slip this ring on your little finger." Goroba-Dike put the ring on his finger. It fitted perfectly. King Hamadi said, "And *you* must marry my daughter."

Kode Ardo began to weep and said, "I won't marry such an ugly, dirty man, a man from the country." The king said: "It was your own will. Now you must marry the man." Kode Ardo wept all day long, but she had to marry the dirty Goroba-Dike. The marriage was celebrated the same day. That night Goroba-Dike slept with his wife. The next day Kode Ardo wept. She wept the whole day and said, "Oh, what a dirty man my father married me to!"

One morning the Burdama (Tuareg) rode into the land and stole all King Hamadi Ardo's cattle and all the cattle of Sariam. The herders came running and said: "The Burdama have stolen all the cattle. Pursuit! pursuit!" Everyone snatched his weapons. Goroba-Dike lay idle in a corner. King Hamadi Ardo went to him and said, "Won't you take horse and ride to war with us?" Goroba-Dike said: "Climb on a horse? I've never sat on a horse in my life. I'm a poor man's son. Give me a donkey. I can stay on a donkey." Kode Ardo wept. Goroba-Dike climbed on a donkey and rode not after the warriors but in the other direction. Kode Ardo wept and wept. She said, "Father, Father, what misery you have brought upon me!"

Goroba-Dike rode to the farmstead where he had left his horse, his weapons and his bard. He jumped down from the donkey and said, "Ulal, I have married!" The Mabo said: "What? You have married?

Whom have you married?" Goroba-Dike said, "I have married the proudest maiden in the town, Kode Ardo, the daughter of Hamadi Ardo, the king." The bard said: "What? You were as lucky as that?" Goroba-Dike said: "Yes. But today there is something else to attend to. The Burdama have stolen my father-in-law's cattle. Now, be quick with my clothes and weapons; saddle me a horse. Then I can take a shortcut across country." Ulal did as he was told and asked, "May I go with you?" Goroba-Dike said, "No, not today." And then he rode off as fast as his horse would carry him.

Soon he overtook the others and rode parallel with them, some distance away. Hamadi Ardo's two sons-in-law and the other Fulbe saw him coming and said: "That must be Djinar, the devil. Let us win him to our cause. Then we'll be victorious and the recovery of the cattle will be assured." A few rode over to him and asked: "Where are you riding? What do you want?" Goroba-Dike said, "I ride to battle and will help him whom it pleases me to help." The men said, "So you are Djinar?" Goroba-Dike said, "Of course, I am Djinar." The men said, "Then will you help us?" Goroba-Dike said: "Why should I not help you? How many of King Hamadi Ardo's sons-in-law have you in your ranks?" The men said, "Two of them." Goroba-Dike said, "If each of them gives me one of his ears in payment, I will help you." The men said: "But that is impossible! What would people say in the town?" Goroba-Dike said: "That is very simple. All the two sons-in-law need to say is that they lost their ears in battle. They held their heads so—and received only a glancing blow. And that is honorable." The men rode back and reported to the king's two sons-in-law. At first they did not agree but finally each let an ear be cut off. Then they sent the ears across to Goroba-Dike. He put the ears in his wallet and then rode over and put himself at the head of the warriors. He told the Fulbe, "You may not say that Djinar helped you." The Fulbe said, "No, no, we won't tell."

They met the Burdama. They fought the Burdama. Goroba-Dike killed more and more and won their horses. These he gave to the king's sons-in-law. The Fulbe won the battle. Thereupon they drove the herds of cattle back towards Sariam. But Goroba-Dike rode off in another direction and returned to the farmstead where his bard waited for him. Here he dismounted, laid aside weapons and clothing, donned the old rags, swung up on the donkey and rode back to the town. As he rode through Sariam he was seen by the smith who called to him: "Keep away from my doorstep. You are no Fulbe. You are a common, ordinary bastard or a slave, but no Fulbe warrior." The smith's wife heard him and said: "Stop your fool talk. A Fulbe is a Fulbe and you're not so very wise that you could know what there might be behind it."

Meanwhile the victorious Fulbe had arrived with their recovered cattle. All greeted them with joy. Hamadi Ardo, the king, even went so far as to approach them. He said: "That's real fighting. You are still true Fulbe. Are there any wounded?" One son-in-law said: "As I attacked from the flank a tall Burdama struck at my head. I turned my head, the sword took off my ear and I was saved." The other son-in-law said: "As

I attacked on the other flank a small Burdama struck upwards at my throat. I nearly had to pay with my head. But I ducked sideways and only lost an ear. The head was saved." King Hamadi Ardo said: "It is a pleasure to hear such things—and you are heroes both. But, tell me, did anyone see my third son-in-law?" Everyone laughed and said: "See him? Why at the very beginning he rode off in the other direction. No, we did not see him."

From the other direction came Goroba-Dike on his donkey. As he drew near he struck the beast and put it to a gallop. When Kode Ardo saw him coming she wept bitterly and said, "Father, Father, what misery you have brought upon me!"

That evening the well-born young Fulbe sat in a circle and told of the deeds of the day. Goroba-Dike lay in his rags in a corner and listened to what was being said. One said, "As I, the first among the enemy, charged . . ." A second said, "When I captured the horses . . ." A third said: "Yes, you are not like Kode Ardo's husband. You are real heroes all." And the two sons-in-law had to relate again and again how they had lost their ears in the heat of battle. Goroba-Dike sat nearby and heard everything. His fingers played with the two ears in his wallet. As the night drew on he went into his house. Kode Ardo said to him: "You will not sleep with me any longer. You can sleep on the other side of the room."

The next day the Burdama attacked the town in great numbers. As soon as they appeared on the horizon all the warriors prepared for battle. But Goroba-Dike swung himself up on his donkey and galloped off in the other direction, and the people shouted, "There flees the king's third son-in-law!" Kode Ardo broke into tears and said, "Oh, Father, Father, what misery you have brought upon me!" Goroba-Dike rode to the farmstead where he had left his weapons, his horse and his bard. There he leapt in haste from his donkey and said to Ulal: "Quick, quick, saddle my horse, give me my things! Today there is really something doing. The Burdama are attacking in big numbers and there is no one there to defend the town." The bard Ulal asked, "May I ride with you?" Goroba-Dike said, "No, not today." Then he donned his other clothes, seized his weapons, sprang on his horse and galloped away.

Meanwhile the Burdama had attacked Sariam and surrounded it. One group had broken into the town and was pushing towards the king's kraal. Goroba-Dike, coming from the outside, broke through the ranks. To right and left he hurled men from their saddles, put the spurs to his horse and, leaping over all obstacles, reached his father-in-law's courtyard just as a number of Burdama had seized Kode Ardo and were carrying her off. Kode Ardo, seeing the brave Fulbe coming, called to him, "Big brother, help me, for the Burdama are carrying me off and my cowardly husband has fled!" Goroba-Dike struck down the first man with his spear. From the second he received a gaping wound but struck him down, too. Kode Ardo saw that Goroba-Dike was badly wounded. She cried, "Oh, my big brother, you have saved me, but you are wounded." Quickly she tore off half her gown and wound the cloth around Goroba-Dike's bleeding leg. Then Goroba-Dike spurred his horse once more, sprang into the thick of the Burdama, forcing them to scatter in all directions, running them through and hurling them to the ground and filling the enemy with terror. The Burdama rushed out of the town and set off in desperate flight. The Fulbe pursued them.

Goroba-Dike rode off to the farmstead where his bard Ulal waited. There he dismounted, put aside weapons and clothes and, donning his rags, returned to the city on the donkey. As he passed the smithy the smith yelled: "Look at the bastard, the dog of the street, the coward! Get a move on, you, and get away from my house!" The smith's wife said: "Stop your fool talk. The man's a Fulbe, and one should never abuse a Fulbe." The smith said: "Woman, hold your tongue. One cannot but curse a man who ran away just at the moment when every man was needed." Goroba-Dike said: "What do you expect? Ever since I've been here I've always said I was a poor man's son."

Then he put his whip to the donkey and reached the great square at a gallop. There stood King Hamadi Ardo surrounded by many Fulbe speaking of the events of the day. Kode Ardo stood there, too. When she saw Goroba-Dike riding up with such aplomb she began to weep and said, "Ah, Father, Father, why have you made my life so miserable when there are still such brave and gallant men among the Fulbe." Goroba-Dike answered, "I told your father at the very beginning that I was a poor man's son and understood nothing of horses or fighting." But Kode Ardo wept and said: "Oh, coward, miserable coward! Never shall you share my bed again!" Goroba-Dike, with complete indifference, went over and sat in a shady corner.

Till evening the Fulbe sat around and spoke of the events of the day. One said, "As I repulsed a group of the Burdama . . ." Another said, "As I scattered the Burdama there . . ." A third said, "As I put the main body of the Burdama to flight . . ." But many mocked and asked Kode Ardo: "Where was your husband then?" Kode Ardo said: "Oh, let me be. I had rather my father had married me to an ape than to such a coward. Oh, how ashamed I am!"

It was night. The Fulbe went into their houses. Kode Ardo could not sleep. She thought of her cowardly husband and of the brave stranger who had saved her. At midnight she looked over towards her husband's bed on the other side of the room. She saw that his clothes were in disarray, that the rags had fallen from his body, she saw blood! The blood dripped from a bandage around his thigh, and the bandage was a part of her dress. It was the part of her dress which she herself had torn to bind the wound of the brave Fulbe stranger. And now the bandage was around the thigh of her husband, of the man who had come back on the donkey. Kode Ardo rose, went to her husband and said, "Where did you get that wound?" Goroba-Dike said, "You think it over." Kode Ardo asked, "Who tore off her dress and used it to bind you with?" Goroba-Dike said, "Just think it over." Kode Ardo asked,

"Who are you?" Goroba-Dike said, "A king's son." Kode Ardo said, "I thank you."

Goroba-Dike said: "Do not repeat it further for the time being. Now warm up some tree-butter and dress my wound with it." Kode Ardo fetched the butter, warmed it and let it drip on the wound. Then she bandaged the wound. Afterwards she crept out, went to her mother, wept and said: "My husband is no coward—he is no fugitive—he is the man who saved the town from the Burdama today. But do not tell anyone." Then she crept back to her bed.

The next day Goroba-Dike climbed on the donkey and rode back to the farmstead where he had left his Mabo, his horse, his weapons and his clothes. He said to his Mabo: "Today is the day on which we may appear in Sariam in our true colors, the day on which we may pay our respects to the proud Hamadi Ardo. So saddle my horse and yours." Goroba-Dike dressed and took his weapons. He rode into Sariam and his bard followed him. In the great square where all the well-born young Fulbe were gathered he dismounted and his bard drove the hitching pegs into the earth. The pegs were of silver.

Goroba-Dike called his wife. She greeted him and she smiled. Then he turned to the Fulbe and said: "I am Goroba-Dike and this is my wife, Kode Ardo. I am the son of a king and I am he who, yesterday and the day before, put the Burdama to flight." King Hamadi Ardo said: "That I do not believe. We have only seen you riding on a donkey." Goroba-Dike said, "Then ask those who were in the battle." And the men said, "Yes, it is true." Only the king's two sons-in-law said, "It is not certain." Thereupon Goroba-Dike drew the two ears from his wallet and said, "Don't you recognize these ears?" And the two were silent and went away.

King Hamadi Ardo went to Goroba-Dike. He knelt before him and said: "Forgive me. Take my kingdom from my hands." Goroba-Dike said: "King Hamadi Ardo, I am no less than you. For, I, too, am of Ardo blood. And now, if I am king, it is my first order that the smith who insulted me and who is still nothing more than a smith, be given fifty strokes across the buttocks—and with a knotted stick."

And so it came to pass.

The Valiant Goroo-Bâ-Dicko

Another Fulbe, or Fulani, story about the hero
of "The Blue Blood," Goroba-Dike, whose
name is set down here in a different spelling.

In his youth, Goroo-Bâ-Dicko was fighting under the command of a great war chief. Once he arrived, at nightfall, with the rest of the host,

From Birthright of Man, *edited by Jeanne Hersch. Paris, UNESCO, 1969. Reprinted by permission of UNESCO, and of His Excellency M. Boubou Hama, on whose French translation from the original this English version is based.*

at a well near which stood a Fulani woman, as beautiful as an angel. The warriors captured her and carried her off to their camp. The chief wanted her for himself. He commanded the woman to lie down alone, away from the soldiers, where no one could come near her.

Time passed, and all the warriors were haunted by the woman's beauty. Goroo-Bâ-Dicko could not sleep. Despite the chief's orders, he crept away and approached the beautiful prisoner. He carried her off at the risk of his life, took her on his horse, and rode out of the camp. The man and the woman journeyed through the night. The hard nipples of the woman's breasts pressed into the young warrior's back. The warrior, though consumed by desire and even by real love, curbed his passion, quenching the feelings aroused by the contact of the woman. The two riders arrived on their horse at the edge of the well where the woman had been captured. The man bade her dismount, and said, "Do you know this well?" In a voice broken by emotion, the woman replied simply and calmly, "Yes, it is the well of my village."

The warrior, though visibly agitated, steeled himself to say to her, "You are free."

Time passed, and with its passing many changes took place. Goroo-Bâ-Dicko had news at last of the woman, who was the wife of a great warrior. But since his encounter with the woman at the well, the thought of her preyed on Goroo-Bâ-Dicko's mind. He lost his strength, and with it the zest for life. The image of the beautiful woman never left him. He fell ill. Wishing to find a remedy for his malady, he went to consult a soothsayer, who said: "Young man, I see the cause of your malady. One night, you carried off on your horse a young woman of matchless beauty. The hard nipples of her breasts touched your back, arousing all the power of your desire. It is this thwarted desire, the image of which haunts you, that is making you sick. Until you have lain with this woman, you will never recover; you will die of your malady."

Goroo-Bâ-Dicko set out to look for the woman he had met at the well. He went to the village. He had no difficulty in finding where the husband of his former prisoner lived. The first man he asked pointed out the dwelling of the woman's husband, who was also a warrior of renown in his country. He found the woman's husband in the midst of his followers, under a crowded penthouse. Goroo-Bâ-Dicko dismounted and greeted his host, who received him as though he were a prince. His slaves ran up and eagerly took charge of the traveller's horse. When the penthouse was empty, Goroo-Bâ-Dicko said to his host: "One night, our warriors captured a beautiful woman near the well in your village. She was to have gone to the warrior chief commanding us. The same night, I managed to approach the woman, bring her out of the camp, and take her back to the place where our warriors had captured her.

"As we rode, the breasts of the woman, whom I had taken on my horse with me, pressed into my back, arousing all the power of my desire. I fell ill. Seeking a remedy for my sickness, I consulted a soothsayer, who told me that until I had lain with this woman I should never recover; without that I should die."

The woman's husband listened to all his guest had to say. He repressed his first impulse, which was one of righteous anger. He thought for a long time. At last he said, "Would you recognize this woman if you saw her?"

Goroo-Bâ-Dicko said that he would. The woman's husband went on: "Well! She is my wife. This evening, I am supposed to go to spend the night in her house. Put on my clothes and shoes. When suppertime comes, she will bring you various dishes. You must eat no more than two mouthfuls of each, for that is what I do. When you are alone with her, you must keep your garment on. You must wait for my wife to make a gesture. When she desires you, she will undo your garment herself. Be careful to do exactly as I have said. It is essential that she should think she is with her own husband."

Goroo-Bâ-Dicko did all that he was told, and found himself with the beautiful woman from the well, desire for whom was the cause of his sickness.

At last there only remained for him to satisfy his desire. At midnight, the woman did as she was accustomed. But, for the first time, her husband refused her caress. The garment was so tightly fastened that it would not come undone. Four times she repeated her gesture, and each time the man she thought was her husband refused her. Wounded in her pride as a woman who knew she was beautiful and adored by her husband, she took no further notice of the man.

Under cover of the half-light of the approaching morning, Goroo-Bâ-Dicko departed, and the beautiful woman did not realize that she had had to do with a man other than her husband. He went to see the husband of his "mistress" for a night, who asked him calmly, "Now have you had what you desired for so long?"

Goroo-Bâ-Dicko replied promptly, "More than I could ever have hoped for, as you will see from the state the bed is in—broken under the strain of our passionate embraces."

Despite this somewhat uncouth remark, the woman's husband remained perfectly calm; he even showed towards his guest a friendliness that was not feigned. Suppressing all jealousy, he played his part to the end.

But this attitude, dictated no doubt by deep gratitude towards the man who had set his wife free, put Goroo-Bâ-Dicko in a difficult position. Because of the confidence that had been placed in him, his duty, first towards his host and then towards the woman's honor, was to behave with the same magnanimity.

The next night, the husband was alone with his wife in the house. The wife reproached him bitterly for his behavior on the previous night. Indignantly, she accused her husband of having wounded her woman's pride. Goroo-Bâ-Dicko's host therefore realized that the Fula horseman had committed no sin with his wife. The woman's honor was saved; so also was the magnanimity of Goroo-Bâ-Dicko, which was equalled only by the confidence placed in it. The firm courage shown by Goroo-Bâ-Dicko was matched by the calm confidence shown by his host.

Goroo-Bâ-Dicko went back to his village. Time passed, and finally he married. His wife bore him a baby boy, beautiful as the morning star. On the day of the child's baptism, when all was joy and gladness, a horseman with a large and boisterous following appeared before Goroo-Bâ-Dicko. It was the husband of the woman at the well, coming to visit his friend. When the latter saw who it was, he ordered his slaves to attend to the traveller's horse. They hastened to do so; and oxen, sheep, goats and camels were killed in honor of the husband of the woman at the well.

At last his followers left Goroo-Bâ-Dicko's penthouse, and he was alone with his guest, who without further delay explained the reason for his visit. "It is a serious matter," he said, "that brings me here. My wife is sick and at death's door. I have consulted the soothsayers, and they tell me that the only thing that can save her from certain death is the blood of your son. So I have come to ask for your son, whose blood is the only remedy that can restore my wife to health."

Goroo-Bâ-Dicko replied: "Be good enough to wait here. I shall return in a moment." He went and told his wife the tragic story. With superb courage, she said to her husband: "You cannot refuse to give him the child. He has come to you in unquestioning trust. Give him our son, so that he may save the life of his wife with the child's blood."

To the amazement of the assembled villagers, the baptismal ceremony was stopped. The child was placed in charge of the slave who accompanied Goroo-Bâ-Dicko's guest. He, however, had brought with them a sheep, which was tied up outside the village.

Satisfied, the two men departed, the slave carrying the baby. He walked ahead, his master following. When they reached the place where the sheep was tied up, they killed it, and soaked the baby's clothes in its blood. The master told his slave to go back to Goroo-Bâ-Dicko and give him his child's bloodstained clothes. The slave did as he was ordered. When he came into the presence of Goroo-Bâ-Dicko, he delivered his master's message, saying: "Here are the bloodstained clothes of your son. He has been killed, and his blood collected. My master bids me to thank you." When he had given his message, the slave returned to his master. He took charge of the baby again, and the child was secretly taken to the village where the husband of the woman at the well lived. This woman had borne a baby boy at the same time as Goroo-Bâ-Dicko's wife.

The two children, who were like twins, were both entrusted to her care, and she brought them up with the same motherly love. They grew up together, and when they were men they always went to battle together. They were both successful warriors, whose fame reached beyond the borders of their own land. Everywhere they were feared, and everybody talked about the two sons of Goroo-Bâ-Dicko's guest.

One day, Goroo-Bâ-Dicko's friend, accompanied by his "two sons," went again to visit him. The sons, by a fortunate chance, were as like as two peas; they might have been twins. Goroo-Bâ-Dicko's followers, remembering what had happened on the previous occasion, rose up against the visitor. "The first time you came here," they said, "you asked for Goroo-Bâ-Dicko's son, whom you sacrificed so that you could save your wife's life with his blood. What fresh misfortune do you bring us now?"

Goroo-Bâ-Dicko reproved his followers sharply. He ordered his slaves to attend to the strangers' horses. As before, oxen, sheep, goats, camels and so on were killed in honor of the visitors. Goroo-Bâ-Dicko was even more cordial than he had been on the first occasion. He behaved with sincere, wholehearted friendliness, and was delighted to see his friend again.

When his visitor was rested and refreshed, he asked to see Goroo-Bâ-Dicko and his wife. In the presence of the whole village he then said to his host's wife: "Your son is not dead. I only wanted to put you and your husband to the test. The blood you saw on your baby's clothes was sheep's blood. Magnanimous and courageous woman, can you tell which of these young men is your son?" The woman replied: "I could recognize my son anywhere. He has a scar on the right thigh." The first of the young men, when examined, had no such scar. He was the son of the woman at the well, whom Goroo-Bâ-Dicko had set free. When the turn of the second young man came, the revealing scar was found on his right thigh.

Goroo-Bâ-Dicko's wife cried, "This is my son!" She fell on his neck and they clasped each other in an ecstasy of joy, in the sight of the amazed and delighted villagers.

Sayings of the Fulbe (Fulani)

It is not his deserts that a man gets but his destiny.

Six things cannot be trusted: a prince, a river, a knife, a woman, string, and darkness.

No matter how far the town, there is another beyond it.

He who rides the horse of greed at a gallop will pull it up at the door of shame.

From Hausa and Fulani Proverbs, *by C. E. J. Whitting. Farnborough (England), Gregg, 1940.*

If death encircles the mortar, it wants not the mortar but the
    pounder.

Alive he was insufficient, dead he is missed.

A dark night brings fear, but man still more.

A Fulani will lie but he will not make a lying proverb.

The Messenger to Maftam

A SONINKE STORY

There once lived, in a certain place, a poor and unpretentious man
by the name of Mamadi. Yet, though Mamadi owned few worldly goods,
he was much respected wherever men knew of him because it was said
that he never told even the smallest falsehood.

One day Bahene, chief of the Soninke, after having heard a long
conversation about Mamadi, said in an irritated way, "Who is this man
Mamadi who is so full of virtue and cleverness that he never makes a
false statement?"

"He lives in the small village of Ogo," his councillors told him. "He
is known far and wide, because he never says a thing that isn't so."

"I believe this character is an exaggeration," the chief said. "There
is no such man, either in the desert or the plains. Have him brought
here for me to see."

So the messengers brought Mamadi to the chief, and Bahene said to
him, "Mamadi, is it true that you have never lied?"

"Yes, it is true," Mamadi said.

"It is hard to believe," Bahene said. "There is no one alive who hasn't
at some time or other said something that wasn't strictly so. Yet, the

Originally from Les Peuplades de la Senégambie, by Laurent Jean-Baptiste
Bérenger-Féraud. Paris, 1879. This liberally translated version is from The
Cow-Tail Switch, by Harold Courlander and George Herzog, © 1947 by Holt,
Rinehart and Winston, Inc. By permission of Holt, Rinehart and Winston.

people say it is true. But tell me, are you certain that you won't ever tell an untruth?"

"Yes, I am quite certain," Mamadi answered.

"How can one be so sure of such a thing?" Bahene asked. "Isn't it presumptuous to say in advance what one will do, without even considering the circumstances?"

"The circumstances are quite unimportant," Mamadi said, "for I am unable to say what is false."

"Well, you seem to be a virtuous man," Bahene said. "If your tongue is as faithful to your principles as you say, then I'm wrong in thinking there is no man who doesn't lie. But if you do lie, then you will commit an act more offensive than when an ordinary person lies, because the ordinary person makes no such virtue of his tongue. So take care, Mamadi, for the day you do tell a lie will be a bad one for you. If the Soninke people ever catch you in a falsehood, I'll have you beaten!"

When Mamadi had gone back to his village, Bahene said to his councillors: "That village man is putting on airs. He must have some virtue, since his reputation is widespread. But it requires more than virtue to tell no falsehoods, it takes cleverness as well. Mamadi's certainty that he can't tell a lie is arrogant. He needs a lesson."

Early one morning, several days later, Bahene sent for Mamadi again. The village man arrived before Bahene's house to find him and his men standing with their weapons in their hands.

"Mamadi, I need you to do a service for me. Please go to my other house in the village of Maftam to deliver a message to my wife. Tell her that we have gone hunting for antelope, and that we shall arrive at Maftam today at noon. We shall be very hungry and shall want plenty to eat. Wait there, and you will eat with us."

Bahene and his hunters started out as though to hunt, while Mamadi took the trail to Maftam, hurrying so that he would get the message there in time for the chief's wife to prepare food. But as soon as Mamadi was out of sight, Bahene turned around and went back to his house. He put down his weapons, and said to the men in his hunting party: "Well, I have changed my mind. We won't go hunting after all. Nor will we go to Maftam today. This country fellow Mamadi who carries the message to my wife believes that he can't tell an untruth. We'll see. He will tell my wife that we are hunting and that we are going to bring an antelope. He will tell her that we shall arrive at noon, and that we will be very hungry. But none of these things will happen. When we finally get there we shall have a great laugh, for the man's wisdom isn't as great as his virtue. And then Mamadi shall be beaten for his arrogance."

Mamadi hurried to Maftam. It was three hours away on foot. When he arrived he went to Bahene's wife and said to her, "I am carrying an urgent message from Bahene."

"What is it?" she asked him.

"Of that I am not sure," Mamadi said.

"How can you carry a message of which you aren't sure? What are you supposed to tell me?"

"It is likely, rather, or so it seemed, perhaps, possibly, or, on the other hand more or less certainly, probably less than more, or more than less, that Bahene went hunting."

"It's not very clear," Bahene's wife said. "Did he or didn't he?"

"It's the way I said," Mamadi went on. "When I saw him and the hunters they were clearly going hunting. I could tell by the way they stood around with their weapons in their hands. Yet of course people sometimes stand around like that when they have just returned from the hunt. It's not likely that they just returned from the hunt, though, because there wasn't any meat, but of course they could have hunted and not found any game, so I suppose they were going hunting instead of coming back, more or less, to be sure, somewhat, none the less, however, or at least that was the general impression that was to be gained from the conversation, which was fairly explicit, in a way . . ."

"Try not to get excited," Bahene's wife said. "I don't yet understand whether he is going hunting or not. But what other news is there?"

"Well, it would be wise to be prepared to cook an antelope, of some sort, just about, in case they catch one, although certainly that is Bahene's general intention, possibly, most likely, that is, in the event they have gone hunting."

"Of all the available messengers, Bahene had to pick you!" Bahene's wife said in disgust. "What else is there to know, almost?"

"Oh, yes, there won't be much time, it would seem, and Bahene's hunting party will assuredly, in all likelihood, be somewhat, or exceedingly, or conceivably hardly at all, hungry, when they arrive here exactly or approximately at noon, if they do, although it is most probable, and there is no grave doubt that they won't, even though some question arises as to the certainty, of which there could be some doubt, probably . . ."

"Wait! Stop a moment!" Bahene's wife cried out. "So far I haven't learned a thing! Is there something more precise you can tell me?"

"Something more?" Mamadi continued. "Oh, yes. I am to wait for him here until he arrives, if that is possible, or even likely, or otherwise . . ."

"Stop your babbling!" Bahene's wife said. "Is he coming or isn't he? And when will he be here?"

"Well, now, as I said before, more or less clearly than I might have, somewhat, or not altogether, it appears, seemingly, though not conclusively, or even assuredly, that Bahene might, at least ought to, sooner or later . . ."

"Never mind!" Bahene's wife interrupted. "Tell me no more! The more you say the less I know!"

Then Mamadi lay down upon a mat to await the chief's arrival. Noon came and went, but Bahene and his hunters didn't appear. Night came, then morning, and finally the chief arrived in Maftam with his following. They all laughed as they saw their messenger waiting for them in the court.

"Well, our meal is perhaps a little spoiled, but no matter," Bahene said, "for we have proved that even a most virtuous man may allow his tongue to speak a lie, and that this man's arrogance is more noteworthy than his virtues."

"How is that?" Bahene's wife asked.

"Why, he told you that we had gone hunting, when we hadn't, and that we would be here yesterday noon, when we weren't, and that we would bring an antelope, which we didn't. So now he is to be beaten as a lesson to him."

"No," the chief's wife said, "he said that you would do this or you wouldn't, that it was likely or unlikely, or certain or uncertain. He delivered the message, but he gave it with so many qualifications and exceptions that I really didn't get any sense out of him at all."

Bahene was crestfallen. It was he, not Mamadi, who was made ridiculous in public. So he had presents given to Mamadi, and said to him: "I was wrong, Mamadi. You are, in truth, a virtuous and wise man. I know now what others already knew, that you will never tell a lie."

"That is quite true," Mamadi replied. "I never never shall, presumably, it is certain, probably. . . ."

KANEM-BORNU

The Two Traders

A KANURI TALE

Two men were traders inside a town and both made money. One spent his money but the other saved his. They left the town and set off home. The one that had a load put his load in the fork of a tree. His friend, the poor man, said, "I'll take your load for a bit, let us continue our journey to the gate of the city." When they got there, the owner said, "I want my load." The other man said, "I don't understand." The owner said, "I shall complain to the king about you." The king said, "What is the matter?" The owner said the load was his load. Then the king asked the friend, but he made uncouth noises, meaning I am deaf, I don't understand, I am dumb. The king said, "This load belongs to

This tale and the following Kanuri items are from The Languages and Peoples of Bornu, *by P. A. Benton, London, Frank Cass and Co., 1968. Reprinted by permission of the publishers.*

him" [the deaf and dumb man]. The real owner went away and told his
story to a certain old man. The old man said, "Let us go to the king's
seat of justice." They went. They sat down. The king questioned the
real owner, who said, "This old man knows the deaf and dumb language." The king said, "What is the matter? Do you understand the
language?" He said, "Yes, I do." The dumb man made uncouth noises.
The old man said, "He says your mother is a—." The man said, "No, no,
I didn't curse you." The king said, "Oh, you do understand." The king
said, "Take the load and give it to the real owner." The king said, "Flog
the dumb man, flog him with a whip; he is a liar, tie him up."

The Sau Hunter

A KANURI STORY

> The Sau people, according to Kanuri tradition,
> were a race of giants whom the Kanuri found
> in possession of Bornu when they first arrived
> in that region from the east. The legend of
> aboriginal giants is found among many peoples
> in the eastern Sudan, and among the nomadic
> populations of northern Ethiopia. The Mensa,
> for example, speak of giants called Rom who
> once lived in the lands south of the Red Sea.
> They point out old grave sites marked by rings
> or piles of large stones as the grave sites of the
> Rom. The Old Testament, likewise, contains
> fragments of tales of the giants. The David and
> Goliath story features one of these giants. And
> the Israelites encounter a population of giants
> while passing through the wilderness during
> their flight from Egypt.

This story is told of the Sau. Having killed two elephants, a Sau slung
them on a stick which he placed on his shoulder, with one elephant
hanging in front and the other behind. A friend, meeting him, asked,
"What do you have there?" And the first Sau answered, "Just a little
meat."

A Chronology of Kings and Migrations in Kanem-Bornu

AS SET DOWN BY A SCRIBE IN THAT COUNTRY IN THE
EIGHTEENTH CENTURY

The Sar. [Siriki, meaning king of] Bornu and Sar. Fika both originally
came from Yemen. They quarrelled about a gazelle on the shores of the
Tchad. The people of Fika got up from Tchad and went east to Dala,

and stayed there one year. From Dala they went to Kilba, and stayed there one year. They got up from Kilba and went to Biu, and stayed there (length of time unknown, but short). They got up from Biu and went southward to Geri, and stayed there one hundred and two years. From Geri they went to Kami, which is quite close, and stayed there ninety years. From Kami they went to Ngegi, close to the Benue, and stayed there one year. From Ngegi they went to Njimbum, also close to the Benue (length of stay unknown, but short). From Njimbum they went to Mazua, which is west of Njimbum, and away from the river (length of stay unknown, but short). From Mazua they got up and returned to Njimbum, and stayed there one year: the Sar. Borlawa named Donomasha died at Njimbum, and was succeeded by a man called Apa. The Borlawa then got up and went to Kadibu, one day southwest of Fika: Apa died at Kadibu and was succeeded by a man named Barma. The Borlawa then got up and went to Toriwel near Ngalda, close to the river Gongola. Barma died there, and was succeeded by Zommo. From Toriwel they went one day northwards to Chalam. They left Chalam and went to Kadibu Kupti, then to Karajiji, where Zommo died, and was succeeded by Mai Disa Bunowo. They then went to Geldabo, half a day west of Fika: they remained there seven years. They then went to Lariski, then to Daniski, from whence they drove out the Gamawa, and where seven years later Bunowo died, and was succeeded by his son Bunowo, who reigned thirty years, and was succeeded by his son Wainyi

was succeeded by his son Wainyi		"	2 "
"	Barma	"	17 "
"	Gando	"	34 "
"	Langoa	"	17 "
"	Barma	"	1 "
"	Mele Monso	"	17 "
	(Monso his mother's name)		
"	Halgo	"	19 "
"	Ambanga	"	11 "
"	Mama	"	35 "

(Borlawa became Musulmi in his time; in consequence of a visit by Mai Mama to Birni [Gaserregomo, ancient capital of Bornu], he brought a Mallam back with him called Moman Shuwa, whose descendants still live in the town: Mallam Aji Momadu is descended from him in the female line.)

was succeeded by his brother Bawa Kai,		who reigned	10 years	
	(Kai his mother's name)			
"	son	Mele	"	25 "
"	brother	Ibrahima	"	5 months
"	"	Mama	"	6 years
"	"	Adam	"	7 "
"	"	Momadi	"	10 "
"	"	Momadi	"	5 "
"	"	Suliman	"	3 "

was succeeded by his son		Aji,	who reigned	7 years
"	brother	Langoa	"	6 "
"	son	Usuman	"	8 months
"	"	Momadi	"	3 years
"	"	Mele	"	1 "
"	great uncle,	Ibraihima	"	14 "

(Ibraihima got up from Daniski to Fika: he is son of Langoa)

was succeeded by his son		Adam,	who reigned	21 years
"	great uncle	Idrisa	"	13 "

(son of Suliman)

"	son	Momadi	"	10 years & 3 months
"	"	Ismaila	".	4 years & 2 months
"	"	Momadi	"	11 years
"	"	Aji	"	8 months
"	"	Mohama	"	3 years
"	"	Suliman	"	18 "
"	"	Idrisa	"	6 "

still reigns

How The Kanuri Mark the Time of Day

just before cockcrow	tawa
morning	subba
early morning	subba fajer
full day (7–11 A.M.)	balte
midday	kausu dabu
2 P.M.	zuhur
4 P.M.	ashur
3–5:30 P.M.	kajiri
sunset	magarib
evening	lishar
night	{ durtu buni
midnight	dabu bunibe
2 A.M.–5 A.M.	kete
6 A.M.–6 P.M.	dubdo

THE HAUSA

An Account of Their Origin

This account of the origin of the Hausa people
as a distinct society or culture was set down in
the Hausa language early in the twentieth century by a learned malam, or scribe, named
Shaihu. The enterprise was part of the study of
the Hausas then being made by the renowned
student of West African life, Robert Sutherland
Rattray. The account clearly is a written ver-

From Hausa Folk-Lore, Customs, Proverbs, *by R. Sutherland Rattray. Oxford,
The Clarendon Press, 1913.*

sion of Hausa oral traditions. It contains elements of myth-legend, but also a great deal
that can be described as real events remembered or half-remembered. Rattray himself described this document as "a short history, pur-
porting to give the origin of the Hausa nation
and the story of their conversion to the Mohammedan Religion."

In the name of Allah the Compassionate, the Merciful, and may the
peace of Allah be upon him, after whom there is no prophet. This is the
history of the Hausa nation. It has been familiar to everyone from the
time of their grandfathers and grandmothers, and is a thing which has
been handed down from the malamai (learned men) and the elders.
Any account other than this one is not authentic. If a questioner ask of
you, "Where did the Hausa people have their origin?" say, "Truly their
origin was the Barebari and Northerners." And this is the account of
how this came to pass.

The king of Bornu had a horse with a golden horn. This horse did not
neigh just at any time, but only on Fridays. If it neighed you would say
it was a tornado. It was hidden away in a house. Now the king had a son.
He (the son) continually gave him who looked after the horse money
and robes in order that he might persuade him to bring his horse out,
and they should come, and he should mate the horse with his mare. And
it was always thus. And one day the man who was looking after the horse
took the horse out and brought it. The king's son too took his mare out.
They went into the forest and the mare was covered.

Now the king has had previously said that whoever was seen with a
foal from this horse at his house, he would have his throat cut. Things
remained at this, and one day the mare gave birth, and nothing happened till the colt grew up, when one day the king's horse neighed,
then the young horse answered. And the king said, "At whose ever
house they see it let that person be killed, and do not let him be brought
before me." Then the councillors scattered to make search in the town.
They were searching for the young horse. And they came to the house
of the king's son, and behold as it were the king's horse with its golden
horn. Then the councillors said, "The king has said we must come with
you."

Then the king's son lifted his sword. He cut down two men, the
remainder were scattered. Then he saddled up the young horse. He
mounted. The king ordered he should be seized and brought before
him. The whole town mounted their horses and followed him. They did
not come up with him. He has gone his way. The king, moreover, has
given orders that his own horse is not to be mounted, and if not his
horse, then there was not the horse to overtake him. The king's son
went on and eventually dismounted in the country of Daura. He saw
the daughter of the king of Daura, she possessed the town. He stayed

with her. And one day she said she wanted him in marriage and he too said he loved her. So they married. The king's daughter became with child. She bore a child, a son. She weaned it. She was again with child and bore a girl. And that was the origin of the Hausa nation.

The Barebari and Daura people were their ancestors. But the Mohammedan religion, as far as that is concerned, from Bornu it came. Hausas and Barebari and whatever race you can name in the West were at first in early times pagans. Then the malamai (scribes) said that this is what happened: There was a certain man away there at Bornu from among the children of their royal house, his name was Dalama. When he came to the throne he was called Mainadinama, the meaning of that is, "a chief more powerful than any other." After he had reigned for some months then he sent a messenger to the Caliph. Now at this time Abubakari-Sidiku, the blessing of Allah be upon him, he was Caliph. You have seen the beginning of his being sent, referring back to that man Mainadinama, was that he was hearing about Mohammedanism before he succeeded to the kingdom. Behold the name of his envoy whom he sent, his name was Gujalo. At the time when the envoy came he found the Caliph's attention occupied with a war. He said nothing to the envoy. All he said was, "Remain here." Then he did not again remember his words because his mind was so occupied with words of the war of the father of the twins. The messenger remained there till the messenger died.

After three months and a few days then the Caliph Abubakari Sidiku he too died. After some months Umaru Ibunuhutabi was set up. He was the caliph after Abubakari Sidiku. Then he called to mind the report of the envoy and his death. Then they held a consultation, they his friends who remained. They joined their heads about the question of sending an envoy to Bornu. Umaruasi was sent with manuscripts of the Koran. It was said the writing of Abdulahi the son of Umoru the Caliph, and turbans and a sword and spears and shields and the kingly fez and such things and plates; all these presents from the Caliph to Mainadinama. When the envoy drew near he sent to them one to acquaint them of the news of his coming.

The king of Bornu and his men mounted their horses and met him afar off. When he (the envoy) entered his town, then he bound the turban on him, he was established in his right to the kingdom, he was given the name of the king of Bornu, the king gave him everything he was told to give him, because of the presents which the envoy had been sent with for him. He lived among them. He was instructing the people of Bornu in the creed of Allah and the names of His messengers, may the salvation and trust of Allah be assured to them. They continued to honor him, to the extreme that honor could be carried. They sought a blessing by eating the remains of his meals and his food and from the spot he set his feet. Half of them were seeking blessing from the mucus from his nose and his spittle by rubbing it on their persons. They were climbing the roofs in order to see him. They also sought blessing by touching his robes and his slippers and his whip, until it was even said they looked for a blessing from his beasts, and the remains of their fodder and their dung.

Now he wrote manuscripts for them in the writing of his own hand, the blessed one. He lived amid such works up to the very end of his sojourn and this went on till he was informed that, "Other owners of another land are behind you and are wishing for the Mohammedan religion, should they see you they would follow you." He did not give this report credence until he had sent one to spy out the land, his name is unknown. The spy went and travelled over Hausa-land. He made secret inquiries, he heard they were praising the Mohammedan faith and that they wished for it. He returned and gave Umaru Ibunuasi the news. Umaru Ibunuasi told his people. He said they must go and preach the Mohammedan religion. They agreed. Then he made preparations. He sent Abdulkarimu-Mukaila to Kano. About three hundred men, Arabs, followed him. When Abdulkarimu was near to the people of Kano then he sent one to inform them. The messenger came and said, "Tell them the envoy of the envoy has come."

When he came to them he told them what message he had been sent with. They believed him, they received the thing which he had brought. Now at this time Kano was an enclosed town but not a walled town, the name of the man at Kano was Muhamadu Dajakara at the time when Abdulkarimu alighted amongst them. Abdulkarimu wrote them books in the writing of his own hand, the blessed one, because he had not come to them bringing books from Umaru Ibunulasi. And thus it has come to be reported that every one who wished to be able to write well let him set out towards Bornu and remain there till he had learned to write and then return home. But Abdulkarimu continued to instruct them the laws of Allah and the commands of the law until they made inquiries about things which were not to be found in Arabia. He did not know what answer to give them. Then he said to them to leave the matter open till he returned to Arabia. Among the things they were asking about were panthers, and civet cats, and rats, and servals, and tiger cats, and suchlike, whether clean or unclean.

He lived with them many months and every day instructed them well in the Koran and the Traditions, till at length he was informed, "There is another town near this town, it is called Katsina, should the people of the town see you they would believe you and him who sent you." When he heard them speak thus, then he made ready. He set out himself to go to the town. When they got news of his coming, then they met with him afar off. When he alighted among them he taught them about what he had come to instruct them in. He instructed one who was to write books for them. It was said, speaking of him, he did not write the Koran with his own hand, and because of this the Kano people surpass the Katsina in their knowledge of the Koran till today. Then, after the completion of his work at Katsina, he went back, going to Kano, and remained there a short time. Then when he thought of returning to go to Bornu he said to them, "Shortly I shall return to you with the answer to what you were asking about." Then he rose up and went away.

But many among his people did not follow him, only a few among them followed him. The rest remained and continued to perform great deeds in Kano. Their descendants are found and known in Kano until today, till people called them seraphs, but surely they were not seraphs, they were just Arabs. Of a truth Abdulkarimu has set up a judge in Kano, and one to lead in prayers, and one to slaughter livestock, and one who was to instruct the youths in the Koran, and one to call them to prayer. He made lawful for them that which Allah had made lawful, and forbade that which Allah had forbidden. When he returned to go to Umaru Ibunulasi he gave him an account of what they had asked him about. And Umaru Ibunulasi was silent on the subject till he returned to go to the Caliph and then he sent an answer to it after six months had elapsed. He made lawful for them half of it, half he made unlawful. But Abdulkarimu did not return to Bornu after his return to their (Abdulkarimu's) town or to Kano. Thus also Umaru Ibunulasi, but he ruled over Egypt after his return home.

Now the remainder of the towns were coming in, half of them to Kano in order to know about the new religion, and half also to Katsina, until the creed filled all Hausa-land. Now the Kibi country, speaking of them, they refused to adopt the Mohammedan religion, they continued in their paganism. They persisted in it. Their kings, these were their names, Barbarma, Argoji, Tabariu, Zartai, Gobari, Dadafani, Katami, Bardo, Kudamdam, Sharia, Badoji, Karfu, Darka, Gunba, Katatar, Tamu. All these refused the Mohammedan creed after his advent into the land of the Hausas. Then at the time when Zaidu came to the throne he became a Mohammedan and those who were with him. The Kabi country became Mohammedan up to the time of Bata-Musa. These were the kings of Kabi under the Mohammedan régime. The first of them was Zaidu, then Muhamadu, Namakata, Sulaimana, Hisrikoma, Abdulahi, Dunbaki, Alia, Usmanu, Chisgari, Barbarmanaba, Muwashi, Muhamadu-Karfi, Bata-Musa. After them Fumu ruled. He turned Mohammedanism into paganism. These were they who became pagans. The first of them was Fumu, then Kautai, Gunba, Sakana-Murtamu, Kanta, Rataini, Gaiwa, Gado, Masu, Chi-da-gora, Gaban-gari, Maikebe, Marshakoki, Lazimu, Mashirana, Makata. These were they who all continued in paganism. At the time when Kanta ruled he revived the Mohammedan religion and inquired of the learned men the contents of their books. He established the faith in his time and in that of them who followed him, till the whole of the Kabi country became Mohammedan. These were their names, Kantahu, Gofe, Dauda, Hamidu, Sulaimana, Malu, Ishaka, Muhamadu-Nashawi, Amuru, Muhamadu-Kabe, Kantanabaiwa, Muhamadu-Shifaya, Hamidu. All these continued in the Mohammedan faith.

When Barbarma became king he changed the Mohammedan religion and became a pagan. Paganism lasted up to the time of Hudu. He was the one Usmanu the son of Fodio made war against. He drove him out and pursued him till he slew him near to Kebi. Buhari the son of Abdu-Salimi, he it was who slew him. He was the king of Jega. His family are its kings till today. It is finished. But as for Kano in it the faith continued after his, Abdulkarimu's, return home. The faith continued to increase always with force and power. And it lasted on such footing for many years until the time of Mainamugabadi. It was he who changed the order of things Abdulkarimu had set up. He set at naught the law of Mohammed, he made the kingship all-powerful, he disregarded the Mohammedan faith, he exalted fetish worship, and was arrogant. He surpassed all his predecessors in evil. Instructors endeavored to instruct him, but their admonitions were of no avail against him, but he increased in pride. He was vainglorious. He continued thus till he died.

His brother Kunbari reigned in his stead and followed in his ways. He too continued in this evil till the time of Kunfa. He also spread paganism and evildoing. It was he who married a thousand maidens. He instructed people to prostrate themselves and put earth on their heads before saluting him. He said, let not him whose name happened to be the same as that of his parents be called so, but let him be called by some sobriquet. He completely destroyed the creed, he sold free men, he built a palace, the one which the kings of Kano enter today. He did what he wished. And it was so with all the people of Kano except a very few, speaking of them, they kept to the Mohammedan faith, they were not powerful, only the Kano people did not know how to make beer, except a few among them, men in outlying villages. Thus they did not eat any animal that had died a natural death. They removed the clitoris of their women, they covered their heads with a veil. They did nothing else but this. They continued in such conduct until learned men were found in Kano, who had renounced the world, who feared Allah.

Of these learned men one his name was Muhamadu-Zari. He stood up and preached. Rumfa paid no heed to whatever admonitions he admonished them. But they planned to kill him, till at last they did kill him in the night by slaying him from behind, in the road to the mosque, and he lay there murdered, cast aside, till dawn. He was buried about eight in the morning. His grave is known in Kano, it is visited and watched over, he was called "the Kalgo man," blessings are sought by prayers being made for him. Then Abdulahi-Sako stood up to proclaim the creed after him. He was admonishing them but they paid no heed to him, except some people of no importance, but those in authority did not hear. And they frightened him so that he fled to the outlying towns in order to instruct the people of the lesser towns. Then the king sent one to seize him. They seized him, and continually flogged him till he was brought before the king. He was by this time ill and died after a few days. His grave is known, it lies behind the rock known as "the single rock," but it is not visited or watched over.

And so it came to pass that paganism existed till the time of Muhamadu-Alwali. It was he Usmanu, the son of Fodio, made war on, after he had ruled in the kingdom for seventeen years. He (Usmanu-dan-Fodio) drove him out and his men, he fled in the direction of the country on the right and none know where he settled till this day, some say Barnabarna, some say it was not there.

The learned men said that from the coming of Abdulkarimu till the coming of Usmanu, the son of Fodio, there were seventy-six kings. All their graves have remained in the town of Kano, but two of them, that of Bawa and Muhamadu-Alwali, are in Katsina. The creed continued after the return of Abdulkarimu. The faith continued to grow always and took firm hold. Men from Gobir continued to come to Katsina and were adopting the Mohammedan faith with all truth and earnestness, they embraced it, all together. The faith took hold among them also as it had taken hold in Katsina. And so it was until the time of Agarga. He was the first who changed the state of things that Abdulkarimu had established in Katsina. Instructors strove to admonish him. He heard not. He remained in his heathenism till he died. Kaura ruled the kingdom, and then his son; he followed the path his father had taken. Paganism continued till the time of Wari-mai-kworia. It was he who did evil and was most arrogant. He married one thousand maidens. He embraced evil and did not cease.

He sought for medicine in order that he might go on living in the world and not die, till at last a certain wizard deceived him, saying he would never die. That doctor did for him what he did from his knowledge of medicines. This king gave him much wealth, it was said one hundred slaves, one hundred female slaves, a hundred horses, a hundred black robes, and a hundred cattle, cows and bulls a hundred, and a thousand rams, and a thousand goats. He gave him robes which could not be counted by reason of their number, and things of this description, Allah he knows what all. In his reign two learned men made their appearance in Katsina, men who renounced the world and who feared Allah. The name of one was Muhamadu Ibnumusina, the name of the other also was Muhamadu Dunmurna. Each one among them gave instruction, such instruction as enters into the heart. He did not hear them. Then they made them afraid in order to dissuade them from preaching. They did not desist. The kings also did not pay any attention till these learned men died. In Katsina their graves are known till today, where young and old visit and guard, and at which blessings are sought by prayers for them.

Now Wari-mai-kworia, speaking of him, he lived eight years after he had had the medicine made for him to prevent his dying. He died the ninth year after taking it. When he died a quarrel about the kingdom arose among the king's sons. Half were slaying the other half until about one thousand men were killed in the town of Katsina among both free men and slaves. Then the younger brother of Wari ruled after slaying the son of Wari. He again continued in heathenism. And heathenism continued in Katsina till the reign of Bawa-Dungaimawa. It was he Usmanu, the son of Fodio, drove out of Katsina, he and his men, they went to Maradi, they settled there until today. His descendants continue to make war on the descendants of Usmanu, the son of Fodio, till today. But the men of Gobir assembled together and continued in the faith and dwelt in it till the reign of Babari. He was the first who changed the true faith, it became lax, he exalted and set up paganism and was arrogant. The preachers of the faith preached to him but he would not receive their instructions, but persisted in his heathenism till he died.

Bachira ruled over the kingdom, he did what his predecessor had done, he added to the evil he had done, and the harm, the foam from the wave of heathenism rose in the land of Gobir, its kings were proud. They sold free men, they acted as they wished until report had it that every king that ruled married one hundred maidens. But the only redeeming point was they did not know how to make beer, except a few among them, and they did not eat animals that had died a natural death, but when they greeted their kings they poured earth over their heads, they served idols. Some who cleaved to the faith were still among them, at that time only a few and without power or influence among them.

And they continued thus till the time of Bawa-jan-gwarzo. He went on in heathenism. He was arrogant till a learned man was found in his reign, one who had fled from the world, one who served Allah. He was called Alhaji-Jibrilu. It was said, speaking of him, he went from Gobir, he came to Mecca and performed the pilgrimage and resided there twenty years. It was said he lived in Egypt eighteen years. He stayed in Mecca two years, and then returned to Gobir. He instructed them each new day and night, in secret and openly. They refused the message he brought and thought to kill him. All the kings of Hausa plotted to slay him. They could not. The malamai were in Kalawa at that time, but they could not speak from their store of knowledge for fear of the chiefs. Only Alhaji-Jibrilu, speaking of him, he stood fast in preaching and strove openly and they were not able to kill him. He could not, however, prevent them doing the evil they dwelt in. And they continued in evildoing and heathenism in this reign.

Then Usmanu, the son of Fodio, was born at the time when Alhaji-Jibrilu died. Usmanu, the son of Fodio, began to preach little by little till Bawa-jan-gwarzo died. His brother Yaakubu reigned in his stead. Then Usmanu proclaimed his preaching openly till he did what all the world knows he did and finished. We have drawn the history to a close.

Allah, he is the one who knows all. It is finished.

The salvation and blessing of Allah be upon the prophet. Amen.

Hausa Religious Poetry

(EXTRACTS FROM LONG POEMS)

Where is this greatness of yours, and of your lovers? Today you lie in
the tomb.

Where is the protection by those who praised you? Today they carry
you to the place of burial.

Truly it was falsehood they spoke concerning you, they loved you not,
though even had they loved you, you would have no power today.

A line is formed, a prayer is said for you. Alas, you know nothing of what
is done, you fool.

They wash their hands thus, and their feet, they all salute one another.

They scatter in silence, they leave you in the grave. You yourself are
crying, but there is no coming out.

Your goods are divided, rejoicing is made, your goods are given to your
children, each receives something.

You are forgotten, no share is allotted to you. The suffering in the tomb
is sufficient for you.

* * *

My brother, you know that we shall die, let us understand it, let us put
quarreling aside.

For this world is not to be trusted. You escape today, have a fear for
tomorrow.

A false friend will not become true, do not act deceitfully, nor follow
a fool.

My boy, I urge you to be watchful, let the world flee away, refuse to
cling to it.

Accomplish deeds fit for the next world, make much preparation. Leave
alone the things that belong to this world, which will come to an
end.

Give up delaying, saying that it will do when you are old. Death may
come before you are old.

* * *

You who are puffed up with pride because of your relations, your kingdom, or your property, on the day when you meet with the angels
you will be confounded.

From Hausa Superstitions and Customs, by A. J. N. Tremearne. London, John
Dale Sons and Danielson, 1913. Language slightly edited.

This world, you know, is a marketplace; everyone comes and goes, both
stranger and citizen.

* * *

My friend, repent truly, and abandon falsehood, abandon deceit, leave
off drinking beer, and palm wine, and honey-beer.
Repent to God, but cease from repenting like the wildcat, which re-
pents with a fowl in its mouth, it does not put it down.

* * *

The fool would say, "This world is a virgin girl." The wise man knows
that the world is old.

Seidu the Brave

A HAUSA TALE

A man named Seidu lived in the village of Golo. Whenever the men
of his village went hunting and returned with game, Seidu said to his
wife: "Among all the hunters, I was the bravest. Single-handed I fought
with the leopard and chased the elephant. I went forward with my
spear, and the lion fled. I am the bravest of hunters."

His wife, Ladi, replied, "Did no one but you bring back meat?"

Seidu said, "Yes, because of my fearlessness, the others also had good
luck."

Again, when it was said that the enemy was approaching, Seidu went
into the bush country with the men, and when he returned, he hung
his spear on the wall and said to his wife: "The enemy came forward;
I went forward. When I ran at them, they turned and fled. My reputation has spread everywhere. I am the bravest of warriors. What is your
opinion?"

Ladi answered, "It is so."

There was a funeral one time in another village, and some of the
women of Golo wished to go. But the men were working in the fields

and could not leave their work. Ladi told the women: "My husband is the bravest of men. He will take us through the forest."

She went to Seidu, saying: "The women who are going to the funeral agree that you are the one to take them through the forest. Will you go?"

Seidu said: "From one day to another no one mentions my courage. But when courage is needed, people ask, 'Where is Seidu?' Nevertheless, I will come."

He took his spear and went with the women through the forest.

There were warriors of the enemy in the forest. They were hunting game. When they saw Seidu coming with the women, they said, "Look how the man struts like a guinea cock. Let us strike fear into him."

They waited near the trail, and when the people of Golo came, the hunters came out of the brush before them and behind them.

Seidu shouted: "We are surrounded! Run for the trees!"

The women ran among the trees. Seidu ran with them. But there were enemy among the trees, and they seized all the people from Golo.

The leader of the hunters said to Seidu's wife, "What is your name?"

She replied, "Ladi."

He said: "Ladi is a name used by the women of our tribe also. Because you are called Ladi, we shall not hurt you."

He said to another woman, "What is your name?"

Seeing how good it was to be named Ladi, the woman replied, "My name too is Ladi."

The leader of the hunters said, "A good name; we shall not hurt you."

He asked another woman, and she too replied, "Ladi." All of the women were asked, and all of them answered, "My name is Ladi."

Then the leader of the hunters spoke to Seidu. "All the women of your village are named Ladi. It is a strange custom. In our village each woman has a different name. But you, guinea cock who leads the guinea hens, what are you called?"

"I," Seidu said, "I too am called Ladi. My name is Ladi also."

When the hunters heard Seidu's reply, they laughed. The leader of the hunters declared: "No, it is not possible. Ladi is a woman's name. You are a man with a spear. Do not tell me that the men of your village are also called Ladi?"

Seidu said, "No, no, only the women are called Ladi."

The hunters said, "How then are you called Ladi?"

Seidu looked one way and another way, but he saw no chance of escape. He said: "You see, appearances are deceiving. I also am a woman."

The enemy laughed. They could not stop laughing. The women of Golo laughed too.

Seidu's wife spoke. She said: "He speaks badly of himself. He is the courageous Seidu, the famous Seidu."

Seidu said then, "Yes, it is so."

A hunter said, "People say that Seidu claims to be the bravest of all men."

"No," Seidu replied, "it is no longer so. *Formerly* I was the bravest of all men. Today it is different. From now on I shall be only the bravest in my village."

The hunters let them go. Seidu and the women went to the funeral, and they returned afterwards to their own houses. When they arrived in Golo, everyone was laughing at Seidu. Instead of calling him by his name, they called him Ladi. He went into his house and closed the door. Whenever he came out, they laughed. He could not hide from the shame.

At last he sent his wife to tell them this: "Seidu who was formerly the bravest of men was reduced to being the bravest in his village. But from now on he is not the bravest in the village. He agrees to be only as brave as other people."

So the people of Golo stopped ridiculing Seidu. And thereafter he was no braver than anyone else.

Life and Death

A HAUSA TALE

There were two old men who journeyed together. The name of one was Life, and the other was called Death. They came to a place where a spring flowed, and the man who owned the spring greeted them. They asked him for permission to drink. He said: "Yes, drink. But let the elder drink first, because that is the custom."

Life said, "I, indeed, am the elder."

Death said, "No, I am the elder."

Life answered: "How can that be? Life came first. Without living things to die, Death does not exist."

Death said: "On the contrary, before Life was born everything was Death. Living things come out of Death, go on a while, and then return to Death."

Life replied: "Surely that is not the way it is. Before Life there was no Death, merely that which is not seen. The Creator made this world out of the unseen substances. When the first person died, that was the beginning of Death. Therefore you, Death, are the younger."

Death argued: "Death is merely what we do not know. When the Creator created, he molded everything out of what we do not know. Therefore Death is like a father to Life."

They disputed this way, standing beside the spring. And at last they asked the owner of the water to judge the dispute. He said: "How can one speak of Death without Life, from which it proceeds? And how can one speak of Life without Death, to which all living things go? Both of you have spoken eloquently. Your words are true. Neither can exist without the other. Neither of you is senior. Neither of you is junior. Life

Author's collection.

and Death are merely two faces [masks] of the Creator. Therefore you
are of equal age. Here is a gourd of water. Drink from it together."

They received the gourd of water. They drank. And after that they
continued their journey. What say you of these two travellers? They go
from one place to another in each other's company. Can one be the
elder and the other the younger? If you do not know, let us consider
other things.

The Son of the Hunter

A HAUSA STORY

This tale is about a hunter and a chief. There was once a certain man
who had no other work but hunting, both he and his son. One day they
went to the bush. They did not find anything but a rat, and his son threw
the rat away. But they became hungry and the father said, "Roast our
rat for me, let us eat." The boy said, "Oh, but I have thrown it away."
The father cursed him. He lifted his axe and struck the boy. The boy
fell unconscious. The father went his way, and left him. The boy came
round, he rose up, and went home by night. He found them asleep, so
he entered the room and lifted his belongings. He took the road, and
was going to a certain town. When he reached the town it was night;
he entered into the town. Everyone was asleep. He proceeded into the
middle of the town until he reached the chief's house. He entered until
he was right in the house, naked, without clothes, without trousers, and
he met the chief.

The chief said, "From where?"

The boy replied, "From such and such a village."

And the chief said, "Is it well with you?"

The boy said: "Both I and my father went to the bush to walk and
shoot. We did not find anything but one single rat, he gave it to me to
keep, I forgot it somewhere. When we became hungry, then he said,
bring the rat that we may roast it and eat. And I said, I have dropped
it, I do not know where. Thereupon he became angry. He lifted his axe
and struck me. I fainted. When evening came, then I recovered and
rose up, and came here."

Now the chief had gone to war, and his son had been captured and
killed. The chief had no male child. And the chief said, "Now will you
not keep a secret for me?"

The boy said, "What kind of a secret?"

The chief said: "I have no male child. When dawn comes I shall say
you are my son, who was caught at the war, and that you ran away and
came back."

From Hausa Folk-Lore, Customs, Proverbs, *by R. S. Rattray. Oxford, The Clarendon Press, 1913.*

The boy said, "That is surely not difficult."

The chief entered his room and took up his gun and fired it. It was in the middle of the night. And the mother of the house came out and said, "King, lion who causes fear, what is the gun you are firing in the night?"

The chief said, "So-and-so has returned."

Thereupon the mother of the house raised the sound of joy, and the town rose up, they were asking, "What has happened at the chief's house, that they are firing a gun at this time of night?" It was said that the chief's son had come, he who had been caught at the war. And they said, "Indeed! indeed!"

When it was dawn the boy bathed and the chief gave him gifts and he came forth.

Among the councillors some said, "It is not his son." Others said, "It is his son." Now one day the headmen joined their heads together, saying, "Wait, and we shall see if it is really his son." Then they added goods to those their children already had. They put the saddles on the war-horses for them. The children mounted, and the fathers said to them, "Go to the chief's house and call his son, and say you are going to take horse exercise." And they said, "When you have gone and galloped and pulled up, you must dismount, kill your horses, and come home." Each one gave his son a sword and he slung it on his shoulder. They came to the chief's house and called the boy.

Now truly some talebearer has overheard, he went and told the chief. The chief made similar preparation and put the things aside, and said, "If the naked man can dance, much more can the man with the cloak." The chief called the boy, told him. He said, "When you have gone, everything you see they have done, do you also do."

So the boys came, and called the son of the chief, and they set off. As they went they galloped; then they dismounted and killed their horses. So the son of the chief he too galloped, pulled up, dismounted, killed his horse. They went home.

The headmen said, "It is a lie, tomorrow you go back."

When it was dawn they came and called the boy. The chief caused his bodyguard to fasten the saddle on a great horse for him. They went off; as they went they galloped. Then they dismounted, killed their horses. The chief's son also, when he had galloped, then he killed his horse, and they returned home.

Then the sub-chiefs gave their sons slaves, beautiful maidens, and said, "Take them to the midst of the bush and slaughter them."

The talebearer again went and informed the chief, and the chief gave his son two female slaves, saying, "Go, whatever you see they have done, do you do too." They went to the bush. The sons of the headmen killed their female slaves, the chief's son also killed his, they returned home. And people said, "It is his son."

And so time went on, till one day the boy's father came; he was carrying his quiver slung. He met the councillors; he heard all he wished to know, and then passed on till he came before the chief. The boy was sitting by the chief's side. The hunter greeted them. And he said to the boy, "Are you not going to get up that we may go and dig for our rats?"

The boy was silent. Then the chief rose up, entered the house, called them. He said, "Hunter, keep the secret for me, and whatever you wish I will give you." The hunter refused. The chief entreated him. The chief said, "Everything in the world I will give you, one hundred of each." But the hunter refused.

The chief said, "Saddle up for me." They saddled, they saddled a horse for the boy. The chief gave the boy a sword, and slung it across his shoulder. They went off to the bush. The chief halted and said to the boy, "Either you kill me, and take these goods and give them to your father, and return to the town and enter into your kingship; or you kill your father, and you and I will go back and live as before."

The boy was distracted, not knowing what to do.

Now if it were you, O white man, among them whom would you kill? If you do not know whom you would kill, there it is. Off with the rat's head.

The Friend and the Lion

A HAUSA STORY

This story is about some young men who were friends. Some boys made a covenant of friendship; they lived together, and were inseparable. They had their maidens in an outlying village. Always they used to go together and bring them. On one occasion, one of his friends did not go, so only one went to bring the maidens. When he went, he brought back the maids. As they were going along, they met a lion; and it knocked down and lay on one of the girls, but he, he drew his sword and cut at the lion's head. The lion died, and he found the maiden was not dead. And he told her to lie down beneath the lion along with him, and one of them was to go and tell his friend. So she consented, and ran off and found he has begun to sleep. She roused him, and he said, "Where are So-and-so and So-and-so?" And she said, "They are out there, a lion has killed them." And he rose up, he did not take anything with him, he went along and came and reached where the lion was; it was above them. He did not hesitate, but sprang and climbed on the lion. He thought it was alive. Truly it was dead. Then his friend rose up and said, "Rise, So-and-so, you have proved yourself a free-born man." So they lifted up the maiden and went home. Now among them who was better than another? If you do not know, there it is. Off with the rat's head.

From Rattray, ibid.

TWO GIZO TALES

Gizo is the spider trickster hero (or villain) of
the Hausa. His exploits include numerous adventures that are part of the repertoires of
other African tricksters—the spider of the Akan
people, the tortoise of the Yoruba, and the hare
of Central Africa. In addition, the two Gizo
tales given here contain motifs that are widely
dispersed in folklore—the tug-of-war, the
mock sunrise, and the taking back of the feathers.

The Spider and the Crows

This is a story about the spider and the crows. A certain year there
was a famine, above and below there was no food. The crows used to
go to the middle of a river and pluck figs from a tree that stood in the
water and bring them home and eat them. One day the spider heard
about this, and when they (the crows) came back home, then he took
up a piece of broken pot, saying he was going to get some fire. He then
sought for some wax and plastered his testicles with it and went off to
the crows' home. He came on them eating figs, and they were throwing
some down on the ground. Then he went on top of the figs, and sat
down. He greeted them. He rose up. The figs stuck to his bottom. He
drew some hot ashes from the fire and went home. They did not know
what he had done. He took the figs home and put them aside. He put
out the fire, and went back, and sat down on top of the figs; they stuck
to his bottom. He drew out some fire. He took them home and put the
figs aside. He put out the fire and returned again and did so three times.
A crow said: "What kind of way is that to get fire? You are going, and
quenching it on purpose and coming back again." But the spider said,
"No, no, I am not quenching it, it died out itself." The crow said, "It is
a lie; because of these figs you keep coming back." The crow picked out
a fig and gave him, and said, "If it was not for your evil nature, then we
might have gone together to where the fig tree is." And the spider fell
down with sobs: "É! ē! ē! Since my parents have died, we have not made
any friends again. É! ē! ē! No, when my parents were about to die, they
said I must make friends with people; whoever got food was to give his
fellow creature." And the crow said: "Stop crying, go home. When it is
dawn at the very first streak come, we will take you." The spider said,
"It is well." He dried his tears and went home.

When people were having their first sleep then the spider collected
straws and kindled a fire towards the east, and the east became bright.
Then he came and found the crow asleep, and he said, "Early dawn has

From Rattray, ibid.

come." But the crow said: "Come now, spider, it is you who made a fire. Off with you, in the meantime till the fowls have crowed, then you can come." On his going off he slept a little; then he got up and opened the fowl house, and was beating them, and they were crowing. Then he came and met the crow, and said, "You have heard the fowls are crowing." The crow said: "Come now, spider, was not it you who were beating the fowls? Off you go, and not until the muezzin has called to prayer must you come." He, the spider, went off home. On his coming, then he began to call to prayer, "Yallah is yate, yallah is yate." (Allah is great.) Then he went back, and met the crow. And she said: "Oh, no, it was you. I heard you doing it." And she said: "Go home. If it is dawn, I shall come and waken you. Do not come again."

Then the spider had patience. When dawn came then the crow came and roused him. They gave him a feather each, and they rose and went to the middle of the river and climbed the fig tree and were plucking the fruit. But the spider when he saw they were about to pick one of the figs, then he said, "That is my one, I saw it long ago; you must not pluck it." And they desisted, and he came, and plucked it and put it in his bag. And thus he did till he had plucked all the figs and let them get none. The crow who had brought him said, "All right, spider, do not you see the thing I was saying about your bad character?" And they, the crows, got angry, and snatched out their feathers from the spider and rose up and went home, and left him squatting there on top of the fig tree.

He could not think where to go, water in front, water behind. He was there till nearly sunset, and he said, "Wait, I too must jump, for it was merely a jump they the crows gave." So he jumped, but he fell into the river, plump! And it was the home of the crocodile. And the spider said, "There is no God but Allah, this is the place you are." And he commenced to cry. And the crocodiles said, "Where have you come from, that you come and are weeping?" And he said: "Children, leave off asking. Since the days of your grandfather, that you may understand I must tell you I was then a boy, I was lost. I was sought for till they were weary, and have not been seen except today when Allah brought me here." He was weeping, with tears falling splashing, till they said, "Stop crying like this now, for now you have come home." Then they gave him a room where the crocodiles laid eggs.

Now among the crocodiles, one who had all his wits about him said, "Wait, let us see if it is true he is one of our family." So he said: "Let some mud gruel be made and given him. If he drinks it is true what he says, if he does not drink he is telling lies." So they made mud gruel and gave him a calabash full, which they brought him. And he said, "Children, who has shown you this kind of food of the people of long ago?" But he bored a hole in the bottom of the calabash. He dug a hole, he set down the calabash over the hole; all the gruel drained through and went into the hole. And he said, "Children, come and take what is left." And the children came and lifted up the cup, and said, "Truly he is of our family."

Now in the room where he had been put, there were the crocodiles'
eggs, one hundred and one in number. When he was going in to sleep,
then he said: "All right, children, if you have heard pop! you must say,
It is the stranger breaking wind, it is the stranger breaking wind." Of
a truth he had the evil design of eating up the crocodiles' eggs. Then
when night came the spider lifted a crocodile egg and cast it on the fire
and the egg broke pop! when it encountered the heat of the fire. The
children said, "It is the stranger breaking wind, it is the stranger breaking wind." But their parents began to scold the children, but he said,
"Leave them alone, are they not my grandchildren?" Now, every now
and then you heard pop! and, "It is the stranger breaking wind, it is the
stranger breaking wind." And so he went on till he had put all the eggs
on the fire except one solitary one. When it was dawn they were told,
"Children, lift up the eggs and let them be counted." But he the spider
said, "Stop, stop, I have lifted them." Then he went and lifted one, and
marked it. They said, "Set it down here." But he said, "No, no, let me
keep taking them back and returning with another." They said, "All
right," and he kept bringing them backward and forward; it was
marked; and he was going back and licking off the mark they had made
and returning with the same egg. And so on till he had reached one
hundred and one; then they said he had accounted for all.

Things were thus when he said: "I have seen home again. I shall set
out and get your younger brothers and my wives that I may bring them,
and we may all become one family. Whatever a man may seek for there
is nothing to compare with those who bore him." And they said: "It is
well, there is no harm in that. Come back quickly to your grandchildren, come and play with them." He said, "All right." And they said,
"Let him be escorted to the river and taken over." He was escorted and
put in a canoe. He was paddled until he reached midstream. Then one
of the crocodiles who was smart said, "Let us go and look at the eggs."
They went and looked, and saw one single egg was left. And they said,
"Let this stranger be brought back at once." And they went to the edge
of the river and were saying, "Let the stranger be brought back." The
one who was paddling was deaf, he did not hear very well. And when
they said, "Let the stranger be brought back," then the spider said,
"There you are, have you heard? They say: 'Hurry up with the stranger,
as a freshet has come down.' Make haste." And so he said till he was
across; and he went his way. That is it. Off with the rat's head.

Spider Deals with the Famine

This story is about the spider. Once there was a famine, on land and
in the water there was no food. And the spider and his children had
become thin for want of food. And things were in this state, when one
day the spider went to the elephant and said: "Chief, may Allah prolong
your life. The chief of the water, the hippopotamus, sends me to you.
She says I am to tell you to give her one hundred baskets of grain, and

I am to take them to her. When the harvest season has come she will give you a great horse. Moreover, she says these words are only for the ears of the great ones, and you must not allow anyone else to hear." The elephant said, "All right, there is no harm in that." The elephant allowed them to bring one hundred baskets of grain at once, and some youths of the elephants were allowed to lift them and take them to the edge of the river. When they had brought them then the spider said: "Lay them down here, and go back home. I must go into the water and tell the hippopotamus that she may allow her young men to come and lift them. For your part, you have finished the hardest of the work." So the elephant's young men went back home. He indeed (the spider) when they had gone off, went to his home and called his wife and children, and they carried off all the grain, and took it home.

When it was dawn, then he went to the riverbank, and entered into the water. He went to the court of the hippopotamus's house and met the councillors. He went among them, and passed on, and went till he came to where the hippo was sitting, and then he sat down, and said, "May Allah lengthen your days, O chief." The hippo said, "Amen, spider, husband of the koki [female spider], whence came you?" And the spider replied: "Behold me, I was living until just now as usual when the chief of the land, the elephant, sent and had me called to her. I went, and she sent me here to you. She bade me tell you that she has grain foods, but has nothing for making soup with, and you must give her one hundred baskets of fish. When the harvest season has come round she will give you a great horse." The hippo said, "That is all right." And the spider made haste to say: "He says, your words are only for the ears of the great, you must not mention it to anybody, and you, too, you must not ask her any more about all this till she comes and mentions it first to you." The hippo said, "There is no harm in that."

Then the hippo let them bring baskets of fish, one hundred, and boys were made to lift them and bring them to the bank of the river; and they set them down there. Then the spider said, "It is all right, you go back now. I must go and call the elephant's young men to come and lift them." But the hippo's young men said, "If we went off something else might come and eat it up." The spider replied: "As for you, off you all go, there is nothing going to touch them. If you were to stand here, the youths from the elephants would be here, and you know the young men of one chief and the young men of another cannot meet. If you stood and they came, who knows what might happen among you all? And by that time you have put your elders at variance. Boys may eat beans, but it is their elders who get swollen bellies" (i.e., boys may quarrel, but their elders settle the case). Then the eldest of the lads there said, "It is true, let us go home."

They went home. The spider went and called his wife and children, and they removed all the fish and went off home with them, and were eating them, and twisting string. They twisted an immense quantity of string. By the time the harvest season came, they had twisted a long horse rope, as long as from here to Bajimso. Now one day when the bush was burned by the annual bush fires the elephant said, "You must look for and bring the spider." So they went and sought for the spider. He came. They said, "What about the promise we made with you with regard to the hippo?" The spider said: "There is no harm done. I shall go and tell her. The day after tomorrow I shall return." The spider went off; for three days he was gone then he returned. Now what he had done was this. He had gone to the riverbank, and searched out a huge tree, and tied the horse rope to it. He took the end of the rope to where the elephant was and said: "Behold the rope of the horse which the hippo gives you. Tomorrow they are going to take out this horse from the water, and she says you must look for a huge tree to tie the rope to. When it is dawn and if you see this tree shaking, let the boy seize this rope and pull it, for that is this horse pulling the tree." And the elephant said, "Is it really so, spider?" The spider said, "Yes." And the elephant said, "May Allah give us a tomorrow." When the dawn came the elephant assembled the young men.

Now of a truth the spider has gone and told the hippo saying: "The elephant has given me a horse to bring to you, but I am not able to pull it; but its rope is long; I have dragged it along and have brought it to the bank of the river and have fastened it to a tree. When it is dawn let your boys go and pull, for the horse is a rogue." The hippo agreed. When it was dawn the hippo's boys came up from the water and found the tree to which the rope had been tied. It was swaying about as if it was about to be uprooted. Then they seized hold and pulled. The elephant's people also were pulling. When the elephant's people were pulling the hippo's people, then some more people were added. When the hippo's people were pulling the elephant's people, then more persons were added to them. And so it went on till evening came, and they desisted, and lay down.

When it was dawn, very early they rose up and were pulling till the sun was above them. Then the hippo said: "Let them cease, and go and ask the elephant and let them see what kind of a horse she gives me, that had been pulled and pulled and tired everyone out." Now the elephant also said: "You leave off. Let someone go and see what kind of a horse this is that the hippo gives me, that they had pulled and got weary pulling." So the boys went off, and they met in the middle of the bush. Then the youths from the elephant asked the youths from the hippo and said, "Where are you going?" They replied: "We have been sent to the elephant to go and see what sort of a horse she had given to the hippo. Since yesterday they have been pulling at it, till night came, till dawn came." The elephant's youths said: "We too, our errand was with the hippo, that we ask her this same thing. But since things are so let us turn back. You too turn back and go and say what you have seen; say it is a lie that the spider told, and that we have not seen any horse."

So they went away from this place. The hippo's young men went and told her what they had done. The elephant's youths went and told her [the elephant] the news, and the elephant said: "What's all this? I do not owe the hippo, the hippo owes me." And the hippo said: "What's all this? I do not owe the elephant, the elephant owes me." When the affair came to be discussed it became clear it was the spider that had lied, and received their food, and eaten it. Then the hippo sent to the elephant, and said she must not be angry, saying: "Because she is strong, and I also am strong; if we both get angry, the thing cannot be settled. Let us desist, and lie in wait for the spider." And the elephant said, "That is true."

Then they continually sought for the spider. They did not see him. The spider was in hiding, and he did not come out until he had got weak and thin. One day when hunger had overcome his strength, he came out and was looking for food, when he saw the skin of an antelope, which had died—something had eaten it up, and left the skin, and head, and hoofs. Then he lifted it up and went inside. He was walking about when he met the elephant. The elephant saw him and thought he was a decrepit old antelope. Then the elephant said, "You, antelope, will you not look for the spider for me?" And the antelope said: "Is it the spider you are seeking? Keep that your secret. Since we fell out with him he pointed at me his hand and I wasted away. I do not want to see him. Nowadays whoever quarrels with him then he points his hand at him and he pines away." And the elephant asked, "Was it he who made you become like this?" She [the antelope] said, "Yes." The elephant said, "If you have seen him you must not say I was seeking him." The antelope said, "All right." The elephant passed and went on.

Then the spider cast aside the antelope skin, and ran, and met the elephant and said, "Behold me, they say you are seeking me." Then the elephant kept shaking and saying: "I repent. I am not seeking you." He was making water through fear, from a standing position. Then he (the spider) said, "If I hear again that someone is seeking me, I will join with him." He went back, lifted his skin, entered, and was walking along.

Soon he fell in with the hippo. And she said, "You, antelope, perhaps you have seen the spider?" But he said, "This one whom you are searching for, for my part I do not want to hear his name, for he is the cause of my wasting away like this." And the hippo said, "Is that so?" The antelope said, "Yes." The hippo said, "If you have seen him, do not say I was seeking him." So she passed on. Then the spider threw off the skin and returned. He said: "Where is the hippo? Behold me, I am told you are looking for me." On looking behind, the hippo saw him and fell splash into the water. The spider thus saved himself. That is it. Off with the rat's head.

Some Hausa Proverbs and Sayings

One does not need to measure to know that a bridle is too large for a hen's mouth.

If a blind man has scorched his groundnuts once, he will eat them raw next time.

It is when one is in trouble that he remembers God.

The man who is carried on another man's back does not appreciate how far off the town is.

It is by travelling softly, softly that you will sleep in a distant place.

A chief is like a trash heap where everyone brings his rubbish [i.e., troubles and complaints].

A stone in the water does not comprehend how parched the hill is.

The man with one eye thanks God only after he has seen a blind man.

It is not the eye which understands, but the mind.

Faults are like a hill: You stand on your own and talk about those of other people.

Bowing to a dwarf will not prevent you from standing erect again.

Lack of knowledge is darker than the night.

There are three friends in life: courage, sense and insight.

Five things to make a man cautious: a horse, a woman, night, a river, the forest.

A woman's strength is a multitude of words.

Do not gamble for cowries with a blind man, for he is certain to hide one under his feet.

Where a person found a cowry is where he continues looking.

One does not squeeze out his waistcloth before he comes out of the water.

Selected and occasionally rephrased from Tremearne, previously cited, and other sources.

A conscientious man will repay every good deed done for him except the digging of his grave.

Even the Niger River must flow around an island. (No matter how strong one is, he must sometimes turn aside.)

When the drumbeat changes, the dance changes.

FOUR TALES OF THE IMPOSSIBLE

Tall tales are commonplace in the traditions of most African peoples. The protagonists are generally human, and there is no hint, usually, of the supernatural or of magic. Thus, a story in which a person accomplishes great feats by means of magic or medicine, or in which monsters or demons show aptitudes for actions that humans cannot perform, is not considered to be exaggeration. If a man were to use a talisman to fell an enemy, that would be accepted as believable. But if he is said to have felled his enemy by blowing him down with his breath, that would be considered ridiculous and funny. A story of a man who is transported by his juju from one place to another would be listened to seriously. But if he is said to have slipped on a wet path and skidded from one town to another, that would be considered the grossest of exaggerations. The humor lies in the narrator's stretching of believable reality. Sometimes the pattern of the tall tale becomes immediately apparent, with one exaggeration following on the heels of another. Sometimes the exaggeration is saved for a surprise ending. Following are four Hausa and Mende "impossible" stories.

Contest at the Baobab Tree

A HAUSA STORY

This story is about a test of skill. A certain chief had three sons. He wanted to know which of them had the greatest prowess. He called his councillors to assemble and he sent for his sons. Now, near the gate to the chief's house there was a huge baobab tree. The chief asked his sons to mount their horses and show their skills where the baobab tree was

---

From Hausa Folk-Lore, Customs, Proverbs, *by R. S. Rattray. Oxford, The Clarendon Press, 1913.*

standing. So they mounted their horses and rode off to a certain distance.

Then the eldest son came riding at a gallop. He thrust his spear at the baobab tree. The spear passed through the tree, and the young man and his horse followed the spear through the hole made by the spear. He rode on.

Then the second son came riding. When he came near the baobab tree he pulled up on the bit and the horse leaped over the tree. He rode on.

Then the youngest son came riding. He grasped the tree with his hand and pulled it out of the ground by the roots. He rode to where the chief was sitting and waved the tree aloft.

Now, I ask you, who excelled among the chief's sons?

If you do not know, that is all.

Three Friends Cross the Water

A HAUSA STORY

This tale is about some youths. Certain young men went to an outlying village where some young girls were. They went on, and came to a stream. There was practically no water in the ford. The water came only up to their ankles. They passed on. They came to where the maidens were, and came and greeted them, and carried them off. They came to the stream and found it filled up with water. Then they said, "Ah, when we passed this water, it was not so." And they said, "How is this?" One among them said, "Let us turn back." The rest said, "No, we do not go back." Now they were three, the king of wrestlers, the king of bowmen, and the king of prayer.

And they said, "Let each try and get out of the difficulty by resorting to his own particular skill." They said, "Let the one who is strong in prayer commence." So he prostrated himself, spat on his staff, and struck the water; and the water opened and he with his maiden passed over. Then the water returned to where it was. Next the prince of bowmen drew out his arrows from his quiver, he set them in a line on the water, from one bank to another; he returned and lifted up his maiden. They stepped on the arrows and passed over. Then he came back and picked up his arrows. There remained the king of wrestlers. He too sought for what he should do; he could not find a way. He tried this way and failed, he made that plan and failed, until he was weary. Then he got in a rage, and seized his maiden and with a wrestling trick twisted his leg round hers and they jumped and rose in the air, and did not fall, except on the edge of the far bank. Now among them who was better than another? If you do not know who was least, there you are. Off with the rat's head.

From Rattray, ibid.

The Strong One

A MENDE STORY

There was once a strong young man named Kassa Kena Genanina. He often proclaimed that he was the strongest man alive and that he was not afraid of anything.

One day Kassa went hunting in the forest with two other young men named Iri Ba Farra and Congo Li Ba Jelema. Iri Ba Farra and Congo Li Ba Jelema carried guns to hunt with, but Kassa carried a pole of forged iron.

Iri Ba Farra and Congo Li Ba Jelema hunted and hunted, but they found no game. Kassa, who was swift as well as strong, killed twenty large antelopes with his iron pole, and he brought them into the clearing where Iri Ba Farra and Congo Li Ba Jelema waited.

"Here is the meat," Kassa said. "Now who will go into the forest to get firewood?"

But both Iri Ba Farra and Congo Li Ba Jelema were afraid to go into the forest alone, so Kassa said to Iri Ba Farra: "You stay and guard the meat so that it won't be stolen by the animals of the jungle. Congo Li Ba Jelema and I will get the firewood."

Kassa and Congo Li Ba Jelema went into the forest, and Iri Ba Farra was alone. And while he watched, a huge bird came flying down from the sky and said to him: "I am hungry. Shall I take you or shall I take the meat?"

The huge bird was frightening, and Iri said, "By all means take the meat!"

The bird took one of the antelopes and flew off with it. When Kassa and Congo came back Iri said: "While you were gone a huge bird came down and said, 'Shall I take you or the meat?' I said, 'Take the meat!' "

Kassa was scornful. "You shouldn't have given him an antelope. You should have said, 'Take me!' "

The next day Kassa went again into the forest to get firewood, and this time he took Iri with him and left Congo to guard the meat.

And when they were gone the huge bird came sailing down from the sky again and said to Congo Li Ba Jelema: "I am hungry. Shall I take you or the meat?"

Congo was frightened, and he said, "If you're that hungry, then take the meat!"

The bird took one of the antelopes and flew away. When Iri and Kassa returned from the forest Congo told them what had happened. "The huge bird came back and said, 'Shall I take you or the meat?' And I said, 'Take the meat!' "

From The Cow-Tail Switch and Other West African Stories, *by Harold Courlander and George Herzog,* © *1975 by Harold Courlander. Based on a story taken by Leo Frobenius, included in Vol. 8 of his* Atlantis, Volksmärchen und Volksdichtungen Africas.

Kassa said: "You shouldn't have said that, you should have said, 'Take me.' Tomorrow I shall stay and guard the meat."

So the next day Iri and Congo went together into the forest for firewood, and after they were gone the huge bird sailed down to the clearing and said to Kassa: "I am hungry. Shall I take you or the meat?"

Kassa sprang up.

"I am Kassa Kena Genanina, the strongest man alive!" he shouted. "You shall take nothing, neither the meat nor me!" He seized his forged iron pole and threw it at the bird. It struck her as she flew, and she fell dead upon the ground.

But a tiny feather came loose and floated in the air. It floated downward gently and settled upon Kassa's shoulders. It was heavy. It pushed him to the ground. He lay upon his stomach, and the feather was still on him, and it was so heavy he couldn't move. He struggled to get up, but the feather held him to the earth.

After a long while a woman carrying a child on her back came by, and Kassa said to her: "Call my comrades from the forest so they can help me!"

She went into the forest and found Iri and Congo, and they came running to where Kassa lay. First Congo tried to lift the feather from Kassa, then Iri tried, but it was too heavy. Then they tried together, but they couldn't budge it.

The woman stood watching them. Finally she bent forward and blew the feather off Kassa's shoulders with her mouth.

Then she picked up the dead bird from the ground and gave it to the child on her back for a toy, and went away.

Three Fast Men

A MENDE STORY

Three young men went out to their fields to harvest millet. It began to rain. One of the men carried a basket of millet on his head. The earth was wet from the rain, and the man slipped. His foot skidded from the city of Bamako to the town of Kati. The basket of millet on his head began to fall. The man reached into a house as he slid by and picked up a knife. He cut the tall reed grass that grew along the path, wove a mat out of it, and laid it on the ground beneath him. Spilling from the falling basket, the millet fell upon the mat. The man arose, shook the millet from the mat back into the basket, and said, "If I had not had the presence of mind to make a mat and put it beneath me, I would have lost my grain."

The second young man had forty chickens in fifteen baskets, and on the way to his millet field he took the chickens from the baskets to let

From African Genesis, *by Leo Frobenius and Douglas C. Fox. Harrisburg, Stackpole, 1937. By permission of the publishers.*

them feed. Suddenly a hawk swooped down, its talons ready to seize one of the chickens. The man ran swiftly among his chickens, picked them up, put each one in its proper basket, covered the baskets, and caught the swooping hawk by its talons. He said, "What do you think you are doing—trying to steal my chickens?"

The third young man and the first young man went hunting together. The first man shot an arrow at an antelope. The other man leaped forward at the same instant, caught the antelope, killed it, skinned it, cut up the meat, stretched the skin out to dry, and placed the meat in his knapsack. Then he reached out his hand and caught the first man's arrow as it arrived. He said, "What do you think you are doing—trying to shoot holes in my knapsack?"

Lion of Manding

A WOLOF EPIC

> This is a narrative about a fabulous child hero, Sunjata Kayta, as told and sung by a Wolof gewel, or bard. The Wolof have been strongly influenced by Islam, but beneath the conspicuous overlay of Muslim belief is a basic pre-Mohammedan culture. In pre-European days the Wolof comprised various large kingdoms named Cayor, Walo, Baol and Jolof. Many of the songs sung by bards today are in memory and praise of early warrior kings. Although this Sunjata Kayta narrative appears to be essentially an enfant-terrible tale, there are elements in it suggesting that it is a heroic recollection of persons who really lived.

Recorded by David Ames in the Gambia village of Ballanghar in 1950. The story was told and sung by Ali Sawse, a gewel or bard of that village, accompanying himself on a halam, a five-stringed plucking instrument known under various names throughout a wide stretch of the African continent. Included by kind permission of Dr. Ames.

This is the story of Sunjata Kayta, a powerful ruler who lived in Manding.

Sunjata's mother was Sira Nyading, and his father was Suxlu Nyamadu, who was the ruler of Manding. The capital town of this country was Pai Kawraw, and in this town lived the most famous jinn in Manding. When Sunjata's hunchback mother was eight years pregnant, his father consulted this jinn, who lived in a big gui tree. He told the jinn that he was amazed that his wife had been pregnant for eight years, and that he believed she must be sick.

The jinn told Suxlu Nyamadu that his wife was not sick, but that she had a great king in her womb. The jinn said that the baby came out of her womb each night and returned to it at dawn. The only way the child could be captured was this: Suxlu Nyamadu should call his wife to his house on a Thursday night, instructing her to cover her mortar with a cloth and leave it on her bed, so that when their son returned he would enter the mortar thinking it to be her womb.

Suxlu Nyamadu did as the jinn told him, and the following morning they heard a baby crying in the mortar. An old lady, who was the griot [a gewel or bard] of Sunjata Kayta's mother, called Sira Nyading, and told her that her child was crying. Sira Nyading did not tell the old lady or anyone else how the child had been born. When people came the next day to congratulate the parents they were told only that the Lion of Manding had arrived. The father named the child Sunjata, meaning Our Lion. Because Sunjata had been growing so long in the womb of his mother, she carried him on her back for only seven months and weaned him at the same time.

When Sunjata was about six he gathered together all the hunters in the district. He instructed them not to shoot a lion with a white spot on his forehead, for that lion was Sunjata. Their bullets could not hurt him, but if they shot at him he would kill them. Suxlu Nyamadu became fearful of his son because of the miraculous things he was doing. He was afraid Sunjata would kill him or take over the rule of Manding. So he went to the jinn in the big gui tree and asked him to get rid of Sunjata. The jinn said: "I told you he would be a great ruler. There is nothing you can do to prevent it. All I can do for you is to paralyze him." The father asked the jinn to do it. And Sunjata was paralyzed for seven years.

In the seventh year Sunjata told his father he knew his sickness did not come from God but from his brothers. Sunjata knew it was not the fault of his brothers, but of his father, but he was ashamed to say it. Suxlu Nyamadu told the jinn what Sunjata had said. The jinn said Sunjata knew who was responsible. He said: "Sunjata is a great ruler. Even I am afraid of him."

Suxlu Nyamadu regretted what he had done. He asked the jinn to take away Sunjata's paralysis. The jinn agreed to untie the knotted vein, but he said that before Sunjata could stand he must have a metal staff to help him. The father had his blacksmith make an iron staff, but when Sunjata tried to use it it broke. The blacksmith welded it together again, but again the staff broke under Sunjata's weight. The father returned to the jinn. The jinn said, "He is so great he needs a staff of gold." So Suxlu Nyamadu went to his gold box and took out much gold and gave it to his blacksmith. The smith made the gold staff and it was taken to Sunjata. All that night Sunjata used the gold staff. At dawn he threw down the staff and walked through the town. The people came to congratulate and honor him. His father announced, "The Lion of Manding can walk again." His brothers, however, objected to this. They said Suxlu Nyamadu should not call Sunjata a lion because they were his elders and were as brave and strong as he. But Suxlu Nyamadu said that this was not true, that Sunjata was truly the Lion of Manding.

Now that Sunjata was able to walk again he went out into the forest to collect firewood for his mother as youngest sons are supposed to do. There he commanded the animals of the forest, who feared him, to fill his mother's house with firewood. They did so. When he returned to the town he said, "Let no one say that Sunjata Kayta cannot get firewood for his mother." He then commanded his wild animal helpers to bring wood to those who had helped his mother when he was paralyzed.

After that Sunjata went into the forest to a place where there was a gui tree that bore fruit only when a new king was to be named. Whoever succeeded in eating this fruit was the one who would be selected. So potential successors to the throne always went to this gui tree and tried to shoot down the fruit. When evening came, Sunjata Kayta read a special verse from the Koran, then he spat the words on his hand. With this same hand he pushed down the gui tree. He took leaves from the tree to his mother, saying: "Now you can make lalo.[1] Give some to the women who helped you when I was sick. They will know you have a son who can gather leaves from the gui tree."

His father was amazed and alarmed. He went to the jinn and asked him to paralyze Sunjata again. But the jinn said he could not do it. "I told you when Sunjata was in the womb of his mother that he would be a very great ruler." Sunjata's brothers also were amazed and alarmed. They contributed money to hire twelve witches in their village to attack him. That night the twelve witches went to the king's compound to capture Sunjata. They captured a boy, but it was not Sunjata. They took him to a place of three lakes—one white lake, one black lake and one red lake. They transformed the boy into a cow, killed him and divided the meat. Then Sunjata appeared and asked them, "Whom did you kill?" The witches answered, "Sunjata Kayta." He told them they had made a mistake, for he was Sunjata, and the powers of witches were not enough to capture him. He gave each witch a bush cow to replace the meat that had been divided, and told them to bring the boy back to life. They did as he instructed, each replacing what he had taken. The witch that took the head replaced it on the neck. The one that took the skin put the skin back on the body. After the body was

---

1. A staple made of cooked leaves mixed with pounded grain.

put back together, the chief of the witches put a medicine horn on the nose of the cow, and it stood up and ran off to the east. Sunjata told them not to do such a thing again.

The following morning Sunjata told his mother he wanted to visit a friend in a town called Kabu. His mother said he had never had a friend in Kabu since the time he was born, and that he had never been to that town. But Sunjata insisted on going to Kabu, so his mother gave her permission and he departed. When Sunjata's brothers heard that he had gone away they said that he had fled. They took back the gold they had given to the witches and sent it to one of Sunjata's friends, instructing him to make bullets out of it to kill Sunjata. But Sunjata knew what they were planning, because he was *ya bopa*, meaning that he had the ability to see things that ordinary people cannot see. He went to the place of a certain smith and there he met his friend with the gold. He tied his friend's hands and took the gold home and showed it to his brothers. Sunjata said: "I know what this gold has been used for. First you gave it to twelve witches to kill me. Then you gave it to my friend to make gold bullets to kill me. Now I will keep the gold for myself."

Sunjata's father became alarmed again. He went to the jinn and asked him to make Sunjata leave. The jinn said: "I can give you an amulet which you must burn in the center of your compound on Friday. Then blow the ashes away in the breeze and he will leave."

Suxlu Nyamadu took the amulet and did as the jinn advised. On Friday as evening fell Sunjata went out into the bush of Manding.

When Sunjata went into the bush his mother wept very hard. After a while she and Sunjata's sister, called Heliya Kayta, went out to find him. But they could not find him. Sunjata's mother was crying, so his sister called all the hunters of the town to assemble. She reminded them that the lion with the white spot was really Sunjata, and she asked if anyone had seen him. One hunter said yes, he had seen the lion but had not shot at him. Heliya Kayta then went into the bush with four hunters to find Sunjata. They came to a place where a number of lions were lying in a circle, their legs straight forward and their heads towards the center where Sunjata, in the form of a lion, was sleeping. The lions were about to attack Heliya and the hunters, but Sunjata awoke and restrained them, telling them to allow his sister to approach him. Heliya spoke of how his mother was weeping over him, but Sunjata said he would not live in his father's house again. He would live the rest of his life in the bush. When she heard this, his sister cried. Sunjata told her to return home. She answered that she could not go home and tell her mother that Sunjata would not come back. Rather than this she would stay with Sunjata in the bush.

So Sunjata asked the hunters to remain with his sister because she would need protection when he was out hunting, and he promised to reward them when he became king of Manding. The names of those hunters were Jili Sikanta, Jaba Kinte, Sara Mbai and Biram Mbai. They remained seven years in the bush with Sunjata's sister. During these seven years Sunjata killed eight hundred elephants to feed them. He also killed eight thousand lions, but this was because he fed only from their livers and did not eat the rest of the meat. Because Sunjata killed so many beasts the people knew where he was in the bush by looking to see where the vultures were flying.

In the seventh year the jinn sent for Suxlu Nyamadu. He said that the ruler of Manding would die in a month. He told Suxlu Nyamadu to bring Sunjata back from the bush, for Sunjata was the bravest of his sons and should become king. Suxlu Nyamadu said, "But I do not know where to find him." The jinn answered, "I will tell you where he is because it was I who told him where to go." The jinn told his only son, Dun Ndun Boye, to leave the gui tree and enter the hut that stood below, where all their medicine was kept. He instructed him to bring back their most powerful medicine, which was called dantoma, and to tie it on the great vulture called Duga. When the medicine was tied to the Duga, the vulture arose and flew into the bush and alighted on a tree where many other vultures were resting. Under this tree sat Sunjata, his sister and the four hunters. The vulture cried out, and Sunjata recognized it as the Duga. He saw the medicine tied around its neck. He awakened his sister and said that they must go home. She wanted to know why they must go home. He pointed to the vulture with the medicine amulet that had revealed to him that it was time to return. The hunters asked Sunjata if he knew the way home, because they had been in the bush so long they had forgotten. Sunjata called the vulture down to where he was sitting. He took the amulet. The amulet spoke, saying that Sunjata was to carry it and consult it whenever he wanted to know the way.

Because they had lived in the bush for seven years, Sunjata and his sister and the hunters had only rags to wear. These they had taken from travellers who had come through the bush. And their hair was long and hung down their backs. They walked towards the town. Whenever they came to a fork in the trail, Sunjata put the amulet on the ground. Whichever way it jumped, that was the trail they followed. As they approached the town, Sunjata said they would go to the house of his maternal uncle who would cut their hair and give them clothes. But Heliya Kayta objected. She said they should not do this. If they were to do it, she said, the children of their maternal uncle would later on, in some future time, remind Sunjata of how he had been driven away by his father and how he had to come to their father for help. This would arouse Sunjata's anger, she said, but he would be helpless to do anything about it because those who angered him would be the children of his mother's brother. She suggested, instead, that they should go to Sunjata's brothers, because they were afraid of him and would not remind him of their father's deed.

They passed the gui tree where the jinn lived. The jinn asked Sunjata who his companions were. Sunjata explained. The jinn said he wanted to speak to Sunjata alone. Sunjata refused, saying: "I have lived in the bush and eaten with these people for seven years. Whatever is to be said can be said in their presence. If it cannot be said in their presence I do not wish to hear it." So the jinn spoke to Sunjata before all of them. He asked Sunjata if he had feared anything in the bush. Sunjata said no. The jinn called on Sunjata to prove this statement by shooting a silver arrow through seven plates of gold. Sunjata's silver arrow penetrated six gold plates but did not penetrate the seventh. The jinn declared that because the arrow had not penetrated the seventh plate, Sunjata had lied to him. Sunjata's sister spoke. She told the jinn that Sunjata had never feared anything.

But Sunjata declared that in fact he had one fear. It was the fear he had inherited from his mother when a jinn appeared before her to make her deliver. And the jinn answered: "I shall take away this fear from Sunjata by having him read a verse from the Koran, spit on his hand, and place this hand on his chest. This way the fear will leave him." Sunjata did these things. He read a verse, spat on his hand, and placed his hand on his chest. When he did this he no longer had any fear. He tried again with the arrow and the plates. This time he drew the arrow seven yards from the bow, and it pierced the seven plates and went through a bentenki tree and was lost. The tree split from the topmost branch to its roots and fell in two pieces. The jinn commanded the tree to stand up again, and it did. But Sunjata commanded it to fall again, and it fell. They countermanded each other this way for a long time. Then both of them ran to the tree. Sunjata arrived there first and made the tree fall between him and the jinn.

The jinn declared that Sunjata had disgraced him, which was not right because he had been there since the time of Sunjata's ancestors to protect the town. The jinn prayed that Sunjata would have much trouble throughout his reign. Sunjata answered, "That is fine, because I am a man of trouble." He and his companions went on to the house of Sunjata's father. Suxlu Nyamadu received Sunjata. He washed Sunjata, cut his hair and gave him clothes.

Sunjata lived with his father for only one month. Then his father died.

When Suxlu Nyamadu died, the eldest and strongest among his thirty children gathered around. The people thought that either Sunjata or Mamodu Kata would become king. The people wanted Mamodu Kata because they knew him. They did not know Sunjata because he had lived so long in the bush. But all the jinns in the district wanted Sunjata. Sunjata and Mamodu Kata argued. The people made a proposal. They asked the Duga to fly with the king's ring and drop it over a well where the two men would be standing. Whoever should catch the ring and put it on his finger would be the ruler. The vulture took the ring and flew so high they could not see him. He dropped the ring. Sunjata, with his relatives and his bards standing behind him, caught the ring and placed it on his finger. He held out his hand in front of his bards, so that they could see it and praise him. The royal drums of Manding played, and Sunjata marched through the town to his father's house. He sat on the king's bed and told the people that from this day on he would be their king and that they should trust him. He asked them if they believed in him. They said they neither believed nor disbelieved, because he was their ruler. But they told him they would believe if he would perform a miracle.

So Sunjata offered to kill a certain beast that was despoiling their crops. Other persons had tried to kill the beast but had been unable to do so. A month passed, and Sunjata went out to perform this deed. Now the beast was an old woman who sometimes took on an animal form. One of her sons had been ambitious and had been killed by Sunjata's father. For this reason she turned herself into an animal and persecuted the people.

Sunjata went to the town of Falilinjala where the woman lived. He took eighty cows with him, and in his pockets he carried two white kola nuts and sixteen shillings. On his way he met a blind man, to whom he gave a kola nut. The man asked if he was Sunjata. Sunjata said yes. The man complained how empty his pockets were. He asked for the other kola nut, and Sunjata gave it to him. Then the blind man said Sunjata would find the old woman at the edge of town winnowing with a broken calabash, a bundle of wood beside her. He instructed Sunjata to give the old woman eight shillings, to wait for her, and to stay in her house. Sunjata went on. He came to where the woman was winnowing, and he dropped eight shillings in her calabash, saying it was for charity. When the old woman asked what his name was, he said it was Mamadu Jara. He said he had come with four shepherds from a town called Gidibene, and that he was on his way to sell cows. He proposed that they stay at the old woman's house. She answered that she was old and had no one to cook for them. But Sunjata persisted, saying that she was the first person he had met on the journey and that he was going to stay with her. He said: "My men can cook for us, or I will do the cooking myself. My mother, also, was very old, and I cooked for her."

So the old woman agreed. When they came to her house she said it was so small she didn't see how they could all sleep in it. Sunjata said he would sleep in the house and the four shepherds would sleep behind the house with the cattle. The next day Sunjata killed a cow and gave a portion of it to the old woman. The rest he took to town to sell. Every night he called the young men of the town to the house and talked with them. Every night Sunjata slept with the woman and squeezed her body. On the eighth day the woman again asked Sunjata his name, and he gave her a false name as he had before.

She said: "Sunjata, I know who you are, and I know that you want to kill me. Because of your good behavior I will give you my life." She gave him some shells, some powder, an egg, some rice and some charcoal and instructed him what to do. At a certain time, which was Friday evening, he was to go between the three lakes of Manding. She said: "Light the powder and put the shells over the smoke. Then call all the people of Manding to gather, but the men must climb into trees, otherwise I will kill them. You will see a beast with six horns coming from the east to drink at the lakes. Do not shoot at it, for it will not be me. After it has drunk it will cry three times and then go away. Another beast, having twelve horns, will come and drink from the lakes. After that it will go away. Do not shoot at it, for it will not be me. I will be the third beast to come. All the bush will shake when I am coming, but do not be afraid. I will have sixteen horns, and an eye on my forehead. Do not be afraid. I will come at dawn and drink at the first lake. That is the time that you should shoot at me. I will also drink at the second lake. Keep shooting. You must prevent me from drinking at the third lake or I will kill you. I will try to attack you. Throw the rice on the ground and it will turn into a dense jungle of bamboo. If I penetrate the bamboo and come after you, throw the charcoal between us. It will turn into a great fire. I will enter the fire and spit some of the flames at you. Do not run away. If I penetrate the fire, throw the egg between us and it will turn into a great sea. There I will die. Bury me in a place where people do not go."

Sunjata returned home. He told his people that on Friday he would kill the beast. On the designated day he went to the lakes. He did everything the old woman had told him to do. And when at last the beast was dead, Sunjata told the men of Manding to come out of the trees and bury it. They came down, took the body and buried it in a hollow gui tree.

Then Sunjata, ruler of Manding, went to his town and rested.

The King of Sedo

A WOLOF TALE

In the town of Sedo, it is said, there was a king named Sabar. Sabar's armies were powerful. They conquered many towns, and many people paid tribute to him. If a neighboring chief passed through Sedo, he came to Sabar's house, touched his forehead to the ground, and presented gifts to the king. As the king grew old, he grew proud. His word was law in Sedo. And if his word was heard in other places, it was law there too. Sabar said to himself: "I am indeed great, for who is there to contradict me? And who is my master?"

There came to Sedo one day a minstrel, and he was called on to entertain the king. He sang a song of praise to Sabar and to Sabar's ancestors. He danced. And then he sang:

> "The dog is great among dogs,
> Yet he serves man.
> The woman is great among women,
> Yet she waits upon her children.

From The King's Drum and Other African Stories, © 1962 by Harold Courlander. Reprinted by permission of Harcourt Brace Jovanovich, Inc.

> The hunter is great among hunters,
> Yet he serves the village.
> Minstrels are great among minstrels,
> Yet they sing for the king and his slaves."

When the song was finished, Sabar said to the minstrel,"What is the meaning of this song?"

The minstrel replied, "The meaning is that all men serve, whatever their station."

And Sabar said to him, "Not all men. The king of Sedo does not serve. It is others who serve him."

The minstrel was silent, and Sabar asked, "Is this not the truth?"

The minstrel answered, "Who am I to say the king of Sedo speaks what is not true?"

At this moment a wandering holy man came through the crowd and asked for some food. The minstrel said to the king, "Allow me to give this unfortunate man a little of the food which you have not eaten."

Sabar said, "Give it, and let us get on with the discussion."

The minstrel said, "Here is my harp until I have finished feeding him." He placed his harp in the king's hands, took a little food from the king's bowl, and gave it to the holy man. Then he came back and stood before Sabar.

"O king of Sedo," he said, "you have spoken what I could not say, for who contradicts a king? You have said that all men serve the king of Sedo and that he does not serve. Yet you have given a wandering holy man food from your bowl, and you have held the harp for a mere minstrel while he served another. How then can one say a king does not serve? It is said, 'The head and the body must serve each other.'"

And the minstrel picked up his harp from the hands of the king and sang:

> "The soldier is great among soldiers,
> Yet he serves the clan.
> The king is great among kings,
> Yet he serves his people."

The Song of Gimmile

A GINDO TALE FROM MALI

Once there was Konondjong, a great king of the Gindo people.

One day a singer from Korro came to Bankassi, where Konondjong lived. He went to the king's house and sang for him. He played on his lute and sang about famous warriors and their deeds, about things that had happened in the world, and about the accomplishments of the chiefs of former times. King Konondjong was entertained by what he heard. When the singing was finished, Konondjong asked the singer what he wanted in Bankassi. The bard replied, "Oh, sir, all I want is a small gift from you."

The king said in surprise, "You ask the king of the Gindo people for a gift?"

"Only a small gift, a token in exchange for my singing," the bard answered.

"Ah!" Konondjong said with exasperation. "Here is a homeless bard who presumes to ask the king of the Gindo for a present! Many famous bards come and sing for the honor of being heard, but this man asks for something in return! Whoever gave me such disrespect before? Take him away and give him fifty lashes."

So King Konondjong's servants took the bard and beat him with a knotted rope for punishment. The singer then made his way home to Korro.

In Korro there lived a man by the name of Gimmile. Gimmile heard the story of what happened to the bard who sang for King Konondjong. So he composed a song of contempt about the king. It went:

> "Konondjong, king of the Gindo,
> He is fat, his neck is flabby.
> Konondjong, king of the Gindo,
> His teeth are few, his legs are swelled.
> Konondjong, king of the Gindo,
> His knees are bony, his head is bald.
> Konondjong, king of the Gindo."

This was the song made by Gimmile. He went out where the people were, taking his harp with him, and he sang his song. Gimmile's voice was good. The music of his song was catching. Soon other people of Korro were singing this song. It became popular among the people and the bards. Travellers who came to Korro took the song away and sang

A *rephrasing of a tale from* Atlantis: Volksmärchen und Volksdichtungen Afrikas, *by Leo Frobenius, Jena, Eugen Diederichs, 1921–24, in* The King's Drum and Other African Stories, *©1962 by Harold Courlander. Reprinted by permission of Harcourt Brace Jovanovich, Inc.*

it elsewhere. It was heard at dances and festivals. Among the Gindo people it was known everywhere.

> "Konondjong, king of the Gindo,
> He is fat, his neck is flabby.
> Konondjong, king of the Gindo,
> His teeth are few, his legs are swelled.
> Konondjong, king of the Gindo,
> His knees are bony, his head is bald.
> Konondjong, king of the Gindo."

Women sang it while grinding corn. Girls sang it while carrying water. Men sang it while working in the fields.

King Konondjong heard the people singing it. He was angered. He asked, "Who has made this song?"

And the people replied, "It was made by a singer in Korro."

Konondjong sent messengers to Korro to the bard whom he had mistreated. The bard came to Bankassi, and the king asked him, "Who is the maker of this song?"

The bard replied, "It was made by Gimmile of Korro."

The king gave the bard a present of one hundred thousand cowry shells, a horse, a cow, and an ox. He said, "See to it that Gimmile's song is sung no more."

The bard said: "Oh, sir, I was whipped with a knotted rope when I sang for you. Even though you are a king, you cannot retract it. A thing that is done cannot be undone. A song that is not composed does not exist; but once it is made, it is a real thing. Who can stop a song that travels from country to country? All of the Gindo people sing it. I am not the king. If the great king of the Gindo cannot prevent the song of Gimmile from being sung, my power over the people is certainly less."

The song of Gimmile was sung among the people, and it is preserved to this day, for King Konondjong could not bring it to an end.

The king was not compelled to beat the bard, but he did, and then it could not be undone.

Gimmile did not have to make a song about the king, but he did, and it could not be stopped.

The Gluttonous Ansige

A KARAMBA STORY

There was a man whose name was Ansige. Ansige was rich, for he had inherited much wealth from his father, but he was a miserly man and an incredible glutton. He had a wife named Paama and many servants and slaves. But he was a trial to them all. To Paama he was always complaining: "I never have enough to eat. You don't provide for me the way a wife ought to." Ansige was perpetually ill-mannered. He felt that the slaves and servants were eating too much, and robbing him besides. But they were really getting very little to eat, for Ansige hoarded his property so well that no one ever got anything out of him. The people of Maku thought that he was the most impossible man they had ever known.

Ansige abused Paama with his complaints until she couldn't stand it any longer. So she went to him one day and said: "I think I shall visit my father's village for a while. My family needs me." She took her things and left Maku for her home.

Now Ansige was more unhappy and more petulant than before. His meals were prepared by the servants, who cared for him less than his wife had. Whereas his food had been, in fact, rather good before she went away, now it was really bad, and there was less of it. The more he complained to the servants and slaves the worse things got, because they were quite tired of his greed and his gluttony.

One morning, after Paama had been away for a long while, Ansige said to himself: "This is certainly a cruel situation. My wife ran away to her parents two years ago. Now I have to pay fabulous wages to ungrateful servants to prepare my meals, and they only cheat me and give me bad things to eat. I am practically dying of hunger. I shall get Paama and bring her home."

So he started out, and after a long journey he came to the village where his wife's parents lived. He went to their home, and there he was greeted by Paama's father. As a gesture of hospitality Paama's father gave Ansige a young goat.

Ansige's mouth began to water. Forgetting everything else, he immediately took his goat out into a field, where he killed it and cooked it. He was very worried that someone might come along and want to share his meal with him. Even before it was quite done he began to gulp it down. He ate and ate. Before long the meat was all gone.

But Ansige was still hungry. He saw a large sheep grazing in the field. He caught it and killed it, and carried it to where his fire was burning.

He had been away from the village a long time, however, and Paama began to wonder where he was and what he was up to.

Based on a tale set down by Leo Frobenius in Atlantis, *Vol. 6. This version is from* The Cow-Tail Switch, *by Harold Courlander and George Herzog, © 1975 by Harold Courlander.*

"I know my husband," she said to herself. "I had better go to see what kind of trouble his gluttony has gotten him into."

She went out to the field and found Ansige getting ready to cut the sheep up.

"What's this?" she said. "That isn't the goat my father gave you! It's a sheep that belongs to the chief!"

"Don't act as if you didn't know me," Ansige said petulantly. "I ate the goat your father gave me, but it wasn't enough. Then I saw this sheep, so I decided to round off my meal with him."

"Well, now you're in trouble," Paama said. "The chief will have you punished for killing his sheep. However, I'll get you out of it."

She made Ansige carry the dead sheep to where the chief's wild horse was tied, and they laid it down close by. Then they went back to the village. Paama stopped at the chief's house and reported to him that they had seen the sheep lying by the wild horse, and that the horse had kicked him and killed him. The chief sent a man out to see. "Yes," he told the chief when he returned, "the sheep must have been killed by the horse. It's an unfortunate accident."

The next day Paama said to her father, "If I know Ansige, he brought a great hunger along with him from Maku. What can I give him to eat that will satisfy him?"

"Why don't you give him some young roasted corn?" her father said. "That ought to quiet his hunger."

So Paama went out to the cornfield and gathered a large basket of corn. There was enough corn for twenty men. She roasted it and took it to her husband.

Ansige ate it all. Not a single kernel was left. But his appetite was not stilled, it was simply aroused. He wanted more. So he went out to the fields. There he began breaking off ears of corn. When it was nearly dark Ansige picked up all that he could possibly carry and started off for the village.

He had trouble finding the trail, however, and it was getting darker and darker. At last he came out of the cornfield, but he couldn't see a thing, only the lights of the village. He started towards them, but between him and the village was a well. And when he came to the well Ansige fell into it with all his corn.

Meanwhile Paama, at home in her father's house, said to herself: "I know my husband. I guess I had better see what he is doing. I wonder what kind of predicament his stomach has gotten him into now."

She went off to look for him, a torch in her hand. When she came to the well she heard him calling for help. She looked down with her torch, and there was Ansige, corn floating all around him.

"What are you doing down there?" she asked him.

"Don't act as though you didn't know me!" Ansige shouted. "I was just looking for something more to eat! People are trying to starve me to death! Get me out of here!"

"You certainly are in trouble! The people won't like it that you've been stealing their corn. But never mind, I'll help you out of this."

She went to where the cattle were, and chased them into the field where Ansige had been so busy. After the cows began to graze there Paama began to shout. People came running from the village.

"What is happening?" they said.

"A misfortune!" Paama said. "My husband was taking a walk when he saw the cattle in the field, trampling the stalks and breaking off the ears of corn! He chased them and picked up the ears that had fallen off, but he is a stranger who doesn't know the trails, and he has fallen into the well!"

"Well, never mind," the people said. "It's not so bad. We'll get him up."

They chased the cows from the field and brought lights and ropes to pull Ansige out of the well. The first thing he did was to hurry back to the house for his dinner.

The next day Paama's father said to her, "Today prepare something extranice for your husband to eat, something that he likes very much."

"I'll make millet dumplings," Paama said.

She put the millet in the wooden mortar and pounded it until it had become meal. Ansige looked on from a distance, hungrily. Four times she filled the mortar and made meal. There was a huge amount of it. She then mixed it with water and made the dumplings. When the dumplings were finished she brought them to Ansige. There was enough for twenty men.

But Ansige ate everything. And when the last speck of it was gone, he began to look longingly at the mortar in which the millet had been ground.

"Perhaps there is a little meal left in it!" Ansige said to himself. He went to the mortar and looked down into it. Halfway down he saw some meal clinging to the side. He put his head inside to lick the meal off with his tongue. There was a little more in the bottom. He pushed his head as far down as he could. But when he tried to take his head out he couldn't budge it. It was wedged fast.

Just about this time Paama was thinking: "I know my husband. I ought to see what he is doing now. I'm sure his gluttony has gotten him into some new kind of trouble."

She went to the house and looked around, but Ansige wasn't there. Then she went out into the court, and there she saw her husband head-down in the mortar.

"What's going on?" Paama said.

"Don't stand there and ask me what's going on!" Ansige said angrily from down in the mortar. His voice sounded hollow and muffled. "I just stuck my head in here to get a little more of the meal! Now I'm wedged tight! Do something!"

"All right, all right," Paama said. "I'll get you out."

She shouted for help, and the village people came to see what was the matter.

"Ah, what bad luck!" Paama said. "And it's all my fault! I told my husband he has a thick head, and he said no, he doesn't have a thick head. I said his head was too thick to go in the mortar, and he said no it wasn't. Then he put his head in the mortar to show me and it got caught. It's all my fault!"

"Well, it's not so bad," the people said. They had to laugh, seeing Ansige bottom-side-up in the mortar. "But you must be right, he evidently does have a thick head!"

They sent for an axe, and with it they broke the mortar apart and got Ansige out. The whole village was amused. But Ansige was angry. He didn't like to have people laughing at him. He was so angry he took his things and went back to his village of Maku.

When he arrived there he remembered that he had been so busy eating that he had forgotten to tell Paama to come back with him. So he sent a servant to her to tell her to return at once.

But Paama simply sent the following message to Ansige, "Don't act as though I didn't know you."

The Cow-Tail Switch

AN ILLUSTRATED PROVERB OF THE JABO PEOPLE OF LIBERIA

Proverbs are plentiful throughout most of Africa, and a great many of them have self-evident meanings requiring no explanation. But a proverbial saying may be the distillation of a principle established in a particular tale or parable. Thus, a story may explain or rationalize why a man should confide a certain thing to his best friend but not to his wife; or why he should accompany a friend on a journey if asked to do so. This Jabo story illustrates the idea that a dead person lives on in the minds of those who knew him.

In the village of Kundi there lived a hunter by the name of Ogaloussa.

One morning Ogaloussa took his weapons down from the wall of his house and went into the forest to hunt. His wife and his children went to tend their fields, and drove their cattle out to graze. The day passed, and they ate their evening meal of manioc and fish. Darkness came, but Ogaloussa didn't return.

From The Cow-Tail Switch and Other West African Stories, *by Harold Courlander and George Herzog,* © 1975 by Harold Courlander.

Another day went by, and still Ogaloussa didn't come back. They talked about it and wondered what could have detained him. A week passed, then a month. Sometimes Ogaloussa's sons mentioned that he hadn't come home. The family cared for the crops, and the sons hunted for game, but after a while they no longer talked about Ogaloussa's disappearance.

Then, one day, another son was born to Ogaloussa's wife. His name was Puli. Puli grew older. He began to sit up and crawl. The time came when Puli began to talk, and the first thing he said was, "Where is my father?"

The other sons looked across the ricefields.

"Yes," one of them said. "Where is father?"

"He should have returned long ago," another one said.

"Something must have happened. We ought to look for him," a third son said.

"He went into the forest, but where will we find him?" another one asked.

"I saw him go," one of them said. "He went that way, across the river. Let us follow the trail and search for him."

So the sons took their weapons and started out to look for Ogaloussa. When they were deep among the great trees and vines of the forest they lost the trail. They searched in the forest until one of them found the trail again. They followed it until they lost the way once more, and then another son found the trail. It was dark in the forest, and many times they became lost. Each time another son found the way. At last they came to a clearing among the trees, and there scattered about on the ground lay Ogaloussa's bones and his rusted weapons. They knew then that Ogaloussa had been killed in the hunt.

One of the sons stepped forward and said, "I know how to put a dead person's bones together." He gathered all of Ogaloussa's bones and put them together, each in its right place.

Another son said, "I have knowledge too. I know how to cover the skeleton with sinews and flesh." He went to work, and he covered Ogaloussa's bones with sinews and flesh.

A third son said, "I have the power to put blood into a body." He went forward and put blood into Ogaloussa's veins, and then he stepped aside.

Another of the sons said, "I can put breath into a body." He did his work, and when he was through they saw Ogaloussa's chest rise and fall.

"I can give the power of movement to a body," another of them said. He put the power of movement into his father's body, and Ogaloussa sat up and opened his eyes.

"I can give him the power of speech," another son said. He gave the body the power of speech, and then he stepped back.

Ogaloussa looked around him. He stood up.

"Where are my weapons?" he asked.

They picked up his rusted weapons from the grass where they lay and gave them to him. They then returned the way they had come, through the forest and the ricefields, until they had arrived once more in the village.

Ogaloussa went into his house. His wife prepared a bath for him and he bathed. She prepared food for him and he ate. Four days he remained in the house, and on the fifth day he came out and shaved his head, because this was what people did when they came back from the land of the dead.

Afterwards he killed a cow for a great feast. He took the cow's tail and braided it. He decorated it with beads and cowry shells and bits of shiny metal. It was a beautiful thing. Ogaloussa carried it with him to important affairs. When there was a dance or an important ceremony he always had it with him. The people of the village thought it was the most beautiful cow-tail switch they had ever seen.

Soon there was a celebration in the village because Ogaloussa had returned from the dead. The people dressed in their best clothes, the musicians brought out their instruments, and a big dance began. The drummers beat their drums and the women sang. The people drank much palm wine. Everyone was happy.

Ogaloussa carried his cow-tail switch, and everyone admired it. Some of the men grew bold and came forward to Ogaloussa and asked for the cow-tail switch, but Ogaloussa kept it in his hand. Now and then there was a clamor and much confusion as many people asked for it at once. The women and children begged for it too, but Ogaloussa refused them all.

Finally he stood up to talk. The dancing stopped and people came close to hear what Ogaloussa had to say.

"A long time ago I went into the forest," Ogaloussa said. "While I was hunting I was killed by a leopard. Then my sons came for me. They brought me back from the land of the dead to my village. I will give this cow-tail switch to one of my sons. All of them have done something to bring me back from the dead, but I have only one cow tail to give. I shall give it to the one who did the most to bring me home."

So an argument started.

"He will give it to me!" one of the sons said. "It was I who did the most, for I found the trail in the forest when it was lost!"

"No, he will give it to me!" another son said. "It was I who put his bones together!"

"It was I who covered his bones with sinews and flesh!" another said. "He will give it to me!"

"It was I who gave him the power of movement!" another son said. "I deserve it most!"

Another son said it was he who should have the switch, because he had put blood in Ogaloussa's veins. Another claimed it because he had put breath in the body. Each of the sons argued his right to possess the wonderful cow-tail switch.

Before long not only the sons but the other people of the village were talking. Some of them argued that the son who had put blood in Ogaloussa's veins should get the switch, others that the one who had given Ogaloussa's breath should get it. Some of them believed that all of the sons had done equal things, and that they should share it. They argued back and forth this way until Ogaloussa asked them to be quiet.

"To this son I will give the cow-tail switch, for I owe most to him," Ogaloussa said.

He came forward and bent low and handed it to Puli, the little boy who had been born while Ogaloussa was in the forest.

The people of the village remembered then that the child's first words had been, "Where is my father?" They knew that Ogaloussa was right.

For it was a saying among them that a man is not really dead until he is forgotten.

Preachments of the Animals

SAYINGS OF THE GREBO PEOPLE OF LIBERIA

Alligator says, "We know the war canoe from the peace canoe."
  (One can distinguish between hostility and goodwill.)

Red deer says, "If you are a coward your horns will not wear."
  (One who meets challenges can be identified; so can he who avoids them.)

Snake says, "Do not strike at me after I have passed you."
  (Do not indulge in gratuitous actions.)

Monkey says, "If you keep your child in front of you, you can see what is the matter with it."
  (You are responsible for your own affairs.)

Boa constrictor says, "After eating, one's skin shines."
  (A person's successes are apparent.)

Hog says, "Muddy roads are plentiful."
  (If one is not successful in going one way, he tries another.)

Chicken says, "We follow the one with something in her mouth."
  (If you need a thing, go to the place where it is to be found.)

Mosquito says, "If you want a person to understand you, speak in his ears."
  (Don't send a message but go yourself if you want to be persuasive.)

Dog says, "An old man begs not by words but with his eyes."
  (A person's face says as much as his words.)

Colobus says, "It is for wisdom that people travel together."
   (An interchange of views produces wise actions.)

Sheep says, "To report a thing promptly avoids embarrassment."
   (Don't wait to have the unfavorable facts dragged out of you.)

Ant says, "Nothing surpasses a swarming crowd."
   (There is safety and strength in numbers.)

Cock says, "If there is no one to praise you, praise yourself."
   (One must speak up on his own behalf.)

Kru War Song

> Because many West African languages are
> tonal they can be simulated on instruments
> such as signal drums and horns. This war song
> was played on a horn. It was "translated" into
> Kru, one of the languages spoken in Liberia,
> and then into English.

On guard! The battle is coming!
Whoever runs away will get the whip!
The warriors say go quickly to the military!
Bring in all the women from the fields!
The enemy are coming on the right side!
They are now on the other side of the river!
Gather warriors on the left! Prepare! They are approaching!
They are not falling back! They are coming!
Come here quickly, quickly! Run, run, run, quickly!
The guns, the guns fire! The guns are firing now!
Good! They get them! They get them!
They get them! They get them! They are getting them now!

Hammer and Chisel Rhythm

MANO TRIBE, LIBERIA

From one end of Africa to another, wherever sustained effort is required for work, one may expect motion to be converted into rhythm

---

*From Folkways Records Album No. 8852, African Music, © 1957. By permis-
sion. Word text has been slightly edited.*

and rhythm into music. For it is taken for granted, and sometimes articulated, that music makes the task lighter; and even beyond that, music is conceived as part of the fabric of labor. Men walking great distances sing; women winnowing sing; people pounding grain in mortars sing, and use their pestles rhythmically to provide percussive sounds. Whenever the tools of work, such as bush knives, axes or hammers, give off repeated sounds, there is the probability that the sounds will be transformed into music.

Among stonecutters, the sound of hammer on steel suggests not only rhythm in complicated forms, but also melodic line and sonority. The hammers and chisels of a group of Mano stonecutters produced the following score:

THE AKAN PEOPLES OF GHANA

The Akan peoples of Ghana are those who speak the Twi language and its related dialects. Prior to its independence, Ghana—then called Gold Coast Colony—included some seventy Akan states, a number of which had histories going back to the thirteenth century. Rulers of some of the states can be traced back for several hundred years. Fante was founded about the year 1300, and the Bono state a little earlier. But the Akan, as they are now known, were not a single tribe and they did not derive out of a common racial stock. Various clans and groups moving into the region superimposed themselves on resident populations, and subsequently received immigrating settlers who were unrelated to either. The Akan or Twi language appears to have been introduced into the region by people from Kumbu in the west. In time it became widespread, and in some of the states, such as Ashanti, it became dominant. But it is not merely language that binds the Akan peoples. Living in close proximity they absorbed much from one an-

other, and today, despite regional differences, there is considerable
cultural unity.

Akan Poetry

This discussion of Akan poetic forms is extracted from an essay by J. H. Kwabena Nketia.

In Akan society—the Ashanti, Fanti, Akim and other [peoples] of
Ghana—literary activity has until recently been carried on largely by
word of mouth. The texts of Akan poetry, therefore, occur as language
events, and some forms of it are not always readily recognized as poetry
by those not thoroughly acquainted with our poetic tradition. Moreover, the use of poetic expressions is not peculiar to the poem. The very
names and the praise appellations which are given to people in Akan
society have the feel of poetry:
"One who is restive until he has fought and won."
"Dwentiwaa's husband, and a man of valor."
"Daughter of a spokesman who is herself a spokesman."
"Karikari that weighs gold and gives it away, the benevolent one."
These and many others have a highly evocative power for the Akan. No
one says "The chief has died" if he knows [Akan] poetic habits. He says
"The chief has gone to his village." Incidence of hardship is described
in terms of fire in the house going out.
Similarly, the use of proverbs is not confined to the poem; they are
quoted in many situations—in the home, at work, at the court. They are
considered a mark of eloquence and wit, and anyone who is able to
quote or use proverbs habitually may be regarded as a poet of a sort.
Like other African peoples the Akan are particular about their social
greetings. These usually consist of a short sentence or two and lack the
marks of a literary form. On the other hand, the same material could
be worked out in a literary form, as in the following text of greetings
to the chief of an Akan state on the occasion of the new year:

> The year has come round.
> I have come to greet you,
> To shower blessings on you.
> Live long, live long, live long,
> Live to a good old age.
> The drummer of the talking drums says
> He showers his blessings on you.
> Live long, live long, live long,
> Live to a good old age.
> The God of old says

From "Akan Poetry," by J. H. Kwabena Nketia, in An African Treasury, *by
Langston Hughes, New York, Crown, 1960. By permission of Professor Nketia.*

He showers his blessings on you.
Live to a good old age, chief,
The Earth Amponyinamoa says
She showers her blessings on you.
Live to a good old age.
Live long, live long, live long,
Live to a good old age.
May years be added to your years.

Such utterances are rather like the texts of ordinary social greetings
—"Live long, may years be added to your years"—but in a more elaborate form, and with additional expressions and repetitions not common
in everyday greetings. There is a definite pattern which unfolds itself
as the text enlarges. In the way it is arranged, it carries a far greater
emotional force and esthetic merit.

The development of the poetic tradition of the Akan appears to have
followed four distinct courses, each one giving rise to a distinctive style
of arrangement or delivery.

ORAL POETRY. First there is the tradition of oral poetry, or poetry
which is recited and not sung. The greatest use of this is in connection
with chiefship. At state functions special poems of praise are recited by
minstrels to paramount chiefs. In these poems allusions to past successes
in war, particularly the decapitations of enemy chiefs and potentates,
are made. They are intended to remind the chief of his former enemies,
to remind him of his power as war leader and to incite him to deeds of
bravery:

He is one who hates to see an enemy return victorious.
He is bulletproof: when you fire at him, you waste your ammunition.
He catches priests and snatches their bells from them.
He is not to be challenged. If anybody dares him, the one is sure to lose
    his head.
He is like the tough tree as well as the old, wet half-dead tree, neither
    of which can be cut.

The delivery of the poems is very dramatic and expressive. There
may be an introductory exclamatory lead, "He is the one *(Ono no)*, or
a simple interjection for calling attention, *"Odee e!"*

Oral literature has tended to give prominence to persons, interper-
sonal relationships and attitudes and values derived from our conception of the universe. We do not spend time on the daffodils or the
nightingale or on reflections on abstract beauty, the night sky and so on
as things in themselves, but only in relation to social experience. Our
poetry is full of animals and plants, but these are used because they
provide apt metaphors or similes, or compressed ways of stating bits of
social experience.

RECITATIVE. The second tradition is that of verse which is half-
spoken and half-sung—the recitative style used in dirges and the poetry

of hunters' celebrations. A number of references are made which can be grouped around a few themes: the ancestor, the deceased or any particular individual, the place of domicile.

LYRIC POETRY. The third tradition of poetry is lyric: the use of the song as a vehicle for poetry. This tradition constitutes the bulk of Akan poetry. There is no uniformity of themes, for the songs are used in different contexts. Songs of worship and songs for particular ceremonies make their peculiar references, but the cultural value of these songs is not merely that they provide such data; they are statements of the poet, reflections of his vision. They are first and foremost poetry.

The structure of lyric poems in Akan society is greatly influenced by the musical requirements. Songs performed by individuals tend to have a sustained verse form with the minimum of wholesale repetitions, whereas those sung by solo and chorus tend to have some phrases repeated over and over again. Poems in this tradition fall into various lyric types:

Songs of prayer, exhilaration and incitement.

Cradle songs. Introduction to poetry begins very early in life, long before one is able to understand the language. The tune, the sound sequences which form the words, and most important of all the rhythm evoke responses from the child, responses of excitement or of calm and repose, which lull it to sleep. There are, however, cradle songs which build up statements of wider meaning to the mother of older infants. In these songs there is always scope for the reflections of the mother or nurse, for allusions to the co-wife of a polygamous marriage, allusions to the treatment meted out to the woman by the husband:

> Little child, come for a feed.
> If you divorce me, you cannot take away my child.
> Little one, come for a feed.
>
> Someone would like to have you for her child
> But you are my own.
> Someone wished she had you to nurse you on a good mat;
> Someone wished you were hers: she would put you on camel
>   blanket;
> But I have you to rear you on a torn mat.
> Someone wished she had you, but I have you.

Songs from folktales.

Warrior songs.

Maiden songs. In Akan society maiden songs are sung on moonlight nights by women who form themselves into little performing groups for this purpose. The women in a group stand in a circle and clap their hands as they sing. Each one takes a turn at leading the verses.

The songs are used mainly for praising or making references to loved ones, brothers or other kinsmen or outstanding men in the community. In the past, anybody who was thus honored was supposed to give the women presents the following day.

> He is coming, he is coming,
> Treading along on camel blanket in triumph.
> Yes, stranger, we are bestirring ourselves.
> Agyei the warrior is drunk,
> The green mamba with fearful eyes.
> > Yes, Agyei the warrior,
> > He is treading along on camel blanket in triumph,
> > Make way for him.
> He is coming, he is coming,
> Treading along on sandals [i.e., on men].
> Yes, stranger, we are bestirring ourselves.
> Adum Agyei is drunk.
> The Green Mamba, Afaafa Adu.
> > Yes, Agyei the warrior,
> > He is treading along on camel blanket in triumph,
> > Make way for him.

The fourth tradition is the POETRY OF HORNS AND DRUMS.

Drum Poetry of the Akan Peoples

The development of the poetic tradition has not been confined to the spoken voice. A great deal of Akan heroic poetry is conveyed through the medium of horns, pipes and drums. Although drums are used in Akan society for making a limited number of announcements, they are also vehicles of literature. On state occasions poems of special interest are drummed to the chief and the community as a whole. These poems run into many scores of verses and fall into four groups.

First there are the poems of the drum prelude called the Awakening, *Anyaneanyane.* When a drummer is playing these poems he begins by announcing himself, closing the opening with the formula: "I am learning, let me succeed" or "I am addressing you, and you will understand."

He then addresses in turn the components of the drum—the wood of the drum, the drum pegs, strings, the animal that provides the hide of the drum: the elephant or the duiker.

Next he addresses the earth, God, the witch, the cock and the clockbird, ancestor drummers, and finally the god Tano. The cock and the clockbird are frequently referred to in drum texts because of the alert

From Nketia, ibid. *Slightly abridged. By permission of Dr. Nketia.*

they give. They are like drummers who have to keep vigil while others
are asleep.

> When I was going to bed, I was not sleepy.
> When I felt like sleeping, my eyes never closed.
> All night he stood in his coop,
> While children lay in bed asleep.
> Early in the morning he was hailed:
> "Good morning to you, Mr. Cock."
> The Cock crows in the morning.
> The Cock rises to crow before the crack of dawn.
> I am learning, let me succeed.
> Kokokyinaka Asamoa, the Clockbird,
> How do we greet you?
> We greet you with "Anyaado,"
> We hail you as the Drummer's child.
> The Drummer's child sleeps and awakes with the dawn.
> I am learning, let me succeed.

The second group of texts are in the nature of panegyrics or eulogies.
Abridged forms incorporating the names, praise appellations of individuals and greetings or messages are used in social situations—for
example, in a dance arena. The chief use of these eulogies, however, is
for honoring kings and ancestor kings on ceremonial occasions when
their origin, parentage and noble deeds are recalled against a background of tribal history.

The third group of poems are those used for heralding the movements of a chief, for greeting people, for announcing emergencies and
so on. When a chief is drinking at a state ceremony, the drummer drums
a running commentary. If it is gin, he drums as follows:

> Chief they are bringing it.
> They are bringing it.
> They are bringing it to you.
> Chief you are about to drink imported liquor.
> Chief pour some on the ground.
> He is sipping it slowly and gradually.
> He is sipping it in little draughts.

The last group of poems are the proverbs. These may be used separately or they may be incorporated into other poems or into drum
pieces intended for dancing. Here are some proverbs of the Akantam
dance:

> Rustling noise by the wayside
> Means what creature?
> The wood pigeon, the wood pigeon.
> Wood pigeon Seniampon,

He goes along the path eating grains of millet.
Condolences, wood pigeon.
> *Duiker Adawurampon Kwamena*
> *Who told the Duiker to get hold of his sword?*
> *The tail of the Duiker is short,*
> *But he is able to brush himself with it.*

"I am bearing fruit," says Pot Herb.
"I am bearing fruit," says Garden Egg.
Logs of firewood are lying on the farm,
But it is the faggot that makes the fire flare.
> *Duiker Adawurampon Kwamena*
> *Who told the Duiker to get hold of his sword?*
> *The tail of the Duiker is short,*
> *But he is able to brush himself with it.*

"Pluck the feathers off this tortoise."
Tortoise: "Fowl, do you hear that?"
> *Duiker Adawurampon Kwamena*
> *Who told the Duiker to get hold of his sword?*
> *The tail of the Duiker is short,*
> *But he is able to brush himself with it.*

The origin and storehouse of Akan poetry is the individual member of Akan society brought up on the traditions of his people, the individual who from childhood has been taught or has learned through social experience to use certain words and expressions, to regard some as beautiful, deep, proper, improper, correct, bad and so on; the individual who has been taught to understand and use the proverbs in his language, who has been taught to sing cradlesongs, dance songs, war songs and love songs, to drum and dance or to appreciate drumming and dancing; the individual who under emotional stress would quote a proverb, a familiar saying, a line or two of traditional oral poetry. But the function of the individual was not merely to act as a carrier of a tradition. He was also to maintain it by using it, by re-creating it, for each time he performed his set pieces he was in a sense giving the poetry of his people a new life.

Drum Poems to Onyame, the Supreme Deity

The supreme deity of the Ashanti and other Akan peoples is named Onyame (or Nyame) and is also known as Onyankopon and Odomankoma. These names are said to represent different manifestations of the deity, who is regarded (by some Akan) as a triad or trinity. In some traditions Onyame is considered as male in character, in others as female, and in still others as androgynous. Those who make distinctions between Onyame and Onyankopon say that Onyame is the female element, symbolized by the moon, while Onyankopon, symbolized by the sun, is the male element and the soul *(kra)* of Onyame. Another

explanation is that Onyame represents the natural universe; Nyankopon, experience and life; and Odomankoma, the creative force that
constructed the visible world. Odomankoma, say some Akan, made the
earth and the sky by pressing down one and raising up the other. Where
the distinctions are not made between the three names of the deity, it
is maintained that Onyame created himself (or herself), the universe,
lakes and rivers, mountains, all living things and the part of the world
that is invisible. Onyame, under the name Odomankoma, also created
death. It is said that after he created death, death claimed him, though
he lived on in a different form. This tradition explains, in an indirect
way, the Akan belief in the continuation of life, in a different form and
place, for ancestors of the family.

A more simplistic explanation of Onyame's residence in the sky is that
he once lived on earth among humans. One day Onyame was vigorously
jolted by the pestle of a vigorous old woman pounding palm kernels in
her mortar. Each time her pestle came down it jolted Onyame upward,
until at last he reached the sky, and there he decided to remain.[1]

In addition to Onyame in his various forms there are, in Akan belief,
various lesser deities, such as Asaase Afua, a daughter of Onyame and
the goddess of fertility and procreation; Asaase Yaa, also known as
Aberewa, goddess of the barren places of the earth; and two sons of
Onyame, Tano and Bia. Tradition says that when Tano and Bia grew to
manhood, their father decided to give them gifts in accordance with
their merits. To Bia, who had been an obedient son, Onyame determined to give the most fertile and pleasing portions of the land, which
was the country of Ashanti, while to Tano he would give the dreary
forest land of the frontier.

Onyame told the goat, Akua Abirekyi, who was his trusted servant,
of what was in his mind, and he told the goat to inform his two sons that
they should come the next day for his gifts. But the goat preferred Tano
to Bia, so when he delivered the message he advised Tano to come very
early in the morning disguised as Bia. To Bia he said there would be no
need to hurry. When Tano arrived disguised as Bia, Onyame was deceived. He gave Tano all that land through which the River Tano now
flows. When Bia arrived, Onyame understood what he had done, but he
could not undo it. So he gave Bia the land that was left, the poor soil
and the forests.[2]

Onyame is a distant deity. He is too remote to be supplicated directly.
So when humans want to speak to him they do so through the lesser
gods, the spirits that inhabit various trees, caves, rivers and lakes, and
the dead ancestors.

The following drum poem speaks of Odomankoma's (Onyame's)
great creations—the Herald or Court Cryer, the Drummer and the
Executioner. The Herald symbolizes order in the universe. The Poet-

1. A. A. Y. Kyerematen, Panoply of Ghana, London, Longmans, 1964.
2. A. W. Cardinall, Tales Told in Togoland, Oxford, 1931.

Drummer is the preserver of knowledge and tradition. And the Executioner, here called Touch-and-Die, is death.

> Odomankoma
> Created the thing.
> Borebore [the Architect]
> Created the thing.
> He created what?
> He created the Court Cryer,
> He created the Poet-Drummer,
> He created Touch-and-Die
> As principals.[3]

To Odomankoma

The following drum poem to Odomankoma, like the previous one, stresses that before the physical world came into being there was nothing but the deity himself. It poses a question, similar to a riddle, but here the answer is self-evident and needs no pondering:

> The stream crosses the path,
> The path crosses the stream.
> Which of them is the oldest?
> Did we not cut a path
> To meet the stream?
> The stream had its beginning
> Long long ago.
> The stream had its origin
> In Odomankoma.
> He created the Thing.[4]

Drum Poem to Nyankopon

In the following drum poem the deity Nyankopon is referred to by one of his many praise names, Twiaduampon, which is believed to mean, freely translated, Lean-on-a-Tree, Fall-Not. Various English translations of the poem have appeared, but the following seems closest to the original:

> The sky is wide, wide, wide,
> The earth is wide, wide, wide.
> The one was lifted up,
> The other was set down

---

3. J. B. *Danquah*, The Akan Doctrine of God, *London, 1944.*
4. *From* Ashanti, *by R. S. Rattray, London, Oxford University Press, 1923.*

In ancient times, long, long ago.
Nyankopon, Twiaduampon,
We serve you.
When Nyankopon teaches you something
You profit by it.
If we wish "white" we get it;
If we wish "red" we get it.
Twiaduampon,
God, good morning.
God of Saturday, good morning.[5]

Flute Poem in Praise of River Deities

This praise recitation by the durugya flute gives thanks to the river spirits for their help in providing for the needs of the people.

River Adutwum, in you we bathe, and from you we quench
    our thirst.
From you we take the water to wash our clothes.
Asante Kotoko, our children and our grandchildren,
But for you what would we have done?
Sakyiakwa River, lady born on Tuesday,
River Adutwum Amponkuru,
Asante Kotoko, we carry a dart thrower without a dart, a
    bow without an arrow.
Mighty one, condolences.[6]

Akan Sayings About Nyame (Onyame)

The earth is wide but Nyame is chief.

The order [that] Nyame has settled, living man cannot subvert.

All men are Nyame's offspring. No one is the offspring of the earth.

No one teaches forging to a smith's son. If he knows it, it is Nyame who
    taught him.

---

5. *From Rattray*, ibid.
6. *From* Panoply of Ghana, *by A. A. Y. Kyerematen, Accra, Longmans, Green and Co., 1964 for Ghand Information Services. By permission of Ghana Information Services Department and Dr. Kyerematen.*
From Twi Mmebusem Mpensa-Ahansia Mmoaano (A Collection of Three thousand and six hundred Tshi Proverbs in use among the Negroes of the Gold Coast speaking the Asante and Fante (i.e., the Akan) language), *by J. G. Christaller, Basel, 1879, and other sources.*

The hawk says, "All that Nyame did is good."

No one points out Nyame to a child.

When a fowl drinks water it shows it to Nyame.

There is no way around Nyame's destiny.

If living man knocks over your cup of wine, Nyame will refill it.

Unless you die of Nyame, let living man kill you and you will not perish.

To save fraud, Nyame gave each person a name.

If you would tell Nyame, tell the wind.

Could Nyame die, I would die.

When all the world makes Nyame its burden, no one becomes hump-backed.

Deceiving the crab is exposing one's buttocks to Nyame.

The Drum-History of the State of Mampon

I

Kon, kon, kon, kon,
Kun, kun, kun, kun,
Spirit of Funtumia Akore,
Spirit of cedar tree, Akore,
Of cedar tree, Kodia,
Of Kodia, the cedar tree,

From Ashanti, *by R. S. Rattray,* © *1923 Oxford University Press. By permission of The Clarendon Press, Oxford. Rattray's text includes occasional words in parentheses to make the meaning more clear. These words are retained here, though the parentheses signs have been dropped.*

The divine drummer announces that
Had he gone elsewhere in sleep
He now has made himself to arise;
As the fowl crowed in the early dawn,
As the fowl rose up and crowed,
Very early, very early, very early,
We are addressing you,
And you will understand;
We are addressing you,
And you will understand.

II

Spirit of Earth, sorrow is yours,
Spirit of Earth, sorrow is yours,
Earth with its dust,
Spirit of the Sky,
Who stretches to Kwawu,
Earth, if I am about to die
It is on you that I depend.
Earth, while I am yet alive,
It is upon you that I put my trust.
Earth who receives my body,
The divine drummer announces that,
Had he gone elsewhere in sleep,
He has made himself to arise.
As the fowl crowed in the early dawn,
As the fowl rose up and crowed,
Very early, very early, very early.
We are addressing you,
And you will understand.
We are addressing you,
And you will understand.

III

Spirit of the mighty one, Ankamanefo,
He and the drummers will set out together,
Spirit of the mighty one, Ankamanefo,
He and the drummers will return together.
You of mighty bulk, Gyaanadu, the red one
The swamps swallow thee up oh, elephant,
Elephant that breaks the axe,
Spirit of the elephant, the divine drummer declares that
He has started up from sleep,
He has made himself to arise;
As the fowl crowed in the early dawn,
As the fowl rose up and crowed,

Very early, very early, very early.
We are addressing you,
And you will understand;
We are addressing you,
And you will understand.

IV

Spirit of the fiber, Ampasakyi,
Where art thou?
The divine drummer announces that,
Had he gone elsewhere in sleep,
He has made himself to arise,
He has made himself to arise;
As the fowl crowed in the early dawn,
As the fowl rose up and crowed,
Very early, very early, very early.
We are addressing you,
And you will understand;
We are addressing you,
And you will understand.

V

Oh, pegs, made from the stump of the ofema tree,
Whose title is Gyaanadu Asare,
Where is it that you are?
The divine drummer announces that
Had he gone elsewhere in sleep,
He has made himself to arise,
He has made himself to arise.
As the fowl crowed in the early dawn,
As the fowl rose up and crowed,
Very early, very early, very early.
We are addressing you,
And you will understand;
We are addressing you,
And you will understand.

VI

Kokokyinaka bird,
How do we give answer to thy greeting?
We salute thee "Anyado,"
We salute thee as the drummer's child,
The drummer's child sleeps,
He awakes with the dawn,
Very early, very early, very early.

We are addressing you,
And you will understand;
We are addressing you,
And you will understand.

VII

Oh, witch, do not slay me, Adwo [term of respect],
Spare me, Adwo,
The divine drummer declares that,
When he rises with the dawn,
He will sound his drums for you in the morning,
Very early,
Very early,
Very early,
Very early.
Oh, witch that slays the children of men before they are fully
   matured,
Oh, witch that slays the children of men before they are fully
   matured,
The divine drummer declares that,
When he rises with the dawn
He will sound his drums for you in the morning.
Very early,
Very early,
Very early,
Very early.
We are addressing you,
And you will understand.

VIII

Spirit of Asiama Toku Asare,[1]
Opontenten Asi Akatabaa [strong names],
Asiama who came from the God of the Sky,
Asiama of the Supreme Being,
The divine drummer declares that,
Had he gone elsewhere in sleep,
He has made himself to arise,
He has made himself to arise.
As the fowl crowed in the early dawn,
As the fowl rose up and crowed,
Very early,

---

1. *Asiama Toku Asare was the first Queen Mother of the Beretuo clan; mythology has it
that she descended from the sky on a chain. Her blackened stool is preserved and has the
central place of honor at the Adae ceremonies. She was the head of the Beretuo clan before
they migrated to Mampon. She ruled over the clan at the village of Ahensan in Adanse.*

Very early,
Very early.
We are addressing you,
And you will understand.

IX

Oh, Boafo Anwoma Kwakyie,
Kwakyi, the tall one,
Kwakyi Adu Asare,
Whence camest thou?
Thou camest from Mampon-Kontonkyi, the place where the rock
    wears down the axe.
Mampon Kontonkyi Aniampam Boafo Anwoma Kwakyi.
Kon!
Who destroys towns, Firampon,
Alas!
Alas!
Alas!

X

Friend of the Shield,
We gave thee a Shield,
Friend of the Shield,
We gave thee an Afona (sword)
The Shield which we gave was so terrible,
That in just three days,
It devoured backbones.[2]
Oh, Obirempon Antiedue,
Son of Antiedu Gyedu Asare,
Antiedu, the short one,
Kon!
Antiedu, the short one, Firampon,
Alas!
Alas!
Alas!

XI

Shield with its dust (of tramping feet),
Gyirampon Agai and Ampam,
Agai Boaete, Maniampon,
The dust of whose battle caused the little Kukuban to fall from its
    tree,
Giving thee the strong name of "Kukuban 'Birempon,"

---

2. Bremmo *is also the center part of the framework of a shield—its backbone.*

Whence was it that thou camest?
Thou camest from Mampon Kontonkyi, where the rock wears down
    the axe.

XII

Oh, Adu Boahen,
Boahen Kojo,
Whence was it that thou camest?
Thou camest from Mampon Akurofonso,
The place where the Creator made things.
Adu Gyamfi with an eye like flint, whose title is Ampafrako.

XIII

The Shadows were falling cool,
They fell cool for me at Sekyire.[3]
The day dawned,
It dawned for me at Sekyire,
Who is Chief of Sekyire?
The Chief of Sekyire is Kwaitu,
Kwaaye knows Afrane Akwa,
Boatimpon Akuamoa,
Akuamoa,[4] whom we even grow weary of thanking for his gifts,
Akuamoa, you were of the royal blood since long long ago,
Thou camest from Mampon Kontonkyi, where the rock wears away
    the axe.
Kon!
Akuamoa Firampon,
Alas!
Alas!

XIV

Oh, Otieku Amosoansan,[5]
Atakora the elder,
Whence was it that thou camest?
Thou camest from Mampon Kontonkyi, where the rock wears down
    the axe.
Kon!
Atakora, Firampon,
Alas!

---

3. *Sekyire is the name given to the country comprising Mampon, Nsuta, Effiduase, Ejura,
and Jamasi.*
4. *The sixth ruler of the Beretuo clan.*
5. *The seventh ruler of the Beretuo clan, Amosoansan (he who declares war and does not
turn back).*

XV

Kra hi gede gede gede gede gede kra hi ka,
Kra hi kata kata kata kata kata kra hi ka,
Kra hi kra hi kre,
Kra hi kra hi kre,
The Creator made something,
What did he make?
He made the Herald,
He made the Drummer,
He made Kwawuakwa, the Chief Executioner,
They all, they all, declare that they came from one Ate pod,
Konimsi Amoagye,
Gyaneampon Amoagye,
Esene Konini Amoagye,
Come hither, oh, Herald, and receive your black monkey-skin cap.
What was your heritage?
Your heritage was a good master,
Your heritage was the death dance, Atopere,
Gyaneampon Sakyi Amponsa,
Asumgyima 'Birempon,
Kon!
Asumgyima[6] Firampon,
Alas!
Alas!
Alas!
Alas!
Alas!
Alas!
Alas!

XVI

Osafo, the tall one,
Osafo, the tall one,
Gyamfi Agyai,
Osafo Gyamfi Akwa,
Osafo the red,
The child of Osai Tutu,
Osafo Gyamfi Agyai, whence camest thou?
Thou camest from Coomassie whose title is Aduampafrantwi.
Oh, Path thou crossest the River,
Oh, River thou crossest the Path,
Which of you is the elder?
We cut a Path, and it went and met the River,
This River came forth long long ago.

---

6. *Asumgyima, eighth ruler of the Beretuo clan, was the son of a herald called Amoagye.*

It came forth from the Creator of all things.
Kon!
Gyamfi Agyai Firampon,
Alas!
Alas!
Alas!
Alas!
Alas! Osai,
Alas! Osai,
Alas! Osai,
Alas! Osai.

XVII

Oh Asiase Pepra,[7]
Okwawuo, the slayer,
Drummer Pepra,
Where art thou?
Thou camest from Mampon Kontonkyi, where the rock wears down
        the axe,
Boafo who fought, fought, fought, fought, fought, fought.
Pepra Firampon,
Alas!
Alas!
Alas!

XVIII

We salute thee as Chief, with the title Kwa,
We salute thee as 'Birempon, with the title Kwa,
Chief, Kwa,
'Birempon, Kwa,
Who is Chief?
He is Chief who is worthy of the title "master,"
He is 'Birempon who is worthy of the title "master,"
Yerefie and Ampasakyi, man among men,
Atakora the hero,
Atakora the Royal of Royals.
Atakora Kwaku Firampon,
Alas!

XIX

Yerefi Ankamafo Akyaw Wusu,
Akyaw 'Birempon,
Owusu the last-born,

---

7. *Asiase Pepra, the tenth ruler of the Beretuo.*

Child of Osai Tutu,
Owusu Akwasi,
Owusu Sekyire,[8]
Onoborobo Osai Kojo 'Birempon,
Child of Osai Tutu.

XX

Osafo[9] the tall,
Osafo the tall,
Gyamfi Agyai,
Child of Osai Tutu,
Thou camest from Mampon Kontonkyi, where the rock wears down
the axe.

XXI

We salute thee as Chief with the title Kwa,
We salute thee as 'Birempon Kwa,
Chief Kwa,
'Birempon Kwa,
Who is Chief?
Who is Chief?
He is Chief who is worthy of the title of "master."
He is 'Birempon who is worthy of the title "master."
Yerefie and Ampasakyi, man among men,
Atakora the hero.
Atakora, the Royal of Royals.

XXII

Kra hi gede gede gede gede kra hi ka,
Kra ka ka hi,
Kra hi gada gada gada gada,
Kra ka ka hi,
Gada gada kra ka ka hi,
Kra hi kra hi kre kra hi ka,
Ka ka ka hi kra hi kra ka ka hi,
Two or three Potopodie birds to one he fought,
What part will the Vulture eat?
The Vulture will eat the head,
Oboadu Gyabaa Antwi,[10]
Gyaba the man of great bulk,

---

8. *The eleventh ruler of the Beretuo.*
9. *The twelfth ruler of Mampon.*
10. *Antwi Abunyawa was thirteenth ruler of the Beretuo clan.*

The divine Drummer,
Okwawuakwa the Chief Executioner.

XXIII

Boafo Fosu,
Boafo Aduanwoma,
Boafo Badu,
Boafo Aduanwoma,
Ofosu, who in a fit of anger took his wife and gave her to a slave,
Child of Oduro, the elder,
Kwaante Bosomtwe,
A white fowl is a fit offering for Lake Bosomtwe [whose day of
     observance is a Sunday].

XXIV

We salute thee a Chief with the title Kwa,
We salute thee a 'Birempon with the title Kwa,
Chief Kwa,
'Birempon Kwa,
Who is Chief?
He is Chief who is worthy to be called "master,"
He is 'Birempon who is worthy to be called "master,"
Yerefie and Ampasakyi, man among men,
Atakora Kwaku,[11]
Thou camest from Mampon Kontonkyi, from Botaase.

XXV

Ofie Banyin Agyepon Ntara,[12]
Agyepon the last-born,
Agyepon Ntara whence came he?
Agyepon Ntara came from Mampon Kontonkyi where the rock
     wears down the axe.
Agyepon Ntara, thou wert a hero,
Thou wert ever a man.

XXVI

Atakora the warrior,
Whence camest thou?
Thou camest from Mampon Botaase,
Atakora, if we are going to fight anywhere,
We speak of it to thee.

---

11. Atakora was the sixteenth ruler.
12. Seventeenth ruler of the Beretuo.

XXVII

Apia Kusi,[13]
Kusi Oboadum,
Apia Kusi,
Thou wert a hero,
Thou wert ever a man.
Boafo who fought, and fought, and fought.

XXVIII

Berefi Ankamafo Akyaw Wusu,
Owusu the last-born,
Owusu Sekyire,[14]
Thou camest from Mampon Kontonkyi where the rock wears down
    the axe.
Boafo who fought, and fought, and fought and fought.

XXIX

Onoborobo Osai Tutue,
Bonsu[15] who fought and seized kings,
Osai Tutu 'Birempon,
Thou art a warrior,
Thou art ever a man,
You whose motto is "Were I alone, I should go and fight,"
    Onoborobo Osai Tutu,
The hero who holds a gun and a sword when he goes to battle,
Bonsu who fought and seized kings,
Osai Tutu 'Birempon.

CHIEFDOM AMONG THE ASHANTI

Chiefdom among the Ashanti is considered an office with heavy responsibilities to the people. The chief, called Ohene or Omanhene, is

---

13. *The nineteenth ruler of Mampon.*
14. *The twentieth ruler of Mampon.*
15. *The twenty-first ruler of Mampon.*

regarded as a sacred personage descended from an ancient clan founder through the female line. In former times the Omanhene was credited with supernatural powers, for which reason he acted as intermediary between the people and the ancestral dead. His decisions and judgments were thought of as coming from the ancestors, and accordingly his words were sacred. Nevertheless, he had to rule in conformity with clearly defined principles, and his personal behavior and his attitude towards his subjects were subjected to minute scrutiny. On the occasion of his enstoolment, his senior councillors made known to him through his spokesman or "translator" what was expected of him:

> "Tell him [they said] that
> We do not wish that he should disclose the origin of any person.
> We do not wish that he should curse us.
> We do not wish greediness.
> We do not wish that his ears should be hard of hearing.
> We do not wish that he should call people fools.
> We do not wish that he should act on his own initiative.
> We do not wish things done as in Kumasi.
> We do not wish that it should ever be that he should say, 'I have
>   no time, I have no time.'
> We do not wish personal abuse.
> We do not wish personal violence."[1]

Thus, as noted by Rattray: "To all outward appearance and to superficial observers, who included the populace, the Chief was an autocrat. In reality every move and command which appeared to emanate from his mouth had been discussed in private and been previously agreed upon by his councillors, to whom every one in the tribe had access and to whom popular opinion on any subject was thus made known."[2] Such was the ideal, at any rate, and serious infringement of the custom could lead to destoolment.

Another admonishment to the new chief to behave well was given by the Stool Okyeame, or Caretaker of the Stool, of the Ashanti state of Bekwai. He declared, on behalf of the councillors:

> "Because the Ko'ntire and the Akwamu say I must give you the
>   Stool.
> Because the Advance-guard say I must give you the Stool.
> Because the Gyase say I must give you the Stool.
> Because the Rear-guard say I must give you the Stool.
> Because the men and women of Bekwai say we must give you the
>   Stool.
> When a sickle breaks, we put a new shaft in it. Today your uncle

---

1. From Ashanti Law and Constitution, by R. S. Rattray, London, Oxford University Press and International African Institute, 1956. By permission of The Clarendon Press, Oxford.
2. Rattray, ibid.

lay down and did not rise up, so we have brought his gun to give you. Today the Bekwai people consulted together, and they say that you are their choice, they declare that we must give you the Stool of Aguyeboafo.
Do not take it and go after women.
Do not take it and drink spirits.
Do not take it and make civil war.
When we give you advice, listen to it.
Do not take the Stool and abuse your elders.
Do not take it and gamble with the people.
We do not wish shame.
We bless the Stool, *Kuse! Kuse! Kuse!*
The elders say we are to take this Stool and give it to you."[3]

Following this admonishment the new chief answered with a pledge of good behavior:

"I beg pardon of Sunday, the forbidden name of which I speak; I implore Small-pox, the forbidden name of which I speak; I supplicate the great forbidden name, the name which I speak, saying that: Today, you, the people of Bekwai, have taken my grandsire's gun which you have given me; I am the grandchild of Aguyeboafo, whose gun you have this day given me; if it is not a good government with which I govern you, or if I gamble with my grandsire's town; if I go after women; if I do not listen to the advice of my councillors; if I make war against them; if I run away; then I have violated the great forbidden names of Sunday and of Small-pox."[4]

In an enstoolment rite in Juaben, another Ashanti state, the new chief was instructed:

"Do not seduce the wives of your elders.
Do not seduce the wives of your young men.
Do not disclose the origin whence your people came.
Let your ears hear our advice.
Do not act foolishly towards your subjects, or your clan, or your children.
Be humble.
Do not spoil the Stool heirlooms."[5]

After each admonition the new chief answered, "I agree to that," or "I have heard."

---

3. *Rattray, ibid. By permission of The Clarendon Press, Oxford.*
4. *Rattray,* ibid. *By permission of The Clarendon Press. These forbidden names relate to the deaths of certain chiefs. Yao Kofo died on a Sunday, and Boakye Yam died of smallpox in a war against the Fanti.*
5. *Rattray,* ibid.

A Song for the New Chief

AN ASHANTI TALE

It is said that there was a chief of Agona, and the people had grown accustomed to him. He ruled many years, he grew old, he died. The royal family selected another chief to replace him. His name was Adoko.

The procession that brought him to the chief's house was long, as long as from the town of Kibi to the town of Koforidua. Drummers marched in front of the procession, playing on their drums. What their drums said was, "Our Chief is great; Adoko is wise." In the city there was a great celebration. Musicians beat gongs and drums, and the people danced. When Adoko arrived in his hammock, carried by his slaves, he was taken three times around the city, then they brought him to his house. The royal stool was set in front of the house, and he sat there to watch the festivities.

Many bards were in the city for the celebration. They came before the new chief and sang songs. The last of the bards to appear was the oldest of them all. In his lifetime he had seen many chiefs come and go, and it was he who knew how to recite the history of Adoko's family from the very beginning. They brought him before Adoko and asked him to sing. He tuned his lute and sang this song:

> "Our new father is Adoko,
> He is great indeed,
> But our former chief had no greatness.
>
> Our new father is Adoko,
> He is wise,
> But our last chief understood nothing.
>
> Our new father is Adoko,
> He is generous,
> Even though our last chief was stingy.
>
> Adoko is our father,
> He cares for the welfare of all,
> But our last chief did not care.
>
> Nana Adoko is here,
> He will judge our lawsuits with justice,
> Our former chief cared little for such things.

From The King's Drum and Other African Stories, © *1962 by Harold Courlander. Reprinted by permission of Harcourt Brace Jovanovich.*

> Our former chief is gone,
> He only slept and grew fat
> Until he was claimed by death.

> But Nana Adoko sleeps little,
> He is our good father
> Who watches over our affairs."

When Adoko heard this song of praise, he thought: "Indeed, I am the great Adoko. Who has ever said it so well? And my cousin, the chief who has gone, was he not truly the poorest of rulers? How sharp and understanding these people are! How wise is this old bard!"

To the bard who had seen so many chiefs come and go, he said: "This song, it is good. It is a fine song. I shall make you the first singer of Agona as long as I live."

He ordered his servants to distribute gifts among all the people at the celebration and had palm wine given out.

Then he asked the old bard, "Who is the maker of the song you sang? He must be a great singer indeed. Are you the maker of this song?"

"Oh, no," the old bard answered. "I am not the composer. This song was made in ancient times, and we sing it each time a new chief is appointed over us. We merely change the name of the chief."

And when Adoko grew old and died, a bard sang to the new chief:

> "Our new father is Mahama,
> He is great indeed,
> But our former chief had no greatness."

Some Ashanti Proverbs

One does not tell stories to Intikuma.

> (Intikuma is Anansi's son, and through a compact with Nyame, the Sky God, Anansi is the owner of all stories. Intikuma presumably is familiar with all of Anansi's tales. This proverb is used when someone imparts knowledge or news to those who already know it.)

From a compilation by Daniel A. Osei-Cobbina, and other sources.

One head cannot go into consultation.

> (This proverb derives from a story about Anansi, who had collected all the wisdom of the world and placed it in a knapsack. He decides to take the wisdom into the treetops to hide it, but as the knapsack is hanging in front he is unable to climb. His son Intikuma keeps telling Anansi to put the knapsack on his back, but Anansi ignores the advice and finally falls to the ground, scattering his collection of wisdom.)

It is the fool who proclaims, "The insults are not meant for me but for my colleague."

If you swear an oath alone in a pit, still it leaks out.

It is the hunter whose kill is over the fire.

It is not strange to see someone who feeds on the shell of a crab enjoying a broken piece of calabash.

It is with the aid of the tree that a tree-climber makes contact with the sky.

It is hard to fell a tree that is leaning against a rock.

One doesn't dream when he is awake.

I Will Do It Later On is a brother to I Didn't Do It.

If someone calls out "Witch, Witch" and you are not a witch you will not turn around.

No sensible person leaves a stream to drink from a pool.

If the chief orders your execution there is no use drawing lots.

The stranger says he saw no one in the town; the people he met say they did not see anyone come.

It is because of man that the blacksmith makes weapons.

The goldweights (mrammuo) of the asantehene (king) are heavier than those of the ordinary man.

> (Special circumstances have special requirements. The asantehene's weights are expected to be heavier so that there will be an extra margin of gold dust to defray costs of maintaining the court. In some of the Akan states gold was conceived to be state

property, so that the heavier weights of the chiefs were, in effect, a means of taxation.)

A dog's incentive is in his heart, not his head.

If one is fortunate people say he has been to the diviner; if he is destitute they say he is hopeless.

If one does not live in heaven he must live on earth among ordinary men.

Lizard says, "If a man were to achieve everything he would lose his mind."

Justice today, injustice tomorrow, that is not good government.

The slave is naturally the guilty party.

Sayings as Guides to Good Social Behavior

Respect for seniority

Even though you may be taller than your father you still are not his equal.

If you want someone more knowledgeable than yourself to identify a bird, you do not first remove the feathers. (That is, when you want an advised judgment on something, do not withhold important facts.)

Rewards for merit

When a child learns to wash his hands before he eats, he dines with his elders.

If a child conducts himself like an adult at a funeral, he is given a white kola nut. (Kola nuts are chewed by mourners to kill hunger, and the white nuts are more costly than the red ones.)

Against selfishness

If you alone drink a medicine for long life, or to stave off death, you will be left alone in the wasteland.

From Panoply of Ghana, *by A. A. Y. Kyerematen. Accra: Longmans, Green and Co., 1964, with occasional rephrasing.*

If you do not allow a friend to get a nine, you yourself will never get
a ten.

Against obstinacy

If a friend who has asked you to accompany him somewhere says you
should return, you do not argue with him.

If you reach the shrubs and they turn into a forest, you have to turn
back.

Riddle

> He Went Far Away;
> He Went Long Ago;
> He Went Before Anyone Came.
> Which of them is the oldest?

FOUR ASHANTI TALES

The Coming of the Yams

There were not always yams in Ashanti. In ancient times, it is said,
there were none, and the people often found it hard to raise enough
food to last them the year round.

But one day a traveler came through the country carrying a yam
among his possessions. This yam was seen by an Ashanti named Abu. It
made him think. "If we had this yam growing in our country, we would
have something really worthwhile," Abu told his friends. "We wouldn't
have to fear famine the way we do now." And Abu decided to search
for yams so that his people could plant them.

He took his weapons and began his journey. He walked for many
days. Everywhere he. went, he asked people if they knew where he
could find the country where the yams grew. Sometimes they told him

---

From The Hat-Shaking Dance and Other Ashanti Tales from Ghana, © *1957*
by Harold Courlander. Reprinted by permission of Harcourt Brace Jovanovich.

it was this way; sometimes they told him it was the other way. It was a long journey. But at last he found it. He looked at the fields and saw yams growing everywhere. He asked people where he would find the king, and they directed him. He went to the king's house and explained why he had come.

"In my country there are no yams," Abu said, "and the people are often hungry. If you could give me some yams to take back we could plant them, and there would be no more hunger."

The king listened and considered. He said, "I will think about it." And he had Abu put up and cared for in his guesthouse.

After several days, the king sent for Abu and said: "I would like to help your people, but when they are well fed and strong, they may think of going to war against their weaker neighbors."

"This would not happen," Abu said, "because my people are peaceful. And is it not true that people who are hungry may go to war to relieve their misery?"

"Still, if they are ambitious, I would be risking a great deal to help you," the king said. "However, if you will bring me a man from your tribe to live here as a hostage, I will give you the yams."

So Abu returned to Ashanti, and he went to his father's house and told him what he had learned. He said: "Father, you have many sons. Send one of them as a hostage to the king of the yam country, and then we can have yams to feed the people."

But the father could not bring himself to send any of his sons into exile, and he refused. Abu went next to his brothers and told them of the offer of the king of the yam country. He asked them to send one of their sons as a hostage, but like their father they turned away and refused.

So in desperation Abu journeyed again to the yam country and told the king he couldn't find anyone to act as a hostage. The king was firm. He said, "Then I am sorry, but I can't give you the yams without security."

Abu returned home sadly, for he saw no solution. And when he came again to his village, he remembered his sister, who had only one son. He went to her and told her the story. She said to Abu, "I have only one son, and if he should go, I would have none."

Abu said: "Then we are lost. You are the last hope. In many lands there are yams. Here there are none, and the people are doomed to be hungry." His sister listened while he told how yams would change the life of the people. At last Abu's sister consented.

Then he returned to the king of the yam country with his sister's son and gave him as a hostage. The king took the boy into his own house, and he gave Abu yams to take home in exchange.

When Abu came back to Ashanti, he gave the people yams to plant, and they were glad. The yams grew and were harvested, and there was plenty to eat. The yam became the most important of all the crops grown in Ashanti.

As for Abu, he declared: "My father refused to send a son as hostage in exchange for the yams. Each of my brothers refused to send a son. Henceforth I will have nothing further to do with my father or my brothers. It was my sister who gave a son so that we might not go hungry. She will be honored. When I die, all of my property will be given to my nephew who lives in the yam country, for he is the one who made it possible for us to eat."

And so it was that when Abu died, his cattle and his land passed on not to his son or his brothers, but to his nephew, the child of his sister.

As for the people of Ashanti, they said: "Abu has done a great thing for us in bringing the yams to our country. We shall therefore do as Abu has done, in memory of his great deed."

And from that time onward, when a man died he left all he owned to his sister's son.

In honor of Abu, the Ashanti people now call the family by the name *abu-sua*, meaning "borrowed from Abu."

This is how it came about among the Ashanti people that boys inherit property not from their fathers but from their [maternal] uncles.

Journey to Asamando, Land of the Dead

Among the Ashanti, a young man was living there. His name was Kwasi Benefo. His fields flourished, he had many cattle. He lacked only a wife to bear children for him, to care for his household, and, when the time should come, to mourn his death. Kwasi Benefo went looking. In his village he found a young woman who greatly pleased him. They married. They were content with each other. But soon the young woman faded, and death took her. Kwasi Benefo grieved. He bought her an amoasie, a piece of silk-cotton cloth to cover her genitals, and beads to go around her waist, and in these things she was buried.

Kwasi Benefo could not forget her. He looked for her in his house, but she was not there. His heart was not with living anymore. His brothers spoke to him, his uncle spoke to him, his friends spoke to him, saying: "Kwasi, put it from your mind. This is the way it is in the world. Find yourself another wife." At last Kwasi Benefo comforted himself. He went to another village. He found a young woman there and made arrangements. He brought her home. Again he became contented with living. The woman had a good character. She took good care of the household. She tried in every way to please her husband. Kwasi Benefo said, "Yes, living is worthwhile." But after she had been pregnant for some time, the young woman became ill. She grew gaunt. Death took her. Kwasi Benefo, his heart hurt him. His wife was dressed in her amoasie, she was buried. Kwasi Benefo could not be consoled. He sat in his house. He would not come out. People said to him: "People have died before. Arise, come out of the house. Mingle with your friends as

Narrator: Kingsley Kwarteng. Author's collection. Compare with the Angola story, "King Kitamba Kia Xiba," p. 293.

you used to do." But Kwasi Benefo did not desire life anymore. He remained in his house.

The family of the young woman who had died heard about Kwasi Benefo's grief. They said: "He is suffering too much. This man loved our daughter. Let us give him another wife." They sent messengers to Kwasi Benefo, and they brought him to their village. They said to him: "One must grieve, yes, but you cannot give your life to it. We have another daughter, she will make a good wife for you. Take her. This way you will not be alone. What is past is past, one cannot go there anymore. What a man has loved is in his heart, it does not go away. Yet the dead live with the dead, and the living with the living."

Kwasi Benefo pondered on it. He said, "Now, how can I take another wife when the one who has died calls to me?" They answered: "Yes, that is the way a person feels. But in time it will be different." Kwasi Benefo went home. He resumed working in his fields. And after some months he returned to the village where his wife's family lived. He said, "The daughter you spoke of, I have been thinking of her." They said: "Yes, our daughter will make a good wife. She has a good character. She will do well for you." They talked, they made arrangements. At last Kwasi Benefo arose, and with his new wife he returned to his house. They went on living. The young woman conceived, and a boy child was born. There was a celebration in the village. People danced and sang. Kwasi Benefo gave out gifts. He said: "My life is good. When has it ever been so good?"

One day Kwasi Benefo was working in his fields. Some women of the village came crying that a tree had fallen. Kwasi Benefo ceased his hoeing, saying, "Who cries over a falling tree?" Then darkness covered his spirit. He said, "Is there something left unspoken?" They said: "Your wife was coming back from the river. She sat beneath the tree to rest. A spirit of the woods weakened the roots and the tree fell on her." Kwasi Benefo ran to the village. He went to his house. His wife lay upon her mat without life in her body. Kwasi Benefo cried out. He threw himself on the ground and lay there as if life had departed from him also. He heard nothing, felt nothing. People said, "Kwasi Benefo is dead." The medicine men came. They said: "No, he is not dead. He lingers between here and there." They worked on Kwasi Benefo. They revived him. He stood up. He made the arrangements that were necessary. There was a wake, and the next day his wife was buried in her amoasie. After that, Kwasi Benefo brooded. He thought: "Evil is working against me. Each of my wives has died. I do not want another wife, yet if I did, what family would trust me with its daughter?" What was in Kwasi Benefo's thoughts was also in the minds of other people. They said, "It is not good to be a wife of Kwasi Benefo."

Kwasi Benefo said: "Of what value are my fields and my cattle? They are nothing to me." He took his boy child and left the village. He abandoned his house, he abandoned his farm. He carried his son to the place where his wife's family lived and left him there. He went out into the bush. He walked for many days, not caring where he was. He

arrived at a distant village, but he departed from it at once and went
deeper into the bush country. At last, at a wild place, he stopped. He
said, "This place, far from people, I will stay here." He built a crude
house. He gathered roots and seeds to eat. He made traps for small
game. Thus he lived. His clothing turned to rags, and he began to wear
the skins of animals. In time he almost forgot that his name was Kwasi
Benefo, and that he had once been a prosperous farmer. His life was
wretched, but he did not care. This is the way it was with Kwasi Benefo.

A year passed, then another. Little by little the desire for life came
back to Kwasi Benefo. Once again he began to farm. He burned the
brush and planted corn. He built a new house. He travelled to a distant
village and acquired cloth, and he clothed himself. His farm began to
prosper. He acquired cattle. And once again he yearned to have a
woman to care for his house and bear children. Thus he sought once
more a wife. He married again. Things were going well for Kwasi
Benefo until this wife, his fourth, became sick and died.

This time Kwasi said, "How can I go on living?" He abandoned his
farm, his house and his cattle and journeyed back to the village where
he was born. People were surprised because they had thought of him
as dead. His family and his friends gathered to celebrate his return, but
Kwasi Benefo said: "No, there is to be no celebration. I have come back
only to die in my own village and be buried here near the graves of my
ancestors." He settled again in his old house, which was now open to
the weather and falling down. But he made no effort to repair anything,
nor did he go out to his fields, which were grown up with brush. He
lived on this way, thinking of all his wives, tormented by the thought
that when his time came to die there would be no one to mourn his
death and sing praise songs for him.

One night as he lay sleepless the thought came to him that he should
go to Asamando, the Land of the Dead, and see the four young women
who had shared his life. He arose. He went out of his house and departed from his village. He went to the forest place called Nsamandow,
where the dead were buried. He reached it, he went on. There were
no paths to follow. There was no light. All was darkness. He passed
through the forest and came to a place of dim light. No one was living
there. There were no sounds in the air. No voices of man, no birds, no
animals broke the stillness. Kwasi Benefo went on, until he came at last
to a river. He tried to ford the river, but he could not do it, for the water
was too deep and it was running too fast. He thought, "Here my journey
comes to an end."

But at this moment he felt the splash of water on his face. Sitting on
the far bank was an old woman with a brass pan at her side. The pan
was full of women's loincloths and beads. By this sign Kwasi Benefo
knew her to be Amokye, the person who welcomed the souls of dead
women to Asamando, and took from each of them her amoasie and
beads. This was the reason why women prepared for burial were
dressed as they were, so that each could give her amoasie and beads to
Amokye at the river crossing. Amokye said to Kwasi Benefo, "Why are

you here?" And he answered: "I have come to see my wives. I cannot live any longer, because every woman that stays in my house, death takes her. I cannot sleep, I cannot eat, I want nothing that the living world has for the living." Amokye said to him: "Oh, you must be Kwasi Benefo. Yes, I have heard of you. Many persons who came through here have spoken of your misfortune. But you are not a soul, you are a living man, therefore you cannot cross." Kwasi Benefo said, "Then I will remain here until I die and become a soul."

Amokye, the guardian at the river, took compassion on Kwasi Benefo. She said, "Because of your suffering I will let you come across." She caused the water to run slowly. She caused it to become shallow. She said: "Go that way. There you will find them. But they are like the air, you will not be able to see them, though they will know you have come." Kwasi Benefo crossed the river, and he went on. Now he was in Asamando. He came to a house, he entered. Outside the house he heard the sounds of village activities. He heard people calling to one another. He heard hoeing in the fields, the clearing of brush, and grain being pounded in mortars.

A bucket of water appeared, and washcloths suddenly came into view before him. He washed off the dust of his journey. Outside the house, now, he heard his wives singing a song of welcome. The bucket and washcloths disappeared, and in their place he saw a gourd dish of food and a jug of water. While he ate, the voices of his wives went on singing Kwasi's praises. They told of what a kind husband he had been in the land of the living, and spoke of his gentleness. When he was through eating, the dish and the jug disappeared, and then there was a sleeping mat for Kwasi. His wives invited him to rest. He lay down on the mat. His wives sang again, and in their song they told Kwasi to continue living until his natural death, when his soul would come to Asamando unencumbered by a body. When this time arrived, they said, they would be waiting for him. Meanwhile, they said, Kwasi should marry again, and this time his wife would not die.

Hearing these sweet words from the women he loved, Kwasi Benefo fell into a deep sleep. When at last he awoke he was no longer in Asamando, but in the forest. He arose. He made his way back to his house in the village. He called on his friends to come and help him build a new house. When that was done, he sent messengers to the people who belonged to his fraternal society, saying that on such and such a day there would be a clearing of his fields. The men gathered on that day. They cleared and burned his fields, they began the hoeing. Kwasi Benefo planted. His crops grew and he cultivated. Again he mingled among people. In time he found a wife. They had children. They lived on. That is the story of Kwasi Benefo. The old people told it that way.

O the World!

There was a certain village called Nyamempesa, the name of which signifies God-does-not-like-so.

In Nyamempesa lived a hunter named Kwabena Mpeasem, the meaning of which is Kwabena-does-not-like-matters. His wife was called Yaa Ohia, meaning Yaa Poverty.

Because he made his living at hunting, Kwabena Mpeasem went to distant places in the forest to find game, along with his servant, Kofi Suro, whose name means Kofi Afraid. The hunter was away from his home weeks and months. He came, he went, and he was in the forest as much as he was in his house.

Yaa Ohia, the hunter's wife, did not mind his absences. She had three lovers in the village. Sometimes she entertained one of them in her bed, sometimes another. One of these men was known as Ewiase, because he had written on the truck he owned the word Weiase, meaning The World. The second of Yaa Ohia's lovers was the village chief. And the third was Opanying Ko Somuah, the chief's linguist. As for Ewiase, it was understood that he would come to visit Yaa whenever he desired, and this he did. For the chief, it was not that easy, for according to custom a chief was forbidden to have intercourse with another man's wife. But whenever the moment was opportune he sent his linguist to tell Yaa to come to his house. As for Opanying Ko Somuah, the linguist, whenever he arrived at the hunter's house with a message for Yaa, he entered and had pleasure with her, after which he brought her to the chief.

The hunter's wife therefore had a full life, if not with one lover, then with another. The linguist knew about the chief, but he did not know about Ewiase. The chief had no knowledge about the doings of his linguist or of Ewiase. And Ewiase had the impression that he alone had access to the hunter's wife. So discreetly was everything done that the other people of the village had no suspicions. But the hunter's servant, Kofi, sensed that all was not as it should have been. He observed that Yaa seemed restless when her husband returned from hunting, and that she seemed contented whenever he went on an expedition for game. Sometimes Kofi asked a question here or a question there, but he learned nothing. Nevertheless, his suspicions grew, and at last he summoned up courage and spoke of the matter to the hunter. Kwabena Mpeasem took no offense, but neither did he take Kofi's comments seriously. He hunted, he returned, he hunted, he returned. That was the rhythm of his life. Little by little, hearing warnings from Kofi, the hunter became uneasy about Yaa.

One day as he and Kofi departed on another expedition to the forest, Kwabena told Yaa that this time he was going to a very distant place and that he would be away longer than usual. As soon as the hunter was

Told by Daniel A. Osei-Cobbina. Author's collection.

gone, Yaa went to tell Ewiase, the linguist, and the chief that she was once more alone. As for Ewiase, he came often. He had more good times with Yaa than the other two did. One evening when Yaa and Ewiase were together in bed Yaa heard a sound at the door. She said, "Ah! Kwabena has returned so soon!" Ewiase said, "How so? He went on a long journey." Yaa answered, "Nevertheless, it is my husband, I am sure of it, for I dreamed last night that he came suddenly!" Ewiase was afraid. He said, "Where shall I go?" And Yaa answered: "There is nowhere to go. Get under the bed. I will urge Kwabena to take a bath, and while he is doing this you can slip away." So Ewiase crawled under the bed and lay there in terror.

When Yaa opened the door she was surprised to see not her husband, but Opanying Ko Somuah, the linguist. The linguist entered, giving the message that the chief wanted Yaa to come secretly to his house. "However," he said, "let the two of us have pleasure first." He offered Yaa ten pounds as a gift, and the two of them went to bed. Underneath the bed Ewiase kept silent. As for the chief, after he had waited for a long time, he went to Yaa's house himself. He knocked on the door, and once more Yaa feared that her husband was about to enter. So she urged Opanying, as she had Ewiase, to get under the bed, saying that she would try to distract her husband with a bath. Opanying went under the bed quickly. There he met Ewiase, and the two of them lay without making a sound.

And this time, instead of the hunter, it was the chief who entered the room. He complained about his linguist, whom he had sent with a message, but Yaa said she had not seen the man. Since it was dark outside, and since he was already at Yaa's house, the chief decided to stay instead of taking her to his own place. And so the two of them had their pleasure, with Ewiase and the linguist lying underneath, after the chief had given Yaa a gift of twenty-five pounds. The chief and Yaa spoke hard words about Kwabena, calling him a man who did not take care of his household.

Even as they abused him the hunter was approaching, because Kofi had persuaded him to return sooner than expected. Kofi was certain that the whole matter would now be revealed. Yaa heard Kwabena and Kofi talking outside. She said to the chief: "Nana, we are at the mercy of God! My husband has arrived from the bush! Have you a rope so that we may hang ourselves?" The chief was too stunned with his misfortune to say a word. The weight of disgrace was too much for him. He lay as though he were dying. But Yaa shook him vigorously and made him crawl under the bed, where he found his linguist and Ewiase. They huddled together, companions in fear.

The hunter entered his house. He greeted his wife. He offered her snails that he had gathered on the hunt. Yaa was anxious for him to go and bathe, so that her lovers could make their escape. She urged him, saying, "When one returns from hunting he should cleanse himself of the taint of his game."

Kwabena Mpeasem said, "Yes, it is so. But first I must rest." He sat down in a chair. He was so weary that he exclaimed, "O Ewiase! O the World!"

Hearing this, the man named Ewiase, thinking the hunter was talking to him, called out: "Oh, Kwabena Mpeasem! Be considerate! I am not the only one under the bed! The chief and his linguist are here also!"

Kwabena looked underneath and saw the three men huddled together. He asked Yaa Ohia for an explanation, but she could not give it. Her tongue would not serve her. She could not say a word. When Kwabena took out his hunting knife, the three lovers of Yaa began to talk at the same time. They begged him to be indulgent with them, and offered an indemnity. The chief sent his linguist to the chief's house, and he returned with one hundred eighty pounds. Kwabena accepted the indemnity. After that Yaa's lovers went out into the night and scattered.

The next day Kwabena Mpeasem took his wife Yaa Ohia to her relatives. He divorced her and left her behind. Yaa became poor and despised, and thus she earned her name Ohia, Poverty. To his servant, Kofi Suro, Kwabena gave a double-barrelled gun and twenty pounds as a reward for his faithfulness.

And in time to come, whenever anyone asked him the reason for his sudden divorce, the hunter always answered:

"O Ewiase! O the world!"

Talk

A farmer went out to his field one morning to dig up some yams. While he was digging, one of the yams said to him: "Well, at last you're here. You never weeded me, but now you come around with your digging stick. Go away and leave me alone!"

The farmer turned around and looked at his cow in amazement. The cow was chewing her cud and looking at him.

"Did you say something?" he asked.

The cow kept on chewing and said nothing, but the man's dog spoke up.

"It wasn't the cow who spoke to you," the dog said. "It was the yam. The yam says leave him alone."

The man became angry, because his dog had never talked before, and he didn't like his tone besides. So he took his knife and cut a branch from a palm tree to whip his dog. Just then the palm tree said, "Put that branch down!"

The man was getting very upset about the way things were going, and he started to throw the palm branch away, but the palm branch said, "Man, put me down softly!"

From The Cow-Tail Switch and Other West African Stories, *by Harold Courlander and George Herzog,* © *1975 by Harold Courlander.*

He put the branch down gently on a stone, and the stone said, "Hey, take that thing off me!"

This was enough, and the frightened farmer started to run for his village. On the way he met a fisherman going the other way with a fish trap on his head.

"What's the hurry?" the fisherman asked.

"My yam said, 'Leave me alone!' Then the dog said, 'Listen to what the yam says!' When I went to whip the dog with a palm branch the tree said, 'Put that branch down!' Then the palm branch said, 'Do it softly!' Then the stone said, 'Take that thing off me!' "

"Is that all?" the man with the fish trap asked. "Is that so frightening?"

"Well," the man's fish trap said, "did he take it off the stone?"

"Wah!" the fisherman shouted. He threw the fish trap on the ground and began to run with the farmer, and on the trail they met a weaver with a bundle of cloth on his head.

"Where are you going in such a rush?" he asked them.

"My yam said, 'Leave me alone!' " the farmer said. "The dog said, 'Listen to what the yam says!' The tree said, 'Put that branch down!' The branch said, 'Do it softly!' And the stone said, 'Take that thing off me!' "

"And then," the fisherman continued, "the fish trap said, 'Did he take it off?' "

"That's nothing to get excited about," the weaver said, "no reason at all."

"Oh, yes it is," his bundle of cloth said. "If it happened to you you'd run too!"

"Wah!" the weaver shouted. He threw his bundle on the trail and started running with the other men.

They came panting to the ford in the river and found a man bathing.

"Are you chasing a gazelle?" he asked them.

The first man said breathlessly: "My yam talked at me, and it said, 'Leave me alone!' And my dog said, 'Listen to your yam!' And when I cut myself a branch the tree said, 'Put that branch down!' And the branch said, 'Do it softly!' And the stone said, 'Take that thing off me!' "

The fisherman panted, "And my trap said, 'Did he?' "

The weaver wheezed, "And my bundle of cloth said, 'You'd run too!' "

"Is that why you're running?" the man in the river asked.

"Well, wouldn't you run if you were in their position?" the river said.

The man jumped out of the water and began to run with the others. They ran down the main street of the village to the house of the chief. The chief's servants brought his stool out, and he came and sat on it to listen to their complaints. The men began to recite their troubles.

"I went out to my garden to dig yams," the farmer said, waving his arms. "Then everything began to talk! My yam said, 'Leave me alone!' My dog said, 'Pay attention to your yam!' The tree said, 'Put that branch down!' The branch said, 'Do it softly!' And the stone said, 'Take it off me!' "

"And my fish trap said, 'Well, did he take it off?' " the fisherman said.

"And my cloth said, 'You'd run too!' " the weaver said.

"And the river said the same," the bather said hoarsely, his eyes bulging.

The chief listened to them patiently, but he couldn't refrain from scowling.

"Now this is really a wild story," he said at last. "You'd better all go back to your work before I punish you for disturbing the peace."

So the men went away, and the chief shook his head and mumbled to himself, "Nonsense like that upsets the community."

"Fantastic, isn't it?" his stool said. "Imagine, a talking yam!"

Gold and Gold Weights

One of the earlier forms of currency among the Akan peoples was iron. Later, brass was used for this purpose and, in time, cowries. Then gold dust, or nuggets, came into use. Gold had a sacred significance among the Akan, and was considered by some to be the symbol of the kra, or soul, of Nyame, the supreme deity. In theory at least, all gold belonged to the king, which is to say it belonged to the state. In some cases the state conducted gold-digging operations on a large scale, with slaves comprising the labor force. But all citizens were permitted to pan gold from the streams or mine it from the ground. A certain portion had to be remitted to the state, in some cases one third or more. In the state of Bono the entire gold output was actually reserved for state use. Thousands of pits found along river courses testify to the enormous effort put into the extraction of gold, as do still other pits and shafts found in mountainous regions.

With the discovery of gold came the gold trade, and with the trade came the counterweights for measuring gold dust. For most of those who dealt in gold, whether buying or selling, the weights were cast in brass, although the weights of some royal personages are known to have been made of gold or silver. The weights belonging to kings were always cast one-third heavier than ordinary weights, the extra amount representing the state's rightful share. The casting of the weights was a function of the goldsmiths, who belonged to a kind of guild or brotherhood and who traced their common ancestry back to a legendary first goldsmith. Their profession had a semisacred character because of the religious significance of gold. Eventually the center of the gold trade came to be the state of Ashanti.

The weights are now recognized as one of the finest artistic creations of the Akan, and in particular of the Ashanti. Some of them—generally regarded as the oldest—are geometric in form, and the designs on them are believed to be symbols derived from religious concepts. Other weights were made in the form of people, animals and objects, many of which represent proverbs and sayings or historical and legendary events. In numerous instances the meanings of the geometric forms and human figures are no longer recalled.

Gold weights (mrammuo)—that is, the brass weights used for weighing gold—were for the most part cast by the lost-wax method. The figures were first fashioned in beeswax and encased in clay, which was then heated sufficiently for the wax to be melted and absorbed. Afterwards, by one of several methods, molten brass was introduced into the cavity. When the metal had hardened, the clay mold was broken and the figure, a unique sculpture, removed. A similar process was used to produce so-called "lost beetle" weights. Instead of making a wax model, a beetle or some other miniature object from nature was enclosed in clay and reproduced in brass. The "lost beetle" weights include facsimile reproductions of such things as grasshoppers, crabs' claws, earthworms, birds' feet, peanuts, and a wide variety of seed pods, at least some of which have symbolic meaning.

A gold trader of prestige included in his paraphernalia numerous weights of different value and design. Sometimes foreign objects found their way into the assortment, perhaps a brass button, a brass bell, a small brass machine part, or a brass key. If a weight came out of the cast a little heavy, a small portion was broken off, or the weight was reduced by filing. If it came out light, a bit of lead was added. A figure of an animal with only three legs is not necessarily a victim of a casting accident, but may be an altered weight. Some gold weights, presumably as a mark of distinction, were plated with white metal, such as tin, zinc, or silver.

Gold weights are no longer functional among the Akan, but they have great value both as art objects and as the bearers of old traditions. Many of them are carefully kept as family heirlooms and treasure.

Ashanti Proverbs and Sayings Cast in Brass

Some gold weights are mnemonic, serving to remind people of proverbs or events without actually depicting them. Others are more pictorial, representing an action or a scene mentioned by a proverb, or by a story from which a proverb or saying is derived. Some of the proverbs are simplistic, others sophisticated and many-layered. Here are some proverbs of the Ashanti people immortalized—*written*, in a sense—in brass.

GOLD WEIGHT	PROVERB
A leopard attacking a hunter	It's better not to shoot at the leopard at all than to shoot and miss.
Two fighting birds	Two birds fighting with their beaks. (A disturbance, but no one gets injured.)
A man with a load of wood on his head	As long as a person has a head he cannot avoid carrying loads on it.
A shield (with or without a covering)	Even when the shield covering wears out the frame survives. (Men do not live forever, but their accomplishments remain behind.)
Birds on a tree	Only birds of the same kind gather together. (Comments on a person's background, his family or his reputation.)
A man scraping bark from a tree	The bark falls to the ground if the one who scrapes has no one to gather it up for him. (One should accept help if he needs it.)
A leopard	When rain falls on the leopard it wets him but does not wash out his markings. (A person's character does not change.)
A man playing a drum	When a drum has a drumhead, one does not beat the wooden sides. (Avoid farfetched actions.)
A chief sitting on a chair or stool	When the head of the household dies, that is the end of the household. (No group can survive without good leadership.)
A scorpion	When a scorpion stings without mercy, you kill it without mercy. (A man responds according to the seriousness of his situation.)
A man with a gun	It is only when a gun has someone to cock it that it can be warlike.
Crossed crocodiles with a common stomach	Two crocodiles having a common stomach nevertheless fight over the food. (Persons with a common interest who compete. Also refers to the well-being of the family or the village.)
A crocodile with a fish in its mouth	If the fish in the water grows fat, it is in the interest of the crocodile.

A porcupine	A man does not rub backs with a porcupine. (Don't get involved with someone who can hurt you.)
An elephant-tail whisk	Short though the elephant's tail may be, he can flick away flies with it. (Handicaps or disadvantages are no excuse for lack of effort.)
A fowl's head protruding from a cooking pot	The head of a bird is recognizable in the soup even if the other parts are not. (Some things can't be covered up.)
A man throwing a stone at a bird in a tree	When a bird sits too long in the tree it may have a stone thrown at it.
A man with a hump on his back	If one has a hump on his chest or his back, there's nothing he can do about it. (Don't rail against what can't be changed.)
A hunter eating a mushroom	When the hunter returns from the forest carrying mushrooms, one need not ask him how he fared.
An elephant	If you follow the elephant you don't have to knock the dew from the grass.
A rooster	Rooster, do not be so proud. Your mother was only an eggshell.
A man holding a head in his hands (an executioner)	After a man has had his head cut off he no longer fears anything.
A man hanging by his neck	All the different forms of death are death.
A rooster and a hen	The hen knows when it is daybreak, but allows the rooster to make the announcement.
A child with his hand on a lion	There are still those who do not know a lion when they see one. (Innocence.)
A man holding his stomach	Intestines do not help the belly. (That is, the belly is filled with intestines, but one can still be hungry.)
A bird caught in a snare	The bird caught in the snare is the one that sings sweetly.

A man smoking a pipe	Even a farmer has time to relax.
A man with a pipe in his mouth and a keg of gunpowder on his head	Because you carry gunpowder is no reason you should not smoke.
An okra fruit	An okra does not show its seeds through its skin. (A man's face does not reveal all he knows.)
A snail	To get at the meat of a water snail you must cut off the top and the bottom of the shell. (Nothing worthwhile is achieved without effort.)
Kola pods	The ant on the kola pod will not pick the kola to eat or sell. (A person who has something he doesn't need but won't let someone else have it.)
A guinea fowl	If a guinea fowl goes after a dead frog its hunger will only increase. (Dead frogs are tabooed. The meaning is that it is foolish to do something that does not have any prospect of success.)
A cartridge belt	The cartridge belt of Akowua was never known to be empty. (Akowua was a famous warrior. The meaning is that even if an enterprising person is in difficulty he will find a way to prevail.)
A clockbird	In his own forest the clockbird is supreme (even if nowhere else).
A canoe	The canoe must be paddled on both sides. (Cooperation makes for success.)
Fowls eating a cockroach	A cockroach has fallen among the fowls. Or: Fowls will not spare a cockroach that has fallen among them. (One who is at the mercy of his enemy should not expect consideration.)
A sankofa bird with turned head, looking backward	Regrets are useless.

A man digging up a stump	A stump that could hurt you is dug out by the roots (not merely cut off at the top).
Doves sitting around the bowl of an oil lamp	After a man has eaten he will drink.
A man with an axe, carrying wood on his head	A poor man must go out and cut firewood.
An antelope with horns sloping far to the back	"Had I known that." (It is futile to regret what has passed.)
A man with gun in hand standing before a trap, a dead monkey slung over his shoulder	If one person had not helped me, another would have helped me. (One way or another one achieves something. If the hunter had not shot the monkey he would have caught game in his trap.)
A man lying on his stomach and a man lying on his back	If I who am lying on my back cannot see the Sky God, how can you, lying on your stomach, do so?
Two old men shaking hands	Represents two friends, Adu and Amoako, once men of wealth, who have met again after years of separation, only to find out that they both are now poor.
A man helping another man climb a tree	A man with no friends has no one to help him up.
A snake with a bird in his mouth	Although the snake has to crawl on his belly, God has given him wings.
A leopard with a porcupine in his mouth	An animal that the leopard has not been able to eat, its carcass will not be eaten by the cat.
Two men, their heads together	One head does not exchange ideas.
A tortoise holding a baby tortoise in its mouth	The tortoise does not have milk to give but it knows how to take care of its child.
A tortoise	If hair is so easy to grow why doesn't the tortoise have any?

The Search for Gold

AN ASHANTI TALE

It is said that one time the chief of the Gurensi people had to make a long journey to the south, but he was concerned about the welfare of his daughter during his absence. He went to his friend named Gold and said to him: "I shall be gone one month, two months—who knows how long? Watch my daughter for me while I am gone. If men come with the hope of marrying her, turn them away; I will speak with them when I return."

Gold replied, "Yes, do not worry; I will see after her."

The chief went on his journey. One month, two months passed, and he did not return. Men came to ask about the chief's daughter. They wished to marry her. But Gold turned them away. When the chief had been gone many months, Gold said: "Something has happened to my friend the chief. He is not coming home."

A young man came to ask for the chief's daughter. Gold said: "Her father went away and never returned. He put her in my charge. So you must make the marriage settlement with me."

The young man and Gold discussed the marriage settlement. They argued. At last they settled the amount. The young man brought many cowries. He brought cloth. He brought copper bars. He brought a horse. He brought many things and paid them to Gold for the marriage settlement. Then the young man took the chief's daughter and went away to another village to the north. Gold said to himself, "Indeed, now I am rich."

A day came when it was said that the chief was returning. Gold said: "He told me to send the suitors away, and I did not do it. His daughter is no more in his house. I thought the chief was dead, but now he returns. I received the marriage settlement for myself. How can I face him?"

Gold took his family and everything he owned and went away. He travelled far, fearing that the chief would come after him and bring him back. He went across the grassy plains. He disappeared from the country.

The chief came back to his village. He came to his house, saying, "Where is my daughter?"

The people said, "Your friend Gold took the marriage settlement and gave her to a suitor."

He replied, "Bring Gold here at once."

They said, "It cannot be done. Gold has fled out of the country."

From The King's Drum and Other African Stories, © *1962 by Harold Courlander. Reprinted by permission of Harcourt Brace Jovanovich. In the original rendition by the narrator, the friend of the chief is named Gold. The King's Drum text gives the name as Money, in accord with the narrator's suggestion. As given here, the name reverts back to the original, Gold.*

The chief said: "Gold has broken his word. He has given my daughter away in my absence. He has taken the marriage settlement for himself. Find him. Bring him back."

They asked, "Wherever shall we look for him?"

He said: "Look everywhere. The matter cannot be closed until he is brought back."

The people looked. When they went hunting, they also sought the chief's friend. When they met Hausa traders from the north they asked, "Have you seen Gold?" And the traders asked in every village through which they passed, "Is Gold here?"

Time passed. The chief of the Gurensi became old and died. Still the people searched. They never stopped. The son of the chief became chief. He grew old and died. Still the search went on.

This is why it is said that people everywhere are always looking for Gold.

ANANSI, TRICKSTER HERO OF THE AKAN

Anansi, the spider, sometimes called Kwaku (Uncle) Anansi, is the paramount trickster hero of the Ashanti and related Akan peoples. He is also a culture hero and, frequently, a buffoon. He is endlessly preoccupied with outwitting the creatures of the field and forest, men, and even the deities. He is an adversary in endless contest with his community. Sometimes seen sympathetically, even as wise, he is more generally characterized as cunning, predatory, greedy, gluttonous and without scruples. Though he may be admired for his frequent victories over those who are larger and stronger than himself, he does not necessarily gain moral approval. In fact, there are moral teachings in many of his defeats, teachings which say, in effect, "This is what Anansi did and, in consequence, how he was shamed, humiliated or punished." If he is generally shrewd, he is also often stupid or an unwitting clown.

As a culture hero, some of his actions and escapades result in the creation of natural phenomena (such as the moon) or the beginning of certain customs, traditions and institutions. Thus, as the stories explain, he is responsible for all men having hoes, for the fact that men have debts, for the fact that greed is found everywhere, for the origin of the human tongue, for the fact that spiders build webs in dark corners and that snakes turn their bellies to the sky when they are killed. He has frequent encounters with the supreme Sky God, Onyame (or Nyanko-pon), and the earth deity Aberewa. As culture hero he owns all tales and stories that are told—anansesem, as they are called—having obtained title to them from Nyame himself.

A great many anansesem are told today in the Caribbean and in other Afro-American communities. Anansi himself is remembered in the New World as Nancy, Aunt Nancy, and Sis' Nancy, while his son In-tikuma lives on as Terrycooma.

Anansi Proves He Is the Oldest

It happened one time that the animals of the fields and the forest had a great argument about which of them was the oldest and entitled to the most respect. Each of them said, "I am the oldest." They argued at great length, and at last they decided to take the case before a judge. They went to the house of Anansi, the spider, and they said to him: "Kwaku Anansi, we are in dispute as to which of us is the most venerable. Listen to our testimony."

So Anansi called his children to bring him a cashew shell, and he sat on it with great dignity, as though he were a chief sitting on a carved stool.

The guinea fowl was the first to speak. He said: "I swear it. I am the oldest of all creatures. When I was born, there was a great grass fire. Since there was no one else in the world to put it out, I ran into the flames and stamped them out with my feet. My legs were badly burned, and as you can see, they are still red."

The animals looked at the guinea fowl's legs and saw it was true: they were red. They said: "Eeee! He is old!"

Then the parrot declared: "I swear it. When I came into the world, there were no tools and no weapons. It was I who made the first ham-mer that was ever used by blacksmiths. I beat the iron into shape with my beak, and it is for this reason that my beak is bent."

The animals looked at the parrot's beak, crying out, "Eeee! The par-rot is old indeed!"

Then the elephant spoke: "I swear it. I am older than the parrot and the guinea fowl. When I was created, the Sky God gave me a long and useful nose. When the other animals were made, there was a shortage of material, and they were given small noses."

The animals examined the elephant's nose and shouted, "Eeeeee! The elephant is truly old!"

This story and the four immediately following—"Anansi Owns All Tales That Are Told," "Anansi's Rescue from the River," "Aberewa's Sword," and "Anansi Borrows Money"—are from The Hat-Shaking Dance and Other Ashanti Tales from Ghana, *© 1957 by Harold Courlander. Reprinted by permission of Har-court Brace Jovanovich.*

The rabbit gave his testimony then, saying: "I swear it. I am the oldest. When I came into the world, night and day had not yet been created."

The animals appaluded the rabbit. They said, "Eeeeee! Is he not really the oldest?"

The porcupine spoke last, and he said: "I swear it. As you will all have to admit, I am the oldest. When I was born, the earth wasn't finished yet. It was soft like butter and couldn't be walked upon."

This was great testimony, and the animals cheered the porcupine. They cried, "Eeeeee! Who can be older than he?"

Then they waited to hear Anansi's judgment. He sat on his cashew shell and shook his head, saying: "If you had come to me first, I would have saved you this argument, for I am the oldest of all creatures. When I was born, the earth itself had not yet been made, and there was nothing to stand on. When my father died, there was no ground to bury him in. So I had to bury him in my head."

And when the animals heard this they declared, "Eeeeee! Kwaku Anansi is the oldest of all living things! How can we doubt it?"

Anansi Owns All Tales That Are Told

In the beginning, all tales and stories belonged to Nyame, the Sky God. But Kwaku Anansi, the spider, yearned to be the owner of all the stories known in the world, and he went to Nyame and offered to buy them.

The Sky God said: "I am willing to sell the stories, but the price is high. Many people have come to me offering to buy, but the price was too high for them. Rich and powerful families have not been able to pay. Do you think you can do it?"

Anansi replied to the Sky God: "I can do it. What is the price?"

"My price is three things," the Sky God said. "I must first have Mmoboro, the hornets. I must then have Onini, the great python. I must then have Osebo, the leopard. For these things I will sell you the right to tell all stories."

Anansi said, "I will bring them."

He went home and made his plans. He first cut a gourd from a vine and made a small hole in it. He took a large calabash and filled it with water. He went to the tree where the hornets lived. He poured some of the water over himself, so that he was dripping. He threw some water over the hornets, so that they too were dripping. Then he put the calabash on his head, as though to protect himself from a storm, and called out to the hornets: "Are you foolish people? Why do you stay in the rain that is falling?"

The hornets answered, "Where shall we go?"

"Go here, in this dry gourd," Anansi told them.

The hornets thanked him and flew into the gourd through the small hole. When the last of them had entered, Anansi plugged the hole with a ball of grass, saying, "Oh, yes, but you are really foolish people!"

He took his gourd full of hornets to Nyame, the Sky God. The Sky God accepted them. He said, "There are two more things."

Anansi returned to the forest and cut a long bamboo pole and some strong vines. Then he walked toward the house of Onini, the python, talking to himself. He said: "My wife is stupid. I say he is longer and stronger. My wife says he is shorter and weaker. I give him more respect. She gives him less respect. Is she right or am I right? I am right, he is longer. I am right, he is stronger."

When Onini, the python, heard Anansi talking to himself, he said, "Why are you arguing this way with yourself?"

The spider replied: "Ah, I have had a dispute with my wife. She says you are shorter and weaker than this bamboo pole. I say you are longer and stronger."

Onini said: "It's useless and silly to argue when you can find out the truth. Bring the pole and we will measure."

So Anansi laid the pole on the ground, and the python came and stretched himself out beside it.

"You seem a little short," Anansi said.

The python stretched farther.

"A little more," Anansi said.

"I can stretch no more," Onini said.

"When you stretch at one end, you get shorter at the other end," Anansi said. "Let me tie you at the front so you don't slip."

He tied Onini's head to the pole. Then he went to the other end and tied the tail to the pole. He wrapped the vine all around Onini, until the python couldn't move.

"Onini," Anansi said, "it turns out that my wife was right and I was wrong. You are shorter than the pole and weaker. My opinion wasn't as good as my wife's. But you were even more foolish than I, and you are now my prisoner."

Anansi carried the python to Nyame, the Sky God, who said, "There is one thing more."

Osebo, the leopard, was next. Anansi went into the forest and dug a deep pit where the leopard was accustomed to walk. He covered it with small branches and leaves and put dust on it, so that it was impossible to tell where the pit was. Anansi went away and hid. When Osebo came prowling in the black of night, he stepped into the trap Anansi had prepared and fell to the bottom. Anansi heard the sound of the leopard falling, and he said, "Ah, Osebo, you are half-foolish!"

When morning came, Anansi went to the pit and saw the leopard there.

"Osebo," he asked, "what are you doing in this hole?"

"I have fallen into a trap," Osebo said. "Help me out."

"I would gladly help you," Anansi said. "But I'm sure that if I bring you out, I will have no thanks for it. You will get hungry, and later on you will be wanting to eat me and my children."

"I swear it won't happen!" Osebo said.

"Very well. Since you swear it, I will take you out," Anansi said.

He bent a tall green tree toward the ground, so that its top was over the pit, and he tied it that way. Then he tied a rope to the top of the tree and dropped the other end of it into the pit.

"Tie this to your tail," he said.

Osebo tied the rope to his tail.

"Is it well tied?" Anansi asked.

"Yes, it is well tied," the leopard said.

"In that case," Anansi said, "you are not merely half-foolish, you are all-foolish."

And he took his knife and cut the other rope, the one that held the tree bowed to the ground. The tree straightened up with a snap, pulling Osebo out of the hole. He hung in the air head downward, twisting and turning. And while he hung this way, Anansi killed him with his weapons.

Then he took the body of the leopard and carried it to Nyame, the Sky God, saying: "Here is the third thing. Now I have paid the price."

Nyame said to him: "Kwaku Anansi, great warriors and chiefs have tried, but they have been unable to do it. You have done it. Therefore, I will give you the stories. From this day onward, all stories belong to you. Whenever a man tells a story, he must acknowledge that it is Anansi's tale."

In this way Anansi, the spider, became the owner of all stories that are told. To Anansi all tales belong.

Anansi's Rescue from the River

When the first of Anansi's sons was born, Anansi prepared to give him a name. But the baby spoke up and said: "You needn't bother to name me. I have brought my own name. I am called Akakai." This name signified "Able to See Trouble."

When the second of Anansi's sons was born, he too announced that he had brought his own name. "I am called Twa Akwan," he said. This name signified "Road Builder."

When the third son was born, he said, "My name is Hwe Nsuo." That meant "Able to Dry Up Rivers."

When the fourth was born, he announced, "I am Adwafo." That meant "The Skinner of Game."

The fifth son said when he was born: "I have been named already. I am known as Toto Abuo." His name signified "Stone Thrower."

The sixth son told Anansi, "I am called Da Yi Ya." That meant "Lie on the Ground Like a Cushion."

One day Kwaku Anansi went on a long journey. Several weeks passed, and he failed to return. Akakai, the son who had the ability to see trouble, announced that Anansi had fallen into a distant river in the middle of a dense jungle.

Twa Akwan, the builder of roads, constructed a highway through the jungle, and the brothers passed through it to the edge of the river.

Hwe Nsuo, who had the power to dry up rivers, dried up the river, and they found there a great fish which had swallowed Anansi.

Adwafo, the skinner of game, cut into the fish and released his father.

But as soon as they brought Anansi to the edge of the river, a large hawk swooped down out of the sky, caught Anansi in his mouth, and soared into the air with him.

Toto Abuo, the stone thrower, threw a rock into the sky and hit the hawk, which let go of Anansi.

And as Anansi dropped towards the earth, Da Yi Ya threw himself on the ground like a cushion to soften his father's fall.

Thus Kwaku Anansi was saved by his six sons and brought home to his village.

Then one day when he was in the forest, Anansi found a bright and beautiful object called Moon. Nothing like it had ever been seen before. It was the most magnificent object he had ever seen. He resolved to give it to one of his children.

He sent a message to Nyame, the Sky God, telling him about his discovery. He asked Nyame to come and hold the Moon, and to award it as a prize to one of Anansi's sons—the one who had done the most to rescue him when he was lost in the river.

The Sky God came and held the Moon. Anansi sent for his sons. When they saw the Moon, each of them wanted it. They argued. The one who had located Anansi in the jungle river said he deserved the prize. The one who had built the road said he deserved it. The one who had dried up the river said he deserved it. The one who had cut Anansi out of the fish said he deserved it. The one who had hit the hawk with the stone said he deserved it. The one who had cushioned Anansi's fall to earth said he deserved it.

They argued back and forth, and no one listened to anybody else. The argument went on and on and became a violent squabble. Nyame, the Sky God, didn't know who should have the prize. He listened to the arguments for a long time. Then he became impatient. He got up from where he sat and went back to the sky, taking the Moon along with him.

And that is why the Moon is always seen in the heavens, where Nyame took it, and not on the earth where Anansi found it.

Aberewa's Sword

There once was a famine, and the only food in the land was in the storehouse of Nyame, the Sky God. Nyame let it be known that he wanted an agent to sell his food supplies to the people. Many creatures went to Nyame's house, thinking to become his agent. But the Sky God told them there was one condition: whoever was appointed as agent would have to agree to have his head shaved, so that everyone would know he was Nyame's servant. No one wanted to submit to this, until Anansi came along. Anansi told the Sky God that he would allow his head to be shaved, and so Nyame made him his official seller of food.

Nyame's servants took Anansi and shaved his head. It hurt him, and when he went out among the people, they jeered at him. But he sold Nyame's food supplies, and the next day he went back for more. Again they took hold of Anansi and shaved his head. Again it hurt him, and again people jeered when they saw him. Every day Nyame's servants shaved Anansi, and at last he couldn't stand it any longer. He took a supply of food from Nyame's storehouse and ran away with it without permitting his head to be shaved. He fled into the bush. He came to the house of the Earth Goddess, named Aberewa, who had powerful magic. He offered her a share of his stolen food in return for her protection from Nyame, and she agreed.

But the Sky God had a herd of warrior cattle who could divine the whereabouts of any creature. Nyame ordered them to seek out the hiding place of Anansi and to bring him back to complete his contract. The warrior cattle sensed the whereabouts of Anansi, and they went into the bush country to get him. They came at last to the house of Aberewa, and they declared, "The Sky God commands Anansi to return."

"He is not here," Aberewa said.

"He is here, and we will take him," the warrior cattle said.

But Aberewa was not called Aberewa for nothing. She had powerful magic. She had a long sharp sword which could fight by itself. When commanded to fight, the sword would fight. When commanded to stop, the sword would stop.

She took the sword from the house and commanded it "Fight." It left her hand and went out to fight with Nyame's warrior cattle. It killed all of them. Then she commanded, "Cool down!" And the sword came to rest.

Thus Anansi was saved. He continued to stay in Aberewa's house. One day Aberewa had to visit another village, and before going she asked Anansi to guard her place while she was away. He agreed. But when she was gone, he stole the powerful sword and fled back to the town of Nyame, the Sky God.

He said to the Sky God: "I broke my contract with you because I couldn't stand having my head shaved every day. But I have come back anyway, because I now have powerful medicine to protect you in case of war."

Nyame accepted Anansi's explanation and did not molest him. Then one day there was trouble in the kingdom. An army came to attack Nyame's town and subdue the Sky God. Nyame ordered the horns blown and the drums beaten. His soldiers heard, and they came at once with their spears and their shields. But Nyame saw that the army of the enemy was larger. So he called on Anansi for help, saying, "Now where is the powerful medicine you have brought?"

Anansi took out the sword, and he commanded it, "Fight!" The sword left his hand and went out to attack the enemy just as they came to the gates of the town. It leaped here and there, cutting and stabbing. The enemy soldiers could do nothing about it, and they fell everywhere. Some tried to flee, but the sword overtook them and cut them down. At last the entire enemy army lay dead on the field.

Then Anansi called to the sword to stop. He said "Stop!" But the sword didn't stop. He said: "Return!" But the sword didn't return. He said: "Rest!" But the sword didn't rest. Anansi had forgotten the words "Cool down" which Aberewa had used, and so the sword heard nothing.

Having no more of the enemy to kill, the sword turned on Nyame's warriors and began to slaughter them. Anansi shouted out commands of every kind, everything but the proper one, "Cool down." And so the sword heard nothing. It kept killing until all of Nyame's army was slain. At last Anansi was alone on the battlefield. Then the sword came and killed Anansi, too.

There was no one left on the field to kill. So the sword stuck itself into the ground and changed itself into a plant called tinni.

And even now, whenever anyone touches the tinni plant, it will cut him and cause the blood to flow. That is because the words "Cool down" were forgotten when they should have been spoken.

Anansi Borrows Money

It happened once that Anansi needed money. He went to his neighbors for help, but because of his bad reputation, no one would lend him anything. He went to the leopard and the bush cow, but they refused him. He went to the guinea fowl, the turtle and the hawk, but they all refused him. Then he went to a distant village where Owoh, the snake, lived. Owoh lent him the money he needed, on condition that it would be returned by the end of twenty-one days.

But when twenty-one days had passed, Anansi had no money to repay the loan. He began to think of ways to get out of his predicament. He went to his garden and dug up a basket full of yams. He put the basket on his head and carried it to the house of Owoh, the snake.

He said to Owoh: "This is the day I was to repay the money you lent me. But there is a small complication. I won't have the money for two or three days yet, and I hope you will be kind enough to wait. In the meanwhile, I have brought some yams to share with you in gratitude for your help."

Anansi used many sweetened words, and the snake agreed to wait three more days for his money. Of the yams he had brought, Anansi gave half to the snake. Owoh shared his portion with his friends. Anansi kept his portion in the basket. Owoh treated Anansi with great hospitality and invited him to stay overnight in his house. So Anansi stayed.

But in the middle of the night Anansi arose from his sleeping mat quietly and went out. He took the yams he had saved for himself away from the house. He carried them into the bush and hid them in the ground. When he returned, he placed his empty basket in front of the house and went back to sleep.

In the morning he came out and said to Owoh, "Where are my yams?" But Owoh knew nothing about the yams. So Anansi took his empty basket and returned home. He went to the headman of the district to make a complaint that his yams had been stolen. The people of the district were very concerned. They said to each other, "What kind of a thief is it who would steal yams from someone who has been as generous as Anansi?"

The headman called for a trial to find the guilty person. The people of all the villages came. Anansi said to them: "There is only one test to prove innocence. I have a magic knife. I will draw it across the skin of each person. It will not cut those who are innocent of this crime. It will cut only those who are guilty."

Then each of the animals came forward for the test. When the guinea fowl came, Anansi drew his knife across the guinea fowl's skin, but he used the blunt edge instead of the sharp edge. He did the same with the turtle, the rabbit, and the other animals. No one was hurt. When the snake's turn came, he said, "Test me."

But Anansi refused, saying: "Oh, no. It is unthinkable that you who have been so good as to lend me money would steal my yams." But Owoh insisted, saying: "I also must have my turn. You were in my house when the yams were stolen. All the others have taken the test. I, too, must prove my innocence." Anansi protested that it was unnecessary, and Owoh protested that he must be cleared of any suspicion of guilt.

"Very well," Anansi said at last. "Since it is your wish, I will let you take the test."

So Anansi drew his knife across the skin of Owoh, but this time he used not the blunt edge but the sharpened edge, and he killed him. The people said, "He has failed the test; he must be guilty!"

As Owoh died, however, he rolled on his back, turning his belly to the sky, as if to say: "Oh, God, look at my belly and see whether I have eaten Anansi's yams!"

It is for this reason that whenever a snake is killed, he turns his belly to the sky, calling upon God to judge his innocence.

Anansi Gives Nyame a Child

Anansi and Nyame, the Sky God, were friends. And it happened one time when they were in conversation that Nyame looked at his children and said, "See how all my children are the same color, all are dark."

Anansi said: "Yes, it is monotonous. I will bring you one of a different color."

Nyame replied: "Well, now, that is something. You make difficulties for yourself, but I will hold you to it."

Anansi left Nyame and went home, thinking, "Where shall I get Nyame a child of a different color?" He looked everywhere, but there

Author's collection. Informant, Kofi Prempeh.

were only children of dark complexion. Time passed. Nyame sent messengers to Anansi. They asked, "Where is the child you promised Nyame?" Anansi spoke to them as though he were offended. He said, "Does one make a baby instantly?" And when the messengers came again, Anansi answered, "Is a baby made in two months?" More time passed. The messengers again came, saying, "Nyame inquires about the child you promised him." Anansi replied, "Since when is a baby born in four months?" Anansi went on looking for a different-colored child. When the messengers from Nyame appeared another time at his house, eight months had passed. He told them: "Surely Nyame does not want a too-early child? The nine months are not yet used up."

Because Nyame had said, "I will hold you to it," Anansi became anxious. He decided to hide himself in the forest so that people would think he had died while hunting. He went out with his weapons and disappeared among the trees. He followed a trail used by hunters. He was gone a long while.

Now there was a woman from a distant village who had given birth to a boy child. The child's appetite was unending. Whatever she gave him, he wanted more. Her milk did not satisfy him. She gave him mush, but that did not fill his stomach. For seven days she devoted herself to feeding him from morning till night, but his hunger was never satisfied. At last she said: "This child is unnatural. He hungers without end. And his color is not the color of others. He is red. Surely this matter is too big to deal with." So she took the infant into the forest and placed him in the crotch of a tree, after which she went back to her village.

Anansi was walking along the game trail. He heard the crying of an infant. He found the baby where the mother had left it. He saw that its color was red, and he rejoiced, saying, "At last I can give birth." He took the baby home. He sent word to Nyame that the nine months were up and the child had been born. Nyame dispatched messengers to Anansi's house. They found Anansi lying on his mat as though he were recovering. He said: "Here, as I promised, is the child of a different color. Why does my friend Nyame reproach me? I have done what I promised."

The messengers took the child to Nyame's house. Nyame saw that its color was red instead of dark and he was pleased. He gave the baby to his senior wife, saying, "Take it, care for it as your own." She gave the child milk, but it cried for more. She asked Nyame's other wives for help. They all gave milk, they all fed the child mush, yet it continued to cry for more. At last Nyame's senior wife complained. She went to Nyame, saying: "It is an impossible thing. He does not stop wanting. He cries. He makes a great disturbance."

Nyame was annoyed. He said, "Who ever heard of such a thing?" But the child answered him. He said, "Where I lived before I ate better than here." So Nyame answered, "Very well." And he began to take care of the baby himself. He ordered milk brought. He ordered boiled plantains and other food. He began to feed the child. Whenever he stopped the child cried for more. Nyame sent word out into the village that all the people should bring food. They brought pots of everything. Whatever they brought, the boy was ready for it. People came from everywhere to watch him eat. Nyame's servants brought huge vessels of water so the boy could wash down his food.

The food and water were gone. The boy looked in one direction and another. He saw that the feeding was ended. In the front of the crowd that was watching him an old man was standing, his mouth wide open in amazement. The boy jumped into his mouth. He became a tongue. It was the first tongue. Because the boy was red, all tongues are red. Because the boy was never satisfied, tongues are never satisfied. If a person's stomach is full or empty, it is all the same to his tongue. The tongue always wants something. So there is a saying: "Even though the stomach has plenty, the tongue wants more." For all this Anansi was responsible.

How Debt Came to Ashanti

In the beginning there was no debt in Ashanti. For the coming of debt, it is said that Anansi was responsible.

Once a hunter named Soko arrived among the Ashanti from another place. The reason for his coming was that he owed money in his own village. He sought to evade his debt, and so he travelled. But where he settled among the Ashanti, people learned of his reasons and became troubled. So some of the old men of the community went to Soko, saying: "Until you came here there was no debt among us. Now, the way it is, we do not like it. You must get rid of debt."

Soko did not know how to get rid of debt. He reflected on it, but he could not think of a way. Anansi heard about Soko's debt. He went to Soko's house one morning when Soko was making palm wine. Anansi wanted palm wine. He said: "Getting rid of your debt is easy. Simply say, 'Whoever drinks my palm wine will take the debt.'"

So Soko said: "Yes, that is the way it is. Whoever drinks my palm wine will take the debt."

"I will take the palm wine," Anansi said.

"Take it," Soko said.

Anansi took the palm wine back to his house. He drank it. He had the debt, and Soko no longer had it. Then Anansi planted grain in his fields, saying, "Whoever eats the grain takes the debt." One day a bird flew down and ate some of Anansi's grain. Anansi said, "Now it is you who has the debt."

The bird went back to her nest, taking the debt with her. She laid some eggs in her nest and said, "Whoever breaks my eggs takes the debt." Then she flew off in search of food. While she was away there came a wind. It broke a branch from the tree that held her nest. The branch fell on the eggs and cracked them. When the bird returned she

---

Author's collection.

said to the tree: "I don't have the debt anymore. It is you who has the debt."

In this way the tree became the owner of the debt. But when the tree grew blossoms on its branches it said, "Whoever eats my blossoms takes the debt." A monkey climbed into the tree and began eating the blossoms, and the tree said: "Now I do not have the debt anymore. It is you who owns the debt."

The monkey said: "Very well. Whoever eats me will take the debt." He went down from the branches, and when he was on the ground he was caught by a lion. The monkey said, "If you eat me you take the debt." The lion ate him, and now the debt was owned by the lion. The lion said as he went here and there, "Whoever eats me takes the debt."

One day Soko the hunter went into the bush looking for meat. He saw the lion. He killed him. He took the meat back to the village and shared it with all the families that lived there. They ate. Thus they acquired debt. And since that time debt has remained with the Ashanti people. For this, Anansi and Soko were responsible.

The Competition for Nyame's Daughter

Nyame, it is said, had a daughter who refused many suitors. Men came from other villages or distant countries in hope of marrying her, but she rejected them all. A time came when Nyame could no longer tolerate her refusals. He said, "I will have to take a hand in the matter." And he spoke to his councillors, saying: "It is right that my daughter should have a husband, but she turns all men away. I have been too lenient. Now something must be done." His councillors asked, "To whom will you give her?" And Nyame replied: "I have decided. The man who can recite her secret name, to such a person will I give her." So messengers went through the village announcing that Nyame's daughter would become the wife of the person who could discover her secret name. Many men thought they knew the answer. They went to Nyame's house and declared that her name was this or that, but Nyame sent them all away.

Anansi, also, wanted Nyame's daughter. When a certain day was becoming dark, Anansi climbed over the wall that surrounded Nyame's courtyard, and he hid in the top of a large kola tree. There he waited until Nyame's daughter came walking with a friend, and when they were below him, Anansi dropped a kola fruit. The friend of Nyame's daughter picked it up, saying, "Oh, Baduasemanpensa! A kola fruit has fallen from the tree." Anansi dropped another one, and the girl said, "See, Baduasemanpensa, a second kola fruit has come down!" Anansi dropped a third fruit and heard the girl say: "Baduasemanpensa, Baduasemanpensa! The kola fruits are still falling!" The two girls sat and ate the fruits. After that they left the court and entered their houses.

Author's collection.

Anansi also departed, saying the name Baduasemanpensa over and over so that he would not forget it. His excitement was great, for he was certain to get Nyame's daughter. He ran to the house of Abosom, the lizard, saying: "I have discovered the name of Nyame's daughter! Tomorrow I will go to Nyame. I will say, 'I have come for your daughter.' He will say: 'What is her name?' Then I will take out my atumpan drum. I will play on it the phrase, 'Baduasemanpensa! Baduasemanpensa! Baduasemanpensa is the name of Nana's daughter!' Nyame will say: 'Yes, surely, it is clear. Anansi has discovered the secret.' Thus, he will give the girl to me. He will say: 'There is no doubt about the matter. Anansi is my son-in-law.' "

The next morning Anansi sent a message to Nyame saying that he would soon come to take the test. On the way, however, he went to the lizard's house. He said, "You, Lizard, come with me and be my witness." So the lizard accompanied Anansi to the place where Nyame lived. A large crowd had already gathered. Nyame came out from his house and sat on his stool. People said to one another, "Today Anansi will reveal the secret name and the affair will be ended."

Anansi took his atumpan drum from his shoulder and began to play on it. He played his phrase over and over. Nyame listened for a while. Then he said to his councillors: "What can the man be playing? It is incomprehensible." To Anansi he said: "If you know the name, say it. The sounds you are making are meaningless." Anansi spoke in reproach, saying, "Do you not recognize the name of your own daughter?" And again he played his phrase, over and over, until Nyame stopped him. "Anansi," Nyame said, "if you know the answer, speak it plainly. If you do not know it, let us bring this event to a conclusion."

Anansi called to his friend, the lizard. He said: "Play the words for me. These people are very stupid. I am tired from so much playing. Take the drum. Give them the phrase." But the lizard did not take the drum. He said, with his own mouth, "The girl's name is Baduasemanpensa." Hearing this, Nyame replied, "Yes, it is so." There was much excitement in the crowd. And Nyame continued: "I promised that whoever revealed my daughter's name would become her husband. Therefore, the lizard will be my son-in-law." Anansi protested, saying: "It was I, Anansi, who discovered your daughter's true name. The lizard was merely my linguist."

Nyame said: "What you played on the drum, Anansi, I could not recognize it. My councillors could not recognize it. The people could not recognize it. Who is there who could recognize anything you played? No one. But we all heard the lizard say plainly, without any ceremony, 'Baduasemanpensa.' Therefore, my son-in-law is he who spoke the word. My daughter henceforth is the wife of the lizard."

After that it was a saying among the people: "If you have important words to convey, do not give them to Anansi's drum."

The Hat-Shaking Dance

If you look closely, you will see that Anansi has a bald head. It is said that in the old days he had hair, but that he lost it through vanity.

It happened that Anansi's mother-in-law died. When word came to Anansi's house, Aso, his wife, prepared to go at once to her own village for the funeral. But Anansi said to Aso, "You go ahead; I will follow."

When Aso had gone, Anansi said to himself: "When I go to my dead mother-in-law's house, I will have to show great grief over her death. I will have to refuse to eat. Therefore, I shall eat now." And so he sat in his own house and ate a huge meal. Then he put on his mourning clothes and went to Aso's village.

First there was the funeral. Afterwards there was a large feast. But Anansi refused to eat, out of respect for his wife's dead mother. He said: "What kind of man would I be to eat when I am mourning for my mother-in-law? I will eat only after the eighth day has passed."

Now this was not expected of him, because a person isn't required to starve himself simply because someone has died. But Anansi was the kind of person that when he ate, he ate twice as much as others, and when he danced, he danced more vigorously than others, and when he mourned, he had to mourn more loudly than anybody else. Whatever he did, he didn't want to be outdone by anyone else. And although he was very hungry, he couldn't bear to have people think he wasn't the greatest mourner at his own mother-in-law's funeral.

So he said, "Feed my friends, but as for me, I shall do without." So everyone ate—the porcupine, the rabbit, the snake, the guinea fowl and the others. All except Anansi.

On the second day after the funeral they said to him again, "Eat, there is no need to starve."

But Anansi replied: "Oh, no, not until the eighth day, when the mourning is over. What kind of person do you think I am?"

So the others ate. Anansi's stomach was empty, and he was unhappy.

On the third day they said again, "Eat, Anansi, there is no need to go hungry."

But Anansi was stubborn. He said, "How can I eat when my wife's mother has been buried only three days?" And so the others ate, while Anansi smelled the food hungrily and suffered.

On the fourth day, Anansi was alone where a pot of beans was cooking over the fire. He smelled the beans and looked in the pot. At last he couldn't stand it any longer. He took a large spoon and dipped up a large portion of the beans, thinking to take it to a quiet place and eat it without anyone's knowing. But just then the dog, the guinea fowl, the rabbit, and the others returned to the place where the food was cooking.

This tale and the one that follows, "Anansi Plays Dead," are from The Hat-Shaking Dance and Other Ashanti Tales from Ghana, © *1957 by Harold Courlander. Reprinted by permission of Harcourt Brace Jovanovich.*

To hide the beans, Anansi quickly poured them in his hat and put it on his head. The other people came to the pot and ate, saying again, "Anansi, you must eat."

He said, "No, what kind of person would I be?"

But the hot beans were burning his head. He jiggled his hat back and forth with his hands. When he saw the others looking at him, he said: "Just at this very moment in my village the hat-shaking festival is taking place. I shake my hat in honor of the occasion."

The beans felt hotter than ever, and he jiggled his hat some more. He began to jump with pain. He said, "Like this in my village they are doing the hat-shaking dance."

He danced about, jiggling his hat because of the heat. He yearned to take off his hat, but he could not because his friends would see the beans. So he shouted: "They are shaking and jiggling the hats in my village, like this! It is a great festival! I must go!"

They said to him, "Anansi, eat something before you go."

But now Anansi was jumping and writhing with the heat of the beans on his head. He shouted: "Oh, no, they are shaking hats, they are wriggling hats and jumping like this! I must go to my village! They need me!"

He rushed out of the house, jumping and pushing his hat back and forth. His friends followed after him saying, "Eat before you go on your journey!"

But Anansi shouted, "What kind of person do you think I am, with my mother-in-law just buried?"

Even though they all followed right after him, he couldn't wait any longer, because the pain was too much, and he tore the hat from his head. When the dog saw, and the guinea fowl saw, and the rabbit saw, and all the others saw what was in the hat, and saw the hot beans sticking to Anansi's head, they stopped chasing him. They began to laugh and jeer.

Anansi was overcome with shame. He leaped into the tall grass, saying, "Hide me." And the grass hid him.

That is why Anansi is often found in the tall grass, where he was driven by shame. And you will see that his head is bald, for the hot beans he put in his hat burned off his hair.

All this happened because he tried to impress people at his mother-in-law's funeral.

Anansi Plays Dead

One year there was a famine in the land. But Anansi and his wife Aso and his sons had a farm, and there was food enough for all of them. Still the thought of famine throughout the country made Anansi hungry. He began to plot how he could have the largest portion of the crops for himself alone. He devised a clever scheme.

One day he told his wife that he was not feeling well and that he was going to see a diviner. He went away and didn't return until night. Then he announced that he had received very bad news. The diviner had informed him, he said, that he was about to die. Also, Anansi said, the diviner had prescribed that he was to be buried at the far end of the farm, next to the yam patch. When they heard this news, Aso, Kweku Tsin and Intikuma were very sad. But Anansi had more instructions. Aso was to place in his grave a pestle and mortar, dishes, spoons, and cooking pots, so that Anansi could take care of himself in the Other World.

In a few days, Anansi lay on his sleeping mat as though he were sick, and in a short time he pretended to be dead. So Aso had him buried at the far end of the farm, next to the yam patch, and they put in his grave all of the cooking pots and other things he had asked for.

But Anansi stayed in the grave only while the sun shone. As soon as it grew dark, he came out and dug up some yams and cooked them. He ate until he was stuffed. Then he returned to his place in the grave. Every night he came out to select the best part of the crops and eat them, and during the day he hid in his grave.

Aso and her sons began to observe that their best yams and corn and cassava were being stolen from the fields. So they went to Anansi's grave and held a special service there. They asked Anansi's spirit to protect the farm from thieves.

That night Anansi again came out, and once more he took the best crops and ate them. When Aso and her sons found out that Anansi's spirit was not protecting them, they devised a plan to catch the person who was stealing their food. They made a figure out of sticky gum. It looked like a man. They set it up in the yam patch.

That night Anansi crawled out to eat. He saw the figure standing there in the moonlight.

"Why are you standing in my fields?" Anansi said.

The gum-man didn't answer.

"If you don't get out of my fields, I will give you a thrashing," Anansi said.

The gum-man was silent.

"If you don't go quickly, I will have to beat you," Anansi said.

There was no reply. The gum-man just stood there. Anansi lost his temper. He gave the gum-man a hard blow with his right hand. It stuck fast to the gum-man. Anansi couldn't take it away.

"Let go of my right hand," Anansi said. "You are making me angry!"

But the gum-man didn't let go.

"Perhaps you don't know my strength," Anansi said fiercely. "There is more power in my left hand than in my right. Do you want to try it?"

As there was no response from the gum-man, Anansi struck him with his left hand. Now both his hands were stuck.

"You miserable creature," Anansi said, "so you don't listen to me! Let go at once and get out of my fields or I will really give you something to remember! Have you ever heard of my right foot?"

There was no sound from the gum-man, so Anansi gave him a kick with his right foot. It, too, stuck.

"Oh, you like it, do you?" Anansi shouted. "Then try this one, too!"

He gave a tremendous kick with his left foot, and now he was stuck by both hands and both feet.

"Oh, are you the stubborn kind?" Anansi cried. "Have you ever heard of my head?"

And he butted the gum-man with his head, and that stuck as well.

"I'm giving you your last chance now," Anansi said sternly. "If you leave quietly, I won't complain to the chief. If you don't, I'll give you a squeeze you will remember!"

The gum-man was still silent. So Anansi took a deep breath and gave a mighty squeeze. Now he was completely stuck. He couldn't move this way or that. He couldn't move at all.

In the morning when Aso, Kweku Tsin and Intikuma came out to the fields, they found Anansi stuck helplessly to the gum-man. They understood everything. They took him off the gum-man and led him towards the village to be judged by the chief. People came to the edge of the trail and saw Anansi all stuck up with gum. They laughed and jeered and sang songs about him. He was deeply shamed, and covered his face with his headcloth. And when Aso, Kweku Tsin and Intikuma stopped at a spring to drink, Anansi broke away and fled. He ran into the nearest house, crawled into the rafters, and hid in the darkest corner he could find.

From that day until now, Anansi has not wanted to face people because of their scoffing and jeering, and that is why he is often found hiding in dark corners.

The King's Drum

The king of the forest once called a meeting of all his subjects. His messengers went out to distant villages, and when the animals heard the king's command, they put on their best clothes and began their trip. But many weeks passed before they arrived.

When they had all gathered before his house, the king said to them: "When a meeting is called, many days pass before we are gathered. This is not good. What if we are in danger? What if the enemy is coming? We must find a way to gather quickly."

Anansi the spider was the king's councillor. He said, "What is needed is a drum. When the royal drum is beaten, it will be heard everywhere. Everyone will come quickly."

The animals applauded Anansi's suggestion. It was agreed that there should be a drum. The king ordered that a drum should be made. The animals were organized into work squads. Each squad was to take its

From The King's Drum and Other African Stories, © 1962 by Harold Courlander. Reprinted by permission of Harcourt Brace Jovanovich.

turn at the making of the drum. First, one squad went out and cut a tree. Another squad went out to trim the tree. Another squad took adzes and cut the tree into the shape of a drum. The drum was hollowed. After that, carvers were set to work to decorate the drum. Only the monkey did not do any work. While the others labored, the monkey found a shady place and slept, or he went off looking for berries. When they came back to the village, the animals sang:

> "Life is labor,
> We are tired,
> We are hot,
> It is for the king we labor."

The monkey also sang:

> "Life is labor,
> I am tired,
> I am hot,
> It is for the king I labor."

But Anansi saw that the monkey shirked and rested while the others labored. He said nothing.

A time came when the drum was finished. The king announced: "Let the drum be brought in. There will be a ceremony. The drum will be initiated. After that, the assembly will be ended. When the people are wanted again, the royal drum will be sounded."

Anansi said: "Yes, the drum shall be brought in. There is only one problem remaining. Who shall carry the drum?"

The drum was very large. It was heavy. The distance was great. No one wanted to carry it.

The leopard said, "Let the lion receive the honor."

The lion said, "No, it is the antelope who should carry it."

The antelope declared, "No, it is more fitting for the elephant to do it."

Each animal suggested that another should have the honor.

Anansi said: "It appears that each person wants someone else to do the carrying. Therefore, I suggest that the person to carry the drum is he who is most lazy."

The king said, "Yes, that is the way to do it."

The animals considered the question. They looked at each other. They tried to think who was the laziest. First, one looked at the monkey, then another looked at the monkey. The monkey looked here, looked there. Everywhere he looked, he saw people looking at him.

He went to the middle of the crowd and said: "I wish to make a statement. I refuse to carry the drum. Never, never will I carry the drum. That is all I have to say."

All the animals laughed. The antelope said: "Why are you here? No one mentioned your name."

The porcupine said: "Why do you speak? No one asked you to carry the drum."

The crowd called out, "Yes, no one said even a word to him."

Once more the monkey said: "I want it to be made clear. I will not carry the drum. These are my words."

Again the animals laughed.

Anansi said to the king: "No one mentioned the monkey's name. People were thinking to themselves, 'Who is the laziest?' They could not make up their minds. But the monkey was sure. He came forward. He said, 'I want it made clear that I will never carry the drum.' Thus he confessed that he is the laziest. With his own mouth he has said it."

The animals answered, "It is true, the monkey is the laziest of all!"

And so when at last the great drum was brought from the forest to the king's house, it was the monkey who carried it.

The Wall of Millet

A TALE OF THE TOGO PEOPLE

Before our times there lived in the kingdom of Seno, in a village called Tendella, a man of wealth whose name was Kaddo. This man owned many fields and gardens. He flourished in every way. When it was time to clear and turn the earth in the fields, the men of Tendella gathered and did what was necessary. When it was time to plant seed, the women of Tendella came together and sowed for Kaddo. What was gathered from the fields at harvesttime was far more than an ordinary man's granary would hold. Kaddo had many granaries in which to store his harvested grain. Travellers who passed through Tendella marvelled that one person should be the owner of so much food, and they told the story of Kaddo wherever they went. Kaddo's reputation spread far beyond the frontiers of Seno. His wealth became a legend in far-off places.

Kaddo pondered a great deal about what he should do with all the grain kept in his storage places. And one day he called a meeting of the village to discuss the matter. When the people assembled, Kaddo said:

Based on a story in Atlantis, Volksmärchen und Volksdichtungen Afrikas, Vol. 6, by Leo Frobenius, Jena, 1921.

"My granaries are heavy with grain. My family cannot possibly eat it all. What should be done about this matter?"

The people listened. They considered. An old man said: "Yes, Kaddo, you have a great wealth of millet grain. Your fields produce more and more. The solution is clear. There are many families in the village for whom life is hard. They have nothing to eat a great part of the year. Share your millet with them. When you have done that you will still be a man of wealth, and your generosity will be praised."

Kaddo, however, said: "No, there will be no satisfaction in that. It doesn't suit me."

Another person said: "There is another way. You could lend grain to families that have no seed to plant. When their crops are grown they can repay you. That would keep poverty away from the village. Your name would be praised."

Kaddo replied, "No, it doesn't please me."

A man said: "Sell some of your millet then, and buy cattle. That would relieve the weight of your granaries."

"No," Kaddo answered, "the suggestion does not please me."

Other persons suggested things that Kaddo might do with his grain to relieve him of his burden. But nothing that was said pleased Kaddo. And after a while he said: "I have made a decision. I will have the grain ground into meal. Tomorrow send me all the girls of the village with their mortars."

The people dispersed. They were provoked by Kaddo's attitude. But the next day they sent girls with mortars to grind Kaddo's millet, thinking that perhaps he would give meal to those who were in need. The grinding began. All day long the sound of pestles was heard as they pounded in the mortars. There was a pile of meal. It grew. The grinding went on for seven days. And when the last of the grain had been turned into meal, Kaddo ordered water brought from the spring. He instructed that the water and meal be mixed to make mortar, and out of the mortar bricks were made and left in the sun to dry. "When the bricks are dried," Kaddo said, "I shall have a wall built around my house."

When the people of the village heard what Kaddo intended to do, they came to his house and protested. "In what place was it ever heard," they said, "that a man built a wall of millet around his house?" And they said, again, "Kaddo, this flaunting of food in the face of those who are hungry is not right." And they said, "In all the history of our ancestors no one has ever used food to build a wall."

Kaddo answered: "Is not the millet mine? Was it not grown in my fields? Who has ever said that a man may not do what he wants with his own grain? It is my right."

And so when the bricks were dried, Kaddo had the people of the village begin the erecting of a wall around his house. The wall grew higher. When the last brick was laid, Kaddo had the people stick cowries into the wall to give it beauty. At last everything was done. Kaddo admired his wall. It gave him pleasure. He said, "Surely now, people everywhere will know my name and praise it."

The people of the village shook their heads. They did not think well of Kaddo for what he had done. Yet he continued to be influential in the village because he was, indeed, a man of wealth. When people came to see Kaddo they had to stand by the gate in the wall of millet bricks until they were invited to enter. When Kaddo gave instructions to the people who worked his fields he sat on his wall and talked down to them from his high place, and they stood below and looked up to him. The story of Kaddo's wall travelled to faraway regions, for who before him had ever had a wall of millet?

The village lived on, and then one year there was not enough rain and there was a bad harvest. The earth dried up. Kaddo's grain did not grow. From all the many fields he owned, Kaddo did not harvest anything. So Kaddo and his family ate the seed grain that had been saved for planting. The next year he had to buy seed for his fields, but that year also there was drought. And so it continued, one year after the other. Kaddo sold his cattle and horses to buy food. Year after year no grain grew in Kaddo's fields. His relatives grew lean. They died, or they left the village and went to other regions of Seno. Kaddo's servants and slaves also departed because he was unable to feed them. Kaddo's part of the village became deserted. Those who continued to live there were only Kaddo, his daughter, and a donkey.

To feed his own hunger, Kaddo one day scraped some millet meal from his wall and ate it. The next day he did the same. Little by little Kaddo's wall grew lower, and a time came when the wall no longer existed. Kaddo wondered who could help him. The people of Tendella no longer had dealings with him because when he had had wealth he had refused to share even a little of it with those who were hungry. Kaddo thought of Sogole, king of Ghana, a man famous for his generosity. So he and his daughter mounted his donkey and they rode seven days to reach the place where Sogole lived. Sogole received them. He had a skin placed on the ground for them to sit on, and he had millet beer brought to them. But Kaddo could drink only a little, for his stomach had shrunk from hunger. Sogole listened to Kaddo's story of the famine in Tendella. He said: "Things have indeed been hard in your village. But there is plenty of everything here. I shall give you whatever you need."

After a while the king of Ghana pressed Kaddo for details of life in Tendella. He said: "Yes, I have heard often of your village. The famine came and drove people out, so it was said, just as you tell it. People say that there was a rich and powerful man in Tendella called Kaddo. Is Kaddo still alive?"

"He is still alive," Kaddo answered.

"I have heard," Sogole went on, "that Kaddo built a wall of millet meal around his house, and that when he talked to ordinary people he sat on his wall next to his gate. Is this story true?"

"It is so," Kaddo replied. "He built a wall of bricks made of millet meal."

Sogole asked, "Is he still a man of wealth, with many cattle?"

Kaddo answered: "No, his cattle are all gone. His wall is gone. His servants and slaves are gone. Only his daughter is left."

"It is a story full of sorrow," Sogole said. "Were you one of Kaddo's relatives?"

And Kaddo answered: "Yes, I was indeed part of Kaddo's family. Once I was rich. Once I had many cattle. Once I had many growing fields. Once my granaries were heavy with grain. Once I was Kaddo, the famous personage of Tendella."

Sogole said, "What? You yourself are Kaddo?"

Kaddo said: "It is so. Once I was a man of wealth and respect, the lordly Kaddo. Now I am only a beggar in need of help."

Sogole pondered on the downfall of Kaddo. He said, "What can I do to help you?"

"Great king of Ghana," Kaddo said, "give me some seed so that I may go back to Tendella and plant my fields once more."

Sogole ordered his servants to bring bags of millet seed and load them on Kaddo's donkey. Kaddo thanked Sogole with humility. And when he and his daughter were rested they began the return journey to Tendella. On the way, Kaddo became hungry. He took a little of the seed grain given to him by Sogole and ate it. He gave some to his daughter. Because they were starving, their hunger would not depart. They ate more and more of the seed grain. They arrived at Tendella. They slept. They arose and ate again. Kaddo no longer cared that the grain was for planting. He could not stop eating. His stomach was not used to it. Kaddo became ill. He lay on his bed and cried out in pain. And before long, Kaddo died.

Kaddo's descendants in Seno have remained poor to the present time. And to those who are well off but who are reluctant to share their good fortune, people sometimes say, referring to Kaddo, "Is it right to build a wall of millet meal around your house?"

DAHOMEY, THE KINGDOM BUILT IN DA'S BELLY

The kingdom of Dahomey emerged early in the seventeenth century out of the conquest of the city states of Calmina and Abomey by the king of Allada. The extent of the kingdom was considerably less than that of present-day Dahomey. Including Allada and the territory surrounding Abomey, the kingdom covered perhaps some four thousand square miles. It was greatly respected by neighboring peoples for its military prowess, which was frequently commented upon by European chroniclers. The first European contacts with the Dahomeans, who also called themselves Fon, were in the closing years of the seventeenth century, and there followed numerous accounts of exotic and bloody traditions of the country's rulers. One institution that fascinated European visitors was the women's army set up by King Agadja early in the eighteenth century, and which a century later had become a conspicuous Dahomean establishment. To Europeans it recalled the mythical Amazons, and by this name they were called in the chronicles.

Dahomean military capability was frequently tested, for the kingdom often found itself at war with the Mahi, the Yoruba and other neighboring states. In some of those tests the Dahomeans were bested by their adversaries. In 1738, for example, Abomey was captured by an army from the Yoruban city state of Oyo, and for many years thereafter Dahomey had to pay tribute to its conqueror. But continuing conflicts with the Yoruba, and much taking of slaves on both sides, had cultural as well as military consequences. Ideas as well as slaves were taken from one another. By the time West Africa was under colonial rule the Dahomeans and the Yoruba had religious systems that in many respects were remarkably similar. Dieties in the Dahomean and Yoruban pantheons paralleled each other in function, character and sometimes name, and the two peoples shared a highly developed system of divining.

The name Dahomey means In Da's Belly. In the year 1625, it is said, Da, king of Abomey, complained of the harassments of Dako, king of Allada, saying, "You will soon be building in my belly." When Dako conquered Abomey he referred to the complaint by naming his new kingdom In Da's Belly. Here is how the event was recorded by the English chronicler Robert Norris in his book, *Memoirs of the Reign of Bossa Ahadee, King of Dahomey, an Inland Country of Guiney,* London, 1879:

"The Dahomans, but little more than a century ago, were an inconsiderable nation; formidable however to their neighbours, for their valour and military skill: they were then known by the name of Foys [Fons]; and the town of Dawhee, which lies between Calmina and Abomey, was the capital of their small territory.

"Early in the last century, Tacoodonou [another name for Dako], chief of the Foy [Fon] nation, basely murdered, in violation of the sacred laws of hospitality, a sovereign prince his neighbour, who made him a friendly visit to honor one of his festivals: he then attacked and took Calmina, the capital of the deceased: strengthened by this acquisition, he ventured to wage war with Da, king of Abomey, whom he besieged in his capital, which he soon reduced; and in consequence of a vow, that he made during the seige, put Da to death, by cutting open his belly; and placed his body under the foundation of a palace that he built in Abomey, as a memorial of his victory; which he called Dahomy, from Da the unfortunate victim and Homy his belly; that is, a house built in Da's belly.

"Tacoodonou after this conquest fixed his residence at Abomey, and assumed the title of King of Dahomy; of which the cruel circumstance just mentioned gives the true etymology; and from thence also the Foys, his subjects, are generally called Dahomans: in the country indeed the old name of Foys prevails; but to Europeans I believe, they are only known by the name of Dahomans."

From Dahomean Narrative, *by Melville J. and Frances S. Herskovits. Evanston, Northwestern University Press, 1958. By permission of Northwestern University Press*

The Gods of Dahomey: Their Exploits

The mythology of the Fon, or Dahomean, people includes a vast repertoire of tales about the voduns, gods and demigods sprung from the androgynous Mawu-Lisa. Mawu is the female aspect of Mawu-Lisa and is represented by the moon; Lisa is the male aspect, represented by the sun. Other voduns appear to have come into being as the result of the deification of ancient ancestors. The exploits of the voduns and their conflicts with one another, and the special characteristics and powers with which each is endowed, provide the rationale, both moral and amoral, of Dahomean religious belief. As in ancient Norse belief there are gods representing phenomena and elements of nature, but there are also gods representing abstract concepts, such as Legba, spirit of accident and unaccountability. The following tales about the voduns are taken from a large collection gathered by Melville and Frances Herskovits. Some were told by priests of the Hevioso, Sagbata and other cults.

DRAMATIS PERSONAE

SAGBATA, the Earth pantheon
MAWU, the Creator; the female portion of the androgynous Great God Mawu-Lisa; the moon
LISA, the male portion of Mawu-Lisa; the sun
DA ZODJI, firstborn of Mawu; chief of the Earth pantheon
NYOHWÈ ANANU, female twin and wife of Da Zodji
SO, second-born of Mawu; androgynous deity, chief of the Thunder pantheon
SOGBO, another name for So
HEVIOSO, another name of So; popular general term for Thunder pantheon
AGBÈ, third-born of Mawu; chief of Sea pantheon
NAÈTÈ, female twin and wife of Agbè
AGÈ, fourth-born of Mawu; deity of the Hunt
FA, cult of divination; personified as principle of foretelling destiny; master of Legba
GU, fifth-born of Mawu; deity of Iron, War, Weapons and Tools
DJO, sixth-born of Mawu; god of the Air
LEGBA, seventh and youngest born of Mawu; divine trickster, linguist of the gods
AZÕ, another name for Sagbata
KU, Death
WUTUTU, a bird; messenger of Sogbo
AÏ, Earth; another name for Sagbata

AIDO-HWEDO, Rainbow serpent
AGBLO, first man to issue from the earth
CHEYI, first human to make contact with the Ruler of the Earth; first priest
AWÈ, first human to learn magic; "chief of magic"
SEGBO, king of the gods; early ruler of the world of men; lit. "supreme soul"; also called Da or Dada Segbo, "King Segbo"

To Each Is Given His Dominion

Sagbata comes from Mawu and Lisa. Mawu is one person but has two faces. The first is that of a woman, and the eyes of that part which belongs to the woman is the Moon. That face takes the name of Mawu. The other side is the side of a man. That face has for its eyes the Sun, and it takes the name of Lisa. The part called Mawu directs night. Where the Sun is, Lisa directs the day.

Since Mawu is both man and woman, she became pregnant. The first to be born were a pair of twins, a man-child called Da Zodji, and a woman-child called Nyohwè Ananu. The second birth was So, who had the form of his parent, man and woman in one. The third birth was also of twins, a male, Agbè, and a female, Naètè. The fourth to be born was Agè, a male; the fifth Gu, also male. Gu is all body. He has no head. Instead of a head, a great sword is found coming out of his neck. His trunk is of stone. The sixth birth was not to a being, but to Djo, air, atmosphere. Air was what was needed to create men. The seventh to be born was Legba. Mawu said Legba was to be her spoiled child, because he was the youngest.

One day Mawu-Lisa assembled all the children in order to divide the kingdoms. To the first twins, she gave all the riches and told them to go and inhabit the earth. She said the earth was for them.

Mawu said to Sogbo he was to remain in the sky, because he was both man and woman like his parent. She told Agbè and Naètè to go and inhabit the sea, and command the waters. To Agè she gave command of all the animals and birds, and she told him to live in the bush as a hunter.

To Gu, Mawu said he was her strength, and that was why he was not given a head like the others. Thanks to him, the earth would not always remain wild bush. It was he who would teach men to live happily.

Mawu told Djo to live in space between earth and sky. To him was being entrusted the life-span of man. Thanks to him also, his brothers would be invisible, for he will clothe them. That is why another name for vodun is djo.

When Mawu said this to the children, she gave the Sagbata twins the language which was to be used on earth, and took away their memory of the language of the sky. She gave to Hevioso the language he would speak, and took from him the memory of the parent language. The same was done for Agbè and Naètè, for Agè, and for Gu, but to Djo was given the language of men.

Now she said to Legba: "You are my youngest child, and as you are spoiled, and have never known punishment, I cannot turn you over to your brothers. I will keep you with me always. Your work shall be to visit all the kingdoms ruled over by your brothers, and to give me an account of what happens." So Legba knows all the languages known to his brothers, and he knows the language Mawu speaks, too. Legba is Mawu's linguist. If one of the brothers wishes to speak, he must give the message to Legba, for none knows any longer how to address himself to Mawu-Lisa. That is why Legba is everywhere.

You will find Legba even before the houses of the vodun, because all beings, humans and gods, must address themselves to him before they can approach God.

The Rule of Sky and Earth Delimited

Originally Sagbata was not called Sagbata. He comes from Ananu and was called Azõ. He was always disobedient. His parents sold him. At the place where he was sold, he behaved as always. He never obeyed. Those people took him and sold him to Death. They said when they sold him, "Now if Death buys you and you begin the same tricks, if you refuse to obey him, then we will see what happens to you."

So Death bought him. He said, "Now, I will show you how people behave here." He said, "We never permit insults here." So Death planted millet. Death said when the birds came to eat this millet, he must drive them away.

He said: "I, I don't want to do this. I am not one to drive away the birds who come to eat millet."

Death said: "You are my slave. Why don't you want to go?"

Then Death and he began to quarrel. So Azõ said, "Here's a man with long eyelashes who insults me."

Death asked: "Do you know what we do here with a man like you? You shall see."

He said: "What will you do to me? Nothing."

At night Death put him in a locked room. He said: "Now you will eat nothing. You will die here of hunger."

Now, it was settled that the moment Azõ fell asleep, he would be killed by Death. So he did not sleep. He knew it. He did not sleep for seven days. The seventh day Death came to open the door. He thought the man was asleep. But he was not asleep. Death said: "This man cannot stay here. He will destroy my house if he stays." He went and sold him to another.

So Death sold him to another country, and this country was quite close to Azõ's own home. So Azõ escaped and went home.

Now, as no master would keep him, but bought him and sold him, bought him and sold him, he had sores all over his body. People said, "Ah, Azõ, why have you sores like this?"

He said, "It is because they sell me and resell me."

So his brothers said to him, "You have become like a mound of earth that is gradually worn down and down until it is all flattened out." They mocked him. But they were not sold like he had been sold.

As they were in the house, he joked with his brothers, and one day he said to them: "One does not insult Death. But I, I insulted him. Now I am called Keledjegbè Kutõ. I am greater than Death. Death has millet, but he cannot chase away the birds."

Before he was sold, Hevioso was his friend. When he was away, they took Hevioso, his friend, and made him family head. After he came home and all the sores were healed, he was a fine-looking man. He was asked to become king. So he and Hevioso began to quarrel. Hevioso said, "Now, what they gave me, you cannot take away from me." But he took away the kinship from Hevioso, and he became king.

So this happened when he became king and Hevioso was nothing. He commanded a field to be cleared, and he told his people to cultivate it for him. They planted corn. When the time came for the rains, so that the grain might come, Hevioso stopped all rain. There was no longer any rain. So the season became dry. The animals died; men died, too. There was no water to drink.

Everybody began to berate Sagbata. They said, "So, that evil man has come back again to us."

So he had all the people come. The people came and the animals, too, Eagle, Vulture, Cat, Chameleon. Sagbata had much magic. He had white cotton and black. He took the white and black cotton to his mouth, talked to it and had it ascend to the sky.

He said to the creatures, "I'm going to send you to Hevioso to ask for water."

He asked who would be the first to go. Eagle said, "I." When Eagle climbed up halfway to the sky, Hevioso killed him.

The cat said, "Now it is my turn." He almost reached the same place, when lightning crushed him. So Chameleon, who belongs to the Sun-god Lisa, said, "Now it is my turn." He left.

Sagbata said to him: "Now go to Hevioso and tell him to send water that the people and animals and the harvest may thrive. Here on earth all are almost dead."

Chameleon went slowly, slowly. He went almost halfway. When Hevioso wanted to kill him, he curled up and hid under the thread.

Now Hevioso sends his thunderbolts, then goes into his house. He returns and sends another, then goes back to his house. So when he hurled the thunder and went in, Chameleon was at his door. Now there were guards there, and they asked Chameleon, "What do you want here?"

He said, "I am looking for Hevioso." So one guard went to tell Hevioso that there was a man to see him.

He said, "Who sent him?" The man said it was Sagbata.

Chameleon said, "Sagbata sends me to tell you that pigs, goats, men, homes, harvests, all are dying." He said, "He begs you to send water that man might find water to drink."

Hevioso said: "All right. I'll send him water." So he led Chameleon behind his door and gave him a new jar and a new calabash. He said: "Now, give these two things to Sagbata, and tell him to bring all his people together before his door. He must make a hole, and put the jar inside." He said also: "All right, I'll send him water. But tell him beginning today, he is not to command the people in the sky, and I will not command the people below." He said: "All right. Now that I shamed him before his people, I do not ask any more to rule below."

When Chameleon came before Sagbata and said all that Hevioso had said, they had all the people assemble. So they made the hole and put in first the closed calabash, and then the jar on top. So they put earth over this and said, "If someone goes for water, the first water he finds, he must throw over this mound of earth."

Before this there was no earthen mound which they call Aizan. If Hevioso had not ordered Sagbata to make this earthen mound, the rain would not fall. From then on, when it did not rain, one put water on Aizan, and the rain fell. Before this quarrel, there was no trouble, because Hevioso gave water.

Sogbo Becomes Master of the Universe

Sagbata and Sogbo are brothers. We are told that the Creator did not work any more after she created the world, but delegated her children, Sagbata and Sogbo, to rule the world for her. The two quarrelled. Sagbata, the elder, decided to leave the sky and go down on earth. He took with him, since he was the eldest, all his heritage, which included everything of his mother's. The younger brother, who was the more brutal, remained in his mother's kingdom, and he took the name of fire —Miyomiyo, or Sogbo.

Before leaving for the earth, their mother said to them, she would not justify the claim of either in a quarrel. They must be together like a closed calabash and the world must exist inside them. She said that since Sagbata was the elder, he should be the lower part and that Sogbo should be the upper. The mother told them both to go and live in the world. Sogbo refused. He would not leave his mother.

When Sagbata descended, he could not get back on high. He, therefore, descended lower and lower. Sogbo, who was near the mother, won all the confidence of his mother and of the gods who surrounded her. Then one day Sogbo caused the rains to stop. Rain came no longer.

Now in the world below, Sagbata had had himself chosen as king, and the people came to him and said: "Since you came among us and we made you king, there is no longer any rain. We are dying of hunger." He said, "Yes, it is so, but in a few days you will have rain."

A year went by and no rain. Two years went by and no rain. For three years, no rain. Now, two men came down from the sky. Those men fell down in a country called Fe. They preached. They preached the writing of Fa, Destiny. They travelled everywhere.

It is said that at that time the world had no more than a thousand people.

Now, people came to tell Sagbata that two men came from the sky and preached something called Fa. He said they should come. When they came, they spoke to Sagbata the language spoken in the sky, and Sagbata knew at once [that they told the truth]. He asked them why there was no rain.

They said they did not know. Their errand was to preach Fa. What they did know was that his little brother was angry.

Sagbata asked, "Why is he angry?"

They said they did not know, but with Fa, which was the writing of Sagbata's mother, they would know at once. They took the divining seeds, and, throwing them, asked why the rain did not fall in this country. The first combination of Fa that fell was called Yeku Gbuloso. At once they told Sagbata that there was a dispute between two brothers, who both wanted the same thing, and that the elder should submit to the younger to bring about a reconciliation.

Sagbata said that now the sky was too far away and that he no longer had the power to climb up. He said that before going down to earth, his mother had given him the right to take with him all the riches. These he put in his sack. He said that it was he himself who had refused to take along water, because he could not take it in his sack. But arriving on earth, the water which he had left behind had become very necessary. The two men said that water was now under control of his brother. Sagbata asked these men what was to be done to have the rain fall.

The two men then said to him if he wished to make the sacrifice, he must give a portion of all the riches on earth and confide this to the bird Wututu, the great friend of Sogbo. They said, "When Wututu goes up there to talk to Sogbo, Sogbo will never refuse her."

Sagbata heard. He gathered up a portion of all of his riches, and he had Wututu called. He said to Wututu: "Go tell Sogbo that now I, Sagbata, surrender the Universe. I shall let him have the country, and the compounds, and the houses. He may take the sons and the father; the children and the mother. He, Sogbo, is to dwell up high and guard those below."

Once she was up high in the air, Wututu, in a voice which Sogbo knew at once, began to sing: "The earth, Ai-Sagbata, charged me with a commission for you. Do you hear, So?" And Wututu sang: "He said that he leaves you the Universe. He leaves you the country. You are to have the compounds and all the houses. He lets you have the sons and the father; the children and the mother."

When he said this, Sogbo recognized the voice of Wututu from on high. He told his sons to behave, that a stranger was coming. He sent a bolt of lightning. As the lightning flashed, he saw it was Wututu. Sogbo said to let him come.

When Wututu came up, Sogbo said: "Go and say to my elder brother Sagbata that though he is the elder who inherited all the wealth of our mother, he had been foolish to leave behind the two things that are the power of the Universe. With these two things, I, the younger, can control all the wealth of Sagbata."

Those two things are water and fire.

He told Wututu to return, and before even reaching earth, he would see what followed. Wututu flew away towards the earth. When he reached halfway between sky and earth, a great rain began to fall.

Wututu arrived. Sagbata was very happy. And he commanded that Wututu was never to be killed. Should someone kill him by accident, a great ceremony is to be given. This ceremony consists of removing the head-pad, because it was he who had carried on his head the message from Sagbata to Sogbo.

That day the brothers were reconciled. And that is why each year thunder visits the earth. On that day Hevioso gave himself the new name Djato-gbedji-gbezō Djato-megi-mete Kutjo-amu-susu-nokloso.

> Fallen on the grass, the grass puts forth shoots;
> Fallen on mankind, mankind becomes fertile,
> The sprinkling dew gives glory to So.

Sagbata's Control of Earth Stabilized

When they were about to choose the child who was to rule the earth, Hevioso was the first to offer to go. Mawu said as the earth was too far from the sky, the oldest had better go. So Sagbata went. When he came there, Hevioso stopped rain from falling. He waited for men to entreat his mother to send him instead. The people complained. They said [of Sagbata]: "This king is not good for the earth. Since his coming, we find nothing to eat; we find nothing to drink. We have nothing."

One day Mawu sent Legba to earth to see what was happening. He went to see Sagbata, and Sagbata told him Hevioso was keeping the rain from falling. Legba said: "All right. That is nothing." He climbed back into the sky, promising Sagbata to send him a bird who would tell him of Mawu's decision. On his arrival there, Legba sent a bird named Wututu to Sagbata with the message that a fire, so great that the smoke would mount on high, should be kindled at once.

Now Legba had himself suggested that Hevioso cause the rains to stop. To accomplish his purpose, Legba had gone to Mawu with a tale that there was no water in the sky, and that everyone was dying of thirst. Mawu, on hearing this, had given orders that not a drop of rain should leave the sky, so that all the water might be retained there for those in the heavens. But now, after visiting Sagbata on earth, Legba had told the bird Wututu that when Sagbata lit the great fire and the smoke began to rise on high, Wututu should begin to sing.

Thus when Wututu came to earth with his message, Sagbata kindled the fire he had been told to light and, as the smoke rose, Wututu began to sing. Legba then hurried to Mawu and said that he had not been able to go to earth himself, but had sent his "little assistant," Wututu, who, because there had been no rain on earth and the heat had so dried everything that the trees and all else were burning, was on the verge of being consumed. He said, also, that all the sky risked being destroyed in the flames, if rain was not at once made to fall and extinguish the fire. Mawu at once gave Legba orders to command Hevioso to cause the rain to fall, so that Wututu should not be burned. And rain fell abundantly and the earth was saved.

All this time Mawu did not know about the quarrel between the brothers, Sagbata and Hevioso, and to this day knowledge of their quarrel has been withheld from her. Because of what occurred, however, Mawu decreed that all rain should be regulated from the earth, since the danger of a universal conflagration lies there. For this reason Wututu was sent to live on earth, and when this bird finds that the ground is too hot, he cries out, and the rain comes down. Later, Legba effected a reconciliation between the two brothers, so that today man lives without fear of another such severe drought.

Sun God Brings Iron to Man

I do not know if Mawu is a man or a woman. History tells that Mawu created the world. Then when the world was created, Mawu withdrew from the earth and went to live in the sky. After living in the sky, Mawu did not care to come down and live on earth again. But on earth nothing went well. Human beings did not understand how to do things for themselves. They quarreled. They fought. They did not know how to cultivate the fields, nor how to weave cloth to cover their bodies.

So Mawu sent her only child down to earth. This child's name was Lisa. Now, Gu is not a god. Gu is metal. Now, to her son Lisa, Mawu gave metal, and she told Lisa to go down to the earth and cut the bush with this metal, and teach men how to use it to make useful things.

So he came down, and with him he took Gu, this metal given by his mother. With the help of Gu, Lisa cut down trees, and cleared the bush, and got the fields ready. Then he built houses. And when all was done, he said to all men that his mother's words were, "Without metal men cannot live." So Lisa remade the world; and he told all men, "To overcome obstacles, you must learn to use metal." When he said this, he went back to the sky.

Lisa returned to his mother and gave her back the cutlass called gugbasa, which was made of iron.

Mawu said: "Gold is a costly metal. All other metals are dear, too. But iron must serve all mankind." And Mawu said that as Lisa was a good son, and had carried out his mission well, he would have as his reward the Sun to live in. From there Lisa keeps watch over the universe. Gu went with Lisa to the Sun, to serve as his sword. This was a gift from

Mawu to Lisa so that Lisa might do his work in the world.

From that day onwards this cutlass has been called Ali-su-gbo-gu-kle, The-road-is-closed-and-Gu-opens-it.

Serpent as Headrest for an Overburdened Earth

There are some who say the world is a machine. Somebody made it, but if there was one Mawu or many, history does not tell us. Aido-Hwedo, the serpent, is a vodun, but is not of the family of the gods. They say he is not the son of the Great Mawu, because Aido-Hwedo existed before any of the children of Mawu; before Sogbo. They say that Aido-Hwedo came with the first man and the first woman of the world.

Now, when the Creator made the world, she had Aido-Hwedo with her as her servant. Aido-Hwedo carried her in his mouth everywhere. We do not know if the world was there already. We know the earth was the first created, because the world is like a calabash. The top is put on last.

Wherever the Creator went, Aido-Hwedo went with her. That is why the earth is as we find it. It curves, it winds, it has high places, and low places. That is the movement of the serpent Aido-Hwedo. Where Mawu and Aido-Hwedo rested there are mountains, because the mountains were made by the excrement of Aido-Hwedo. That is why we find riches inside mountains.

Now, when the work was finished, Mawu saw that the earth had too much weight. There were too many things—too many trees, too many mountains, elephants, everything. It was necessary to rest the earth on something. So Aido-Hwedo was told to coil himself into a circle and rest as a carrying pad underneath the earth.

Now, Aido-Hwedo does not like heat, so Mawu made water for him to live in. So he is in the sea. But it is not he who commands the sea. It is Agbè, a son of Mawu, who commands there, because those who command must be of royal blood.

Now, when Aido-Hwedo stirs, there is an earthquake.

The People Who Descended from the Sky

Tradition tells that in very ancient times, a man and a woman came down from the sky to the district of Somè in Adja. This was the first family on earth. The man and woman brought with them a long wand and a calabash. They wore long shirts, much longer than those worn today.

It rained the day they came from the sky, and it rained for seventeen days more. All this time they did not speak. They only called out, "Segbo, Segbo, Segbo . . . !" This was the name of the one who had sent them on earth. After seven days, another man and woman came down from the sky. This man and woman wore the beads we know even today as lisaje, "Lisa's beads."

Then they began to teach the worship of Mawu and Lisa. We are told that the first temple they raised for Mawu-Lisa still exists in Adja. On the day they were to offer sacrifices to Mawu and to Lisa it rained once more. Many people came down from the sky with the rain to help them carry out the ceremony. But as soon as the ceremony was over, these went back to the sky.

This ceremony of giving offerings to Mawu and Lisa was carried out three or four times. Then the man and the woman who had brought the beads returned to the sky. They left their beads behind them. They also left a daughter on earth. Four shrines had by then been established, one for Mawu, one for Lisa, one for Gu and one for Agè. For Mawu they killed a sheep, for Lisa a white goat and a white chicken. For Gu they gave a white cock, and to Agè a dog was given. We make the same sacrifices today, because that is what these people had done who came from the sky to teach the worship of Mawu to man.

Then the woman gave birth to two children, the first a son and the second a daughter. Each child was born with a small wand in the hand, and the wand grew as the child grew. The children always had their wands with them. They were never lost. Then seven years later, the mother and father of the children returned to the sky. The children carried on the teaching of the worship of the sky gods. Since what they taught was good, the worship of these gods spread everywhere in Dahomey.

The first pair who came from the sky was accompanied by a chameleon. The chameleon went everywhere the man and woman went, just as a dog goes with his master. The chameleon was sent by Lisa to protect them. Lisa knew that when they taught about Mawu and Lisa, there would be people who would refuse to receive their teaching, and who would conspire against them. But the chameleon, who was always in front, reflected on his smooth skin everything that happened behind their backs as they went about.

Any move by an enemy to strike them from behind was mirrored on the body of the chameleon. For the chameleon's body is like Lisa's, smooth as a mirror. This is why the chameleon is the animal sacred to the god Lisa.

Origin of the People of the Agblo Quarter

This was in very ancient times. There was a heavy rain. A great cloud of smoke came up from the earth. In those times, the region of Abomey was all big bush. There were no people living there. The cloud of smoke came from inside this bush. When the smoke cleared, a man followed by a woman were visible. Each carried a sack of okra seeds.

The following day it rained again, and again smoke came from inside the bush. When everything cleared, there were sixty-six people there, thirty-six women and thirty men. These people began to cut down the trees and to clear the land for planting. They prepared the fields and planted the okra seeds they had brought in their sacks.

The name of the first man was Agblo. Agblo mated with the woman who accompanied him. The people who came with the second rain also mated. They had children, and these grew up and mated, and in time their descendants peopled the region.

Agblo and his wife died, he in the morning, she the same afternoon. The others mourned the two who, they said, had founded their family. A ram was sacrificed to their spirits, and this was buried with them in the hole in the earth from where they had come.

When the founders of the family were buried, and the hole from which they had come was filled in, these people had no gods to worship. Then later, a man named Cheyi began to dig a well. When he had dug to a depth of twelve to fourteen meters, he saw a road along which many people were passing.

He followed along this road, and soon met an old woman. The woman asked him why he had come. He said he was digging a well and had found this road. The woman said the place where he had been digging was sacred to the Earth. She said he must come before the ruler of this place.

Cheyi was brought to a temple where he heard a voice say he was now in the house of Sagbata. He saw no one, but the voice went on speaking. The voice said Sagbata had caused him to choose the spot for the well to bring him to this country so that he might learn how to worship the earth gods and take this knowledge back to his people.

Then Cheyi was told to return to his home. He was instructed to close the hole where he had dug and build a temple for Sagbata over it. He was told to raise another temple for Mawu and Lisa, the gods of the sky, not far from the Sagbata temple. Then he was commanded to tell his people to worship these three deities as their tohwiyo [clan founders]. He was told how Sagbata "eats" the male goat, Lisa the female goat, and Mawu the sheep. He was taught the cult of these three gods.

Cheyi did as he was told. He closed the hole he had dug, and built the house for Sagbata over it. Then he built the houses for Mawu and Lisa. He called all the people together to tell them what had happened to him and what he had been told. Then the first ceremony was held. Everything Cheyi was told to do he did. The first sheep and goat sacrificed to Mawu and Lisa were accepted. A heavy rain fell, thunder was heard, and in an instant the animals disappeared. When the goat for Sagbata was brought to the house of Sagbata, the earth opened and swallowed it.

Cheyi knew the animals to sacrifice to these gods, but he did not know how to worship them. That is why, later, a man named Agamu came out of the earth to teach Cheyi how to "establish" the gods, how to sprinkle their altars with the blood of the animals sacrificed to them. For sixteen days he stayed with Cheyi teaching him about the gods.

Cheyi was the first human to learn about the cults of the great gods.

He became the first priest of these gods. When he was very old, the earth opened and he disappeared. But he had taught what he knew to others, and the worship of Sagbata and Mawu-Lisa has continued.

How Legba Became Chief of the Gods

Long ago, Legba was the last of the gods. One day Mawu said to the gods he would show them something. He would show them who would be their chief. Mawu then gave them a gong, a bell, a drum, a flute and said whoever took all the instruments, and played the four together and also danced to them would be their chief.

Hevioso said: "I am very strong. I can do all." So he tried. But he failed.

Mawu called on Gu and Agè to try. Agè said: "I am a hunter. I have great strength. I can do everything." He tried and failed. Gu came. He said he had much strength. He had fire. He made many things. He would do it. He tried, and he, too, failed.

Now Mawu called all the gods together and asked Legba to try. Legba tried and did all. He struck the drum; he played the gong; he rang the bell; he blew into the flute, and [at the same time] made all the gestures of the dance. Mawu said to him, "Now I will give you a woman whose name is Konikoni." And Mawu said to the other gods that Legba was to be first among them.

Now Legba said he would sing, and he sang:

> If the house is peaceful
> If the field is fertile,
> I will be very happy.

Now Legba had knowledge, and he began to make magic charms. He was the first to make them. He made a serpent. Then he put the serpent down on the road to the market, and he commanded the serpent to bite the sellers and the buyers. Once the serpent bit them, Legba came and said to them, "Give me something, and I will cure you." If they gave him something, he went away to buy acasa, and palm oil and drinking water. Then he ate all and drank all.

One day someone asked Legba, "What is that," pointing to the serpent, "that which bites people?"

Legba answered him, "It is magic." Legba said to this man, "Bring me two chickens and eighty cowries and some straw and I will make one for you." So Legba began to make magic charms for this man.

Legba led this man down the road to the market, and he told him all that had to be done to make this magic charm. When Legba said to throw the liana, the liana became a serpent, and began to bite people. Then, Legba gave him the medicine to cure these people. This man was called Awè, and it was Legba who gave magic charms to Awè.

Now magic charms spread everywhere. Legba began to give him

other charms so that if someone needed a charm he came to Awè, and Awè called Legba to his house. They made the charms inside the house, and then carried them outside to give to those who came for them.

Now, Mawu was angry. She called Legba and said to Legba, "Now if someone does not see you, you will not do this again." [That is, Legba was made invisible.]

Now, Legba is forever a vodun. Awè is a man. So he continued to make charms. Awè became chief of magic. When someone wished to make a charm, he came to him and brought all that was needed, and Awè took the place of Legba. So Awè went everywhere and asked who wanted to make charms. Then he gave them charms and disappeared.

He gave the magic charms to everyone. He also gave charms to those who do evil. He gave charms to pregnant women that the child should not come. Then when the woman was having a difficult time, they called Awè, and they had to give him many things before he was satisfied. Then only would he give medicine that the child might come.

The kings of many lands came to Awè to ask for charms. If Awè met a child he would drop medicine on its body, and the body of the child became a ball.

Awè now said: "I am going to see the world. Now there is enough magic." One day he bought cotton thread and silk, and all one night he rolled the cotton into a ball. He did this from six o'clock in the evening until six o'clock the next morning. He left it. During the day he took the silken thread, and he rolled it until night. He measured both and he discovered that they were both the same length.

One day he climbed an anthill, and he'threw the cotton and silken threads towards the sky. Mawu caught both threads. Then holding on to these two threads, Awè reached the sky. Mawu said to him, "What are you looking for here?"

Awè said to Mawu: "My knowledge is great. I now seek to measure my knowledge with Mawu."

Mawu said, "Show me what is your knowledge." Awè cut down a tree. He began to make a human figure. He made the head very well, the face, the hair, the arms, all the members. But the statuette could not talk. It did not breathe. It could not move. Mawu said to him: "Your knowledge is not enough. Wait, I'll show you."

On the same day Mawu took a grain of corn, traced a row and sowed it. The grain sprouted, and the same day they ate the ripe corn. They removed the corn from the cob, put it in the mill, brought the flour home, and prepared the dish that Awè ate.

Mawu left Awè, and Awè went back to earth. But Mawu sent Death to follow him. Mawu said to Death: "Men are evil. If someone does evil, it is necessary to kill him."

Awè tried a charm, and attacked Death. In those days, wood would not burn, for there was no fire. It was impossible to cook. So Mawu said to Death and Awè, "If you, Awè, attack Death, then whoever will prepare his food will find that food raw again." So Awè let Death go, in order that, among men, one could put food to cook, and it would cook quickly, and people could eat. Mawu said to Awè: "If someone is ill, you are to take good care of him. But if I like, I will send Death to kill him."

Awè mastered Legba's knowledge, and he became a practitioner of magic. Awè and Death are the two friends of the world.

EXPLOITS OF THE ALADAHONU DYNASTY

According to Melville and Frances Herskovits, from whose superb narrative collection these stories are taken, the Dahomean distinguishes between heho, or tales, and hwenoho, "history." In the Dahomean mind the term hwenoho signifies tradition, traditional history and ancient lore. A storyteller in Abomey explained: "We in Dahomey say that heho tell of things which never existed and are inventions of people. Hwenoho is the true story, and the life of Dahomey is based on hwenoho." Hwenoho thus include the following narrative types: myths, which are chiefly stories of the beginning of things or about the deities; clan myth-chronicles, which tell of the origin of important families or clans, and of their adventures and exploits and sometimes of the origin of ritual behavior and taboos; and verse sequences which are sung by professional narrators as aids in remembering events and genealogies. The following hwenoho belong to the category of clan myth-chronicles.

DRAMATIS PERSONAE

ADJAHUTO, a ruler of Adja, son of a male leopard, founder of the dynasty
AGASU, brother of Adjahuto
TE AGBANLI, brother of Adjahuto
AWISU, an ancient king of Allada
HWEGBADJA, a king of Allada
KAKPOKPOLEKESE, father of one of Hwegbadja's servants
A NAGO
BEHANZIN, also called DEGENO, a king of Dahomey, reigned 1889–1894, until the French exiled him to Martinique
GLELE, a king of Dahomey, reigned 1858–1889
TOFA, brother of Glele

From Dahomean Narrative, *by Melville J. and Frances S. Herskovits. Evanston, Northwestern University Press, 1958. By permission of Northwestern University Press.*

AGOLIAGBO, brother of Behanzin
ADJAHOSU (ADJAHUTO?), a king of Adja

Origin of the Royal Sib

In the early days, a male leopard came out of a river, and lay with a wife of the king of Adja. The king alone knew this secret. He told it to his principal wife. This wife was childless.

Now this wife spread the news, and the people did not want these leopard children to be kings of Adja. So the three brothers born to the "wife of the leopard" killed their enemies and escaped to Allada. Here they became rulers over the Aizonu, who lived there.

The three brothers could not live together without quarrelling. The blood of their animal father brought about their separation. The hunter, Agasu, and his followers went north. Adjahuto stayed in Allada. And Te Agbanli, the third brother, went south. His descendants came to rule over the land of Porto Novo. The leopard favored Agasu more than the other two, because, as we see, it was his descendants who came to rule ancient Dahomey, Adja, Allada, and many other kingdoms.

Now the father of Adjahuto, Agasu, and Te Agbanli was a warrior and a lover of human blood. But their mother wanted peace and had taught them peaceful ways. So to carry out their mother's wishes, they conquered an enemy kingdom southwest of Allada. Here they commanded the people to live forever at peace, and in this way to act for them.

How the Aladahonu Kings Came to Rule Abomey

This happened in ancient times before our people came to this country [the Plateau of Abomey]. In the days of our forefathers, if a man died, the custom was not to bury him. They took the body and put it in the hollow of a tree. Then the dead man's enemies removed the head, and sang and danced. In those days there was no cloth. To cover the body, they took bark and beat it.

At that time there were many kings who ruled the country, not one. Each one had his district. Awisu was a big king. He took the throne for a year, and the following year another village took the throne. So it was. When one king ruled, he made a law. The following year another king made another law.

Our ancestors were kings in Allada before they came here. Then in the days of our ancestors, when Hwegbadja lived, the family had many men. So people said he should become king. They liked him very much. In those days, when anyone was to become king, he had to go to Awisu's gate to be confirmed. If you were to become king anywhere, they would call a council meeting. That was all. Nobody gave them food.

When Hwegbadja called the first meeting, he ordered much food to be cooked. But the carriers who were bringing the food were a little late. The people were so impatient for the food that the food was spilled. Now the people said to Hwegbadja: "If you want to call a meeting, call it at your house. This way food goes to waste. You do not have to go to Awisu's gate."

Then, when Hwegbadja was king, he called the second meeting at his own house. Everybody came to his gate, not Awisu's gate. Then he showed them how to spin cotton. He did it first, and then gave it to the women. They began to make cotton thread. Then they made cloth. But it was too white. They did not know how to make colors. Everything was white.

Hwegbadja commanded one of his servants to make a white cloth. Then, this servant's father died. The father's name was Kakpokpolekese. So when the father died, Hwegbadja ordered him to take the cloth he wove for his father's burial.

The man said, "I will make another one for you. I will start on it today." So he took the cloth and wrapped his father's body in it. Then they went to prepare the earth. They dug the grave.

Then, the people to whom the country belonged [the autochthonous people], told Hwegbadja: "All right. We never did this before. But if you want to bury a person in the earth, you must pay. You must buy the land from us." They said, how much would they pay them? They said they wanted two hundred francs in cowries. The man who received this money was a very rich man. Hwegbadja paid before they dug the grave, and buried him.

Several days after the man's father died, his mother died. The people of the country began to denounce him. They said: "We did not bury people. No sooner do you begin to bury people, than they begin to die off." Then the people began to quarrel about it.

Hwegbadja assembled all the other kings, and said: "Now I tell you people, during my command here, nobody must throw away the dead; nobody must put them inside trees. All must bury the dead. If this is not done, I will kill him who disobeys."

He gave them another law, and said: "If a man puts fire to another man's house; or, if someone who does not like me burns my house, then he who catches him in the act should kill him, and bring his head to show me, saying, 'That man burned your house. I saw him do it, and I killed him.'"

Then he told them: "If a man has an enemy and cuts off the head of an innocent man, and brings it, then if I find out that the man is lying, I will kill him."

Then he said: "If someone deflowers a young girl, not yet of age, I will kill him." He said: "Let no one seize people who pass by with loads on their heads and sell them. If someone does this, and I find out, I will kill him."

He said: "If there is a minor chief who persecutes a poor man, let the poor man come to me, and I will summon the chief and investigate, and tell him not to trouble the poor man." He said: "If any man takes a load and escapes with it to another country, if I catch him, I will kill him."

He said he wished all men to remain [not to flee the country].

He said, no one is knowingly to poison another. If there is a dispute and quarreling, they must inform the chief, and it must be settled. Whoever is to be put in prison will be put in prison. But no one is to poison another man. Whoever is to be flogged, will be flogged. But no one is to poison another man.

Everybody liked these laws against bad people.

Then the minor chiefs, whom he told about these laws, would not agree [to obey them]. When there was a death in the districts ruled over by the other kings, the people hurried to Hwegbadja, and said: "When my father dies, you will bury him for me. It is not good to put the dead inside trees." When people died, each one of the other kings would say: "All right, you must pay. If you pay, they can bury them." So people from another country came to Hwegbadja, and said: "Our father died. Pay the money, and let us go bury him." But that king, if he did not like the man [who appealed to Hwegbadja for the burial fee], would flog the man, and dig up the grave and cut off the head. So the man came to tell Hwegbadja.

Hwegbadja said: "Ah, I went and paid the money, and you did this! I will kill you." He went and made war, and he killed the king.

So he began making war on all the kings. If a man came to say that his king did this, he [Hwegbadja] would say: "All right. I will go and make war on him. I will kill the king. I will catch him."

The people liked this very much. They said: "All right. We like you. We will make you king for all time."

For that reason, he told the whole country. He said: "Now, I will die. When I am dead, my son will succeed me. After I am dead, and before my son becomes king, he must pay that money." For that reason, before a king is enthroned, he distributes much money among the people, because he must buy the land. Everybody gets money. A woman gets some. A man gets [some].

Everybody says: "I am Hwegbadja's slave. Hwegbadja paid for me."

The King and the Nago

There was once a king. And there was a young girl. A wall separated the king's houses from the outside, and the girl lived outside this wall. The king asked to have intercourse with the girl. The girl refused. He offered her a thousand francs. He promised if he could have her once, she would then be free. The girl refused.

On the third day, he had the girl brought to him, and he made her the same offer. He begged to have relationship with her. The girl again refused. The king said, "Good."

The king went to find an azondato, a man who makes evil charms. He began to use such a charm against the girl. On the seventh day the girl died. The dead body of the girl lay there. That night, the chief in charge of burial was behind the house. Two men were digging the grave. The king came and had intercourse with the dead girl, and went away.

Now a Nago man saw the king do this. The king ran away. The Nago said: "All right. Why do you run away? Come here."

The king said, "I beg you, do not tell anyone."

The Nago said, "If I tell no one, what will you give me?"

The king said, "I will make you a present of six girls, whom you can marry, and I will add four thousand francs."

The Nago said: "Good. I drank too much today. I will come and see you tomorrow at four o'clock." The next day the Nago went to the king, and said, "I want nothing from you. I ask only to command you."

The king said: "No, you cannot live here. If people come to me to pass judgment, what will I do?"

The Nago said: "All the worse for you. That does not trouble me. All I know is that I desire to command you." The king pleaded with the Nago. The Nago would not listen. To all the king's entreaties, he said, "No."

The day of the king's court, the Nago came and stood behind the king. They judged, and the subchiefs came and said: "We have finished judging. Speak. Give us the verdicts."

The king wished to speak. The king said, "I say . . ."

But the Nago rose and said, "Enough, my chief." The king fell silent. The king ordered the subchiefs to leave. They were all astonished.

The people went out talking. They said: "What does it mean, the king cannot speak? A worker of magic commands here? That cannot be."

Arrived at the house, the king said to the Nago: "Please, I beg you, I will give you ten thousand francs. I will give you a village."

The Nago said: "No, I do not want that. I will remain here, wearing my old clothes, and I will command you. If they say in the city, 'Here's a poor man who commands a king,' it is enough for me."

Again the day came when the king was to hold court. They went to the courthouse. The Nago sat down behind the king. They judged. The chiefs brought the verdicts to the king. The king wanted to speak. He said, "I say . . ."

The Nago said, "Enough, my patron."

The king said again, "Go back to your houses." All the chiefs of the district went to see the king at his house.

The chiefs asked: "What have you done, that you cannot confess, so that a poor magician can command you so? Have you killed?"

One chief said to him: "If a man wishes to be king, he steals, he kills, he has intercourse with the dead, he sells slaves. All that is forbidden to do, he does, before becoming king." Good. After he said this, he asked again: "Why does a poor man annoy the king in his own kingdom? If the king gives a command in court, the others will throw themselves at the Nago."

The king said to them, "Yes. It is true." He gave four thousand francs to this chief for his advice. He gave them drinks, and they drank till they were drunk.

The Nago did not know that they had made a conspiracy. The Nago came and sat down in the same place. They finished hearing the cases, and then the chiefs came to the king to learn his decisions. The king said, "I say . . ."

The Nago arose, and said, "Enough."

The king said: "Silence, my people. I wish to speak. Listen to me." He followed the advice of the chief. He said: "Why does this Nago disturb me every day? This is the third time he has annoyed me in this council. I am not in his district here." The king said: "If one wishes to be king here, one steals, one kills, one sells slaves, one has intercourse with the dead, one does all the evil. I did all before becoming king. This Nago troubles me. Take him and kill him."

The Nago escaped. They ran after him, ran after him till they caught him. There were two very tall trees. There was a small wheel. A long, sharp nail was put into the tree, with a very sharp head. Everybody was there. They put the rope about the neck of the Nago. The king commanded them to have the Nago lifted up to the nail. The nail was placed so that it would enter his head. They raised up the man till the nail entered his head. The Nago died.

The king said, "All right. I'll make him climb up to the flag."

This tells that here in Dahomey a Nago must not command a king.

How Behanzin Fought Against the Whites

There is a village called Wefi which is found behind Porto Novo. Wefi belonged to King Tofa. Tofa had his wife there, his mother and father-in-law, his children. But the people of Wefi did not want to obey Tofa.

Tofa and Glele were brothers. Tofa sent a "commission" to Glele to say that there was a village in his province that did not obey him. Glele sent back a reply asking what he wanted him to do to these people. And Tofa replied that he wanted him to make war against them.

At this, Glele came with the people of Abomey, and made war there. He killed, and caught slaves there, and took the slaves to Abomey. At this, Tofa sent a message that among those people he had taken were his own children, his father-in-law, his mother-in-law, his wife. He asked for those people.

But these people were already with Prince Behanzin—Degeno was his name then—for his father had given them to him, when he returned to Abomey. So Tofa called on Behanzin to bring back the slaves that were of his house.

Behanzin said to Tofa's messengers he was wrong to ask this for it was not he who had bought the powder that Glele had used in capturing these slaves. He said he would never return the slaves that his father had caught. He [Tofa] had no right to ask to share the slaves. And he said if Tofa was not careful, he would one day make war against him.

When Glele died and Behanzin became king, he sent a message to Tofa to say that he was now ready to make war; that war was near. Behanzin brought together all the people of Abomey and gave each a gun with which to make war against Tofa. In this war, [Behanzin] could not quite kill Tofa, but he took an arm and part of one side. But Tofa is not yet dead. He escaped from Porto Novo, and stayed at Agosa, where his uncle was.

When Behanzin arrived in Porto Novo, he killed all the people he found there, and cut down all oil palms. At this, Tofa sent a message by Hazoume to the French. Because in France Tofa had a friend. He told Hazoume to speak to his friend in France, and tell him the king of Abomey had come to break Porto Novo. He begged the French to come and make war, so that Dahomey might belong to him.

Behanzin did not know that the messenger had been sent to France.

Soon after, the whites, many whites with their guns, landed in Cotonou. They had all sorts of weapons with them, and they sent a message to Behanzin, who was in Abomey, that they were going to amuse themselves.

Behanzin sent a message back that he was ready for everything. And that very evening, Behanzin brought together all the people of Abomey and told them he had received a message from the whites, and that they must leave the following morning at cockcrow.

When they left for Cotonou, the war began. They killed all the whites, and the few who remained fled, leaving their guns. These whites did not return to France. They were on the sea, in their vessels, and from there they sent a message to France.

Much later, many, many landed. Now, the whites sent another message to Behanzin saying that they had come once more, and that they were going to take their coffee in three days, with the sugar that was in his house. So Behanzin started towards Cotonou to make war. But the whites had separated their army into two parts. One remained in Cotonou. The other was already in Abomey. But Behanzin did not know it.

As Behanzin continued his travels to the coast, the other whites followed him. They began the war at Cotonou. They did nothing but kill. They killed the whites; they killed the blacks. But as the whites were stronger than Behanzin, the Dahomeans retreated. But they did not know that there was a white army behind them.

As Behanzin marched towards Abomey, one of his children who had been in Abomey, and had seen the whites, came to warn him. He came to say to Behanzin that the whites were in Abomey now. Behanzin was not yet in Kana when he received this message. Behanzin sent the same child back with the message that all houses were to be burned, that none should be left for the whites.

With this news, his wives and children escaped to Agbadogudo, and Behanzin changed his route, not passing by Kana.

So the whites, who were in Abomey, believed that the whites in Cotonou had killed all the Dahomeans. And those in Abomey descended to Cotonou and said that all were dead.

But the whites in Cotonou said that when you break a country you must get the king, and that they wanted Behanzin. So they returned to Abomey to catch Behanzin. They searched for him for three months.

If the whites, who were looking for Behanzin, thought they had him in a certain house, he would change into a cat. Once he changed into a vulture. He changed into a lion, into a panther. But the whites bothered his family in Abomey so much that Behanzin finally said, "Well, I will go and give myself up."

When he arrived, he went before the door of his dead father, and asked for all the whites to come, saying he wanted to speak to the commander and his aide. He shook the hand of the general and his next in command, and said, "If you go, you will die, since I have shaken hands with you." And so, when the two of them arrived in Cotonou, they died.

He said: "I myself [of my own free will] want to go to France. If I did not wish to go, you could go on looking for me for many years without ever finding me. If I did not wish to be caught, not one of you could catch me." So he said, "Go on." He had the whites go before him, and he walked behind, as he wished.

He told one of his brothers, Agoliagbo, that he should stay in Abomey while he was in France. He entrusted his wives to Agoliagbo, and he said that if one of his wives wished to find another husband, Agoliagbo should look for one for her. He forbade his brother to marry his wives.

He said it was Tofa who had brought the whites, and that he would go to Porto Novo and greet Tofa before he embarked for France. Tofa sent a message that he did not want him to come to Porto Novo, that he should depart for France from Cotonou, because, if Behanzin had come there, Tofa would have been killed.

So the whites came here because Glele broke Wefi.

Seeking Poverty

The king of Adja, Adjahosu, had everything. One day when he went to see his diviner, he said: "You must divine something for me. I am too rich and do not know what it is to be poor. I want to know what it is to be poor."

The diviner told him, after he divined, to bring a drum, a gong and rattles. "When you have them, tell your hunters to catch a giraffe."

When he returned home, he ordered a drum, a gong and rattles to be made, and he commanded his hunters to catch a giraffe for him. When they brought the animal, he gathered all the things the diviner had told him to get, and took them to him.

The diviner instructed them to tie the gong, drum and rattles about the neck of the giraffe, and told the man to get on its back. Then they took a cloth and tied him in place, and the diviner gave him a little stick to strike the drum with. When he beat the drum, the giraffe ran away with him into the bush.

They passed through brush and thorny bushes until they were in the middle of the forest, when the cloth became so torn that the king fell off the animal. He did not know where his house was; he was completely lost.

As he could find no place to sleep, he climbed a tree and stayed there during the night. He was in the bush three months. The third month he came on an old woman looking for leaves of the indigo plant. Now the man had already lost an eye, so when the old woman looked at him, and she saw a man who looked to her as though he were blind, she led him to her house. And every five days, when the woman went to market to get cloths to dye and to sell those she had dyed, she put her load on the head of the man she had found, and led him to market.

This she did for three years.

In the meantime, the children of the king of Adja did not know what had happened to him. One fine day, however, the woman went to one of the king's fields to sell something to one of his sons. As usual, the man carried the cloths. When they reached the field of Adjahosu, his sons looked at the man who was with the old woman. He had only one eye, but he resembled their father, and each asked the other if this was not he.

He had put down his load, and while he was sitting there, someone called, "Adjahosu, come and sell me some wood."

When the sons came home, they said to the eldest brother: "Look, we were at a market in the field of Adjahosu, and we saw a black man whom they call Adjahosu. And an old woman commanded him to sell wood." The older brother said, "Good, we will go to the next market there."

So he went early to market and arrived before the woman came. He placed himself where his younger brothers had been, and after a time saw an old woman accompanied by a man, who was carrying her cloths. When the man put the cloths down, he took his bush knife and entered the forest nearby. In a short time, he saw the man returning with wood, which he put down beside his mistress. After this, the woman said, "You can eat," and gave him something to eat.

As he was eating, his son approached him. When he recognized his child, he began to cry, and the son did, too.

The son led his father to the old woman and asked her, "Where did you find this man?"

She answered: "I was looking for indigo leaves. One day I saw him alone in the bush."

The son took the man and said, "Now you will sell him to me."

She said, "If I sell him now, who will carry my load to my house?"

The son said, "I will buy him and give you the money, and you can buy another carrier with this money."

"Let me be! This old one here, what will you do with him?"

The son replied: "This is not an old one to me. He is my father. I beg you to sell him to me."

The old woman said, "Since he is your father, take him."

So his son took Adjahosu home, and bathed him and gave him fresh clothes. After that Adjahosu summoned all his people before him to speak to them. He said: "Because I myself am very very rich, I wanted to know what is poverty. Now I say to you, my sons and my family, never

ask to be poor. Because poverty eats nothing, drinks nothing."
And so, a man must not seek poverty.

Two Dahomean Songs for the Dead

I

I came to drink with my friend,
And find him I could not.
O Death, who taketh away Life
And giveth no day at court,
A day will come and I shall see him again.
Aye, I shall see him . . .
For I too am going towards death.

II

I see it,
There is no enjoying beyond Death,
And I say to all of you say,
That which your senses taste of Life,
Goes with you.

I say to you say
The wives you have,
The passion you know of them
Goes with you.

I say to you say
The drinks you drink,
The pleasure of them
Goes with you.

I say to you say
The meats you eat,

From The New Republic, *84, September 4, 1935. Translated from the Fon original by Frances S. Herskovits. By permission of* The New Republic.

The relish you have of them
Goes with you.

I say to you say
The pipes you smoke,
The quiet they bring
Goes with you.

Come, then
Dance all the colors of Life
For a lover of pleasure
Now dead.

Some Dahomean Riddles

The Dahomean riddle is expressed with economy. Its appeal lies not only in the hidden meaning of the solution, but more especially in its double entendre, the play on words that is so important an element of Dahomean everyday communication.

A period of riddling prefaces all storytelling sessions. For the adults it is a warming-up time, a keying to attention, that keeps them occupied until latecomers arrive. For the children it has the special function of memory training, and is so recognized by the adults. To be present at one of these children's storytelling sessions, presided over by one of their age mates, and listen to the answers to the riddles coming with lightning rapidity is like hearing a drill in the multiplication table. Of the double entendre the children get nothing, though at certain points they will laugh in imitation of their elders. It is this double entendre that gives the riddle its importance in the rites for the dead. For the dead, who are being sent away from the world of the living, must savor all that gave them pleasure when alive; so at wakes the old men show their mastery in introducing riddles with the broadest innuendo, the greatest subtlety, and the sharpest suggestiveness. Some of these elements, unfortunately, are blurred or lost in translation.

Substance taken from Dahomean Narrative, *by Melville J. and Frances S. Herskovits. By permission of Northwestern University Press.*

Hole within hole, hair all round, pleasure comes from inside. (Answer: A flute being played by a bearded man.)

A thing leaves the house bent over and returns home straight. (Answer: A water jar.)

A thing is naked going out, but returning, the body is covered with clothes. (Answer: Corn.)

My father eats with his anus and he defecates through his mouth. (Answer: A gun.)

One throws a thing across the hedge, and it falls in one heap. (Answer: A frog.)

A large hat in the midst of weeds. (Answer: A latrine.)

One thing falls in the water with a loud voice, another falls in the water with a soft voice. (Answer: A bottle of oil, a carrying basket.)

Some Dahomean Proverbs

The big do not eat out of the hand of the small.

He who makes the gunpowder wins the battles.

War lies in wait on a narrow path.

A snake bit me; I see a worm and I am afraid.

If one wants to catch a large fish he must give something to the stream.

Mawu [the creator] sent sickness into the world but he also sent medicine to cure.

When one is at sea he does not quarrel with the boatman.

The fish trap that catches no fish is brought back to the house.

THE YORUBA

The Yoruba people, of whom there are probably more than ten million, occupy the southwest corner of Nigeria along the Dahomey border, and a branch of the Yoruba—the Anago—extends into Dahomey itself. To the east and north the Yoruba culture reaches its approximate limits in the region of the Niger River, though there are ample reasons to believe that ancestral cultures directly related to the Yoruba once flourished well north of the Niger.

Portuguese explorers "discovered" the Yoruba cities and kingdoms in the fifteenth century, but it is believed that Ife and culturally related Benin may have been standing at their present sites at least four or five hundred years before the European arrival. Benin was a creation of the

This introduction, slightly altered, and the stories about the deities which follow are from Tales of Yoruba Gods and Heroes, © *1973 by Harold Courlander, and are reprinted here by permission of Crown Publishers.*

Edo-speaking people of that region, but its history and traditions were intricately intertwined with those of the Yoruba cities and kingdoms. Archeological evidence indicates that a technologically and artistically advanced people—possibly proto-Yoruba—were living somewhat north of the Niger in the first millennium B.C. Sophisticated terra-cotta art found at Nok, about three hundred miles north of Ife, has a stylistic relationship with later Yoruba art. The Nok terra-cotta was made about 300 B.C., and the Nok people were then already working iron.

Tradition says that Ife was the first of all Yoruba cities, and that the kingdoms of Benin and Oyo came into being later. Oyo and Benin probably grew and expanded as a consequence of their strategic locations at a time when overland trade became increasingly important in West Africa. The city of Benin was accessible by river from the sea, which gave it added importance as a link in the trade routes. Ife, unlike Benin and Oyo, never developed into a true kingdom. But though it remained a city-state it had paramount importance to Yoruba as the original sacred city and the dispenser of basic religious thought.

Until relatively recent times the Yoruba did not consider themselves a single people, but rather as citizens of Oyo, Owo, Yagba and other cities, regions or kingdoms. Oyo regarded Lagos and Owo, for example, as foreign principalities, and the Yoruba kingdoms warred not only against the Dahomeans but against each other. The name Yoruba was applied to all these linguistically and culturally related peoples by their northern neighbors, the Hausa.

The old Yoruba cities typically were urban centers with surrounding farmlands that extended outward as much as a dozen miles or more. Some of them had earthworks around their perimeters for defense, either mound walls or ditches, or a combination of both. Ijebu-ode, for example, is described as having had a forty-foot-high earthwork, comprised of a ditch and a bank, enclosing an area of some four hundred square miles.

Both Benin and Oyo are said to have been founded by Ife rulers or descendants of Ife rulers. Benin derived its knowledge of brass casting from Ife, and the religious system of divining called Ifa spread from Ife not only throughout the Yoruba country but to other West African cultures as well. A common Yoruba belief system dominated the region from the Niger, where it flows in an easterly direction, all the way to the Gulf of Guinea in the south.

Deeds and Adventures of the Yoruba Gods

The orishas—that is to say, the gods—the nearly orishas and the heroes of Yoruba tradition are innumerable. There are literally hundreds of orishas, ranging from the original and supreme sky deity Olorun to the local protective deities of regions, towns and villages. Best known and most widely served where traditional religious life survives are a dozen or so "greater" orishas who, under the supreme Olorun,

were active in earthly affairs after dry land had been created by
Obatala, whose name signifies King of the White Cloth. Some of the
greater orishas played roles in the ordering of human life on earth, and
some are personifications of natural forces and phenomena.

Thus Obatala is the shaper of infants in the wombs of humans and,
by extension, the special protector of all who are malformed. Ogun is
the essence of iron and the patron of all who depend on iron. Shango
is the owner of lightning and the wielder of the thunderbolt. Sonponno
is the force of smallpox. Olokun is the ruler of the sea and the marshes
where the sea has intruded. Some of the greater orishas represent more
abstract forces and ideas. Orunmila, the eldest son of Olorun the Sky
Deity, is the archdiviner who, through the reading of palm nuts or
cowries, perceives the meanings and intentions of Olorun. Stated differently, he is a personification of fate. Counterbalancing Orunmila is
Eshu, the essence of uncertainty and accident. He is the force of ran-
domness and whim that defies certainty and turns fate aside. When
Eshu appears there is a flaw in the sequence of events, a disruption of
heavenly intention that causes men to turn into unforeseen trails and
trials.

The "lesser" orishas have more limited gifts, sometimes specialized
but more often general in character. They may be invoked for many
types of services to humans—for health, fertility, good crops and protection against enemies. At some point down the scale some of the minor
orishas may become scarcely distinguishable from a category of beings
who are less than orishas but more than humans. And this category of
beings, in turn, blends into the order of epic human heroes and other
persons who have performed memorable deeds.

In short, at the top of the hierarchy are those who are great orishas
beyond dispute. At the bottom are humans who have distinguished
themselves in life but who have remained members of the human
family. And in between are those whose exact nature may be less definite. But all have power in human affairs because it is considered that
dead ancestors live on, unseen, and continue to be interested in the
fortunes and behavior of those who are physically alive. Just as the
orishas are invoked and placated, so are the ancestral dead and, in-
directly, those not yet born. Not only must these various forces be dealt
with by the living, but also random spirits of many other kinds.

Traditions about the orishas may be argued among regions and cults.
An orisha may have one name in one place and another elsewhere.
There sometimes are differences as to which orisha performed a particular deed, or how he first appeared or how he ultimately gave up his
physical form and became an invisible force. An account given in Oyo
may not correspond to one heard in Ife, Benin or Lagos, all of which
have preserved their own interpretations of ancient events, whether
historical or legendary.

The major orishas are generally believed to have existed at the beginning of things, when dry land was created below the sky by Obatala (or,
in the Ife account, by Oduduwa). The creation myth says that after the

land was made by Obatala numerous orishas who had been living in the sky decided to go down and live among humans. But as the legends point out, most deities did not originate in the sky but on the earth. While the creation myth says that Obatala (or, alternately, Oduduwa) founded Ife, some recorded accounts based on oral tradition say that the city was first settled by people who came from the north or east, and that it was their leader who turned the ground solid and who later came to be considered an orisha.

There are ample reasons to believe that the orishas—other than Olorun himself—were not invented, but were either rulers of ancient city-kingdoms or persons who performed deeds of distinction and came to be deified after death. The process of deification becomes clear in stories depicting the emergence of minor orishas. Moremi became a sacred personage after she saved the city of Ife from predatory raiders. A local diviner, Olosun, became sacred and was treated as an orisha after becoming a benefactor of the town of Ikere. Some of the orishas may have been imported, along with the appropriate legends, from neighboring cultures. What the circumstances were that made some humans orishas and others merely heroes, we shall probably never know.

Parallels between various Yoruba myths and those of the Norse and the Greeks are obvious. Like the Greek gods, the Yoruba orishas are deeply involved in the affairs of humans when they are not preoccupied with their own affairs. They are receptive to pleas for intervention in human life; their virtues or vanities are human attributes raised to godly stature; and they can be fallible, arbitrary or whimsical in their attitudes and actions. If a human oba were to give way to the passion and fury frequently indulged in by Shango (See "Shango and the Medicine of Eshu"), he would not be thought well of; but because Shango is more than human his violent outbursts are judged not so much as flaws of behavior as phenomena in nature. This of course does not preclude a silent judgment about acts of injustice. No Yoruba can hear how Shango plotted against the heroes Gbonka and Timi (See "How Shango Departed from Oyo") without recognizing that he is doing reproachful things. But who can reason with an orisha acting out of base motives? The only answer for humans is placation.

The stories that follow are fragments out of a rich and still-living Yoruba oral literature. They contain elements of a half-remembered past and a still more ancient past that has become blended and diffused with myth. And most of them are reflections of religious belief and of the Yoruba concept of man's relationship to the countless forces among which humans have had to live since the beginning.

CAST OF CHARACTERS

OLORUN (Owner of the Sky), the supreme orisha, ruler over the sky and the earth beneath the sky. Called variously Oba-Orun (King of the

Sky), Olodumare (Owner of Endless Space), Eleda (Creator), Oluwa (Lord) and Orisha-Oke (Sky God).

ORUNMILA (The Sky Knows Who Will Prosper), the eldest son of Olorun, and the deity of divination. He is widely known by the name Ifa, the word that designates divining and the paraphernalia of divining. Because he has the knowledge of this art, which in a sense reveals the intentions of Olorun, he has the authority to speak to humans for the Sky God.

OBATALA (King of the White Cloth), said by some to be Olorun's second son, by others to be merely one of Olorun's favorite orishas. He is the one authorized by Olorun to create land over the water beneath the sky, and it is he who founds the first Yoruba city, Ife. Obatala is Olorun's representative on earth and the shaper of human beings. He is known to some Yoruba as Orisha-Nla or Olufon.

OGUN, the deity of iron, and consequently the patron orisha of all humans for whom iron has particular significance, such as smiths, hunters and warriors. Also known as Ogun Onire (Ogun, Owner of the Town of Ire).

ESHU, the orisha of chance, accident and unpredictability. Because he is Olorun's linguist and the master of languages Eshu is responsible for carrying messages and sacrifices from humans to the Sky God. Also known for his phallic powers and exploits. Eshu is said to lurk at gateways, on the highways and at the crossroads, where he introduces chance and accident into the lives of humans. Known by a variety of names, including Elegbara.

SHANGO, the orisha of the thunderbolt, said to have ruled in ancient times over the kingdom of Oyo. Also known as Jakuta (Stone Thrower) and as Oba Koso (The King Does Not Hang).

OYA, one of Shango's wives, orisha of the Niger River.

OSHUN, one of Shango's wives, orisha of the Oshun River.

OLOKUN (Owner of the Sea), female deity of the sea and marshes. Some Yoruba believe Olokun to be male rather than female.

SONPONNO, deity of smallpox and related diseases. Also called Olode (Owner of the Public), Ile-Gbigbona (Hot Ground) and Ile-Titu (Cold Ground).

ORISHA-OKO, the orisha of agriculture, patron of farmers.

OLU-IGBO (Owner of the Bush), orisha of the bush and jungle.

OSANYIN, an orisha of curative medicine and divining.

ODUDUWA, according to Ife tradition, that city's first ruler. Called the Father of Ife and, by many, of all Yoruba. Regarded in Ife as the orisha who created dry land and performed feats elsewhere attributed to Obatala.

ORANMIYAN, a son of Oduduwa who ruled over Benin and later, on his father's death, over Ife. Considered, like his father, an orisha, Oranmiyan also is sometimes called Father of Ife. Sometimes he is referred to as Oranyan.

YEMOJA, deity of the Ogun River, and in some accounts identified as a wife of Ogun.

The Descent from the Sky

In ancient days, at the beginning of time, there was no solid land here where people now dwell. There was only outer space and the sky, and, far below, an endless stretch of water and wild marshes. Supreme in the domain of the sky was the orisha, or god, called Olorun, also known as Olodumare and designated by many praise names. Also living in that place were numerous other orishas, each having attributes of his own, but none of whom had knowledge or powers equal to those of Olorun. Among them was Orunmila, also called Ifa, the eldest son of Olorun. To this orisha Olorun had given the power to read the future, to understand the secret of existence and to divine the processes of fate. There was the orisha Obatala, King of the White Cloth, whom Olorun trusted as though he also were a son. There was the orisha Eshu, whose character was neither good nor bad. He was compounded out of the elements of chance and accident, and his nature was unpredictability. He understood the principles of speech and language, and because of this gift he was Olorun's linguist. These and the other orishas living in the domain of the sky acknowledged Olorun as the owner of everything and as the highest authority in all matters. Also living there was Agemo, the chameleon, who served Olorun as a trusted servant.

Down below, it was the female deity Olokun who ruled over the vast expanses of water and wild marshes, a grey region with no living things in it, either creatures of the bush or vegetation. This is the way it was, Olorun's living sky above and Olokun's domain of water below. Neither kingdom troubled the other. They were separate and apart. The orishas of the sky lived on, hardly noticing what lay below them.

All except Obatala, King of the White Cloth. He alone looked down on the domain of Olokun and pondered on it, saying to himself: "Everything down there is a great wet monotony. It does not have the mark of any inspiration or living thing." And at last he went to Olorun and said: "The place ruled by Olokun is nothing but sea, marsh and mist. If there were solid land in that domain, fields and forests, hills and valleys, surely it could be populated by orishas and other living things."

Olorun answered: "Yes, it would be a good thing to cover the water with land. But it is an ambitious enterprise. Who is to do the work? And how should it be done?"

Obatala said: "I will undertake it. I will do whatever is required."

He left Olorun and went to the house of Orunmila, who understood the secrets of existence, and said to him: "Your father has instructed me to go down below and make land where now there is nothing but marsh and sea, so that living beings will have a place to build their towns and grow their crops. You, Orunmila, who can divine the meanings of all things, instruct me further. How may this work be begun?"

Orunmila brought out his divining tray and cast sixteen palm nuts on it. He read their meanings by the way they fell. He gathered them up and cast again, again reading their meanings. And when he had cast many times he added meanings to meanings, and said: "These are the things you must do: Descend to the watery wastes on a chain of gold, taking with you a snail shell full of sand, a white hen to disperse the sand, a black cat to be your companion, and a palm nut. That is what the divining figures tell us."

Obatala went next to the goldsmith and asked for a chain of gold long enough to reach from the sky to the surface of the water.

The goldsmith asked, "Is there enough gold in the sky to make such a chain?"

Obatala answered: "Yes, begin your work. I will gather the gold." Departing from the forge of the goldsmith, Obatala went then to Orunmila, Eshu and the other orishas, asking each of them for gold. They gave him whatever they had. Some gave gold dust, some gave rings, bracelets or pendants. Obatala collected gold from everywhere and took it to the goldsmith.

The goldsmith said, "More gold is needed."

So Obatala continued seeking gold, and after that he again returned to the goldsmith, saying, "Here is more metal for your chain."

The goldsmith said, "Still more is needed."

Obatala said, "There is no more gold in the sky."

The goldsmith said, "The chain will not reach to the water."

Obatala answered: "Nevertheless, make the chain. We shall see."

The goldsmith went to work. When the chain was finished he took it to Obatala. Obatala said, "It must have a hook at the end."

"There is no gold remaining," the goldsmith said.

Obatala replied, "Take some of the links and melt them down."

The goldsmith removed some of the links, and out of them he fashioned a hook for the chain. It was finished. He took the chain to Obatala.

Obatala said, "Now I am ready." He fastened the hook on the edge of the sky and lowered the chain. Orunmila gave him the things that were needed—a snail shell of sand, a white hen, a black cat, and a palm nut. Then Obatala gripped the chain with his hands and feet and began the descent. The chain was very long. When he had descended only half its length Obatala saw that he was leaving the realm of light and entering the region of greyness. A time came when he heard the wash of waves and felt the damp mists rising from Olokun's domain. He reached the end of the golden chain, but he was not yet at the bottom, and he clung there, thinking, "If I let go I will fall into the sea."

While he remained at the chain's end thinking such things, he heard Orunmila's voice from above, saying, "The sand."

So Obatala took the snail shell from the knapsack at his side and poured out the sand.

Again he heard Orunmila call to him, saying this time, "The hen."

Obatala dropped the hen where he had poured the sand. The hen began at once to scratch at the sand and scatter it in all directions. Wherever the sand was scattered it became dry land. Because it was scattered unevenly the sand formed hills and valleys. When this was accomplished, Obatala let go of the chain and came down and walked on the solid earth that had been created. The land extended in all directions, but still it was barren of life.

Obatala named the place where he had come down Ife. He built a house there. He planted his palm nut and a palm tree sprang out of the earth. It matured and dropped its palm seeds. More palm trees came into being. Thus there was vegetation at Ife. Obatala lived on, with only his black cat as a companion.

After some time had passed, Olorun the Sky God wanted to know how Obatala's expedition was progressing. He instructed Agemo the chameleon to descend the golden chain. Agemo went down. He found Obatala living in his house at Ife. He said: "Olorun instructed me this way: He said, 'Go down, discover for me how things are with Obatala.' That is why I am here."

Obatala answered, "As you can see, the land has been created, and palm groves are plentiful. But there is too much greyness. The land should be illuminated."

Agemo returned to the sky and reported to Olorun what he had seen and heard. Olorun agreed that there should be light down below. So he made the sun and set it moving. After that there was warmth and light in what had once been Olokun's exclusive domain.

Obatala lived on, with only his black cat for a companion. He thought, "Surely it would be better if many people were living here." He decided to create people. He dug clay from the ground, and out of the clay he shaped human figures which he then laid out to dry in the sun. He worked without resting. He became tired and thirsty. He said to himself, "There should be palm wine in this place to help a person go on working." So he put aside the making of humans and went to the palm trees to draw their inner fluid, out of which he made palm wine. When it was fermented he drank. He drank for a long while. When he felt everything around him softening he put aside his gourd cup and went back to modeling human figures. But because Obatala had drunk so much wine his fingers grew clumsy, and some of the figures were misshapen. Some had crooked backs or crooked legs, or arms that were too short. Some did not have enough fingers, some were bent instead of being straight. Because of the palm wine inside him, Obatala did not notice these things. And when he had made enough figures to begin the populating of Ife he called out to Olorun the Sky God, saying, "I have made human beings to live with me here in Ife, but only you can give them the breath of life." Olorun heard Obatala's request, and he put breath in the clay figures. They were no longer clay, but people of blood, sinews and flesh. They arose and began to do the things that humans do. They built houses for themselves near Obatala's house, and in this way the place Obatala named Ife became the city of Ife.

But when the effects of the palm wine had worn off Obatala saw that some of the humans he had made were misshapen, and remorse filled his heart. He said: "Never again will I drink palm wine. From this time on I will be the special protector of all humans who have deformed limbs or who have otherwise been created imperfectly." Because of

Obatala's pledge, humans who later came to serve him also avoided palm wine, and the lame, the blind and those who had no pigment in their skin invoked his help when they were in need.

Now that humans were living on the earth, Obatala gave people the tools they needed to perform their work. As yet there was no iron in the world, and so each man received a wooden hoe and a copper bush knife. The people planted and began the growing of millet and yams, and, like the palm tree, they procreated. Ife became a growing city and Obatala ruled as its Oba or Paramount Chief. But a time came when Obatala grew lonesome for the sky. He ascended by the golden chain, and there was a festival on the occasion of his return. The orishas heard him describe the land that had been created below, and many of them decided to go down and live among the newly created human beings. Thus many orishas departed from the sky, but not before Olorun instructed them on their obligations. "When you settle on the earth," he said, "never forget your duties to humans. Whenever you are supplicated for help, listen to what is being asked of you. You are the protectors of the human race. Obatala, who first descended the chain and dried up the waters, he is my deputy in earthly affairs. But each of you will have a special responsibility to fulfill down below." As for Obatala, he rested in the sky for some time. After that, whenever he wanted to know how things were going at Ife, he returned for a visit. The city of Ife lived on.

But Olokun, the orisha of the sea on whose domain land had been created, was angry and humiliated. And so one time when Obatala was resting in the sky Olokun decided to destroy the land and replace it again with water. She sent great waves rushing against the shores and flooded the low ground everywhere, causing marshes to reappear on every side. She inundated the fields where humans were growing their crops and drowned many of the people of Ife. All that Obatala had created was disappearing, and mankind was suffering. The people called for help from Obatala, but he did not hear them. So they went to the orisha Eshu, who now lived on earth, and begged him to carry to Obatala word of the disaster that was overwhelming them.

Eshu said to them, "Where is the sacrifice that should accompany the message?"

They brought a goat and sacrificed it, saying, "This is the food for Obatala."

But Eshu did not move. He said, "Where is the rest?"

The people said: "We do not understand you. Have we not brought a sacrifice for Obatala?"

Eshu answered: "You ask me to make a great journey. You ask me to be your linguist. Does not a person make a gift to the lowliest of messengers? Give me my part, then I will go."

So the people gave a sacrifice to Eshu, after which he left them and went up to the sky to tell Obatala what was happening to the land and the people over which he ruled.

Obatala was troubled. He was not certain how to deal with Olokun.

He went to the orisha Orunmila to ask for advice. Orunmila consulted his divining nuts, and at last he said to Obatala: "Wait here in the sky. Rest yourself. I will go down this time. I will turn back the water and make the land rise again." So it was Orunmila instead of Obatala who went down to Ife. As Orunmila was the oldest son of Olorun, he had the knowledge of medicine, and he had many other powers as well. He used his powers in Ife, causing Olokun's waves to weaken and the marshes to dry up. The waters of the sea were turned back, and at last Olokun's attempt to reclaim her territory came to an end.

Having accomplished all this, Orunmila prepared to return to the sky. But the people came to him and asked him to stay because of his knowledge. Orunmila did not wish to stay in Ife forever. So he taught certain orishas and men the arts of controlling unseen forces, and he also taught others the art of divining the future, which is to say the knowledge of how to ascertain the wishes and intentions of the Sky God, Olorun. Some men he taught to divine through the casting of palm nuts. Others he taught to foretell the future by the casting of cowry shells or sand or chains. Afterwards, Orunmila went back to the sky and, like Obatala, he frequently made visits to the earth to see how things were going among human beings. What Orunmila taught men about divining was never lost. It was passed on by one generation of babalawos, or diviners, to another.

Earthly order—the understanding of relationships between people and the physical world, and between people and the orishas—was beginning to take shape. But all was not yet settled between Olokun, the orisha of the sea, and the supreme orisha Olorun. Olokun considered ways in which she might humiliate or outwit the Sky God. The powers of the sky deities had proved to be greater than her own. But Olokun had the knowledge of weaving and dyeing cloth, and she had cloths of delicate textures and brilliant colors. She believed that in this respect she excelled all other orishas, including Olorun himself. So one day she sent a message to Olorun, challenging him to a contest to show which had the greater knowledge of clothmaking.

Olorun received the challenge. He thought: "Olokun seeks to humiliate me. Nevertheless, she has unequaled knowledge about the making of cloth. Yet, how can I ignore the challenge?" He thought about the matter. Then he sent for Agemo, the chameleon. He instructed Agemo to carry a message to Olokun. Agemo went down from the sky to the place where Olokun lived. Agemo said to Olokun: "The Owner of the Sky, Olorun, greets you. He says that if your cloth is as magnificent as you claim, he will enter the contest. Therefore he asks that you show me some of your most radiant weaving so that I may report to him on the matter."

Because Olokun was vain she could not refrain from showing her cloths to Agemo. She put on a skirt cloth of brilliant green and displayed it to the chameleon. As Agemo looked at it his skin turned the exact color of the skirt. Olokun then put on an orange-hued cloth, and Agemo's skin turned orange. When Olokun brought out a red skirt cloth,

Agemo's skin turned red. Olokun was perturbed. She tried a cloth of several colors and saw the chameleon's skin reproduce it perfectly. Olokun thought: "This person is only a messenger, nothing more. Yet in an instant he can duplicate the exact color of my finest cloth. What, then, can the great Olorun do?"

Seeing the futility of competing with Olorun, the orisha of the sea said to Agemo: "Give my greetings to the Owner of the Sky. Tell him that Olokun acknowledges his greatness."

Thus Olokun withdrew her challenge to the Sky God, and Olorun remained supreme in all things.[1]

Iron Is Received from Ogun

The orishas and the people were living there in the land created by Obatala. They did the things that are required in life, orishas and humans alike. They hunted, cleared the land so that they could plant, and they cultivated the earth. But the tools they had were of wood, stone or soft metal, and the heavy work that had to be done was a great burden. Because there were more people living at Ife than in the beginning, it was now necessary to clear away trees from the edge of the forest to make more room for planting.

Seeing what had to be done, the orishas met to discuss things. It was said: "Let one of us begin the great task by going out to fell trees and clear the land. When this has been done we can plant our fields."

All agreed except for Olokun, who said: "Do what you want, but it has nothing to do with me, for my domain is the water. The land and the trees were not my doing."

Osanyin, the orisha of medicine, said, "I will clear the first field." He took his bush knife and went out to the trees and began his work. But his bush knife was made of soft metal and it would not cut deeply. After a while it became twisted and bent and it would not cut at all. He returned and said to the other orishas: "I began the work, but the wood is too hard. My bush knife is defeated."

So Orisha-Oko, the orisha of the open fields, spoke, saying: "My bush knife is strong. I will cut the trees." He went out. He worked. The sharpness went out of his bush knife. He returned. He said: "Yes, it was the same with me. My bush knife is dull and twisted."

Then Eshu with the powerful body took up his bush knife and went into the bush. He remained there for a while, and when he returned they saw that his bush knife was broken and bent. He said: "I cleared brush and dislodged stones, but the metal of my bush knife is not hard enough, it lacks spirit."

---

1. *This episode, with Olokun challenging the Sky God to a contest in weaving and dyeing, recalls a Greek tale in which Arachne, a young Lydian woman, challenges Athena to a weaving competition. In the Grecian story, Athena, angered by the perfection of Arachne's work, tears her cloth to shreds. Arachne hangs herself, but Athena loosens the rope and saves her life. The rope turns into a spiderweb, however, and Arachne into a spider.*

One by one the other orishas went out and tried, but the metal of their knives was too soft. They said: "What kind of a world are we living in? How can we survive in this place?"

Until now Ogun, who had been given the secret of iron, said nothing. But when the other orishas had tried and failed he took up his bush knife and went out. He slashed through the heavy vines, felled the trees and cleared the forest from the land. The field grew larger, the edge of the forest receded. Ogun worked on until the darkness began to fall. Then he returned. When he arrived he displayed his bush knife. It glittered even in the greyness that precedes the night. It was straight and its edge was sharp.

The orishas said, "What is the wonderful metal lying within your knife?"

Ogun answered: "The secret of this metal was given to me by Orunmila. It is called iron."

They looked at his knife with envy. They said, "If we had the knowledge of iron nothing would be difficult."

Ogun constructed a forge in his house. Because he was a hunter he forged an iron spear for the killing of game and a knife to cut away the hides. Because he was a warrior he also forged weapons of war. As for the other orishas, neither their hunting weapons nor their battle weapons were good. They had to rely on traps to catch their game, and often, when their luck was not good, they had no meat at all.

The orishas discussed Ogun's secret on and on, saying, "If we had the knowledge of iron we would be equal with Ogun." And afterwards they would say to Ogun, "Give us iron so that we too can be great in hunting and war."

Ogun always answered: "The secret of iron was entrusted to me by Orunmila. He said nothing about giving it to others." And so for a long time Ogun remained the sole master of the spear, the bush knife and other weapons.

The orishas did not give up importuning Ogun. At last they came to his house and said: "You, Ogun, are the father of iron. Be our father also. We need a chief. Become our ruler, and in exchange for our loyalty and service give us the knowledge of making iron."

Ogun considered everything. One day he announced that he would accept what they were offering. So they made him their ruler. He became the Oba of orishas in Ife and all the surrounding territories. Ogun taught them the making of iron. He built forges for them and showed them how to make spears, knives, hoes and swords. Soon every orisha had iron tools and weapons. Then humans began to come from distant places asking for the secret of iron. Ogun gave them the knowledge of forging. A time came when every hunter and warrior had an iron spear.

But though Ogun had accepted the chieftaincy over the orishas, he was above all else a hunter. And so when the knowledge of the forge had been given out, he clothed himself in the skins of animals he had killed and returned to the forest to get game. He was gone many days. Life in the forest was hard. He slept on the ground or in trees. He pursued the animals a great distance, arriving at last at a place called Oke-Umo, near where the city of Ilesha now stands. There he caught up with his game. He killed many animals, skinned them and cut up the meat. After that he returned home. When he came out of the forest he was dirty, his hair was matted, and the skins he wore were smeared and spotted with the blood of his game.

The orishas saw him arriving. They said: "Who is this dirty stranger coming from the forest? Surely it is not Ogun, whom we selected to be our chief?" They were displeased with Ogun. They said: "A ruler should appear in dignity. His clothes should be clean. His hair should be oiled and combed. How then can we acknowledge this unclean person as the one who rules us?"

The orishas turned away from Ogun. They went to his house, saying to him: "We expressed faith in you by making you our Oba. But now you are indistinguishable from the lowliest hunter, and the air around you reeks of dead flesh. What we gave we now take away. You are our Oba no longer."

Ogun said: "When you needed the secret of iron you came begging me to be your chief. Now that you have iron you say that I smell of the hunt."

The other orishas went away. Ogun took off his hunting clothes made of animal skins. He bathed, and when he was clean he put on clothes made of palm fronds. He gathered his weapons and departed. At a distant place called Ire he built a house under an akoko tree, and there he remained.

The human beings who had received the secret of iron from Ogun did not forget him. In December of every year they celebrate, in his honor, the festival of Iwude-Ogun. Hunters, warriors and blacksmiths, and many others as well, make sacrifices to Ogun as their special protector. They offer food at the foot of an akoko tree. They call him Ogun Onire, meaning Ogun the Owner of the Town of Ire. And they display animal skins and palm fronds in memory of how Ogun was rejected by the other orishas after he had given them the knowledge of the forge.

Oranmiyan, the Warrior Hero of Ife

In Ife tradition it is Oduduwa, rather than Obatala, who is credited with coming down from the sky to create dry land, found the city of Ife, and become the first ruler of that city. This story about Oranmiyan, the son of Oduduwa, belongs to Ife, and it is given here without any attempt to reconcile it with the tradition that says Obatala was the city's first ruler.

Oduduwa ruled long over Ife. Orunmila, it is said, went to rule over Benin, where he remained for some time. But after a while Orunmila tired of his life there and returned to the sky. Affairs in Benin did not go well after Orunmila departed. The people sent messengers to Oduduwa asking him to come and take charge of Benin. Oduduwa was reluctant to leave Ife. He said, "If I go to Benin to give it a father, then Ife will have no father." The people of Benin continued to implore Oduduwa for help. At last he agreed to go to Benin. He took his son Oranmiyan with him to that city. He took charge of Benin's affairs, and he remained there until he heard he was much needed back in Ife. Oduduwa named Oranmiyan as ruler of Benin, after which he returned to govern Ife again. But Oduduwa did not live forever. When he knew he was going to die he sent for Oranmiyan. Oranmiyan made his own son ruler over Benin and returned to Ife, and as Oduduwa wanted him to do he became the oni, or oba, of that city.

By this time there were numerous kingdoms scattered across the earth, and war had come among humans. Because Ife was the first of all cities and because it was great in the minds of men it was envied everywhere. For this reason the obas of other places sought to vanquish Ife and diminish its reputation. But just as Ife's name was great, so was the name of Oranmiyan. For he was fierce and valorous in war. Whenever the enemy came to attack, Oranmiyan led Ife's warriors into battle. Wherever the heat of the battle was, that was where Oranmiyan was to be seen. Warrior heroes of many other cities came face to face with Oranmiyan in the fields and were slain. The sunlight flashing from Oranmiyan's long sword struck terror into the hearts of those who sought to destroy Ife. Oranmiyan was the first on the battlefield and the last to leave, and his path could be seen by the corpses left behind by his weapons. The heroes of those times were numerous, but Oranmiyan was the greatest of them all, and while he lived Ife could not be subdued.

But Oranmiyan grew older. A time came when he knew that death would take him. He called the people together. He said: "Soon I must go. When I am no longer here, continue to live as heroes. Do not let our enemies make Ife small in the minds of men. Continue to be courageous so that Ife will go on living."

The people said to him: "Oranmiyan, you are the father of Ife. Reject death and remain here with us."

He answered: "No, it is not possible. Nevertheless I will not forget Ife. If great trouble comes to the city call me. I will give the old men the words to say, and when these words are spoken I will come back to help you."

He called the elders of Ife together and gave them the words. Then he went to the marketplace, all of the people of Ife following him. He arrived there. He struck his staff into the earth. It stood upright in the center of things. Oranmiyan said: "This is my mark. It will stand here forever to remind you of the courage of heroes." The staff turned into a shaft of stone which the people named Opa Oranmiyan, Oranmiyan's Staff.

Then the warrior hero Oranmiyan stamped his foot on the ground. The earth opened. He descended into the earth and it closed behind him. This was how Oranmiyan departed from his people.

Word reached far-off places that Oranmiyan no longer lived. The oba of a distant city said: "Well, now, he is gone and Ife is defenseless. It is time to bring Ife to its knees." He gathered a force of warriors and sent them to destroy Ife. When the people of Ife saw the enemy approaching they went to the old men to whom Oranmiyan had given the secret words, saying, "Send for Oranmiyan quickly or Ife will die." The old men went to the marketplace and called Oranmiyan for help. There was a thunderous noise and the earth shook. The ground opened and Oranmiyan came out, his weapons in his hands. He led the warriors of Ife into battle. When the enemy saw Oranmiyan's weapons flashing in the sunlight terror overcame them. Those who were not killed turned and fled. The warriors of Ife pursued them until at last no living enemy was visible. Then they returned to the city. Oranmiyan stamped his foot on the ground of the marketplace. The earth opened. He descended. The earth closed over his head.

After that for many years Ife was not molested. People in other places said, "Ife remains great because although Oranmiyan is dead he is not truly dead."

There was a festival in Ife. There was drumming, dancing and singing. People feasted and drank much palm wine. Many of them became drunk. Darkness came. The festival went on. Someone said, "Oranmiyan should be here to dance and sing with us." Others said, "Yes, let us bring him out to lead us in our enjoyment." They went to the marketplace where Oranmiyan's staff was standing. They called on Oranmiyan to come out of the ground and join the festivities, but he did not appear. Someone said, "He will not come unless the secret words are spoken, the words that only the old men know." So they went through the city and found some of the elders to whom the words had been entrusted. They brought the old men to the marketplace and asked them to do what was necessary to bring Oranmiyan out of the ground.

The old men protested, saying: "No, it is not a good thing to molest Oranmiyan because of a festival. Let him rest. He should be called on only in times of great need. Those were his instructions."

But the people persisted, saying, "Do what is necessary, old men, for we want Oranmiyan to lead us in the dancing and singing."

The old men continued to protest. Yet at last they said the words: "Come swiftly, Oranmiyan. Ife is in danger."

The ground thundered and opened. Oranmiyan emerged, his weapons in his hands, his face fierce with the courage of a warrior. Because it was dark Oranmiyan could not distinguish one person from another. He believed that the men in the marketplace were the enemy who had come to destroy Ife. He began fighting, thrusting with his spear and slashing with his sword. He struck at anything that moved, killing many men of Ife. The city was in turmoil. People ran in every direction, Oranmiyan pursuing. The killing went on.

The dawn came. Light fell on the city. Now Oranmiyan could clearly see the corpses lying on the ground. He saw the tribal scars on the cheeks of the dead, and he knew then that he had been slaughtering his own people. Grief overcame him. He threw his weapons down. He said: "I was asked to come quickly because Ife was in danger. Therefore I came, and in the darkness of night I killed many of the people of Ife. Because of this terrible deed I will not fight again. I will return to the place from which I came. There I will remain. I will never again come to Ife."

He stamped on the earth. The earth trembled and opened. Oranmiyan went down, and the earth closed behind him. Never after that was he seen in Ife.

His staff, in the form of a shaft of stone, still stands at that place, reminding people of the great warrior hero who once ruled over Ife, and of the slaughter that occurred because he was asked to help when the city was not really in danger.

Orunmila's Visit to Owo

In the place where he was then living, Orunmila decided one day to make a journey to Owo. Before beginning the journey he cast his sixteen divining nuts to reveal the safety or the hazards of the road, which is to say the intentions of the Sky God Olorun. The first time Orunmila cast the divining nuts they said to him, "What is to happen the diviner will not know." He cast again, and the divining nuts said, "Even the Father of Diviners cannot perceive it." Now, Orunmila should have pursued the matter, because the truth had not been made clear, but he was impatient to go to Owo and so he put his divining nuts away and began his journey.

The distance to Owo was long, and Orunmila was five days on the road. On the first day of his journey he met his friend Eshu who was going the other way, returning from Owo. They greeted each other and parted. On the second day Orunmila again met Eshu coming from the opposite direction. Eshu said, "Yes, I am returning from Owo." Orunmila pondered on this and wondered about it, for it was strange that two persons going in opposite directions should meet twice on the road. On the third day, as well, he met Eshu coming from Owo. Orunmila was troubled about the meaning of these events. But he did not stop to consult his divining nuts because he was eager to arrive in Owo as soon as possible.

On the fourth day Eshu lurked on the outskirts of Owo. When he saw Orunmila approaching he placed some fresh kola fruits on the trail and left them there. He went forward and greeted Orunmila again.

Orunmila said: "Eshu, my friend. Are you just coming once more from Owo?"

Eshu answered: "Need friends doubt one another? What is, is."

But Orunmila was not satisfied that all was well. Nevertheless, he was almost in sight of Owo. He thought: "Only a little distance and I am there. There is no need to consult the divining nuts."

He went on. He found the kola fruits left on the road by Eshu. Because he was tired by his long journey he picked up the kola fruits and began to eat to refresh himself. At this moment a farmer of Owo appeared, carrying his bush knife in his hand. He said, "You, whoever you are, are eating kola fruits from my tree."

Orunmila answered: "No, I found the kolas on the trail. I saw no tree. Therefore I took the fruits to refresh myself."

But the farmer was angry and spoke harshly. He attempted to take the kolas away from Orunmila. There was a struggle, and in the fighting the farmer's bush knife cut the palm of Orunmila's hand. Orunmila turned back from Owo and sat by the side of the road, thinking: "This is an evil thing. When have I ever taken something that was not mine? Yet in Owo it will be said that I am a stealer of kolas."

Night came. Orunmila slept on the ground. But Eshu, who had seen everything, went into the city when everyone there was asleep. He went into every house. With his knife he cut the palm of every sleeping person, even that of the Oba himself. Then he went out of the city to the place where the farmer who had fought with Orunmila lived, and cut his palm also.

On the fifth day Orunmila awoke. He resumed his way to Owo. At the entrance of the city he met Eshu. Eshu greeted him, but Orunmila was reproachful. He said: "Eshu, the matter becomes clear. We are friends, yet you have made my way hard."

Eshu said: "Orunmila, we are truly close friends. Do not hesitate. Enter the city. If there is trouble I will speak for you. You will not receive injury in Owo. On the contrary, good things will come to you."

Orunmila and Eshu entered Owo together. The farmer, he who had claimed the kola fruits, was there. He saw Orunmila coming. He went to the Oba and complained, saying that the robber of his kola tree was approaching. He demanded that Orunmila be punished. So the Oba had Orunmila brought before him.

The farmer made his complaint again, and described the struggle over the kola fruits.

After that Eshu spoke for Orunmila. He said: "A stranger comes to Owo with trust. He suspects nothing, for he has no enemies. He asks for nothing, because he already has everything. Yet Owo accuses him of a crime. Where is the evidence? And how can a thief of the kolas be identified?"

The farmer answered: "We struggled on the road. My bush knife carved a wound in the palm of his hand. Therefore let the man show his hand, because that is where the evidence is."

The Oba said to Orunmila, "Yes, open your hand so that everyone may see the truth."

Eshu, speaking for Orunmila, said: "This stranger who has not committed any offense has been singled out. Although many persons could have stolen kola fruits, only he is accused and questioned. Therefore let every citizen of Owo also reveal the palm of his hand."

The Oba said, "Yes, let it be done."

So Orunmila opened his hand and held it out, and the people of Owo did likewise. And every hand in Owo, including that of the Oba and the complaining farmer, had a fresh red cut.

Eshu said, "If a mere cut is the mark of guilt, then all of Owo is guilty."

The Oba agreed, saying: "It is true. This stranger is innocent. He should be indemnified for the false accusation against him."

The people of Owo brought gifts of every kind, including chickens, goats, kola fruits, palm wine and cowries, and gave them to Orunmila.

Why Eshu did what he did to his close friend Orunmila is not said. It is said only that Eshu, being what he is, could not refrain from doing it.

Shango and the Medicine of Eshu

The orisha Shango ruled firmly over all of Oyo, the city and the lands that surrounded it. He was a stern ruler, and because he owned the thunderbolt the people of Oyo tried to do nothing to displease or anger him. His symbol of power was a double-bladed axe which signified, "My strength cuts both ways," meaning that no one, even the most distant citizen of Oyo, was beyond reach of his authority or immune to punishment for misdeeds. The people of Oyo called him by his praise name, Oba Jakuta, the Stone Thrower Oba.

But even though Shango's presence was felt everywhere in Oyo, and even beyond in other kingdoms, he wanted something more to instill fear in the hearts of men. He sent for the great makers of medicine in Oyo and instructed them to make jujus that would increase his powers. One by one the medicine makers brought him this and that, but he was not satisfied with their work. He decided at last to ask the orisha Eshu for help. He sent a messenger to the distant place where Eshu lived. The messenger said to Eshu: "Oba Jakuta, the great ruler of Oyo, sends me. He said: 'Go to the place where the renowned Eshu stays. Tell him I need a powerful medicine that will cause terror to be born in the hearts of my enemies. Ask Eshu if he will make such a medicine for me.'"

Eshu said: "Yes, such a thing is possible. What kind of power does Shango want?"

The messenger answered: "Oba Jakuta says, 'Many makers of medicine have tried to give me a power that I don't already have. But they do not know how to do it. Such knowledge belongs only to Eshu. If he asks what I need, tell him it is he alone who knows what must be done. What he prepares for me I will accept.'"

Eshu said: "Yes, what the ruler of Oyo needs, I shall prepare it for him. In return he will send a goat as sacrifice. The medicine will be ready in seven days. But you, messenger, do not come back for it yourself. Let Shango's wife Oya come for it. I will put it in her hand."

The messenger went back to Oyo. He told Shango what he had heard from Eshu. Shango said, "Yes, I will send Oya to receive the medicine."

On the seventh day he instructed Oya to go to the place where Eshu was living. He said: "Greet Eshu for me. Tell him that the sacrifice will be sent. Receive the medicine he has prepared and bring it home quickly."

Oya departed. She arrived at the place where Eshu was living. She greeted him. She said: "Shango of Oyo sends me for the medicine. The sacrifice you asked for is on the way."

Eshu said: "Shango asked for a great new power. I have finished making it." He gave Oya a small packet wrapped in a leaf. He said: "Take care with it. See that Shango gets it all."

Oya began the return journey, wondering: "What has Eshu made for Shango? What kind of power can be in so small a packet?" She stopped at a resting place. As Eshu had presumed she would do, Oya unwrapped the packet to see what was inside. There was nothing there but red powder. She put a little of the powder in her mouth to taste it. It was neither good nor bad. It tasted like nothing at all. She closed the medicine packet and tied it with a string of grass. She went on. She arrived at Oyo and gave the medicine to Shango.

He said: "What instructions did Eshu give you? How is this medicine to be used?"

Oya was about to say, "He gave no instructions whatever." As she began to speak, fire flashed from her mouth. Thus Shango saw that Oya had tasted the medicine that was meant for him alone. His anger was fierce. He raised his hand to strike her but she fled from the house. Shango pursued her. Oya came to a place where many sheep were grazing. She ran among the sheep thinking that Shango would not find her. But Shango's anger was hot. He hurled his thunderstones in all directions. He hurled them among the sheep, killing them all. Oya lay hidden under the bodies of the dead sheep and Shango did not see her there.

Shango returned to his house. Many people of Oyo were gathered there. They pleaded for Oya's life. They said: "Great Shango, Oba of Oyo, spare Oya. Your compassion is greater than her offense. Forgive her."

Shango's anger cooled. He sent servants to find Oya and bring her home. But he still did not know how Eshu intended for him to use the medicine. So when night came he took the medicine packet and went to a high place overlooking the city. He stood facing the compound where he lived with all his wives and servants. He placed some of the medicine on his tongue. And when he breathed the air out of his lungs an enormous flame shot from his mouth, extending over the city and igniting the straw roofs of the palace buildings. A great fire began to burn in Oyo. It destroyed Shango's houses and granaries. The entire city was consumed, and nothing was left but ashes. Thus Oyo was leveled to the ground and had to be rebuilt. After the city rose again from its ashes, Shango ruled on. In times of war, or when his subjects displeased him, Shango hurled his thunderbolts. Every stone he threw was accompanied by a bright flash that illuminated the sky and the earth. This, as all men knew, was the fire shooting from Shango's mouth.

The sheep that died while protecting Oya from Shango's thunderstones were never forgotten. In their honor, the worshippers of Oya have refused to eat mutton even to the present day.

Obatala's Visit to Shango

The great orisha Obatala, who had dried up the watery wastes and shaped human beings out of clay, decided one day to visit Shango, who ruled in Oyo. "Prepare things for me," he said to his wife, "so that I can make a journey. I want to see my friend Shango, the Stone Thrower."

His wife prepared food for Obatala to take with him on the journey. She instructed that Obatala's clothing should be washed and made spotless. Obatala had no drummers to go ahead of him and announce his coming. He was known everywhere by the white clothing he wore, and thus he was called the King of the White Cloth. But when his wife slept that night she dreamed that although Obatala's white clothing was washed again and again, dark spots appeared on it whenever it was dry. When she awakened she said: "Obatala, do not go to Oyo. In my dream the white cloth would not become clean."

Obatala answered: "But the cloth is indeed clean, whatever you dreamed. I will begin my journey to Oyo."

Nevertheless, before he started the journey Obatala went to the house of Orunmila, the orisha of divining, and asked him whether the visit to Oyo would be a good one. Orunmila brought out his divining tray and cast his palm nuts. When he had finished he said, "Do not go to Oyo, for misfortune will meet you there."

Obatala said: "How can misfortune meet me in Oyo? It is my friend Shango who rules in that place." He returned to his house. He put on his white clothes. He began the walking.

On the road to Oyo he met the orisha Eshu sitting under a tree. They greeted each other. Obatala said, "Why do you sit here waiting?"

Eshu said, "I am waiting for someone to place this bowl of palm oil on my head so that I can carry it."

Obatala helped Eshu lift the bowl, but as he did so the oil spilled over and stained his white robe. Seeing this, Obatala did not continue towards Oyo but returned home and changed to fresh clothing. After that he began the journey again.

On the road he met Eshu once more, and again Eshu asked for help in getting the bowl to his head. Obatala, whose good deeds were many, could not deny help to Eshu. So he helped lift the bowl of palm oil. Just as before, the oil spilled and made spots on Obatala's robe. For the second time Obatala turned back and went home for fresh clothing.

Once again he met Eshu waiting at the roadside. This time the bowl of palm oil was larger than before.

Eshu said, "Obatala, help me raise the bowl to my head."

But the soiling of his white clothing had been a bad omen, and Obatala answered: "No, this time I cannot do it. Twice already my white robe has been stained."

Eshu became angry. He said, "You refuse?"

Obatala said, "Yes, put the bowl up by yourself."

Eshu said no more, but with his hand he splashed oil on Obatala's clothes. Because Eshu was known to do violent things when angry, Obatala did not make an argument. He kept silent and departed. This time, however, he did not turn back but continued on towards Oyo, thinking now of his wife's dream and of the warning given to him by Orunmila.

When he had travelled far and was nearing Oyo he saw a white horse grazing nearby. He thought: "This horse lost in the bush can only be Shango's. I will take him along." He took the horse with him. As he approached Oyo, Shango's servants came looking for the horse. When they saw Obatala they seized him and beat him, saying, "This is the thief for whom we have been looking!" They continued beating Obatala all the way to Oyo, and there they threw him into a prison yard without listening to his explanation.

Time passed. Obatala remained a prisoner. Shango knew nothing of the affair. Many weeks went by, yet no one came to release Obatala. In the beginning Obatala had thought, "Surely someone will come to undo this evil." But no one came, and at last Obatala was overcome with anger. He caused a drought to fall upon Oyo. No rain fell. The fields dried up. The crops did not grow, and the people of Oyo began to feel hunger. Still no one came to release Obatala. So he caused sickness to come into the city. It travelled from one house to another and people began to die.

Seeing the disaster that was overtaking Oyo, Shango sent for his diviners. They cast their palm nuts, their cowry shells and their divining chains, and when they were finished they said to Shango: "An exalted personage wearing a spotted white robe has been imprisoned in Oyo. It is he who has sent us drought and disease. Unless he is released there will be no rain, no food, and no life remaining in the city."

So Shango began a search of his prison yards, and in one of them he found Obatala, King of the White Cloth. Obatala's whiteness was soiled with dirt, his beard was unkempt, and his skin was covered with dust. Though he considered himself the greatest of all rulers, Shango prostrated himself before Obatala like an ordinary person, saying, "You, Obatala, who made all things possible, what terrible fate brought you here?"

Obatala replied: "I came only to visit Shango, ruler of Oyo. On the way I first met Eshu, who soiled my clothing and twisted accident into my journey. I found your horse in the bush and led him to the city. But I was treated as the lowest of criminals, placed here and forgotten."

Shango said, "Great Obatala, it was not known to me."

Obatala answered, "Can a ruler be said to truly rule if he does not know what his servants do with the authority he has given them?"

Shango said, "A thing like this will not happen in Oyo again."

Because Obatala was the creator of humans it grieved him to see them suffering. He caused the rain to come again and the crops to grow, and the sickness fell away from Oyo.

It was Eshu who caused things to go badly with Obatala. Misfortune came to the King of the White Cloth because Eshu stained his clothing with oil. And in memory of this event people who are going on a long journey still say, "Eshu who splashed oil on the clothes of Obatala, please do not soil my white clothing with oil."

How Shango Departed from Oyo

Shango lived on in Oyo. It was a time of wars among the Yoruba cities, and little by little Oyo's influence spread, until Shango was master of the whole country. His armies had subdued everyone who opposed him, and all the other Obas acknowledged Oyo as supreme. Only after this was there peace. As he had in war, Shango now governed with a strong hand, though some say he ruled with a force that was no longer required.

Among the warriors who had fought in Shango's armies there were many heroes, but the greatest of them all were Timi and Gbonka. Because of their valorous deeds they were known everywhere. People remembered this battle and that battle in which the two heroes had fought, and recalled their accomplishments.

Shango could not escape hearing these recollections. He thought: "I am the Alafin of Oyo, the Oba of Obas. My armies have conquered everything. Other obas recognize the supremacy of Oyo. Yet it is not me that people praise. People everywhere are saying 'Timi-this' or 'Gbonka-that.' " Shango brooded. He began to consider how he might rid Oyo of the two heroes.

One day he sent a messenger to instruct Timi to come to the royal house. When Timi arrived he was accompanied by a drummer who beat out sayings of praise for the hero. A crowd of people followed, some of them dancing. This was the way things were done when a great hero went from one place to another. Now, Shango felt gratitude for the loyalty of Timi in the wars, and his jealousy and his gratitude wrestled within him. But the sight of so many people celebrating Timi's great deeds made Shango's heart hard. He decided to send Timi away.

He said: "In the city of Ede things are not good. The people there do not show the proper respect for Oyo. They forget that they are the servants and I am the master. Go and rule over Ede. Grind down those who seek trouble. Bring order out of disorder. Remain there, be Ede's father."

Timi said: "Great Shango, I will do what you ask. When have I ever failed to strike a blow for the honor of Oyo? Do not doubt it, Ede will praise you and be your servant."

He went to his house and prepared for his journey. He hung his medicine bundles and his talismans around his neck and his arms. He took the bow and the flaming arrows he used in war. He mounted his horse and with only a few warrior companions he rode away to Ede.

Shango thought: "Now I have disposed of one of the heroes. He will surely meet his end trying to take Ede." But then news began to come back to Oyo that Timi and his companions had fought the finest warriors of Ede and defeated them. When that was done, Timi became the ruler of the city and all the lands around it. Timi's name had become greater than before. And, as time went on, Ede grew in strength and reknown. Shango was eaten by anger. He devised a new plan to be rid of Timi.

He sent for the second hero, Gbonka, and instructed him in this manner: "Go to Ede for me, where Timi has taken the seat of the Oba. When he departed he promised to make Ede the servant of Oyo. Instead of that he has made Ede proud and vain, as though Oyo were merely a village of no consequence. When you reach Ede challenge Timi, defeat him and bring him back. Because you have powerful medicine you cannot fail in this matter."

Gbonka listened. He felt no anger for Timi, only close comradeship. He said: "Great ruler of Oyo, I hear what you want me to do. But Timi and I fought side by side through the bloodiest of Oyo's wars. When one of us bled, both bled. When one struck down an enemy, so did the other. We have relieved our thirst from the same cup. How can I now fight with Timi? For one of us will surely die."

Shango answered: "Yes, I have thought of it. But your medicine is powerful. It will prevail over Timi without causing anyone to die." Yet in his mind Shango was thinking, "When two heroes like Timi and Gbonka meet in battle one must die. If it is Timi I will have only Gbonka to deal with. If it is Gbonka I will have only Timi to dispose of."

Gbonka said to Shango: "I will go to Ede. I will talk to Timi as to my companion of many wars. I will persuade him to return." He went to his house. He placed his medicine bundles and his talismans on his arms and around his neck. He took his antelope horn in which was kept the most powerful of his jujus. Then he rode away to Ede, his drummer walking in front. The drummer beat out Gbonka's praise names and the great deeds he had performed in battle.

The people of Ede, in time, heard the drumming. They went to the edge of the city to see who was coming. They were overcome with awe at the sight of Gbonka. He was strong and fierce, and his body was nearly covered with leather medicine bundles. So many talismans hung from his head that his face was nearly obscured, but behind them his eyes shone like sparks in the darkness. He carried a long spear, and on his shield were the marks that all men knew to be the sign of Gbonka of Oyo.

The Ede people ran to Timi's house, calling out that Gbonka was coming dressed for battle. When Gbonka arrived there Timi was standing at his door waiting. Gbonka dismounted. He said: "Timi, my companion in war, Shango has sent me to bring you back to Oyo. Let us prepare for the journey."

Timi said: "You, Gbonka, who rode by my side to do great deeds, you are welcome to Ede. But I cannot go back to Oyo with you, for I am the Oba in Ede now."

They spoke this way, two friends one to the other, and gave their arguments.

Timi said: "Gbonka, you must return to Oyo alone. Time has changed many things. Shango sent me here to control Ede. Here I must stay."

Gbonka said: "Shango did not send me merely to ride here and ride there. He said, 'Bring Timi back to Oyo.' He said, 'If Timi does not choose to come, bring him by force.'"

Timi said: "Likewise, when Shango sent me here he did not say, 'Go to that place and return.' Therefore I do not return."

Gbonka said, "If I cannot persuade you by words, then we must fight to decide the matter."

Timi said: "Gbonka, can you use your weapons against me? I am your friend and your companion of many wars."

Gbonka answered, though his heart was sick: "Yes, it is that way. Therefore prepare yourself to fight."

Timi entered his house. When he came out his arms and chest were covered with medicine bundles and talismans. In his hands he held his bow and his flaming arrows.

The people of Ede pleaded with the heroes, saying: "You men are closer than brothers. What you are doing is not right."

But Timi said to the people, "Stand back and do not come between us." So they backed away. Timi's drummer began to play Timi's praise names. Gbonka's drummer began to play Gbonka's praise names. Timi placed a flaming arrow in his bow. But Gbonka did not raise either his spear or his shield. He held only his medicine horn in his hand. He sang a song that ended with the words:

"When a child sleeps he drops whatever he holds in his hands.
Sleep now, Timi, and let go your bow and flaming arrows."

Instantly Timi fell into a deep sleep. His weapons dropped from his hands and he fell to the ground. Gbonka approached him with his spear poised. But when he looked on Timi's still face, Gbonka put his spear down. He ordered the people to put Timi on his horse. Gbonka mounted his own horse and rode away, taking Timi with him to Oyo. When he arrived he went directly to Shango's house and put Timi on the ground. He said to Shango: "We fought, but before he could release his arrow I put him to sleep. As you wanted me to do, I have brought him back to Oyo."

The people who had gathered in Shango's courtyard demanded that

Timi be awakened. Gbonka awakened him. Timi stood up. The people ridiculed him with phrases and laughter. Gbonka turned away silently and went to his own house and entered.

Shango was deeply troubled, for once again he had the two heroes in Oyo. He thought about the matter for some days. Then he sent for Timi and said to him: "Things did not go well. I foresaw that you would defeat Gbonka. Instead, he put you to sleep with his power of medicine. Now the people of Oyo ridicule you. Of all heroes you are the greatest, and your medicine is more powerful than Gbonka's. Therefore injustice has been done. Will you leave the matter there? You cannot live from day to day hearing people say, 'There goes Timi, once great, but now humiliated by Gbonka of Oyo.' In Ede even now you can hear it said, 'Timi who made himself Oba of Ede, he fell asleep in the face of a single warrior.' If you choose to fight Gbonka again I will announce it to the city."

When they had faced each other in Ede, even with their weapons in their hands, Timi had felt like a brother to Gbonka. But now his shame choked him and he longed to fight. He said, "Yes, I will meet Gbonka once more, and may death come to one of us."

Shango sent criers out through the city. They called: "Atoto-o! Atoto-o! Two warrior heroes meet! Gbonka and Timi are going to fight!"

The next morning the two men appeared before Shango's compound prepared to fight. Everyone in Oyo was there. The heroes faced each other calling out taunts back and forth. Their drummers beat out their praise names. There was great excitement. Timi released a flaming arrow from his bow. As the arrow began its flight, Gbonka pointed to the east with his medicine horn. The arrow turned and went to the east. Timi released another flaming arrow from his bow. Gbonka pointed his medicine horn westward. The arrow turned to the west. Timi sent arrow after arrow at Gbonka, but Gbonka's medicine horn turned them all aside. And when Timi's arrows were nearly gone, Gbonka sang the same song he had sung in Ede. The final words of the song came from his mouth:

"When a child sleeps he drops whatever he holds in his hands.
Sleep now, Timi, and let go your bow and flaming arrows."

By the time Gbonka had finished singing, Timi lay sleeping on the ground. The people praised Gbonka. He awakened Timi and left the place of the combat.

Shango was not satisfied, because both heroes still lived. One day he sent for Gbonka. He said to him: "The tree has been bent, but still it continues to grow. You have bent Timi, but still he lives. The contest was never finished. Therefore you must fight again."

Anger seized Gbonka. He said to Shango: "Twice I fought with Timi to please you. Twice I defeated him, but you will not let the matter rest. What can it mean except that you will not be satisfied while the two of us remain alive? Very well. I will fight a last fight with Timi. When that

is done the contest will be between you and me. Either you or I will
have to leave Oyo forever."

And so the two heroes met again in combat. A great crowd gathered
from all the countryside around Oyo. Musicians beat out the praise
names of Gbonka and Timi on their drums. Shango sat on a chair placed
on a leopard skin. There was much excitement. The fighting began. Just
as he had done before, Gbonka felled Timi to the ground with sleep.
But this time Gbonka took his sword from his scabbard and cut off
Timi's head. He turned and threw the head in Shango's lap, saying,
"Here is the head you wanted so much." People cried out in dismay that
Gbonka behaved with such contempt for Shango. Shango stood up, his
eyes red with anger, letting the head fall to the ground. He ordered his
guards to seize Gbonka and put him to death.

They built a large fire there where the fight had taken place. They
tied Gbonka with heavy cords and threw him into the flames. The
people gathered around to watch Gbonka die. But instead they saw him
standing in the fire, his eyes fixed on Shango. When the cords that
bound him had burned away, Gbonka walked from the flames unharmed. The people of Oyo fled in terror. Only Shango and his wife Oya
remained. Gbonka approached Shango and struck him with his medicine horn, saying: "Now, Shango, you are finished in Oyo. You must
leave within five days. Never will you return."

Shango opened his mouth and a great flame shot out and enveloped
Gbonka. But Gbonka withstood the flame and was unharmed. And then
Shango knew that Gbonka could not be conquered.

Four days went by. The people turned away from Shango and sang
praise songs for Gbonka. In the evening of the fourth day Shango made
ready to leave Oyo, and in the darkness of night he and his wife Oya
went out of the city, travelling towards Nupe.

Thus it was that Shango abandoned the kingdom over which he had
ruled. He never reached Nupe, however. As he and his wife went
through the bush country, Oya became more and more disheartened
about the exile from Oyo. Shango hardly spoke. He was afflicted with
shame that he had been driven out by Gbonka. They stopped after a
while to rest.

Oya said in despair: "I cannot go any farther. Oyo is my home. In
Nupe I will be a stranger without friends."

Shango answered: "I have been deserted by all of Oyo. The people
are like leaves that move with the wind. I, Shango, ruler of everything,
have been abandoned. Only Oya accompanies me on the road. But now
Oya wants to go back to Oyo."

Shango left Oya sitting there and went into the forest. He prepared
a rope, tying it to the limb of an ayan tree, and he hanged himself.

Oya waited for him to return. When she was rested she went to look
for him. She found Shango's double-bladed axe lying on the ground. She
went farther, and she saw Shango's body hanging from the ayan tree.
She fled back to Oyo, crying out that Shango had hanged himself in the
forest. People were sent to get Shango's body so that it could be prop-

erly buried. They found the double-bladed axe where Shango had left it. Farther on they found the ayan tree and saw the rope hanging from it, but Shango's body was not there.

They returned and reported what they had seen. The subchiefs of Oyo met in council to discuss the mystery. Some said that since Shango's body could not be found he probably was not dead. Others argued that he must have killed himself, because Oya had seen him hanging from the ayan tree. The weight of opinion was that Oya had reported the truth. "Oba so," people said, meaning, "The Oba hangs." But suddenly the sky darkened and the wind began to blow. A storm enveloped Oyo, and a great bolt of lightning cleaved the air. The lightning struck again and again. Thunderstones rained down on the city and many houses burst into flames.

Then a loud voice proclaimed: "I, Shango, do not hang! I have merely returned to my place in the sky!"

The people prostrated themselves on the ground. They cried out to one another, "Oba koso! Oba koso!" meaning: "The Oba does not hang! The Oba does not hang!" After this the thunderstones stopped falling on the city of Oyo.

From his place in the sky Shango kept watch over the goings-on in Oyo and punished those who spoke evil against him. Anyone struck by lightning was adjudged to be one of Shango's enemies, and he was not buried near other graves but in a separate and isolated place. The ayan tree, from which Shango departed the earth, became sacred, and from that time on people have made sacrifices to Shango at its foot. And whereas formerly he had been known as Shango or as Jakuta, the Stone Thrower, he now was also called Oba Koso, The Oba Does Not Hang.

As for his wife Oya, she did not remain in Oyo. She once again departed from there and travelled northward toward Nupe. After many days she arrived at the great river that separated the land of the Yoruba from the country of the Nupe people. She looked across the water. She said: "In that place I will be an exile. People will forever say to each other, 'See, there stands Oya of Oyo. Once she was the wife of the great Shango, but now she is the most miserable of women.' Can a person go on living this way?"

Oya did not try to cross the river. Instead, she went into the water and disappeared. She became the spirit of that river, which thereafter was called by her name.

YORUBA WARRIORS, KINGS AND HEROES

Ogbe Baba Akinyelure, Warrior of Ibode

There was a time when war was everywhere in the land, and in those days there were many warrior heroes. Among all the heroes whose names were heard in the mouths of men, none was more famous than Ogbe, a man who lived in the town of Ibode in the west. When Ogbe went into battle only the great champions of other cities came forward to fight and test his weapons. And all those who challenged Ogbe in war, who remembers them now? For they felt the weight of Ogbe's sword, the blood of their lives ran out on the battlefield, and their names faded away and were forgotten.

In the times in which Ogbe lived it was said that a warrior should not drink palm wine when his country was at war, for drinking made a man's arms heavy and slowed his spear. It was said: "If one drinks, let him drink. If he fights, let him fight. But the two cannot live together in the same house." Yet Ogbe was swift and he was strong. More than once he went out fighting with the warmth of palm wine inside. It did not make his arms heavy or slow his weapons.

Ogbe had many wives, as befitted a great champion, and he had many children in Ibode. Of all his sons he loved Akinyelure best. Perhaps this was because of all his wives it was Akinyelure's mother who was dearest to him. And the sign of his affection was that he called himself Ogbe Baba Akinyelure; Ogbe, Father of Akinyelure. By this name he was known in far-off places.

Now, one day Ogbe returned from fighting at a distant frontier. In Ibode there was a festival celebrating his victories. Drumming, dancing and singing went on all day and into the night. The people sang of Ogbe's prowess and the war horns signaled Ogbe's praise names. When the first celebration ended another began. Day after day the warriors of Ibode celebrated, and many cups of wine were drunk. During these festivals Ogbe drank mightily. Because he was a great hero no one said the words: "If one drinks, let him drink. If one fights, let him fight."

While the town was just beginning to stir one morning a messenger came with word that an enemy force was approaching Ibode. Ogbe and the other warriors of the town prepared for battle. Seeing his father taking up his weapons, the young Akinyelure said to him, "This time I too will go out to repel the enemy." Ogbe looked at his son. He saw that Akinyelure was now a man. He answered: "Yes, prepare yourself also. Take your spear. Take your battle-axe. We shall stand and fight together, side by side, and rain death on those who want to conquer Ibode."

This story and the two which follow—"The Burning of the Elekute Grove" and "Ogedengbe's Drummers"—are from Tales of Yoruba Gods and Heroes, © *1973 by Harold Courlander, and are reprinted by permission of Crown Publishers.*

The warriors went out to meet the enemy. The fighting was great. The feet of the fighting men stirred up the dust and made a dark cloud hang over the battle. Ogbe and Akinyelure moved together. Where one fought the other fought. The sun moved across the sky and still the battle went on. Ogbe's battle-axe glistened, and the enemy in front of him melted away. They turned their backs and fled into the bush. The men of Ibode called out, "The enemy flees!" It was only then that Ogbe saw that Akinyelure was not at his side. He searched across the fields and found Akinyelure lying dead among the dead. A great grief descended upon Ogbe. The exhilaration of battle ebbed from his body. He dropped his weapons on the ground.

When the other warriors of Ibode gathered their dead and prepared to return to the town, Ogbe merely stood looking at the corpse of his son. They said, "Ogbe, let us return."

But he answered: "No. You return to Ibode. I will stay here. How can I go back now? How can I face the wife whose son I allowed to die on the battlefield?"

His friends said: "This is not the way it is with a hero. Men fight, men die, but one must go on living."

Ogbe refused to return to Ibode. He stood on the battlefield. He sang:

> "I, Ogbe, Father of Akinyelure,
> Possessor of many wives,
> Father of many children,
> Champion of many wars,
> Slayer of many enemies!
> In all my days until now
> No shame has fallen on me!
> How could I know Akinyelure
> Could not strike before and behind,
> To one side and the other?
> I brought him to the battle
> And I gave him no shelter under my spear.
> How can I now speak to his mother
> Who is dear to me, saying merely,
> 'One must go on living'?"

His friends urged him again, pleading with him, "Ogbe, take up your weapons and return with us."

He said: "No, leave me here. I would go to another country, but I would only hunger for the love of my wife whose son I allowed to die. No, here I will stay and take root, for I have nowhere else to go."

When Ogbe said these words he took root where he stood and became an iroko tree.

Although he never returned to Ibode he was never forgotten. From that time on the people of Ibode offered sacrifices at the foot of the iroko tree once each year in memory of Ogbe Baba Akinyelure.

The Burning of the Elekute Grove

Near the town of Owon in early times there was a sacred grove called Elekute. In this grove, filled with trees and wild brush, ceremonies and sacrifices took place, and it was here that ritual dancers came to put on their masks and costumes. Because the grove was so sacred to the people of Owon, the elders of the town took special measures to preserve it from destruction. It was the custom for farmers to burn their fields before planting them, and there was concern that Elekute might be destroyed by spreading flames. The council of elders in Owon discussed at length what the penalty should be for burning the grove, and they agreed at last that the punishment should be death.

Among the men who sat in council and deliberated on the question was a person named Akuko. His family was well known and greatly respected in Owon for its generosity and the many good deeds it had done in behalf of the town. Akuko himself was industrious. His fields were well kept. He often gave corn to those who were in need. He shared the responsibilities of defending the town. And whenever men gathered to discuss important matters he was listened to.

This respected man Akuko was walking one day on a trail outside the town. He saw two small boys huddled together crying, and he stopped to ask them about their trouble. At first they were unwilling to speak, but he urged them, quoting the proverb, "Even a large tree is felled by the woodcutter," meaning that no difficulty is too large to be overcome.

At last the older of the boys said: "We were going from Owon to our father's farm. We were carrying embers so that our father could have fire out there. We walked along this trail as we have always done in the past. And a wind came up and blew sparks from our embers into the Elekute Grove and set it afire. Now we will be punished. As everyone knows, we will be hanged."

Akuko was troubled. He thought, "Surely the town will not demand punishment for these boys, who meant no harm to the sacred grove." But again he thought, "Yet it was definitely agreed that the penalty would be the same for any guilty person, whether man or woman, adult or child." He thought: "I am a man. I am capable of defending myself. Can these small boys stand before the people and plead their case? All they will be able to say is, 'A wind blew sparks from our embers into the Elekute Grove.' "

After some thought he said to the boys: "When you return to the town say nothing about the burning. I will speak of it my own way. Give me the embers and go on to your father's farm." He took the embers and went back into the town. Already word was going from mouth to ear: "The Elekute Grove has been burned! The Elekute Grove has been burned!" Akuko went to the house of the chief. He said: "An unfortunate thing happened. I was carrying embers to my fields and a wind came up and blew sparks into the Elekute Grove. I came directly to you so that you would hear the story exactly as it occurred. I meant no harm to the town."

The chief answered: "This is an important matter. It belongs to the entire town. It was my family of councillors who decreed the burning of the grove to be a serious crime." The chief sent messengers through the town to call his councillors together. He addressed them, saying: "Akuko comes to me. He says, 'It was I who burned the Elekute Grove, but I had no evil intent. I was walking along the trail carrying embers. A wind came up and blew sparks into the bush. This was how it happened.'"

The councillors said, "Let Akuko himself speak about it."

Akuko said: "All the people of Owon know my family. We have never done any mischief in the community. We carry no shame for anything, for we have never injured anyone. I, Akuko, was going out to my fields carrying embers. The wind came up and blew sparks. Am I a master of the wind? I did not leave the trail. I did not approach the grove. The wind took sparks and carried them there. Have I ever done anything against Owon's welfare? Let us forget this matter and go on living."

But an elder replied: "Slowly, slowly. Let us consider things. The councillors met and discussed this question. They agreed it would be a serious crime to burn the Elekute Grove. It was decreed that whoever should commit this crime would die by hanging. You, Akuko, were you not there among us? Did you not concur in what was decided? You said, 'Yes, I agree with everything.' Now you say, 'Let us forget the matter and go on living.'"

Another man spoke. He said: "Akuko tells us this and that. He says, 'My family is respected.' An elephant is large but he can walk gently. An important family also should walk gently. Akuko was carrying embers, but it was his responsibility to see that no sparks escaped. When we agreed on the penalty was it said by anyone that the punishment would be for one kind of person and not for another? Did Akuko himself say, 'If the wind comes up we will forget the matter'?"

Many persons spoke in this fashion. Then one of the councillors said: "Yes, the council agreed on everything, and Akuko has acknowledged what he did. There is no dispute on these things. However, Akuko has been generous in Owon. Many persons have accepted seed from Akuko's granaries to plant in their fields. And who here has not sat drinking palm wine with Akuko? Has not Akuko given out gifts at one festival and another? When the enemy comes does he not take up his weapons like the rest of us? What is there to say against Akuko except that sparks rode the wind from his hand to the Elekute Grove? Let us consider this question in moderation."

They talked back and forth. At last there was a decision. Because of his good name Akuko would be allowed to pay a fine of 2,400,000 cowries. If he did not present this many cowries to the town by the fifth day of the week, Ojo-Obatala, he would be hanged instead.

Akuko's spirits were heavy. He said: "Never has my family owned such wealth. Where will I ever obtain so many cowries? Could even an oba pay a fine like this?"

He went to his relatives for help. They gave him all the cowries they had, but it was not even a beginning. He went to other people in Owon asking for loans, promising to repay with interest. Some people had no cowries to give him. Others refused, saying: "No, Akuko, you could never repay such a large sum of money. Where would you find it?" Still others answered in a hostile manner. They said: "Because you come from a good family, that does not excuse your crime. If someone else in Owon caused the Elekute Grove to be burned would it be said of him, 'He never did anything like this before. Let us excuse him'? No, it would be said, 'Hang him quickly.' "

Ojo-Obatala, the fifth day, came. Akuko went to the chief and said: "My family has given all its wealth. My friends have given everything they can. But it is not even a beginning. Where could anyone find 2,400,000 cowries?"

The chief answered, "In that case the sentence must be carried out."

People seized Akuko, tied his arms behind him and began marching him towards the place of execution, which was on the far side of the river.

Akuko said, "Have all you people forgotten the generosities of my father and my grandfather?"

They answered: "Do not plead for your life, Akuko! Be courageous in the face of death!"

Akuko saw that the people wanted him to die. He said: "I see that you really intend to hang me. But now listen to what I have to say. I always wanted good things for the town of Owon, yet Owon wishes me evil in return. If you execute me it will bring great misfortunes on Owon. The crops in the fields will sicken, and never again will food be plentiful. Never again will a native of Owon prosper, no matter how hard he works."

People said: "Akuko, you are talking too much! Prepare to hang!"

Akuko went on: "If I am hanged the men of Owon will grow impotent before their time and be unable to procreate. The town will wither away."

People called back, taunting Akuko, "Hang, Akuko, hang!"

While they marched Akuko towards the place of execution in a procession, Oge, the chief drummer of the town, walked ahead, making his drum say: "Akuko hangs! Akuko hangs! Akuko hangs!"

Akuko addressed the drummer, saying: "You, Oge, whose drum speaks these vengeful words, if I am hanged you will be among the first to die in the next battle with Owon's enemies."

People shouted: "Akuko, your curses are meaningless! Bring your talking to an end!"

Akuko called out: "May the river run uphill and return to the place from which it came!"

People laughed. They said: "Rivers never run uphill! Rivers never run uphill!"

The procession reached the ford in the river. The people looked in awe. "Look!" they said to one another. "The water flows the wrong way! It is running from the low ground to the high ground!" What they saw increased their hostility towards Akuko. They tied a cloth around his mouth so that he could not speak any more words. They began to ford the river. In the middle of the crossing, Akuko stopped for a moment and washed his legs. People wondered about this, but they kept pushing and tugging Akuko until they reached the other side.

And there, at the execution place, Akuko was hanged to a tree.

People said: "Well, the matter is finished. He who burned the Elekute Grove is dead," and they returned to their homes.

But the matter was not yet really finished, for Akuko's curses on the town of Owon were alive. The next time the warriors of Owon went out to fight the enemy, Oge, the drummer whose drum had said: "Akuko hangs! Akuko hangs!" was among the first to die. As time went on the town's fields dried up and the crops diminished. The men of Owon became impotent at an early age and were unable to have offspring. For this reason the population of Owon decreased. Owon was once a thriving place but it was withering now. After a while all the families of Owon became poor. They had nothing and they no longer hoped for anything.

Owon's river continued to flow the wrong way. People gave sacrifices at its banks, imploring it to reverse its course, but their supplications were never answered. To this day the river flows the wrong way, a reminder of Akuko's execution.

As for Akuko, he was reincarnated as a cock. And even now, after so many generations have lived and died, great care is taken to wash the legs of a cock before it is killed. This is in memory of Akuko's stopping in the river to wash his legs before he was hanged.

Ogedengbe's Drummers

In the days of constant wars among the kingdoms of the Yoruba, a warrior hero called Ogedengbe lived in the city of Ilesha. Ogedengbe ruled firmly in Ilesha, and in other kingdoms he was feared and respected, for it was said that once he had undertaken war against an enemy he would not relent or turn back until his work was finished. He attacked enemy cities and sacked them, taking gold and slaves as his prize. He pursued his enemies to the most distant places to cut them down. Wherever the fighting was most fierce, there Ogedengbe would be. His name was heard with attention in far-off villages, and, at the rumor that Ogedengbe was approaching, people went away into the bush with their cattle and hid themselves.

In other kingdoms people asked each other: "How can Ogedengbe be disposed of? He is like a plague of ants. He comes out of the bush to eat everything that lies in his path. If Ogedengbe were not loose in the land we could go on living, each man in his fields and each city in its place. But now every city is in danger."

The city of Ibadan was then ruled by another warrior chief called Ogunmola. Ogunmola decided one time that he would attack Ilesha and destroy Ogedengbe. He assembled his army. He prepared for the expedition. And when everything was ready Ogunmola's forces set out. They reached the outskirts of Ilesha.

A great battle began. Ogedengbe's warriors met the army from Ibadan in the fields. When night came they rested, but when the sun rose again the battle resumed. The two armies moved from one place to another. They drifted across the land. Other cities became involved. The war spread, leaving suffering and death in its wake. Finally Ogedengbe defeated Ogunmola, who returned with his shattered forces to Ibadan.

But Ogedengbe's anger was not yet stilled. It was said that the city of Benin had conspired with Ibadan in the attack against Ilesha. So Ogedengbe decided to punish Benin. He began the expedition. As he rode his white horse his drummers went on ahead. Their drums spoke like this:

"Ogedengbe is coming.
Ogunmola is finished,
Now it is Benin's turn.
Benin, prepare yourself,
Prepare to bury your corpses."

The sound of the drums was heard far away. Whenever Ogedengbe's army passed through a village there was no sign of human beings and the fields were empty. For everywhere it was said that Ogedengbe's drums and war horns spoke only the truth. When the drums said that Ogunmola had been defeated, everyone agreed that it must be so.

Word of Ogedengbe's approach came to Benin. The ruler of that city met with his councillors to discuss the situation. They sent a messenger to Ogedengbe. He said: "Our people say there is no need to make war on Benin. Benin has done nothing hostile to you. The people know of your courage and achievements, and they praise you. Ogedengbe, turn back and leave Benin as it stands. This is the message I have brought you."

Ogedengbe spoke harshly. He said: "It is just as I thought it would be. The city of Benin whimpers like a child. Hear my drums, for they speak only what is true. The drums say, 'Now it is Benin's turn.' Return to the city and tell your oba what I have said."

The messenger returned to Benin. He reported Ogedengbe's words. Once again the people of Benin sent a messenger to plead with Ogedengbe not to make war on the city. Again Ogedengbe rebuffed the messenger. His army arrived at Benin, surrounded the city and dug a moat around it to prevent the inhabitants from escaping. Benin was besieged. The oba of Benin, the subchiefs and the councillors discussed their situation. They foresaw that the city would be destroyed and their army defeated. While some said: "Let us go out and fight," others said, "No. Listen to Ogedengbe's drums. They recall his great victories over other cities. They speak only what is true."

After the argument had been going on this way for a long time, one of the elders of Benin said: "Can Ogedengbe's drums say only one thing? What are drums, after all? They are objects made of wood and hide. They say only what drummers make them say. Ogedengbe's drums can say other things. They can speak of Benin's greatness also."

People answered: "Now, Ogedengbe's drummers are dear to his heart, for the words their drums speak remind him to be courageous, and his warriors also take courage from the sound. Why, then, would the drummers make their drums tell of Benin's greatness?"

The elder answered: "I will tell you about this thing. The drummers play what pleases Ogedengbe because he pays them well. Does a musician live who does not play what he is paid for? Very well. Let us be patrons to the drummers."

The people saw merit in it. They collected cowries from whoever had cowries, and the oba and the subchiefs gave the greatest share. They appointed a messenger. In the dark of night the messenger took the cowries and went out of the city to the place where the drummers were resting.

The messenger said to them: "Your drumming has been heard. In the city the people have praised it. They say you are truly great musicians and poets. The tones of your drums are so perfect that no one can mistake their meanings. The people of Benin would like you to drum something for them before the battle begins tomorrow. For this small deed they will give you ten thousand cowries."

The drummers talked among themselves. They agreed. They asked, "What do you want our drums to say?"

"Why," the messenger said, "just a small phrase. Have your drums say, 'When has Benin ever been defeated?' Have them say, 'Never has Benin been walked on by its enemies.'" He gave the drummers the ten thousand cowries and went back to the city.

The light of the morning sun began to be visible. Ogedengbe ordered his warriors to prepare for battle. They made themselves ready for the attack. Ogedengbe mounted his horse. The drums began to play. But instead of reciting Ogedengbe's praise names and recalling his great deeds the drums said:

"When has Benin ever been defeated?
Never has Benin been walked on by its enemies."

All in Ogedengbe's camp heard the drums and were surprised. Anger filled Ogedengbe as he heard the drums say over and over:

"When has Benin ever been defeated?
Never has Benin been walked on by its enemies."

Doubt came to Ogedengbe. He thought: "It is true. Benin has never fallen in war." His fury for battle softened. His warriors with their weapons in their hands, they too were thinking: "Have Ogedengbe's drums ever spoken a falsehood? What they say now is so. Benin has never been beaten to the ground. Although it has many enemies, Benin has only survived and grown greater."

Ogedengbe's eagerness to attack Benin diminished, until at last he ordered his fighting men to withdraw to the outskirts of the city. There he had his drummers executed for making their drums say at the very moment of attack, "When has Benin ever been defeated?" After that Ogedengbe and his army returned to Ilesha.

Olomu's Bush Rat

There was a chief. His name was Olomu. In memory of him there is a saying:

"The smell of the bush rat
Is stronger than words."

It is said that once Olomu was travelling from one town to another. He was hungry, because in the night hyenas had come and eaten his food. Olomu's friends and servants went into the bush to find game. While he waited, he moved this way and that, and he came upon a trap in which a bush rat had been caught. He took the bush rat from the trap, thinking how good it would taste. He did not notice a poor countryman, the owner of the trap, standing nearby. Olomu returned to his camp. He heard his servants and friends coming back. He was ashamed to be seen with game taken from a trap belonging to another man, and he quickly hid the bush rat under his cap. The servants brought meat. They prepared it for the chief. He ate.

Olomu continued his journey. The poor man from whose trap the bush rat had been taken came also. He walked behind Olomu's party singing this song:

"Life is hard.
Poverty oppresses me.
Now a new disaster comes.
I found one cowry.
I spent it to buy a trap.
My trap caught a bush rat.

From Olode the Hunter and Other Tales from Nigeria, © 1968 by Harold Courlander. Reprinted by permission of Harcourt Brace Jovanovich.

Olomu came and removed my bush rat.
Olomu is a thief."

Olomu's servants and followers were surprised. They became angry. They threatened the countryman. But he would not remain quiet. Olomu did not look to the left or the right. He was ashamed. The countryman followed him, singing the song over and over again. When they passed people on the road, he sang more loudly so that they would hear. Olomu, his servants, and his followers arrived at the town. The countryman was still singing. When he was scolded by Olomu's soldiers, he paid no attention. When they threatened to beat him, he paid no attention. He went on singing. The town was in an uproar. Everyone was talking about the matter. The underchiefs came together. They said: "This country fellow is trying to ruin the chief's reputation. He should be punished." Others said: "It is so. But he has made an accusation. It must be looked into." So they went to the countryman, saying: "We have heard what you are saying. Remain quiet now. We will look into it. There will be justice. If what you say is true, it shall fall on Olomu. If it is false, it shall fall on you. The words you have said are grave. If you lie, you shall be beaten and thrown into the bush."

So at last the countryman was silent. He waited. But in the town other people began to sing the song he had composed. The underchiefs ordered guards to watch Olomu wherever he went, so that the bush rat might be found. When Olomu entered his house to sleep, the guards came with him. He did not know what to do with the bush rat. He left it where it was, on his head, and he slept with his cap on. In the morning he arose and went out. He felt the meat grow warm. Soon he could even smell it. He could not take a breath without smelling the bush rat.

Seven days went by. The underchiefs called a council, and they sent for Olomu. He came. He sat down in his place.

They questioned him. He said: "I am Olomu, the chief. Who dares say that I am a thief? Whoever says it, he is a scoundrel. Perhaps he is mad. Whenever has a paramount chief stolen? And whenever has he taken such a thing as a bush rat?" As he talked, the smell of decaying meat spread through the council. The underchiefs stopped asking questions. They stopped listening to Olomu. At last they ordered the guards to search him. One of the guards removed Olomu's cap. There, on top of Olomu's bald head, was the dead bush rat.

Olomu was ashamed. He got up; he walked away into the bush. He did not return, for the disgrace was too great. The countryman was sent for. When he arrived, they paid him from what was in Olomu's house for the loss of his bush rat. They selected a new paramount chief. What happened was not forgotten, for people everywhere knew the song the countryman had sung. And there came to be a saying:

"The smell of the bush rat
Is stronger than words."

THE YORUBA TRICKSTER, IJAPA

The animal trickster hero (or villain) who appears in countless Yoruba stories—Ijapa the tortoise—plays a role in Yoruba lore that is almost identical to that of Anansi the spider among the Ashanti and to that of the hare in other regions of West Africa. Like Anansi, Ijapa is shrewd (sometimes even wise), conniving, greedy, indolent, unreliable, ambitious, exhibitionistic, unpredictable, aggressive, generally preposterous, and sometimes stupid. Though he has a bad character, his tricks, if ingenious enough, can excite admiration. Though he may be the victor in a contest of wits, his success does not teach that bad behavior is justifiable. He exists as a projection of evil forces and bad behavior against which mankind must contend, sometimes winning, sometimes losing. Ijapa himself dies many deaths. While many of his adventures parallel those of other West African tricksters, quite a few seem to be localized among the Yoruba. Ijapa has survived in United States Negro folklore as Brother Terrapin.

In the Yoruba setting, Ijapa is something more than an actor in tales of conflict. He is alluded to in songs (some of which may have come from tales), in sayings, and in proverbs. He is used as a kind of yardstick against which human behavior, human foibles, and moral strength are measured.

How Ijapa, Who Was Short, Became Long

Ijapa the tortoise was on a journey. He was tired and hungry, for he had been walking a long time. He came to the village where Ojola the boa lived, and he stopped there, thinking, "Ojola will surely feed me, for I am famished."

Ijapa went to Ojola's house. Ojola greeted him, saying, "Enter my house and cool yourself in the shade, for I can see you have been on the trail."

Ijapa entered. They sat and talked. Ijapa smelled food cooking over

This story and the four immediately following are from Olode the Hunter, © *1968 by Harold Courlander, and are reprinted here by permission of Harcourt Brace Jovanovich.*

the fire. He groaned with hunger, for when Ijapa was hungry he was more hungry than anyone else. Ojola said politely, "Surely the smell of my food does not cause you pain?"

Ijapa said: "Surely not, my friend. It only made me think that if I were at home now, my wife would be cooking likewise."

Ojola said: "Let us prepare ourselves. Then we shall eat together."

Ijapa went outside. He washed himself in a bowl of water. When he came in again he saw the food in the middle of the room and smelled its odors. But Ojola the boa was coiled around the food. There was no way to get to it. Ijapa walked around and around, trying to find an opening through which he could approach the waiting meal. But Ojola's body was long, and his coils lay one atop the other, and there was no entrance through them. Ijapa's hunger was intense.

Ojola said: "Come, do not be restless. Sit down. Let us eat."

Ijapa said: "I would be glad to sit with you. But you, why do you surround the dinner?"

Ojola said: "This is our custom. When my people eat, they always sit this way. Do not hesitate any longer." The boa went on eating while Ijapa again went around and around trying to find a way to the food. At last he gave up. Ojola finished eating. He said, "What a pleasure it is to eat dinner with a friend."

Ijapa left Ojola's house hungrier than he had come. He returned to his own village. There he ate. He brooded on his experience with Ojola. He decided that he would return the courtesy by inviting Ojola to his house to eat with him. He told his wife to prepare a meal for a certain festival day. And he began to weave a long tail out of grass. He spent many days weaving the tail. When it was finished, he fastened it to himself with tree gum.

On the festival day, Ojola arrived. They greeted each other at the door, Ijapa saying: "You have been on a long journey. You are hungry. You are tired. Refresh yourself at the spring. Then we shall eat."

Ojola was glad. He went to the spring to wash. When he returned, he found Ijapa already eating. Ijapa's grass tail was coiled several times around the food. Ojola could not get close to the dinner. Ijapa ate with enthusiasm. He stopped sometimes to say: "Do not hesitate, friend Ojola. Do not be shy. Good food does not last forever."

Ojola went around and around. It was useless. At last he said: "Ijapa, how did it happen that once you were quite short but now you are very long?"

Ijapa said, "One person learns from another about such things." Ojola then remembered the time Ijapa had been his guest. He was ashamed. He went away. It was from Ijapa that came the proverb:

> "The lesson that a man should be short came
>   from his fellowman.
> The lesson that a man should be tall also came
>   from his fellowman."

Ijapa Cries for His Horse

It happened one time that Ijapa the tortoise owned a fine white horse with beautiful trappings. When Ijapa sat on his horse, he felt proud and vain because he was the center of all eyes. Instead of working his garden, he rode from place to place so that everyone could see him. If he came to a town on market day, he rode his horse through the crowded market so that he might hear people say: "What a distinguished stranger! What an important person!" If he came to a village in the evening, he rode before the headman's house so that his presence would be properly noted. And because Ijapa appeared so distinguished on his white horse, the headman would provide him with food and a place to sleep and then send him on his way with dignity. Never had life been so good for Ijapa.

One day Ijapa arrived at the city of Wasimi. As he rode through the streets, he attracted great attention. People said, "He appears to be an important merchant," or, "He looks like a hero returning from battle." Word went to the compound of the oba, or king, that an important personage had arrived. When Ijapa appeared at the oba's palace, he was welcomed with courtesy and dignity. The oba's family took him to the guesthouse and brought him food. When night fell and it was time to sleep, they said: "We shall take care of the horse."

But Ijapa said: "Oh, no, I will keep him here with me in the guesthouse."

People said, "A horse has never before slept in the guesthouse."

Ijapa said: "My horse and I are like brothers. Therefore he always shares my sleeping quarters." So the horse was left in the guesthouse with Ijapa, and the oba's household slept.

In the middle of the night, Ijapa heard his horse groan. He arose, lighted a torch, and went to see what was the matter. His horse was dead.

Ijapa cried out: "My horse! My horse!" Ijapa's cries awakened everyone. The oba's servants came. They tried to console Ijapa and quiet him. But he would not be consoled. He kept crying out: "My horse! My fine white horse! He is dead! He is dead!"

Members of the oba's family came. They said: "Do not cry out so. In their time, all horses die. Be consoled."

But Ijapa went on mourning the death of his horse in a loud voice that was heard everywhere. At last the oba himself came to the guesthouse. He listened to Ijapa's cries, and he said: "Do not cry anymore. To soothe your misery, I will give you one of my own horses."

One of the oba's best horses was brought into the guesthouse. Ijapa stopped crying. He thanked the oba. People went back to their beds. Once more, the night was quiet. Ijapa kept the torch burning so that he could see his new horse. Then, suddenly, he began to cry again: "Oh, misfortune! Oh, how awful it is! See how I am suffering! Who has brought this terrible thing to happen!"

The servants came back. The oba's family came back. They couldn't quiet Ijapa. Then the oba appeared. He said: "Why do you continue this way? Your lost horse has been replaced."

Ijapa said: "Sir, I cannot help crying out when I think of my bad fortune. The horse you gave me is a fine one. So was my own white horse that died. If he had not died, how lucky I would have been, for I now would have two fine horses instead of one." And again Ijapa broke into loud cries: "Oh, misery! Oh, misfortune! How awful it is!"

They could not stop him. So the oba said: "Very well, if it is only your need for two horses that keeps the city awake, think no more about it. I will give you another horse." The servants brought another horse. Ijapa stopped crying. He thanked the oba for his kindness. Everyone went back to bed. They slept. Only Ijapa couldn't sleep. He kept thinking about his good fortune. He had come with one horse. Now he had two.

Then his eyes fell upon the dead horse. He began to cry: "Oh, great misfortune! Oh, terrible thing! How awful it is! Bad luck falls on my head! Oh, misery!" He went on crying.

Again the household was awakened. Again they came and tried to console him. Again the oba himself had to come. The oba said: "This grief for a dead horse is too much. Many men have horses. Their horses die. But men cannot grieve forever."

Ijapa said: "Sir, I cannot help it. I looked at my dead white horse. I realized that only a few hours ago he was alive. Had he not died, I would own three fine horses and be the most fortunate of men!"

The oba was tired. He was cross. But he ordered another horse be brought for Ijapa. "You are now the most fortunate of men," the oba said. "You own three fine horses. Now let us all sleep." The family and the servants returned to their beds. They slept.

And then, just when everything had become quiet, Ijapa began crying out in grief again: "Oh, misery! Oh, misfortune! What a terrible thing has happened!" It went on and on. The oba called his servants. He gave them instructions. They went to the guesthouse and took the oba's three horses away. They took Ijapa to the gate and pushed him out.

He had no horse at all now, and he went on foot like ordinary people. He returned to his own village in shame, for he had ridden away like a distinguished person and now his legs were covered with dust.

Ijapa and the Oba Repair a Roof

It came to the attention of a certain oba, or chief, that while other people came, as they were supposed to, to mend his fences and cultivate his gardens, only Ijapa the tortoise did not fulfill his obligations. The oba made it a principle that everyone should perform some kind of duty. There were some who served as soldiers. There were others who came several days each year to cultivate the ground or make bricks or build houses on the oba's lands. But Ijapa did not appear. So the oba sent for him. Ijapa came. He lay down on the ground as a mark of respect for the chief. The oba was stern. He said: "Ijapa, I am displeased. You do not respect me. Others have come to do their work. Only you have failed to appear."

Ijapa said: "Great oba, it is not disrespect. The only reason I did not come is that I felt I would be worthless."

The oba was not taken in by Ijapa's words, for Ijapa had a reputation for clever talk. The oba said: "Now that you are here, do not remain as motionless as a tree. Go and cut thatch leaves to mend the roof of my house."

As Ijapa went off to fetch leaves, people said: "Look, there is Ijapa. At last he has to work for the oba like other people."

Ijapa said: "It is not I who works for the oba, it is the oba who works for me."

There was laughter. People said, "Ijapa's mouth cannot control itself."

Ijapa gathered the leaves and went to the house where the roof had to be repaired. Other people loitered nearby to watch him take orders from the oba. The oba himself was particularly offended by Ijapa's manner. He decided to see to it that Ijapa did his work properly, so he stood before the house and watched. He noticed that Ijapa was moving very slowly. He said, "Ijapa, begin the mending!"

Ijapa said, "Great oba, I am beginning." He quickly climbed to the roof. "See," he said, "I am commencing the work." Now, Ijapa should have removed his waistcloth before going up, and he should have placed the newly cut thatch leaves on the roof before going up. When he arrived on the roof, he removed his waistcloth and said to the chief: "Great oba, now I am beginning. Since you are there, have the kindness to take my waistcloth and hang it on the tree over there."

The oba took Ijapa's waistcloth and hung it on a tree limb.

"You see, I am making progress," Ijapa said. "Now, if you will pass the thatch leaves up to me, the work will be half done."

The oba was impressed with Ijapa's methodical and serious approach to repairing the roof. He picked up a bundle of thatch and passed it to Ijapa. "We progress, we progress!" Ijapa said. "Now another bundle!" The oba was pleased at so much progress. He picked up another bundle and gave it to Ijapa. Then he picked up the third bundle. "One moment, great oba," Ijapa said. "Hold it for a moment." The oba held the bundle. At last Ijapa said he was ready, and the oba raised the bundle over his head and Ijapa took it.

All the people who loitered near the house saw the oba take care of Ijapa's waistcloth and hand up the bundles of thatch one by one. They said: "Indeed, it is not Ijapa who works for the oba, but the oba who works for Ijapa!"

Because they liked what they saw, the people made a proverb:

"The day an oba puts a person to work, that is the day he also should be put to work."

Ijapa and Yanrinbo Swear an Oath

As it is known to all, Ijapa was shiftless and did not tend his own garden. His wife Yanrinbo spent all her time making conversation with other women, sometimes in the market, sometimes on the trail, sometimes at the stream where the laundering was done. Between the two of them, nothing was ever put away for a time of need. There came a drought in the country, and food was scarce. Other people did not have enough food supplies to spare anything for Ijapa and his wife. They were faced with hunger.

Ijapa said: "Our neighbor Bamidele has a storage house full of yams. It is not right that he has yams while we have none."

He made a plan. And early one morning, before daylight, he awakened Yanrinbo. She took a large basket, and the two of them set out for Bamidele's place. When they approached the storage house, Ijapa ordered Yanrinbo to sit on his shoulders. She did this and placed the basket on her head. Then he went to the storage house. There they filled the basket with yams, and with his wife sitting on his shoulders and the basket on her head, he returned the way he had come. When they arrived home, they emptied the basket and returned for more. The second time, like the first, Yanrinbo sat on Ijapa's shoulders with the basket on her head. They made many trips this way, until they had enough.

A few days later the neighbor, Bamidele, discovered that a large portion of his yams was missing. He saw footprints leading towards Ijapa's house. He inquired here and there. And at last he brought Ijapa and Yanrinbo before the chief and accused them of taking his yams.

Now, it was the custom to take persons accused of a crime to a particular shrine, where they would either admit their guilt or swear their innocence. If they confessed their misdeeds, they were punished according to the law. If they swore their innocence, they then drank a bowl of agbo, an herb drink prepared by the shrine priest. If the oath they had sworn was true, it was said, nothing would happen to them. But if they had sworn to a falsehood, the agbo would cause them to fall sick. In this way their guilt or innocence would become known.

The chief ordered Ijapa and Yanrinbo to appear before this shrine. The whole village came to watch the trial. Ijapa and Yanrinbo kneeled before the shrine while the priest made the agbo. When all was ready, Ijapa was called upon to swear his oath. He swore: "If I, Ijapa, the husband of Yanrinbo, ever stretched up my hand to remove yams from Bamidele's storage house, may I fall sick instantly and die."

Then Yanrinbo swore: "If I, Yanrinbo, wife of Ijapa, ever used my legs to carry me to Bamidele's storage house to steal yams, may I fall sick instantly and die."

The priest then gave Ijapa and Yanrinbo a large bowl of agbo to drink.

They drank. They did not fall ill. Nothing at all happened. Seeing this, the chief said: "Their oaths were true. Therefore, release them." So Ijapa and Yanrinbo were released.

What they had sworn was not false, for Yanrinbo had not used her legs to get to the storage house. She had ridden on Ijapa's shoulders. And Ijapa had not raised his hands to carry away the yams. It was Yanrinbo who had raised her hands to balance the basket on her head.

Ijapa and the Hot-Water Test

It is said that one time Ijapa was called upon to come and help harvest the chief's fields. The idea interested Ijapa because he had neglected to care for his own fields, which therefore had produced nothing, while the chief's fields were full of yams. He thought about how he might use the occasion to fill his empty storehouse. A plan came to him. In the night he went to the chief's fields and dug a deep hole. He made the opening small at the top, and he sprinkled leaves and grass around the opening to disguise it. Then he carried away the dirt from the hole and threw it into the bush.

Morning came. Ijapa went to the chief's house, saying, "Here I am." Opolo the frog was already there, as were Ekun the leopard, Ekute the bush rat, Ewure the goat, Agbonrin the deer, and many others. They went out to the chief's fields to dig yams. Now, the other workers put the yams they dug into their baskets and carried them to the chief's storehouse. But Ijapa, he put a yam into his basket, then dropped a yam into the hole he had dug the night before. He put another yam into his basket and dropped another one into the hole. For each one he put in the basket he put another in the hole. Some of the workers scolded him for being slow, but Ijapa said: "I have great respect for the chief's yams. I handle them gently so as not to bruise them." The work went on. At last all the yams were harvested. The workers went home.

That night when darkness came, Ijapa took his wife and children to the place where he had hidden the yams. They went back and forth many times, each carrying as many yams as he could, until the hole was empty. Ijapa's storehouse was full. He was pleased.

But when daylight came, servants of the chief found Ijapa's hole. They found the path he and his family had made while going back and forth. They followed the path to Ijapa's storehouse. There they saw the yams, and they returned to report their discovery to the chief. The chief sent for Ijapa. He spoke sternly. "Ijapa, it is reported that you have taken yams from my field."

Ijapa said: "Oh, great chief, I came to help you with your harvest. I labored in the hot sun. I brought yams to your storehouse. Then I returned home. Now you reproach me. It is not I who has taken your yams."

The chief said: "Ijapa, your habits are widely known, and in addition there is a path from my fields to your storehouse."

Ijapa said: "Oh, sir, I went to your fields to work for you, I returned. Could this little walking have made a path? If there is such a path, it was made by others to discredit me. Were there not other persons in the fields also?"

The chief said: "There are no paths from my fields to their houses, only to yours. Therefore, suspicion falls on you. If you are innocent, we shall discover it. Let us prepare for the hot-water test. Tomorrow the people will assemble. We shall come to the truth of the matter."

The next day the people gathered in front of the chief's house, where a large pot of water was heating over a fire. When the water began to boil, the chief said: "Ijapa has been accused of stealing yams. He denies it. For this reason he will take the test. He will drink a bowl of the boiling water. If he is guilty, he will feel great pain. If he is innocent, he will not be harmed. In this way we shall know the truth. Let us begin."

Ijapa spoke, saying: "Oh, sir, though I will be proved innocent, you still will not know who has taken your yams. There were many persons there. Let them all be tested."

The chief considered it. He said: "This is good advice. Let everyone who was in the fields take the test."

Ijapa now became very helpful, as though he were the chief's assistant. He ordered that the pot be removed from the fire. "Place it here," he said, "so that the chief may see it from where he sits." They moved the pot of water from the fire as Ijapa directed.

"Because I am the youngest," Ijapa said, "it is I who should serve the water."

The chief agreed. So Ijapa took the bowl, filled it with hot water from the pot, and served it to Opolo the frog. Opolo drank. The hot water burned him inside. He cried out in pain. Ijapa filled the bowl again. He presented it to Ekute the bush rat. Ekute drank. The water scalded his mouth. He cried out. Tears came to his eyes. Ijapa refilled the bowl and handed it to Ewure the goat. Ewure drank. He cried. Ijapa gave hot water to Ekun the leopard. Ekun drank. He moaned in pain, and tears flowed from his eyes. Each person drank; each person suffered.

Then it came to be Ijapa's turn. The chief said: "All these persons have taken the test. All share the guilt. Now it is Ijapa's moment for guilt or innocence."

Ijapa said: "I, Ijapa, am innocent. Yet I am the one who was accused. Therefore, I shall drink the largest portion of the hot water. In this way I shall prove beyond doubt that I did not commit the crime. The bowl is too small. Therefore, bring me a large calabash."

The chief sent for a calabash. Ijapa filled it to the brim. He carried it to the chief, saying: "See it, great chief, see how full the calabash is!"

The chief replied: "I see it. You do well, Ijapa."

Ijapa carried the calabash back and forth, saying, "Family of the chief, see how full the calabash is!"

The chief's family called out: "We see it. You do well, Ijapa!"

"Men of the village," Ijapa chanted, "see how full the calabash is!"
The men of the village called out: "We see it. You do well, Ijapa!"
"Women of the village," Ijapa sang, "see how full the calabash is!"
The women of the village answered: "We see it. You do well, Ijapa!"
"Boys of the village," Ijapa chanted, "see how full the calabash is!"
The boys chanted back: "We see it. You do well, Ijapa!"
"Girls of the village," Ijapa chanted, "see how full the calabash is!"
"We see it. You do well, Ijapa!" the girls replied.

Ijapa showed his calabash of water to this one and that one, each in turn, as evidence of the large amount of hot water he would drink. They could see that Ijapa was not shrinking from the ordeal. But Ijapa spent a great deal of time at this business, and the entire village was constantly singing, "We see it. You do well, Ijapa!"

Meanwhile, the water in the calabash was getting cool. At last the chief said: "Ijapa, we have declared ourselves enough. You do well. But now let us get on with it."

So Ijapa drank. Because the water had become cool, it did not pain him. He emptied the calabash. The chief nodded his approval. Ijapa said: "You have seen it. I did not cry out. Tears did not come from my eyes. How then can I be guilty?" And as an additional proof of his innocence, Ijapa jumped into the pot from which the water had come. The water in the pot also was cool. Ijapa made sounds of pleasure. Then he came out. He said to the chief: "As you see, it was not I who committed the crime. Surely it must be Opolo, and Ekute, and Ewure, and Ekun, and Agbonrin who are guilty, for it was they who felt the pain."

The other creatures protested, but the chief agreed with Ijapa. Thus it was that the chief found all of them except Ijapa guilty of the theft of his yams.

Since then, whenever a person tries to absolve himself of a bad action by putting the fault on others, people say:

> "When Ijapa accuses the whole community,
> He himself must have something to hide."

Ijapa Goes to the Osanyin Shrine

Of Ijapa it is said again and again, "Though he has no legs on the ground he has wisdom in his head." But what is wisdom? It is like one side of an embroidered cloth: on one side is one thing; on the other, something else again. The other part of Ijapa's character is gluttony and greed. And so Ijapa is looked up to and down upon. His shrewdness pierces like a sharp blade, while his avarice cannot restrain itself.

It is said that Ijapa used to wander from farm to farm seeking the most abundant crops on which to feed. Now, surely Ijapa could not eat every-

From Tales of Yoruba Gods and Heroes, © *1973 by Harold Courlander, and reprinted by permission of Crown Publishers.*

thing he found on the poorest of farms, yet his gluttony drove him to the richest of farms. He believed that where the crops were most luxuriant he would nourish himself better. And so it happened one time that he came to a farm near Oyo that was green with yams, beans, and okra, and he decided that he would stay in that vicinity until he had consumed everything.

He went among the yams and began digging them from the ground. He made a pile here and a pile there. He made bundles of the yams and put them on his back. His load was heavy, but still he put more yams on his back, not wanting to leave behind anything that he had dug from the ground. At last he was finished and he tried to depart from the field. But the load was so heavy he could not move. He struggled with his legs. His feet scraped at the earth and raised a cloud of dust, but his body remained where it was. Ijapa could have removed some of the yams, but he was unwilling to relinquish any of them. He became angry at the yams for pressing him to the ground. He scolded them. He threatened them. Still he could not move.

Darkness came. Then the sun rose again. Ijapa had been struggling all night and he had dug himself into a hole. The man who owned the farm came to take care of his crops. He saw a pile of yams on the ground. He said, "Someone has been trying to steal my yams." He picked them up and put them in a bag. On the very bottom he found Ijapa. He said, "So you are the thief!" and he put Ijapa in the bag with the yams and carried it home. When he arrived there he took the tortoise and was about to kill it. He raised his bush knife to sever the tortoise's head, but Ijapa pulled his head into his shell. Then the man took a stone in his hand, but from inside the shell Ijapa sang:

> "Not with a stone is Ijapa killed.
> Bury him instead under a pile of grain."

So the farmer poured a basketful of millet over Ijapa and covered him with a large earthen pot. He placed a heavy stone on the pot and went away to let Ijapa die.

The next morning the farmer returned to see what had happened to Ijapa. He removed the pot. Ijapa was not dead. He had eaten all the millet, and he was, for the moment, very contented. The farmer said, "Surely there is some way to be rid of this predator."

At that moment Ijapa saw a priest of the Osanyin cult approaching. So he sang:

> "A passing stranger will take him away.
> In this way Ijapa will be disposed of."

The Osanyin priest arrived. The farmer greeted him. He said: "It was told to me that I should give this tortoise to a passing stranger. Therefore I give it to you." The Osanyin priest accepted it. He went on after putting the tortoise in his knapsack. Ijapa was satisfied the way things were. Each step the priest took carried Ijapa farther from the farmer who wanted to kill him.

But the Osanyin priest was out gathering things to sacrifice to the orisha Osanyin at a special festival. He said to himself: "The orisha Osanyin has never asked for tortoise meat. Yet it must mean something that this tortoise was put in my hands while I was on the way to the shrine. It cannot be seen any other way. Osanyin desires that a tortoise be sacrificed."

He arrived at the shrine. He prepared the sacrifice. He killed Ijapa and offered his meat to Osanyin. Osanyin was pleased. He accepted the offering, and in return he brought good fortune to the priest and his shrine. For this reason tortoises have been sacrificed to the orisha Osanyin ever since.

And so, though Ijapa is wise, it is also said of him, "When Ijapa is doing something he will not stop until disaster falls upon him."

Ijapa in Yoruba Proverbs

Ijapa's character—his boastfulness, greed, miserliness, cleverness or stupidity in crucial situations, his insensitivity to the feelings of others, and his bad manners—make him an easy peg on which to hang sayings and proverbs such as these:

> Ijapa said, "It emerges!"
> His son replied, "I grasp it!"
> Ijapa asked, "What do you grasp?"
> His son asked, "What did you say is emerging?"

(A ridiculous statement elicits another ridiculous statement; a ridiculous question prompts a ridiculous answer.)

> It is a meticulous person like the tortoise who can see a tortoise in the bush.

(An alert person is aware of the trickery of others.)

> If the medicine (magic) of Ijapa is so powerful, why can't he cure himself?

(A boastful person should demonstrate his prowess at home before offering his services to others.)

> A person who is not like Ijapa still may wear embroidered cloth.

Provided by Ezekiel Aderogba Adetunji, of Ilesha.

(If favor can be shown to a person who does not deserve it, why should a person who deserves good treatment be deprived of it? The "embroidered cloth" alludes to the pattern on the tortoise's back.)

When Ijapa was paying a visit to his wife's relatives he was asked about when he planned to return home. He replied, "When disgrace has stepped in."

(Refers to a person who refuses to halt a dishonorable action before it is too late.)

Though Ijapa has no legs on the ground he has wisdom in his head.

(Refers to a person who behaves more sensibly than is expected of him.)

One morsel for the mouth, one morsel for the pocket, the proverb of Ijapa.

(Refers to a person who behaves in a dishonest manner. One time when Ijapa was attending a feast, he hid his son in his pocket. As he ate, he first placed food in his own mouth, then slipped food into his pocket for his son. When observed in this strange action, Ijapa said he always ate this way, "one morsel to the mouth, one morsel to the pocket." His pocket was examined and his son discovered. Thus his dishonesty was exposed.)

There is no offense if a question is asked with advance permission; proverb of Ijapa.

(One cannot complain about something said or done if he has given permission for the action in advance. Once when Ijapa was in a foreign city, he asked to be permitted to ask a question. Permission was granted, and he asked, "Why is it that the nose of your oba (king) is so pointed?" The people regarded Ijapa's remark as an insult and prepared to punish him. But Ijapa said: "I asked your permission to ask a question. You gave me permission. Therefore I did not commit an offense." The people accepted Ijapa's reasoning.)

Nearness doesn't kill a bird; proverb of Ijapa.

(A near miss is not the same as accomplishment.)

As Ijapa arrived at his in-laws' house he exposed his penis, saying, "Nobody knows who might like to have a look."

(An action that is not in the interest of one part of the community may be in the interest of another part of the community.)

The Worship of Twins Among the Yoruba

In Yoruba tradition, twins—called ibejis—are a category of children quite apart from others, and are believed to have been sent among humans by monkeys. Ibejis are thought to have special powers to bring good or bad fortune to their families, and for this reason they are catered to in a way that other children are not. Parents do everything possible to please twins, responding to whims and wants which, if expressed by other children, would be ignored. It is felt by the parents that if they should fail to do so the ibejis might be disheartened or angered, in consequence of which misfortune rather than good fortune would come to the family. In particular, the orisha Ibeji, the protector deity of twins, might punish the parents by causing sickness or death to come, or crops to fail, or other disasters to fall upon the household. Yet the arrival of twins is always welcomed because of their power to better the lot of the parents. As stated in the following praise song, ibejis are considered to be special patrons of the poor:

> Fine-looking twins, natives of Ishokun,
> Descendants of treetop monkeys.
> Twins saw the houses of the rich but did not go there.
> Twins saw the houses of great personages but did not go there.
> Instead they entered the houses of the poor.
> They made the poor rich, they clothed those who were naked.

Various other praise songs emphasize the importance of treating ibejis well, as in this example:

> Unimportant objects in the eyes of the mother's rivals [co-wives],
> They are Two-at-a-Time in the eyes of their mother.
> Generous children who bring good luck to their father.
> Generous children who bring good luck to their mother.
> Slight me and I will follow [harass] you,
> Praise me and I will part from [not molest] you.

Another praise song says:

From Tales of Yoruba Gods and Heroes, © *1973 by Harold Courlander. By permission of Crown Publishers.*

Taiyewo [the first twin to arrive] asked me to greet you, and I
    do so.
Kehinde [the second to arrive] asked me to greet you, and I do
    so.
The ibejis asked for you to be fortunate.
The ibejis asked for you to be wealthy.
Had I known I would have followed the monkeys [who created
    the first twins] to Ishokun [the place where twinning began].

The orisha Ibeji is worshipped or supplicated only by parents who
have twin children, but he is widely respected by others because of his
readiness to punish anyone who slights or abuses twins. If a mother
takes her twin infants to the marketplace (sometimes accompanied by
a drummer who sings praise songs) and solicits gifts for them, people are
likely to give something lest the orisha Ibeji become offended. The
desires of infant ibejis are sometimes learned through consultations
with a babalawo, or diviner. Ibejis may want their mother to beg in the
market, to dance in public, or to give parties for them. The mother will
fulfill such wishes as a matter of course.

The ibeji cult is widely believed to have begun at Ishokun, now
merged with Oyo. Numerous accounts say it was to a home in this town
that the monkeys sent the first twins. Some versions say the mother was
the wife of a poor farmer, while others say she was the wife of the oba,
or town chief, who ruled Ishokun. But the totemic relationship of twins
to monkeys is usually indicated. Some of the praise names or nicknames
of twins are references to monkeys—Edun, for example, meaning monkey, and Adanju-kale, meaning Glittering-Eyes-in-the-House.

Some variant Yoruba explanations of twins, however, make no reference to monkeys, and may reflect traditions and attitudes of cultural
groups outside the Yoruba area, or possibly some regional, perhaps
rustic, traditions among the Yoruba themselves. Among the Iyagba
Yoruba, on the northern fringe of the Yoruba area, it is said that the first
twins came as a result of competition between two wives of a certain
oba. Neither the iyale (the senior wife) nor the iyawo (the junior wife)
had given birth to a male child. Both recognized that whichever of
them could produce a male heir for the oba would have an enhanced
position in the household. So they went regularly to a certain shrine and
supplicated the orishas for boy children. One day the iyale would go to
the shrine, the following day the iyawo. Through their supplications the
two wives became pregnant and produced male children at about the
same time. But the orishas were particularly sympathetic to the
younger wife because she was badly treated by the older wife. And so
they gave her male twins, which was understood by the oba to be a sign
of heavenly favor for her. The iyawo's status in the household thereby
became enhanced.

While among the Yoruba twins are generally regarded as good fortune, among some other West African cultures (and possibly in early-
day Yoruba culture) twins were once considered to be omens of ill

fortune. One Yoruba tale reflects this contrary interpretation. It tells of a certain orisha-oba who suspects one of his wives of stealing his cowries. He lines them up and forces them to "draw straws," by which process he discovers the guilty one. This wife subsequently gives birth to twins as punishment for her crime.

Though twins began, according to some renditions of the dominant legend that follows, as abikus—children who die and come back again and again to torment their parents—the connection seems to have become vague and uncertain. Whether there was a higher mortality rate among twins than among nontwins—as would seem likely—there is no way of knowing. But the existence of an enormous number of ibeji carvings, some double, some single must mean something about the mortality rate for twin children. For the ibeji figures are records of twin children who died at an early age. These carvings form one of the most prolific categories of Yoruba wood sculpture.

Each ibeji carving represents a twin child, but it is more than a record or representation. It is considered a repository or home of a twin spirit, the object through which communication with a dead twin is achieved. If a twin dies in infancy the parents have an ibeji figure carved to "replace" it. If both twins die a set of two carvings is made. The carvings are not portraits. Except for sexual characteristics—and sometimes tribal marks or hairstyling—all the figures made by a particular carver are quite similar. If a family has some special distinction or attribute, some small variant may be indicated in the carvings. With few exceptions, the dead twins are conceived by the carver (and therefore by others) as adults, with adult sexual development and adult features. Carvings made in a particular community by various sculptors tend to have a common style, and by its style the origin of a carving frequently can be established.

The ibeji carvings are treated as though they were living. If one of the infant twins is dead the mother carries its wooden representation wherever she carries the living survivor. When she feeds the living twin she also puts the spoon to the mouth of the carving. If both twins are dead the mother tends both carvings. She may give a party for dead twins just as she would have if they were living, inviting children to come and enjoy refreshments and play games. Dead twins are not referred to as having died, but as having gone to another place, perhaps to a thriving commercial center somewhere from which place they will send money or other good fortune to their parents.

The continuing necessity for pleasing the ibejis, whether living or dead, and for placating the orisha who is their guardian can be and usually is costly. But the expenditures of effort and money are weighed against the harm that displeased ibejis can do and the good luck that satisfied ibejis can bring. Out of this endless pursuit of the goodwill of twins comes the Yoruba saying, "Dead ibeji expenses are expenses for the living."

There is a general belief, in Yoruba tradition, in rebirth. It is thought by many that a person who dies will be reborn, sometimes in the same family, sometimes in a far-off place. If a male child born after his father's death greatly resembles his father he may be named Babajide or Babatunde, meaning Father Comes Again. If a mother dies in childbirth a female infant born to her may be named Iyabo, meaning Mother Returns. It is not certain to what extent naming a child in this manner may be considered merely a token of affection for the departed parent. But in the case of abikus, previously referred to, the Yoruba do not doubt that these children die and come back again at the next pregnancy. Parents try in various ways to break the cycle of death and rebirth of abikus. They try to divert or discourage a presumed abiku child from dying. Sometimes they will disfigure it in some fashion so that its spirit companions will not want it to return to them. It may be given a name such as Kokumo (Do Not Die Again), Igbekoyi (The Bush Rejects This), Kotoyesi (One Who Does Not Deserve Honor), or Malomo (Don't Go Again).

How Twins Came Among the Yoruba

In ancient times in the town of Ishokun, which later became a part of Oyo, there was a farmer who was known everywhere as a hunter of monkeys. Because his fields produced good crops, monkeys came from the bush and fed there. The monkeys became a pestilence to the farmer. He tried to drive them away. But they came, they went, they returned again to feed. The farmer could not leave his fields unguarded. He and his sons took turns watching over the fields. Still the monkeys came and had to be driven away with stones and arrows.

Because of his desperation and anger the farmer went everywhere to kill monkeys. He hunted them in the fields, he hunted them in the bush, he hunted them in the forest, hoping to end the depredations on his farm. But the monkeys refused to depart from the region, and they continued their forays on the farmer's crops. They even devised ways of distracting the farmer and his sons. A few of them would appear at a certain place to attract attention. While the farmer and his sons attempted to drive them off, other monkeys went into the fields to feed on corn. The monkeys also resorted to juju. They made the rain fall so that whoever was guarding the fields would go home, thinking, "Surely the crops will be safe in such weather." But the monkeys fed while the rain fell. When the farmer discovered this he built a shelter in the fields, and there he or one of his sons stood guard even when water poured from the sky. In this contest many monkeys were killed, yet those that survived persisted.

The farmer had several wives. After one of them became pregnant an adahunse, or seer, of the town of Ishokun came to the farmer to warn him. He said, "There is danger and misfortune ahead because of your

From Tales of Yoruba Gods and Heroes, © 1973 by Harold Courlander, and reprinted by permission of Crown Publishers.

continual killing of the monkeys. They are wise in many things. They have great powers. They can cause an abiku child to enter your wife's womb. He will be born, stay a while, then die. He will be born again and die again. Each time your wife becomes pregnant he will be there in her womb, and each time he is born he will stay a while and then depart. This way you will be tormented to the end. The monkeys are capable of sending you an abiku. Therefore do not drive them away anymore. Cease hunting them in the bush. Let them come and feed."

The farmer listened, but he was not persuaded by what the adahunse had told him. He went on guarding his fields and hunting monkeys in the bush.

The monkeys discussed ways of retaliating for their sufferings. They decided that they would send two abikus to the farmer. Two monkeys transformed themselves into abikus and entered the womb of the farmer's pregnant wife. There they waited until the proper time. They emerged, first one then the other. They were the original twins to come among the Yoruba. They attracted much attention. Some people said, "What good fortune." Others said, "It is a bad omen. Only monkeys give birth to twins."

Because the twins were abikus they did not remain long among the living. They died and returned to reside among those not yet born. Time passed. Again the woman became pregnant. Again two children were born instead of one. They lived on briefly and again they departed. This is the way it went on. Each time the woman bore children they were ibejis, that is to say, twins. And they were also abikus who lived on a while and died.

The farmer became desperate over his succession of misfortunes. He went to consult a diviner at a distant place to discover the reason for his children's constantly dying. The diviner cast his palm nuts and read them. He said: "Your troubles come from the monkeys whom you have been harassing in your fields and in the bush. It is they who sent twin abikus into your wife's womb in retaliation for their suffering. Bring your killing of the monkeys to an end. Let them eat in your fields. Perhaps they will relent."

The farmer returned to Ishokun. He no longer drove the monkeys from his fields, but allowed them to come and go as they pleased. He no longer hunted them in the bush. In time his wife again gave birth to twins. They did not die. They lived on. But still the farmer did not know for certain whether things had changed, and he went again to the diviner for knowledge. The diviner cast his palm nuts and extracted their meaning. He said, "This time the twins are not abikus. The monkeys have relented. The children will not die and return, die and return. But twins are not ordinary people. They have great power to reward or punish other humans. Their protector is the orisha Ibeji. If a person abuses or neglects a twin, the orisha Ibeji will strike such a person with disease or poverty. He who treats the twins well will be rewarded with good fortune." The diviner again threw the palm nuts and read them. He said, "If the twins are pleased with life, good luck and prosperity will come to their parents. Therefore, do everything to make them happy in this world. Whatever they want, give it to them. Whatever they say to do, do it. Make sacrifices to the orisha Ibeji. Because twins were sent into the world by the monkeys, monkeys are sacred to them. Neither twins nor their families may eat the flesh of monkeys. This is what the palm nuts tell us."

When the farmer returned to Ishokun after consulting the diviner he told his wife what he had learned. Whatever the twins asked for, the parents gave it. If they said they wanted sweets they were given sweets. If they said to their mother, "Go into the marketplace and beg alms for us," the mother carried them to the marketplace and begged alms. If they said, "Dance with us," she carried them in her arms and danced.

They all lived on. The farmer's other wives also gave birth to twins. Prosperity came to the farmer of Ishokun and his family. He was fortunate in every way.

Because of their origin twins are often called edun, meaning monkey. Likewise they are referred to as adanjukale, meaning "with-glittering-eyes-in-the-house." The first of a set of twins to be born is considered the younger of the two. He is named Taiyewo, meaning "Come-to-Taste-Life." The second to be born is named Kehinde, meaning "Come-Last." He is the older of the two. It is said that Kehinde always sends Taiyewo ahead to find out if life is worth living.

It was the ancient confrontation with the monkeys at Ishokun that first brought twins into the world.

Two Tales from Benin

One of the traditional institutions for the transmission of stories among the Bini of Nigeria is the ibota, a family gathering in the early evening after the routine daily tasks have been completed. The content of the narratives is considered to be "history." Many tales concern the lives and fortunes of kings and chiefs, oth-

This introduction and the two Bini tales that follow are from "Story Telling in Benin," by Daniel Ben-Amos, in African Arts, Autumn 1967, *reprinted here by permission of Professor Ben-Amos and the Regents of the University of California.*

ers the adventures of ordinary villagers. According to Daniel Ben-Amos, a scholar in the field of Bini oral literature:

The art of telling Benin history involves both singing and speech. The songs are interspersed between the narrative episodes and often are an integral part of the plot. For example, in the story of "Ozolua and Izevbokun" the song serves a reflective function, enabling one of the main heroes to meditate upon the course of events. Similarly, in the tale of "Igioromi" one song is actually a commentary by a secondary character upon the nature of the hero. These songs provide a respite in the flow of actions. The second song in this tale, however, is an essential narrative dialogue put into rhythmical language and music. The audience takes part in the chorus and in this way participates in the storytelling itself. The narrator does not resort to any dramatic impersonation of the characters or to any external effects, such as gestures, in order to impress the listeners. He relies mainly upon the actual wording of the story and the sheer effect of the unfolding of the events. In that sense, Benin storytelling is more a verbal than a dramatic art.

Benin narratives do not have any required opening and closing formulae. The storyteller may start with the phrase ox'okpa ke do re, a story is coming, or ox'okpa siensiensien, this is a nice story. Then he introduces the main characters in the tale. In other cases he may begin with the main song and thus prepare his audience in a more active manner for what follows. For the conclusion the teller simply signifies evba ni oxa nan ya de wu, here the story dies.

The second story centers upon a common theme in Benin tradition, namely, the rivalry between the oba's sons. Succession to the throne followed the rule of primogeniture, but due to polygamy there was often more than one claimant to the throne.

The first tale, "Igioromi," is about a local hero who excelled in the favorite Bini sport of wrestling. Although the Bini consider Igioromi to be a historical figure, it is hardly surprising to find similar tales in other West African traditions.

Igioromi

> Solo: Do not wrestle with them, O
> Chorus: Igioromi, Omigior[1]
> Solo: Do not wrestle with them
> Chorus: Igioromi, Omigior
> Solo: You have wrestled all over the world
> Chorus: Igioromi, Omigior
> Solo: Now you are going to the spirit world
> Chorus: Igioromi, Omigior
> Solo: Nobody in the world could defeat you
> Chorus: Igioromi Omigior
> Solo: The spirits will not be able to defeat you
> Chorus: Igioromi, Omigior
> Solo: Kere Kese[2]
> Chorus: Igioromi, Omigior
> Solo: Kiri Kisi
> Chorus: Igioromi, Omigior

Igioromi was a very devilish person. He was so clever that he could wrestle and no one had ever thrown him to the ground. Whenever he would come to any place where a wrestling contest was going on, he would defeat every wrestler with only one hand. He would knock them all down; he wrestled on and on. Then one day he took a rope and climbed a palm tree, although he had been warned never to do so. When he saw that his father and mother had gone to the farm, he began to climb palm trees, one after the other. As he was climbing one tree, he looked down and saw that they were wrestling in the spirit world. He said, "Ho! Why am I wasting my time here? Look at that wrestling contest." He climbed down the tree, and when he reached ground he ran as quickly as he could along the road holding up his pants. At that moment his brother Ekpofi turned himself into a bluebottle fly and followed him. Igioromi reached the spirit world and descended into it. When he had arrived there, he began to follow the spirits. He lifted up one of them and threw him down. He lifted another and threw him down. When his brother saw this, he said: "What! Woe is me! How can I make him return home?" He started to sing:

> Solo: Do not wrestle with them, O
> Chorus: Igioromi, Omigior
> Solo: You have wrestled all over the world
> Chorus: Igioromi, Omigior
> Solo: Now you are going to the spirit world
> Chorus: Igioromi, Omigior
> Solo: Nobody in the world could defeat you

---

1. *The name Igioromi with a reverse syllable order.*
2. *Kere Kese and Kiri Kisi: Onomatopoeia imitating the sound of a calabash rattle.*

> Chorus: Igioromi, Omigior
> Solo: Kere Kese
> Chorus: Igioromi, Omigior
> Solo: Kiri Kisi
> Chorus: Igioromi, Omigior

Igioromi caught another one, swung him around his head, and threw him down. That one died like the others. In the spirit world any person who hits the ground must die. So he died also. As Igioromi gripped another spirit, his brother began to sing.

> Solo: Don't wrestle with them, O
> Chorus: Igioromi, Omigior
> Solo: Do not wrestle with them, O
> Chorus: Igioromi, Omigior
> Solo: You have wrestled all over the world, O
> Chorus: Igioromi, Omigior
> Solo: Now you are going to the spirit world, O
> Chorus: Igioromi, Omigior
> Solo: Nobody in the world could defeat you
> Chorus: Igioromi, Omigior
> Solo: The spirits will not be able to defeat you
> Chorus: Igioromi, Omigior
> Solo: Kere Kese
> Chorus: Igioromi O, Omigior
> Solo: Kiri Kisi
> Chorus: Igioromi O, Omigior

Igioromi lifted another of them, swung him around his head, and threw him down. He grasped another one and hit him in the same way. This was the fourth one he killed. There remained three more with whom he still had to wrestle. His brother broke into song:

> Solo: Do not wrestle with them, O
> Chorus: Igioromi, Omigior
> Solo: Do not wrestle with them, O
> Chorus: Igioromi, Omigior
> Solo: You have wrestled all over the world, O
> Chorus: Igioromi, Omigior
> Solo: Now you are going to the spirit world, O
> Chorus: Igioromi, Omigior
> Solo: Nobody in the world could defeat you, O
> Chorus: Igioromi, Omigior
> Solo: The spirits will not be able to defeat you, O
> Chorus: Kere Kese
> Solo: Kiri Kisi
> Chorus: Igioromi O, Omigior

Igioromi did it again. There were only two left. He followed one of the two, who was the sixth among them. They began to shake each other, holding one another by the upper arms.[3] Again his brother broke into song:

> Solo: Do not wrestle with them, O
> Chorus: Igioromi, Omigior
> Solo: Do not wrestle with them, O
> Chorus: Igioromi, Omigior
> Solo: You have wrestled the world over
> Chorus: Igioromi, Omigior
> Solo: Now you go to the spirit world
> Chorus: Igioromi, Omigior
> Solo: Nobody in the world has defeated you
> Chorus: Igioromi, Omigior
> Solo: The spirits will not be able to defeat you
> Chorus: Igioromi, Omigior
> Solo: Kere Kese
> Chorus: Igioromi, Omigior
> Solo: Kiri Kisi
> Chorus: Igioromi, Omigior

Igioromi lifted him and threw him down. After that he followed Ugbogiorinmwin, the seven-headed monster.[4] It grasped Igioromi and with just one hand threw him up and Igioromi fell flat on the ground and died. "Oh!" his brother exclaimed, "Woe is me! Didn't I tell him this would happen!"

The seven-headed monster plucked a leaf from the roadside, ground it up and used it to revive all the six spirits that Igioromi had killed. It woke them up, every one of them. When all of them had gotten up it said, "Look at the person who killed you." It said, "Look at him. I killed him." They said, "Well done. Aren't we going to eat him now?"

Some of them left to fetch water, others went to bring pepper and others to bring salt. The rest said they were going to bring other materials which were necessary for cooking. They divided the work among themselves. The Ugbogiorinmwin who killed Igioromi went to look for the *unien*,[5] which gives flavor to food. All of them went away. They left the dead body lying on the ground. When the monster left, Ekpofi, Igioromi's brother, carefully went down. He took the leaf with which Ugbogiorinmwin had awakened the others not very long ago, and, whispering a charm, revived his brother with it. When Igioromi woke up he told him: "Don't you see in what trouble you are now? Didn't I

---

3. *This is the first phase in wrestling, called sikan. After that the partners let go of each other and the real match starts.*
4. *The monster who lives in the spirit world. It breathes flames, blood, and smoke. It is considered as a king of bogey and there is no belief in it.*
5. *A fruit of the tree of* Xylopia aethiopica. *It is used as an ingredient in pepper soup.*

tell you not to go and you didn't listen! Let us escape."

They ran away as fast as they could.

Those who had gone to bring firewood and water encountered Igi-oromi on the road. They looked him over. "This is like an elephant, like an elephant's leg!" The boy Igioromi began to sing:

Solo: It isn't I, father. Yesterday I went to war. Today I am
         coming back.
Chorus: Safe return[6] home!

He passed by them. When another met him he said:

Solo: This is like the hand
         I left dead on the ground
         This is like the leg
         I left dead on the ground.
Chorus: It isn't, it isn't, father.
         Yesterday I went to war.
         Today I am coming back.
         Safe return home!

He let him pass on. After Igioromi walked some distance another one asked him these questions and he answered likewise, and so he passed by. It happened like this several times. He travelled on and on. When he approached home another stopped him and said: "He is just like the one I killed on the ground, like the one I put on the ground." The boy jumped forward.

Solo: It isn't, father.
         Yesterday I went to war.
Chorus: Today I am coming back.
         Safe return home.

And he passed by. When he went farther on he met Ugbogiorinmwin. The monster looked him up and down and said, "This is the man I killed." The boy began to sing:

Solo: It is not I, it is not I, father.
Chorus: Yesterday I went to war.
         Today I am coming back.
         Safe return home!

In this way he got past them all and began to run. He approached his house. Just as he drew near his house the spirits returned from their errands and realized that he had run away. Then they asked the one-

---

6. *Lyare, a formula used for blessing the warriors on going out to war and welcoming them back.*

legged spirit to go and fetch him. He said, "All right. But if you send me, by the time I have managed to hobble this way and that, won't he have reached home?" The two-legged spirit said, "By the time I have branched out this way and that, won't he have reached home?"

"You, three-legged, go after him!"

"By the time I have panicked this way and that, won't he have reached home?"

The four-legged said, "Before I have defecated this way and that, won't he have reached home?"

The five-legged said, "Before I have jumped this way and that, won't he have reached home?"

The six-legged said, "Before I have bent this way and that, won't he have reached home?"[7]

Ugbogiorinmwin said that he himself would go after him. It placed one leg on the crossroads between the spirit world and earth and placed its other leg at the gate of the boy's home. The boy quickly ran inside. The monster tried to catch him, but only managed to scratch some skin off his back with its thumbnail. The monster said: "This is very tasty. My share in the common feast would never have been so large." Then it went back. When it got there it told them that it had been able to lay hands on Igioromi and showed them its thumb. "Look at the thumb that I used in scratching him." They began to lick its thumb one after the other and licked and licked until the thumb became very small.

Evba ni oxa nan ya de wu.

Here the story dies.

Ozolua and Izevbokun

This is a story about Ozolua and Esigie and all the people of Benin. Oba n'Osa, who created man, also made Esigie. Esigie was the senior brother, Izevbokun came next, and Ozolua was the youngest. They were brought up in Urorla. They were sent to the place called Urora. There they were nourished. There they were brought up. When they reached maturity, the earth ate chalk.[1] The people sent for them, so that Izevbokun could be made oba of Benin. Ozolua said that he would accompany him part of the way. They prepared themselves and started on the road to Benin. All the children of the oba followed them. Yes, so it was. As they approached Benin, the people said: "What is this? Two children of the oba are coming to be kings of Benin?" "What is this?" they said, "Izevbokun is not worthy to be the oba. Ozolua is the one who is fit for the throne."

---

7. *This dialogue is based on word play constructing the verbs which designate each action upon the number of legs of each character. "Okpa-one, kpa-to hobble (onomatopoeia); eva-two, va-to branch into side roads; eha-three, ha-to panic; even-four, nen-to defecate; isen-five; san-to jump; ehan-six, han-to bend.*

1. *Oto ri'orhue, a euphemistic expression referring to the burial of the oba.*

"So that is the case." Izevbokun had been told that Ozolua would bring trouble.

The people began to follow Ozolua. Izevbokun started to sing. He sang:

Solo: I did not ask my brother to follow me
Chorus: Ighi do
Solo: I did not ask my brother to follow me
Chorus: Ighi do
Solo: Eguanran[2] cleared some farmland in Oka
Chorus: Ighi do
Solo: The yam pickers picked yam and planted it in his farm
Chorus: Ighi do
Solo: The owner of the yam is the owner of the land
Chorus: Ighi do
Solo: I did not ask my brother to follow me

They passed by those people. After they went on for some time, other onlookers came to watch them. They said, "What! Is this the person who is coming to be oba?"

Izevbokun said, "Yes."

They said, "What!" They said, "The other one is worthy to be oba. It is he whom we will crown as king."

They moved on a little farther and Izevbokun began to sing again. They went on until they reached the Ikpoba river. When they arrived there, they called at the house of the priest of Ore.[3] The priest gave Ozolua two hundred men and two hundred women.[4] He who was supposed to be the king was not recognized at all.

Izevbokun remarked bitterly, "So it has already started."

They went on and Izevbokun sang:

Solo: I did not ask my brother to follow me
Chorus: Ighi do
Solo: I did not ask my brother to follow me
Chorus: Ighi do
Solo: Ezoro cleared some farmland in Oka
Chorus: Ighi do
Solo: Ozolua picked yam and planted it in his land
Chorus: Ighi do
Solo: The owner of the yam is the owner of the land
Chorus: Ighi do
Solo: I did not ask my brother to follow me
Chorus: Ighi do

2. A proverbial giant.
3. Another name for Ikpoba river.
4. A formulistic number used in describing the procession of the oba.

They went on. They walked until they reached Okedo.[5] The people there repeated what the other groups had said before. They said, "Izevbokun is not worthy to be oba."

They said, "Ozolua is the one who is fit for the throne." When they reached Benin, the chiefs of the city repeated what the people on the road had said. They proclaimed, "Ozolua is the one whom we will crown as oba." They made Ozolua the oba of Benin. They sent Izevbokun to rule over Ogbe.[6] The Ikhimwin[7] tree of Ezoti[8] is still there today.

How Bronze Castings Were Made at Benin

According to tradition, the art of bronze or brass casting was brought to maturity in the city of Ife, from whence the knowledge spread to other kingdoms. This is not to say that the Ife artisans possessed a secret unknown to other peoples in the region. But Ife was, clearly, a center renowned both for the excellence of its art and for the great skill with which its craftsmen transformed wax sculptures into bronze. Benin, famous in the field of art for its bronze sculptures, is said to have acquired its casting techniques from Ife. Bini tradition says that it was Igueghae, a great craftsman from Ife, sent by the king of that city-state, who brought the sophisticated bronze technology to Benin. Igueghae is thought to have arrived in Benin during the reign of King Oguola during the closing years of the fourteenth century. The style of art developed in Benin was highly stylized in contrast to the naturalistic, even idealized, sculpture of Ife. The Bini court art followed its own course, but its bronze-casting technology derived considerable benefits from

5. *The first quarter within the city wall.*
6. *A quarter near the palace.*
7. *This tree is believed to be the oldest tree in the world and is used in the worship of Osa, the High God. It is identified as* Newbouldia Caevis.
8. *An oba. According to Jacob U. Egharevba,* A Short History of Benin *(Ibadan, 1960), pp. 21–23, 75, Ezoti preceded Oba Ozolua.*

the knowledge made available by Ife. Following herewith is a description by a Hausa tribes-
man—undoubtedly a craftsman himself—of
how the now-famous Benin bronzes were
made.

In the name of Allah the Compassionate, the Merciful. This account
will show how the figures are made. This work is one to cause wonder.
Now this kind of work is done.with clay, and wax, and red metal [cop-
per], and solder [zinc], and lead, and fire. The first thing to be done if
one of the figures is to be made, is to get clay and work it most
thoroughly, and get the little stones which are in it worked out. It is well
worked in the hands. Next the shape of the top of a head is constructed
[from the clay], and then the jaws on the same piece as the top of the
head. Then the nose is shaped, and the eyes and the lips made. Then
a certain stick which has been shaped like a knife is put [against the
model] and it is smoothed [with this]. A very little water is put on when
it is being thus smoothed until it is perfect; then it is set in the sun to
dry. Next wax is melted and poured over it [the clay model, and] then
it is gone over [again] with the knife. As it [the wax] hardens it is
smoothed over. When it has been well done, then a fire is kindled, [and]
a knife put in the fire. When it is slightly warm it is taken up and pressed
over the wax in order that it may adhere well [to the clay foundation].
The eyes get the finishing touches, [and] the eyebrows, and mouth and
chin and beard. Then this stick like a knife is got out [and] dipped in
water [and] pressed against the wax, [and] passed over it—it is well
smoothed [and] shines [all over]. If the model is of a woman's head then
the hair adornment is put on. How the adornment of the hair is made,
is as follows. Wax is rolled out till it is like a string—water is used; it
forms a long piece. Then he [the smith] cuts it into pieces [and] fastens
them on top of the head. Then he takes a razor [and] cuts [them the
required length]. Next he cuts off other short pieces of wax [and] sticks
them along the head. Then he rolls out another bit of wax with water,
making it long like a rope. He divides it in two [down the middle, not
across], lays them side by side, and puts them on the top of the first
upright pieces and sticks [the whole] on. The part left over he cuts off
[and] casts aside. Then he prepares a certain broad piece of wax and
makes ears out of it [and] fixes them on. But whenever he is about to
stick any piece on, first he puts the knife in the fire and presses it against
the wax. Then he sits down—this [part of the work] is completed. There
remains the pouring in of the metal. When he has finished [the part just
described] he takes up mud [and] covers the whole head with it, leaving
only a small hole. He puts it in the sun to dry—this part is finished.
There remains the pouring in of the metal.
  This description is of the pouring in of the metal. The way the metal

The description is reprinted from Hausa Folk-Lore, Customs, Proverbs, *by R. S. Rattray. Oxford, The Claredon, Press, 1913.*

is poured in is [as follows]. When the fire has been brought it is poured into the melting-furnace, [and] the bellows are set to work [and] the fire blown [and] charcoal poured in. Then the model is lifted [and] placed on the fire. Water is poured into a pot or cup. When the model has become heated then the wax inside melts. Then it is taken up, the tongs, or some [take] a stick, are placed across the pot [of water], and the figure put on top, and the wax keeps dropping out. And it is held so till all the wax has melted and dropped into the water. Then a great quantity of charcoal is poured [into the furnace]. The figure [in clay] is set on the fire. Bars of metal are continually being cut with a hammer; many pieces are broken up in this way, [and] put in the smelting-pot. Then they scrape out a hole in the charcoal and put the smelting-pot in, replace the charcoal again, [and] cover up. The [mud] figure is brought and set. [It is set] on the fire. They keep blowing the bellows, and this clay lump is turned till red-hot. Then the metal has melted, then the figure is taken up, a hole is dug, [and] it is placed in it so that it is firmly set. The hole left in the clay is cleared out and the melted metal poured in. If it is filled, that is well; if not, more is added to fill it. If full then [the work] is finished. Next it is set aside to cool, then [the outside covering of clay] is broken off. Then you see a beautiful figure. That is it. The work . . . is completed.

Onugbo and Oko

A POEM OF THE IDOMA PEOPLE OF NIGERIA

This is a sacred poem about Oko, one of the ancestors of the Idoma people. The Idoma are agriculturalists living along the Benue River about a hundred miles east of the Niger. The story tells of two inseparable brothers, Oko and Onugbo, who go on an extended hunt together. As the story develops it is seen that Oko is a great hunter, but that he displays his prowess to an excess. After Oko drinks at a certain water hole a spirit horse muddies the water, and Onugbo believes it is Oko who has committed this offense. Out of jealousy and anger Onugbo kills Oko, but he is filled with remorse when he finds out that the mischief at the water hole was done by a bush spirit. Back in the village the people accept Oko's death as a hunting accident, but Onugbo cannot forgive himself. He turns himself into a bird who goes about endlessly calling the name of Oko. The story

From text accompanying the record album, Music of the Idoma of Nigeria, by Robert G. Armstrong. Sponsored by the Institute of African Studies, University of Ibadan, and UNESCO. By permission of Asch Records, New York.

thus explains why the evening bird known as
onugbo gives the call "okoe." It is also an implicit comment on the rivalry of brothers.
Above all, it is part of the Idoma people's recol-
lection of their ancient past.

Eleelele, (mother) who bore me,
    My father, O!
Ajeega and Oko, Onugbo and Oko,
What caused the trouble between
    Onugbo and Oko?
Oko, Ajeega Joogwugwu,[1]
What caused the trouble between
    Onugbo and Oko?
Oko, Ajeega!
If Onugbo did not see Oko he would not go.
If Oko did not see Onugbo, his brother,
    He would not go!
What did cause the trouble between
    Onugbo and Oko, now?

Eleeee ye!
When Oko went hunting,
Oko said, "Onugbo, my brother!"
    Onugbo the brother of Oko,
Onugbo and Oko went as a pair:
"Let us go as a pair in case of trouble!"
As Oko has gone hunting,
Onugbo and his brother Oko
    have gone hunting.
Oko killed fourteen lions,
Oko killed fifteen leopards.

Oko was about to go to the stream,
On turning sharply to go there to the stream
Oko killed seven mongooses,
Then it was that Oko made his ogwu.[2]
As Oko pushed on
They hunted long
On the third day,
On the fourth day
Oko and Onugbo his brother hunted
    from early morning
Oko's gun spoke kpitii!!

1. *Ajeega Joogwugwu: Oko's title.*
2. *Ogwu: The acclamation for a brave deed.*

Oko had killed an elephant!
Despite the elephant Oko had killed,
    Oko went on hunting.
Oko saw a water pond,
    A pond which was at the foot of a tree there.
An evil spirit is going to cause trouble
    Between Onugbo and Oko his brother!
Eleelele, a white horse is not easy to ride.
As Oko left off (hunting)
As Oko Ajega turned away
Oko drank his fill.
Oko called out,
    "Onugbo, my brother,
    Onugbo, brother of Oko, come oh!
    Come, water is here oh!"
Ah, because Oko saw water,
That is why he asked . . .
    Went to call Onugbo, his brother.

Agabi Idoma![3]
When Oko had drunk his fill,
    As he had come,
    Then Onugbo came to drink water
Idoma, Father who begot me!
An evil spirit had stirred up the water.
A white horse came to drink water
    And stirred the water up completely.
    Then he stole away.
Onugbo began to call Oko, his brother.
"Oko!
Why have you spoilt the water for me?"
Onugbo asked Oko,
    "Oko, why have you spoilt the water for me?"
Oko said: "Onugbo, my brother,
    It was not I who muddied the water.
It was an evil spirit that muddied the water here.
Onugbo, brother of Oko,
    The water which I saw just now,
Agabi Idoma!
That is the reason why I shouted
    Calling you!"

Anger boiled in the heart of Onugbo, brother of Oko.
Oko went on, Oko,
Oko went on hunting.

---

3. *Agabi Idoma: the legendary ancient home of the Idoma people. Used as an exclamation.*

"Onugbo, my brother,
    Though the water was muddied,
    Still you should cool your heart!
    When we have hunted for a while
    We should come upon another pond."

Anger boiled in the heart of Onugbo, brother of Oko.
Though Onugbo had turned away,
    Elee, Oko started on his hunt again.
Then Oko called,
    "Onugbo, my brother,
      Come a while! Come a while!"
Then Onugbo changed,
    Raising his gun,
    "Oko, Oko, my brother it is you who muddied that water!"
Oko said, "It was not I who muddied the water."
Oko, Oko said, "It was not I who muddied the water."
Eleee!
Oko said: "Onugbo, my brother,
    If you don't see me, you don't go;
    If I don't see you, I too don't go!
    What has caused this trouble?
    It was a bad spirit that muddied the water
    Onugbo, brother of Oko,
    I am sorry! Do not be angry!"

Then Oko turned away,
Oko began to hunt, [saying]
    "Onugbo, come!"
Oko!
Oko's gun spoke kputuu!
Oko had killed a leopard!
    The mongoose which . . .[4]
Because of the leopard Oko had killed
    He shouted:
    "Onugbo, my brother, come quickly, oh
    Come and cleanse my face with honor for the leopard."
The honor-cleansing of the leopard
    That Onugbo has come to wash from Oko's face, now!
    Eleeee!
Onugbo came up close to Oko
    There.
Then Onugbo said, "Oko, it is you who muddied the water for me!"
Then Onugbo, the brother of Oko, changed.
Oko said, "It was not I who muddied the water!"
Onugbo's gun spoke kputuu!

---

4. *This line difficult of translation. A proverb.*

Now Onugbo had killed Oko, his brother
Eleelelee leele elee!
Then Oko . . . and Oko . . .
    Oko said, "It was not I who muddied the water,
    Onugbo, I am going forever . . ."

Agabi Idoma!
Olodu Bogeena, House of my Father!
After this he then came and saw the white horses in the pond.
They had come to stir up the water in a mess!
Onugbo cried out: "Wooo
    Oko, my brother,
Okoo, Okoo Okajeega ii!
Elee! Had I but known!"
"Had I but known" is a late-born child,
It is not a first-born child.
Then he went back.
The council gathered together,
    The lineage of the father who begot
    Onugbo and Oko.
Ogeba, father who begot me!
Oko was a real man,
    Onugbo was a weakling.
Ah, oh!
Longing for Oko was dawning upon Onugbo.
The council assembled,
And the answers that Oko would give before the council of his
    father
Onugbo could not give.
And Onugbo was angry, "Oko, my brother,
It was an evil spirit that caused trouble between us."
And Onugbo said: "I can no longer bear
    The ill treatment by the people at home.
    Oko, my brother has gone.
    Instead of continuing I will fly up
    To become a bird in the bush!"
This is the cause of the longing,
    Why Onugbo seeks Oko.
Onugbo calls Oko,
    When the sun rises early in the morning
Onugbo seeks his brother, Oko,
    When the sun is low in evening
When the sun is disappearing
    And the ancestral spirit-masks go home
Onugbo seeks Oko,
Onugbo calls, "Oko, Oko!
Ajega, my brother, oh, Oko!
Oko!

Oko!
Oko of Onugbo!"
This is the cause of the longing,
Why Onugbo seeks Oko!

THREE ISOKO SONGS FROM ILUE-OLOGBO

**The Isoko-speaking peoples, of Edo and Ibo
origins, live in the northwestern region of the
Niger Delta. The Isoko songs that follow are
from the village of Ilue-Ologbo, bordering on
Urhobo country.**

I Dance Despite Death

I dance despite death, mother,
I dance despite death.
On my father's side is death;
On my mother's side is death.
I dance despite death, mother,
I dance despite death.
Whatever happens, I accept it.

Let Me Drink Wine

Let me drink wine.
We don't come twice to this world, my brother.
That of today is what I know;
That of tomorrow I cannot know.
He took plantains and went to Igbo-land;
With my ears I heard that Death killed him.

From "Isoko Songs of Ilue-Ologbo," by Philip M. Peek and N. E. Owheibor,
African Arts, *Winter 1971. By permission of Philip M. Peek and the Regents of
the University of California.*

Let me drink wine.
We don't come twice to this world, my brother.

Destiny! O Death!

Umubu now weeps.
"My daughter who is married at Aka,
Two days ago she was ill,
Yesterday she is dying;
Those who come from Aka bring the death news.
Death ho! ho! ho! ho!"
Umubu weeps, "My life is this?
My daughter has reached the other world."
Umubu, do and go, marriage fails you.
Awokererie ran to the scene, choking sobs.
"My life is this?
Destiny! O Death!"

THE EKOI PEOPLE OF THE CALABAR COAST:
THEIR TRADITIONS ABOUT ORIGINS OF THINGS

Obassi Nsi and Obassi Osaw

> The following is a dialogue that took place be-
> tween a well-known specialist in the field of
> Ekoi traditions, P. Amaury Talbot, and an Ekoi
> elder on the nature of Obassi, the Ekoi su-
> preme deity.

"Who is Obassi Nsi?"
"He is Obassi who is kind to us."
"Where does he live?"

This dialogue and the origin stories which follow are from In the Shadow of
the Bush, *by P. Amaury Talbot. London, Heinemann, 1912.*

"Under the earth. There is a world beneath the earth whose king is Obassi Nsi."

"Which do you think the more powerful—Obassi Nsi or Obassi Osaw?"

"Both are powerful, but Osaw is cruel and Nsi kind and good."

"Why then do you pray to Obassi Osaw?"

"Obassi Nsi told us to do so, that Osaw might spare our lives, for the latter always seeks to kill us."

"How do you know that Osaw is fierce and cruel?"

"Because he tries to kill us with thunder and in many other ways. Also, he is not so loving and near to us as Obassi Nsi, for he cannot receive our offerings. We sometimes throw things up into the air for him, but they always fall back again to the earth. Obassi Nsi draws them down; that shows he is more powerful."

"How do you know that Obassi Nsi is good?"

"He never shows us terrifying things as Osaw does, such as thunder or lightning, nor the sun which blazes so hot as to frighten us sometimes, and the rain which falls so heavily at others as to make us think there will be no more sunshine. Nsi ripens our yams, cocos, plantains, etc., which we plant in the ground. When we are dead we are buried in the ground, and go to the world under the earth, to our Father Obassi Nsi."

"What do you think happens to you when you are buried?"

"When a man's body decays, a new form comes out of it, in every way like the man himself when he was aboveground. This new shape goes down to its Lord, Obassi Nsi, carrying with it all that was spent on its funeral in the world above."

"You said that Obassi Nsi told you to make offerings to Obassi Osaw. Why then does he draw them down to himself, as you say he does?"

"He draws them back because he is greater than Osaw. Besides, he wants the latter to come to him, that they may divide the offerings between them. They are, of course, friends."

"Does Obassi Nsi ever want to kill you?"

"No, he would like us to live always; but when Osaw kills us, Nsi takes us to his country under the earth."

"You said that you were told to make offerings to Osaw, in order that he might spare your lives. How then can Nsi, who does not want you to die, partake of these?"

(Hesitation and shy laughter.)

"I told you that they are friends. They talk together and eat together. I think that Obassi Nsi is really our mother and Osaw our father. For whenever we make offerings we are taught to say Nta Obassi (Lord Obassi) and Ma Obassi (Lady Obassi). Now I think that the lord is Osaw, and the lady Nsi. Surely Nsi must be a woman, and our mother, for it is well known to all people that a woman has the tenderest heart."

How the First Rain Came

Once, long ago, a daughter was born to Obassi Osaw, and a son to Obassi Nsi. When both had come to marriageable age, Nsi sent a message to say: "Let us exchange children. I will send my son that he may wed one of your maidens. Send your daughter down to my town, that she may become my wife."

To this Obassi Osaw agreed. So the son of Nsi went up to the heavens carrying many fine gifts, and Ara, the sky maiden, came down to dwell on earth. With her came seven men-slaves and seven women-slaves, whom her father sent that they might work for her, so that she should not be called upon to do anything herself.

One day, very early in the morning, Obassi Nsi said to his new wife, "Go, work in my farm!" She answered: "My father gave me the slaves so that they should work instead of me. Therefore send them." Obassi Nsi was very angry and said: "Did you not hear that I gave my orders to you. You yourself shall work in my farm. As for the slaves, I will tell them what to do."

The girl went, though very unwillingly, and when she returned at night, tired out, Nsi said to her: "Go at once to the river and bring water for the household."

She answered: "I am weary with working in the farm; may not my slaves at least do this while I rest?"

Again Nsi refused, and drove her forth, so she went backward and forward many times, carrying the heavy jars. Night had fallen long before she had brought enough.

Next morning Nsi bade her do the most menial services, and all day long kept her at work, cooking, fetching water, and making fire. That night again she was very weary before she might lie down to rest. At dawn on the third morning he said, "Go and bring in much firewood." Now the girl was young and unused to work, so as she went she wept, and the tears were still falling when she came back carrying her heavy burden.

As soon as Nsi saw her enter he called to her: "Come here and lie down before me. . . . I wish to shame you in the presence of all my people. . . ." On that the girl wept still more bitterly.

No food was given her till midday on the morrow, and then not enough. When she had finished eating up all there was, Nsi said to her, "Go out and bring in a great bundle of fish poison."

The girl went into the bush to seek for the plant, but as she walked through the thick undergrowth a thorn pierced her foot. She lay down alone. All day long she lay there in pain, but as the sun sank she began to feel better. She got up and managed to limp back to the house.

When she entered, Nsi said to her: "Early this morning I ordered you to go and collect fish poison. You have stayed away all day and done nothing." So he drove her into the goat pen, and said, "Tonight you shall sleep with the goats; you shall not enter my house."

That night she ate nothing. Early next morning one of the slaves opened the door of the goat pen, and found the girl lying within, with her foot all swollen and sore. She could not walk, so for five days she was left with the goats. After that her foot began to get better.

So soon as she could walk again at all, Nsi called her and said: "Here is a pot. Take it to the river, and bring it back filled to the brim."

She set out, but when she reached the waterside, she sat down on the bank and dipped her foot in the cool stream. She said to herself, "I will never go back; it is better to stay here alone."

After a while one of the slaves came down to the river. He questioned her: "At dawn this morning you were sent to fetch water. Why have you not returned home?"

The girl said, "I will not come back."

When the slave had left her she thought: "Perhaps he will tell them, and they will be angered and may come and kill me. I had better go back after all." So she filled her pot and tried to raise it onto her head, but it was too heavy. Next she lifted it onto a tree trunk that lay by the side of the river, and, kneeling beneath, tried to draw it, in that way, onto her head, but the pot fell and broke, and in falling a sharp sherd cut off one of her ears. The blood poured down from the wound, and she began to weep again, but suddenly thought: "My father is alive, my mother is alive, I do not know why I stay here with Obassi Nsi. I will go back to my own father."

Then she set out to find the road by which Obassi Osaw had sent her to earth. She came to a high tree, and from it saw a long rope hanging. She said to herself, "This is the way by which my father sent me."

She caught the rope and began to climb. Before she reached halfway she grew very weary, and her sighs and tears mounted up to the kingdom of Obassi Osaw. When she reached midway she stayed and rested a while. Afterwards she climbed on again.

After a long time she reached the top of the rope, and found herself on the border of her father's land. Here she sat down almost worn out with weariness, and still weeping.

Now, one of the slaves of Obassi Osaw had been sent out to collect firewood. He chanced to stray on and on, and came to the place near where the girl was resting. He heard her sobs mixed with broken words, and ran back to the town, crying out: "I have heard the voice of Ara. She is weeping about a mile from here."

Obassi heard but could not believe, yet he said, "Take twelve slaves, and, should you find my daughter as you say, bring her here."

When they reached the place they found that it was Ara for true. So they carried her home.

When her father saw her coming he called out, "Take her to the house of her mother."

There one of the lesser wives, Akun by name, heated water and bathed her. Then they prepared a bed, and covered her well with soft skins and fine cloths.

While she was resting, Obassi killed a young kid and sent it to Akun, bidding her prepare it for his daughter. Akun took it, and after she had washed it, cooked it whole in a pot. Also Obassi sent a great bunch of plantains and other fruits, and these also they set, orderly upon a table before the girl. Next they poured water into a gourd, and brought palm wine in a native cup, bidding her drink.

After she had eaten and drunk, Obassi came with four slaves carrying a great chest made of ebony. He bade them set it before her, opened it and said, "Come here; choose anything you will from this box."

Ara chose two pieces of cloth, three gowns, four small loincloths, four looking glasses, four spoons, two pairs of shoes (at £I), four cooking pots, and four chains of beads.

After this Obassi Osaw's storekeeper, named Ekpenyon, came forward and brought her twelve anklets. Akun gave her two gowns, a fu-fu stick and a wooden knife.

Her own mother brought her five gowns, richer than all the rest, and five slaves to wait upon her.

After this Obassi Osaw said, "A house has been got ready for you, go there that you may be its mistress."

Next he went out and called together the members of the chief "club" of the town. This was named Angbu. He said to the men: "Go; fetch the son of Obassi Nsi. Cut off both his ears and bring them to me. Then flog him and drive him down the road to his father's town, with this message from me: 'I had built a great house up here in my town. In it I placed your son, and treated him kindly. Now that I know what you have done to my child, I send back your son to you earless, in payment for Ara's ear, and the sufferings which you put upon her.'"

When the Angbu Club had cut off the ears of the son of Obassi Nsi, they brought them before Obassi Osaw, and drove the lad back on the earthward road, as they had been ordered.

Osaw took the ears and made a great juju, and by reason of this a strong wind arose, and drove the boy earthward. On its wings it bore all the sufferings of Ara, and the tears which she had shed through the cruelty of Obassi Nsi. The boy stumbled along, half-blinded by the rain, and as he went he thought: "Obassi Osaw may do to me what he chooses. He had never done any unkind thing before. It is only in return for my father's cruelty that I must suffer all this."

So his tears mixed with those of Ara and fell earthward as rain.

Up till that time there had been no rain on the earth. It fell for the first time when Obassi Osaw made the great wind and drove forth the son of his enemy.

How the Moon First Came into the Sky

In a certain town there lived Njomm Mbui (juju sheep). He made great friends with Etuk (antelope), whose home was in the bush.

When the two animals grew up they went out and cut farms. Njomm planted plantains in his, while Etuk set his with coco-yams.

When the time came round for the fruits to ripen, Njomm went to his farm and cut a bunch of plantains, while Etuk dug up some of his coco.

Each cleaned his food and put it in the pot to cook. When all was ready they sat down and ate.

Next morning Etuk said: "Let us change. I saw a bunch of plantains in your farm which I would like to get. Will you go instead to mine and take some coco?"

This was arranged, and Etuk said to Njomm, "Try to beat up fu-fu." Njomm tried, and found it very good. He gave some to Etuk. The latter ate all he wanted, then took the bunch of plantains and hung it up in his house.

Next morning he found that the fruit had grown soft, so he did not care to eat it. He therefore took the plantains and threw them away in the bush.

During the day Mbui came along and smelt plantains. He looked round till he found them, then picked up one and began to eat. They were very sweet. He ate his fill, then went on, and later met a crowd of the Nshum people (apes). To them he said, "Today I found a very sweet thing in the bush."

In course of time Etuk grew hungry again, and Njomm said to him, "If you are hungry, why don't you tell me?"

He went to his farm and got four bunches of plantains. As he came back he met the monkey people. They begged for some of his fruit, so he gave it to them.

After they had eaten all there was, they in their turn went on, and met a herd of wild boars (Ngumi) To these they said, "There is very fine food to be got from Njomm and Etuk."

The Ngumi therefore came and questioned Etuk, "Where is coco to be had?" and Etuk answered, "The coco belongs to me."

The boars begged for some, so Etuk took a basket, filled it at his farm, and gave it to them.

After they were satisfied, they went on their way and next morning met Njokk (elephant).

To him they said, "Greetings, Lord! Last night we got very good food from the farms over there."

Njokk at once ran and asked the two friends, "Whence do you get so much food?" They said, "Wait a little."

Njomm took his long machete and went to his farm. He cut five great bunches of plantains and carried them back. Etuk also got five baskets full of coco, which he brought to elephant. After the latter had eaten all this, he thanked them and went away.

All the bush beasts came in their turn and begged for food, and to each the two friends gave willingly of all that they had. Lastly also came Mfong (bush cow).

Now not far from the two farms there was a great river called Akarram (The One-Which-Goes-Round). In the midst of it, deep down, dwelt crocodile. One day Mfong went down into the water to drink, and from him crocodile learned that much food was to be had nearby.

On this crocodile came out of the water and began walking towards the farms. He went to Njomm and Etuk and said, "I am dying of hunger, pray give me food."

Etuk said, "To the beasts who are my friends I will give all I have, but to you I will give nothing, for you are no friend of mine;" but Njomm said, "I do not like you very much, yet I will give you one bunch of plantains."

Crocodile took them and said: "Do not close your door tonight when you lie down to sleep. I will come back and buy more food from you at a great price."

He then went back to the water and sought out a python, which dwelt there. To the latter he said:

"I have found two men on land, who have much food." Python said, "I too am hungry. Will you give me to eat?"

So crocodile gave him some of the plantains which he had brought. When python had tasted he said: "How sweet it is! Will you go back again and bring more?" Crocodile said, "Will you give me something with which to buy?" and python answered, "Yes. I will give you something with which you can buy the whole farm."

On this he took from within his head a shining stone and gave it to crocodile. The latter started to go back to the farm. As he went, night fell and all the road grew dark, but he held in his jaws the shining stone, and it made a light on his path, so that all the way was bright. When he neared the dwelling of the two friends he hid the stone and called, "Come out and I will show you something which I have brought."

It was very dark when they came to speak with him. Slowly the crocodile opened his claws, in which he held up the stone, and it began to glimmer between them. When he held it right out, the whole place became so bright that one could see to pick up a needle or any small thing. He said, "The price of this that I bring is one whole farm."

Etuk said: "I cannot buy. If I give my farm, nothing remains to me. What is the use of this great shining stone if I starve to death?" But Njomm said: "I will buy—oh, I will buy, for my farm full of plantains, for that which you bring fills the whole earth with light. Come let us go. I will show you my farm. From here to the waterside all round is my farm. Take it all, and do what you choose with it, only give me the great shining stone that, when darkness falls, the whole earth may still be light."

Crocodile said, "I agree."

Then Njomm went to his house with the stone, and Etuk went to his. Njomm placed it above the lintel, that it might shine for all the world; but Etuk closed his door and lay down to sleep.

In the morning Njomm was very hungry, but he had nothing to eat, because he had sold all his farm for the great white stone.

Next night and the night after he slept full of hunger, but on the third morning he went to Etuk and asked, "Will you give me a single coco-yam?" Etuk answered: "I can give you nothing, for now you have nothing to give in exchange. It was not I who told you to buy the shining thing. To give something, when plenty remains, is good; but none but a fool would give his all, that a light may shine in the dark!"

Njomm was very sad. He said: "I have done nothing bad. Formerly no one could see in the nighttime. Now the python stone shines so that everyone can see to go wherever he chooses."

All that day Njomm still endured, though nearly dying of hunger, and at nighttime he crept down to the water, very weak and faint.

By the riverside he saw a palm tree, and on it a man trying to cut down clusters of ripe kernels; but this was hard to do, because it had grown very dark.

Njomm said, "Who is there?" and the man answered, "I am Effion Obassi."

The second time Njomm called, "What are you doing?" and Effion replied, "I am trying to gather palm kernels, but I cannot do so, for it is very dark amid these great leaves."

Njomm said to him, "It is useless to try to do such a thing in the dark. Are you blind?"

Effion answered, "I am not blind. Why do you ask?"

Then Njomm said: "Good; if you are not blind, I beg you to throw me down only one or two palm kernels, and in return I will show you a thing more bright and glorious than any you have seen before."

Effion replied: "Wait a minute, and I will try to throw a few down to you. Afterwards you shall show me the shining thing as you said."

He then threw down three palm kernels, which Njomm took, and stayed his hunger a little. The latter then called: "Please try to climb down. We will go together to my house."

Effion tried hard, and after some time he stood safely at the foot of the tree by the side of Njomm.

So soon as they got to his house, Njomm said, "Will you wait here a little while I go to question the townspeople?"

First he went to Etuk and asked: "Will you not give me a single coco to eat? See, the thing which I bought at the price of all that I had turns darkness to light for you, but for me, I die of hunger."

Etuk said: "I will give you nothing. Take back the thing for which you sold your all, and we will stay in our darkness as before."

Then Njomm begged of all the townsfolk that they would give him ever so little food in return for the light he had bought for them. Yet they all refused.

So Njomm went back to his house and took the shining stone, and gave it to Effion Obassi, saying: "I love the earth folk, but they love not me. Now take the shining thing for which I gave my whole possessions. Go back to the place whence you came, for I know that you belong to the sky people, but when you reach your home in the heavens, hang up my stone in a place where all the earth folk may see its shining, and be glad."

Then Effion took the stone, and went back by the road he had come. He climbed up the palm tree, and the great leaves raised themselves upwards, pointing to the sky, and lifted him, till, from their points, he could climb into heaven.

When he reached his home, he sent and called all the Lords of the Sky and said, "I have brought back a thing today which can shine so that all the earth will be light. From now on everyone on earth or in heaven will be able to see at the darkest hour of the night."

The chiefs looked at the stone and wondered. Then they consulted together, and made a box. Effion said, "Make it so that the stone can shine out only from one side."

When the box was finished, he set the globe of fire within, and said: "Behold, the stone is mine. From this time all the people must bring me food. I will no longer go to seek any for myself."

For some time they brought him plenty, but after a while they grew tired. Then Effion covered the side of the box, so that the stone could not shine till they brought him more. That is the reason why the moon is sometimes dark, and people on earth say: "It is the end of the month. The sky people have grown weary of bringing food to Effion Obassi, and he will not let his stone shine out till they bring a fresh supply."

How All the Stars Came

Ebopp (the lemur) and Mbaw (the mouse) were making a tour in the bush. They looked for a good place to cut farm. When one was found they cut down the trees, and took two days to clear enough ground. After this they went back to the town where the other animals were living. Next morning Ebopp said, "Let us go back to our new farms and build a small house." This they did. Ebopp made his, and Mbaw his.

Now before a new town is begun, a little shed called Ekpa Ntan (House Without Walls) is made where the Egbo house is to stand. Ebopp and Mbaw accordingly set to work and built an Ekpa Ntan. Then they went back to their old town and rested for two days.

On the third day they went to work again. Ebopp worked on his farm, Mbaw on his. That night they slept in the huts they had built, and at dawn started to work once more. When night came, Ebopp lighted a lamp and said: "I do not want to sleep here. If we sleep here we shall sleep hungry. Let us go back to our old town."

When they got there their wives cooked for them. Ebopp said to Mbaw, "Come and join together with me in eating." So his friend came and ate with him.

Afterwards Mbaw said, "Let us go to my house and have food too." So they went thither.

After they had eaten up all that Mbaw had cooked, Ebopp went home.

Next morning he went to call his friend and said, "Go and get young plantains to plant in the farm." Both of them collected a great basket full of these, and went to the place where the new farms were, Ebopp to his, and Mbaw to his.

Both worked hard. At midday Ebopp said, "Let us rest a little while, and eat the food we have brought." To this Mbaw agreed, but after some time they set to work again.

About five o'clock Ebopp called, "Let us go back now to the old town, for it is very far off."

So they left off working and went back, but before they could get there night fell.

Next morning they took more young plantains, and again worked hard all day. When it was time to go back, Ebopp asked, "How many remain to plant of the young plantains?" Mbaw answered,"About forty." On which Ebopp said, "Of mine also there remain about forty."

At dawn next day they went to their old farms to get some more plantain cuttings. Then they went on to the new farms and began planting. So soon as he had finished, Ebopp said, "I have finished mine." To which Mbaw replied, "Mine also are finished."

Ebopp said, "My work is done, I need only come here for the hunting."

Then they both went back to the old town and told their wives: "We have finished setting the plantains. We hope that you will go and plant coco-yams tomorrow. Try, both of you, to get baskets full of coco-yams for the planting."

To this the women agreed, and when they had collected as many as were necessary they set out for the new farms.

When they arrived, Mbaw's wife asked the wife of Ebopp, "Do you think we can finish planting all these today?" Ebopp's wife answered, "Yes, we can do it."

All day they worked hard, and at night went home and said, "We have finished planting all the coco-yams." Ebopp said, "Good, you have done well."

Now his wife's name was Akpan Anwan (Akpan means firstborn). She and her sister Akandem were the daughters of Obassi Osaw. When she got home she started to cook the evening meal for her husband. When it was ready she placed it upon the table, set water also in a cup, and laid spoons nearby.

They were eating together when a slave named Umaw ran in. He had just come from the town of Obassi Osaw. He said, "I would speak to Ebopp alone." When Akpan Anwan had left the room, the messenger said, "You are eating, but I bring you news that Akandem is dead."

Ebopp called out aloud in his grief, and sent a messenger to call his friend Mbaw.

So soon as the latter heard he came running and said: "What can we do? We are planting new farms and beginning to build a new town. There is hardly any food to be got. How then can we properly hold the funeral customs?"

Ebopp said, "Nevertheless, I must try my best." When Umaw got ready to return, Ebopp said: "Say to Obassi Osaw 'Wait for me for six days, then I will surely come.'"

Next morning he said to Mbaw, "Come now, let us do our utmost to collect what is necessary for the rites of my sister-in-law."

They went round the town and bought all the food which they could find. Then Ebopp went back and said to his wife: "I did not wish to tell you before about the death of your sister, but today I must tell you. Get ready. In five days' time I will take you back to your father's town to hold the funeral feast."

Akpan Anwan was very grieved to hear of this and wept. Ebopp said to Mbaw: "We must get palm wine for the feast, also rum for libations. How can we get these? I have no money and you also have none." Mbaw said, "Go round among the townsfolk and see if any of them will lend you some."

Ebopp said, "Good," and began to walk up and down, begging from all his friends, but none would give to him, though it was a big town. At last he went down to the place where they were making palm oil by the river. Near to this lived Iku (water chevrotain). Ebopp told his trouble and begged help, but Iku said, "I am very sorry for you, but I have nothing to give."

Ebopp was quite discouraged by now, and turned to go away full of sorrow. When Iku saw this he said: "Wait a minute, there is one thing I can do. You know that I have the 'four eyes.' I will give you two, and with them you can buy all that you need."

From out of his head he took the two eyes with which he used to see in the dark. They shone so brightly that Ebopp knew they were worth a great price. He took them home and showed them to his wife and his friend Mbaw.

The latter said: "From today you are freed from all anxiety. With those you can buy all that is needed."

Next morning they gathered together all that had been collected, the plantains and the two shining eyes. Ebopp, Mbaw and Akpan carried the loads between them. They set out for the dwelling place of Obassi Osaw.

When they got to the entrance of the town, Akpan Anwan began to weep bitterly. She threw down her burden, and ran to the spot where her sister lay buried. Then she lay down on the grave and would not rise again.

Ebopp carried his own load into the house where the dead woman had dwelt. Then he went back and got his wife's load which she had left behind.

The townsfolk said to Ebopp: "You have come to keep your sister-in-law's funeral customs today. Bring palm wine. Bring rum also for the libations, and let us hold the feast."

Ebopp said: "I have brought nothing but plantains. All else that is necessary I mean to buy here."

Now there was a famine in Obassi Osaw's town, so Ebopp put all his plantains in the Egbo house. Next day he sent to Obassi Osaw to bring his people, so that the food might be divided among them. Each man got one.

Then Osaw said: "All that you brought is eaten. If you can give us no more, you shall not take my daughter back with you to your country."

Ebopp went to find his friend, and told him what Obassi had said. "Shall I sell the two eyes?" he asked. "They are worth hundreds and hundreds of plantains, and many pieces of cloth, but if I sell them now, the people are so hungry, they will only give a small price."

Mbaw said: "Do not mind. See, I will teach you how to get more sense. You hold one in your hand, and it is a big thing like a great shining stone, but if you put it in a mortar and grind it down, it will become, not one, but many, and some of the small pieces you can sell."

This Ebopp did, and ground up the great bright stones which had been Iku's eyes till they became like shining sand.

Then they went and got a black cap, which they filled with the fragments.

Mbaw said, "Now go and look round the town till you find someone who can sell what we need."

Ebopp did so, and in the house of Effion Obassi he saw great stores hidden—food and palm wine, palm oil in jars, and rum for the sacrifice.

Ebopp said to Effion, "If you will sell all this to me I will give you in exchange something which will make all the townsfolk bow down before you."

Effion said, "I will not sell all, but half of what I have I will sell you."

So Ebopp said: "Very well. I will take what you give me, only do not open the thing I shall leave in exchange till I have got back to my own country. When you do open it, as I said before, all the townsfolk will bow down before you."

So the funeral feast was made, and the people were satisfied.

When the rites were finished, Obassi said: "It is good. You can go away now with your wife."

So Ebopp said to Mbaw and Akpan Anwan: "Come, let us go back to our own town. We must not sleep here tonight."

When they had reached home once more, Ebopp sent a slave named Edet to Effion Obassi with the message: "You can open the cap now. I have reached my town again." It was evening time, but Effion at once sent to call the townspeople and said, "I have a thing here which is worth a great price." They cried, "Let us see it." He answered, "My thing is a very good thing, such as you have never seen before."

He brought the cap outside and opened it before them. All the shining things fell out. As they fell a strong breeze came and caught them and blew them all over the town. They lay on the roads and on the floors of the compounds, each like a little star.

All the children came round and began picking them up. They gathered and gathered. In the daytime they could not see them, but every night they went out and sought for the shining things. Each one that they picked up they put in a box. At length many had been got together and shone like a little sun in the box. At the end of about a month nearly all had been collected. They could not shut down the lid, however, because the box was too full, so when a great breeze came by it blew all the shining things about again. That is why sometimes we have a small moon and plenty of stars shining round it, while sometimes we have a big moon and hardly any stars are to be seen. The children take a month to fill the box again.

When the sparkles were scattered about the town, Effion sent a messenger to Ebopp to ask, "Can you see the things shining from your town?"

At that time earth and sky were all joined together, like a house with an upstairs.

Ebopp went out and looked upward to the blue roof overhead. There he saw the small things sparkling in the darkness.

Next day he went to Iku and said: "Will you please go into a deep hole? I want to look at your eyes."

Iku went inside the hole. Ebopp looked at his eyes. They were very bright, just like the sparkles which shone in the sky.

The cause of all the stars is therefore Ebopp, who took Iku's eyes to Obassi's town.

Iku's eyes are like the stars.

The moon shines when all the fragments are gathered together. When he shines most brightly it is because the children have picked up nearly all the fragments and put them into the box.

How the Rivers First Came on Earth

In the very, very, very ancient time, an old man named Etim 'Ne (Old Person) came down from the sky, he alone with his old wife Ejaw (Wildcat). At that time there were no people on the earth. This old couple were the very first to go down to dwell there.

Now up to this time all water was kept in the kingdom of Obassi Osaw. On earth there was not a single drop.

Etim 'Ne and his wife stayed for seven days, and during that time they had only the juice of plantain stems to drink or cook with.

At the end of that time the old man said to his old wife, "I will go back to Obassi Osaw's town and ask him to give us a little water."

When he arrived at the old town where they used to dwell, he went to the house of Obassi and said: "Since we went down to earth we have had no water, only the juice which we sucked from the plantain stems. For three nights I will sleep in your town, then when I return to earth I hope that you will give me some water to take with me. Should my wife have children they will be glad for the water, and what they offer to you in thanksgiving I myself will bring up to your town."

On the third morning, very early, Obassi Osaw put the water charm in a calabash, and bound it firmly with tie-tie. Then he gave it to Etim 'Ne, and said: "When you wish to loose this, let no one be present. Open it, and you will find seven good gifts inside. Wherever you want water, take out one of these and throw it on the ground."

Etim 'Ne thanked Lord Obassi, and set out on his way earthward. Just before he came to the place where he had begun to cut farm, he opened the calabash, and found within seven stones, clear as water. He made a small hole and laid one of the stones within it. Soon a little stream began to well out, then more and more, till it became a broad lake, great as from here to Ako.

Etim 'Ne went on and told his wife. They both rejoiced greatly, but he thought: "How is this? Can a man be truly happy, yet have no child?"

After two days his wife came to him and said: "Obassi is sending us yet another gift. Soon we shall be no longer alone on earth, you and I."

When the due months were passed, she bore him seven children, all at one time. They were all sons. Later she became pregnant again, and this time bore seven daughters. After that she was tired, and never bore any more children.

In course of time the girls were all sent to the fatting-house. While they were there Etim 'Ne pointed out to his seven sons where he would like them to build their compounds. When these were finished, he gave a daughter to each son and said: "Do not care that she is your sister. Just marry her. There is no one else who can become your wife."

The eldest son dwelt by the first water which Etim 'Ne had made, but to each of the others he gave a lake or river—seven in all.

After one year, all the girls became pregnant. Each of them had seven children, three girls and four boys. Etim 'Ne said, "It is good." He was very happy. As the children grew up he sent them to other places.

Now the seven sons were all hunters. Three of them were good, and brought some of their kill to give to their father, but four were very bad, and hid all the meat, so that they might keep everything for themselves.

When Etim 'Ne saw this, he left the rivers near the farms of his three good sons, but took them away from the four bad boys. These latter were very sad when they found their water gone, so they consulted together and went and got palm wine. This they carried before their father and said: "We are seven, your children. First you gave the water to all. Now you have taken it away from us four. What have we done?"

Etim 'Ne answered: "Of all the meat you killed in the bush you brought none to me. Therefore I took away your rivers. Because you have come to beg me I will forgive you, and will give you four good streams. As your children grow and multiply I will give you many."

After another year the sons had children again. When the latter grew up they went to different places and built their houses.

When these were ready Etim 'Ne sent for all the children and said: "At dawn tomorrow let each of you go down to the stream which flows by the farm of his father. Seek in its bed till you find seven smooth stones. Some must be small and some big like the palm of your hand. Let each one go in a different direction, and after walking about a mile, lay a stone upon the ground. Then walk on again and do the same, till all are finished. Where you set a big stone a river will come, and where you set a small stone a stream will come."

All the sons did as they were bidden, save one alone. He took a great basket and filled it with stones. Then he went to a place in the bush near his own farm. He thought: "Our father told us, if you throw a big stone a big river will come. If I throw down all my stones together, so great a water will come that it will surpass the waters of all my brothers." Then he emptied his basket of stones all in one place, and, behold! water flowed from every side, so that all his farm, and all the land round about became covered with water. When he saw that it would not stop but threatened to overflow the whole earth he grew very much afraid. He saw his wife running, and called to her, "Let us go to my father." Then they both ran as hard as they could towards the house of Etim 'Ne.

Before they reached it the other children, who had been setting the smooth stones in the bush, as their father had told them, heard the sound of the coming of the waters. Great fear fell upon them, and they also dropped what remained and ran back to Etim 'Ne.

He also had heard the rushing of the water and knew what the bad son had done. He took the magic calabash in his hand and ran with his wife to a hill behind their farm. On this there grew many tall palm trees. Beneath the tallest of these he stood, while his children gathered round one after the other as they got back from the bush. Etim 'Ne held on high the calabash which Obassi had given him, and prayed, "Lord Obassi, let not the good thing which you gave for our joy turn to our hurt."

As he prayed the water began to go down. It sought around till it found places where there had been no water. At each of these it made a bed for itself, great or small, some for broad rivers, and some for little streams. Only where the bad son had emptied his basket it did not go back, but remained in a great lake covering all his farm, so that he was very hungry, and had to beg from his brothers till the time came for the fruits to ripen in the new farm which he had to cut.

After many days Etim 'Ne called all his children around, and told them the names of all the rivers, and of every little stream. Then he said, "Let no one forget to remember me when I shall have left you, for I it was who gave water to all the earth, so that everyone shall be glad."

Two days afterwards he died. In the beginning there were no people on the earth and no water. Etim 'Ne it was who first came down to dwell with his old wife Ejaw, and he it was who begged water from Obassi Osaw.

The Egbo Secret Society

This description of the Egbo secret society of
the Ekoi and Efik peoples of the Calabar Coast
region of West Africa has considerable intrinsic
interest in that it conveys something of the importance such groups once played, not only in
regulating social life, but in carrying out functions of government. It was written by P.
Amaury Talbot early in the century, since
which time, of course, much has changed. The
importance of Egbo among the peoples of the
Calabar Coast is indicated by its survival in the
New World until very recent times among descendants of African slaves in Cuba.

The whole country is honeycombed with secret societies, among
which the Egbo Club is the most powerful. Before the coming of the
white man this institution ruled the land, and even now it has more
influence in many ways than government itself, and has caused endless
difficulty to administrators.

The Ekoi claim to have originated the whole idea of such clubs, which
have existed among them for centuries, and are mentioned in some of
their very old folklore tales. Later on, the Ododop and other tribes near
Iffianga, Akwa and Efut in the South Cameroons, started a similar society, which gradually became more powerful than the original Ekoi
one, and therefore more costly to join. The Efiks of Calabar were not
slow to perceive the advantage of such institutions, and so founded the
Ekkpe Club, which, with the growing importance of their town through
the coming of white men, soon became the wealthiest of all Egbo
Societies.

As the Efiks held the monopoly of the Calabar trade they and their
club obtained great influence over the Ekoi, who found it advisable to
adopt many Efik customs and laws. This was especially the case with the
Ekoi who live to the south of Oban, and therefore nearest to Calabar.
Those to the north still keep their old Egbo practically unchanged,
except the inhabitants of Ndebbiji, who have adopted that of the Ododop people, which is almost the same as the Efik one.

Calabar was practically the only place whence the Ekoi could obtain
guns and gunpowder. To reach it, they had to pass through Efik territory. The roads were picketed by the latter people, and it was impossible to reach the factories save by their goodwill. Even if some men from
the interior managed to reach a white official and attempted to lay their
grievances before him, the Efik interpreter took care that the true state
of things should not be translated. If a case was tried in the Calabar
courts the only chance which a "bush man" had of winning it was to

From In the Shadow of the Bush, *by P. Amaury Talbot, London, Heinemann,*
1912.

enlist the help of some powerful Efik, and often the only way of doing this was to promise to become his "member." The arts by which Efik traders entrapped first one man and then the whole family, as slaves, were often cruel in the extreme. The only holds possessed by the Ekoi over their persecutors were that the Efiks feared their jujus and wanted the dried meat killed and preserved by Ekoi hunters. The establishment of a native court at Oban did not much improve matters. Indeed, in some ways, it made them worse, as the clerk who ruled it was always an Efik and arranged that judgment should be given in favor of his own people.

It is natural that the most powerful society should be called by the name of the most dreaded denizen of the bush, for "Egbo" is supposed to express to the Efik "Ekkpe" and the Ekoi "Ngbe," i.e., Leopard.

Possibly among the Ekoi, where totemism is still an article of belief, though most of them will deny the existence of any such idea, the Leopard Society originally consisted only of those who belonged to this totem. On account of the superior craft and power of the animal it would naturally draw to itself the largest following. Later, as totemism began to lose force, first one, then another prominent individual who was not, properly speaking, a "Leopard soul" might be allowed to join, until it gradually became open to all.

There are many indications which seem to place beyond doubt the fact that some form of totemism still enters into the ritual of the Egbo Society. For instance, at some of the bigger "plays," while the principal performers (or "images" as they are called) run up and down, now to the right, now to the left, the lesser personages form a circle, and keep time to a monotonous chant. In one case they sang:

"Okum ngbe ommobik ejennum ngimm, akiko ye ajakk nga ka ejenn nyamm."

The Egbo cannot walk straight, he is driven hither and thither by the movement of the beast.

On another occasion a prominent member of the Egbo, who had the reputation of knowing more Nsibidi—a primitive secret writing much used in this part of the world—than any man now alive, was asked to give me a little help in the study of this script. He refused point blank, though a good remuneration had been offered for his services. He added as an aside to another member of the society, with no idea that his words could be understood by [me], "If I taught him Nsibidi, he would know all the Egbo signs, and the secrets of the animals." He refused to give any further information, and soon after went away.

The importance of the society is obvious even to the most careless visitor to any land where it has gained a foothold, for the clubhouse is the principal building in every town. Even the smallest village has its Egbo shed, and when a town decides to migrate the first thing done, as soon as the fresh site is cleared, before even new farms are cut, or the land divided up, is to fix the position of the clubhouse. A small shed, called Ekpa Ntan (the house without walls) is erected to mark the spot where the Egbo house is to stand.

The many-sided character of Egbo may be judged from the immense powers which it has arrogated to itself in almost every direction. Under native rule it usurped practically all functions of government, made trade almost impossible for nonmembers, and exercised a deep influence on the religious and mystic side of the nation.

The ritual is certainly very ancient, and in it many juju cults are mixed. The name of Obassi is invoked before every sacrifice, and an oblation of food and drink laid in front of the Etai Ngbe (leopard stone), the cut stone usually found before the second pillar of the clubhouse.

It is difficult to discover more than the merest fragments of the secrets of Egbo, as any known informant would meet with a speedy death. Still from what has been gathered—mostly, as in the case already quoted, from snatches of song sung at different plays—there seems to be a close resemblance between these secrets and the Eleusinian and ancient Egyptian mysteries. Certainly a considerable amount of hypnotism, clairvoyance, and spiritualism is taught, and only too many proofs have been given, that some of the powers of nature are known and utilized by initiates, in a way forgotten or unknown to their white rulers.

For instance, some of the esoteric members seem to have the power of calling up shadow forms of absent persons. Once an exhibition of this nature given in the central court of the compound of one of the head chiefs of Oban, was described to me.

It was midnight, and a bright moon was shining. Within the open space in the center of the compound a fire was burning. On this from time to time medicine was thrown, which caused clouds of smoke to rise. These died down, save for isolated puffs, which after a time assumed definite shape.

The spectators sat on the ground in a half-circle behind the fire, and facing a low mud wall, beyond which, against the background of the moonlit sky, dark silhouettes began to pass, each clearly recognizable as that of some person known to be absent at the time. There was no sign of any artificial means of producing these shapes, which continued to pass for about a quarter of an hour, at the end of which time they grew faint and at length faded.

The chiefs claimed to have the power of calling up the shadow shapes of white men, but no case in which this had actually been done was cited.

There are seven grades which the aspirant must pass before he can be admitted to the deeper teaching or the revelation of any save the lesser mysteries. All may be entered by young boys, should their fathers be rich enough to pay the necessary fees, but the secrets are not unfolded till middle age has been reached.

1. EKPIRI NGBE. Small Egbo.

2. EBU NKO (an old word, the meaning of which is not known). At a dance given by this grade, members must always wear their best

clothes. Aspirants to each of these are marked with white chalk on both arms.

3. MBAWKAW (old Ekoi word adopted by Efiks). Aspirants to this are marked on the forehead with ekui (camwood dye). These three grades are called collectively Abonn Ogbe, i.e., Children of the Egbos. They are neither important nor expensive to enter.

4. NDIBU (old word, meaning unknown, equivalent to Efik Nyampke). This is the second division, and one to which it is accounted a great honor to belong. It is often called "The Mother of the Grades." Its president holds the second place in the whole society. If it was found necessary to expel a member who had reached this grade, death followed as a matter of course, lest any of its secrets should be revealed by the outcast.

When a man joins Ndibu the head chiefs and officials stay in the Egbo house, while the young men dance and play round the town. The best friend of the aspirant brings forward a calabash containing a leg of meat, and two bottles of palm wine. The postulant then enters the clubhouse, and sits down before the chief, who puts powder on his head, and recites all the names of the Egbo. The new member next rises and invokes the names in his turn, while after each the chiefs call out "Owe," i.e., Our Own. He then goes out and dances with the young men. The play is carried on for about eight days, during which time palm wine and meat are supplied to all.

At the present day at Oban, entrance to this grade costs about thirty pounds, which must be paid before full membership is allowed.

5. OKU AKAMA (The Priest Consents). This is not very expensive to enter, nor considered of much account, but it must be passed before further grades can be reached. The postulant is marked with yellow dye (ogokk) on the abdomen and the back of his shoulders.

The old Ekoi grade was called Asian, but when Oban adopted the Calabar Egbo, the Efiks insisted on this being suppressed.

6. ETURI (Metal or Brass Rod), Efik Okpokgo. In the old days during a play, all fires had to be extinguished and no noise of any kind was permitted in the town. Formerly very few men succeeded in reaching this grade, but now it is usually passed on the same day as

7. NKANDA, the highest and final grade. Oban took this from the Efiks, who again insisted on the destruction of the old Ekoi equivalent "Isong," and of another old grade "Mutanda," of slightly lesser importance.

Nkanda is more expensive than any other grade, and most men only enter late in life. When a man has succeeded in joining this high grade, he is rubbed on head and chest with yellow powder (ogokk). Five rings are made on front and back. Two yellow, one round each breast, a white one in the center some few inches below, and, beneath this again, two more yellow ones, forming a square with those on the breasts.

On the back the rings are arranged in the same way, but the central one is yellow and the four outer ones white. The arms are ornamented with alternate stripes of white and yellow, and till the last rite is finished, the man goes bare save for a long loincloth which reaches from waist to feet.

The chief of Nkanda is the president of the Egbo Lodge, and by far the most powerful man of the town. His office is sometimes hereditary, and only free-born chiefs can aspire to it. In olden days a slave could not join Egbo, lest he should reveal its secrets to a new master. He could, however, be present at most of the ceremonies if his owner was a member of Egbo, and permitted.

One of the chief insignia of the Nkanda grade is called the Ekabe (Efik Ekarra) Nkanda. This is a kind of hoop, covered with bright-colored cloth. The attendant whose duty is to carry this, performs many curious evolutions with it. He is obliged to hold back the Okum (or image) by its means if the latter, in a state of excitement, seems about to show himself to a nonmember, particularly a woman, at a time when this is not permitted. Should the Okum succeed in evading the vigilance of the Ekabe bearer, a cow is killed, and a feast provided for the members at the expense of the defaulting official.

Another symbol, used by Nkanda and Ebu Nko alike, is the Effrigi, a sort of wooden fan on which Nsibidi signs are inscribed.

The head priest of the whole Egbo Society is called Iyamba, the old Ekoi equivalent for which was Musungu.

Other officials are Murua, who carries the rattle during "plays," and Isua, the master of ceremonies for the Abonn Ogbe. The head of each grade is called Ntui (chief) and acts as treasurer.

Those who belong to the four higher grades, and have paid the fees in full, may join in another ceremony called Mariba, or Etem-I-Ngbe (The Bush Leopard). This is performed in the depths of the forest and with the greatest secrecy. It is during the Mariba that the successive mysteries are unveiled. The ceremony may also be performed at the funeral "customs" of very great chiefs.

The danger run by nonmembers on such occasions, before the coming of white rule, may perhaps be better understood by a case which happened not long before my arrival to start the District.

During the Mariba the sacred images, etc., are carried to a part of the bush where a little hut of green boughs has been built to receive them. Sentries are posted to keep all intruders from coming within a mile of this spot. On this occasion, however, two young girls, sisters, happened to have missed the patrol, and trespassed unwittingly within the sacred precincts, probably in search of nuts or bush fruits, which abound everywhere. They were caught by the sentries, brought before the Egbo, condemned to death, and hanged almost immediately. Their brother, who was a member of the highest grade of the society, was allowed, as a great favor, to be present at their death and afterwards to carry home the bodies to his family. Of redress, in such a case, there could be neither hope nor thought.

Sometimes rich and influential women are permitted to become honorary members of all grades, but they are never allowed to be full members, nor to know any of the mysteries.

Each grade has its particular dances and tunes, and each its own Okum Ngbe or Egbo image, which is never supposed to come out and show itself unless under direct inspiration to do so.

The so-called image is a figure robed from crown to heel in a long garment, of the color proper to the grade, and pierced with eyeholes. It usually bears on its head a wooden framework covered with skin and shaped like a human head, often with two faces, one male and the other female. This represents the omniscience of the Deity looking both ways, into the future and back to the past, as also the bisexual character shown in the oldest conceptions of Obassi Osaw and Obassi Nsi, Sky Father and Earth Mother.

The Okum runs up and down accompanied by two attendants clothed in gorgeous, close-fitting, knitted garments, usually of red, yellow and white. One of these carries a rod or whip, the symbol of the power of the society, with which, under native law, he had the right to flog to death any nonmembers who had seriously offended against its rules. The other bears the symbolic green boughs, which play so great a part in the lives of the Ekoi. At almost every important occurrence, from birth onward, green leaves of the kind proper to the event are used, and at the last are gently drawn over the face of a dying man, that his spirit may pass peacefully and without pain from this world to the next.

There is great rivalry between the different towns as to which can produce the most gorgeous robes for images and members. The financial state of a place can be told by a glance at one of the plays, as the local resources are strained to the utmost in the hope of outdoing neighboring towns. The chiefs of Oban volunteered the information that the play was so much finer on the second New Year after my arrival than formerly, because the opening of a government station had brought them an increase of wealth.

The most interesting figure in last New Year's dance, however, wore nothing either rich or attractive. This was the Ekuri Ibokk (Efik "Axe-Medicine"). It is a very old Ekoi juju, but was renamed a few years ago when the axe was placed between its jaws in addition to the other insignia.

The image was robed in a long gown of dark blue cloth, daubed with mud from the riverbed. This, to the Ekoi, as formerly to performers in the Greek Mysteries and to Flamen Dialis, is in itself a great juju. Over the robes of the image dark-spotted juju leaves were fastened here and there. On its head it bore a crocodile mask, carved in wood, perhaps a representation of Nimm herself. It was attended by two hunters armed with flintlock guns, a third bore a fishing net, and a fourth a curious earthen trumpet covered with leopard skin. The image was supposed to be deaf to human voices, and to hear only those of the bush beasts, save when awakened by the call of the trumpet. Ekuri Ibokk is the great "hunting juju" of the Ekoi, and had never before appeared to a European. It is the juju that is supposed to have the power of "smelling out" all others, and the axe in its jaws is a sign of its special fierceness.

Powerful as it is, however, it is not proof against the very human weakness of wishing to have its photograph taken, and appeared, on this inducement, among its less exclusive brothers.

At such "plays" all the principal characters carry wands or whips, the symbol of the power of the society, which, as has already been mentioned, could be used to flog to death nonmembers who ventured outside their houses during an Egbo performance, or seriously offended in any way. Minor offenses were punished by fines, and from these the main revenues of the club were derived.

One great advantage to be gained from membership in the old days was the facility offered for the recovery of debts. A creditor brought his case before the Egbo Lodge in the debtor's town. The council considered the matter, and if the claim was thought justified, the club drum would be beaten through the streets, and the defaulter ordered to pay. He was also bound to provide a "dash" for the Egbo Society. Should he be unable to comply with both demands, his goods were seized, and, other means failing, himself or some of his family reduced to the position of slaves, in order to make good all liabilities.

There are many stories to account for the coming of Egbo, but perhaps the following is the best known.

How the First Egbo Image Came

One day Nki (Dormouse) went into the bush to gather palm kernels. He cut down a great cluster from which one fell. This rolled down a crab's hole, right through to the ghost town, where the son of one of the chiefs found and ate it.

Nki climbed down from the palm tree, and went in search of his kernel. He followed it till he came to the ghost town. There he saw the young chief and guessed what he had done. So he went before the head chief and said: "Will you give me back the palm kernel which your son has eaten?"

The old chief answered: "Here is a drum. Take it and beat upon it. It will repay you for what you have lost."

Nki did as he was told. Hardly had he struck the drum when a calabash full of fruit appeared. The chief said, "Take the drum with you," so Nki took it and went on his way.

When he reached home he called to his wives and said: "Weep no more. I bring you food in plenty."

He beat the drum, and the calabash appeared as before. He ate of the fruit, and gave some to all his family.

After this there was always much chop in his house, for he needed only to strike the drum to obtain a fresh supply. He grew rich, and hired people to work for him instead of working himself as formerly.

One day he hired the men of the town to go and cut crops for him. All of them went save Ngbe (Leopard) alone. Each day Nki cooked twelve great calabashes of chop for his workers.

When the farm was cleared he hired the women to plant it, and prepared food for them as he had done for the men. The wife of Ngbe took her portion home. Her husband seized it and ate it up, whereon she said: "When the others went to cut farm for Nki, you refused to go with them. Why then do you eat my chop?"

One day Nki went to visit his farm. He put the magic drum into an inner room and locked the door. Then he gave the key to Lame Boy and said, "If anyone should come and ask for this do not give it."

As soon as he was out of sight Ngbe came and demanded the key. The boy refused to give it up, but Leopard said, "I will kill you if you do not give it to me." So the boy gave it.

Ngbe opened the door, seized the drum and bounded with it into the bush. There he made a small clearing, set up the drum and began to beat it. So strongly did he strike, that almost at once several calabashes appeared full of sweet things. There was too much for one to eat alone, so Ngbe ate what he could and left the rest, then broke up the drum and threw away the pieces. Afterwards he went off to his house.

When Nki came home, he asked Lame Boy for the key of the inner room, whereon the boy told him all that Ngbe had done.

Nki was sad over his loss. After a while he went out into the bush as before. Again he cut palm kernels, but, as none of them fell, he looked round for a crab hole, threw a kernel into it, and pushed it down with a long stick. He then followed it through the hole till he came again to the ghost town. Here he saw a chief and said: "One of your sons has taken my palm kernel. Give it back to me."

On this the chief gave him Egyuk, the long kind of drum which we now find in Egbo houses. Nki took it and went on his way.

When he reached the bush where he had cut the kernels he set down the drum and began to beat it. Out sprang the Egbo [demon] image and started to flog him with the whip which it held in its hand.

Nki went on beating the drum, and after a while the image went back into it. Then he took up the drum and went home.

Next day Nki went out as if he were again going to farm. No sooner was he out of sight than Ngbe came as before and demanded the key from Lame Boy. This time the boy gave it without resisting, as his master had told him to do.

Ngbe opened the door of the inner room where the drum was, took it, and sprang into the bush as before. He started to play with all his might, and so furiously did he strike that seven Egbo images sprang out, each armed with a whip, and began to flog him.

Full of anger and fear, he broke the drum, and threw the pieces into the bush. The images could no longer go back to their home in the drum, so they ran into the town, and beat all who came in their way.

That is the reason why the images run up and down to this day, and beat those who cross their path. It is because Ngbe broke the first long drum which was brought from the ghost town, and in which they used to dwell.

The reason we call them Egbo is because Nki gave that name to the first image that came out of the magic drum.

How the Efik Learned to Cook Their Meat

This Efik explanation of how it happened that people came to eat cooked meat is a type of rationalizing story once removed from legend. It involves no heroic or supernatural elements whatever. Its conception is rooted in the experiences of everyday life, as though the original narrator said to himself: "Our legends do not contain the answer. How, then, might it have happened that people now cook their meat?" And his answer was strikingly similar to Charles Lamb's speculation in his essay on the subject of roast pig.

In the beginning, when Efik did not possess fire, an old woman wanted to crack a palm kernel. She looked for her stone pestle but couldn't find it so she used an old machete blade. She placed the kernel on a grinding stone and struck at it with the machete blade. The blade missed the kernel but struck the stone and flashed fire. She called her husband who came, repeated the act, and set fire to palm husk fibre. But the Efik did not yet know cooking. One day after a chief left the house his child accidentally set fire to the cooking shelf. The fire spread to the roof and eventually burned the entire compound killing many pigs. When the chief returned he collected the dead animals in one place, cut off some meat and tasted it. He found the meat tasted very nice. Beginning from that day the Efik cooked food until the Europeans came. Then the Efik stopped hitting two stones together or hitting a machete on stone to make fire.

From "Specimens of Efik Folklore," by D. C. Simmons, in Folklore, *Vol. LXVI,* 1955.

An Efik Lamentation

This song was sung by the eldest daughter of a family on the death of the mother. Each line of the song was followed by the wailing of the mourners.

Oh, our dear mother, you have left a big loneliness for us.
Today we have lost one who gives advice from our midst.
Today we have lost our right hand.
What is life good for?
Oh, death, what a loss you have given us.
Why do you have a strong heart against us in this way?
Today you have taken our mother to ghost town.
Mother good-bye, greet relatives in that region for us.
Please our mother do not forget us.
Remember us as you used to.
Our beloved mother, safe journey.
The good woman whose gait is admired, safe journey.
Our mother with sweet speech, safe journey.

The Feast

A BAMUM TALE FROM CAMEROON

A chief who ruled over many villages decided to give a great feast for all of his people. So he sent messengers to the villages to announce the event. His messengers told the people that the feast would take place on such and such a day and asked each of the men to bring one calabash of palm wine.

The day of the festival came. People bathed and dressed in their best clothes. They walked to the chief's village. Many hundreds of men and their families were on the roads and paths. They converged on the

From Simmons, ibid.
From The King's Drum and Other African Stories, © *1962 by Harold Courlander. Reprinted by permission of Harcourt Brace Jovanovich. Original source, Gilbert Schneider, Bamenda.*

house of the chief. There was drumming and dancing. Each man, as he entered the chief's compound, went with his calabash to a large earthen pot, into which he poured the liquid refreshment that he had brought.

Now there was one man who wanted very much to attend the feast, but he had no palm wine to bring. His wife said, "Why don't you buy palm wine from so-and-so, who has plenty?"

But the man replied: "What! Spend money so that I can attend a feast that is free? No, there must be another way."

And after a while he said to his wife: "Hundreds and hundreds of people will pour their wine into the chief's pot. Could one calabash of water spoil so much wine? Who would know the difference?"

And so he filled his calabash with water and went with the others to the chief's village. When he arrived, he saw the guests pouring their wine into the big pot, and he went forward and poured his water there and greeted the chief. Then he went to where the men were sitting, and he sat with them to await the serving of the palm wine.

When all the guests had arrived, the chief ordered his servants to fill everyone's cups. The cups were filled, and each of the men awaited the signal to begin to drink. The man who had brought only water was impatient, for there was nothing so refreshing as palm wine.

The chief gave the signal, and the guests put the cups to their lips. They tasted. They tasted again. And what they tasted was not palm wine but water, for each of them had thought, "One calabash of water cannot spoil a great pot of good palm wine." And each of them had filled his calabash at the spring. Thus the large earthen pot contained nothing but water, and it was water they had to drink at the chief's feast.

So it is said among the people: "When only water is brought to the feast, it is water that must be drunk."

Brass Casting Among the Bamum

The ancient art of brass (or bronze) casting by the cire perdu technique remains alive in Africa, even though the periods of great art creations are in the past. The lost wax method is still employed by craftsmen in Ghana, Dahomey, Nigeria, Ivory Coast and Cameroon to create brass objects of various kinds, most of which are in the category of folk art. Gilbert Schneider, who spent many years in Cameroon, documented the process of making brass figures there. Following is his description of the technique employed by a Bamum craftsman, Umaru Njasi, in the environs of Bamenda.

Extracted from "Brass-Casting, An Ancient Art," in United Nations Review, April 1957. By permission of the U.N. Department of Publications.

The materials and tools necessary for casting are: a supply of wax, refined clay, horse dung, charcoal, a raffia bamboo spatula about four to six inches long for marking and forming wax models, raffia bamboo tongs for handling hot molds, a supply of brass, files to smooth and clean the castings. Large figures, masks, small houses, pipes, bells and brace-lets all have a core, made from local clay which has been worked fine and mixed with horse dung. Slightly warm wax is worked over the core into the desired shape. The model is marked and smoothed with a short raffia bamboo spatula made from the outer part of the bamboo. Many smaller figures and articles are modelled wholly in wax.

After the wax model has been completed it is usually allowed to harden, after which a mixture of clay and horse dung is gently worked around it. When small figures are being made it is possible to work several of the figures into one large mold, and at the top a shallow bowl-shaped receptacle is formed. From this basin small bamboo sticks lead to the top of the individual wax models. The mold is dried slowly in the shade and sun. The bamboo sticks leading to the models are removed and when the mold is sufficiently dried it is laid in the fire, the bellows is operated by a young apprentice and a medium heat is gene-rated. During the process the wax in all the smaller models is lost into the substance of the surrounding clay mixture. In the larger models a small wax residue is poured off and used again.

The brass is now prepared for the mold. Umaru takes the brass rod which is twenty-four to thirty-six inches in length and coils it around a bamboo pole. The coil is placed in the fire and heated for some time. He takes it from the fire with bamboo tongs and places it on a stone. A stone hammer is used to strike the coil; as the brass is now brittle, it shatters into many short crescent-shaped pieces.

The fragments of brass are then placed in the shallow bowl-shaped receptacle forming the top of the mold. A mixture of clay and horse dung is then carefully sealed over the brass fragments, enclosing them completely. This moist clay shell is then allowed to dry.

The mold, when thoroughly dried, is placed in the charcoal fire with the bowl-shaped receptacle filled with its brass pieces at the bottom. Charcoal is heaped around the mold and the fire is gradually brought to an intense heat. Umaru claims that he can tell by sight and by smell when the molten metal is ready for pouring. When the metal is ready the mold is picked up by the bamboo tongs and inverted, and the brass runs into the casts.

The mold is allowed to cool. After cooling, it is broken open and the various figures are removed. The surface of the casting on removal from the mold is slightly rough and copperish-red, but filing restores the natural brass color. Leaving some portions of the surface unpolished produces two-toned effects.

Some Cameroon Sayings in Pidgin English

Pidgin English came to Africa, as it did elsewhere, with English traders, and in the late eighteenth century it was well established in various regions. Missionaries as well as traders used this "baby talk" language, travelling, as they frequently did, in areas where the tribal languages were not known. In time Pidgin English was used by Africans as a lingua franca in various parts of the continent. The development of large plantations, which employed workers speaking a variety of languages or dialects, encouraged the use of Pidgin English, and although the logic of Pidgin over a simplified standard English has mystified many, it is still spoken and considered worthwhile in numerous parts of Africa.

The following proverbs and sayings from Cameroon in Pidgin English are in the revised typewriter script commonly used for accurate phonetic transcription of "exotic" languages. Most letters have traditional English values. Those with special phonetic values are: *a*, as in m*a*m*a*; *æ*, as in c*a*t; *č*, *ch* sound as in *ch*ur*ch*; *e*, *ay* sound as in French *é*; *ɛ*, short *e* as in g*e*t; *i*, as in French, *ee*; *ɪ*, short *i* as in d*i*n; *ŋ*, nasal as in lo*ng*; *ɔ*, short *o* as in s*o*ng; *o*, long as in m*o*te; *š*, *sh* sound as in *sh*all; *u*, as in f*oo*d; *ʊ*, as in f*oo*t. A colon (:) extends the length of a preceding letter.

na dæso amɛn-amɛn yu fɪt ænsa?
Can you only answer "amen"? (Is joining the chorus all you can do?)

awʊf no gɛt bon.
A bribe does not have a bone. (Taking a bribe does not require willpower.)

ayən no də hat wɛ: de no pʊt-am fɔ: faya.
Iron won't get hot unless you put it in the fire. (There is a logical explanation for everything, or a particular thing.)

tek mɔni bay-am mɔni.
Take money, buy money. (One bribes with money to earn more money.)

mɔŋki də wə:k, bæbun də čap.
The monkey works, the baboon eats. (The black man works, the white man eats. Or can refer to any situation in which some profit on the labor of others.)

trəbu no də rɪŋ bɛl.
Trouble does not ring a bell. (Trouble comes without forewarning.)

Proverbs and sayings are from Cameroons Creole Dictionary, *in manuscript, by G. D. Schneider, mimeographed in Bamenda, 1960.*

wuman də kəm-awt bet mɪmbo no də kəm-awt.
A man can do without a woman but not without wine.

mɔf no də fɪa.
Your mouth will say whatever you let it say.

səm_əns no bi jəj.
A summons is not a judge. (To serve someone a summons does not mean
you have won the case.)

mɔŋki no sæbi wəːk fɔː i tel, sote: mæn kət-am.
The monkey doesn't appreciate his tail until it is cut off. (People don't
appreciate good fortune until they lose it.)

wuman i dinay mæn, i mɛri tɔrəki.
If a woman refuses to marry a good man she will have to marry a poor
one.

akwara-wuman no də jæm bɛd.
A prostitute does not lack for a bed. (Hard-working people do not have
to do without the essentials of life.)

The Journey of the Afo-A-Kom

Kom is the name of a small kingdom in West Cameroon somewhat
north of the town of Bamenda. It was only one of numerous African
kingdoms, and few persons, except those who were familiar with the
country's grasslands tribes, knew of its existence. But Kom became
prominent in 1973 when *The New York Times* published a series of
articles about a sacred statue that had been stolen from the royal storage
house and transported across the Atlantic, where it came into the
possession of a New York art dealer. The investigative reporting of *The
New York Times* made Kom better known to its readers than the names
of many of Africa's more significant kingdoms and tribes.

The stolen statue, called the Afo-A-Kom, or, alternately, Mbang, was
a century or more old. It was brought out from its storage quarters on
great ritual or state occasions, such as the enstooling of a new fon, or
king. It was the figure of a man, completely covered with beadwork,
almost life-size. That it was a fine piece of art was only incidental to the
Kom, if, indeed, they thought of it in such terms. Above all, it was a
symbol of the power and lineage of Kom kings, of the unity of the Kom
people, of good fortune and of tranquillity in the land.

Then, one dark night, the Afo-A-Kom was stolen. The Kom say the
thieves were relatives of the Fon. The statue was wrapped in a grass
mat, carried down the mountainside—probably by two men—to a place
where it was loaded into a taxi. The thief-in-charge at this point, a
dealer, represented the mat-covered figure as a corpse that was being

taken home for burial. Eventually the Afo-A-Kom reached the town of Foumbon, and from there, in some manner or other, it was taken to Douala, some three hundred miles away. Its itinerary thereafter is not clear, but in time it reached New York, where a prominent art gallery put it up for sale at a price of sixty thousand dollars.

In Kom, the loss caused consternation. Not only were there recriminations on high levels, tranquillity and unity among ordinary people began to erode. It was said that people did not get along well anymore, that they did not cooperate in the tasks of life as they had before. The king ordered a new statue to be made to replace the old one. A carver of a neighboring tribe, the Babanki, made a new Afo-A-Kom. The new statue esthetically fell short of the almost classical grace of the old one. But it was not this shortcoming that made the Kom people dissatisfied with it. They simply declared that it was an imitation, and that only restoration of the real Afo-A-Kom would bring the force of harmony back to the kingdom.

When it was discovered that the sacred statue was in the possession of a New York art dealer, *The New York Times* began printing a series of articles about the affair. By implication the articles seemed to place much blame on the dealers who received stolen art treasures without questioning the manner in which they had been acquired. The publicity given to the Afo-A-Kom produced results. Private contributors offered money to purchase the statue from the dealer. The State Department became involved, and so too did the Museum of African Art in Washington. The dealer gave up the Afo-A-Kom, and it was taken back in state to its original home. In Kom its return was a joyous and festive occasion, and there were many who expressed the feeling that the country would surely return to unity, good fortune and tranquillity.

The Origin of the Kom Kingdom

ACCORDING TO POPULAR TRADITION

Long, long ago the ancestors of the Kom people left their home in Ndobo along the Mbam River and went to Bamessi. They lived there for many years in peace, but then there was trouble. The Kom people began to outnumber the Bamessi people.

So the Fon of Bamessi came to the leader of the Kom and said, "Let us each build a house with only one door, and we will put all our old men inside and set the houses on fire to do away with excess people." The plan was agreed upon and one day all the old men from Bamessi entered one house and all the old men from Kom entered another without knowing the reason. The doors were fastened and the houses set aflame.

As told to Sandra Blakeslee and printed in The New York Times, *December 14, 1973. © 1973 by The New York Times Company. Reprinted by permission.*

But the Bamessi chief was treacherous. He had built an escape tunnel for his people. The Kom perished, but the Bamessi lived. The leader of the Kom was furious. He went up to the other chief and bashed him on the head with his harp. And then, after instructing his people to watch for the track of a python, he hanged himself.

The track of a large snake did appear one day and, under a new leader, the remaining Kom followed it. It led them first to Jottin, where they settled temporarily. Next they moved to Ajung, where a lookout was established to watch for the python track. It reappeared and led them to Laikom, where it vanished into the ground. That sacred spot is where the palace compound is today.

THE A-MBUNDU OF ANGOLA

The following description of the A-Mbundu, a
Bantu people, and their way of life was written
by Heli Chatelain, a linguist and commercial
agent at Loanda, Angola, in the 1880s and early
1890s. The A-Mbundu (not to be confused with
the Ovi-Mbundu) include a number of sub-
groups speaking dialects of Ki-Mbundu. The
stories that follow—collected by Heli Chatelain—are exceptional not only for their content
but for their literary style as well. Even in translation, they preserve the imagery and the
rhythm of the Ki-Mbundu narrations and a
particular lyric quality.

The introductory description and the Mbundu tales are taken from Folk-Tales
of Angola, *by Heli Chatelain, American Folk-Lore Society Memoirs, 1894.*

Every native community however small or large, inhabiting one place, that is, forming a village or town, is governed by a chief who is elected and controlled by the body of the elders.

In an old community the chief is generally chosen in one family according to the tribal law of succession, provided the lawful heir be deemed fit for the office. If he is not, the dignity passes to the next heir. In new communities—as is the case of fugitives meeting in the bush and building together—the community by mutual consent organizes itself in accordance with its needs, traditional preferences and superstitions, and the council of the elders bequeaths to the following generation the constitution which they have framed.

The form of government is neither purely monarchical, oligarchic nor democratic, but a happy combination of all three. The council of the elders, which might be called the parliament and forms the legislative and controlling power, is composed of all the adult and free males who show any ability. It delegates the executive power to a chief, whose selection is determined by definite traditions and rules, and who is constantly controlled by the leading elders, whom he has to consult in every important matter. Within the limits of the tribal constitution or traditional laws, the chief or king has absolute power over his subjects' lives and property. His chief officers are: (1) his premier, who often is his presumptive successor, and whose title is Ngolambole. He is the chief's right hand, represents him in his absence, and is regent during the interim between the chief's death and the inauguration of his successor. (2) The secretary, called Tandala, Muzumbu, or Sakala, who corresponds to the foreign secretary or minister of foreign affairs in European states. He is the chief's mouthpiece, publishes his orders, receives and introduces strangers and attends to the official correspondence, if he can write.

Besides these two standing officers, Angolan chiefs have, according to their importance and tribe, a larger or smaller number of accessory officers who carry out the chief's orders and keep him posted on the state of things; thus, the captain of the militia, the collector of this or that tax, the superintendent of roads or markets and others.

In some tribes, the chief may be either a female or a male; and in most tribes the head wife of the chief has great power, even under the reign of his successor.

The Ki-Mbundu title of the chief is generally Soba. A vassal chief is called a Kilamba of his suzerain. A suzerain of many vassals is called in some tribes Faka (Portuguese, jaga), in others Ndembu. The latter name prevails among the independent chiefs between the Nzenza (Bengo), Ndanji (Dande), and Loji rivers, where a soba used to be an inferior chief. It is from this title of Ndembu that the whole district derived its official name "Dembos." The independent Ndembu form a federation.

In former times every tribe had a head chief or king; now the only tribe which still has one great head is that of Ngola. It is still absolutely independent, and enjoys an elaborate system of elective and hereditary nobility. In Angola there is no trace of the military despotic system of the Ama-Zulu.

The social organization of the family in Angola is similar to that of most Bantu peoples. As fatherhood is never absolutely certain, while there can be no doubt about motherhood, it is the mother, not the father, that determines consanguinity or kinship, and succession or heredity. The father's relation to his children is as loose as, with us, that of a stepfather to his stepchildren. Of course, affection is commensurate with the belief in consanguinity. Therefore, the closest relation is that of mother and child, the next that of nephew or niece and uncle or aunt. The uncle owns his nephews and nieces; he can sell them, and they are his heirs, not only in private property, but also in the chiefship, if he be a chief.

Polygamy is honored, although its evil concomitants are not ignored. In the absence of metal or paper money to represent capital, a large number of wives, of children, and hence a wide circle of blood connection and influence, is considered the best investment and most substantial element of wealth. Each wife occupies a separate house and tills her own fields. She provides her husband with food and tobacco; he builds her house and procures her clothing. The money and other things given by the suitor to the girl's parents are not the "price" of the girl, as is often said, but the "pledge" and symbol of the contract thereby executed. If he treats her unmercifully he may lose the money; if she proves untrue or unfruitful the parents have to return the gifts. Impotence in men and barrenness in women are the greatest misfortunes that may befall them. Blindness and lameness are trifles compared to that, so great is the abomination in which these infirmities are held.

One of the most important institutions is that of the tambi, or funeral and mourning. The moment one dies, all those who are in the house and all those who soon come in, raise the most heart-rending wail, and this is repeated daily at stated hours, and for weeks and months by the nearest relatives. The corpse is wrapped in a mat and carried on a pole to the grave, followed by howling men and women who march in the quickest trot. Broken pottery and other objects are placed on the grave. On the grave of a hunter a mound of stones is raised, or skulls of wild animals are placed on the trimmed limbs of a dead tree.

In Loanda, the nearest relative of the deceased stays for months unwashed and unkempt in the bed just vacated; the windows are closed, the room kept unswept, and the mourner can break his or her silence only for the funeral wail. The greatest thing about the mourning, however, is the gathering of all the relatives and friends from afar for the mourning dance, and the regular Irish wakes they keep up at the expense of the successor and next of kin, as long as money lasts.

Circumcision is very widely practiced, but obligatory among only a few tribes.

Slavery and its unavoidable concomitant, the slave trade, are practiced all over Angola. It is based on three facts: (1) The right of the uncle to dispose of his nephews and nieces as merchandise, (2) the absence of penitentiaries, (3) war. If a man is unable to pay a debt, or has committed a crime and cannot otherwise pay the fine, he is sold himself or he sells his nephew or niece in his stead. Prisoners of war are reduced to slavery and sold to the highest bidder. As a rule, the slaves of "uncivilized" natives are not worked hard, nor cruelly treated; and they have a chance to redeem themselves. "Civilized" masters and the plantation owners, on the contrary, make the slaves' yoke a galling one, and sometimes thrash them to death.

This brings us to the subject of jurisprudence. Whenever natives quarrel, one party or both call one or more umpires, generally old men, to settle the case. If it is an important case it is also brought before the chief. In vital questions, such as that of witchcraft, the case is decided by the poison test, in which case the medicine man is practically the judge, and frequently the executioner as well.

The ever-repeated assertion that Africans are fetishists, that is, worshippers of inanimate objects, is utterly false, or else all superstitious people are fetishists. The Angolans have the same religious system as the Bantu generally. They are not idolaters in the strict sense, nor atheists, nor fetishists, nor polytheists, but superstitious deists. They believe in one great, invisible God who made all things and controls all things. But they confess they know very little about his character. Tradition says men have offended him, and he has withdrawn his affection from them. They do not formally worship God, nor do they ever represent him in any visible form, or think he is contained in a fetish of any sort. That is, inasmuch as they are purely native. They do, however, carve wooden images which they call gods; but the images thus called are always in the shape of a crucifix, and every native knows that the image does not represent their own great, invisible God, but the God or fetish of the whites. True fetishism I have found, in Africa, among ignorant Portuguese, who do assert and believe that this or that image is God, does work miracles and must be worshipped, not as a mere symbol of its spiritual prototype, but as the actual incarnation or embodiment of it, equal in all respects to the original.

What other figures the natives have are not idols, for they have no connection with the Deity; they are simply charms, amulets or talismans, to which the medicine man has, by his incantations, imparted certain virtues emanating from an inferior spirit.

These inferior spirits of Bantu mythology are generally, but without foundation, called African gods. It would be as rational to call the native chiefs gods because they are saluted by the most worshiplike prostrations. In their various attributes and powers, these spirits (ma-bamba) correspond pretty closely to the gods of classical antiquity, and to their modern substitutes, the saints, minus their intercessory office. Each spirit or demon represents some force of nature, is morally no better than sinful men, and, according to his capricious passions, deals with men in a friendly or unfriendly manner. The friendship of the demons must be secured and maintained by presents, offerings, sacrifices, and in these consists the only visible worship or cult of the Bantu. The media between demons and men are the professional medicine men or women, the diviners, and any individual having the gift of possession or inspiration. These media constitute a kind of secret order, and have much influence individually; but they are not organized into a hierarchy, nor do they exert any combined effort. A few of the genii, or demons, are: Kituta or Kianda, who rules over the water and is fond of great trees and of hilltops; Muta-Kalombo, who is king or governor of the woodland; hence of the chase and of the paths, and is to be propitiated by hunters and travelling traders; Lemba, to whom pertains the mysterious province of generation, gestation, birth, and childhood. The belief in the reality of these entities and in the power of their media is so deep, that even the civilized natives, whatever their position in the state, the church, the army, or commerce may be—though nominally Christians or professed rationalists and materialists conversant with Comte, Spencer, Renan—will secretly resort to them as soon as they find themselves in great straits. Yea, not a few whites, after prolonged intimacy with native women, have been found to become secret adepts of those heathen superstitions. The spirits or shades of mortals are never confounded in the native mind with the genii of nature; but their enmity is dreaded as much as that of the genii, and they are propitiated by the same or similar rites.

All the natives of the interior, that is, outside the cities of Loanda and Dondo, are supposed to know the rudiments of certain arts. For instance, all women must know something of midwifery, washing, cooking, trading, tilling, sewing, carrying on the head or back, etc. Every man must have learned something about building a house, hunting, carrying loads, cooking, trading, medicine, etc. In small, isolated communities a man has to be a jack-at-all-trades; in large settlements, division of labor produces specialties, and increases the exchange of commodities, that is, trade. The principal crafts or trades of native Angola are:

(1) *Medicine and Divining.* This has already been referred to under the subject of religion.

(2) *Hunting.* This has to be pursued as a specialty in order to be profitable, for since the introduction of firearms the game has become both scarce and wary.

(3) *Fishing.* This is, on the coast, one of the most important crafts, as the fish attracts the farthest inland tribes to the coast. But for its famous dried fish, Loanda would scarcely be visited by any inland caravans. The quantity of dried fish sold yearly from Loanda to the far interior is truly astounding, and the quantity of fresh fish daily consumed in the capital is not less amazing. The nets, the canoes and the sails used in this fishing business are all of native manufacture. A large proportion of the cotton thread is spun in Kisama and sold in Loanda. The fish of the rivers and lagoons of the interior is also dried and sold far away from where it was caught. Dried "bagres" stuck in a slit of a stick are to be seen for sale in most marketplaces.

(4) *Wood Carving.* Spoons, tubs, drums, mortars, stools, images for charms, ornamental clubs, smoking pipes, scepters of chiefs, plates,

bowls, snuffboxes, combs and a variety of other objects are produced by native sculptors in wood. As a rule every tribe has its own pattern or design.

(5) *Pottery.* Clay is found everywhere, and is used in the manufacture of cooking pots of all sizes, of water jugs resembling the amphoras of the ancients, of pipes, lamps, dishes, clay figures and, in some parts, of adobes for house building.

(6) *Spinning and Weaving.* The African loom is well known. The material used in weaving is either palm fiber or cotton thread. The cotton tree thrives all over Angola; and among all tribes spinning and weaving are carried on to some extent. All native textiles are very strong and durable. With the palm fibers natives make mats, which were, of old, the principal garment, and formed, with the cowry shells of Loanda, the currency which European cloth and coined money have not yet quite superseded. Mats are still manufactured and sometimes beautifully dyed, around the headwaters of the Lukala and Ndanji rivers and around Pungo Andongo; cotton mantles, hammocks, and loincloths are still woven for export to neighboring tribes by the people of Kisama.

(7) *Smelting and Smithing.* This trade is chiefly in the hands of wandering smiths whose original home is found in Luangu north of the Congo River. They still speak their Luangu dialect along with Ki-Mbundu. Their largest settlements are found between the Mbengu and Lufuni rivers, in the country of the independent Dembos. The articles they chiefly manufacture are: hoes, with single or double handles; hatchets, either for cutting or for ornament and cult; knives; needles for basket and mat making; arrowpoints; heads of spears; arm rings and anklets; earrings of brass or copper; and any object that may be ordered of them.

(8) *Basket, mat and rope making.* All Angolans sleep and eat on mats; the walls, doors and shutters of many huts are made of mats. This alone gives an idea of the quantities of mats that must be continually produced to replace the worn and torn. Angolan mats are principally of three kinds: (a) The coarse papyrus mat (ngandu); (b) the fine and large grass mats (ma-xisa), made of disenu grass; (c) the fine and small palm mats (ma-bela), used as clothing, for sacks, for covering tables or for the ornamentation of rooms. Baskets are made of all sizes, shapes and qualities: for carrying earth or stones; for holding flour and corn; for winnowing and for sifting; for carrying loads either on head, shoulder or back; for holding mush or cassava meal, and so on. The baskets are made of mateba palm leaf and fibrous grass. The former material is also used for sacks, fans, brooms and ropes. The baobab fiber is used for skirts (among the Kisamas), for ropes, sacks and caps. Hats are made of straw or mateba fiber by the Mbaka tribe. . . .

The internal native commerce of Angola is almost exclusively that of barter, one commodity being exchanged for another.

The Kisama people have salt, wax and honey, cotton cloths, orchilla weed, some game, cattle and agricultural produce to export to the north bank of the Quanza, where they receive in exchange guns, powder, Manchester cloth, blankets, rum, and minor articles.

The Lubolo tribe exports chiefly slaves, its greatest market being Dondo. As long as the trade in human beings continues, there is little hope of the Lubolos tapping the exhaustless resources of their spontaneous vegetation, fertile soil and minerals. Though in relatively small quantities, they do, even now, bring some food produce to barter for European goods.

The Songo tribe trades to some extent in rubber and wax; and some of the men earn a living by carrying loads between Malange and Dondo.

The Mbondo tribe gets its very limited requisite of European goods in exchange for cattle, food and scraps of rubber and other produce from the Kuangu River.

The Ngola tribe has only recently entered the labor field as carriers from Malange and Cazengo to Dondo or to the far interior. Most of the resources of the country are still untapped, and trade with the whites is on a very small scale.

The Mbamba people of the Malange district obtain what they want of European articles by carrying loads and hammocks for the whites of Malange and Pungo Andongo. As this suffices for their modest requirements, they do not produce anything. The bulk of the Mbamba, however, around the headwaters of the Lukala and Loji rivers, produce coffee.

The great Mbaka tribe displays its best qualities away from home. They used to be active agriculturists; and their peanuts (groundnuts) were exported to Europe in great quantities. But the extortions of some Portuguese "chefes" discouraged them from producing, and scattered them to the neighboring districts and to the farthest interior, where they are doing well as farmers, traders, tradesmen, secretaries of chiefs, clerks and servants of whites, and generally as pioneers of civilization. It is not the Portuguese, nor the Germans or Belgians, but the black Ambaca people, who have opened up the Kuangu, Kuilu and Kassai basins. They are the only people in Angola who cultivate rice. Their tobacco, too, is greatly appreciated. The main native produce of the districts of Cazengo, Golungo Alto and Dembos is coffee, nearly all of which is exported via Loanda.

MBUNDU HUMAN TALES:
KINGS, HUNTERS AND HEROES

King Kitamba kia Xiba

> The protagonist of this story, Kitamba kia Xiba,
> is believed to have been the twentieth king of
> Kasanji. Kalunga, to which the medicine man
> goes on his unique mission, is the land of the
> dead. When people die they go to Kalunga and
> "live" on, much in the way they did in the
> upper visible world. According to A-mbundu
> belief, people residing in Kalunga have yet to
> die another death, after which they enter the
> kingdom of Mbulu a Maminiu, where they re-
> main till the end of time.

Mbanza (King) Kitamba kia Xiba, a chief who was at Kasanji, had built
his village; he lived on. When he was thus, his head wife, Queen
Muhongo, died. They buried her; they wailed the mourning; it ended.

Mbanza Kitamba said: "Since my head wife died, I shall mourn; my
village too, no man shall do anything therein. The young people shall
not shout; the women shall not pound; no one shall speak in the village."
The headmen said: "Master, the woman is dead; thou sayest, 'In village
they shall not speak; I will not eat, not drink; not speak'; we never yet
saw this." He, the king, said, "If you desire that I laugh, that I talk, that
in the village they talk, it shall be that you bring me my head wife,
Queen Muhongo." The headmen say, "King, the person is now dead;
how can we fetch her?" He said: "If ye cannot fetch her, I am in
mourning; in my village, no person shall talk."

The headmen consult among themselves, saying: "Let us seek a medicine man." They send for the medicine man; the calling-present to the
doctor is a gun. The doctor has come; his cooking is a cow. The doctor
said, "Tell, what you sent me for." They said: "The head queen
Muhongo is dead; King Kitamba says, 'I will mourn; in the village no one
shall talk; if you want to talk, you must fetch me my head wife, Queen
Muhongo.' Therefore it is we sent for thee, thee, the doctor, that thou
fetchest her, the head queen, from Kalunga; that the people may rejoice."

The doctor said, "All right." He went through the country gathering
herbs; he set a medicine mortar outside, saying: "The king, he shall
come and wash; all the people shall wash." The chief washed; all the
people washed. The doctor said, "Dig ye a grave in my guest hut, at the
fireplace." They dug the grave; it is done.

He entered the grave with his little child, which had come with him.
He told his wife, saying: "All days, do not wear a girdle; thou shalt tuck
in only. All days thou shalt constantly put water on the fireplace here."
The woman assented. The doctor said, "Cover ye it up." They filled it

up, with the doctor and his child; they rammed it down as when there was the fireplace itself. They lived on. The wife always puts the water on the fireplace, all days.

The doctor, when he got into the grave, there opened a large road. He starts on the road; he goes ahead; his child walks behind. They walk awhile; they arrive beside a village; that is at Kalunga-ngombe's. The doctor looks into the middle of the village; Queen Muhongo is yonder; she is sewing a basket. He arrives where Queen Muhongo is; Queen Muhongo turns her eyes. She sees a man who is coming, she says, "Thou, who art coming, whence comest thou?" The doctor said: "Thou, thyself, I have sought thee. Since thou art dead, King Kitamba will not eat, will not drink, will not speak. In the village they pound not; they speak not; he says, 'If I shall talk, if I eat, go ye and fetch my head wife.' That is what brought me here. I have spoken."

The head queen said: "Very well. Come look at that one; who is it sitting?" The doctor said, "I know him not." The head queen said, "He is Lord Kalunga-ngombe; he is always consuming us, us all." She said again: "He yonder, who is he? who is in the chain." The doctor said, "He looks like King Kitamba, whom I left where I came from." The queen said: "He is King Kitamba. He is in the world not any longer; there lacks how many years, the chief will die. Thou, doctor, who camest to fetch me, we, here in Kalunga, never comes one here to return again. Take my arm ring, that they buried me with; that when thou goest there, they accuse thee not of lying, saying, 'thou wentest not there.' The chief himself, do not tell it him, saying, 'I found thee already in Kalunga.' " She paused. She said again: "Thou thyself, doctor, I cannot give thee to eat here. If thou eatest here, thou canst return no more." The doctor said: "Well." He departed.

He arrives at the place where he got into the grave with his child, that he went with. The woman, who stayed on earth, kept putting water on the fireplace. One day, she looks at the fireplace: there are cracks breaking. A while, she looks: the head of the doctor has come out. The doctor throws his arms outside; he gets out; he is on ground. He takes the child by the arm; he sets him on ground. The child looks at the sun; he faints. The doctor goes to the bush; he gathers herbs. He comes; he washes him. The son comes to. They slept.

In morning, the doctor says, "You, headmen of the town, who fetched me, come here that I report where I went." The headmen all come; he reports everything that the head queen had told him. The doctor said: "Finished. Pay me now." The headmen said, "Well." They took two slaves; they paid him. The doctor went to his home.

The headmen reported to the chief, saying: "The doctor reported, saying, 'I went to Kalunga-ngombe's. The chief's wife, I found her, said: "Since thou didst die, the chief does not eat, does not drink; come, let us go." The queen returned to me, saying: "We, here, there comes not a person, to return anymore. This my arm ring, take it along, that they see thee not with lies." ' That is what the doctor reported to us. Thou, king, we have spoken. The ring is here, which they buried the queen with." The chief said, "Truth; it is the same."

When they spent a few days, the chief, he eats; the chief, he drinks. They spent a few years, the chief died. They wailed the funeral; they scattered.

King Kitamba kia Xiba in Kasanji left this story.

The Young Man and the River

> This tale tells of a boy indentured, or given into slavery, by his uncle, who cannot pay a debt of one ox. Because the boy's relatives die, there is no one to buy his freedom. In the end, the river comes to his aid by giving him the gift of medical knowledge.

A young man was given as a pledge by his uncle, the pledge of an ox. They lived on.

His uncle died; there is none to redeem him. His father died; there is none to redeem him. His relatives all died; no person was able to redeem him. In bondship, there he hoes; he cuts wood; he gets water. Now they beat him. His masters of bondship, they do not dress him at all. He goes about in rags, to walk and cry to himself in the bush. He says: "I am seeing great misery, because of lacking a relative of mine, who can redeem me." He lived on. When his uncle gave him as a pledge, he was a child; but now he has become a young man. He keeps on doing his slavery work.

One day, he goes to sleep; he dreams a dream, that the River is speaking to him, saying: "Tomorrow in morning, when the people have not opened yet, be early at the landing. Three things, that thou shalt find there, whichever pleases thee, take. The best is the ngonga-basket; as to the other two things, they are inferior." The young man awakes from sleep: it is a dream. He thinks, says, "The dream, that I dreamt, it meant what?" He kept quiet.

He spent three days; on the fourth, he dreamt again, the River saying: "Thou, I have told thee, saying, 'tomorrow in the morning, be early at the landing. The thing that pleases thee, take.' Now, because of what didst thou not go there?" The River paused.

The young man awakes: a dream. Outside it was just beginning to dawn. He gets up; they all have not yet opened. He enters the road; arrives at the landing. He stands at the side of the water. A moment, he sees a bundle of guns that is coming on top of the water. The muzzles are downward under the water, the butt ends are looking upwards; he keeps quiet. He looks again; two bales of cotton cloth are coming on top of the water; they pass by. A moment again, he looks: a small basket is coming; it arrives where he stands. It also stands still. He takes it;

returns home. He arrived at the side of the house; he cut a small twig. He struck the basket; he hid it in the grass wall of the house. He went into the house; kept quiet.

His masters said: "Devil, take up the hoe; go to till. When thou leavest the tilling, thou shalt come with a bundle of fire sticks." He took up the hoe; he went to the fields. He hoed; he left hoeing. He cut wood; he bound it. He took it up; he arrived at home. He laid down the fire sticks; kept quiet; slept.

Morning, he says, "I will look first inside of the basket." He opens it: medicine things all complete are in it. He closed it again; laid it aside. He went to cut wood; came, laid it down. They say, "Go to the landing." He went, bailed; came, set down. The sun died; he goes to sleep. He dreams that they are showing him the plants of medicine, saying: "When thou goest to cure such diseases, the plants are such. Whoever has sores, his plant is such a one. The medicine of chiefs, thou shalt make it this way and this way." They are silent; he wakes up: a dream.

He gets up; goes to the fields. He has worked; has come home. He slept two days. In village, there have come two persons who are seeking a doctor. He is in the house, the two persons are speaking with his master of bondship.

His master says: "We, here, there is not a doctor. Go ye, and seek elsewhere." He, the young man, goes out of the house; asks the two men, saying, "Gentlemen, which sickness is ailing him for whom you come to seek a doctor?" The two men said, "The sickness, thou shalt find it thyself." He says, "Ye give me the calling fee." They say, "The fee is how much?" He said, "A piece" "[i.e., a piece of trade cloth]. They said, "We agree." They give him the piece. His master of bondship said: "This one is presumptuous. Thou indeed, ever since we are two, the plant of the thread-worm thou knowest it not; the medicine to cure the sick man, where wilt thou find it?" He said, "Master, I am learning only." His master of bondship told the two men, saying, "If he does not master it, beat him; because he was presumptuous." They started with him; they arrived at house where was the patient.

They tell the patient, saying, "The doctor, we have come with him." He, the doctor, looked at the patient, said, "I can cure him." He begins to doctor every day. Where it fails him, he is shown in sleep. In twenty days, the patient is safe. The doctor says, "The patient is already well; pay me, that I may go." They say, "Thy pay, how much?" Says he, "A heifer." They agree, because all the doctors had given him up, but he mastered him. They paid him; he returned to his home.

He finds his master of bondship. His master asks him, saying, "The medicine, couldst thou do it?" Says he, "I could; the patient is cured; they paid me a heifer." His master says, "All right." He took his heifer. They lived on some days.

There came again people to seek a doctor. He went with them; he cured; they paid him again a heifer. He came home; now he is famous in all the land. They say, "He is a doctor of truth."

He spent three years; he is already at six cattle. He considers, says, "I will redeem myself now." He asks his master of bondship, saying, "I want to go wherever I choose; I shall redeem myself for how much?" His master said, "Bring three mother cows." He gave him them; he left there. He went to another country that pleased him. He built; married; lived on, practicing medicine. In six years he has a herd of many cattle; he has come to be a rich man.

Our friend, who had been put in bondship, and had to see much misery, River gave to him medicine. He earned the cattle; he redeemed himself; he soon became a great man, celebrated. "Wealth came from medicine" [i.e., "Knowledge is the source of prosperity."].

I have told stories and stories; if you have heard, hush! In mouth there remain tongue and teeth. He who has cut wood, binds; he who has done hoeing, leaves work. He who came to go, says, "I am going." Finished.

[Towards the end of this story, Heli Chatelain introduces a non-African literary saying, which the editor has eliminated.]

Kingungu A Njila and Ngundu A Ndala

"They quarrelled in the bush; witnesses,
We get them from (their) tongues."

Kingungu a Njila took up his gun, saying, "I will go a-shooting." He arrived in forest; he is stalking the elephants. He approached them; he shot one elephant; it fell on ground.

Ngundu a Ndala heard the gun of Kingungu a Njila. He is looking, "Who has shot here?" He arrives where is the elephant of Kingungu a Njila. He too shot it again, saying, "The elephant is mine."

Kingungu a Njila came; said: "This is my elephant; thou foundest me with it. Thou, why speakest thou, saying 'the elephant is mine'?" Then they begin a quarrel about the elephant. They say, "Let us go home; there let us plead!"

Kingungu a Njila went to So-and-So; he accused. They call Ngundu a Ndala; they say, "Plead ye." Kingungu a Njila explained how he killed the elephant. Ngundu a Ndala pleaded too. So-and-So said: "The case, how shall I judge it? There is no witness who saw which one spoke the truth and which one spoke untruth." Says: "Go ye home. The case, tomorrow I shall decide it; because my wife is not here." They separate; the sun goes down.

Kingungu a Njila went to his elephant; Ngundu a Ndala came too. Kingungu a Njila begins to cry, saying, "This, this elephant is my elephant!" Ngungu a Ndala too begins to cry, saying: "This elephant is my elephant! This elephant is my elephant!" He cried one hour. He went away.

Kingungu a Njila still kept on crying: "This elephant is my elephant! This elephant is my elephant!" He laid all night there crying.

The morning shone. They call them, "Come now to plead." Kingungu a Njila pleaded the same as he pleaded yesterday. Ngundu a Ndala pleaded falsely. So-and-So asks the messengers, saying, "You, who stayed overnight with Kingungu a Njila and Ngundu a Ndala, now who laid all night crying until dawn?" The messengers said: "Kingungu a Njila, he laid all night crying. Ngundu a Ndala yesterday cried one hour."

So-and-So says, "Kingungu a Njila is going to win." They have come to decide the case. So-and-So says: "Thou, Kingungu a Njila art right; thou, Ngundu a Ndala art wrong. The other wanted to take wrongly his elephant."

Thus far, that we have heard it. The end.

Two Men, One Woman

An elderly man had one daughter; her name was nga Samba. This daughter, a number of men wanted her. Her father would not give her. When there comes a man, her father demands of him a living deer. The men, each and all, who wanted his daughter, then they refuse, saying, "The living deer, we cannot get it."

One day, there appear two men, saying, "We have come to the old man who owns a daughter, nga Samba." The man then comes out, and they greet each other. He asks them, saying: "What is it you wish?" One of them says to him, "I have come to ask for thy daughter, whom I want." He turns to the other; he asks him also what brought him. The other tells him, saying, "I have come to ask for thy daughter; I want her, that she be my consort."

Then her father says: "The girl is one. You have come to ask her, two of you. I now am possessor of one daughter only; I have not two children. He, who brings me the living deer; the same, I will give him my daughter." And they go away.

On the road, on which they were walking, one speaks, saying, "Tomorrow, I will seek the living deer in the forest." Then the other: "I too, tomorrow I will go to seek the deer. Where shall we meet tomorrow, to go and seek the deer?" The other then says to him, "Tomorrow we will meet at the muxixi-tree, outside the forest." And they go, each one to his home. And they sleep.

In early morning, they rise, dress, with their machetes; and they go to meet for seeking the living deer. When they found each other, then they go until they are in the forest.

They come across a deer; they begin to pursue it. One pursued, got tired; he cannot run anymore. Says: "That woman will destroy my life. Shall I suffer distress because of a woman? If I bring her home, if she dies, would I seek another? I will not run again to catch a living deer. I never saw it, that a girl was wooed with a living deer. I will await my comrade, whether he gives up, that we may go."

When he had spent a while, he sees the other, who comes with a deer bound. When he had completed approaching, he says, "Friend, the deer, didst thou catch it indeed?" Then the other: "I caught it. That girl delights me much. Rather I would sleep in forest, than to fail to catch it."

And they go to the man who begat the young woman. They bring him the deer. Then the old man: "The deer, keep ye it; eat, please. Directly we will talk the matter over." And he orders to cook the food for them.

When they had done eating, this old man, who begat his daughter, then calls four old men, and says to them, saying: "I have one daughter; I did not beget a son. I need a good son-in-law, gentle of heart. Therefore I always demand a living deer. These gentlemen came yesterday, two of them, to ask for my daughter, and I told them saying, 'I am possessor of one daughter; he who wants her let him bring me a living deer.' Today these have come with it. They two came to ask for the girl; one only brought the deer. The other, what has moved him, that he did not come with a deer? You, aged men and neighbors, to you indeed I have given my daughter. Choose ye our son-in-law among these two."

The aged men, they ask these two gentlemen, saying: "Yesterday you came to ask for the girl, two of you; today, one came with the deer; the other, what has caused him not to come with it?"

Then one of the gentlemen said: "We went into the forest to seek deers, both of us, and we saw them. My comrade pursued and gave up; I, your daughter charmed me much, even to the heart, and I pursued the deer till it gave in. And I caught it; I bound it; and joined my comrade where he got tired. My comrade, he came only to accompany me."

Then the aged men say: "Thou, sir, who gavest up the deer, what crime caused thee to get tired of catching the deer, if thou didst want our daughter?" "I never saw, that they wooed a girl with a deer. I went with my comrade to seek a deer, perhaps I might catch it. When I saw the great running, I said: 'No, that woman will cost my life. Women are plentiful.' And I sat down to await my comrade, to see whether he would give up chasing the deer, and come, so that we might go. I saw my companion coming with the deer bound. I have only come to accompany him. I have not come again to your daughter."

Then the aged men: "Thou, who gavest up catching the deer, thou art our son-in-law. This gentleman, who caught the deer, he may go with it; he may eat it or may sell it; for he is a man of great heart. If he wants to kill, he kills at once; he does not listen to one who scolds him, or gives him advice. Our daughter, if we gave her to him, and she did wrong, when he would beat her, he would not hear one who entreats for her. We do not want him; let him go. This gentleman, who gave up the deer, he is our son-in-law; because, our daughter, when she does wrong, when we come to pacify him, he will listen to us. Although he were in great anger, when he sees us, his anger will cease. He is our good son-in-law, whom we have chosen."

A Father-in-Law and His Son-in-Law

One day at night, a father-in-law and his son-in-law were outside spending the evening. The darkness grew great and the father-in-law stood up whence he sat, saying: "My son-in-law, let us go to sleep! There is a darkness like the gloom of a blind eye." His son-in-law then remained with shame, for he was dead of one eye; but he kept quiet.

One night, when moonshine had come, they are again gossiping outside, both the father-in-law and the son-in-law. The son-in-law then tells his father-in-law, "O sir, let us go to sleep; for there is a moonlight of bald-head shine! that will do us harm outside, where we are."

The father-in-law then goes into his house. He will no more wish good-bye nicely to his son-in-law. His son-in-law also then goes away into his house.

In three days, the father-in-law calls six aged men, seven with himself. Says, "I want to be heard about the insult, which my son-in-law gave me." The aged men then send to call the son-in-law. When he came, the father-in-law then spake: "You, gentlemen, they are wont to say this proverb, 'Where is a bought one, do not there refer to it.' But, my son-in-law, one day, we were outside spending the night, he sees the moonlight set in, he will not speak to me, saying, 'let us go to sleep'; he speaks to me, with a heart to offend me, saying, 'there is a moonlight of bald-head shine! let us go to sleep, my father-in-law, for this moonlight, it will do us harm.' Therefore, until today let him be with my daughter; but I am not his friend, because of insults which he gave me. I am bald-headed, he said 'bald-head shine.' Me, did he not insult me? Therefore I reject the friendship with him."

Then the son-in-law: "I would not have said it, if my father-in-law had not been first in insulting me. One day, after dark, we are outside gossiping, my father-in-law told me, saying: 'Come let us go to sleep; for there is a darkness as the gloom of a blind eye.' I am dead of one eye; did he not insult me thus, you gentlemen?" "Truth; he insulted thee. Why! thy son-in-law, who is dead of one eye, thou comest to say this saying about the darkness! If he said the moonlight of bald-head shine! he returned what thou begannest to tell him. Thus be not in enmity, both son-in-law and father-in-law. Thou, father-in-law, hast no son; thy son, [he] is thy son-in-law. Thou thyself wast first in offending him; he then retorted to thee also. Be ye friends. This affair, do not go away with it; take it out of your heart. Because thou, the aged, wast the first, the younger he paid thee back. We will not hate each other because of these things. Bring rum; let us drink. We will have no bad words like those. Thou thyself hast said it, 'Where is a bought one, do not refer to it.' Thou knewest that thy son-in-law is one-eyed; thou didst refer to it; now when he pays it back, shall it be a crime?"

They then remained in friendship, both the son-in-law and the father-in-law.

The Young Man and the Skull

A young man started on a journey; he arrived in middle of the path. He finds a skull of the head of a person. They all used to pass it by there. But he, when he arrived there, he struck it with staff, saying, "Thou, foolishness has killed thee." The skull said, "I, foolishness has killed me; thou, soon smartness shall kill thee." The young man said: "I have met an omen; where I was to go, I will not go, but return hence at once. The head of a person has spoken to me!"

And he returned; arrived at home. He finds others, old men, says, "You, gentlemen, I have met an ominous wonder." The old men said, "What omen?" He says, "The head of a person has spoken to me." The people say: "O man, thou hast told a lie. We all of us, at same place we are wont to pass by the head. We never yet heard it speak; how has the head spoken to thee?" He said: "Let us go. When I beat it with staff, if it does not speak, I, cut off my head." They say, "All right."

The crowd starts with him; they arrive at the place; they found it. The young man beat it with his staff, "Foolishness has killed thee." The head kept silent. He beat it again, the second time, saying, "Foolishness has killed thee." The head kept silent. The crowd say: "O man! thou didst tell a lie." They cut off his head. When they finished cutting it off, the skull said: "I, foolishness has killed me; thou, smartness has killed thee." The people said: "Why, we killed him unjustly; the head of a person has spoken."

The young man found the head of a person, and he beat it, saying, "Foolishness has killed thee." The head of the person said, "Thou, soon smartness shall kill thee." Wits and foolishness, all are equal. The young man, his wits killed him.

Finished.

The White Man and the Negro

Two men, a white man and a Negro, had a discussion.

The white man said: "I, in my house there is lacking nothing. I have all things." The Negro said: "Untruth! In thy house, I look for a thing, I do not find it." The white man said: "You, Negroes, you lack all things; I have to look for nothing."

The Negro assented; went to his house. He spent a month. He wove his mat; he is sewing it. He arrives in the middle of the mat; the cords give out. There is no more a place where he can take the dry cords. He says: "How shall I do? I will go to the house of the white man, that he give me the cords, that I may finish the mat."

He arose; arrives at the white man's, says, "Sir, I am in need at the place whence I come." The white man says: "What needest thou?" He says: "I was weaving a mat; it gave out. I said, 'I will go to the house, in which are all things; the white man that he give me a few cords, that I may finish my mat.'"

The white man looks at him; he laughs. He goes into the store; he looks in it: there are no cords in it. He says: "Negro, thou art lucky." He takes a hundred macutas; he gives them to the Negro.

The discussion, that the white man had with the Negro, the Negro won it, the white man lost it.

The Past and the Future

Two men were walking on road. They arrived in midst of road; they found a tapper of palm-wine; they say, "Give us palm-wine!"

The tapper says, "If I give you palm-wine, tell me your names!" The first said, "I am Whence-we-come." He who remained behind said, "I am Where-we-go." The tapper of palm-wine said: "Thou, Whence-we-come, hast a beautiful name; thou, Where-we-go, spakest evil. I will not give thee palm-wine."

They began to quarrel; they go to be judged. They find So-and-So; they plead. So-and-So says: "Where-we-go is right, the tapper is wrong; because, where we have already left, we cannot thence get anything more. The thing that we shall find, is where we are going to."

Finished.

MBUNDU ANIMAL TALES

The animal tale in African tradition amuses and entertains, provides explanations, and frequently, as an obvious or subtle parable, comments on human foibles and values. If the protagonist of the story is the trickster hero, the main theme may be the victory of shrewdness over stupidity, but the narrative may also include an implied social commentary or moral preachment. The relevance of the story to human behavior, even though unstated, is usually clear. The animal tale is therefore important as a carrier of deeply rooted attitudes about what is good or proper and what is not.

These tales are from Chatelain, ibid.

Squirrel and the Kingship

"Squirrel," the people said, "directly, we will give him the kingship." He said, "It shall be today." The people said, "We are looking for the insignia of the kingship." Squirrel said, "I, it shall be today, at once." The people said: "He, we only told him, saying, 'we are going to get the insignia.' He says, 'it shall be today'; why, we will give it to him no more. If we gave him it, he could not govern the people."

Squirrel, they talked of giving him the kingship. He said, "It must be today." It remained among the people, "Today at once deprived Squirrel of the kingship."

I have told the little story. Finished.

Dog and the Kingship

Mr. Dog, they wanted to invest him with the kingship. They sought all the things of royalty: the cap, the scepter, the rings, the skin of mukaka [a rodent]. The things are complete; they say, "The day has come to install."

The headmen all came in full; they sent for the players of drum and marimba; they have come. They spread coarse mats and fine mats. Where the lord is going to sit, they laid a coarse mat; they spread on it a fine mat; they set a chair on. They say: "Let the lord sit down." He sat down. The people begin to divide the victuals.

He, Mr. Dog, on seeing the breast of a fowl, greed grasped him. He stood up in haste; took the breast of the fowl; ran into the bush. The people said: "The lord, whom we are installing, has run away with the breast of the fowl into the bush!" The people separated.

Mr. Dog, who was going to be invested with the kingship, because of his thievery, the kingship he lost it.

I have told my little tale. Finished.

Dog and Lizard

Mr. Dog played friendship with Lizard. Dog goes to entertain Lizard all days.

This day, Mr. Dog went to entertain his friend Lizard. Lizard says, "You, dogs, who are always with men, you go to catch the game in the bush; you always eat much meat." Mr. Dog says, "We do not often eat meat." Lizard says, "You always go to hunt game, you dogs; you catch the game." Dog says: "The day after tomorrow we are to go a-hunting. Thou, Lizard, when we come from hunting, shalt climb on thy tree, where we usually divide the game. I, when I shall take a bit of meat, thou shalt see that they give me the staff on my head." They slept twice.

Day breaks in morning; the men call the dogs, "Let us go a-hunting!" They arrive on game-ground; they kill game; they come where they are used to divide. They are dividing. Dog lifts a small bit of meat. They give him a heavy clubbing. Mr. Dog he yelled, "Ué! ué!"

He looked with his neck up to the tree; his friend nods with his head: "Why, truth, what thou didst say."

Dog and Jackal

Jackal used to be in the bush with his kinsman, Dog. Jackal then sends Dog, saying: "Go to the houses, to fetch some fire. When thou comest with it, we will burn the prairie of grass; so as to catch locusts and eat." Dog agreed.

He started; arrived in the village. He enters a house; finds a woman, who is feeding her child with mush. Dog sat down; fire, he will not take it. The woman has fed her child; she scrapes the pot. She takes mush; she gives it to Dog. Dog eats; thinks, saying: "Why, I am all the time just dying with hunger in the bush; in the village there is good eating." The Dog settled there.

Jackal, behind where he stayed, looked for the other, who was sent for fire; he does not appear.

The Jackal, whenever he is howling, people say, "The Jackal is howling, tway!" But no; he is speaking, saying: "I am surprised, I, Jackal of Ngonga; Dog, whom I sent for fire, when he found mush, he was seduced; he stayed for good."

The people, when they were in villages, had not any dogs. What brought the dogs, Jackal sent Dog to fetch fire in the village. Dog, when he came to the village, found food there; it pleased him. Now he lives with the people. Finished.

The House-Hog and the Wild Boar

Boar used to be with his kinsman, Hog, in the forest. As they were, Hog said, "I am going to the village, to live with the men." Boar said, "To the village, do not go there; there they hate the animals." Hog said, "I will go to the village; I shall always eat the food, that men eat; in the bush there are bitter plants."

Hog started; he arrives in the village. They built him a sty; he entered; stayed. He bred in the village; they seized him. Now they kill him; because he has already left seed.

Whenever the hog squeaks, when they kill it, it is speaking, saying: "Boar, he told me, saying, 'in the village, do not go there'; I said, 'to the same I will go.'"

When it is left already with little life, it says, "I die, I die, I, Hog."

People, when they were, they had no hogs; what brought the hogs to the habitations is that the food, which the people are wont to eat, is good.

Finished.

Partridge and Turtle

I will tell of Partridge who had a discussion with Turtle.

Partridge said: "Thou, friend Turtle, never canst run away. When the fire is coming into the land, thou art always burnt." Turtle said: "I cannot be burnt. Thou art burnt, thou, Partridge." Partridge said: "I have my wings; I fly. Thou canst not fly, canst not run; thou shalt burn just here, in this very same place." They were silent.

They spent days; the dry season came. The fires begin over the country. The bush, where are Turtle and Partridge, it is set on fire. The fire approaches where Turtle is; Turtle gets into an anthill. It comes where Partridge is; Partridge runs; it will not do. The fire comes nearer him; he begins to fly from the fire. The fire catches him; he is burnt.

The fire came to end in country. The hunters, who had come to the fire-hunt, have scattered. Turtle comes out of the anthill; he looks on ground; Partridge is burnt! He says: "What! comrade Partridge, I had with him that discussion, he saying 'thou shalt be burnt;' but he himself was burnt."

Turtle took him by the leg; he took off from him a spur. He begins to play with the spur of Partridge, saying:

> "Little horn of Partridge,
> Partridge is dead,
> The little horn is left."

Partridge had a discussion with Turtle; Partridge was burnt; Turtle escaped.

Lion and Wolf

Lion roared, saying: "In the world there is not another equal to me in strength; only my friend, Elephant Ngola 'Aniinii and Red-ant of Malemba, whose touch is pain, they are equal to me."

But the Wolf, who had lurked in the thicket, then gets up; moves off a short distance, says: "Lion, thou toldest a lie, saying 'in the world there is no other equal to me.' The Know-much [i.e., Man] is stronger." He walks a little, says again, "The Hang-arms is stronger!"

Lion looks at Wolf. Anger takes him, and he chases him; he gives him up.

Therefore it is they hate each other; because Lion once told a lie; but Wolf, he exposed him.

Frog and His Two Wives

I will tell of Frog Kumboto, who married two wives. This wife, he built for her on the East; the other, he built for her on the West. He, his favorite place was in the middle.

The wives cooked mush, both of them; it was done at the same time. The head wife took a messenger, saying, "Go and fetch your father!" The inferior wife also took up a messenger, saying, "Go and fetch your father!"

The messengers started; they arrived at the same time. One said, "They sent for thee." The other said, "They sent for thee." Frog said, "How shall I do? Both wives sent for me. If I begin by going to the superior, the inferior will say, 'thou wentest first to the head wife'; but if I begin by going to the inferior, the superior will say, 'thou wentest first to thy sweetheart.' " Frog began to sing, saying:

"I am in trouble! I am in trouble!
I am in trouble! I am in trouble!"

Frog had married two wives; they cooked mush at the same time. They sent for him at the same time. Frog said, "How shall I do?" He whenever he is croaking: Kuó-kuó! kuó-kuó! people say, "The frog is croaking." But no; he is speaking, saying:

"I am in trouble!"

Variants of the story of frog and his two wives are known elsewhere in Africa. In the version given here, as in the others, there is an implied commentary on the difficulties sometimes raised by the practice of polygamy. In numerous African stories the plot hangs on the competition between wives or on the failure of the husband to resolve that competition.

Dinianga dia Ngombe and Deer

Dinianga dia Ngombe took up his gun, saying, "I will go hunting." He arrived in the bush; he found Deer, who was eating mudia-mbâmbi. He set up a tree-seat; he returned home.

He awaited the hour when Deer eats, and said, "I am going now!" He takes up the gun; he arrives at the tree-seat. He climbs into it. He spends a while; Deer comes.

He sets the gun to the shoulder; he cocks it; he fires. Deer falls on ground. He gets down. He grasps Deer by a leg; he finishes it with the hatchet; it is dead. He takes the knife from waist; he is flaying the Deer.

Deer is done being flayed; he pulls the hide from under Deer; Deer stands up!

It runs away in haste. It reaches a distance; stands. The Hunter, who remained with hide in hands, says: "What is this ominous wonder, that I meet with? The deer that I killed, it leaves the hide in my hands!" He says: "Thou, Deer, shame will seize thee, when thou shalt arrive at thy father's and thy mother's; they will ask thee, 'Thou comest naked; the skin, thou didst leave it where?'"

Deer says: "Shame is thine, Nianga, as shame is mine, Deer. Thou, when thou shalt arrive at home, and findest thy people and thy wife, thou sayest, 'I went to lurk; I shot a deer. It died; I flayed it. The deer stood up; it left the hide in my hands.' Shame will seize thee."

Deer has spoken; Dinianga does not reply to him again. He says, "I am going home." He took up his gun; he went home. He found his folks and his wife. He says: "I met with an ominous wonder! I went to lurk. Deer came; I shot it; it died. I skinned it; Deer stood up; it left me the hide in my hands." The others laugh at him.

Thus Deer won; Nianga lost.

NZAMBI AND NZAMBI MPUNGU

Among various related peoples of the lower stretches of the Zaire (Congo) River the name Nzambi designates a supreme god comparable to Nyame among the Ashanti and the Yoruba deity Olorun. But according to some students of Bakongo customs, there were in fact two major gods in that region—Nzambi Mpungu, a male sky god, and his daughter, Nzambi, who ruled the earth. Whereas Nzambi Mpungu is remote from the affairs of men, the earth goddess Nzambi is ever-present and frequently invoked for assistance. One explanation says that Nzambi Mpungu created the earth and sent Nzambi down to take charge of his creation, after which he came down, married her, and became the father of the human race. The following stories are about encounters with the two deities, or about the gods themselves.

These tales are from Folklore of the Fjort, *by R. E. Dennett. London, 1898.*

The Bird Messengers

All the towns in Ncotchi were suffering terribly from the awful
scourge or evil wind (smallpox). And the chief prince called the princes
and people together and asked them if it were not time to ask Nzambi
Mpungu why he was so cross with them? And they all agreed that it was
so. But whom were they to send? They said that the ngongongo was a
wonderful bird, and could fly in a marvelous way. They sent him with
a message to Nzambi Mpungu; but when he got there, and cried out,
"quang, quang, quang," it was evident that Nzambi Mpungu did not
understand his tongue. So he flew back back to Ncotchi and reported
his failure.

Then Ncotchi sent the rock pigeon (mbemba), but he could not make
Nzambi Mpungu understand, and he also returned to Ncotchi.

Then the prince sent the ground dove (ndumbu nkuku), and she went
and sang before Nzambi Mpungu:

> "Mafuka Matenda is dead,
> Vanji Maloango is dead,
> Vanji Makongo is dead;
> This is the news that I bring."

And Nzambi Mpungu heard what the dove had said, but answered
not.

Nzambi Mpungu's Ambassador

Nzambi Mpungu heard that someone across the seas was making
people who could speak. This roused his ire, so that he called the ox, the
tiger, the antelope, the cock, and other birds together, and after telling
them the news, he appointed the cock his ambassador.

"Tell the white man that I alone am allowed to make people who can
talk, and that it is wrong of them to make images of men and give them
the power of speech."

And the cock left during the night, passing through a village about
midnight, and only a few of the people got up to do honor to Nzambi
Mpungu's ambassador, so that Nzambi Mpungu waxed wroth, and
turned the inhabitants of that village into monkeys.

Who Beats Nzambi's Drum?

Nzambi was in her town resting, when she was called to settle a palaver
in a town nearby. She and her followers went, and after the usual
preliminary formalities, commenced to talk the palaver. While they
were yet talking, Nzambi heard the drum beaten in her own town, and
wondered greatly what the matter could be. She sent the pig to see what

the disturbance was, and to find out who had dared to beat her Ndungu zilo, or great drum, during her absence. But the pig returned, and said, "Princess, I did not see anyone in the town, and all was quiet and in order."

"Strange!" said Nzambi, "but I distinctly heard the beating of my drum."

They continued the palaver until Nzambi again heard her drum beating.

"Go immediately, O antelope!" said Nzambi, "and find out who is beating my drum."

The antelope went and returned; but he had not seen nor heard anything. They continued the palaver, and just as they drew it to a close, Nzambi heard the drum a third time.

"Let us all go and find out," said Nzambi, "who has thus dared to disturb us."

They went, but saw nothing.

"Hide yourselves in the grass round about the town, and watch for the intruder!"

Then they saw the crab coming out of the water. Breathlessly they all watched him. They saw the crab creep stealthily up to the drum and beat it. Then they heard him sing:

"Oh, Nzambi has gone up to the top of the mountain, and left me here all alone."

Then the people rushed out of the grass, and caught the terrified crab and dragged him to Nzambi.

And Nzambi rebuked him saying: "Thou hast acted as one without a head, henceforth thou shall be headless, and shalt be eaten by all men."

Nchonzo Nkila's Dance Drum

Nzambi Mpungu made the world and all the people in it. But Nzambi had made no drum for her people, so that they could not dance. Nchonzo Nkila, a little bird with a long tail, fashioned like a native drum that seems always to be beating the earth, lived in a small village near to the town that Nzambi had chosen as her place of residence. This Nchonzo Nkila set to work, and was the first to make a drum. He then called his followers together, and they beat the drum and danced. And when Nzambi heard the beating of the drum she wanted it, so that her people might also dance. "What!" she said to her people, "I, a great princess, cannot dance, because I have no drum, while that little wagtail dances to the beat of the drum he has made. Go now, O antelope, and tell the little wagtail that his Great Mother wants his drum."

And the antelope went to wagtail's town and asked him to send Nzambi his drum.

"Nay," answered the wagtail, "I cannot give Nzambi my drum, because I want it myself."

"But," said the antelope, "the Great Mother gave you your life; surely you owe her something in return."

"Yes, truly," answered wagtail, "but I cannot give her my drum."

"Lend it to me then," said the antelope, "that I may play it for you."

"Certainly," said the wagtail.

But after beating the drum for a short time, the antelope ran away with it. Then wagtail waxed exceeding wroth, and sent his people after him. And they caught the antelope and killed him, and gave him to their women to cook for them.

After a while Kivunga, the hyena, was sent by Nzambi to see why the antelope was so long away. And he asked Nchonzo Nkila what had become of the antelope. And Nchonzo Nkila told him.

"Give me then some of his blood, that I may take it to our Mother, and show her."

Nchonzo Nkila gave him some, and Kivunga took it to Nzambi, and told her all that had occurred. And Nzambi was grieved at not being able to secure the drum. Then she addressed the Mpacasa, or wild ox, and besought him to get her the drum. But Mpacasa tried the same game as the antelope, and met with the same fate. Kivunga came again, and was told by the wagtail that Mpacasa had been killed by his people for trying to steal the drum. Kivunga returned to Nzambi, and told her how Mpacasa had tried to run away with the drum, and had been killed. Nzambi grieved sorely, and would not be comforted, and cried out to her people, praying them to get her Nchonzo Nkila's drum.

Then Mfiti (the ant) stood out from among the people and volunteered, saying, "Weep not, O Nzambi, I will get the drum for you."

"But you are so small a creature, how will you secure the drum?"

"From the fact of my being so small I shall escape detection."

And so the ant went out to wagtail's town, and waited there until all were asleep. Then he entered the house where the drum was kept, and carried it away unperceived, and brought it to Nzambi. And Nzambi rewarded the ant and then beat the drum and made all her people dance.

Then Nchonzo Nkila heard the noise, and said: "Listen! they are dancing in Nzambi's town. Surely they have stolen my drum."

And when they looked in the house for the drum, they found it not. So Nchonzo Nkila became very angry and called all the birds together; and they all came to hear what he had to say, save the Mbemba, or pigeon. Then they discussed the matter and decided upon sending Nzambi a messenger, asking her to appoint a place of meeting where the palaver between them might be talked. And Nzambi promised to be in Neamlau's town the next day to talk the palaver over before that prince.

Then Nchonzo Nkila and his followers went to Neamlau's town and awaited Nzambi. Two days they waited, and on the third Nzambi and her people arrived.

Then Nchonzo Nkila said: "O prince! I made a drum and Nzambi has taken it from me. It is for her to tell you why; let her speak."

Nzambi arose and said: "O prince! My people wished to dance, but we had no drum, and therefore they could not. Now I heard the sound of a drum being beaten in the village over which I had set Nchonzo Nkila to rule. I therefore first sent the antelope as my ambassador to Nchonzo Nkila, to ask him for the drum; but his people killed the antelope. I then sent Mpacasa for the drum; but they killed him also, as Kivunga will bear witness. Finally I sent the ant; and he brought me the drum, and my people danced and we were happy. Surely, O prince, I who brought forth all the living in this world have a right to this drum if I want it."

Then Kivunga told them all he knew of the palaver.

Neamlau and his old men, having heard all that was said, retired to drink water. When he returned, Neamlau said: "You have asked me to decide this question, and my judgment is this: It is true that Nzambi is the mother of us all, but Nchonzo Nkila certainly made the drum. Now when Nzambi made us, she left us free to live as we chose, and she did not give us drums at our birth. The drums we make ourselves; and they are therefore ours, just as we may be said to be Nzambi's. If she had made drums and sent them into the world with us, then the drums would be hers. But she did not. Therefore she was wrong to take the drum from Nchonzo Nkila."

Nzambi paid Nchonzo Nkila for the drum, and was fined for the mistake.

Then both Nzambi and Nchonzo Nkila gave presents to Neamlau and went their way.

Nzambi's Daughter and Her Slave

Nzambi had a most beautiful daughter, and she took the greatest care of her. As the child grew up, she was kept within the house, and never allowed to go outside, her mother alone waiting upon her. And when she arrived at the age of puberty, her mother determined to send her to a town a long way off, that she might be undisturbed while she underwent her purification in the paint-house.

She gave her child a slave; and unnoticed these two left Nzambi's town for the distant place where the paint-house was situated.

"Oh, see there, slave! what is that?"

"Give me your anklets, and I will tell you," answered the slave.

The daughter of Nzambi gave the slave the anklets.

"That is a snake."

And then they walked along for some time, when suddenly the daughter of Nzambi said: "Oh, slave, what is that?"

"Give me your two new cloths, and I will tell you."

She gave the slave the two cloths.

"That is an antelope."

They had not gone far when the daughter again noticed something strange.

"Slave, tell me what that thing is?"

"Give me your bracelets."

The girl gave the slave her bracelets.

"That thing is an eagle."

The princess thought it wonderful that the slave should know so much more than she did; and when she caught sight of a thing rising gently from the ground, she turned to her again and asked: "And what is that?"

"Give me your coral necklace."

The girl gave the slave the coral.

"That is a butterfly."

The next time she asked the slave for information, the slave made her change her clothes with her; so that while she was nearly naked, the slave was dressed most beautifully. And in this fashion they arrived at their destination, and delivered their message to the prince.

After the proper preparations they placed the slave in the paint-house, with all the ceremony due to a princess; and they set the daughter of Nzambi to mind the plantations. In her innocence and ignorance the daughter of Nzambi at first thought all this was in order, and part of what she had to go through; but in a very short time she began to realize her position, and to grieve about it. She used to sing plaintive songs as she minded the corn, of how she had been mistaken for a slave, while her slave was honored as a princess. And the people thought her mad. But one day a trade caravan passed her and she asked the trader where he was going, and he answered, "To Nzambi's town."

"Will you then take a message to Nzambi for me."

The trader gladly assented.

"Then tell her that her daughter is as a slave watching the plantations, while the slave is in the paint-house."

He repeated the message; and when she had said that it was correct, he went on his way and delivered it to Nzambi.

Nzambi and her husband immediately set out in their hammock, accompanied by many followers, for the town where she had sent her daughter. And when she arrived she was greatly shocked to see her daughter in that mean position, and would have punished the prince, had she not seen that he and his people were not to blame.

They called upon the slave to come out of the paint-house. But she was afraid, and would not. Then they entered, and having stripped her of all her borrowed plumes, they shut her within the house and burnt her.

The Creation of Lake Bosa

Some women were busy planting in a country where water was scarce, so that they had brought their sangas, containing that precious fluid, with them. As they were working, a poor old woman, carrying a child on her back, passed by them, hesitated for a moment, and then walked back to them and asked them to give her child a cup of water.

The women said that they had carried the water from afar, and needed it for themselves, as there was no water just there.

The poor old woman passed on, but told them that they would one day regret their want of charity.

Noticing a man up a palm tree, she asked him if he would mind giving her baby a little palm wine, as the poor little thing, she was afraid, was dying of thirst.

"Why not, mother?" he replied, and straightway came down the tree and placed a calabash at her feet.

"But I have no cup," she said.

"Nay, mother, let me break this spare calabash, and give the child a drink."

She thanked him, and went her way, saying: "Be here, my son, at this time tomorrow."

He wondered what the old woman meant; but such was the impression her words had made upon him, that he could not sleep at all that night, and felt himself obliged, when the morrow came, to proceed to the place.

"Surely this cannot be the place," he said, as he came near to the palm tree where he had met the old woman. "There was no water where the women were at work yesterday, yet surely that is a great lake."

"Wonder not, my son," said the old woman, as she approached him, "for thus have I punished the women for their want of charity. See my son, this lake is full of fish, and you and all men may fish here daily, and the abundance of fish shall never grow less. But no woman shall eat the fish thereof, for as sure as she eats the fish of this lake, so surely shall she immediately die. Let the lake and its fish be kazila [taboo] for women. For I, Nzambi, have so ordered it." Nzambi then loaded the young man with many gifts, and told him to depart in peace. The name of this lake is Bosi, and it is situated a few miles inland behind a place called Futilla.

How the Spider Won and Lost Nzambi's Daughter

Nzambi on earth had a beautiful daughter; but she swore that no earthly being should marry her, who could not bring her the heavenly fire from Nzambi Mpungu, who dwelt in the heavens above the blue roof. And as the daughter was very fair to look upon, the people marvelled, saying: "How shall we secure this treasure? and who on such a condition will ever marry her?"

Then the spider said, "I will, if you will help me."

And they all answered, "We will gladly help you, if you will reward us."

Then the spider reached the blue roof of heaven, and dropped down again to the earth, leaving a strong silken thread firmly hanging from the roof to the earth below. Now, he called the tortoise, the woodpecker, the rat, and the sandfly, and bade them climb up the thread to the roof. And they did so. Then the woodpecker pecked a hole through the roof, and they all entered the realm of the badly dressed Nzambi Mpungu.

Nzambi Mpungu received them courteously, and asked them what they wanted up there.

And they answered him, saying: "O Nzambi Mpungu of the heavens above, great father of all the world, we have come to fetch some of your terrible fire, for Nzambi who rules upon earth."

"Wait here then," said Nzambi Mpungu, "while I go to my people and tell them of the message that you bring."

But the sandfly unseen accompanied Nzambi Mpungu and heard all that was said. And while he was gone, the others wondered if it were possible for one who went about so poorly clad to be so powerful.

Then Nzambi Mpungu returned to them, and said, "My friend, how can I know that you have really come from the ruler of the earth, and that you are not impostors?"

"Nay," they said; "put us to some test that we may prove our sincerity to you."

"I will," said Nzambi Mpungu. "Go down to this earth of yours, and bring me a bundle of bamboos, that I may make myself a shed."

And the tortoise went down, leaving the others where they were, and soon returned with the bamboos.

Then Nzambi Mpungu said to the rat: "Get thee beneath this bundle of bamboos, and I will set fire to it. Then if thou escape I shall surely know that Nzambi sent you."

And the rat did as he was bidden. And Nzambi Mpungu set fire to the bamboos, and lo! when they were entirely consumed, the rat came from amidst the ashes unharmed.

Then he said: "You are indeed what you represent yourselves to be. I will go and consult my people again."

Then they sent the sandfly after him, bidding him to keep well out of sight, to hear all that was said, and if possible to find out where the lightning was kept. The midge returned and related all that he had heard and seen.

Then Nzambi Mpungu returned to them, and said, "Yes, I will give you the fire you ask for, if you can tell me where it is kept."

And the spider said: "Give me then, O Nzambi Mpungu, one of the five cases that you keep in the fowl-house."

"Truly you have answered me correctly, O spider! Take therefore this case, and give it to your Nzambi."

And the tortoise carried it down to the earth; and the spider presented the fire from heaven to Nzambi; and Nzambi gave the spider her beautiful daughter in marriage.

But the woodpecker grumbled, and said: "Surely the woman is mine; for it was I who pecked the hole through the roof, without which the others never could have entered the kingdom of the Nzambi Mpungu above."

"Yes," said the rat, "but see how I risked my life among the burning bamboos; the girl, I think, should be mine."

"Nay, O Nzambi; the girl should certainly be mine; for without my help the others would never have found out where the fire was kept," said the sandfly.

Then Nzambi said: "Nay, the spider undertook to bring me the fire; and he has brought it. The girl by rights is his; but as you others will make her life miserable if I allow her to live with the spider, and I cannot give her to you all, I will give her to none, but will give you each her market value."

Nzambi then paid each of them fifty longs of cloth and one case of gin; and her daughter remained a maiden and waited upon her mother for the rest of her days.

Litigation Among the Fiote People

Lawsuits and criminal indictments among the tribes of the Lower Congo region, as elsewhere in Central Africa, were far from perfunctory processes. The rules for litigation were laid down in custom and common law. The presiding officer of a legal dispute might be the headman of a village, the chief of a district or the ruler of a tribe. In a minor dispute, litigants might go to a respected village elder for a decision, and such cases were disposed of quickly. But where cases were brought before a chief or other tribal official they sometimes lasted for several days. The testimony given by litigants consisted not only of facts (as they represented them to be), but of moral principles as contained in songs, proverbs and sayings. In short, the litigants not only had to prove what happened, but to cite the values under which they claimed justice. Sometimes the litigants had counsel to speak for them. And sometimes, in a heated dispute, friends of the litigants gave approval of the arguments by singing songs, to the accompaniment of drumming, that supported the testimony of one or the other of the

From Dennett, ibid.

parties. The following description is of Fiote
[Fjort] litigation as seen by a non-African ob-
server, R. E. Dennett, in the late nineteenth
century.

It has struck me, as it must have struck all residents in Africa, that the
force of reason and logic, as illustrated in his many palavers, plays no
mean part in the life of the Fjort.

A discussion takes place between two natives which leads to a quarrel. Each party relates his side of the question to some friend, these
friends enter into the discussion, but fail to settle the question in dispute. A bet is then made between the two in the following way: one
offers the other a corner of his cloth (a dress), and the other taking his
knife cuts it off. Or a stick is broken into two parts, each keeping his part
until the palaver is settled. The dispute is then referred to a prince, in
whose presence it is "talked out." This prince decides the matter, and
is paid for his trouble. This the Fjort calls "Ku funda nKana," that is to
plead and circumstantiate a cause.

Palavers of the above kind of course are easily settled, but the more
serious questions, such as those of shedding blood and intertribal dispute, are far more imposing and formal. It matters not whether the
tribes have had recourse to arms in their endeavors to settle the
palaver; no question is considered finally settled until it has been properly and judicially talked out. In wars of this kind the stronger may gain
the day, but the weaker, if not entirely annihilated, will bide his time,
and bring the palaver up again on some future and more favorable
occasion, and probably be successful in getting right given to him after
all. The palaver settled, the fine inflicted paid, the whole question is
closed forever.

The princes before whom the palaver is to be talked are generally
seated near the trunk of some wide-spreading, shade-giving tree. The
audience sit opposite to them—the defendant and plaintiff and their
followers on either side, the space left being thus formed with a hollow
square.

If the palaver is one of great importance, and the parties opposed to
each other are wealthy, they will employ their pleaders or Nzonzi (who
know how to speak). The plaintiff states his case. The defendant states
his. The simple hearing of the supposed facts of the case may take days,
for each has to trace back the palaver to its origin. "If you want to catch
a rat," says the Fiote, "go to its hole." Then the Nzonzi of the plaintiff
argues the case, showing that under each head his party is in the right,
illustrating his speech by well-known comparisons, proverbs, truisms
and songs. The Nzonzi of the defendant, on the other hand, takes up
each heading and argues against it. The followers on each side emphasize each conclusion drawn by the Nzonzi by repeating his last sentence, by clapping their hands, or by joining in the chorus of the song
that the Nzonzi has sung to illustrate his case. If this song is a stirring
one and does not tell much either way, princes and audience as well as

both sides join in it until by a terrific grunt the presiding prince silences the court.

This kind of thing goes on for many days, perhaps, until the two have as it were talked themselves dry, then, after leaving the court to drink water (as they say), the princes, having decided upon the guilt of the litigant, return. The presiding prince then, going through the counts once more, gives his judgment. Song after song is sung, hands are clapped, and telling words are repeated, until as the prince nears the end of his discourse the whole court is led by pure reason to admit the justice of his words and judgment.

Then a great uproar ensues, the last song is sung with terrible enthusiasm, men jump up and twist themselves about, dancing and waving their spears and guns above their heads. The condemned is fined and given so many days to pay, or if the punishment be death, he is immediately tied up and either killed or ransomed according to his position. If the dispute has been between two tribes, after the fine has been paid an agreement is made between the two parties, and a slave killed, to seal the compact.

Litigation Among the Bambala

Among the Bambala of the western Congo, a litigation between two parties consists not of references to court decisions and Blackstone, but of songs, epigrams and proverbs which are the repository of tribal higher knowledge. When a disagreement arises between members of the clan or village in connection with hunting, women, fighting or ownership of property, the disputants refer the matter to the chief, who convokes a tribunal on a set day. The entire community assembles, not only as a social gathering, but to listen to the "evidence," and to assure that the judgment of the chief conforms to tradition, custom and justice. The parties to the dispute come with their friends, and each has a spokesman to represent him and put forward his arguments. The village drummers are also present. When the chief has called the litigation to order, one of the disputants or his spokesman stands and presents his argument. When he has finished for the moment he sings an allegorical song which he believes contains proof that justice must be on his side, and in this song he is accompanied by the drummers and friends who are present. Then the other litigant, or his spokesman, arises and gives his arguments, attempting to show that his adversary is wrong or has contradicted himself, following which he sings another allegorical song of his choice to drive the point home.

Speaking first, the defendant describes himself as an innocent party upon whom the litigation has been forced. He declares:

From On Recognizing the Human Species, *by Harold Courlander. New York, One Nation Library, 1960.*

"I was in my house and would have liked to stay. But he has come and wants to argue the matter in public. So I have left my house and that is why you see me here."

Then he sings, accompanied by the drums:

"I am like a cricket.
I would like to sing,
But I am prevented
By the wall of earth around me.
Someone has forced me
To come out of my hole,
So I will sing."

He continues his argument:

"Let us debate these questions, but slowly, slowly. If we do not come to a decision we will have to take the matter to the tribunal of the white people. I have been forced to come, so I shall speak out. When the sun has set we shall still be here debating."

He sings:

"I am like the dog
That stays before the door
Until he gets a bone."

The opponent stands and declares:

"Nobody goes both ways at the same time. You have said this and that. One of the two must be wrong. That is why I am attacking you."

Then, in song, he accuses the defendant of associations which reflect badly on his character:

"A thief speaks with another thief.
It is because you are this way
That I attack you."

Thus, each of the disputants gives evidence and cites the "law" under which he pleads his case. When the chief's decision comes, it is supported by another song or proverb.

Mnemonics for a Yombe Song

So accustomed are we to the total mastery by singers of their texts, even in long historical or epic song-poems, that the use of mnemonics appears as a novelty, as in the case of this song taken down in a Yombe village at the turn of the century. The Yombe people live along the Zaire (Congo) River above the region inhabited by the Kongo tribe. The significance of the song is not clear, no exegesis having been provided by the collector, but in characteristic fashion it alludes to certain persons and events known to the listeners, and contains within it sayings and proverbs of the Yombe people. The mnemonics are numerous small objects fastened along the length of a string. One end, the beginning, is held by the singer, the other end by an assistant. The singer feels the first object on the string, a small rounded stick, and sings the line it represents, after which the line is repeated by others who are present. The singer's fingers move to the second object, a peanut shell, and sings the line it calls to his mind. The call and response song goes on until no more mnemonics are left.

IN ORDER, THE OBJECTS AFFIXED TO THE STRING	SONG TEXT INDICATED BY THE OBJECTS
A piece of rounded stick about one inch long:	Shoots of the silk-cotton tree come from Sundi,
A peanut shell:	And peanuts, which are not very common, also come from Sundi.
A small rounded stick with two notches:	O Mother Ngombi, dance the Nquanga.
Two pieces of rounded stick (two wives) and a small bundle of cloth (the dead husband):	Tie up the corpse in grass cloth.
A piece of rounded stick of a certain wood:	The man who does not wish to hear the word turns his face to the grass.

From appendix notes by Mary H. Kingsley in Notes on the Folklore of the Fjort, by R. E. Dennett, London, 1898.

Two pieces of stick of different woods:	Ngoma [Truth] and Mavungu [Falsehood] are present at all palavers.
A piece of calabash:	Tell us openly the thing you have in your heart.
Two pieces of stick, one piece of mandioca [manioc], one piece of a palm-kernel husk:	Two young women made up with takula [body paint] go to visit their lovers.
One piece of rounded stick:	Buketi keeps going to town [because she is pregnant], may she bring forth her child well.
A piece of stick with a string tied round it:	Nganga [fetishist doctor-priest] Nsassi is sick.
A piece of stick of a particular wood:	[A man on the other side of the river calls] "Buyali, Buyali, bring your canoe here, I want to cross over." [Buyali answers] "I am pushing my canoe along with my bamboo; my child is at the bottom of the river."
A rounded piece of calabash, a crescent-shaped piece of calabash:	The sun is always marching, and meets the new moon on the beach.
One small round stick without markings, one round stick with two notches, and a small bundle of cloth:	The blacksmith makes the hoe by beating; he beats and beats the iron until his hammer [too hot to hold] drops to the ground. [His friend says] "Take this piece of cloth to hold your hammer with, and go on beating and make your hoe."
A small wooden cross (representing a man with a drum between his legs):	[He says to the drummer] "Take your drum and put it between your legs and beat the drum."
A round piece of a particular wood, a smaller piece of the same wood, a bit of leaf from a maize stalk:	When a man in town is old and eats maize, he leaves some on the cob; the corn he leaves, his son is forced to finish it.
A flat bit of wood representing tree bark:	How is it my family no longer respects me?

Round stick with a string tied about the top:

Someone has touched my birth juju and it has lost its power.

Round piece of stick with one notch, smaller bit of stick:

My child is sick, fetch the ngoma [small drum].

A flat bit of stick, like a spoon:

Let me eat malandu [a fruit] and remember the whole palaver,

Two small bits of tobacco stem:

[Put] tobacco in the pipe, liamba [hemp] in the calabash,

A small flat stick:

To think deeply, with a frown on one's forehead, about the palaver.

A longish stick, with forked sticks tied round the top (representing Father Makuika, a prisoner):

Father Makuika, who is a prisoner, is saluted by his sons and answers, "Don't salute me; can't you see the yoke on my neck?"

Small piece of smoking pipe:

An old pipe left by a relative must not be thrown away.

A small rounded stick tied round the middle:

Renowned muamba [a tree] is our medicine tree.

A small piece of grass:

Xizika [a grass with strong roots] is the old man [wise head] of the road.

A shell:

The laughter hears good words and goes on laughing.

A bit of wood shaped like a comb, another like a hand mirror:

When you comb your hair, hold the glass before you.

A round stick tied to string one-quarter length from end:

Stumps on the road keep hurting one's toes.

Bit of buffalo skin:

The buffalo fights until his head falls off.

Hair from elephant tail:

The elephant has a tail [whose hairs are valuable], but the porcupine has spines.

Bit of skin of the big antelope:

The sungu [name of a large antelope] eats on the top of large hills.

Tail feather of parrot, tail feather of pheasant:

The parrot perches on a branch, the pheasant sings his song.

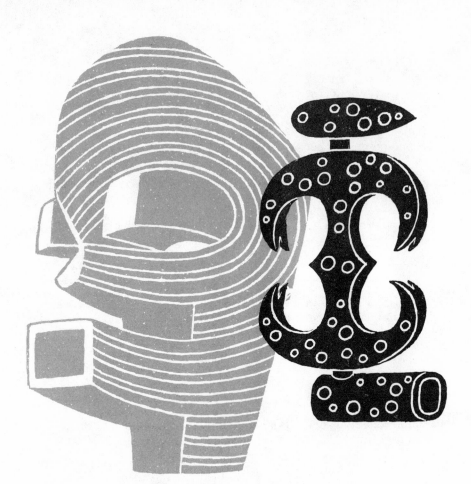

The Mwindo Epic

NYANGA TRIBE, ZAIRE

This epic story, called a karisi by the Nyanga, is about a fabulous human hero with great gifts and powers. He is called Mwindo, and is frequently referred to by the epithet Kabut-wa-kenda, the Little-one-just-born-he-walked. Physically he is small, and some versions of the epic say he was born by parthenogenesis, while in others he is depicted as having emerged from his mother's middle finger. Among his super-

The text is from The Mwindo Epic, from the Banyanga, *edited and translated by Daniel Biebuyck and Kohombo C. Mateene, Berkeley, University of California Press, 1971. Reprinted by permission of the Regents of the University of California.*

natural gifts are the the ability to move about
on land, in the water, under the earth and in
the air; magic objects; the capability of destroying evil forces; premonition; and alliance with
powerful superhuman beings and elements
such as lightning, bats, spiders and the spirit of
his paternal aunt. Mwindo is an enfant terrible
whose dimensions raise him almost to the stature of a culture hero.

The narration—or, more properly, performance—of the Mwindo story contains within it
a great variety of literary forms known to the
Nyanga: prose, poetry, songs, proverbs, riddles,
praises, prayers, blessings and, among other
things, improvised remarks and asides of the
narrator which include, at the very end, a
moral summation. The epic was taken down in
1956 by Daniel Biebuyck. It was recited over a
period of twelve days by a bard named She-
karisi (title of a devotee of the spirit Karisi)
Candi Rureke. For the bards who know and
narrate the Mwindo story, in whatever version,
it has religious significance. They believe that
the spirit Karisi wanted them to learn the story
and to perform it, and that the performance
gives the narrator protections against disease
and death.

The Nyanga, who are primarily food-gather-
ers, trappers and cultivators, number no more
than about 27,000; compared to the Luba or
the Yoruba they are indeed a small and insignificant tribe. But they have produced and preserved an epic of great stature in this story of
Mwindo. And beyond the narrative itself, the
epic contains within it a prolific record of
Nyanga culture and beliefs. The original publication of the Mwindo epic has numerous foot-
notes and exegeses that cannot be included
here. Even without these aids the Mwindo
story stands solidly on its own.

Long ago there was in a place a chief called Shemwindo. That chief
built a village called Tubondo, in the state of Ihimbi. Shemwindo was
born with a sister called Iyangura. And in that village of Shemwindo
there were seven meeting places of his people. That chief Shemwindo
married seven women. After Shemwindo had married those seven
wives, he summoned together all his people: the juniors and the seniors,
advisors, the councillors, and the nobles. All those—he had them meet
in council. When they were already in the assembly, Shemwindo sat
down in the middle of them; he made an appeal, saying: "You my wives,
the one who will bear a male child among you my seven wives, I will

kill him/her; all of you must each time give birth to girls only." Having made this interdiction, he threw himself hurriedly into the houses of the wives, then launched the sperm where his wives were. Among his wives there was a beloved-one and a despised-one. The despised-one had her house built next to the garbage heap and his other wives were in the clearing, in the middle of the village. After a fixed number of days had elapsed, those seven wives carried pregnancies, and all at the same time.

Close to the village of Shemwindo there was a river in which there was a pool, and in this pool there was a water serpent, master of the unfathomable. In his dwelling place, in the pool, Mukiti heard the news that downstream from him there was a chief who had a sister called Iyangura; she was always glistening like dew like sunrays because of beauty. After Master Mukiti had heard the news of the beauty of that young woman Iyangura, he went in pursuance of her in order to court her. Mukiti reached Tubondo; Shemwindo accommodated him in a guesthouse. When they were already in twilight, after having eaten dinner and food, Mukiti said to Shemwindo: "You, my maternal uncle, I have arrived here where you are because of this one your sister Iyangura." Shemwindo, having understood, gave Mukiti a black goat as a token of hospitality and, moreover, said to Mukiti that he would answer him tomorrow. Mukiti said: "Yes, my dear father, I am satisfied." When the night had become daylight, in the morning, Mukiti made himself like the anus of a snail in his dressing up; he was clothed with raphia bunches on the arms and on the legs, and with a belt made of bongo antelope, and he also carried an isia crest on the head. In their homestead, Shemwindo and his sister Iyangura also overstrained themselves in dressing up. The moment Mukiti and Shemwindo saw each other, Mukiti said to his father-in-law, "I am astonished—since I arrived here, I have not yet encountered my sister." Hearing that, Shemwindo assembled all his people, the councillors, and the nobles; he went with them into secret council. Shemwindo said to his people, "Our sororal nephew has arrived in this village looking for my sister; and you then must answer him." The councillors and nobles, hearing that, agreed, saying, "It is befitting that you first present Iyangura to Mukiti." They passed with Iyangura before Mukiti. Mukiti, seeing the way in which Iyangura was bursting with mature beauty, asked himself in his heart: "Now she is not the one I expected to see; she is like a ntsembe-tree." Iyangura, indeed, was dressed in two pieces of bark cloth imbued with red powder and mbea oil. Seeing each other, Mukiti and Iyangura darted against each other's chests; they greeted each other. Having greeted each other, Iyangura said to Mukiti, "Do you really love me, Mukiti?" Mukiti told her, "Don't raise your voice anymore, my wife; see how I am dancing, my back shivering like the raphia-tree larva, and my cheeks contain my laughing." After Mukiti and Iyangura had seen each other in this manner, the councillors and nobles of Shemwindo answered Mukiti, saying: "We are satisfied, Mukiti, because of your word; now you will go to win valuables; whether you win many, whether you win few, from now on you win them for us." After Mukiti had been spoken to in that way, he returned home with soothed heart. Returning home, they fixed him seven days for bringing the valuables.

After Mukiti was home, he assembled his people and told them that he was just back from courting, that he had been assigned nine thousand, and a white goat, and a reddish one, and a black one, and one for sacrifice, and one for the calabash, and one for the mother, and one for the young men. The councillors and the nobles, hearing that, clapped their hands, saying to their lord that they were satisfied, that they could not fail to find that payment of goods enough, because this maiden was not to be lost. After the seven days were fulfilled, in the morning, Mukiti took the marriage payments to go, and his people remained behind him; they went to Shemwindo's to give him the payments. On leaving his village, he went to spend the night in the village of the Baniyana. The Baniyana gave him a ram as a token of hospitality. The Banamukiti and Mukiti himself slept in that village, being like a blister because of repletion. In the morning, Mukiti woke up; he went to throw himself into the village of the Banamitandi; the Banamitandi gave Mukiti a goat as a token of hospitality; he spent the night there. In the morning, he set out from one of the ways out of the village together with his people, and went to arrive at long last in the village of his fathers-in-law, in Tubondo, at Shemwindo's. When they arrived in Tubondo, Shemwindo showed them a guesthouse to sleep in and also gave them a billy goat as a present of hospitality. In the late evening, Iyangura heated water for her husband; they went together to wash themselves. Having finished washing themselves, they anointed themselves with red powder; they climbed into bed; Iyangura put a leg across her husband. In the morning, there was a holiday. Shemwindo assembled all his people; they sat together in a group. When all the Banashemwindo were grouped together, Mukiti came out with the marriage payments and placed them before his fathers-in-law. His fathers-in-law were very satisfied with them. They told him, "Well, you are a man, one who has his nails cut." After they had completely laid hold of the marriage payments, the Banashemwindo told Mukiti to return to his village; they would conduct his wife to him. Hearing this, Mukiti said, "Absolutely all is well; what would be bad would be to be deceived." He returned to his village. When he was already in his village, Mukiti had his people prepare much food because he was having guests come. When Shemwindo, who had remained in his village, realized that Mukiti had been gone a day, in the morning, he set out to follow him; they went to conduct Iyangura. While going, the attendants carried Iyangura, without allowing her foot to set on the ground, in mud, or in water. When the attendants arrived with the incoming bride at Mukiti's, Mukiti showed them to a guesthouse; they sat down in it. They seized a rooster "to clean the teeth." In this guesthouse they had Iyangura sit down on an utebe-stool. When she was already seated, she took out the remainder of the banana paste from which she had had breakfast in her mother's house in their village. She and her husband Mukiti ate it. When her husband had finished eating from that piece of paste, they had still more banana paste with taro leaves prepared for them. When the paste and the leaves were ready in the house, they told Mukiti to sit down on an utebe-stool; and they placed the paste between both of them. When they were grouped like that, they told Iyangura to grasp a piece of paste in her right hand and make her husband eat it together with a portion of meat. Iyangura took a piece of paste from the dish; she had her husband eat it; and her husband took a piece of paste, and he too had his wife eat it. After both husband and wife had finished eating the paste, the councillors of Mukiti gave Shemwindo a strong young steer as a gift of hospitality.

After they had finished eating this young steer, they answered Mukiti, saying, "Don't make our child here, whom you have just married, into a woman in ragged, soiled clothing; don't make her into a servant to perform labor." After they had said this, in the early morning right after awakening, they went, having been given seven bunches of butea money as a departure gift by Mukiti. When the bridal attendants arrived in Tubondo, they were very happy, along with their chief Shemwindo. Where Mukiti and his people and his wife Iyangura remained, he made a proclamation saying: "You, all my people, if one day you see a man going downstream, then you will tear out his spinal column, you Banamaka, Banabirurumba, Banankomo, Banatubusa, and Banampongo; however, this path here which follows the flow of the river, it is the great path on which all people pass." After he had passed this interdiction regarding these two paths, and while in his village there lived his Shemwami called Kasiyembe, Mukiti told his big headman Kasiyembe: "You, go to dwell with my wife Iyangura at the borders of the pool; and I Mukiti shall from now on always reside here where all the dry leaves collect in flowing down, where all the fallen tree trunks are obstructed in the middle of the pool."

Where Shemwindo lived in Tubondo, together with his wives and all his people, they were very famous there; his fame went here and there throughout the entire country. When many days had passed that his wives had remained pregnant, one day six of his wives pulled through; they gave birth merely to female children. One among them, the preferred-one, remained dragging herself along because of her pregnancy. When the preferred-one realized that her companions had already given birth, and that she remained with her pregnancy, she kept on complaining: "How terrible this is! It is only I who am persecuted by this pregnancy. What then shall I do? My companions, together with whom I carried the pregnancy at the same time, have already pulled through, and it is I who remain with it. What will come out of this pregnancy?" After she had finished making these sad reflections, reawakening from her thoughts, at the door then there was already a bunch of firewood; she did not know from where it had come; lo! it was her child, the one that was inside the womb, who had just brought it. After some time had passed, looking around in the house, there was already a jar of water; she did not know whence it had come; all by itself it had brought itself into the house. After some time had passed, raw isusa vegetables also arrived there at the house. When the preferred-one saw it, she was much astonished; lo! it was the child in her womb who was performing all those wonderful things.

When the inhabitants of the village saw that the preferred-one continued to drag on with her pregnancy in her house, they got used to sneering at her: "When then will this one also give birth?" Where the child was dwelling in the womb of its mother, it meditated to itself in the womb, saying that it could not come out from the underpart of the body of its mother, so that they might not make fun of it saying that it was the child of a woman; neither did it want to come out from the mouth of its mother, so that they might not make fun of it saying that it had been vomited like a bat. When the pregnancy had already begun to be bitter, old midwives, wives of the councillors, arrived there; they arrived there when the preferred-one was already being troubled with the pains of the pregnancy. Where the child was dwelling in the womb, it climbed up in the belly, it descended the limb, and it came out through the middle finger. The old midwives, seeing him wailing on the ground, were astonished, saying: "It's terrible; is the child now replacing its mother?" When they saw him on the ground, they pointed at him, asking, "What kind of child is it?" Some among the old midwives answered, "It's a male child." Some of the old midwives said that they should shout in the village place that a male child was born. Some refused, saying that no one should shout that it was a boy who had just been born, because when Shemwindo heard that a boy had been born, he would kill him. Where the councillors were sitting together with Shemwindo, they shouted, asking, "What child is born there?" The old midwives who were sitting in the house kept silent, without giving an answer. After the birth of the child, the midwives gave him the name Mwindo, because he was the first male child who followed only female children in order of birth.

In that house where the child had been born that day, there was a cricket on the wall. Where Shemwindo was staying, after he had asked what child was born and the midwives were unwilling to give him an answer, the cricket left the house where the child had been born and went to say to Shemwindo: "You, chief, a male child was born there; his name is Mwindo; that is why those who are in that hut there have not answered you." When Shemwindo heard that his preferred-one had given birth to a boy, he took up his spear; he rubbed it on a whetstone; he sharpened it; he went with it where the child had been born. The moment he prepared to throw it into the birth hut, the child shouted from where it was; it said: "May this spear end up at the bottom of the house pole; may it never end up where these old midwives are seated here; may it neither arrive at the place where my mother is." Shemwindo threw the spear into the house six times, each time reaching nothing but the pole. When the old midwives saw that extraordinary event they stormed out of the house; they fled away, saying to one another that they should not go to die there. When Shemwindo had become exhausted from running back and forth with his spear and had completely failed to kill Mwindo, he spoke to his councillors, saying that they should dig a grave in order to throw Mwindo into it, because he did not want to see a male child. When the councillors had heard the order of the lord of their village, they did not disagree with him; they dug the grave. When the grave was finished, they went to fetch the child Mwindo; they carried him; they went to bury him in the grave. Mwindo howled within the grave, saying: "Oh, my father, this is the death that you will die, but first you will suffer many sorrows." While Shemwindo was hearing the sound of the Little Castaway, he scolded his people, telling them to cover the grave right away. His people went to fetch fallen plantain stems; they placed them above him and above the plantains they heaped much soil. Lo! at his birth, at that very moment, Mwindo was born with a conga scepter, holding it in his right hand. He was also born with an adze, holding it in his left hand. He was also born with a little bag of the spirit of Kahombo, wearing it slung across his back on the left side; in that little bag there was a long rope. Mwindo was born laughing and also speaking.

When the day had ended, those who were sitting outdoors, seeing that where Mwindo had been thrown away there was light as though the sun were shining there, went to tell the men about it and the latter also arrived there; they saw the place; they could not bear to stay a moment "which is long as what?" because the great heat, which was like fire, burned them. Each time they did as follows: as one passed by, he cast his eyes there and proceeded on. When they already were in the first vigil, when all the people were already asleep, Mwindo got out of the grave; he went to sneak into the house of his mother. As Mwindo was wailing in the house of his mother, and when where he was sitting Shemwindo began to hear the way in which the child was wailing in the house of the preferred-one, he was very much astonished, saying: "This time what was never seen is seen for the first time; again a child cries in that house. Has my wife just given birth to another child?" Shemwindo died of indecision whether or not to stand up, because of fear. Owing to his virile impetus, Shemwindo stood up; he went into the house of his wife, the house of the preferred-one, slithering like a snake, without letting his steps be noisy. He arrived at the hut; he peeked through the open door, casting an eye into the house; he saw the child sleeping on the floor; he entered the hut; he questioned his wife, saying: "Where does this child come from again; did you leave another one in the womb to whom you have given birth again?" His wife replied to him, "This is Mwindo inside here." Where Mwindo was sitting on the ground, he kept silent. Shemwindo, witnessing this marvelous event, his mouth itched to speak but he left the house without having retorted another word. Where he went, he went to wake up the councillors. Arriving there, he told them, "What is there behind me, is what is there; it is astounding." He told them also: "Tomorrow, when the sky will have become day, then you will go to cut a piece from the trunk of a tree; you will carve in it a husk for a drum; you will then put the hide of a mukaka antelope in the river to soften." When the sky had become day, all the people assembled together; they went to see Mwindo in the house of his mother. Mwindo was devoured by the many longing eyes. After they had looked at him, the councillors went to the forest to cut a piece of wood for the husk of the drum. They arrived in the forest; they cut it; they returned with it to the village. Arriving in the village, they carved the wood; they hollowed it out so that it became a husk. When the husk was finished, they went again to fetch Mwindo; they carried him; they stuck him into the husk of the drum. Mwindo said: "This time, my father has no mercy; what! a small baby is willingly maltreated!" The Banashemwindo went to get the hide for the drum; they glued it on top of the drum; they covered the drum with it. When Shemwindo had seen how his son had been laid in the drum, he declared to all his people that he wanted two expert divers, swimmers, to go the next day and throw this drum into the pool where nothing moves. After the divers, swimmers, had been found, they picked up the drum; all the people abandoned the village; they went to throw Mwindo. When they arrived at the pool where nothing moves, the swimmers with the drum entered the pool, swimming in the river. When they arrived in the middle of the pool, they asked in a loud voice, "Shall we drop him here?" All those who were sitting on the edge of the river answered "Yes," all saying together: "It is there, so that you will not be the cause of his return." They released the drum in the middle of the pool; it sank into the depths. The waves made rings above the place where the drum had entered. After the swimmers had thrown him into the pool, they returned to the shore. Shemwindo was very pleased with them, "You have performed good work!" He gave each swimmer a maiden; thus those two got married because of receiving a gift for their labor. That day, when Mwindo was thrown away, earth and heaven joined together because of the heavy rain; it rained for seven days; hailing left the earth no more; that rain brought much famine in Tubondo.

After they had thrown Mwindo away, they returned to Tubondo. When they arrived in the village, Shemwindo threatened his wife Nyamwindo, saying, "Don't shed tears weeping for your son; if you weep, I shall make you follow up where your son has been thrown away." That very day, Nyamwindo turned into the despised-one. Unable to weep, Nyamwindo went on merely sobbing—not a little tear of weeping!

Where Mwindo dwelt in the pool where he had been thrown away, when he was in the water on the sand, he moaned inside the drum; he stuck his head to the drum; he listened attentively; he said: "I, to go downstream the river, and this without having warned my father and all his people who have thrown me away so that they hear the sound of my voice—well then, I am not Mwindo." Where the drum was in the water on the sand, it arose all alone to the surface of the water. When the drum was at the surface of the pool—in its middle—it remained there; it did not go down the river; neither did it go up the river.

From Tubondo, from the village where the people dwelt, came a row of maidens; they went to draw water from the river at the wading place. Arriving at the river, as soon as they cast their eyes towards the middle of the pool, they saw the drum on the surface of the water, which was turning around there; they said inquiringly to one another: "Companions, we have dazzling apparitions; lo! the drum that was thrown with Mwindo—there it is!" Where Mwindo dwelt inside the drum in the pool, he said, "If I abstain from singing while these maidens are still here drawing water from the river, then I shall not have anybody who will bring the news to the village where my father is in Tubondo." While the maidens were in the act of drawing water and still had their attention fixed there towards the drum, Mwindo, where he dwelt in the drum in the pool, threw sweet words into his mouth; he sang:

> I am saying farewell to Shemwindo!
> I am saying farewell to Shemwindo!
> I shall die, oh! Bira!
> My little father threw me into the drum!
> I shall die, Mwindo!
> The councillors abandoned Shemwindo;
> The councillors will become dried leaves.
> The councillors of Shemwindo,
> The councillors of Shemwindo,
> The councillors have failed in their councilling!
> My little father, little Shemwindo,
> My little father threw me into the drum
> I shall not die, whereas that little-one will urvive!
> The little-one is joining Iyangura,
> The little-one is joining Iyangura,
> Iyangura, the sister of Shemwindo.

When the girls heard the way in which Mwindo was singing in the drum in the pool, they climbed up to the village, running and rushing, after they had left the water jars at the river, behind them, in disarray. When they arrived within the inhabited area, the men, seeing them appear at the outskirts running and rushing, took their spears and went, believing that they were being chased by a wild beast. Seeing the spears, the maidens beseeched their fathers: "Hold it! We are going to bring the news to you of how the drum that you threw into the pool has stayed; it is singing: 'The councillors of Shemwindo, the councillors have failed in their councilling; the councillors will become dried leaves.'" When he heard that, Shemwindo told the girls that they were lying: "What! the drum that we had thrown away into the pool arose again!" The maidens assented to it, "Mwindo is still alive." They had seen him with their own eyes, and he really was still alive. When Shemwindo heard that, he assembled again all his people; the village remained empty; everybody deserted the village for the river carrying spears, arrows, and fire.

Where Mwindo dwelt in the river, after he had seen the way in which the maidens had cleared the river for the village, he also stopped his singing for a while; he said that he would sing again when the people arrived, because these girls had just witnessed his astonishing deed. All the people of the village, children and youngsters, old people and young men, women, when they arrived at the river, seeing the drum in the middle of the pool, grouped together looking attentively at the drum. When Mwindo noticed them waiting in a group on the shore, he threw sweet words into his mouth; he sang:

> I am saying farewell to Shemwindo;
> I shall die, oh, Bira!
> The councillors abandoned Shemwindo.
> Scribe, move on!
> The councillors will turn into dried leaves.
> What will die and what will be safe
> Are going to encounter Iyangura.

When Mwindo had finished singing like that, saying farewell to his father and to all the Banashemwindo, the drum sank into the pool; the waves made rings at the surface. Where Shemwindo and his people were standing on the shore, they were very perplexed; they nodded their heads, saying: "How terrible it is! Will some day then be born what is never being born?" After they had witnessed this extraordinary event, they returned to the village, Tubondo.

Where Mwindo headed inside the water, he went upstream; he went to the river's source, at Kinkunduri's, to begin it. When he arrived at Kinkunduri's, he lodged there; he said that he was joining Iyangura, his paternal aunt, there, whither she had gone; the news had been given him by Kahungu. He began the trip; he joined his aunt Iyangura downstream; he sang:

> Mungai, get out of my way!
> For Ikukuhi shall I go out of the way?
> You are impotent against Mwindo,
> Mwindo is the Little-one-just-born-he-walked.
> I am going to meet Iyangura.
> For Kabusa, shall I go out of the way?
> You are helpless against Mwindo,
> For Mwindo is the Little-one-just-born-he-walked.
> Canta, get out of my way!
> Canta, you are impotent against Mwindo.
> I am going to encounter Iyangura, my aunt.
> For Mutaka shall I go out of the way?
> You are helpless against Mwindo!
> I am going to meet Iyangura, my aunt.
> For Kitoru shall I get out of my way?
> You see, I am going to encounter Iyangura, my aunt.

I stated that:
For Mushenge shall I get out of my way?
You are impotent against Mwindo!
See, I am going to encounter Iyangura, my aunt,
Iyangura, sister of Shemwindo.
For Nyarui, shall I get out of my way?
Whereas Mwindo is the Little-one-just-born-he-has-walked.
I am going to encounter Iyangura, my aunt,
Sister of Shemwindo.
For Cayo shall I get out of my way?
You see, I am going to encounter Iyangura, my aunt,
Sister of Shemwindo.
Look! You are impotent against Mwindo,
Mwindo the Little-one-just-born-he-walked.
He who will go up against me, it is he who will die on the way.

Each time Mwindo arrived in a place where an aquatic animal was, he
said that it should get out of the way for him, that they were powerless
against him, that he was going to his aunt Iyangura. When Mwindo
arrived at Cayo's, he spent the night there; in the morning he went
right after awakening; he sang:

> For Ntsuka shall I go out of the way?
> You see that I am going to encounter Iyangura.
> You see that you are powerless against Mwindo.
> Mwindo is the Little-one-just-born-he-walked.
> For Kirurumba shall I go out of the way?
> You see that I am going to encounter Aunt Iyangura.
> You see that you are powerless against Mwindo,
> For Mwindo is the Little-one-just-born-he-walked.
> For Mushomwa shall I go out of the way?
> You see I am going to encounter Aunt Iyangura.
> You see that you are powerless against Mwindo.
> For Mwindo is the Little-one-just-born-he-has-walked.

Musoka, the junior sister of Mukiti, had gone to live upstream from
Mukiti:

> For Musoka shall I go out of the way?
> You are powerless against Mwindo
> Mwindo is the Little-one-just-born-he-walked.

When Musoka saw Mwindo arriving at her place, she sent an envoy to
Mukiti to say that there was a person there where she was, at Musoka's,
who was in the act of joining Iyangura. The envoy ran quickly to where
Mukiti was; he arrived there and gave the news: "There is a person back
there; he is in the act of joining Iyangura." Mukiti replied to that envoy
that he should tell Musoka that that man should not pass beyond her

place; "If not, why would I have placed her there?" That envoy arrived at Musoka's; he announced the news of how he had been spoken to by Mukiti. Musoka kept on forbidding Mwindo like that, without knowing that he was a child of Mukiti's wife, Iyangura. Musoka replied to Mwindo, saying: "Mukiti refuses to let you pass; so it is your manhood that will permit you to pass; I here, Musoka, I am placing barriers here; you will not find a trail to pass on." Mwindo answered her, softening his voice: "I, Mwindo, never am I forbidden to pass on a trail; I will thrust through there where you are blocking." Mwindo hearing this pulled himself together; he left the water above; he dug inside the sand; and he went to appear in between Musoka and Mukiti. After Mwindo had passed Musoka, having broken through the dam of Musoka, he praised himself, "Here I am, the Little-one-just-born-he-walked; one never points a finger at me." When Musoka saw him anew downstream, she touched her chin, saying: "How then has this tough one here gotten through? If he had passed above me I would have seen his shadow; if he had passed below me, I would have heard the sound of his feet." Musoka complained a lot saying that she would be scolded by Mukiti because she had let somebody pass.

After Mwindo had passed Musoka, he began a journey to go to Mukiti's; he sang:

> In Mukiti's, in Mariba's dwelling place!
> For Mukiti shall I get out of my way?
> You see I am going to encounter Iyangura,
> Iyangura, sister of Shemwindo.
> Mukiti, you are powerless against Mwindo.
> Mwindo is the Little-one-just-born-he-walked.

When Mukiti in his dwelling place heard this, he moved, asking who had just mentioned his wife. He shook heaven and earth; the whole pool moved. Mwindo on his side said, "This time we shall get to know each other today, we with Mukiti; for I Mwindo never fear an insolent child, so long as I have not measured myself against him." When Mwindo heard that, he said, "This time, the husband of my aunt is lying; it is I Mwindo who am being forbidden the road to my aunt!" Mwindo pulled himself together; he went to appear at the knot where Mukiti was coiled up. When Mukiti saw him, he said, "This time it is not the one whom I expected to see; he surpasses expectation!" He asked, "Who are you?" Mwindo referred to himself saying that he was Mwindo, the Little-one-just-born-he-walked, child of Iyangura. Mukiti said to Mwindo, "How then?" Mwindo answered him saying that he was going to encounter his paternal aunt Iyangura. Hearing that, Mukiti said to Mwindo: "You are lying; here never anybody passes, who would have crossed over these logs and dried leaves; so, then, you never go to sleep thinking! You alone are the man who in spite of all will be able to pass here where I am!" While Mukiti and Mwindo were still talking to each other like that, maidens went from Iyangura's place to draw water; at

Mukiti's place, there it was that the water hole was. As soon as the
maidens witnessed the way in which Mwindo constantly mentioned
Iyangura saying she was his aunt, they ran to Iyangura; they arrived
there and said to Iyangura: "Over there, where your husband Mukiti
is, there is a little man saying that Mukiti should release him, that he
is Mwindo, that he is going to encounter Iyangura, his paternal aunt."
When Iyangura heard that news, she said, "Lo! that is my child, let me
first go to where he is." Iyangura climbed up the slope; she went to
appear at the water hole; she looked to the river that she first might see
the man who was mentioning that she was Iyangura. As soon as Mwindo
in his place saw his paternal aunt coming to see him, he sang:

> I am suffering much, Mwindo.
> I will die, Mwindo.

While his aunt Iyangura was then descending the slope, he went on
singing looking in the direction from which his aunt was coming.

> Aunt Iyangura,
> Mukiti has forbidden me the road.
> I am going to meet Aunt Iyangura,
> I am going to encounter Iyangura,
> Sister of Shemwindo.
> For Mukiti shall I go out of the way?
> I am joining Iyangura,
> Sister of Shemwindo.
> For Mukiti, my father, shall I go out of the way?
> You are powerless against Mwindo,
> Katitiiri and Mpumba
> And Rintea and Sheburenda!
> My father, I shall die, Mwindo!
> Aunt Iyangura howled, she said,
> Aunt Iyangura "of the body."

Iyangura said: "If the sororal nephew of the Banamitandi is in this
drum, let it arrive here so that I can see it before me." When the aunt
cited the Banamitandi in this way, the drum refused to move in the
direction of Iyangura. Inside the drum, Mwindo complained that this
time his aunt missed the mark. His aunt spoke again: "If you drum, if
you are the sororal nephew of The-one-who-hears-secrets, come here;
draw near me." When his aunt had mentioned in that way Those-who-
hear-secrets, the drum still refused to draw near her. His aunt said
anew: "If you really are the nephew of the Baniyana, come here before
me." When Mwindo heard that, he went singing, in leaving the pool:

> I am going to my Aunt Iyangura,
> Iyangura, sister of Shemwindo.
> Kabarebare and Ntabare mountain,

Where the husband of my senior sister sets byoo traps.
And a girl who is nice is a lady,
And a nice young man is a kakoma pole.
We are telling the story
That the Babuya have told long ago.
We are telling the story.
Kasengeri is dancing wagging his tail;
And you, see! this tail of nderema fibers.
Nkurongo bird has gone to court mususu bird;
Muhasha bird has contracted asthma.
If I am at a loss for words in the great song,
If it dies out, may it not die out for me there.
I cannot flirt with I-have-no-name;
They are accustomed to speak to Mukiti with bells.
The tunes that we are singing,
The uninitiated-ones cannot know them.
I cannot be given mburu monkey and still eat a lot,
I would remain satisfied with my flat belly.
I have seen a rooster cock-a-doodle-dooing;
I also saw muntori bird pointing him out.
The little guardian of the rice field
Is never confused about
When sky has become day.
I see that meditations kill;
They killed the couple, otter and his mother.
If little pot travels too much,
It means little pot looks for a crack.
He who one day ate ntsuka fish does not sojourn long.
It is as though he had eaten the heart of the plunger.
If Nyabunge coils like the whirlpools,
Then she loses her way home.
I learned that a catastrophe happened:
One suffering from frambesia and a leper on a bed.
If you hear the uproar of an argument,
It means the old woman has gotten more than the young mother.
I always sit down thinking about myself,
As in the game "throat and top."
I have cultivated bananas for the dragon
So heavy that a cluster had no one to carry it.
The muhangu animal that tries to make the first banana fruits drop.
If the mother of the girl dies because of the young man,
It means an atumbu insect falls from the ntongi tree.

When Mwindo was still in the act of going down the river, the moment he joined his aunt he went to arrive before her where she was. His aunt seized the drum; her people gave her a knife; she slashed the drum; removing the hide, she saw the multiple rays of the rising sun and the moon. That is the beauty of the child Mwindo. Mwindo got out of the drum, still holding his conga scepter and his axe, together with his little bag in which the rope was. When Kahungu saw Mwindo meeting with his aunt, he went to bring the news to the mutambo elder who had been given to Iyangura to keep watch over her continually. He arrived there, he gave him the news, "You, you who are here, it is not merely a little man who appears over there; he is with many stories and feats; you are dead." Hearing this news, Kasiyembe said: "Envoy, go! When you will have arrived at Mwindo's, tell him he should not even try to pass this side; otherwise I shall tear out his spinal column; I here am setting up traps, pits and pointed sticks and razors in the ground, so that I shall know where he will step." Seeing that, Katee went to appear where Mwindo was and told him: "You, Mwindo, your mates are holding secret council against you; they are even preparing pit traps against you, and pointed sticks and razors. I am Katee, don't you always see me on the ground, in the depth of the earth?" Mwindo answered him, "Yes, I always see you; it is on the ground that you live." After having given Mwindo the news of that danger there in order to warn him, Katee also told him, "I am going to have a road go by, so that it emerges from the place where you are, and I want to make it come out inside the house of your aunt, at the base of the house pole." Mwindo said "Yes" to him. Mukei began to dig in the ground, inside it. Mwindo told his aunt Iyangura: "You, Aunt, proceed ahead; you be already on your way home; I shall meet you there; and that Kasiyembe threatening me over there, I shall first meet up with him; if he really has force, I shall deal with him today." He also said to his aunt, "Tell him, the one who is threatening me there, that he should prepare himself." Master Spider also emerged from within the pits, he was building bridges; he made them come out above the pits; the pits became merely bridges; he said to himself that it was there that Mwindo was going to play. "As far as I, Master Spider, am concerned, Mwindo cannot completely perish, since we are there." After his aunt had thus been told by Mwindo to proceed going, she did not tergiversate; she went home. Back there where Mwindo had remained, he took the road made by Katee; he came out in the house of his aunt, at Iyangura's, thanks to his kahombo [i.e., good fortune]. When Kasiyembe saw him, he said, "Mwindo is already over here; now, from where has he emerged?" The people of his village said that they did not know from where he had emerged.

When Iyangura saw that her son Mwindo had already arrived, she said to him: "My son, don't eat food yet; come first to this side, so that we may dance to the rhythm of the drum." After Mwindo had heard the words of his aunt, he left the house and appeared where his aunt was outdoors; he told his aunt that there he was, that he was going to dance without having eaten food, that he was going to faint with this drum. His aunt replied to him: "Not at all! Dance all the same, my son; and as for me, what shall I do then, since the one whom I was given to take care of me is saying that you must dance? What then shall we do? Dance all the same!" Hearing the word of his aunt, Mwindo said: "Oh!

Right you are; let me first dance; hunger never kills a man." Mwindo sang; he howled, he said:

> Kasiyembe, you are powerless against Mwindo,
> For Mwindo is the Little-one-just-born-he-walked.
> Kasiyembe said, "Let us dance together."
> Shirungu, give us a morceau!
> If we die, we will die for you.
> Kasengeri is dancing with his conga scepter,
> Conga scepter of nderema fibers.
> I am saying farewell to Mpumba,
> My Mpumba with many raffia bunches.

Mwindo went round about in the middle of the pits; he marched with the body bent over the pits, without even being injured by the razors; he passed and passed everywhere where Kasiyembe had placed traps for him, without injuring himself. After Mwindo had passed and passed where traps had been set up for him, he danced; he agitated his conga scepter to and fro, singing:

> It is Katee who is crackling of dried leaves,
> And it is Kantori who is Shebireo.

He also pointed out the Banamitandi, saying:

> You have seen that I am a follower of the Banamitandi.
> May Kahungu go to see now.
> May I see over there Shemumbo's village.
> I am seeing that among the chimpanzees of the ficus tree,
> The one who is repleted comes down.

Iyangura told her son to eat some food, saying that since the time he arrived he had not spit his saliva while eating food. Iyangura gave her son a bovine as a token of hospitality; he/she felled it. Eating it were those who were on the side, the maidens, who ate from it for several days; he did not put it in the mouth trying to eat from it. After Mwindo had eaten the hospitality gift of the bovine, which his aunt had offered to him, together with the maidens, Kasiyembe, the man of hatred, persisted in trying to kill him, saying: "Is this the boy against whom I shall be impotent, whereas I heard that he came from the inside of a drum?" Kasiyembe implored Nkuba, the lightning-hurler, saying, "You, Nkuba, you will have to come down; may you cut Mwindo into two pieces, in the house here where he is together with all these maidens who are with him here." When Mwindo heard the way in which Kasiyembe threatened him, over and over again, he told the maidens sitting with him in the house to sit down on one side with him because Kasiyembe wanted to bring lightning down on him. Then Mwindo said threateningly to Master Nkuba: "You, Nkuba, since you come down, you must come down on one side of the house; don't come down on the side where Mwindo is." Master Nkuba, on hearing the voice of Kasiyembe, descended onto the house where Mwindo was; Mwindo pointed him out, saying: "You too will die the same death; you are climbing on a hard tree." Master Nkuba came down seven times; each time he descended onto one side of the house in which Mwindo was, he did not come close to the place where he was; the fire burned on one side; that side became merely ashes. Where Iyangura, aunt of Mwindo, was sitting, tears rolled from her eyes and reached her legs, she saying that lo! her son was dying and that she had not even seen him well. Mwindo then came out of the house together with the maidens; he presented himself before the crowd of people; he declared about himself that there he was, the Little-one-just-born-he-walked. He said to his aunt to come close to where he was so that he could speak to her; his aunt came close to him; Mwindo spoke to her, "No more crying; it is you, my aunt, who are the reason Kasiyembe made this evil test come over me; in the day of tomorrow, if you will see me no more, it means that I am not worthy of Mwindo." He told his aunt that within the twinkling of an eye, the mop of hair of Kasiyembe would already be burning. Where Kasiyembe was, people were all of a sudden struck by the fact that in the mop of hair of Kasiyembe the fire was already flaring up; the tongues of flame rose into the air; all the lice and all the vermin that were nestled on his head, all were entirely consumed. When they saw the mop of hair of Kasiyembe burning, the people of Kasiyembe thought about fetching water in the jars in order to extinguish the fire on the head of Kasiyembe. When they arrived at the jars, in arriving there, there was no water left; all the water had dried up in the jars, there was not a drop of water left in them. They went straight to the herbaceous stalks of the plantains; they arrived there when they were already dried up, without a drop of water in them. They said: "What then! Spit some saliva on his head!" Saliva was lacking among all the people; their mouths were wanting of saliva. When they experienced this, they said: "This Kasiyembe is about to die. Go and look for help for him at his master's; it is at Mukiti's that there is a pool." They went there. Arriving there, they found Mukiti with butterflies and flies flitting about him; for him, too, the water had dried up; the whole pool had dried up, without even a drop in it. When his aunt saw that, she went to beg before her son: "Widen your heart, you my son 'of the body,' you only child. By any chance did you come here where I am in order to attack us? Set your heart down; undo my husband together with his mutambo elder, this one Kasiyembe; heal them without harboring further resentment against them." After the aunt had finished humbly imploring her son, Mwindo had his heart go down; he woke up Kasiyembe, waving his conga scepter above him; he sang:

> He who went to sleep wakes up.
> You are impotent against Mwindo,
> Mwindo is the Little-one-just-born-he-walked.

"Wake up thanks to my conga here of nderema fibers."

> He who went to sleep wakes up.
> Look, I am playing with my conga scepter.

Suddenly, Kasiyembe was saved. And the jars, water returned again in them; and the herbaceous stalks of all the plantains, in them again was water; and there where Mukiti was, the water came back again for him; the river was full again. When they saw that feat, they were much astonished, saying, "Lo! Mwindo, he too, is a great man." Kasiyembe gave Mwindo a salute, saying, "Hail! hail! oh! Mwindo." And Mwindo answered, "Yes." After he had accomplished that deed, Mwindo said to his aunt that tomorrow he would be going to Tubondo to fight with his father, because his father had thrown him away twice; now he would in his turn go to stand up against him. The aunt told him: "Oh! my father, you will be impotent at your father's, in Tubondo; you, just yesterday's child, born just a while ago, is it you who will be capable of Tubondo, village with seven meeting places? Iyangura! I had you taken out from within the drum; as far as I am concerned, I say 'No,' strongly; never again try to go alone; the lonely path is never nice." When Mwindo heard the way in which his aunt was speaking, he refused; he wiped out his aunt's words by humming to himself. The aunt told him: "You, my young man, to give birth to a son is to rest. Do not go to fight with your father; if you go, at any rate, then I also shall go with you to see how your father will be cutting you into pieces." She went to tell the maidens to pack up her household objects, so as to go with Mwindo, because the lonely path is not nice; it never fails to find something that could kill a man. When the sky had become daylight, they had breakfast before the journey of returning back to Tubondo. Mwindo went together with his aunt, together with his servants who were chanting the refrain. Mwindo sang:

> Ntiriri-liana has become mubanga-rope,
> And musara-liana has become a mukendo-bag.
> Scribe, march!
> I am going over there to Tubondo;
> I shall fight over there in Tubondo,
> Even though Tubondo has seven entries.
> We are saying, oh, Bira!
> Aunt, give me advice
> To fight with the people downstream;
> They carry spears and shields.
> In Ihimbi where dwelt Birori,
> I shall die today, Mushumo.
> On Ntsuri hill where dwelt Ruronga,
> In Munongo where dwelt Shecara,
> Bitumbi hill of Shemene Ndura,
> And the old ones fight because of a wind.

On Mbare hill where dwelt Karai,
He was the one who gives much tribute of words.
Mbare hill is together with Irimwe hill, his kinsman,
Tunkundu hill is together with Nteko hill, his kinsman.
May I mention Mabura Banyore,
Homeland of my mothers,
Kabotyo Munyangoro
Nyabuke Kamwikoti.
Big legs ravaged Mpurwa,
And the baboon ruined Kamuri.
Sky became day, I was still speaking
Like the sound of Mukuki.
The sky in this village takes a long time to become day:
It is the single man who is cooking hard-to-cook food.
Mikere river is together with Mboru river, his kinsman,
And Batoi river is together with Tua river, his kinsman.
Who will take me to Bukuca, to Ngara?
Mbuhi is of both Mutatea and Mwindo,
Kirambo is of Mamboreo.
May the people of Ntande not regret the lack of meat,
For they have had a woman who fishes with a net.
Mpinga is land
Whereas Nkasa is the natal village of Burongo
And of Mwindo.
May the Batembo not regret the lack of meat.
They hold Mutumba and Kunju.
And Birere hill of Rukobakoba;
I cannot fish with the Baroba.
From Europe there come all kinds of things!
The sun is setting downstream
From the Batika-Rukari.
Maere, little girl of Rukunja,
Maere, what did you eat when you came?
I have not eaten anything extraordinary;
I have eaten a goat for sharing purposes,
And I also ate mususa vegetables picked in the village.
They were full of sand and slime.
To a trap that is not well set
Katiti pigeon only leaves its tail.
The nkurongo birds of this village are mean;
The nkurongo birds, as soon as they have seen people,
Flutter their tails.
In Kumbukumbu of the Batobo
Where dwelt Nkuru and Rukari.

Mwindo sang:

Scribe, march!
I am going with the aunt.
The Little-one has slept all prepared for the journey.
Oh! my father, the Little-one set out right after awakening.
I warn you we are already under way, we,
To Bat of the Baniyana.

During this journey that Mwindo was making in spite of all with his aunt, evening went to find him at his maternal uncles, the Baniyana. He slept there after they had killed a goat of hospitality for him. After he, together with his paternal aunt and the servants of the aunt, had eaten that goat, Mwindo said to his maternal uncles, "I am going to fight Shemwindo in Tubondo; forge me, you blacksmiths of large light spears, you my uncles." The Baniyana said that they were going to forge him. They dressed him in shoes made entirely of iron and pants of iron; they also forged him an iron shirt and a hat of iron. They told him, "Since you are going to fight your father, may the spears that they will unceasingly hurl at you go striking on this iron covering that is on your body." After the uncles had finished forging him, they said that they could remain no more; they would be going with him so that they might see the way in which they would knead him. In the morning, Mwindo began the journey together with his uncles and his aunt Iyangura, and the servants of his aunt. Mwindo went singing; he howled, he said:

I shall fight over there at Shemwindo's.
The cattle that Shemwindo possesses,
May they join Mwindo.
Oh! scribe, march!

Mwindo and his party arrive on the outskirts of Tubondo, at the foot of the mountain. Mwindo sends his uncles against the town, but they are killed. Then he goes alone to Tubondo, and after being insulted he calls down lightning that destroys the whole town. His father, Shemwindo, flees, enters the ground beneath a fern, and escapes into the subterranean world. After miraculously reviving his uncles, Mwindo pursues his father. He also enters beneath the fern and begins his underworld journey. He arrives at Muisa's house, and through his understanding of things and his magical powers, avoids the disasters Muisa has in mind for him. Eventually he overcomes Muisa and catches his father, Shemwindo. Mwindo and Shemwindo return to the upper world.

In leaving Muisa's village, Mwindo began the trip; he and his father went home; they went to appear where they had entered at the root of the kikoka fern. When Mwindo and Shemwindo arrived at the entrance of Tubondo, those who were in the village, Iyangura and the uncles of Mwindo, swarmed in the village like bees; they went to greet Mwindo and his father at the entrance; they met them. Seeing Mwindo, Iyangura and the uncles of Mwindo lifted him up into the air; they carried him on their fingertips. When they traversed the village of Tubondo, Mwindo told them to let him down. They put him down in the middle of the village place; they went to take a lot of spearheads, and it is on them that Mwindo sat down—they stood for the utebe stool. His maternal uncles put him to the test like that in order to know if perhaps their nephew was still as they had forged him. When Mwindo was on the stool in the middle of the village, he gave his aunt the news from where he had come and the way in which he had fought, searching for his father. He sang:

When I descended with the rope,
Aunt,
I met with Kahindo.
Kahindo shouted and said:
"Mwindo, let me charge you with the following words:
If you see Muisa,
What Muisa will say,
You should refuse it."
Mwindo said:
"I go to the village, the village place
Where Muisa lives,
If I am not victorious
Where Muisa remains."
When I arrived in the village of Muisa,
Muisa shouted and said:
—Muisa brought out a chair—
"Mwindo, sit down here."
Mwindo shouted, complaining,
Saying, "This is your head, Muisa."
Muisa shouted and said,
"Councillors, give me some little beer
So that I may give it to Mwindo."
And Mwindo shouted, complaining,
"A father's urine a child never drinks."
Muisa said, "Let us fight together."
I have kneaded Muisa.
I was already going.
I arrived in Ntumba's cave,
In the cave of Ntumba Munundu.
Ntumba said, "Let's fight together."
I kneaded Ntumba,

I who had kneaded Muisa.
You too, Ntumba, are powerless against Mwindo,
Mwindo, the Little-one-just-born-he-walked.
I kneaded Ntumba so that I got tired.
Already I was hurrying in Sheburungu's house;
When I arrived there at the entrance of Sheburungu's—a god—
The youngsters howled, saying,
"Oh, Mwindo, we are hungry."
I sent pastes over there;
The youngsters ate the pastes.
Already I was on my way to Sheburungu's,
Together with the youngsters.
Sheburungu said: "Let us play wiki together."
I said: "You, Sheburungu,
You are powerless against Mwindo, the Little-one-just-born-he-
     walked.
Who made Muisa and Ntumba fail."
I shouted, complaining,
I, saying, "Give me my father here."
Sheburungu shouted, saying,
"Mwindo, you are helpless in the wiki-game against Sheburungu,
Which has beaten Heaven and Earth."
We took a handful of mbai seeds.
Mwindo shouted and said,
"Sheburungu, you are helpless against Mwindo.
Give me Shemwindo,
You see, I have already beaten you."
Kahungu notified Mwindo;
Kahungu showed me Shemwindo.
It is I who seized Shemwindo,
My little father, the dearest one.
We were already on the return trip;
"Shemwindo, let us go home,
Let us go up to Tubondo
Where remained Aunt Iyangura."
What Shemwindo accomplished!
I arrive at the peak in Tubondo.
You see, I am carrying Shemwindo;
I am carrying my little father, the dearest one.

Iyangura gave her son the order, "Since you have arrived with your
father, bring him first into the iremeso hut to let him rest there." They
carried Shemwindo into the iremeso hut; he settled down in it. In giving
hospitality to his father, Mwindo killed for him the goat that never
defecates and never urinates; they cooked it, along with rice, for his
father. He said to his father: "Here are your goats! It is you who were
wrong in vain; you made yourself awkward to Mwindo, the Little-one-
just-born-he-walked, when you said that you did not want boys, that you

wanted girls; you did a deliberate wrong in the way you desired. Lo! you did not know the strength of the blessing of Mwindo." After Mwindo had given food to his father as a hospitality gift, Iyangura said to him: "You, my son, shall we go on living always in this desolate village, we alone, without other people? I, Iyangura, I want you first to save all the people who lived here in this village; when they have resuscitated, it is then only that I shall know to ask our young man, Shemwindo, to tell me some of the news of the ways in which he acted, all the evil that he did against you." Mwindo listened to the order of his aunt to heal those who had died. His uncles, the Baniyana, beat the drum for him while he, Mwindo, was dancing because of the joys of seeing his father. They sang. Aunt shouted and said,

> My father, eternal savior of people.

Mwindo said:

> Oh, father, they tell me to save the people;
> I say, "He who went to sleep wakes up."
> Little Mwindo is the Little-one-just-born-he-walked.
> My little father threw me into the drum.
> Shemwindo, you do not know how to lead people.
> The habits of people are difficult.
> My little father, eternal malefactor among people,
> Made bees fall down on me,
> Bees of day and sun;
> I lacked all means of protection against them.

While Mwindo was healing those who died in Tubondo, he continued on in the following way: when he arrived at the bone of a man, he beat it with his conga so that the man would then wake up. The resuscitation was as follows:

Each one who died in pregnancy resuscitated with her pregnancy;
each one who died in labor resuscitated being in labor;
each one who was preparing paste resuscitated stirring paste;
each one who died defecating resuscitated defecating;
each one who died setting up traps resuscitated trapping;
each one who died copulating resuscitated copulating;
each one who died forging resuscitated forging;
each one who died cultivating resuscitated cultivating;
each one who died while making pots and jars resuscitated shaping;
each one who died carving dishes resuscitated carving;
each one who died quarreling with a partner resuscitated
     quarreling.

Mwindo stayed in the village for three days resuscitating people; he was dead of weariness. The people and all the houses—each person resuscitated being straight up in his house. Tubondo filled itself again with the people and the goats, the dogs, the cattle, the poultry, the male and the female ewes, the teenage boys and girls, the children and the youngsters, the old males and females; in the middle of all those people were the nobles and the councillors and the Pygmies and all the royal initiators; all those also were straight up. All the descent groups that formerly dwelt in Tubondo resuscitated; again they became as they were before, each person who died having things of a certain quantity, resuscitated still having his things. Tubondo again became a big village with seven entrances. When the people were resuscitated, Iyangura began to speak in the middle of the crowd of people, saying: "You, Shemwindo, my brother, in the middle of the whole country of yours, have them prepare much beer and cows and goats; let all the people meet here in Tubondo. It is then that we shall be able to examine in detail all the palavers and to redress them in the assembly." After Shemwindo had heard the voice of his sister Iyangura, he uttered a cry, high and low, to all his people, saying that they should bring beer together. After one week had passed, all groups within his state swarmed into Tubondo, together with beer and meats. On the morning of the eighth day, all the people of all the villages of Shemwindo's state pressed together in the assembly. After all the people, the children and the youngsters, the adults and the elders, had thronged about, Mwindo dressed himself and became [clean] like the anus of a snail. His aunt Iyangura, she too threw on her clothes, those famous ones of Mukiti's. His father Shemwindo, he too dressed himself from top to bottom: tuhuhuma bark clothes on which were red color and castor oil, ndorera fringes, masia hair ornaments. He too became something beautiful. After the people had grouped themselves in the assembly, servants stretched mats out on the ground, there where Mwindo and his father and his aunt would pass. All the people in that assembly kept silent, pi! There was sacred silence. Those three radiant stars, Mwindo and his father and his aunt, appeared from inside the house. They went into the open to the assembly; they marched solemnly. Those who were in the gathering of the assembly gave them the gift of their eyes: there where they appeared, that is where their attention was focused. Some among them surmised, saying, "I wonder, is Shemwindo born with another young man?" Some answered, "Shemwindo is there with the chief of Shekwabahinga, together with his wife." Some said, "No, Shemwindo is there with his sister, Mukiti's wife, and with Mukiti himself." The remainder said that Shemwindo was with his sister Iyangura, Mukiti's wife, together with his son Mwindo, the Little-one-just-born-he-walked, the man of many wonders, the one who was formerly martyrized by his father. Shemwindo and Mwindo and Iyangura went in a line, while appearing in the middle of the gathering of the assembly. Mwindo beseeched his friend Nkuba, asking him for three copper chairs. Nkuba made them come down. When they were close to the ground, being close to the ground, they remained suspended in the air about five meters from the ground. Mwindo and his father and his aunt climbed

up onto the chairs; Iyangura sat down in the middle of both, Shemwindo
on the right side and Mwindo on the left side. When all the men had
finished grouping themselves together in the assembly and had finished
becoming silent, Mwindo stood up from his chair; he raised his eyes into
the air, he implored Nkuba, saying, "Oh, my friend Nkuba, prevent the
sky from falling!" Having spoken like that, he lowered his eyes towards
the ground, down upon the mass of people; he said, he lauded them,
saying, "Be strong, you chiefs." They approved of it. He said: "You
councillors, be strong." They approved of it. Then he, "You seniors, be
strong." They approved. Mwindo praised the council, holding all the
things with which he was born: conga, axe, the little bag in which the
rope was; he also held an ancient stick to praise the council. After
Mwindo had finished praising those who were in the council, he made
a proclamation, "Among the seven groups that are here in Tubondo,
may each group be seated together in a cluster; and the chiefs and the
seniors of the other villages, may they also be seated in their own
cluster." After he had finished speaking like that, the people grouped
themselves in an orderly manner, each group in its own cluster.
Mwindo also ordered that all his seven mothers be seated in one group
but that Nyamwindo, the mother who gave birth to him, should separate herself somewhat from his little mothers. After he had spoken like
that, his mothers moved to form their own cluster; his mother who gave
birth to him moved a short distance away yet remaining near her
cospouses. Mwindo also ordered: "Now you, my father, it is your turn.
Explain to the chiefs the reason why you have had a grudge against me;
if I have taken a portion larger than yours, if I have borne ill will against
you because of your goods, if I have snatched them away from you, tell
the chiefs the news so that they may understand." Where Shemwindo
was sitting, he was flabbergasted: sweat arose from his big toe, climbed
up to his testicles, went to arrive at the hair on his head; in his virile
impetus Shemwindo got up. Because of the great shame in the eyes of
Shemwindo, he did not even praise the chiefs anymore; he spoke while
quivering, and a little spitting cough clung to the centipede of his
throat, without warning: all this caused by the great evil of destruction.

Shemwindo said:

"All you chiefs who are here, I don't deny all the evil that I have done
against this, my offspring, my son; indeed, I had passed an interdiction
on my wives in the middle of the group of councillors and nobles, stating
that I would kill the one among my wives who would give birth to a son,
together with her child. Among all the wives, six among them gave
birth only to girls, and it was my beloved-one who gave birth to a boy.
After my beloved-one had given birth to a boy, I despised her; my
preferred wife became my despised-one. From then on, I always looked
at the soles of her feet. In the middle of all this anger, I armed myself
with a spear; I threw it into the birth hut six times; I wanted to kill the
child with its mother. When I saw that the child was not dead, I made

an agreement with the councillors and the nobles; they threw this child away into a grave. When we woke up in the morning, upon awakening, we saw the child already wailing again in its mother's house. When I noticed that, I asked myself in my heart, I said: 'If I continue to fail to kill this child, then it will oust me from my royal chair; now I, here, have seen all these amazing things that he is doing, so this child will cause me a big problem.' It's only then that I carried him into the drum and that I threw him into the river. Where this child went, I believed that I was harming him, whereas I was only making him stronger. From there it is that this child's anger stems. When he came out of the river he marched right up against me; he attacked me here in Tubondo; it is from that point on that I began to flee, all my people having been exterminated. Where I fled, I rejoiced, saying, 'I was safe,' thinking that where I was going, there was salvation, whereas I was casting myself into the thorns of rambling around throughout the country counting tree roots, sleeping in a filthy place, eating bad foods. From that moment on, my son set out in search of me; he went to take me away in the abyss of evil in which I was involved; he went to seize me at the country's border. I was at that time withered like dried bananas. And it is like that that I arrive here in the village of Tubondo. So may the male progeny be saved, because it has let me see the way in which the sky becomes daylight and has given me the joy of witnessing again the warmth of the people and of all the things here in Tubondo."

Iyangura spoke to the men who were sitting in the assembly, reproaching openly their young man here, Shemwindo:

"Here I am, aunt of Mwindo, you chiefs, in your presence. Our young man here, Shemwindo, has married me out to Mukiti; I got accustomed to it thanks to the confidence of my husband. Thanks to my labor and to getting along with him, my husband placed me high up, so that he loved me above all the wives he had married. So then—you chiefs, may I not bore you; let me not carry you far off in a long line of many words. Suddenly, this child appeared where I lived; Mukiti was then on the verge of killing him because he did not know that he was my child; but his intelligence and his malice saved him. It is from then on that I followed him and followed him to point out to him the way to Shemwindo's, and also because of my desire to see him. It's there that Mwindo's fights with his father began, because of the anger caused by all the evils that his father perpetrated against him. He subdued this village, Tubondo; his father fled. Where he fled, Mwindo went in search of him, saying that his father should not go to die in the leaves. When he joined him, he seized him; it is that, that Mwindo has made his father return again to this village, Tubondo. So it is that we are in this meeting of the assembly of the chiefs."

She also said:

"You, Shemwindo, acted badly, together with your councillors and nobles. If it were a councillor from whom this plan of torment against Mwindo had emanated, then his throat would be cut, here in the council. But you are safe, it being yourself from whom this plan sprang. You have acted badly, you Shemwindo, when you discriminated against the children, saying that some were bad and others good, whereas you did not know what was in the womb of your wife; what you were given by Ongo, you saw it to be bad; the good thing turned into the bad one. So, there is nothing good on earth! But nevertheless, we are satisfied, you notables, because of the way in which we are up on our feet again here in Tubondo, but this Shemwindo has committed an iniquitous deed. If the people had been exterminated here, it is Shemwindo who would have been guilty of exterminating them. I, Iyangura, I finish, I am at this point."

After Iyangura had finished speaking, Mwindo also stood up; he praised the assembly, he said:

"As for me, I, Mwindo, man of many feats, the Little-one-just-born-he-walked, I am not holding a grudge against my father; may my father here not be frightened, believing that I am still angry with him; no, I am not angry with my father. What my father did against me and what I did against my father, all that is already over. Now let us examine what is to come, the evil and the good; the one of us who will again start beginning, it is he who will be in the wrong, and all those seniors here will be the witnesses of it. Now, let us live in harmony in our country, let us care for our people well."

Shemwindo declared that as far as he was concerned, the act of giving birth was not repugnant in itself. He said that here where he was, no longer was he chief, that now it was Mwindo who remained in his succession, that against the one who would insult Mwindo in this land the seniors would clap their hands. When Mwindo heard his father's voice, he answered him: "You, father, just sit down on your royal chair; I cannot be chief as long as you are alive, otherwise I would die suddenly." Where the councillors and nobles were seated, they assented to Mwindo; they said to Shemwindo: "Your son did not speak wrongly; divide the country into two parts; let your son take a part and you a part, since, if you were to give away all authority, you would again be immensely jealous of him, and this jealousy could eventually trouble this country in the long run." Shemwindo said: "No, you councillors and nobles, I am not on that side; but I want my son to become chief. From now on I shall always work behind him." The councillors told him: "You, Shemwindo, divide your country into two parts, you a part and your son a part, since formerly you always used to say that you alone were a man surpassing others; and what you said happened: that is why we witnessed all these palavers; we had no way of disagreeing with you because you inspired fear. Lo! if the chief cannot be disagreed with, then it is too great foolishness." Shemwindo said: "Since you, my councillors and my nobles, come to give this advice, so I am ready to divide the country into two parts: Mwindo a part and I, Shemwindo, a part, because of the fear you inspire; but in my own name I had wanted to leave the country to Mwindo, and from then on I would always have been eating food after my son Mwindo, because I have felt and do feel much shame in the face of my son and of all the people."

After Shemwindo had spoken like that, he conferred the kingship upon his son: he stripped himself of all the things of kingship which he bore: a dress dyed red and two red belts; he also gave him butea watukushi to wear on his arms when he would pile up the bsebse meat, and butea to wear on the legs; he also gave him a ncambi belt; he also gave him a kataba belt; he also gave him a kembo hat; he also gave him the hide of a white goat. Shemwindo dressed Mwindo in all those things while Mwindo was standing up, because a chief is always being dressed in such things while standing. The councillors went to fetch the chair imbued with ukaru powder and castor oil; they gave it to Shemwindo; Shemwindo made Mwindo sit on it. Shemwindo handed over to Mwindo the scepter of copper on which there were lamels imbued with ukaru powder and castor oil. Shemwindo handed these things over to him when he was already seated on the chair. When he stood up, his father also handed over to him the wrist protector and the bow; he also gave him the quiver in which there were arrows. Shemwindo also handed Pygmies over to his son; he gave him the bandirabitambo initiators: mwamihesi, mushonga, mubei, mushumbiya, muheri, shemumbo, councillors, nobles. They dressed him in all these things in the guesthouse. After Shemwindo had enthroned his son like that, Mwindo shouted that he now had become famous, that he would not want to act as his father had so that only one descent group would remain on earth. "May all the descent groups establish themselves in the country; may boys and girls be born; may there be born deaf and cripples, because a country is never without some handicapped ones." After Shemwindo had dressed his son in the chiefly paraphernalia, he distributed beer and meat for the chiefs who were there; each group took a goat and a cow. They also gave Iyangura one cow for returning to her husband Mukiti. The chiefs and the councillors who were there said, "Let Mwindo remain here in Tubondo and let Shemwindo go to dwell on another mountain." Hearing this, Shemwindo clapped his hands; he was very satisfied. During Mwindo's enthronement, his uncles, the Baniyana, gave him a maiden, and Shamwami also gave him a maiden; Mwindo's father, he too, gave him a maiden called Katobororo and the Pygmies gave him one. During Mwindo's enthronement, he was given only four women; he went on getting himself married while he was crossing the country. In each place where he made a blood pact he carried off a maiden. During Mwindo's enthronement, the convives grew weary; some of them defecated on their heels. After Mwindo had been enthroned, the assembly dispersed: all those who came from somewhere returned there; Shemwindo also took possession of his mountain; he left to his son Tubondo. When Iyangura, aunt of Mwindo, returned to her husband, she anointed Mwindo in the middle of the group saying:

Oh, Mwindo, hail!
Blessing, here, hail!
If your father throws you into the grave, hail!
Don't harbor resentment, hail!
May you stand up and make your first step, hail!
May you be safe, may you be blessed, hail!
And your father and your mother, hail!
May you bring forth tall children, boys and girls.
Be strong, my father; as for me, there is nothing ominous left, hail!

When Mwindo took leave of his father, his father also gave him a blessing. Mwindo handed over to his aunt two councillors to accompany her; he also gave her four goats and a return gift of twenty baskets of rice and five little chicken baskets.

> After some time has elapsed, Mwindo goes on a dragon hunt with a party of Pygmies. He conquers the dragon and liberates all the people whom the monster has swallowed. Then Mwindo goes on a sky journey where he endures great ordeals and gains new wisdom. He visits the domains of Lightning, Rain, Hail, Moon, Sun and Star. Before departing from the sky he is instructed to never again kill an animal, and to accept Lightning as his guardian. After his return to earth he relates his celestial experiences to his people.

After Mwindo had taken rest, he assembled all his people. They arrived. He told them: "I, Mwindo, the Little-one-just-born-he-walked, performer of many wonderful things, I tell you the news from the place from where I have come in the sky. When I arrived in the sky, I met with Rain and Moon and Sun and Kubikubi-Star and Lightning. These five personages forbade me to kill the animals of the forest and of the village, and all the little animals of the forest, of the rivers, and of the village, saying that the day I would dare to touch a thing in order to kill it, that day the fire would be extinguished; then Nkuba would come to take me without my saying farewell to my people, that then the return was lost forever." He also told them, "I have seen in the sky things unseen of which I could not divulge." When they had finished listening to Mwindo's words, those who were there dispersed. Shemwindo's and Nyamwindo's many hairs went say "high as that" as the long hairs of an mpaca ghost; and in Tubondo the drums had not sounded anymore; the rooster had not crowed anymore. On the day that Mwindo appeared there, his father's and his mother's long hairs were shaved, and the roosters crowed, and that day all the drums were being beaten all around.

When Mwindo was in his village, his fame grew and stretched widely. He passed laws to all his people, saying:

May you grow many foods and many crops.
May you live in good houses; may you moreover live in a beautiful village.
Don't quarrel with one another.
Don't pursue another's spouse.
Don't mock the invalid passing in the village.
And he who seduces another's wife will be killed!
Accept the chief; fear him; may he also fear you.
May you agree with one another, all together; no enmity in the land nor too much hate.
May you bring forth tall and short children; in so doing you will bring them forth for the chief.

After Mwindo had spoken like that, he went from then on to remain always in his village. He had much fame, and his father and his mother, and his wives and his people! His great fame went through his country; it spread into other countries, and other people from other countries came to pay allegiance to him.

Among children there are none bad; whether he be disabled, or whether he not be disabled, he must not be rejected. So then there is nothing bad in what God has given to man.

Heroism be hailed! But excessive callousness either pushes a man into a great crime or brings him a great one, which normally he would not have experienced. So, whosoever in a country is not advised will one day carry excrements—and to experience that is terrible.

Mutual agreement brings about kinship solidarity; the one who will save his companion is unknown; it is like the chief and his subordinates. So, the world is but made of mutual aid. So, then, may the chief safeguard his subordinates and the subordinates safeguard the chief. Kingship is the stamping of feet; it is the tremor of people.

Even if a man becomes a hero to surpass the others, he will not fail one day to encounter someone else who could crush him, who could turn against him what he was looking for.

SOME SONGS OF THE LUBA PEOPLE

Football

A SONG SUNG BY SCHOOLBOYS

> Football! Yes,
> Football is a good thing
> To play every day.
> A football, I had one,
> I put it in my bag,
> But when I arrived at my destination,
> Football had been left behind.

Recorded and translated from the Tshiluba by the Rev. Jeroom Callebaut at Gandajika, Zaire, 1966.

Whence I came, football remained behind.
Whence I came, football remained behind.
Whence I came, éé!
Whence I came, éé!

Grasshopper-Hunting Song

**SUNG WHILE THE BOY IS CREEPING ON HANDS AND KNEES IN THE
GRASS IN PURSUIT OF A GRASSHOPPER**

I'll catch it!
I'll catch it!
I'll catch it!
I'll catch it!
It is so! I'll keep it! I'll eat it!

(The grasshopper leaps again, the boy follows.)

Wi! Wi! Wi!
This grasshopper makes me much trouble!
But this time it will die!
First I'll sing a song for it!
Let us see!

(He sings his song to the hunting spirits, that they may grant him
successful hunting.)

Nkuma wa Nkuma, our Nkuma! [name of this kind of grasshopper]
Your mother says, our Nkuma,
Prepare a small manioc ball
With a rathead [for meat]
And offer it to the spirits!
Pearl of Tshibuji [a place name]
Never seen, éé! [the phrase is an exclamation]
Our Nkuma!
Beaten and turned,
Turned into a grasshopper!

(He catches the grasshopper, which is of the Tshibutelu variety.)

Tshibutelu mpompo, éé!
From here to the river!

(His hunting has been successful, and as he returns to the village he
sings a song that names all the different kinds of grasshoppers.)

The dear grasshoppers,
Dear grasshoppers whose wings I have plucked!
The Lutente, male and female as well!
The Tshibutela, male and female as well!
The Dinzela, male and female as well!
The Ntenga, male as well as female!
The Nkuma, male as well as female!
The Tshibutu, male as well as female!
The Mukuku, male as well as female!

Praise Song in Mourning for a Dead Person

> (Sung in praise of Tshiumbula Kayembe by his
> son. The song alludes to the dead man's origins
> by tribe, clan, family and region, and speaks of
> his various descendants as well. Statements of
> praise are made in the form of proverbs, meta-
> phors and cryptic allusions whose meanings
> are clear to the Luba but esoteric for the out-
> sider.)

Dear father, native of Mutombo, of the clan of Yumba;
Tshiumbula Kayembe, of those who dig pits on the road;[1]
Handle of the basket among the blacksmiths;[2]
Native of Lusamba, those who live on the land of Kasongo of
     Ngandu, slippery frog;[3]
Ntombolo [colobus] will not sleep where mbala [wildcat] fears to get
     his fur plucked;[4]
Father of Kela of Kabamba, those who wound with knives for fear
     that spears should hurt their hands;[5]
Father of Biyoyo and Tumpula Kabeya, of Nsana Muketa, husband
     of Musangu, Mashinda's daughter;
Father of Yakusu, Mutombo's wife, he [her husband] is a native of
     Mudiayi where blacksmiths live;
Father of Kanyinda, nsenji [big rat] with open loins;[6]
Father, born at Tshitumbi's, Kabeya's son;

---

1. "... those who dig pits on the road"—Refers to the traps dug by hunters to trap game,
and by warriors to trap the enemy. Implies shrewdness and courageousness.
2. The subject of the song was a blacksmith when he was alive. "Handle of the basket"
refers to an adage that says the handle is the most important part of a basket, because
a basket without its handle is thrown away. "Handle of the basket among blacksmiths"
means that the deceased person was a renowned blacksmith.
3. "slippery frog"—an esoteric compliment.
4. A proverb whose meaning is apparent. The man was prudent.
5. "... those who wound with knives ..." etc.—Ironic. "Those who use knives" refers to
quarrelsome people in ordinary situations who are less than courageous in war.
6. "... with open loins"—Signifies "fat." Thus, a fat bush rat, used in a complimentary
sense.

Tshitumbi, the vindictive [whose heart keeps hatred], who was
hated in his country but liked in others, like the mukenge
[genet] running about in the millet [fields].[7]

Young People's Courting Song

(Boys and girls stand facing each other in two
lines. While they sing, a boy leaves his line,
goes forward, selects a girl and brings her back
to his line. Then a girl from the other side approaches the boys' line, selects a partner and
returns to her line.)

Choose, choose!
Choose yours,
Your husband
Whom you love,
With whom you will go away
Even to death,
Even to the angels!

Choose, choose!
Choose yours
To go away with him,
Even to Europe!
If you love him
And if he loves you
You both will be glad!

Choose, choose!
Even if they beat you,
Even if they insult you,
Always be glad
And you will stay
Until you go to Father,
To Father, our Creator!

---

7. *The man is compared to the genet which people try to kill if it invades their grainfields.
Refers to bad relations that Tshiumbula had with people in his own country, but does
not explain.*

A Lullaby

(While the mother is away, one of the baby's
elder sisters picks it up and tries to sing it to
sleep.)

Cry, child, cry, child! Yes!
Cry, child, cry, child! Yes!
I found my child in the high grass!
I found my child in the high grass!
Yowela, my child!

The Supreme Deity of the Luba

Among the Luba people living in the Kasayi region of Zaire, God, the
Creator, is known by a name widespread among the Central African
Bantu, Nzambi. In the Luba concept, Nzambi is supreme and unique.
There is no pantheon as found in the religious systems of some other
African peoples. In the opinion of those intimately familiar with Luba
culture, the Lubas are monotheistic. Although there are believed to be
a variety of demons and other supernatural creatures, only Nzambi is
a deity. He is called by such names as:
   Mvidi (or Mvidie), meaning The Spirit;
   Mvidi (or Mvidie) Mukulu, meaning The Eldest Spirit;
   Mulopo, meaning The Lord; and
   Muena Kulu, meaning The One from Above.
Nzambi is also given such honorific titles as:
   Nkole, meaning The Strong One;
   Nkole Muena Bintu, meaning The Strong One Who Has All Things;
   Mvidi Mukulu Wa Tshimpanga, meaning The Eldest Spirit, the
      He-goat (refers to the image in the Luba saying, "Mulume wa
      tshimpanga, tungunuja mikoko"—"The he-goat makes the other
      goats follow him");
   Mulopo Maweja Nnangila, meaning God Who Loves Us; and
   Maweja Lulamangani, meaning God the Conserver.
Attributes of Nzambi are expressed in such sayings as:
   Muntu kayi mufuka kudi Mvidi? Nkayende mudipangile.—Isn't
      man created by God? By himself he (man) would fail to do it.
   Bintu bionso bidi bia Mvidi, Mvidi Mukulu wafukile.—All things
      are God's, he created them.
   Mikombo wa Kalewo mudifuke.—God created himself.
   Mvidi, tshibi lumona kubidi.—God is a door that looks two ways.
      (That is, he is like a closed house door, one side facing the
      visible outside world, the other side facing the invisible
      world within.)

Provided by the Rev. Jeroom Callebaut.

How I Shall Be Admired

A BENE-MUKUNI TALE

This is what that man did.

He went to the court to report. "Listen!" he said. "At the place where I come from I have found an enormous snake. I should say, my lords, that, if you had it brought here, all your honorable friends would assemble to come and look at it."

The king, hearing that, said, "I am going to call all the people of the land together."

He had them called, then held an assembly where he said, "I am the king, bring me the thing that is over there, that I too may come and see it with my own eyes in a hut."

Of course those people went. As they reached the place, they gathered together outside, trying to go and peep inside. Then, finding the thing still asleep, they started singing:

"How I shall be admired!
[Chorus]: How I shall be admired!
Come out that we may look at you!
[Chorus] That we may look at you!
If I come out, you will be afraid of me!
[Chorus] By [your] mother! You will be afraid of me!
That is what was done by your fathers!
[Chorus] By your fathers!
They even left their bows here!
[Chorus] Even their bows!"

Those people ran away leaving their bows there and came and said, "As for us, O Chief, that is more than we can do."

The king then said, "Go and give birth to children."

The following day, when they gave birth to children and these went, as soon as they reached the place, they too surrounded the hut, but said,

From Specimens of Bantu Folk-Lore from Northern Rhodesia, by J. Torrend. London: Kegan Paul, Trench, Trubner & Co., 1921. By permission of the publishers.

"It is you, your very own self, that we have come for, you who are in the house."

Bacu! They put the snake on their shoulders, the tail hanging behind. Then, having brought it outside, they dragged it along, singing the while:

"How I shall be admired!" (etc.)

Then, as they took that thing to the court and reached the place, the king said: "You my wives, all of you, go and fetch water to whitewash the hut."

So, having gone to fetch water, the women came and whitewashed the hut.

And, when they had finished whitewashing, the brute itself was brought in.

Then the king came over also to have a look at it. And, having seen it, he said: "You people of my realm, disperse and go away, all of you. I do not care in the least for such things. To me, such as I am, what have you brought but an ugly snake?"

The Story of Mukana-lwewo

LAMBA TRIBE, ZAMBIA

One day some people went from the village of the chief for a walk, and came suddenly upon the house of a blacksmith. They found that there was but one house and a smithy. They found the owner working the bellows. When he had finished blowing, he arose and took the iron, and began to hammer; and then again put back the iron. And those people were amazed, when they saw what the smith did. Those people arose, and returned to the village. When they reached the village, they said: "Sir, where we went, we found a man forging hoes and small axes in an extraordinary way. He himself forged, and one and the same man blew the bellows!" Then the chief said, "Tomorrow you must take an elephant's tusk." Then indeed in the morning, they went and carried the tusk; and reached the place. They found the owner forging. When

From Lamba Folk-Lore, *by Clement M. Doke,* Memoirs of the American Folk-Lore Society, *Vol. XX, New York, 1927. Reprinted by permission of the American Folklore Society.*

he saw them, he said, "Greetings, friends!" And they answered, "Greetings!" And they said: "The chief has sent us, saying, 'Go to that smith; I want friendship!' " And he said, "All right!" And he entered the house and took a bundle of hoes, and a bundle of axes, and tied them up for them, "Go! and I am coming behind (later)!" Then indeed they arose and went.

When they reached the chief yonder, they put down the bundles saying, "These are what your friend has put aside; and he himself is coming behind." Then indeed they put those hoes inside. Then his friend, where he remained, after some days gathered together bundles of hoes and of axes, and set out, saying, "Just let me, too, see the chief!" He reached the chief there, and arrived thus in the bush, and sat down. The people said, "Don't you see the friend of the chief yonder has arrived today?" Then indeed the chief went out, and took him to a good house. And he arrived and entered. In the evening he undid his bundles of hoes, and took hoes and axes to the chief. The next morning he remained over. But the following morning he went to the chief and said, "Now, sir, I am going home today!" Then the chief gathered together goods for him, and he arose and went. And he went and reached home, and began his work of forging; and he himself alone to hammer.

Again many days after, the chief again sent his people with an elephant's tusk, saying, "Take it to my friend!" And they indeed arrived and put down the tusk, saying, "This tusk has come from the chief; he told us to take it to his friend!" And he was pleased, and said, "I am very grateful to my chief!" And he entered the house, and took bundles of hoes and of axes, and gathered them together for them saying, "Go!" And then off they went, and reached the chief with the hoes and axes.

Many days later Mukana-lwewo arose, and off he went, and reached the chief, and he showed him to a house. When morning dawned, he said, "Now I am going today, sir, I am in a hurry!" And the chief took a slave, and gave to him to help him. And he received him, and went, and reached home.

Again after some days the chief began a journey, and Mukana-lwewo too arose saying, "Let me see the chief, I am longing for him!" And he arrived. They told him that the chief was gone away. The principal wife of the chief came, and gave him a house. When darkness fell the principal wife came, and talked for a very long time. That Mukana-lwewo said, "Go along now, mother, and let me shut the door!"

[*The following paragraph was given by the original translator in Latin, being deemed too vulgar for the English language.*]

But the first wife refused to go. "I don't want to," she said. "I want you to sleep with me." Mukana-lwewo said, "I don't want to because you are the chief's wife, and I am afraid he will do harm to me." The first wife said: "Do not be afraid. Give in to the pleasure of a woman." "I agree," he said, "but the fault is yours." She said, "I burn for your love every day." Then they copulated. In the middle of the night the first wife went home. Before dawn Mukana-lwewo went to her and said,

"Now I am going home." She answered, "I order you to stay; I want to see you." Thus, after copulating with her for five days he went home. Many days later when the first wife was pregnant the chief returned. On the day he arrived he sent for all his wives. "Come," he said, "I have in mind to inspect your wombs." When all his wives had gathered he examined them and found the younger ones all right. But after inspecting the first wife's belly, he asked, "First wife, who did that to your womb?" She answered: "I am not pregnant. My belly was injured and it swelled." The chief said, "You are lying. If you don't tell the truth I will kill you." Then the first wife confessed. She said, "Mukana-lwewo made me pregnant. When you left he came here and for five days he slept with me. Thus he made me pregnant."

Then the chief was very angry, and said, "Bring him, and let us kill him!" Then there went people to Mukana-lwewo, and arrived and caught him, saying, "It was you who made the wife of the chief pregnant!" And Mukana-lwewo said, "Let us go!" And he added, "Take me to my uncle that I may bid farewell!" Then indeed those people agreed to take him. And they reached his uncle there, and the uncle said, "What has this man done?" They said, "He lay with the chief's wife!" The uncle said, "Right, let him kill him! Who are his relations?" But his wife said, "What man! to let them kill your relative?" He said: "Yes, let them kill him! He denied me long ago. He never comes here. I don't want to see him at all!" Then his wife said: "You don't play the game! Won't you redeem your relative?" And he refused, saying: "No, have I wealth? He himself is the wealthy one!" Then night fell, and she gave them food. In the middle of the night, his uncle's wife came out, with a loin slip, and found him asleep in the midst; and she roused him, saying, "Wake up!" And he awoke; and she gave him the loin slip, saying, "Wear this [woman's] loin slip. When you reach the chief, ask for a hammer. Whilst forging, let your calico [waistcloth] drop down. You will see that the chief will save you!"

Then indeed morning dawned; they arose and went. And they reached the chief. And the chief said, "Have you brought Mukana-lwewo?" They said, "Yes, sir, we have brought him!" He called the principal wife, saying, "Wife, come here!" He said, "Where is he who lay with you?" She said, "This very one, sir!" Mukana said: "No, sir, I lay not with the wife of the chief, she is telling lies about me!" The chief said, "Right, we shall kill you in the morning!" Then indeed they put him in a house.

When morning dawned, he said, "Bring forth Mukana-lwewo, and let us kill him!" Then indeed they brought him forth. But he said: "Give me a hammer, sir, let me forge, and bid myself farewell!" Then indeed the chief agreed, and gave him a hammer. He went to the smithy, and began to blow the bellows. And the chief sat down. And the smith borrowed the hammer, and Mukana-lwewo took the big hammer, and began to hammer. He said, "He who denies the charge, how is he to deny it?"

[*Again a paragraph from the Latin*]

And he let his waistcloth fall [revealing the woman's loin slip]. The chief said to him, "Please come here." Mukana-lwewo went forward and stood without moving. The chief then called his principal wife. He said: "This is not the person who lay with you, whoever she may be. It was somebody else. As for it being this one, it is clear that you lied."

The principal wife replied, "It must have been another who changed himself into this one, because this one is indeed a fellow woman of mine!"

Then the chief was much ashamed, and said to Mukana-lwewo: "I am ashamed, friend Mukana-lwewo, because I lied about you. And so I want to give you much wealth!" Then indeed he took a great quantity of goods, and said, "Carry these for my friend!" Then Mukana-lwewo arose, and said to those people, "Come, let us pass by my uncle's!" And they went right to his uncle, and he gave him all the goods, and profusely thanked his uncle's wife, saying, "And the wealth that is at my home I shall bring it all to you!" Then he went home; all the goods that were at his house, he picked up, and took to the wife of his uncle. And that was how Mukana-lwewo escaped.

TEACHINGS OF THE CHAGGA ELDERS

Moral and ethical values are woven into many types of African tales and are frequently made explicit by a concluding proverb or epigram. But the teaching of good behavior is not left to good example and chance. Why a person should do one thing and not another is explained in persuasive detail by parents, uncles and tribal authorities, as in these teachings of the Chagga people of Tanzania.

From Die Stammeslehren der Dschagga, *by B. Gutmann, Munich, C. H. Beck, 1932–38. The English translation appeared in* Birthright of Man, *edited by Jeanne Hersch. By kind permission of C. H. Beck'sche Verlagsbuchhandlung and UNESCO.*

Nothing on Earth Is Cleverer than the Female Sex

See, my grandchild! As I teach you, and you children in the older class teach each other, you think: We men are clever. If you see womankind and watch how four or five of them sit together and tell each other things, you think: Instead of chatting here, they ought to get up, go home and cut grass. As you talk like this to each other, you think in your own minds: They are stupid and ignorant. See, my grandchild, they are not stupid. Nothing in the whole world is cleverer than the female sex. Know this, if you are as other men, you are not as intelligent as a woman. It is only that she is given into your charge. If it were you who were given into her charge, she would surpass you in intelligence. Therefore I tell you: a woman will hold a thing in her head better than you. See, my grandson, you live together and she is your wife. Drive a cow into the house and let her milk it. Now if you feel a bit hungry during the night, because you have not eaten your fill, then you say to her: If only you had cooked a milk dish, we would have easily eaten our fill! And she says to you: Oh, no, there was not enough to cook a dish with. Get some more!

See, my grandson, you must realize that a woman is intelligent. For she wants to keep the milk until it is sour, so that when she puts it into the food it is strong enough to give a good taste to it. But you just listen and say nothing. The next day, when the sun rises she says to you: Help me and put out a piece of banana branch for the cow, so that it can chew it slowly, while I go to fetch grass. Then while you are cutting that piece of banana branch, you think: All right, I'll examine the calabash to see whether she was deceiving me when she said there was no more milk in it, or if there really isn't any in it. When you have cut the piece of banana branch, you seize the calabash, you pick it up like that and then put it down again. You don't drink any of it, Oh, no! When she comes, you say nothing, get up and go out to where the men are. See, my grandson, the woman seeks out the calabash and thinks: I wonder whether when he had cut the piece of banana branch, he took up and looked at the calabash? She goes, finds it and notices that you have turned it round, put it down in another position and were unable to set it down as she did.

If you do this four times, the woman will speak of it behind your back. Then if you are a little rude to her she will go to her family; and if you and they then discuss the matter, and the woman is not properly trained—no one has told her "You must not say such things"—her education having been neglected, she says: Get up and go away from here, monster, you who lift up women's calabashes. With such words she brings you into great disrepute and you are hated among men. They curse you and say: What is the point of touching women's calabashes? And the women speak of you and say: I should not like to be married to a man who lifts women's calabashes!

See, my grandson, as a man you are not capable of setting down anything anywhere so that you can see, as a woman can, whether it has been touched.

Therefore I tell you: a woman is clever. And if you respect what is women's business your reputation will not suffer. And your wife will honor you, because she knows that you have learnt to keep quiet like other men.

We Are Little Snails Who Seek Refuge Behind the Fronds of the Banana Tree

See, my grandchild, I see from your hand which you hold outstretched, so that you may acquire cattle which will multiply. The Heaven Man helps to increase it for you, so that it may fatten you. But you puff yourself up and think, "There is nothing that can vie with me any longer." You look at the elders around the chief and think, "I am as big as they!" Eventually, when you see the chief himself, you think, "Bah!" So that he, watching you, perceives that you hold everyone in contempt. And they speak of this and say, "So-and-so no longer recognizes anyone as his superior." Another answers: "Oho! He no longer even acknowledges the chief!" And the chief declares, "A trap must be set for him and he must be plundered!" But another declares: "He has become too big for that. If he goes off with all his kith and kin, it will upset the whole country. As long as he does not curse the chief, let things be, let him stay here and let us watch him."

But after this there is an epidemic on your farm and your livestock die. For livestock mean vicissitudes, my grandchild. They are subject to ups and downs. Then you sit down and think to yourself, "Hmm, what about things?" and you sigh. As you sit thinking, illness comes to you, too; you die and leave behind orphans. But the tribe you held in such contempt now says: "He was a really violent man and no longer acknowledged the worth of others. Let him depart!" If they speak in this way when you have left orphans, starvation will come upon your family. When there comes starvation, which licks people up [that is, exterminates them like flies], then we are snails, and our haunt is behind the fronds of the banana trees, where we hide so as to stay alive. If you want to understand that we are really like snails, then watch when it becomes hot in the kilning month. For this month brings hunger to the snails, and when you look for one you can find none. But if you break a frond from the banana bush, you find many of them hidden behind it. But in the rainy season they thrive, and as many of them as have survived the heat come out into the open; and we human beings too are like snails and live by the grace of the great, who are chiefs. Should you leave behind an orphan, the chief will take it in and give it shelter, just like those snails that took shelter behind the banana leaves and stayed alive. The chief is man's banana leaf. And therefore I tell you, my grandchild, do not elbow your way through life pushing your way past people, and acknowledging no master. Lie low and be humble. And keep an open mind, so that your mind is aware of its surroundings. Then if you leave an orphan, it will find its hiding place behind the fronds of the chief. The chief will bestow honors on the orphan and it will come to greatness as you formerly were great. And the Heaven Man will bestow other cattle, because the chieftain took over responsibility for the child, because you showed yourself so accommodating, and he did not avoid your company.

Chiefs Are like the Rain

Look you, my grandson! Chiefs are like the rain, there is no telling the day when they start to hate each other. If you are suffering from the heat and your plants, which you have tended, wither, so rain falls on the earth on the day the Heaven Man wishes and your plants are saved. And this is how chiefs are too. Today they choose to fall out and before very long you will see them join forces.

And you decide to set off and go to the other chiefs. Yet meanwhile, as you are setting off from home, they happen to defy each other. One thinks to himself, "If someone just gave me one of his men, I would kill him, so that he should come and we would fight each other and all would see who is a man and who is a woman."

At the place you are going to the chief has consulted with his men and said, "Let us block the way so that he [the other chief] should notice it, become angry and we fight each other."

When he has spoken, one man goes and tells it to his wife. He says to her, "We have been commanded to block the road to Moschi tomorrow." She asks him, "What are you going to do to block the way?" He says to her, "If we see a man coming from Moschi, we are to kill him, so that they know we harbor enmity towards them."

The woman thinks to herself, "Heh, heh, a man could come along who has sealed a bond of blood brotherhood with my father or with my stepfather and should he be killed?" So she decides: "I'll go and cut grass by the wayside. Should I see someone, I shall bid him turn back. Man is man; whatever happens I shall bid him turn back so that his life shall be spared." And the woman takes up her fiber bonds and goes to cut grass by the wayside. But they are lying in ambush near where the chief lives. And you come briskly walking along, proceeding as the mood takes you, until you come to the woman cutting grass. You wish to go past and are not even inclined even to greet her. She raises her head and sees you. And she asks you: "Mister, where do you come from that you should go past on the way without any greeting? Where do you come from, my father-in-law?" You are in a hurry and quickly say to her, "I come from Moschi." But she asks you, "Do you know then the story about the eastern country that you should go by on your way in this manner?"

On hearing this, think hard and may that which I have told you come into your head. Turn back and flee; do not mind the woman. If you do,

you put her in danger of being found out. And should you meet someone else, bid him turn back too.

Look you, my grandson, they later fall upon someone and kill him,
but you have been saved. Once they have fought each other and one
of them [i.e., one of the chiefs] has been defeated and sued [for peace],
they make peace. And people go to and fro as before and visit one
another. But you think to yourself, "Look, look, were it not for the
woman, I would very likely have been killed." And then they rejoice
likewise, when things have thus been settled.

That is what I mean when I tell you they are like the rain. You would
have died and they would then have made peace. But you would have
been lost.

Eating Alone Brings Ruin

Listen, my grandchildren! You are the four sons born to one woman
and you have grown up together. And you are one of the four and you
think to yourself, "I will be cleverer than the others!" and so as to be
smarter than they are, you decide to eat all by yourself.

But what you eat alone you are robbing your kith and kin of. They,
your brothers, have no knowledge of all this. They continue to treat you
well. One of them has a goat to spare and invites you to come along.
When he kills his goat, which came with the last litter, he calls you, the
four of you. He invites you so that his brothers can eat their fill and carry
their supper home with them.

You are the one among them who gives himself airs and comes before
them. And the one who has saved the goat wishes you to be his father,
as you are the firstborn among them. If God took your father away from
you and he is no more, so you are their father, and he [the brother in
question] reserves the piece of breast that goes to the father for you. So
you get the piece of breast, and after you, your younger brothers share
the carcass piece between them [consisting of the first three ribs.] The
fourth one though takes the rest of the carcass. That will be your marriage support [i.e., for his children].

If there is another brother of yours there, who is not the offspring of
your father, he gets a hind leg and shares it with his neighbor who is
helping to guard the home. And the brother who chose the goat will
have a word with you and say: "Look you, my older brother, as I had
got this goat, I invited you all here and have now been your marriage
support, just as you have left this piece of rib for me. If, however, there
is someone left who wants to do us harm, that is your affair and is no
longer any concern of mine [i.e., I have done my duty and, for my part,
arranged matters between us after our father's death on a new foot-
ing]." But you leave them; they have made you important and you
come home and get a fat belly.

You have given someone a goat to look after. You kill it there and
bring its flesh home. Someone sees you on the way, stops to make sure

it's you, and tells your brothers. When your brothers learn this, they say to one another, "Our brother has killed a goat." They keep it in their heads and are silent about it.

Then you brew some beer, invite them and they come. You place a jar ready on one side with an infusion of bananas and water down the beer with it. And they say to you, "This beer is very thin." You answer them, "Yes, there was only a little eleusine corn." With troubled thoughts they go home. They are not lighthearted as one normally is on taking leave of one's brother. It is as though they were taking leave of just anyone.

Look you, my grandson, when you have something to eat, ask an old man who takes precedence of you: "Pray for us to the Heaven Man and to our tribal ancestor. Say: 'We beg you, our ancestor, come together with the Heaven Man so that He should look down upon us. Should we keep food from each other, will you then, O Heaven Man! O chief! look down upon us and crush us. But if we show proper regard for each other, then let us rise up like the steam from brewing, so that we prosper. O Heaven Man let us thrive!' "

When you have done that and you, my grandson, then eat and keep things back [from the others], the Heaven Man will fix His eyes on you and not allow you to continue to thrive.

The seclusion in which you secretly eat and deprive your brothers will rather lead to your extinction [i.e., to your being robbed of your children].

And soon afterwards you yourself will disappear from the tribe. The solitariness to which your stomach has led you will be to blame.

Therefore I say to you, my grandson: if your brothers think you honest, don't go and leave their midst and eat alone. Solitude leads to much harm and an early death.

This I forbid you and say: let it be. Rather share honestly with your brothers. Let them see [everything] as they let you see [everything].

The Head of a Man Is a Hiding Place, a Receptacle

The teacher sings:
  Yes, indeed, man, yes, indeed, you man with the shield!
  Yes, indeed, man, yes, indeed, you man with the shield!
  The head of a man, indeed, yes, is a long-term store!
  It is a crack in the rock used for storage.
  If you notice that some uninitiated boy, immature as a red plum, is a chatterbox, hide everything in your head.
  Ha, indeed, the child's nurse, she too is talkative. But your head is the crack in the rock for storage. Ah, yes! Ha, surely one of the children will tell tales to you and say, "Your mother spoke of you behind your back," or say, "That uninitiated girl of yours spoke of you."
  Then your head is the long-term container to store this away. Let us

tell the child in his lessons, the head of the flute player is a crack in the rock for storing what is said.

The assistant teacher explains:

Mark well, my younger brother, beware of the idle chatter which goes round the farm.

See, when you bring back meat, then perhaps you will cut a large piece off for a small child. When it has eaten it, out of sheer joy it will tell you about home; saying, "This woman cursed you and swore."

But you have a head in which to store things; do not fly at the woman. That child surely invented the whole story, when it was so pleased with the meal which you gave it as a sign of love. See, whether it heard the woman saying something other than it claimed, or really heard her curse you, store it in the back of your mind and do not burn down your farm.

Or another time you come home, and another child says to you when you are alone: "Papa, I have something to say to you: when you had gone away she got together with her mother-in-law, and they swore about you and said: 'The lazy fellow, he goes off early in the morning from the farm and is making slaves of us. We do not sleep in the bushes, but we are his swine!'" If you heard that you would surely be tempted to hit her and your mother-in-law. But if you hit her, your home life is doomed. For this reason the old teacher tells you: The head of a man is a storage place, a loft! Do not listen to the idle chatter of little children. When you are grown up and have acquired serenity, you must store everything that people say to you in your head and not blurt it out in anger. Store it in your head until you have made your decision. And about what you notice yourself, question her carefully, in your own home. But if you beat your wife in anger about tales told behind your back, and later find out that they are untrue, and you become a continual irritation to her, and afterwards she comes to you, argues with you and wins the argument, she will be lost to you; she will bear another man's children, and keep another man's house and the old teacher is left alone with his teaching which you have scorned and wasted. And for this reason the old teacher says to you: Keep quiet! Store what you hear from others in your head and wait until your father and mother ask you about it, and they will tell you, let it be; she is our young mother who looks after the household; we will guide her back to the right path.

SOME TRADITIONS AND STORIES OF THE GANDA

The First King of Uganda

From the earliest times in the history of Uganda there has been a king (kabaka) with despotic powers. The first king was Kintu, and with him the early history and development of the country are bound up. Prior to Kintu, there were a few aborigines who dwelt in isolated communities or clans; each clan was governed by its chief, who owned allegiance to no other chief. Kintu came either from the north or the northeast, and began at once to subdue and amalgamate these clans, and to form them into a nation. He appears to have been of a different stock from the aborigines, and also of superior intellect to the people who came

From The Baganda, an Account of their Native Customs and Beliefs, *by John Roscoe, London, Frank Cass and Co., 1911.*

with him; the latter held him in great esteem, and looked upon him as belonging to a different race from themselves. From Kintu the royal family trace their descent, and with him the history and traditions of the country commence. The history previous to his reign is lost; the one established fact is that the country was inhabited. From Kintu to the present king [1911] there have been thirty-two generations, which in round numbers cover a period of about a thousand years. . . .

Many legends gather round Kintu, for he was supposed to be descended from the gods. He married a woman named Nambi, of the Colobus Monkey Clan. Tradition says that he lived alone for some time, and that this woman was then given him by the god Gulu out of compassion. Further, tradition runs that, when he was an old man, he went into the forest and disappeared. As it was unlawful to say that the king was dead, the chiefs said that he had disappeared. The burial took place secretly, a pit was dug behind the enclosure of the house, and the body of Kintu wrapped in a cowhide was placed in it, and left. No earth was thrown into the pit, but thorns were put round it and over the body, as a protection against wild animals, and the medicine man visited the grave from time to time, until he was able to work the jawbone away. He then took the bone, and after cleansing and decorating it, he put it in the temple which was built on the Magongo hill in Singo. Rain gradually filled in the grave by washing in the sides, and no further notice was taken of it, except that all persons were prevented from walking near it.

The Legend of Kintu

When Kintu first came to Uganda he found there was no food at all in the country; he brought with him one cow and had only the food which the animal supplied him with. In the course of time a woman named Nambi came with her brother to the earth and saw Kintu; the woman fell in love with him, and wishing to be married to him pointedly told him so. She, however, had to return with her brother to her people and father, Gulu, who was King of Heaven. Nambi's relations objected to the marriage because they said that the man did not know of any food except that which the cow yielded, and they despised him. Gulu, their father, however, said they had better test Kintu before he consented to the marriage, and he accordingly sent and robbed Kintu of his cow. For a time Kintu was at a loss what to eat, but managed to find different kinds of herbs and leaves which he cooked and ate. Nambi happened to see the cow and recognized it, and complaining that her brothers wished to kill the man she loved, she went to the earth and told Kintu where his cow was, and invited him to return with her to take it away. Kintu consented to go, and when he reached Heaven he was greatly surprised to see how many people there were with houses, [and] cows, goats, sheep and fowls running about.

When Nambi's brothers saw Kintu sitting with their sister at her house, they went and told their father, who ordered them to build a house for Kintu and said they were to give him a further testing to see whether he was worthy of their sister. An enormous meal was cooked, enough food for a hundred people, and brought to Kintu, who was told that unless he ate it all he would be killed as an impostor; failure to eat it, they said, would be proof that he was not the great Kintu. He was then shut up in a house and left. After he had eaten and drunk as much as he wished, he was at a loss to know what to do with the rest of the food; fortunately he discovered a deep hole in the floor of the house, so he turned all the food and beer into it and covered it over so that no one could detect the place. He then called the people outside to come and take away the baskets. The sons of Gulu came in, but would not believe he had eaten all the food; they therefore searched the house, but failed to find it. They went to their father and told him that Kintu had eaten all the food.

He was incredulous, and said Kintu must be further tested; a copper axe was sent by Gulu, who said: "Go and cut me firewood from the rock, because I do not use ordinary firewood." When Kintu went with the axe he said to himself: "What am I to do? If I strike the rock, the axe will only turn its edge or rebound." However, after he had examined the rock he found there were cracks in it, so he broke off pieces and returned with them to Gulu, who was surprised to get them; still he said Kintu must be further tried before they gave their consent to the marriage.

Kintu was next sent to fetch water and told he must bring dew only, because Gulu did not drink water from wells. Kintu took the waterpot and went off to a field where he put the pot down and began to ponder what he was to do to collect the dew. He was sorely puzzled, but upon returning to the pot he found it full of water, so he carried it back to Gulu. Gulu was most surprised and said, "This man is a wonderful being; he shall have his cow back and marry my daughter." Kintu was told he was to pick his cow from the herd and take it; this was a more difficult task than the others, because there were so many cows like his own he feared he would mistake it and take the wrong one. While he was thus perplexed a large bee came and said: "Take the one upon whose horns I shall alight; it is yours." The next morning he went to the appointed place and stood and watched the bee which was resting on a tree near him; a large herd of cows was brought before him, and he pretended to look for his cow, but in reality he watched the bee, which did not move. After a time Kintu said, "My cow is not there." A second herd was brought, and again he said, "My cow is not there." A third, much larger, herd was brought, and the bee flew at once and rested upon a cow which was a very large one, and Kintu said, "That is my cow." The bee then flew to another cow, and Kintu said, "That is one of the calves from my cow," and so on to a second and third which he claimed as the calves that had been born during the cow's stay with Gulu.

Gulu was delighted with Kintu and said: "You are truly Kintu, take your cows; no one can deceive or rob you, you are too clever for that."

He called Nambi and said to Kintu, "Take my daughter who loves you, marry her and go back to your home." Gulu further said, "You must hurry away and go back before Death (Walumbe) comes, because he will want to go with you and you must not take him; he will only cause you trouble and unhappiness." Nambi agreed to what her father said and went to pack up her things. Kintu and Nambi then took leave of Gulu, who said, "Be sure if you have forgotten anything not to come back, because Death will want to go with you and you must go without him."

They started off home, taking with them, besides Nambi's things and the cows, a goat, a sheep, a fowl, and a plantain tree. On the way Nambi remembered that she had forgotten the grain for the fowl, and said to Kintu, "I must go back for the grain for the fowl, or it will die." Kintu tried to dissuade her, but in vain; she said, "I will hurry back and get it without anyone seeing me." He said, "Your brother Death will be on the watch and see you." She would not listen to her husband, but went back and said to her father, "I have forgotten the grain for the fowl, and I am come to take it from the doorway where I put it." He replied: "Did I not tell you that you were not to return if you forgot anything, because your brother Death would see you, and want to go with you? Now he will accompany you." She tried to steal away without Death, but he followed her; when she rejoined Kintu, he was angry at seeing Death, and said: "Why have you brought your brother with you? Who can live with him?" Nambi was sorry, so Kintu said, "Let us go on and see what will happen."

When they reached the earth Nambi planted her garden, and the plantains grew rapidly, and she soon had a large plantain grove at Manyagalya. They lived happily for some time and had a number of children, until one day Death asked Kintu to send one of his children to be his cook. Kintu replied: "If Gulu comes and asks me for one of my children, what am I to say to him? Shall I tell him that I have given her to be your cook?" Death was silent and went away, but he again asked for a child to be his cook, and again Kintu refused to send one of his daughters, so Death said, "I will kill them." Kintu, who did not know what he meant, asked, "What is it you will do?" In a short time, however, one of the children fell ill and died, and from that time they began to die at intervals. Kintu returned to Gulu and told him about the deaths of the children, and accused Death of being the cause. Gulu replied: "Did I not tell you when you were going away to go at once with your wife and not to return if you had forgotten anything, but you allowed Nambi to return for the grain? Now you have Death living with you: had you obeyed me you would have been free from him and not lost any of your children."

After some further entreaty, Gulu sent Kaikuzi, the brother of Death, to assist Nambi, and to prevent Death from killing the children. Kaikuzi went to the earth with Kintu and was met by Nambi, who told him her pitiful story; he said he would call Death and try to dissuade him from killing the children. When Death came to greet his brother they had quite a warm and affectionate meeting, and Kaikuzi told him he had come to take him back, because their father wanted him. Death said, "Let us take our sister too," but Kaikuzi said he was not sent to take her, because she was married and had to stay with her husband. Death refused to go without his sister, and Kaikuzi was angry with him and ordered him to do as he was told. Death, however, escaped from Kaikuzi's grip and fled away into the earth.

For a long time there was enmity between the two brothers; Kaikuzi tried in every possible way to catch his brother Death, who always escaped. At last Kaikuzi told the people to remain in their houses for several days and not let any of the animals out, and he would have a final hunt for Death. He further told them that if they saw Death they must not call out nor raise the usual cry (ndulu) of fear. The instructions were followed for two or three days, and Kaikuzi got his brother to come out of the earth and was about to capture him, when some children took their goats to the pasture and saw Death and called out. Kaikuzi rushed to the spot and asked why they called, and was told they had seen Death; he was angry, because Death had again gone into the earth; so he went to Kintu and told him he was tired of hunting Death and wanted to return home; he also complained that the children had frightened Death into the earth again. Kintu thanked Kaikuzi for his help and said he feared nothing more could be done, and hoped Death would not kill all the people. From that time Death has lived upon the earth and killed people whenever he could, and then escaped into the earth at Tanda in Singo.

Mpobe and Death

A GANDA STORY

There was once a hunter named Mpobe, who was an expert in hunting the edible rat (musu). One day as he was sitting in his house, he saw a friend, Omuzizi, come running towards him, who said, "Come and let us hunt the rat." Mpobe agreed to go and took his hunting net and his dogs, and they went off together to the place where the game was known to abound. Omuzizi told Mpobe to stop at a certain place while he went on to fix the net to catch the animals; when he had fixed it he called to Mpobe to let the dogs loose; the latter then fastened the bells to one dog and turned them loose. The dogs soon started a fine rat and went after it, but it turned and ran to one side where there was no one standing and no net to stop it. Mpobe said, "Never mind, the dogs will catch it," and he followed them, leaving his companions by the net.

Omuzizi waited until sunset for Mpobe and then took the net and went home. The rat ran on and the dogs after it, and Mpobe after the dogs, until it entered a large hole, and the dogs dashed in after it; when Mpobe reached the hole he could hear the bells and followed the sound of them. They went on until the rat came to a number of people: it rushed past them with the dogs close after it. When Mpobe came up, he was surprised to see the people, a large garden, and many houses. He asked the people if they had seen his dogs; they replied that they had, and pointed out the way they had gone. So he followed, though he was afraid, and at length he came upon his dogs with the rat standing near an important-looking person.

Mpobe fell down before him and greeted him, and Death (for it was he) asked him where he came from. Mpobe answered that he came "from above" where he had been hunting, and told him how he had followed his dogs into the hole and on until he reached that spot. Death then asked him what he had seen since he entered his country. Mpobe said he had not had time to look about him, because he was so busy following the dogs. Death then told him to return to his home, and warned him not to tell anyone where he had been, nor to mention what he had seen; he said, "You must not tell your father, mother, wife nor any of your brothers"; Mpobe promised to obey, and said he would not speak about the place. Death threatened him that if ever he did so he would kill him.

Mpobe then returned home with his rat; his wife congratulated him upon his return, and went to cook his food. After the meal she asked her husband, "Have you been in the field all the time since you went away?" He replied, "Yes, I went to hunt the rat and stayed all night hunting it." His father came later on, and asked him where he had been hunting all the time. Mpobe replied, "I was in the field hunting all the time." After some days Mpobe's mother came to see him, and found him alone and asked him: "Were you really in the field all those days? What did you eat and drink?" Her son replied, "As I have said I was there, I am not going to tell you anything further, you can go and ask others and listen to what they say." She answered, "Mpobe, tell me just a little, please do." Mpobe answered, "I will tell you just a little, but do not tell anyone else." His mother promised she would not, so Mpobe told her how he followed his dogs, how he entered into the hole, and came to the land of the dead, where he saw numbers of people. He told her how fearful he was, how he asked the people to tell him the way the dogs had gone, how he had come upon Death and found his dogs and the rat, how he had been sent back with the rat, and how he thanked Death. He further told how Death had asked his name and warned him not to tell anyone his experiences on pain of death. His mother left him after hearing the story and returned home.

In the evening when it was dark Mpobe heard someone calling him, "Mpobe! Mpobe!" and he replied, "I am here. What do you want?" Death said, "What did I tell you?" Mpobe said, "You told me not to tell what I had seen at your place, and, sir, I have only told my mother a little." Death said, "I will leave you time to settle up your affairs, you must die when you have expended your property." Mpobe was silent, he had nothing to answer. Death therefore repeated his words, so Mpobe answered, "Let me sell all I have, and live upon the proceeds before I die." He sold first his child and bought a cow with the money and killed it, and ate it very slowly; a year passed, and indeed many years before he had come to an end of all his property. Death called to him and asked if he had not consumed everything. Mpobe said he had not; he tried to hide away in the forest where Death would not find him, but Death said: "Mpobe! why are you hiding in the forest? Do not think I cannot see you." He tried all kinds of different places wherein to hide, but Death always discovered him.

At last he returned to his house and said, "Let me remain here and let Death come to me, because it is useless to try to hide from him." Death came and asked, "Mpobe, have you finished your wealth?" He replied, "I have finished it all," so Death took him. Hence comes the saying, "To be worried into telling a secret killed Mpobe." If he had not told his mother, Death would not have killed him.

Ndyakubi and Ndalakubi

A GANDA STORY

Once a man named Ndyakubi made blood-brotherhood with another man named Ndalakubi. Ndalakubi said to Ndyakubi, "Come and see me when you can." Ndyakubi agreed to do so, and after a time he went. Ndalakubi told his wife to cook a special meal for the visitor, which she did, and took the food to him, but it was not enough; he said he was still hungry when he had eaten what they supplied. Ndalakubi told his wife to cook a larger quantity of food, so she cooked as much as five men would eat and brought it to Ndyakubi, who ate it and still complained that he had not had enough. Ndalakubi told his wife to go to their friends and ask if they could help them, because all their food was finished. She went and brought back the food, cooked as much as would suffice a hundred men, and still Ndyakubi said he was not satisfied. Ndalakubi said, "I am sorry, but all my food is done." Ndyakubi said, "Very well, brother, I must go hungry, and die by the roadside from starvation."

Some time after this Ndalakubi went to see how Ndyakubi was. When he arrived Ndyakubi sent his wife to cook for the visitor, and she brought the food to Ndalakubi, who ate a little. Later on he asked where he was to sleep. Ndyakubi said, "I will let you have my bedstead." "But," said Ndalakubi, "there is no room for me to stretch myself." Ndyakubi took out a post from the house to make room for Ndalakubi. They then retired to rest, but Ndalakubi called out: "My friend, my feet are still outside," so Ndyakubi sent his wife to his friends and asked for reeds, and made an extension to the house, and they lay down again. Again Ndalakubi called, "My friend, my feet are still outside; the wild animals will eat me." Ndyakubi said: "What am I to do? All the reeds are done and I have no timber to build with." Ndalakubi said: "When you came to visit me I had an immense amount of food cooked for you and you ate it all and still complained, and afterwards said: 'Let me go away and die in the road,' when I failed to satisfy you; what I say now is, Let the wild beasts come and eat me." Ndyakubi said: "No, my friend, curl yourself up and draw your legs inside and do not stretch yourself your full length, and when I come to your house I will eat a little and be satisfied. I am sorry for what I did." Ndalakubi said: "You did not say so before when I told you I was sorry the food ran short, you simply complained and grumbled. Now let me draw up my legs, and when you visit me again, eat properly and do not complain."

> The plot of this story is widely dispersed in Africa, and familiar among the adventures of various trickster heroes such as the Ashanti spider, Anansi, and the Yoruba tortoise, Ijapa. See pp. 135 ff. and 221 ff.

Some Proverbs and Sayings of the Ganda

A grumbler does not leave his master, he only stops others from coming to serve him.

The stick that is at your friend's house will not drive away the leopard.

One who has not suffered does not know how to pity.

The thin cow goes on eating grass while they are asking for the axe to kill it. (A careless man who does not heed a warning is like the thin cow.)

Let me cut the difficult knot as the wizard did at Bubiro. (There was a chief whose son was said to have been killed by witchcraft. A man was caught and accused. He denied the deed and was put to the poison ordeal. Everyone was so sure he was the culprit that they had a fire ready in which to burn him. When the poison was brought to the accused, he refused to drink it. He said, "Let me cut the knot," which he did by jumping into the lake, where he was drowned.)

When it is not your mother who is in danger of being eaten by the wild animal, the matter can wait until tomorrow.

Death is like a wild animal. (It kills a person whenever it can find him.)

He who gets his food with the help of medicine must not be angry because he has many visitors to help him eat it. (Food has come plentifully and should be shared.)

The beautiful woman is the sister of many. (A good-looking woman has many admirers who claim to be related so that they may visit and make love to her.)

A branch of the cassava tree. (A branch of the cassava tree when thrown on the ground will readily take root, grow into a new tree and yield fruit. In the same way, one who is despised and cast aside could bring glory to the tribe.)

Covered with shame like a child who has stolen from its mother.

The king is the lake. (The lake does not differentiate; it drowns the

fisherman who is always in the vicinity and the occasional traveller
as well. Thus, the king does not discriminate in taxes, and all must
pay.)

Sense has left you like a person nodding in sleep before he has spread
his sleeping mat. (Said to, or of, a person who begins a project that
he doesn't have the means to finish.)

A garden without young trees. (Such a garden will soon come to an end,
as will a family without children.)

He who cuts the plantain fiber. (A person who cuts the plantain fiber
scatters the ants that have built there. Meaning: when a wealthy
person dies his dependents are scattered.)

How the Mountains and Rivers Were Made

A TALE OF THE AKAMBA OF EASTERN KENYA

A long, long time ago, a group of men went to the forest to hunt.
Among them was one big man. His bow was immense, as tall as eucalyptus trees, and the bowstring was as thick as three arms put together. He
had only one arrow, which was as long as one hundred arms joined
together. This giant was the leader of the hunting party, and he told the
other men to carry many barrels of oil.

As they went through the forest, the giant gave the men his bow to
carry for him, but after a short distance, he saw that it was proving too
heavy for them. So he carried it. They travelled until they came across
a large herd of rhinoceros, and the men said to the giant, "Here is a herd
of animals, shoot them." But he smiled and said, "Don't bother me with
these little things." Then they went on until they came across another
herd, of elephants. The men urged the giant to shoot them, but again
he smiled and said, "I cannot waste my energy on these tiny animals."
The men wondered, and followed the giant. They reached a large plain,
full of giraffes, and the men asked the giant to shoot them. He smiled
again, and said, "Children, perhaps you are hungry." He stretched his
leg and kicked ten giraffes, knocking them down. The men ate the
meat, while the giant waited for them and watched. They wondered

From Akamba Stories, *by John S. Mbiti,* © *1966 by Oxford University Press.
Used by permission of The Clarendon Press, Oxford.*

what he was going to shoot, because they had by then come across all the animals they had seen or heard of before. The giant told them to go on.

After travelling for many days, they came to a vast plain, and the giant sat down there. He told the men that he was going to wait for an animal called nzangamuyo [a legendary animal whose name suggests delicious meat]. They had never heard of that animal, and they were anxious to see it. The giant's name was Mwooka. When they had rested for one day, Mwooka cut down all the tall grass, and made a large open space about three miles across. He told his men to make four ladders, and to climb on his back, carrying their oil barrels. They were to pour out the oil on his body: his back, his shoulders, his ribs, his chest, and his neck and arms. The giant wanted his muscles to soften. So these men spent one whole day doing as they had been told, and the following day, Mwooka lay down on his belly and basked in the sun.

As the sun was about to go down, Mwooka took his bow and arrow, and practiced pulling the bow. He did so continuously for three hours. He did not feel that he was ready to shoot the nzangamuyo should it appear. So, the following morning he went out and killed about twenty giraffes, and brought them back to the camp. He told his men to light a big fire. They roasted the giraffes, and made oil from their fat. With that oil the men anointed Mwooka, so much that oil was dripping down like rain.

They went on waiting for the big animal, until ten days were gone. They waited on and on for two months, eating meat from animals that Mwooka killed for them. He ate only once or twice during that time, as he said he wanted to become hungry so that he would be able to eat the nzangamuyo when he killed it. When he did eat, he ate eight or ten giraffes at a time.

One day, however, they spotted a tiny column of dust rising out of the plain, from a great distance. They watched it grow bigger and bigger the first day. The next day they noticed that it was moving towards them, and the men told Mwooka about it. He smiled and said, "I think the animal is now coming." The cloud of dust increased and moved closer, and the men watched and waited. Mwooka informed them that it would take about six days before the head of the animal appeared; and so, in the meantime, they were to add more oil on his shoulders and arms and back.

By the morning of the sixth day, the column of dust stretched as high as the clouds, and spread as wide as a vast lake. Then the head of the nzangamuyo appeared, and to the amazement of all, it was exceedingly small. There were four little horns, growing in a line, one behind another. The head was flat, and its width was about ten arms put together. The mouth was situated on top, and always faced the sky. When the animal ate, it ate from the bottom upwards. Its food was boughs of trees and long grass; and as it chewed, it made a noise like running water; and when it swallowed, it made a noise like falling water. It never drank water from rivers or lakes: instead, it merely opened its mouth when

the rain came down, and let water pour in directly. There were four
nostrils, two on either side of the head. Its eyes were fixed on top of the
head, so that it always looked up towards the sky.

When the men saw that head, they became terrified, and wanted to
run away. Mwooka, however, assured them that all would be well. He
took his arrow and began to sharpen its metal head, and put more
poison on it. The men told him to shoot the animal, but he smiled and
said, "I have to wait for four more days before I worry about that!" The
head disappeared that first day, as the animal continued to go by.

On the second day, the neck appeared. It was long and thick, and was
covered with hairs that reached to the ground. The hairs swept away
grass, and knocked down trees, as the animal moved. The shoulders
appeared the third day. As the nzangamuyo passed by, it made a noise
like peals of thunder or the falling of heavy rain. The men felt as if they
were going to become deaf. They continued pouring oil over Mwooka's
body, and towards the evening of that day the giant began to pull his
big bow. At night the men lit a big fire, to warm his back and shoulders,
while he continued to pull the bow.

On the fourth day the ribs appeared, and Mwooka was still pulling his
bow. The animal pounded stones into dust, and boulders into pebbles,
with its feet. Any trees that were on the way were either eaten up, or
crushed into paste. Mwooka now pulled his bow harder than ever
before, and aimed the arrow at the part of the nzangamuyo where he
thought the heart would be. He pulled on and on, and urged the men
to pour more oil on him. At noon he let go the arrow, and there was
a bang that sounded louder than any peal of thunder. The arrow went
right through the animal, and fell out on the other side. For about an
hour, nothing happened, and the animal seemed to continue moving.
Then suddenly there was a rumbling noise as the nzangamuyo collapsed. The noise was like that of a volcano erupting or that of a peal
of thunder repeated ten times. The ground shook as if there was an
earthquake, when the body reached the ground. The band of Mwooka's
fellow hunters was more frightened than ever before, and some of them
fell down in a faint. He ran to the river and scooped up some water,
which he poured on them and revived them. When the big job was
over, Mwooka took a deep breath, and sat down to rest. His companions
went to sleep as well.

Early the next day, Mwooka told the men that they must skin the
animal. For two days they worked hard, and managed to skin a fair
portion, which was all that they wanted. A very big fire was made, and
Mwooka cut up pieces of meat which he roasted for two days. He cut
up other pieces, so that his fellow hunters would carry them back to the
rest of their people at home. He himself was going to remain there
gorging the delicious meat of that animal, until he could stuff down no
more.

When the meat was roasted, Mwooka chewed pieces, and gave them
to the men to eat. It was so tough that those men could not have chewed
it themselves. They enjoyed what he gave them, and they feasted on

it for two days until they had enough. The men decided to go to sleep, but Mwooka warned them to move as far away from him as they possibly could, and to sleep far away, on the windward side. They went and lay down about half a mile away from him, and could not at first understand why he did not want them to sleep so near to him.

By the end of that second day, Mwooka had devoured enough meat to last him a month. He also went to sleep, and slept for three continuous days. At night on the third day there burst a sudden gust of wind from his behind! It flattened all the grass and trees nearby, and even his fellowmen who were sleeping half a mile from him were carried off a few paces. They woke up and realized why he had warned them to keep away from him.

Mwooka woke up, lit another big fire, and roasted more meat. This time he munched for five days, without stopping. Again he fell asleep, and slept for ten days. When he woke up, he decided to ease his bowels. So he bent down, and left huge droppings behind him. These became hills and mountains like Musyau, and Kitumui, and others; and his urine flowed across the plain and became rivers like the Nzeeu, and the Kalundu, and the Tiva. That is how the hills and rivers of Kitui were made.

Wanjiru, Sacrificed by Her People

A KIKUYU TALE FROM KENYA

The sun was very hot and there was no rain, so the crops died, and hunger was great; and this happened one year, and again it happened a second, and yet a third year the rain failed; so the people all gathered together on the great open space on the hilltop, where they were wont to dance, and said each to the other, "Why does the rain delay in coming?" And they went to the medicine man, and they said to him, "Tell us why there is no rain, for our crops have died, and we shall die of hunger?" And he took his gourd and poured out the lot, and this he did many times; and at last he said: "There is a maiden here who must

This group of Kikuyu stories comes from With a Prehistoric People, the Akikuyu of British East Africa, *by W. Scoresby Routledge and Katherine Routledge, London, Frank Cass and Co. Ltd., 1910.*

be bought if rain is to fall, and the maiden is Wanjiru. The day after tomorrow let all of you return to this place, and every one of you from the eldest to the youngest bring with him a goat for the purchase of the maiden."

So the day after the morrow, old men and young men all gathered together, and each brought in his hand a goat. Now they all stood in a circle, and the relations of Wanjiru stood together, and she herself stood in the middle; and as they stood the feet of Wanjiru began to sink into the ground; and she sank to her knees and cried aloud, "I am lost," and her father and mother also cried and said, "We are lost"; but those who looked on pressed close, and placed goats in the keeping of Wanjiru's father and mother. And Wanjiru went lower to her waist, and she cried aloud, "I am lost, but much rain will come"; and she sank to her breast: but the rain did not come, and she said again, "Much rain will come"; then she sank to her neck, and the rain came in great drops, and her people would have rushed forward to save her, but those who stood around pressed into their hands more goats, and they desisted.

So she said, "My people have undone me," and sank to her eyes, and as one after another of her family stepped forward to save her, one of the crowd would give to him or her a goat, and he fell back. And Wanjiru cried aloud for the last time, "I am undone, and my own people have done this thing." And she vanished from sight, and the earth closed over her, and the rain poured down, not, as you sometimes see it, in showers, but in a great deluge, and everyone hastened to their own homes.

Now there was a young warrior who loved Wanjiru, and he lamented continually, saying, "Wanjiru is lost, and her own people have done this thing." And he said: "Where has Wanjiru gone? I will go to the same place." So he took his shield, and put on his sword and spear. And he wandered over the country day and night; and at last, as the dusk fell, he came to the spot where Wanjiru had vanished, and he stood where she had stood, and, as he stood, his feet began to sink as hers had sunk; and he sank lower and lower till the ground closed over him, and he went by a long road under the earth as Wanjiru had gone, and at length he saw the maiden. But, indeed, he pitied her sorely, for her state was miserable, and her raiment had perished. He said to her, "You were sacrificed to bring the rain; now the rain has come, I will take you back." So he took her on his back like a child, and brought her to the road he had traversed, and they rose together to the open air, and their feet stood once more on the ground, and he said, "You shall not return to the house of your people, for they have treated you shamefully." And he bade her wait till nightfall; and when it was dark he took her to the house of his mother, and he asked his mother to leave, and said he had business, and he allowed no one to enter. But his mother said, "Why do you hide this thing from me, seeing I am your mother who bore you?" So he suffered his mother, but he said, "Tell no one that Wanjiru is returned."

So she abode in the house of his mother; and then she and his mother slew goats, and Wanjiru ate the fat and grew strong; and of the skins they made garments for her, so that she was attired most beautifully.

It came to pass that the next day there was a great dance, and her lover went with the throng; but his mother and the girl waited till everyone had assembled at the dance, and all the road was empty, and they came out of the house and mingled with the crowd; and the relations saw Wanjiru, and said, "Surely that is Wanjiru whom we had lost"; and they pressed to greet her, but her lover beat them off, for he said, "You sold Wanjiru shamefully." And she returned to his mother's house. But on the fourth day her family again came, and the warrior repented, for he said, "Surely they are her father and her mother and her brothers." So he paid them the purchase price, and he wedded Wanjiru who had been lost.

The Lost Sister

A KIKUYU TALE FROM KENYA

A long time ago a young warrior and his sister lived together in a hut. They lived alone, for their parents had died when they were children, and the hut stood by itself; there were no other homesteads near. The name of the young man was Wagacharaibu, and the maiden was called M'weru. Wagacharaibu had beautiful hair which reached to his waist, and all the young women admired him greatly, so that he often went away from home to a long distance to see his friends, and M'weru was left quite by herself.

Now one day when he came back after he had been thus away, M'weru said to him: "Three men came here last night when I was all alone, and each had a club and each had a spear, and if you go away and leave me all alone I know that they will come back and carry me off." But Wagacharaibu only said, "You talk nonsense," and he went away again as before. And the three men came back, as M'weru had said, with the three clubs and the three spears, and they took hold of the girl by the neck and by the legs, and they lifted her up and they carried her away.

When Wagacharaibu came home again he went to the house and found it quite empty, and as he went he heard a girl's voice crying from the opposite hillside, and the voice was the voice of his sister, and it said: "Wagacharaibu, men have come and carried me away. Go into the hut, you will find the gruel on the stool." And Wagacharaibu cried aloud and said, "Who will shave the front of my head now you are gone, for we have no neighbors?" And he plunged into the grass after M'weru, and the farther he went the farther she was carried away from him; and he heard her voice and she heard his voice, but they could not see each other; and he followed and followed for one month, and he became very hungry. And he wore a hat such as men used to wear in the old days; it was a piece of goatskin, and it had two holes cut in it and strings to tie under the chin, and the skin stood out over the forehead so that rain could not touch the face; and you may see such hats even now among the mountains where there are many trees and much rain, and among the Masai.

So Wagacharaibu cut a piece of the leather and ate it, for he was very hungry, and he felt strong again; he went on and on a second month, and again a third month, till the hat was all finished; and then he took his garment of skin and he ate that, and so he went on a fourth month and a fifth month, until he had travelled one year and four months, and the cape was finished. Then being again hungry, when he came to a big homestead he went inside, and he saw a woman cooking food and he begged a little; and she gave him some, but she did not hand it to him in a nice vessel, but in a broken piece of an old pot. And that night he slept there, and the next morning he went out with the little son of the woman to scare the birds from the crops, for the grain was nearly ripe, and he took stones and threw them at the birds, and as he threw a stone he would say, "Fly away, fly away, little bird, like M'weru has flown away, never to be seen anymore." And the little boy listened, and he went home, and when Wagacharaibu was not near, he told his mother the words the stranger had said, but she paid no attention to the tale of her son and did not listen to it, and the next day the same thing happened again, and the third day the woman went herself to the fields and she heard the words of Wagacharaibu, "Fly away, fly away little bird, like M'weru has flown away, never to be seen anymore," and the woman's name was M'weru, and she said, "Why do you say those words to the birds?" And he said, "I once had a sister named M'weru, and she was lost, and I have followed her many months and years, but I have never seen her again." And the woman put her hand over her eyes and she wept, for she was indeed his sister, and she said, "Are you truly my brother?" for she had not known him, so changed was he by his long travels, and she said, "Truly your hair is unkempt and your clothes are not as they were, and I did not know you, but you shall be once more dressed as in time past, and I shall see if you are my very brother Wagacharaibu."

So she went to her husband, who had carried her away in the old days, and she got four sheep and three goats, and the four sheep were killed, and Wagacharaibu ate of the flesh and became big and strong once more, and his sister took of the fat and dressed his hair, and put it on his shoulders; and of the three goats two were black and one was white, and she made a cape, and she took a spear and gave it him, and it was the spear which her husband had carried when he came to the little hut when she was alone, and gave it to her brother. She put on his arms brass and iron armlets, and ornaments on his legs and round his neck, and then she said, "Now I see that you are indeed my brother Wagacharaibu." And the husband of M'weru loved Wagacharaibu dearly, and he gave him twenty goats and three oxen, which was much more than the price of his sister, but he gave it because of the affection he bore him, and he built him a hut in the homestead and gave him thirty goats to buy a wife. And Wagacharaibu bought a maiden and brought her to the hut, and the goats of Wagacharaibu increased and multiplied, and he took ten of the goats and his sister's husband gave him twenty goats and he bought a second wife, so that Wagacharaibu did not go back to his old life anymore, but lived with the sister he had lost and with her husband.

Mukunga M'Bura

A KIKUYU TALE FROM KENYA

There was once a small boy who was herding the goats, and his father came and pointed out to him some long and luxurious grass, and told him to take them there to feed. So he pastured them there that day, and took them there again the day following. Now the next day while the goats were feeding, the owner of the pasture appeared, and he said to the boy, "Why are you feeding your goats on my grass?" And the boy said, "It is not my doing, for my father told me to come here." And he said, "This evening I will go to your father's house and talk to him." Now the owner of the grazing ground was a man very big and tall, and his name was Mukunga M'Bura, so in the evening he came to the home of the boy and he said to the father, "Why were your goats eating my grass when you could see I had closed it?" [That is, he had put up signs to show that the pasture was protected by his medicine.]

The father said, "That is my affair." So he said, "As you have done this, I will eat you and all your people," to which the father replied, "You shall do no such thing." So the young men made sharp their swords and got ready their spears, but Mukunga M'Bura was too strong for them, and he ate the father, and the young men, and the women, and the children, and the oxen, and the goats, and then he ate the house and the barns, so that there was nothing left. The only person who escaped was the little boy, who ran away and hid in the grass so that Mukunga M'Bura did not see him.

Now he made himself a bow and shot wild game, and became very strong and built himself a house; and at last he said, when he was full grown, "Why do I stay here? I am big and strong. Mukunga M'Bura, who killed my father and all my people, still lives." So he took his sword and made it very sharp, and went to the district where Mukunga M'Bura lived, and as he drew near he saw him coming up out of the great water where he lived. He shouted to him, "Tomorrow I will come and kill you." And he went back and ate more meat so as to be stronger than ever. The next day he went again, but Mukunga M'Bura was not to be seen; but the third day he met him again, and he said, "You have killed all my people, so I will kill you," and Mukunga M'Bura was afraid and said to the warrior, "Do not strike me with your sword over the heart or I shall die, but open my middle finger," so the warrior did so, and he said, "Make a big hole, not a little one." And the warrior made a big hole, and out came first the father, whom Mukunga M'Bura had eaten, and then the young men, and the women, and the cattle, and the sheep, and the houses, and the food stores just as before. And Mukunga M'Bura said, "You will not now kill me?" And the warrior said, "No, I will spare you for you have restored my father, his people and his goods, but you must not again eat them." And he said, "They shall be safe."

The warrior and his people went back and rebuilt their homesteads, but the warrior thought to himself, "Now this Mukunga M'Bura is big and strong and very bad. He has eaten many people. He may come again and destroy my father."

So he called the young men and asked them to come and fight Mukunga M'Bura with him, and they all made ready for war and went to the home of Mukunga M'Bura. He saw them coming and said, "Why are you here to slay me? Have I not given you back your people?" But the warrior replied, "You are very evil; you have killed and eaten many people; therefore you shall die." Then they all fell upon him and slew him, and cut off his head and hewed his body in pieces. But a big piece separated itself from the rest of the body, which was dead, and went back into the water, and the warrior returned to his home and told his brothers that he had slain Mukunga M'Bura, all but one leg. "But tomorrow," he said, "I will go into the water and get that leg and burn it." And the mother besought him not to go, but the next day he went, and when he got to the place there was no water to be seen, only cattle and goats, for what remained of Mukunga M'Bura had gathered together his children and taken all the water and gone very far, but the beasts he had not taken but left behind. So the warrior went back and brought his people, and they gathered the cattle and goats together, and took them back to their own homestead.

The Making of Iron Among the Kikuyu People

There are ample indications that both the smelting of iron ore and the use of iron were known in both East and West Africa many centuries before the arrival of Europeans, even among cultures that never achieved notice as highly developed kingdoms. The Akikuyu, or Kikuyu people, of Kenya, seem to have had a long tradition of ore extraction, smelting and forging, as revealed in this description written very early in the twentieth century by the anthropologist William Scoresby Routledge.

In the labyrinth of hills that form Kikuyu, the native of today is found smelting iron in a manner so simple that, as we watch the different steps he takes to achieve his end, we feel we are standing beside primitive man before the dawn of history. . . .

Those branches of the Akikuyu that I have been amongst cannot imagine a time when iron was not in use: I have made careful and wide inquiry to establish this point. Their folktales too, though dealing with times so remote that the animals are mythical, nevertheless refer to articles made of iron.

The population may amount to perhaps five hundred thousand. Every individual is the possessor of at least some iron: a child may have less than an ounce, whilst a man or woman may perhaps hold as much as ten or fifteen pounds in different forms, but all, for use or ornament, have a little.

The following is a fairly exhaustive list of the articles in use amongst the Akikuyu that are made of iron:

Spears, swords, scabbard tips, arrowheads, axes or adzes, knives, razors, stilettos, tweezers for extracting the beard, branding irons for cattle, agricultural or digging knives, blacksmiths' hammers and tongs, cattle bells, goat bells, small ornamental ankle rattles, ceremonial thigh rattles, wiredrawers' tools (clamp, drawplate, chisel), wire, large (size of lead pencil), wire, small (size of fine twine), chain, spirals of wire (used as stops on thongs), earrings, necklets, finger rings. . . .

At the lower end of a secluded and narrow gorge of sharp fall, through which flows a perennial stream, the workings are found. They form a continuous exposure of one side of the ravine, as a cliff some one hundred and fifty feet in height, creamy pink in color and devoid of vegetation. The original rock, which is broken down by water to yield the iron-bearing sand, is a much decomposed granite, from which can also be extracted a good deal of micaceous clayey matter strongly stained with iron oxide. A portion of the rivulet, deflected at a point nearer the head of the glen, is led, with steady fall, in an artificial channel, over the surface of the detritus of the cliff. In this way its action can be brought to bear as desired against the material of the glacis at any level, and at any point, throughout the greater part of the length of the gorge.

Thus is excavated, and carried down into the brook below, the ferriferous sand formed from the more disintegrated portions of the rock, whilst those portions that are somewhat harder remain *in situ*, as huge boulders and isolated masses, making a chaotic scene and rendering progress difficult. The bounding cliffs of the ravine being thus gradually deprived of the support of their natural buttress, are constantly breaking away. After this manner have apparently millions of tons of material been removed by the directing hand of man, associated with the action of the torrential rains.

The winning of the ore is done by the women and children of a few families living nearby, as an occasional employment: the cultivation of the soil is still their primary occupation which they have not renounced, to any considerable extent, for the greater gain that would arise from collecting the iron sand.

Selecting a spot by the side of the stream where the ground is hard, or some place in the course of the flume, the native smooths out a shallow pan. Its shape is somewhat that of a scollop shell. Its dimensions are three feet by two feet. At the point where the shell would be hinged to its fellow, and for two feet on either side, he builds a wall a few inches high of sticks and grass, leaving an opening about nine inches wide in the middle. This opening he then temporarily closes with a separate wisp of grass.

Making a pile of about ten quarts of the iron-bearing sand, at the end of the pan farthest from him, and standing with one foot just outside his little grass gate and the other in the stream, he takes a half gourd in his hand and begins work. Holding the gourd by its neck, he scoops up the water and dashes it against the face of the pile with a rapidity and accuracy that is obviously the outcome of practice. The water flows away in a steady stream, turbid with the lighter materials in suspension. Larger pieces he lightly flicks out of the pan with the fingertips as he pauses from time to time. So he continues until most of the pile has disappeared. The sand now covers the floor of the pan, and has assumed a much darker color than formerly, owing to the larger proportion of iron ore mixed with it. Again it is piled up at the same spot in the pan, and again the same process is repeated. From time to time he lifts the wisp of grass that closes the opening in the little fence, and scrapes up with his hands the rich deposit accumulated in front and beneath it, as also that which by now covers the floor of the pan.

This process of alternately piling and washing is repeated some half-dozen times. When the iron grains spread over the floor of the pan fairly mask, by their black color, any sand mixed with them, he scrapes up and puts into his half gourd what he has gained, and moving knee-deep into the stream proceeds to give the final washing.

Time after time he stirs with his hand the contents of his gourd, adds more water and pours it off when turbid. At last the water comes away perfectly clear and he can do no more. The result is a wet mass of black sand, which is, to describe it accurately, a magnetite ore. It consists of a mixture of quartz grains and magnetite, the latter often in well-formed octahedral crystals: a small quantity of ilmenite is present. This wet sand is at once spread out on a flat rock to dry, and is then poured into a gourd bottle ready to be carried home. To gain a pint of well-cleaned ore would take a native a good hour.

The iron smelters are blacksmiths, some half-dozen in number, who live in the neighborhood of the quarry. The collection of the ore is done by their women and children. Today only enough is collected for their working needs, in addition to perhaps an equal amount sold as raw iron. In the past the production must have been much greater, judging from the extent of the old workings, but a knowledge of the political conditions that existed in Kikuyu prior to the advent of the white man, leads me to think that only those Akikuyu resident in the immediate neighborhood of the deposit ever worked it. It is inconceivable that it was ever treated as other than the private, though common, property of the natives in the immediate vicinity. There may, however, have been a much greater local population than now working energetically at it: moreover, the splendid virgin forest existed close at hand until within the last three generations: today it is twenty miles distant. Two out of the thirteen clans into which the Akikuyu are divided do not work in iron. No member of these two clans can become a smith. There is nothing of the nature of a trade guild amongst the ironworkers, nor is the smelting of iron associated with any ceremonial rites. The curse of a smith is, however, considered to be particularly biting and adhesive, and is expensive for him who has fallen beneath its ban to "spit out."

The furnace or "hearth" consists of a hole in the ground lined with tempered clay, similar to that of which pots and bellows' nozzles are made. Its shape is that which a round bowl assumes when lateral compression has reduced its diameter by one-half: the edge becomes depressed at the extremities of the long axis, forming, as it were, two spouts, whilst the sides rise up considerably above their level. The fireclay lining is brought well over the edge, forming a wide, convex, everted border all around. The interior of the furnace has the form of a blunt truncated cone, laterally flattened. The substance of the clay forming the lip, where alone I could observe it, was, I think, about two inches thick. Over the whole was thrown a well-built permanent roof —a circular hut without sides—about fifteen feet in diameter.

The bellows consist of a cone, or foolscap, of sewn goatskins, about four feet long, and six inches in diameter at the large end. Into the apex is whipped a carved wooden pipe six inches in length. This pipe, when the bellows are in use, is securely pegged down to the ground, and over its extremity is loosely fitted the expanded butt of another pipe, made of pottery. This earthenware nozzle is about three feet long, and of the size throughout of a man's wrist. It rests on the lip of the hearth, with its nose directed somewhat downwards. Its distal half is buried beneath the mass of black charcoal that occupies the top of the hearth, but of it the nose alone is in a position of great heat, as is shown by that part alone becoming fused. The circumference of the brim of the leather foolscap, that constitutes the body of the bellows, is roughly divided into three parts. To two of these, on its outside, a straight flat strip of wood is sewn. An adjustable thong is stretched between the two extremities of each stick to form a becket.

Slipping all the fingers of one hand into one loop, and the thumb of the same hand into the other, the lad who works the bellows brings together the butts of the two straight sticks, and rests them upright on the ground. Retaining them there by pressure, he next proceeds to separate his thumb from the fingers and palm, which results in the upper extremity of the sticks becoming separated; in other words, the circular opening of the bag is constrained to assume the form of a V, and through this V-shaped opening the air enters the bellows. Still keeping the sticks vertical, he now brings them together by closing his hand. That done, he depresses them onto the upper surface of the bag in the line of its long axis with a steady squeeze. A blast is thus ejected through the earthen nozzle equal to the capacity of that part of the leather cone, compressed by the two sticks. The continuity of the blast is maintained by the resiliency of the uncompressed portion. Two such bellows are always used simultaneously by the native, one being placed on either hand of the blower, who sits on his heels between them, and works them alternately. The ground is made up so that the bellows, as they rest on it, shall slope gently downwards into the fire. The same form of bellows is used by all Kikuyu smiths. Other instruments incidentally employed are the usual blacksmith's anvil, hammer, and tongs. The only materials made use of are the clean-washed iron sand and charcoal; nothing else whatsoever. The charcoal is made from the wood of a particular tree (mukoiigo).

I have not seen a furnace actually being started: they commence operations at dawn. When I arrived the furnace was full to the top and the bellows working, but, as the mass gradually fell in the center more ore was sifted over it by the handful, and more charcoal added little by little. The top surface of the mass in the hearth always remained black, and kept tending to become concave in consequence of the combustion of the central core. The blast is maintained till sundown. The mass is then left in the hearth for the night to cool.

Next morning all loose charcoal was, as far as possible, scraped away from the top and sides of the mass in the hearth, thereby giving it a semiglobular form. A little water was sprinkled on it: a rope of green banana leaf midribs slipped beneath its greatest diameter, and it was capsized onto the depressed lip of the hearth and so rolled clear. Its appearance was then that of a coherent mass of hot charcoal. More water was now sprinkled on it, and the smith and his crew, with round waterworn boulders in their hands, proceeded to knock it to pieces.

The slag was found distributed throughout the mass as it has flowed, whilst the pure iron had similarly run together into small lumps.

Carefully picking out the pieces of pure iron, the smiths then carried them to the adjoining forge, and heated and beat them into the little "blooms" of Kikuyu commerce. These weigh about two pounds each. Ten quarts of sand, which is about the usual charge, might produce half a dozen such "blooms," whose value in the market would be, today, a small goat.

On examination, the iron thus obtained proves to be a very pure form of steel, that can be drawn into wire or fashioned into cutting instruments. These, though untempered, maintain a keen edge. It is welded without difficulty simply by heating and hammering.

MUSIC AMONG THE BONGO

More than a hundred years ago the German explorer Georg Schweinfurth visited areas of Central Africa previously unseen, or scarcely seen, by other Europeans. Dr. Schweinfurth had an irrepressible urge to description, considerable knowledge of flora and fauna, and a remarkable talent for drawing faithfully whatever he chose to depict of people, animals, plants and objects. Few things escaped being recorded by his sketches or word pictures. His two-volume book, *The Heart of Africa*,[1] is an impressive documentation of his African journeys, beginning in 1868 and ending in 1871.

Schweinfurth's impressions of African life, however, were flawed by concepts and prejudices that afflicted most of the outside world in his time. He measured African culture by European standards that automatically found non-literate peoples wanting. The mystique of "civilization" on one side and the primitive world on the other was the foundation from which he looked upon the Bongo, the Azande, the Betu people and others whom he "discovered" in the course of his explorations. He was impressed by African handicrafts and yet somehow failed to grasp the esthetic dynamics that played so strong a part in tribal life. While his documentation, even of minutest details, was splendid, he documented from a biased European viewpoint. Unfortunately, the science of man and his institutions was itself extremely primitive in those days. Had it been otherwise, the German explorer undoubtedly would have seen Africa and Africans in another light.

Even so, he saw virtues in some individuals and tribes that he considered lacking in others. He sometimes seemed to have a sympathy for Africans that he found embarrassing to acknowledge. He detested the slave trade and hated the Arab slavers with a great passion. If he did not question that some of the tribes he visited were cannibals, or that they had other savage traits, he was sensitive to the brutalities laid on the weak by the powerful.

Schweinfurth's descriptions of African dancing were laced with such familiar terms as "wild," "frenzied" and "chaotic." Dancers all

---

1.The Heart of Africa, Three Years' Travels and Adventures in the Unexplored Regions of Central Africa from 1868 to 1871, *2 vols., New York, 1874.*

too often were "foaming at the mouth," while
the music was "monotonous," drummers
"banged on their tom-toms," and singers
"shouted," "screamed" or "wailed." Yet often
there was reluctant approval or even admiration for the music he did not understand. Following is Schweinfurth's account of a musical
scene among the Bongo people.

The Bongo, in their way, are enthusiastic lovers of music; and although their instruments are of a very primitive description, and they
are unacquainted even with the pretty little guitar of the Niam-niam,
which is constructed on perfectly correct acoustic principles, yet they
may be seen at any hour of the day strumming away and chanting to
their own performances. The youngsters, down to the small boys, are
all musicians. Without much trouble, and with the most meager materials, they contrive to make little flutes; they are accustomed also to
construct a monochord, which in its design reminds one of the instrument which (known as the "gubo" of the Zulu) is common throughout
the tribes of Southern Africa. This consists of a bow of bamboo, with the
string tightly strained across it, and this is struck by a slender slip of split
bamboo. The sounding board is not, however, made of a calabash attached to the ground, but the mouth of the player himself performs that
office, one end of the instrument being held to the lips with one hand,
while the string is managed with the other. Performers may often be
seen sitting for an hour together with an instrument of this sort: they
stick one end of the bow into the ground, and fasten the string over a
cavity covered with bark, which opens into an aperture for the escape
of the sound. They pass one hand from one part of the bow to the other,
and with the other they play upon the string with the bamboo twig, and
produce a considerable variety of buzzing and humming airs which are
really rather pretty. This is quite a common pastime with the lads who
are put in charge of the goats. I have seen them apply themselves very
earnestly and with obvious interest to their musical practice, and the
ingenious use to which they apply the simplest means for obtaining
harmonious tones testifies to their penetration into the secrets of the
theory of sound.

As appeals, however, to the sense of sound, the great festivals of the
Bongo abound with measures much more thrilling than any of these
minor performances. On those occasions the orchestral results might
perhaps be fairly characterized as cat's music run wild. Unwearied
thumping of drums, the bellowings of gigantic trumpets, for the manufacture of which great stems of trees come into requisition, inter-
changed by fits and starts with the shriller blasts of some smaller horns,
make up the burden of the unearthly hubbub which reechoes miles
away along the desert. Meanwhile, women and children by the hundred fill gourd-flasks with little stones, and rattle them as if they were

churning butter: or again, at other times, they will get some sticks or dry faggots and strike them together with the greatest energy. The huge wooden tubes which may be styled the trumpets of the Bongo are by the natives themselves called "manyinyee;" they vary from four to five feet in length, being closed at the extremity, and ornamented with carved work representing a man's head, which not unfrequently is adorned with a couple of horns. The other end of the stem is open, and in an upper compartment towards the figure of the head is the orifice into which the performer blows with all his might. There is another form of manyinyee which is made like a huge wine bottle; in order to play upon it, the musician takes it between his knees like a violoncello, and when the build of the instrument is too cumbrous, he has to bend over it as it lies upon the ground.

Little difference can be noticed between the kettledrums of the Bongo and those of most other North African Negroes. A section is cut from the thick stem of a tree, the preference being given to a tamarind when it can be procured; this is hollowed out into a cylinder, one end being larger than the other. The ends are then covered with two pieces of goatskin stripped of the hair, which are tightly strained and laced together with thongs. At the nightly orgies a fire is invariably kept burning to dry the skin and to tighten it when it has happened to become relaxed by the heavy dews.

A great number of signal horns may be seen made from the horns of different antelopes; these are called "mangoal," and have three holes like small flutes, and in tone are not unlike fifes. There is one long and narrow pipe cut by the Bongo out of wood which they call a "mburrah," and which has a widened air chamber close to the mouthpiece, very similar to the ivory signal horns which are so frequently to be seen in all the Negro countries.

Difficult were the task to give any adequate description of the singing of the Bongo. . . . The commencement of a measure will always be with a lively air, and everyone, without distinction of age or sex, will begin yelling, screeching and bellowing with all their strength; gradually the surging of the voices will tone down, the rapid time will moderate, and the song be hushed into a wailing, melancholy strain. Thus it sinks into a very dirge, such as might be chanted at the grave, and be interpreted as representative of a leaden and a frowning sky, when all at once, without note of warning, there bursts forth the whole fury of the Negro throats; shrill and thrilling is the outcry, and the contrast is as vivid as sunshine in the midst of rain.

Often as I was present at these festivities I never could prevent my ideas from associating Bongo music with the instinct of imitation which belongs to men universally. The orgies always gave me the impression of having no other object than to surpass in violence the fury of the elements. Adequately to represent the rage of a hurricane in the tropics any single instrument, of course, must be weak, poor and powerless, consequently they hammer at numbers of their gigantic drums with powerful blows of their heavy clubs. If they would rival the bursting of a storm, the roaring of the wind or the splashing of the rain, they summon a chorus of their stoutest lungs; whilst to depict the bellowings of terrified wild beasts, they resort to their longest horns; and to imitate the songs of birds, they bring together all their flutes and fifes. Most characteristic of all, perchance, is the deep and rolling bass of the huge manyinyee, as descriptive of the rumbling thunder. The penetrating shower may drive rattling and crackling among the twigs, and amid the parched foliage of the woods, and this is imitated by the united energies of women and children, as they rattle the stones in their gourd-flasks, and clash together their bits of wood. . . .

Schweinfurth Gets to See the Akka Pygmies

What Georg Schweinfurth knew of Pygmies before his journey into Central Africa came from classical mythology and the writings of Greek and Roman historians. That Pygmy peoples lived in the interior of the continent he had no doubt, and the possibility of seeing them excited his imagination. Let other men discover the source of the Nile; Schweinfurth was content to see for himself that the diminutive people referred to in classical literature lived on in the forest belt that nearly spanned the continent. Here and there along the forest belt, from what is now Cameroon to the northeastern regions of what is now Zaire, various Pygmy groups that had been bypassed by the eastward-migrating Bantu peoples continued to live their lives much as they had for many centuries. Their ways were adapted to the forest, and because the Bantu preferred the open country, the Pygmies for long stretches of time remained undisturbed. Sometimes they worked out a modus vivendi with Bantu settlers who established villages nearby, hunting for them in the forest and receiving, in exchange, commodities produced by the villagers. Over the years there was some racial mixing between Bantu and Pygmies, as was evident in Schweinfurth's time, but even today there are Pygmies in Central Africa of pure racial type. The following extract from Schweinfurth's account[1] relates the story of his first contact with the Akka Pygmies while he was staying with the Mangbetu people.

1.Schweinfurth, ibid.

Of the Nile itself, which had the appearance, day by day, of becoming wider as farther and farther we progressed towards the south, [the Nubians] affirmed that it issued from the ocean by which Africa was girt; they would declare that we were on the route which would lead us, like the cranes, to fight with the Pygmies; ever and again they would speak of Cyclops, of Automoli, or of "Pygmies," but by whatever name they called them, they seemed never to weary of recurring to them as the theme of their talk. Some there were who averred that with their own eyes they had seen this people of immortal myth; and these—men as they were whose acquaintance might have been coveted by Herodotus and envied by Aristotle—were none other than my own servants.

It was a fascinating thing to hear them confidently relate that in the land to the south of the Niam-niam country there dwelt people who never grew to more than three feet in height, and who wore beards so long that they reached to their knees. It was affirmed of them that, armed with strong lances, they would creep underneath the belly of an elephant and dexterously kill the beast, managing their own movements so adroitly that they could not be reached by the creature's trunk. Their services in this way were asserted to contribute very largely to the resources of the ivory traders. The name by which they are known is the "Shebber-digintoo," which implies the growth of the disproportioned beard.

I listened on. The more, however, that I pondered silently over the stories that they involuntarily disclosed—the more I studied the traditions to which they referred—so much the more I was perplexed to explain what must either be the creative faculty or the derived impressions of the Nubians. Whence came it that they could have gained any knowledge at all of what Homer had sung? How did it happen that they were familiar at all with the material which Ovid and Juvenal, and Nonnus and Statius worked into their verse, giving victory at one time to the cranes, and at another to the Pygmies themselves?

My own ideas of Pygmies were gathered originally only from books, but the time seemed now to have come when their existence should be demonstrated in actual life.

Legends of Pygmies had mingled themselves already with the earliest surviving literature of the Greeks, and the poet of the Iliad, it will be remembered, mentions them as a race that had long been known:

> "To warmer seas the cranes embodied fly,
> With noise, and order, through the midway sky;
> To pygmy nations wounds and death they bring,
> And all the war descends upon the wing."
> Pope's "Homer's Iliad," iii. 6–10.

But not the classic *poets* alone; sober historians and precise geographers have either adopted the poetic substance of the tradition or have endeavored, by every kind of conjecture, to confirm its accuracy. Nothing, for instance, can be more definite than the statement of Herodotus about the Nasamonians after they had crossed the Libyan deserts: "They at length saw some trees growing on a plain, and having approached they began to gather the fruit that grew on the trees; and while they were gathering it some diminutive men, less than men of middle stature, came up and seized them and carried them away." The testimony of Aristotle is yet more precise when he says plainly: "The cranes fly to the lakes above Egypt, from which flows the Nile; there dwell the Pygmies, and this is no fable but the pure truth; there, just as we are told, do men and horses of diminutive size dwell in caves"; a quotation this, which would seem to imply that the learned Stagyrite was in possession of some exact and positive information, otherwise he would not have ventured to insist so strongly upon the truth of his assertion. Very likely, however, we should be justified in surmising that Aristotle mentions cranes and Pygmies together only because he had the passage of the Iliad floating in his memory, and because he was aware of the fact that cranes do pass the winter in Africa. For my own part, I should be inclined to doubt whether cranes ever reach the Victoria and Albert Nyanza; on the Red Sea I saw them in latitude 20° N., and Brehm observed them in Sennaar; on the White Nile, however, and farther inland, I only found the native Balearic crane, which could hardly have been the species mentioned by Aristotle. But whether cranes were really capable of fighting with Pygmies or not, or whether (as Pauer attempts to prove) the Homeric tradition was derived from ancient Egyptian symbolism, and so was an emblematic representation of the cranes battling with the falling waters of the Nile stream, this is now immaterial; all that concerns us, with regard to the present topic, is that three or four centuries before the Christian era the Greeks were aware of the existence of a people inhabiting the districts about the sources of the Nile, who were remarkable for their stunted growth. The circumstance may warrant us, perhaps, in employing the designation of "pygmy," not for men literally a span long, but in the sense of Aristotle, for the dwarf races of Equatorial Africa.

Throughout the time that I had resided in the Seribas of the Bongo territory, of course I had frequent opportunities of enlarging my information, and I was continually hearing such romantic stories that I became familiarized in a way with the belief that the men about me had really been eyewitnesses of the circumstances they related. Those who had been attached to the Niam-niam expeditions, whenever they described the variety of wonders about the splendor of the courts of the cannibal kings, never omitted to mention the dwarfs who filled the office of court buffoons; every one outvying another in the fantastic embellishment of the tales they told. The general impression that remained upon my mind was that these must be some extraordinary specimens of pathological phenomena that had been retained by the kings as natural curiosities. . . . But that there could be a whole series of tribes whose average height was far below an average never really found a reception in my understanding, until at the court of Munza the positive evidence was submitted to my eyes.

Several days elapsed after my taking up my residence by the palace of the Monbuttoo [Mangbetu] king without my having a chance to get a view of the dwarfs, whose fame had so keenly excited my curiosity. My people, however, assured me that they had seen them. I remonstrated with them for not having secured me an opportunity of seeing for myself, and for not bringing them into contact with me. I obtained no other reply but that the dwarfs were too timid to come. After a few mornings my attention was arrested by a shouting in the camp, and I learned that Mohammed had surprised one of the Pygmies in attendance upon the king, and was conveying him, in spite of a strenuous resistance, straight to my tent. I looked up, and *there*, sure enough, was the strange little creature, perched upon Mohammed's right shoulder, nervously hugging his head, and casting glances of alarm in every direction. Mohammed soon deposited him in the seat of honor. A royal interpreter was stationed at his side. Thus, at last, was I able veritably to feast my eyes upon a living embodiment of the myths of some thousand years!

Eagerly, and without loss of time, I proceeded to take his portrait. I pressed him with innumerable questions, but to ask for information was an easier matter altogether than to get an answer. There was the greatest difficulty in inducing him to remain at rest, and I could only succeed by exhibiting a store of presents. Under the impression that the opportunity before me might not occur again, I bribed the interpreter to exercise his influence to pacify the little man, to set him at his ease, and to induce him to lay aside any fear of me that he might entertain. Altogether we succeeded so well that in a couple of hours the Pygmy had been measured, sketched, feasted, presented with a variety of gifts, and subjected to a minute catechism of searching questions.

His name was Adimokoo. He was the head of a small colony, which was located about half a league from the royal residence. With his own lips I heard him assert that the name of his nation was Akka, and I further learnt that they inhabit large districts to the south of the Monbuttoo between lat. 2° and 1° N. A portion of them are subject to the Monbuttoo king, who, desirous of enhancing the splendor of his court by the addition of any available natural curiosities, had compelled several families of the Pygmies to settle in the vicinity.

My Niam-niam servants, sentence by sentence, interpreted to me everything that was said by Adimokoo to the Monbuttoo interpreter, who was acquainted with no dialects but those of his own land.

In reply to my question put to Adimokoo as to where his country was situated, pointing towards the S.S.E., he said, "Two days' journey and you come to the village of Mummery; on the third day you will reach the River Nalobe; the fourth day arrive at the first of the villages of the Akka."

"What do you call the rivers of your country?"

"They are the Nalobe, the Namerikoo, and the Eddoopa."

"Have you any river as large as the Welle?"

"No; ours are small rivers, and they all flow into the Welle."

"Are you all one people, or are you divided into separate tribes?"

To this inquiry Adimokoo replied by a sudden gesture, as if to indicate the vastness of their extent, and commenced enumerating the tribes one after another. "There are the Navapukah, the Navatipeh, the Vabingisso, the Avadzubeh, the Avagowumba, the Bandoa, the Mamomoo, and the Agabundah."

"How many kings?" I asked.

"Nine," he said; but I could only make out the names of Galeema, Beddeh, Tindaga, and Mazembe.

My next endeavor was directed to discover whether he was acquainted in any way with the dwarf races that have been mentioned by previous travellers, and whose homes I presumed would be somewhere in this part of Africa. I asked him whether he knew the Malagilage, who, according to the testimony of Escayrac de Lauture, live to the south of Baghirmy. My question, however, only elicited a comical gesture of bewilderment and a vague inquiry, "What is that?" Nor did I succeed at all better in securing any recognition of the tribes of the Kenkob or the Betsan, which are mentioned by Kölle. Equally unavailing, too, were all my efforts to obtain answers of any precision to the series of questions which I invented, taking my hints from Petermann and Hassenstein's map of Central Africa, so that I was obliged to give up my geographical inquiries in despair and turn to other topics. But in reality there did not occur any subject whatever on which I obtained any information that seems to me to be worth recording. At length, after having submitted so long to my curious and persistent questionings, the patience of Adimokoo was thoroughly exhausted, and he made a frantic leap in his endeavor to escape from the tent. Surrounded, however, by a crowd of inquisitive Bongo and Nubians, he was unable to effect his purpose, and was compelled, against his will, to remain for a little longer. After a time a gentle persuasion was brought to bear, and he was induced to go through some of the characteristic evolutions of his war dances. He was dressed, like the Monbuttoo, in a rokko coat and plumed hat, and was armed with a miniature lance as well as with a bow and arrow. His height I found to be about 4 feet 10 inches, and this I reckon to be the average measurement of his race.

Although I had repeatedly been astonished at witnessing the war dances of the Niam-niam, I confess that my amazement was greater than ever when I looked upon the exhibition which the Pygmy afforded. In spite of his large, bloated belly and short bandy legs—in spite of his age, which, by the way, was considerable—Adimokoo's agility was perfectly marvellous, and I could not help wondering whether cranes would ever be likely to contend with such creatures. The little man's leaps and attitudes were accompanied by such lively and grotesque varieties of expression that the spectators shook again and held their sides with laughter. The interpreter explained to the Niam-niam that the Akka jump about in the grass like grasshoppers, and that they are so nimble that they shoot their arrows into an elephant's eye and drive their lances into their bellies. . . .

Adimokoo returned home loaded with presents. I made him understand that I should be glad to see all his people, and promised that they should lose nothing by coming.

On the following day I had the pleasure of a visit from two of the younger men. After they had once got over their alarm, some or other of the Akka came to me almost every day. As exceptional cases, I observed that some individuals were of a taller stature; but upon investigation I always ascertained that this was the result of intermarriage with the Monbuttoo amongst whom they resided. My sudden departure from Munza's abode interrupted me completely in my study of this interesting people, and I was compelled to leave before I had fully mastered the details of their peculiarities. I regret that I never chanced to see one of the Akka women, and still more that my visit to their dwellings was postponed from day to day until the opportunity was lost altogether. . . .

A Song of the Twa Pygmies of Rwanda

Transcription by Rose Brandel, from Journal of the American Musicological Society, *Spring 1952. By permission of the American Musicological Society.*

SOME LITERARY TRADITIONS OF THE SOUTHERN BANTU

The most southerly of the Bantu-speaking peoples are those living in the Republic of South Africa, Rhodesia, Botswana, Lesotho and Zambia. Some historians estimate that elements of these southern tribes or clans arrived in the region as early as the fifth century A.D., and that by the thirteenth century they were as far south as the Transkei in Cape Province.[1] There they made contact at various points with earlier peoples to arrive, the Khoikhoi, or Hottentots, and the San, or Bushmen. Some Bantu groups such as the Herero and Berdama were strongly influenced by the ways of these earlier peoples, although most—the Shona, Sotho, Xhosa, Swazi and Shangaan among others—lived much according to the traditions they had brought with them in their migrations from the north, adapting where necessary to their new physical environment. Their way of life gave great prominence and value to the ownership of cattle, which were regarded not only as wealth but as symbols of the benevolence of nature and of contact with natural forces. Cattle were involved in almost every aspect of living, secular and religious. Complicated rules of law regulated the worth of cattle, their ownership, their use as currency in the payment of lobola, or bride price, and of penalties for misbehavior. The importance of cattle remains a conspicuous element in the myths, legends and traditions of the clans and tribes.

Though separated by distance and cultural differences from the Bantu-speakers of the Zaire forest zone, the southern Bantu nevertheless share with them certain literary traditions and esthetic concepts of narrative making. Many of the more commonplace folktales heard in the south have counterparts in Central Africa. Indeed, variants of some are heard over much of the continent. The adventures, whimsies, antics and mischief of the southern Bantu hare trickster-hero are recited throughout a large part of Central and East Africa, and even in West

---

1. *Jan Vansina, "Inner Africa," in* The Horizon History of Africa, *New York, American Heritage Publishing Company, 1971.*

Africa where they are attributed to the spider-trickster and the tortoise-trickster.

But eastern and southern Bantu peoples also share a particular tradition of hero tales which in their most extended and developed form can properly be described as epics. Told sometimes in prose, sometimes declaimed as dramatic poetry, and usually interspersed with songs, these narrations reflect traditions and difficulties of kingship, the surge and recession of kingdoms, wars between tribes and clans, values and aspirations, the search for equity and justice and the ever-present need to deal with evil forces and counteract magic. Some of the hero tales have as their protagonists persons who really lived. But many appear to have been created out of the substance of daily life, the never-ending contest with the forces of nature and magic, and the aspiration to a just balance in the affairs of men. Frequently the hero is a king or the child of a king. Sometimes the hero's trials are precipitated by a king-father's rejection of a son or a wife; or jealousy between brothers, sisters or co-wives; or competition for an inheritance; or an unjust or criminal act. The hero is often an infant or child who, sooner or later, manifests unusual gifts of medicine (magic) that neutralize efforts to harm him. On occasion he is no more than an ordinary hunter or villager. After frightful ordeals and perhaps a series of confrontations with creatures of the bush, magical forces, monsters, witches and evil men, the hero returns home victorious to receive recognition and achieve his proper place (sometimes a kingship) among the people.

Wonder, mystery and magic are woven into the fabric of the tales. If he is a child prodigy, the circumstances of the hero's birth or childhood are awesome. In the story, "The Mwindo Epic" (from the more northerly Nyanga people—see p. 322) the hero is said in some versions to have been born from his mother's middle finger. In the Zulu story, "The King's Child and Ubongopa-Kamagadhlele" (see p. 457), soon after birth the infant hero is placed on the back of an ox, where he lives for the rest of his life.

The adventures of the heroes carry them to far-off places, sometimes to the country beneath the earth, to the land of the dead, even to the kingdom in the sky. While some of their contests are on a human, natural level, others are Gothic and almost cosmic in character. In the narrative, "The Story of Umkxakaza-Wakoingqwayo" (see p. 443), the monster that is encountered has the form of a large range of hills and precipices, with small hills growing from the larger, and great forests and many rivers on its back, which is so large that at one place it is winter and at another place summer. Such are the challenges that the heroes or heroines sometimes have to meet.

Evil and good, cruelties and kindnesses, brutalities and generosities, and life and death weave their way through the hero tales. One discerns through them the hardness of life that these Xhosa, Zulu, Shangaan and others have experienced. One also perceives the spirit to endure and the desire for social order. And one who reads with care will learn much about the traditions and beliefs that have been preserved, and that, in turn, have preserved the clans and tribes of southern Africa to this day.

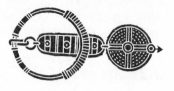

ORIGIN OF THE TSONGA OR SHANGAAN PEOPLE

**AND SOMETHING CONCERNING THEIR TRADITIONS AND CUSTOMS
AS DESCRIBED BY DANIEL P. P. MAROLEN OF DAVEYTON, SOUTH
AFRICA, HIMSELF A MEMBER OF THE SHANGAAN TRIBE**

This is the story of the creation of our first ancestor, as told to me in my ninth year by my maternal grandmother, Madzahisi Nkuna. One day, said my grandmother, N'wari, the bird god, flew down from the mountains to the edge of a river. There N'wari bored a hole in a river reed and laid an egg in it. After time had passed the reed burst, and there emerged from it a man. This man built himself a ntsonga, that is, a mud-daubed hut, its roof thatched with grass. Thus he was the first mutsonga—the first person to live in a hut. In time, this first man married a wife, though it is not said where the woman came from. These two gave birth to many children, who in their turn also had many children. Thus the Tsonga multiplied. First they became a family, then a clan. Then they became a village, and the villages increased until there was a nation. The country came to be known as Vutsonga, the Land of the Tsonga, and it was ruled by a chief. The sons of the chief also became chiefs, and in time there were many chiefs and subchiefs. The Tsonga became a powerful nation, and they subdued their neighbors in what is now called Mozambique. That is the story of the coming of the Tsonga people.

Vutsonga was a land of much food and game, and a nation in the south, the Amazulu, envied the wealth and well-being of the Tsonga. A day came when Vutsonga was invaded by Zulu soldiers led by a general named Zoshangana. The Zulu army conquered the Tsonga and occupied their land, and seized their women and their cattle. The Tsonga in this way became subjects of the Zulu. They obeyed Zulu laws and took over Zulu customs. Thus the Tsonga became known as Mashangana or Shangaan [after the Zulu general Zoshangana], though their language to this day is called Tsonga, and is in fact more Tsonga than Zulu.

This account of the origin of the Tsonga, later known as Shangaan, people, and the following sections on customs and storytelling were contributed by Dr. Daniel P. P. Marolen of Daveyton, Transvaal, South Africa.

The wars of succession fought between Mawewe and Muzila, the sons of Zoshangana, scattered the Tsonga people across the country, as far as southeastern Rhodesia and throughout the eastern part of the Transvaal, from the Lebombo Mountains to the Drakensberg Mountains. That is why the Shangaan are now found in those regions.

Some Customs and Traditions of the Tsonga or Shangaan People

In earliest times, before the arrival of Europeans in this part of the world, the Tsonga people were a civilized nation. They had their own language, their own government, their own legal system, and their own culture. They were one of a number of Bantu tribes whose earliest-known dwelling place was in the vicinity of the great lakes of Central Africa. Because the Tsonga, the Zulu, the Xhosa, the Sotho, the Tswana, the Venda and the Swazi had common beginnings, their languages and customs are similar.

A paramount chief headed the government, and he was the highest judge on the land and leader of the army. Appointed officers of the paramount chief served as subchiefs of regions. All Tsonga males served as soldiers in time of need. Tsonga life was based on family ties and obligations. The man was head of the family, and his wife—or his wives —and children were his dependents. A man could have as many wives as he could afford to pay lobola, or cattle payment, for. The lobola for one wife amounted to one or more head of cattle.

In former days there were no juvenile delinquents among the Tsonga because the children were disciplined early in life to behave according to the ways and traditions of the tribe. Young boys were not allowed to mix with the women and girls. They slept in separate club huts. In work, there was a strict division of labor. The girls helped their mothers run the households. They cooked, cleaned the yards, looked after the smaller children, collected firewood, carried water, and decorated the walls and floors of the huts. The boys took care of their fathers' herds and flocks, helped with housebuilding, hunted with older men, worked at the forge, carved wooden utensils and built granaries—in short, they did the things their fathers did. Tsonga customs regulated life from birth to death. They stressed communal cooperation and welfare rather than individuality and individual well-being. One's actions were guided by what was good for the group. When a man with a family died, his household was "inherited" by his brother; thus widowhood and orphan status, which plague Western societies, were moderated by the customs of the Tsonga. Because of the severe court penalties for breach of approved marriage conduct, there were far fewer divorces among the Tsonga in former days than there are now. Promiscuity and illegitimacy also were far less.

Religious life was centered on placation and supplication of the ancestors. N'wari, the bird god who had created the first man, was the supreme deity. It was N'wari on whom all life ultimately depended. As the good father he gave rain, good harvests, peace and all desirable things. But irritated or angered, N'wari sent disease, famine, droughts, hail, lightning and death. He was so distant, however, that he could not be communicated with directly. It was the dead ancestors who communicated with N'wari for the people. And so the ancestral dead were asked to convey to N'wari the needs and pleas of the living. Yet there was still another intermediary, the cult priest, through whose rituals the living spoke to the dead. The cult priest ("witch doctor") was a powerful and influential member of Tsonga society. He (or she, as the case might be) anointed chiefs and made them potent or powerful; he was herbalist, diviner and prophet; and he had magical powers to counteract disease and ward off death. He had among his many gifts the capability of "smelling out" witches and wizards who imposed sickness, misfortune and death on others—a power and authority under which, no doubt, many "smelled out" but innocent victims may have died.

The Tsonga were highly artistic and had well-developed crafts. They carved wood, modelled clay and forged iron. They developed beadwork into an art. They had their own distinctive music and dances, and a wide variety of musical instruments.

In the period following their conquest by the Zulu general Zoshangana, the Tsonga were called Amashangana, or Shangaan, though their language continued to be called Tsonga.

Shangaan Children's Activities

Chema: This is a guessing game, usually played near the fire where the herdboys are warming themselves under the court tree (under which lawsuits are settled) at the village gate. Sometimes it is played in the boys' clubhouse. In a word, the objective is to locate a single grain of maize. The boys divide into two teams, each possessing a maize seed and a blanket (or a large piece of cloth or animal skin). The first team's members put their hands under their blanket and place the seed in one person's hand. Clenching their fists they remove them from under the blanket, chanting, "Guessing One! Guess! Where is it?" Then a member of the second team touches one after another of the clenched fists, chanting rhythmically the "magical" nonsense words: "Bambala, bambala, bambala, xa maciyo, ciyo, ciyo." He repeats the formula a number of times until he must pause for breath, at which moment he will open the fist he happens to be touching to see if the seed is there, saying, "Here it is!" (He believes that the breath pause should magically indicate the whereabouts of the hidden seed.) If he finds the seed on his first attempt, the teams exchange roles. If he fails, the team members hiding the seed open their hands and shout "Chemaaa!" (That is, "Here is where the chema, or seed, was hidden.") They begin again, the first team continuing to hide the seed and the second team continuing to seek it. Each time a seed is sought and not found counts as a score for the hiding team. When the second team locates the seed, the roles are reversed and the hiding team becomes the seeker. When the game is ended, the winners point all their fingers at their rivals and jeeringly hum, "Whooooo!"

Hojahoja: This is an activity celebrating the "coming out" of a new baby from its mother's nursery hut two weeks after birth. Hojahoja is the name of a mythical cruel animal who is supposed to be responsible for stomachaches and other digestive disturbances that plague newborn infants. Tsonga children believe that Hojahoja really exists, and the activity is directed at driving Hojahoja away so that he does not molest the newly born child.

Shangaan mothers remain in confinement for two or three weeks following the birth of their children, following which there is a ceremonial "coming out" in which they mingle once more with the village people. Early in the morning of the "coming out" day a medicine woman digs up herbs, cooks them and makes a kind of porridge called rikhwere. She instructs the mother to eat some of this and feed some to the infant. She smears mother and child with certain animal fats to scare Hojahoja away. She asks for the maize grains that were boiled the previous night. They are brought to the nursery hut and she blesses them. She throws her divining bones to consult with the ancestral dead. The ancestors say, through the bones, that the new child will grow unharmed by Hojahoja. She takes one or two of the maize grains and drops them into her mouth, after which she spits them into her right hand without chewing them. She throws one of the grains at the stomach of the infant, singing, "Hojahoja, leave my little one alone."

When the village children hear the medicine woman singing they run to the entrance of the hut. She comes out with a bowl of the boiled maize grains, and passes out handfuls to the children, who are dancing and singing. They run around the hut singing, "Hojahoja, leave my little one alone." When they have encircled the building the medicine woman beckons them to enter. They do so, and each child pelts the stomach of the infant with a boiled maize grain. Most of the maize grains they eat. When they depart from the nursery hut they scatter, still singing the song. The singing is heard throughout the day and into the night. Hojahoja has bounced off the infant just as the maize grains have done, and presumably he has been conquered.

Storytelling Among the Shangaan

The traditional storyteller among the Shangaan, as among related Bantu peoples, is the grandmother or elder woman of the family. Others also may tell stories, but it is the grandmother who is the respected and revered transmitter of ancient tales and legends. As darkness falls around the simple grass hut in the rural countryside, the old woman, called Garingani, or Narrator, prepares for the storytelling session by unrolling a mat for herself and one for the children to sit on. At the edge of the household fire she declaims, *"Garingani, n'wana wa Garingani!"* —"I am Narrator, daughter of Narrator!" These are her credentials, testifying to her authority as one who received her stories from a person of the past. Her audience calls back, "Garingani!" signifying that she is accepted as Narrator. This exchange may be repeated several times. Then the woman delivers her first line of poetic narration, and her audience again calls out, "Garingani!" Each line of her story is greeted with the same response. The stories of the Tsonga, like those of the Zulu, the Sotho and other tribes of the region, deal with the conditions of life and the struggles among people. The strands of the stories may be love, violence, hatred, the malevolence of supernatural creatures and demons. The characters are boys, girls, men and women in contest with their own family or village, or with the rigors of the jungle and bush, or with spirits, witches or other beings. Animals, trees and inanimate objects may play roles in the tales. The Garingani spells out the drama with gestures and feeling, as though she herself had been there to witness the struggle. From time to time a little song is interspersed with the action of the narrative, and the children join in the singing. When the Garingani is ready, she resumes the tale. The intermission gives the Garingani time to collect her thoughts about the episodes that follow. It also provides a break in the tension. Sometimes the songs are accompanied by hand clapping, drumming, foot stamping, whistling, or the blowing of a wind instrument. When at last the narration comes to an end, the Garingani spits on the ground to mollify the spirits and makes the sound of a tree branch being placed across the village gate to keep out wild animals and malevolent creatures of the night. While the Garingani is the authoritative transmitter of tales, others also may tell them, but only at night. It is said that a child who tells these stories in daylight will lose his parents to death. But orphans are excepted, as they have no parents to lose. In addition to epiclike adventure tales, the Tsonga have a multitude of animal tales featuring the hare as trickster-hero, and heroic tales based on historic recollections. The historical stories tell of kings, wars, migrations and other old events that have not yet faded from memory.

The Adventures of Papaju

> This Tsonga (Shangaan) adventure story was
> set down and translated into English by Daniel
> P. P. Marolen. "Several decades ago," he re-
> calls, "my maternal grandmother told me, son
> of her eldest son Paul, like all grandmothers
> used to do in the old days, a fireside tale about
> the brave young man named Papaju who lived
> in the jungle long ago."

Narrator: *Hi mina Garingani, n'wana wa Garingani!* (I am Narrator,
             daughter of Narrator!)

Response: (signifying, "We accept you as the Great Narrator") *Garin-*
             gani!

It came about that in a certain country
There was a young king.
This king paid lobola for a wife.
This wife bore a daughter as her first child.
But the king had desired to start with a son
Who would be an heir to his throne.
After a number of years
This wife bore another daughter,
And there were now two daughters.
This did not please the king of the land
Because he was yearning to have a son.
Then the bones were consulted in the family,
And the bones said the king should marry a second wife,
Who would give birth to a son as her firstborn child.
Accordingly the king took cattle and married a young woman
Who indeed came and bore a male child.
Thereafter, the king's first wife
Also bore him a male child.
The king was delighted to have sons
Who were destined to become his heirs.
Then the two sons grew up together.
The elder of the younger wife was called Xigamana;
And the younger one, of the elder wife, was called Papaju.
Because Papaju belonged to the First House
It was proper for him to be the king's successor
If his father happened to die.
Then Xigamana and Papaju grew up together,
And when they had become big young men

---

*Set down by Daniel P. P. Marolen. Used by permission. A Zulu version of this
story under the title, "The Story of Ngangezwe and Mnyamana" appears in the
Odette St. Lys book,* From a Vanished German Colony *(etc.), p. 69 ff.*

Their beloved father died and left them.
After his death matters became difficult,
Because a dispute started in the dead king's family.
It became a problem as to who
Between the two, Xigamana and Papaju,
Would be the dead king's successor.
Xigamana contended that although Papaju
Belonged to the First House by birth,
The kingship belonged to Xigamana because he was older.
But according to the custom of the people
It is the son of the First House
Who should inherit his father's kingship.
Accordingly, although Papaju was the younger of the sons
He was his father's rightful heir.
Nevertheless, Xigamana made himself king.
But Xigamana ruled with fear,
Fear of his brother, Papaju,
Whose kingship he had usurped with Hare's cunning.
Thus Xigamana in his endless fear
Suspected that Papaju might one day arise against him
And try to take the kingship.
Indeed, the kingship was Papaju's.
The councillors of the former king
Confirmed Papaju's right of succession.
Besides which they greatly liked Papaju
Because he was noble and well-behaved.
Xigamana, on the other hand,
Was loved only by the young men
With whom he had conspired against his brother and custom.
Papaju's popularity with the older people
Deepened Xigamana's hatred.
So Xigamana conspired to kill Papaju.
One day Xigamana called Papaju aside secretly
To prepare for his death
So that Xigamana could remain secure
In the kingship of his father.
Then Xigamana said to Papaju in secret:
"My brother, Papaju,
Our father has died and left us.
But at his death he left us a treasure,
The treasure of these two stones that will bring us luck.
On dying, our father said
That you and I must swallow them
So that we will remain lucky in life.
I have already swallowed my lucky stone.
Take this one, yours, and swallow it
And you will always be fortunate."
Saying this, Xigamana handed him the stone

In fulfillment of his evil conspiracy.
Thus poor Papaju unwittingly
Believed all that his brother said,
And took the stone and swallowed it.
But the magical stone stuck in his throat
And would not descend into his stomach.
Thus poor Papaju became mute,
Unable to utter a single word.
He could not even narrate to his people
What had happened to him to impair his speech.
However, he used hand signs instead,
And people came to know that Xigamana had used magic
      against him.
Thereafter, Papaju became an object of laughter in the village,
And those who loved him were pained at heart
Because they admired his noble character.

After living for many months in these circumstances,
One day Papaju left home to seek relief for his plight.
After travelling a long way
He came to a pool at the edge of a big river.
There he met an iguana [an aquatic lizard] basking in the sun,
Basking in the sun on a layer of rock.
Then the iguana greeted Papaju,
But Papaju replied only with hand signs.
Then the iguana asked Papaju, saying,
"Where are you going, Son of My Grandfather?"
But because he could not speak
After Xigamana had made him swallow a pebble,
He replied by signalling with his hand,
Telling Iguana that he was seeking relief.
Now, understanding Papaju's sad situation,
Iguana replied to Papaju, saying:
"Child of My Grandfather, your brother has bewitched you,
And there is no one who can relieve you,
Unless you kill me and skin me.
After killing me, cook and eat my heart.
But keep my skin and gall bladder
To help you whenever bad luck falls on you.
Whenever bad luck meets with you,
Hit the ground with the skin and gall bladder for your safety.
As for my carcass,
Throw it back into this pool of water
So that I may again come to life.
But before you cook my heart,
First go up to the mountain near your home,
Where you will find and dig up an herb.
Then you will cook that herb with my heart.

After eating these things you will be relieved
And you will once again regain your power of speech."
After Papaju had listened to Iguana's instructions
He went some distance from that river,
There he came to a fig tree.
With his axe, he climbed the tree;
With his axe he tapped the gum of the tree;
After tapping the gum, his gourd became full.
Then Papaju carried away that gum
And descended to the river with it.
Then Iguana, seeing Papaju approach,
Sprang at once into the pool and disappeared under the water.
Then Papaju spread the gum on the rock
On which Iguana had been basking in the sun.
Thus Papaju snared his healer, Iguana.
After Papaju had set his gum snare
He went into a thicket some distance away;
There he hid himself, waiting for Iguana to be caught.
As soon as Papaju had gone into hiding,
Iguana came out of the cold water
To bask in the warm sun on the rock;
There he was caught on the gum of the fig tree.
Realizing that he had been caught in a snare,
And life being sweeter than all else,
Iguana tried hard to free himself,
But the fig tree gum refused to let him go.
In a short while Papaju returned,
He found Iguana held by the fig tree gum.
Then Papaju danced gleefully, saying to himself:
"I have trapped Iguana,
Maybe I will again be a human being and speak!"
Then Papaju took his axe and killed Iguana;
Then he skinned poor Iguana;
He then placed the skin aside;
And finally he also took out and put aside the heart,
And cast Iguana's carcass into the pool of water.
Then Papaju remained looking for a while into the pool.
He saw Iguana's carcass tossing about in the water;
He saw Iguana swim across to the other shore of the pool;
He saw Iguana lie on a layer of rock over there.
Then Iguana bade Papaju farewell, saying:
"Son of My Grandfather, you are brave,
And you are not lacking in obedience.
Now go home peacefully.
Do not leave that good heart of mine behind.
Go back to your home as I have advised you;
Go up the mountain and dig up the herb
And cook it together with my heart;

Take these two and eat;
You will be well again."
Then Papaju took the skin, heart and gall bladder
And put them in his bag, carrying them away,
At the same time signalling good-bye to Iguana.
Then he followed the route towards his home.
Then he passed over the mountain, where he dug up his herb.
While he was yet some distance from his home
The sun went down and darkness covered the land.
While he was travelling in darkness
Papaju came to a junction of many footpaths
Where five routes converged, and he did not know which way
     to take.
Then Papaju threw down the skin and gall bladder;
Then the skin and gall bladder showed him the way home.
Then Papaju continued his journey homeward.
Arriving home in darkness when everyone was asleep,
Papaju went into his own house and lit a fire;
Then he took a pot and cooked Iguana's prescription.
As soon as the herb and heart were cooked
He took the pot off the fire and ate Iguana's muti.
Immediately Papaju's throat was open again.
Then, in the dead of night the whole village was awakened
By the loud singing of Papaju
Who had been missing for many days.
Papaju was singing the songs of his happy time of youth.
All the villagers ran towards Papaju's house at once.
Arriving there, they marvelled to hear Papaju speak with
     them
As he had always done before Xigamana bewitched him.
True, most people were glad to find Papaju well again.
But Xigamana and his fellow-conspirators became angry;
They began to hate Papaju more than before,
Fearing he was going to claim his father's kingship.
Papaju saw Xigamana's bitterness in his looks,
He was aware that Xigamana would try again to kill him.
So that night Papaju did not sleep
But stayed awake and ready with his spears at hand.
He also had his axe, his battle club and shield.
Then, when everyone in the village slept,
Papaju attacked Xigamana in his house and killed him.
When daylight came the people were surprised to learn
     Xigamana was dead,
Killed by Papaju the rightful king.
Then the whole country was jubilant about Papaju;
He was installed in the kingship inherited from his father;
He ruled with love, kindness and wisdom.

It came about that after Papaju had ruled for some years
He went out hunting with the men and youths of the village;
They hunted the animals of the plains and the bush.
As they hunted, Papaju heard a honey bird singing,
Seeming to call him to a place where there was honey.
All alone, Papaju followed the honey bird
Thinking it would lead him to honey;
But the honey bird lured Papaju on and on
Until he was separated from the rest of the hunters
Who were pursuing and killing game.
Thus following the honey bird,
Papaju found himself in the depth of a thick forest,
And he could not find his way back to the others.
He went on following the honey bird,
Which lured him into even denser parts of the forest.
His hunting party searched everywhere for the king
With whistling and shouting but they failed to find him.
Then, hoping that he might have gone home,
They returned to the village carrying flesh of their game,
But on arriving they did not find the young king there.
The next day and the next, still they did not find him.
After following the honey bird for a long while
Papaju emerged from the forest
And he saw a village of many beautiful houses.
He was surprised to see such an attractive village there,
And although greatly tired he walked quickly towards it.
Entering the village he noticed that it had no people in
    it;
All was still and there were no human sounds.
Noting the beauty of the first house,
Papaju decided to open its door and enter,
Expecting to find treasure there.
As he stretched out his hand to the door
Papaju heard the honey bird
Warning him not to open it, saying:
"Stand back, My Son!
Do not enter through that door;
Inside that house is your death!
Pass on, pass on, My Son,
You will find pleasure ahead,
Farther on are things worth taking home."
Because Papaju was accustomed to listening to advice
He accepted the warnings of the honey bird;
He refrained from entering that house;
Instead, he continued with his mysterious journey,
Doing what the honey bird instructed him to do.
Then he walked through that attractive village;
Then he arrived at another attractive house,

He found that this house also was tightly closed.
But he wished to enter, as he had with the first;
As he stretched out a hand to the door
Papaju heard the honey bird
Caution him not to open it, saying:
"Stand far back, My Son!
Do not break that house's door;
Inside that house is your death!
Pass on, pass on, My Son,
You will find pleasure ahead,
Farther on are things worth taking home."
Because Papaju was accustomed to listening to advice
He accepted the warning words of the honey bird;
He refrained from entering that beautiful house;
Instead, he proceeded on his unknown journey,
Doing what the honey bird instructed him to do.
Then he walked on through that pretty village;
Then he arrived at another attractive house,
He found that it also was tightly closed.
When he wished to enter it
The honey bird again warned him not to enter.
It happened many times;
Whenever Papaju wanted to enter a house
As he passed through that attractive village,
The honey bird cautioned him against it.
Thus Papaju went through the village of attractive houses
Without ever entering any of them.
Then Papaju walked and walked and walked
Until he came to the goat kraal of the village.
As quickly as Papaju arrived there
The honey bird also arrived there;
The honey bird perched on the kraal.
Papaju was amazed to see such fat goats;
He wished to open the kraal
So that he could drive the goats back to his village;
He was surprised when the honey bird did not prevent him.
Then he drove the entire flock of goats ahead of him,
The honey bird flying overhead showing him the way.
A little distance farther on
Papaju came to a kraal full of fat sheep;
These also he wanted to take.
Perched on the gate, the honey bird
Did not prevent him from taking the sheep.
So Papaju opened the kraal
And drove the sheep and goats homeward,
The honey bird overhead guiding him.
Then Papaju travelled along with his flocks
Until he reached a cattle kraal,

Full of fat, shiny cattle.
Again the honey bird did not prevent him, and he took the
    cattle.
Papaju drove his goats, sheep and cattle ahead of him,
With the honey bird guiding him overhead,
Singing, showing him the way home.
When Papaju came to the far edge of that village
He saw a woven food storage basket on the ground;
It was tightly closed and sealed
And Papaju thought it contained food.
He was indeed very hungry,
And he stretched out his hands to open the basket,
But as he put out his hands
The honey bird warned him not to open it, saying:
"Stand away, My Son!
Do not break the basket's seal,
For inside is your death!"
But because Papaju was indeed very hungry
He disobeyed the advice of the honey bird,
And using all his strength he unsealed the basket.
Instantly there emerged from the basket an old hag with a
    single tooth,
Quarrelsome, dirty, and with sores all over her body.
Lame and fiery-eyed, she sprang on Papaju's shoulders, saying:
"Unmannered boy, what are you doing?
Don't you hesitate to disturb peaceful people?
You don't even fear to take me out of my basket?
And where are you driving my herds and flocks?
Since you have unsealed my basket without provocation
Now you shall have to carry me on your back;
Wherever you go I shall be with you;
You shall never be parted from me
Because of taking me from the basket."
With dirt and smelling sores
The limping one-toothed witch perched firmly
On the back of the frightened Papaju
Who panted like a mouse in the grip of a cat.
Gegetsu was the old hag's name, One Big Tooth.
She ordered Papaju to drive the animals along;
They went towards his home, led by the honey bird.
Papaju was sickened by the bad smell of Gegetsu;
Her weight was too heavy for a man weakened by hunger.
Fearing to refuse to obey Gegetsu,
Fearing that she might peck him with her beaklike tooth,
He drove the herds and flocks,
Gegetsu clinging to him as he walked.
It was a trial of endurance for Papaju,
With the witch riding his back.

In time Papaju conceived a plan
To escape from Gegetsu and her punishment.
Papaju's chance came at last
When he saw a fig tree laden with ripe fruit.
He began to talk to Gegetsu, saying:
"Grandmother, see how ripe these figs are;
I would like you to feast on them.
Alight from my back for a while,
I will climb the tree to get fruit for you."
Because Gegetsu, like Papaju, was hungry
She consented to let him climb the tree.
Papaju climbed the fig tree
And dropped some fruit to old Gegetsu.
She enjoyed the fruit that he threw down,
And Papaju also enjoyed the fruit,
But while he ate he was still thinking of escape,
And he came to a decision.
After sucking the juice from the figs
He kept the refuse in the tree;
Then he shouted down to Gegetsu,
"Grandmother! Grandmother!
See these beautiful ripe figs!"
She looked up to receive them,
And Papaju then threw the fruit waste into her eyes.
Gegetsu was for the moment without sight;
She screamed that Papaju had blinded her.
He went down quickly from the tree;
He drove off the animals quickly;
Gegetsu struggled to get the fruit waste from her eyes;
The honey bird continued to show Papaju the way.
After walking a great distance
Papaju arrived at a flooded river;
He could not cross for fear of drowning.
While he stood there wondering what to do
He looked across the river towards the far bank;
There he saw many young women bathing.
The young women saw Papaju and the animals;
They swam across and brought Papaju over,
Because they were accomplished swimmers;
Afterwards they made his animals swim across.
Thus it was that Papaju and his animals crossed the river.
But beak-toothed Gegetsu was in pursuit.
The pretty young women with spaced teeth
Took Papaju to their village;
They hid him in a certain hut;
Then they told Papaju, saying:
"We are glad you are in the village;
We lack a man to look after us;

Our men were swallowed up by one-toothed Gegetsu,
A witch who often visits this place at night.
She comes, she sniffs around in search of male prey;
When she finds a man she kills him;
That is how our men died.
You, handsome one, if she finds you
You will die, you will be her meat."
So the young women hid Papaju in a certain house
Because they knew how dangerous Gegetsu was,
And Papaju slept there, guarded by a fierce dog.
Gegetsu was now following Papaju and the animals.
Coming to the river she found it in flood,
And she stopped, not able to cross.
Then she composed a song
And she sang while pecking at the water with her beaked tooth,
    saying:

> "Gegetsu,
> I kill with my tooth!
> Gegetsu,
> I kill with my tooth!"

So saying, she pecked at the water of the river,
Pecked it with her mighty tooth.
Immediately the water parted in two,
Forming walls on both sides,
Leaving a dry path across the river.
Then the old woman hobbled along that dry path,
Going straight for the home of the young women.
Arriving there, carrying the leg of a dead man,
Gegetsu began to sniff-sniff around the village
Because she had caught the scent of a man there
And knew that Papaju was hidden in that place.
The young women of the village were frightened;
They pitied Papaju especially,
Fearing that Gegetsu would kill and eat him.
Gegetsu searched all the houses,
She arrived at the place where Papaju was hidden;
Angrily she spoke, saying to him:
"You ran away, leaving me behind?
Haven't I found you now?
You thought to outwit me?
You blinded me with fig waste?
You thought you could escape me?
Whose house is this in which you hide?
Don't you know that this is my house?
Today we are going to sleep together in this house!"
Then Gegetsu with all her sores

Jumped on Papaju, saying,
"Today you will sleep carrying me on your back."
But the fierce dog owned by the young women was near;
The dog sprang towards Gegetsu, frightening her;
Then it bit her all over her body
Until Gegetsu let Papaju alone in fear of the dog.
Then Gegetsu went to sit at the far corner of the house;
She refrained the whole night from molesting Papaju.
In the middle of the night Gegetsu slipped into sleep;
When Papaju heard her deep breathing he was elated;
He ran out at once, leaving her behind.
But before Papaju was far from the village
Gegetsu awoke and pursued him.
Papaju saw her coming behind,
Singing as she came:

> "Gegetsu,
> I kill with my tooth!
> Gegetsu,
> I kill with my tooth!"

The time was mahlambandlopfu, that is to say, dawn.
When Papaju knew that Gegetsu was pursuing him
He ran with all his strength and speed,
But Gegetsu came after him swiftly.
Then the honey bird reappeared,
Pointing the way for Papaju to a baobab tree.
Arriving at the tree, Papaju climbed into it.
Gegetsu also arrived at the tree
But she could not climb it, and there she paused.
After a while she sang her song:

> "Gegetsu,
> I kill with my tooth!
> Gegetsu,
> I kill with my tooth!"

Singing this, she cut down a branch with her tooth,
The branch on which Papaju was perched;
But as that branch was about to fall,
Papaju sprang and perched on another one.
Gegetsu, never tiring,
Went on singing and cutting;
But as the branch was about to break away,
Papaju leaped to the next one.
It continued this way until the tree had no branches,
And when it had no branches
Papaju went quickly to the treetop,

Hoping that Gegetsu could not reach him there.
Then Gegetsu began hewing the tree trunk itself.
But just as the tree began to fall
Papaju thought of his iguana skin and gall bladder;
Then he struck the tree with those magic things
And the tree, where it was severed, stuck firmly in the
    ground.
But Gegetsu continued trying to hew down the tree
With her big beaklike tooth,
Singing all the while as she did so.
But each time the tree was about to fall,
Papaju struck the trunk with his magic things
And the tree stood erect once more.
Yet each time this was done the tree became shorter
And Papaju saw that Gegetsu might succeed in killing him.
Fearing death from Gegetsu,
Papaju remembered his fierce dogs at home,
Especially his favorite dog Makonde.
Then Papaju shouted with a great voice, saying,
"Feee! Feee! Feee! [whistling]
My dog Makonde!
I am in much danger!
Come to my assistance!"
The dog heard and knew it was needed by Papaju,
Papaju who had long been lost on a hunting expedition,
Papaju who was in grave danger.
When Makonde heard his master's voice
He answered with a loud bark, saying,
"Huuu! Huuu! Huuu!"
Then Papaju heard Makonde's answer from afar;
He rejoiced, knowing that his dogs would save him.
Indeed, the dogs were already on the way,
Running straight to the baobab tree on which Papaju was
    trapped.
Papaju went on calling to the dogs for help;
Each time he called, the dogs answered,
Running swiftly to rescue Papaju.
At home, Papaju's people remained wondering,
Not knowing where the dogs had gone;
Some thought the dogs had followed Papaju,
Others feared they might have been devoured by wild
    beasts;
Thus they speculated without knowing the truth.
After Papaju had disappeared during the hunt
There was much loneliness in the village,
And when the dogs disappeared
The lonesomeness became greater than before;
Even the castor-oil plants began to wilt.

Again Papaju called his dog Makonde,
And now Makonde's voice sounded close to the tree;
Then Papaju saw the dogs nearby.
When Gegetsu saw the dogs coming swiftly,
She knew that they were Papaju's dogs;
So she attacked them at once,
Trying to bite with her single tooth, saying:

> "Come! Come! I bite!
> I swallow you!"

Indeed, she swallowed all the dogs of Papaju,
All except Makonde
Who was fierce and vicious.
Then Gegetsu swallowed all of Papaju's animals,
And after that she turned to fight Makonde.
But Makonde was very fierce,
More fierce than Gegetsu herself.
The battle under the baobab tree
Was great and prolonged.
While Gegetsu and Makonde fought
Fiercely under the baobab tree,
Papaju clapped his hands to encourage the determined
    Makonde,
To encourage his dog in the fierce fight against Gegetsu.
Then at last Makonde and Gegetsu were exhausted;
Makonde fell to the ground unconscious,
And Gegetsu also fell unconscious,
But soon they rose up again,
Then the battle was more savage than before,
Until at last Makonde killed Gegetsu.
Then the dog tore open Gegetsu's belly,
And many people came out of it,
People long ago devoured by her;
The goats, sheep and cattle of Papaju came out,
And other animals, and Papaju's dogs came out.
Thus Makonde delivered people from the witch Gegetsu.
Then Papaju descended from the tree;
On reaching the ground he removed Gegetsu's tooth,
And began to rejoice with Makonde
Who had saved him.

Papaju drove his animals before him,
Going towards his home,
Guided on his way by the honey bird.
After a number of days
He arrived at his village.
All of Papaju's people rejoiced to see him;

They marvelled to see his animals,
His many fat cattle, sheep and goats.
Then Papaju told them of his adventures,
Of what had befallen him
To the time he was rescued by Makonde
At the big baobab tree where Gegetsu was destroyed.
The whole country came to hear his story
And to see the brave Papaju and his wealth.
There was a great feast
To celebrate the return of Papaju, the lost king,
Who had returned home in wealth and triumph.
Many cattle were slaughtered and much beer was brewed;
There was dancing, drinking and celebration;
The feasting was great.
Then Papaju told his people he would marry
And have an heir.
He took cattle to lobola a young woman,
One of those who had helped him cross the river
And rescued him from the ferocious Gegetsu.
After some months
Papaju brought his wife home
And there was another great feast.
Then Papaju and his wife ruled,
Ruled with kindness, love and wisdom.

Pthu! Choyoyooo!
I spit! I throw a branch to close the gate!

> *Pthu* is onomatopoeia for spitting. The narrator
> either spits or makes the sound of spitting on
> the ground. This is done to pacify spirits of the
> ancestors and to appease evil or hostile forces
> that made their appearance in the story, so that
> they do not come in the night to harm those
> involved in the narration. *Choyoyooo* is the
> sound of dragging a tree branch and placing it
> across the village gate, normally done to keep
> out wild animals at night; here it serves to keep
> the village safe from evil spirits that may have
> been aroused by the telling of the tale. When
> the narrator has spoken this formula, signifying
> that the story has come to an end, any member
> of the audience may repeat the words and add
> a personal wish such as, "I would like a kraal
> of cattle," or "I would like to be a king."

The Story of Xikhibana

Another Shangaan tale about a young hero
who faced what others feared and thus saved
the life of his father. In the Shangaan tradition,
it is told in a poetic declamatory style, with the
conventional opening and closing.

Narrator: *Garingani-wa-Garingani!* (I am Narrator, daughter of Narrator!)
Response: *Garingani!* (Narrator!)

It happened that there was a beautiful dwelling.
This dwelling was marvellously clean and neat;
There was not the smallest speck of dirt in it.
In the center of this dwelling there was a deep hole,
And this hole was very beautiful.
In the hole in this dwelling there lived a healer,
And this healer was called Masingi.
This Masingi was renowned throughout the land
Because he was a marvellous healer.
No matter how sick a person might be,
Masingi was able to bring him back to health.
Masingi's dwelling was a very deep hole,
There Masingi lived with all his charms.

On a certain day in the household of Maxava it occurred
That a serious illness fell on Maringana,
Maringana the breadwinner and owner of the household.
The family of Maringana tried in many ways
To help Maringana to recover,
But oh, they failed to help him regain his health.
Then they only looked on helplessly with their eyes.
For days and days there was no change.
Only groaning could be heard in this house,
And Maringana was not even able to eat porridge.

Set down by Daniel P. P. Marolen. Used by permission.

Maringana had fathered young men,
Five brave and strong young men.
One day their mother said to them:
"Oh, my children, oh, my young men,
Must we wait until your father's head sinks,
While we look at him and do nothing?
Would it not be good if you went
To call the great healer, Masingi,
So that he can come and revive Maringana?"
The eldest of the sons assented, saying,
"True, Mother, I shall go to Masingi."
Indeed, he then went to the dwelling of Masingi.
But because Masingi dwelt in a deep hole
He could not hear well what was said outside;
Thus everyone who came to his dwelling
Had first to sing Masingi's call song.
On hearing it, Masingi would then emerge,
Emerge from his very deep hole.
So this eldest of the five young men, Ntsalanyana,
On arriving there began to sing, saying:

> "Greetings, O Masingi!
> In your healing, O you excel,
>   O in your healing . . .
> In your healing, O you excel,
>   O in your healing . . .
> In your healing, O you excel,
>   O in your healing!
> Father is seriously ill, O Masingi!
> In your healing, O you excel,
>   O in your healing!
> O come and heal him, Masingi!
> In your healing, O you excel,
>   O in your healing!
> O come and heal him, Masingi!
> In your healing, O you excel,
>   O in your healing!"

When Masingi heard the song
He quickly took up his herb holders,
And he gathered all his herbs and charms.
Then he emerged from his very deep hole.
But when Ntsalanyana saw him,
Instantly he ran home as swiftly as he could
Because fear overcame him at the sight of Masingi the
    Healer,
Masingi the Healer, the great healing snake.
Ntsalanyana went running until he arrived at home,

Breathing heavily from fright,
Because he had been much frightened
At the sight of Masingi, the great snake.
Then his people at home asked him, saying,
"What has happened, O Ntsalanyana,
That you return breathing so heavily
And running so fast and strenuously?"
Then all his people scolded him severely;
They greatly despised him, saying:
"You have done all this knowingly.
How can a person do this to a dying man?
Are you encouraged because your father dies?
Are you looking to inherit your father's belongings?"
Then Ntsalanyana tried desperately to make them understand
The terrible mysteries he had seen,
But they refused to listen to him.
At last Ntsalanyana told them, saying,
"Well, you can send another person there
Because you regard me as a coward."

Then Matirhumi, second oldest of the brothers,
At once made straight for Masingi's dwelling place;
And arriving there, he also sang, saying:

>   "Greetings, O Masingi!
>   In your healing, O you excel . . ." (etc.)

When Masingi heard Matirhumi's song
He quickly got together his herb containers,
And gathered up his herbs and charms.
Then he emerged from his very deep hole.
But when Matirhumi beheld him
He ran in his fright as fast as he could,
Fearing the very sight of Masingi the Healer,
Masingi the Healer, the great healing snake.
Matirhumi ran until he arrived at home
Breathing heavily from fright,
Because he had been greatly frightened
By the sight of Masingi, the great snake,
The terrible great mountain snake.
His people at home asked him, saying:
"What has happened, O Matirhumi,
That you come home breathing so heavily
And running so fast and strenuously?
Are you heartened that your father dies?
Are you eager to inherit his belongings?"
Then Matirhumi tried hard to explain to them
The terrible mysteries he had seen.

But they refused altogether to listen.
At last Matirhumi replied, saying:
"Well, send another one there
Because you believe I am cowardly.
Else, go and see for yourselves."
His people scolded him, saying,
"Oh, you children of nowadays!
You do not love your parents!"

Then they sent Muhunguti, the third son, to Masingi
But he too came back with the same description.
Then they sent the fourth son, Malamulele,
And he came back with the same report.
At last they sent the youngest of the sons, Xikhibana,
Xikhibana, Maringana's favorite son.
But even before Xikhibana left on his dangerous quest
His four elder brothers ridiculed him, saying:
"Have not we, your elders, failed?
Surely Masingi will overcome you with fear."
But Xikhibana did not heed them and he went off to
    Masingi,
Went to Masingi undaunted by his brothers' words.
He travelled until he arrived at Masingi's place;
He stood some distance from the dwelling,
Then he began to sing Masingi's song:

>"Greetings, O Masingi!
>In your healing, O you excel . . ." (etc.)

When Masingi heard Xikhibana's rendition
He quickly gathered all his herb containers,
And he took up all his herbs and charms;
Then he emerged from his very deep hole.
Little Xikhibana looked and saw Masingi
With his charms hanging all over his body,
Saw Masingi sliding along, xololoooo, xololoooo,
Emerging from his deep hole dwelling,
Moving all the time straight toward Xikhibana.
Then Masingi arrived at where Xikhibana was waiting;
Then Masingi wound himself around the little boy,
Beginning at his feet up to his head.
But Xikhibana showed no sign of fear,
And when Masingi saw that he was not afraid
He began to converse, saying,
"Quickly, show me the way to your place;
I have to heal Maringana, your father."
Then the little Xikhibana went with Masingi.
As he travelled, the little boy sang Masingi's song.

At home the people waited anxiously,
Complaining that he did not arrive when expected,
Thinking that he might have been killed by wild beasts.
But when time had passed, Xikhibana arrived,
Arrived suddenly at home with Masingi.
Just at that time the women were cooking food,
But when the people saw Masingi they all fled,
Fled because they feared Masingi the Healer,
Masingi, who was famous in all the land,
The most fearsome snake of the wilderness.
Thus arrived the small boy and Masingi,
Arrived to find Maringana alone in his hut,
Because he could not flee with the healthy ones,
Because he could not escape because of his sickness.
Upon arriving there, Masingi unwrapped his herbs,
He gave medicine to Maringana,
And licked Maringana's skin with his tongue.
At once sick Maringana began to feel better,
He rose and sat upright, tovololooo!
And his eyes began to see better and farther, n'weee!
Then the people who had fled when Masingi arrived
Peered in fear from their hiding places in the bush.
Xikhibana's elder brothers did likewise.
All the people then shouted to the boy, saying,
"What is that snake you have brought home with you?"
And Xikhibana answered them from his father's hut, saying:
"This is Masingi himself, the Healer,
Who is known throughout the land.
Come home, all of you.
Come back and fear nothing.
See, father is now very much better;
He has been saved by the herbs of Masingi the Healer."
The village people returned, greatly surprised.
Thus it was that sick Maringana was brought back to health,
Brought back to life by the courage of the youngest child.

The next day in Maringana's household
Many many cattle were slaughtered and much beer
    brewed,
And there was much feasting and drinking.
The whole country rejoiced at the healing of Maringana.
A few days passed, then Masingi said good-bye to the people.
They gave him many herds and flocks and other presents,
And he was accompanied home by a great multitude,
A multitude that was led by the small boy Xikhibana,
With the snake hanging on him all the way.
When the people once more returned to their homes
Xikhibana went with Masingi as far as his dwelling hole.

Arriving at that place,
Masingi advised the boy, saying,
"If your father's medicines are used up
Or if his illness comes again
Return here and I will give you more herbs."
Thus when Xikhibana returned to his father's house
He gave the message to his father,
And he showed his father gifts given to him by Masingi.
Maringana was pleased with his son;
He made a big feast for him,
And made much beer and slaughtered many cattle for him.
The whole land was proud of Xikhibana
For his great bravery.

Pthu! Choyoyooo!
I spit! I throw a branch to close the gate!

Tendejuva the Handsome

A romantic Shangaan story about a hero whose
outstanding attribute is not heroism but natural physical beauty.

Narrator: *Garingani-wa-Garingani!*
Response: *Garingani!*

It happened that in a certain land
There was a very handsome young man
Whose fine appearance was admired by everyone.
This young man was called Tendejuva.
He prided himself on his natural beauty.
He said to his friends thus,
That he would never offer himself to any young woman,
But that women would offer themselves to him
When he was ready to take a wife,
Come of their own volition

Set down by Daniel P. P. Marolen. Used by permission.

While he remained comfortably in his house.
Tendejuva's mother lived nearby.
She had many fields to till.
On returning from her fields she cooked her food
And brought a share of it to Tendejuva.
On arriving at his dwelling place
She put down the food and returned home
Without waiting to see her handsome son Tendejuva;
For Tendejuva outshone the sun in brilliance
And never came out of his dwelling place.
Many young women in faraway lands
Came to hear of the exceedingly handsome Tendejuva,
And wished to become his wife.

It happened that some young women from the country of
    Makwakwa
Went on a journey to the place where Tendejuva lived,
Each of them hoping to be loved by Tendejuva.
Each of them adorned her body as attractively as possible.
They plaited their hair and smeared their skins with red ocher
    and fat,
Smeared themselves with fat until they shone brightly;
They were immaculate and displayed all their beauty
As if they did not touch the ground.
Thus they went along until they reached the home of
    Tendejuva's mother.
Arriving there, they waited at the gate.
Seeing them, Tendejuva's mother went to the gate, saying:
"Greetings, my children! Greetings, my children!"
The young women from the land of Makwakwa answered,
    saying:
"We hear you, Mother! Greetings, Mother!"
Then Tendejuva's mother asked them:
"Where do you come from, my daughters?"
They replied to Tendejuva's mother, saying to her:
"We come from very far away, from the country of
    Makwakwa."
Then she asked them, saying to them:
"Have you come here on a good mission,
Or are you coming on an unhappy mission?"
They replied together in chorus, saying:
"Yes, Mother, we have come on a good mission;
We are going across the land in search of marriage
And we have heard of a handsome young man in this place,
A young man by the name of Tendejuva.
You, Mother, are you one who knows where he lives?
Perhaps one of us will be fortunate enough
To become a wife of the handsome Tendejuva."

Then Tendejuva's mother answered them, saying:
"Yes, I hear you, my children;
You are not lost, for Tendejuva lives nearby indeed.
But first let me dish out some food for you to eat,
And you can take some of the food to Tendejuva.
Yet, first you should eat
Because you have travelled far from the land of Makwakwa."
The young women declined to eat the food. They said:
"How will it help us to eat before we go to Tendejuva?
Perhaps when we arrive there he will not care for us."
Tendejuva's mother answered, saying:
"My children, do not worry over things.
I am Tendejuva's mother, the mother of the one you seek.
My children, eat the food, fear nothing.
My Tendejuva is indeed a handsome young man.
He does not even leave his dwelling hut
Because he outshines the sun in brightness."
True, even as they spoke to one another this way
Tendejuva sat alone and contented in his house,
Wanting nothing.
Tendejuva's mother said to the young women:
"Let us go now to the dwelling place of my handsome son;
You shall all see and hear for yourselves."
And so Tendejuva's mother and the young women went to
    Tendejuva's place.
Arriving, they stopped at the door of Tendejuva's house.
Each young woman's heart beat with anxiety;
Each young woman wondered if Tendejuva could care for
    her;
In each heart was the wish:
"Oh, may I be the one to be loved by Tendejuva!"
Then Tendejuva's mother said: .
"Listen to my words, my daughters,
I will call him with a song,
And Tendejuva will answer, for he sees you all."
The mother of Tendejuva sang her song, saying:

            "Tendejuva! Tendejuva!
            Oh, your wives, oh!
            Tendejuva! Tendejuva!
            Oh, your wives have come!
            Tendejuva! Tendejuva!
            Oh, they have come to find you!
            Tendejuva! Tendejuva!"

From inside his dwelling hut, Tendejuva answered, singing:

"Oh, my mother!
Tendejuva! Tendejuva!
Oh, my wives!
Tendejuva! Tendejuva!
My wives have come, oh!
Tendejuva! Tendejuva!
Oh, I love them not!
Tendejuva! Tendejuva!
Oh, tell them to go away!
Tendejuva! Tendejuva!
Oh, the one I love is coming!
Tendejuva! Tendejuva!
She is called Nyatinsalwana!
Tendejuvaaaa . . .!"[1]

Then Tendejuva's mother said to those young women:
"You have heard it, my daughters;
You have heard it with your own ears;
You are not loved, there is nothing else;
Tendejuva is waiting for his loved one, Nyatinsalwana.
Return to your homes in peace, my daughters.
Our greetings to all who are there, though we do not know
    them."
So those disappointed young women
Began the journey home to Makwakwa.
They travelled on and on in sadness
Until they arrived in Makwakwa, full of shame.
Upon reaching home they related everything.

In the country of Chayimithi
Were other young women who had heard of Tendejuva.
They also said they would go and try for themselves.
They washed themselves and adorned themselves;
They smeared themselves with fat;
They dressed themselves attractively;
They scented themselves;
They put red ocher on their skin;
They whitened their teeth with ash
Until their teeth were the color of maize flour,
Until it seemed that money would fall from their teeth.
When the young men saw those young women
They threatened to kill themselves if they could not have
    them.
But the young women did not care about those young men;
They were thinking only about Tendejuva.

---

1. *The words "Tendejuva! Tendejuva!" appear to be a choral response made by those listening to the narration.*

They began their journey and travelled on and on
Until they reached the dwelling of Tendejuva's mother.
As was the custom, Tendejuva's mother received them in her
    house;
She dished up food for them to eat;
And when they had eaten, she said to them:
"Let us go to Tendejuva's place, my daughters;
You shall hear for yourselves on reaching there."
They arrived at the entrance of Tendejuva's dwelling;
Each young woman's heart beat with anxiety;
Each one wished to be loved by Tendejuva.
Tendejuva's mother said to them:
"Listen to my words, my daughters,
I will call him with a song,
And Tendejuva will answer, for he sees you all."
Tendejuva's mother sang her song, saying:

> "Tendejuva! Tendejuva!
> Oh, your wives, oh!
> Tendejuva! Tendejuva!
> Oh, your wives have come!
> Tendejuva! Tendejuva!
> Oh, they have come to find you!
> Tendejuva! Tendejuva!"

Then Tendejuva sang back his answer:

> "Oh, my mother!
> Tendejuva! Tendejuva!
> Oh, my wives!
> Tendejuva! Tendejuva!
> My wives have come, oh!
> Tendejuva! Tendejuva!
> Oh, I love them not!
> Tendejuva! Tendejuva!
> Oh, tell them to go away!
> Tendejuva! Tendejuva!
> Oh, the one I love is coming!
> Tendejuva! Tendejuva!
> She is called Nyatinsalwana!
> Tendejuvaaaa . . . !"

Tendejuva's mother said to the young women:
"That is the way it is, my daughters;
You have heard with your own ears;
You are not loved, there is nothing else;
Tendejuva says Nyatinsalwana is coming.
Return to your homes in peace, my daughters;
Greetings to all, although we do not know them."

Then those unfortunate young women
Made their homeward journey to the country of Chayimithi;
They travelled in the grip of sadness;
They went on and on and on
Until they arrived in Chayimithi, chagrined;
And arriving there, they grumbled, saying:
"How could we tolerate Tendejuva?
He does not want a wife;
He does not want to marry;
Are we so ugly that we cannot be loved?
Surely, it is just that he does not want to marry.
Among all the young women of Chayimithi
Can there be not even one to please him?
He will regret it, to be fed by his mother."
Thus the young women told everything about Tendejuva.

Then young women from the country of Nyembani prepared to
    make the journey;
They prepared provisions for the journey to Tendejuva's place;
They washed, adorned themselves and made themselves
    attractive.
Soon after they had left their homes
They saw their younger sisters following them;
Their younger sisters looked very attractive.
The young women turned their younger sisters back, saying:
"Even the most beautiful young women have failed;
So why are you coming, you who are so small?
You will make us disliked by Tendejuva,
Go back at once."
The younger sisters turned back and returned home,
Except for one, named Nyatinsalwana.
The young women caught hold of Nyatinsalwana and thrashed
    her;
Then they left her crying and bleeding, crying bitterly;
After that they continued their journey,
Thinking that the young sister had been left behind.
But after a while they saw her again.
Her elder sister caught her and thrashed her again;
But the other young women said,
"Let her come along with us;
For does she not use her own legs for walking?"
So Nyatinsalwana accompanied them, and they arrived,
Arrived there where Tendejuva's mother lived,
Where Tendejuva's mother received them and fed them.
When they had eaten, Tendejuva's mother took them to
    Tendejuva.
Coming to the entrance of his dwelling place
Tendejuva's mother sang:

"Tendejuva! Tendejuva!
Oh, your wives, oh!
Tendejuva! Tendejuva!
Oh, your wives have come!
Tendejuva! Tendejuva!
Oh, they have come to find you!
Tendejuva! Tendejuva!"

Then Tendejuva sang back his reply, saying:

"Oh, my mother!
Tendejuva! Tendejuva!
Oh, my wives!
Tendejuva! Tendejuva!
My wives have come, oh!
Tendejuva! Tendejuva!
Mine is this one!
Tendejuva! Tendejuva!
She is Nyatinsalwana!
Tendejuva! Tendejuva!
Oh, my mother!
Tendejuva! Tendejuva!
Oh, heat some water, oh!
Tendejuva! Tendejuva!
Pour it for her to wash!
Tendejuva! Tendejuva!
And soothe her wounds!
Tendejuva! Tendejuva!"

Tendejuva's mother sang back to him:

"Tendejuva! Tendejuva!
I have done what you asked!
Tendejuva! Tendejuva!
I have bathed and adorned her!
Tendejuva! Tendejuva!
I have soothed her wounds!
Tendejuva! Tendejuva!
I have taken away her rags!
Tendejuva! Tendejuva!
I have never seen one so beautiful!
Tendejuva! Tendejuva!"

Tendejuva replied to his mother with delight, saying:

"Oh, my mother!
Tendejuva! Tendejuva!
Open up my club hut!

> Tendejuva! Tendejuva!
> Bring out the finest things to wear!
> Tendejuva! Tendejuva!
> And make Nyatinsalwana my bride!
> Tendejuvaaaa . . . !"

And when Tendejuva's mother had done these things
And had adorned Nyatinsalwana
Tendejuva sang again, saying:

> "Oh, my mother!
> Tendejuva! Tendejuva!
> Bring me the one I love!
> Tendejuva! Tendejuva!
> My own Nyatinsalwana!
> Tendejuva! Tendejuva!
> So I may see her with my own eyes!
> Tendejuva! Tendejuva!
> So I can embrace her in my arms!
> Tendejuvaaaa. . . !"

Indeed, the mother brought her to Tendejuva;
And Tendejuva opened his hut dwelling
And took Nyatinsalwana by the hand and embraced her,
And asked her to become his wife.
And Nyatinsalwana accepted
And the two of them were shining.

Then all those who had come from Nyembani
Looked at one another in amazement.
Tendejuva's mother sent the village men
To the dwelling place where Nyatinsalwana had come
    from,
Sending there the cattle for the lobola of their daughter.
The men took with them great quantities of goods,
They took with them Nyatinsalwana and Tendejuva,
Took them to the people of Nyatinsalwana.
They were received with great hospitality;
Indeed, many, many cattle were slaughtered for them.
Then when Nyatinsalwana and Tendejuva had been
    married
And the whole country had witnessed it,
Tendejuva said farewell to these people.
They gave him many gifts and ornaments,
And he returned home with Nyatinsalwana.
There, in that place, another feast was held;
There was drinking, eating and dancing,
And the whole country celebrated the event.

Tendejuva and Nyatinsalwana set up their household;
They became wife and husband;
They started their family;
They loved each other,
Even until they were old.

Pthu! Choyoyooo!
I spit! I throw a branch to close the gate!

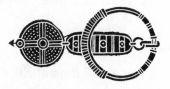

Shinangana's Chronology

> This chronology of events was recited by Shi-
> nangana, a Tsonga tribesman, in 1905, and
> written down by a European student of Tsonga
> life.

Sixty-seven years ago, Shiluvane and the other Tsonga chiefs fled before Manukosi (1838, or 1839?).

Three years later, battle with Matshekwane, Manukosi's general, who pursued the Nkuna (1842).

In the sixteenth year of the era, battle of Gologodjwen, when the Nkuna chief, Shiluvane, fought against the Ba-Pedi of Sekukuni (1855).

In the nineteenth year, Manukosi dies (1858 or 1859? His death may have taken place as early as 1856).

Henceforth each year is known by its principal event:

Expedition of Shihahen (1859).

Beginning of the great war of succession between Manukosi's sons, Muzila and Mawewe. Muzila fled to Spelonken (1860).

Circumcision school at Mudjadji (1861).

We are plundered by Djiwawa [Joao Albasini, the Portuguese commander who for many years was the chief of the Tsonga refugees of Spelonken] (1862).

Djiwawa goes to fight against Mawewe (1863).

We are plundered by the Swazi army (1864).

Shiluvane, the Nkuna chief, settles in the Nyarin country (1865).

From The Life of a South African Tribe, *by Henri A. Junod, 2 vols., London, 1927 (second edition). Junod identified the tribal group as Thonga, a term designating a people in northern Zululand but also used by the Zulu to refer to the Tsonga or Shangaan.*

Djiwawa kills Ribole and Magoro (1866).

The Modjadji army fights with the Nyari clan (1867).

The Swazis plunder Modjadji's country [Buluberi] (1868).

Djiwawa plunders the people of Mashao [Spelonken] (1869).

Muzila's army returns from Mosapa [Gaza], and plunders Spelonken [Bvesha] (1870).

The Swazis plunder Makandju (1871).

Circumcision school of Madosi in Spelonken (1872).

Daiman! [Opening of the Kimberley diamond mines where natives begin to go to work] (1873).

Birth of my child Rihlangana. Death of Shiluvane (1874).

Famine of Magadingele (1875).

Death of Nkambi, son of Mhalamhala, a Khosa (1876).

War of Makhanana of the Loyi country. Refugees come to Spelonken (1877).

The Makandju people kill Ñwashitine of Rikotjo (1878).

Birth of my child Ntitiri (1879).

Circumcision school of Mayingwe (1880).

Djiwawa goes to seize Sekukuni (1881).

War between the Boers and the English (1882).

Year of the comet (1883).

Djiwawa's son, Sambana, becomes chief. Sambana plunders the village of a Venda called Mbekwa (1884).

Phundjululu: the vermin destroy the mealies (1885).

Circumcision school of Ñwamutjungu, a Hlanganu who had come from Spelonken (1886).

A Gwamba chief quarrels with Girifi [Mr. Grieve, an old colonist of Spelonken] (1887).

Sambana [Shinangana's son] beats a policeman (1888).

Death of Djiwawa (1889).

Sambana calls statute laborers (1890).

Death of Sambana (1891).

Circumcision school at Modjadji (1892).

My son Magondjwen starts on a journey (1893).

He returns home (1894).

We are struck by hail. Four people die (1895).

My son-in-law goes away (1896).

Epidemic among cattle. War of Makhube. We accompany the Boers (1897).

Matshona: plague among oxen (1898).

Bahehemuki! The people of Gungunyana take refuge in Spelonken [after the war of Magigwana with the Portuguese] (1899).

The Boers attack Phefu, the Venda chief (1900).

The Whites fight. [Anglo-Boer war] (1901).

The English column chases the Boers away from Pietersburg: Ñwashimbutane! The Son-of-the-Kid! [General Beyers, compared with a kid on account of his swift movements through the country during the guerrilla war.] (1902).

Mugayo! Ndlala! The mealie flour bought from the Whites on account of the famine! (1903).

Daniel Marolen, who contributed the bulk of the materials in this book relating to the Tsonga, comments on the chronology:

"The name Manukusi (Manukosi as given by Junod) was the Tsonga name of the Zulu general, Zoshangana, who invaded the Tsonga domain and conquered the inhabitants in the late 1830s. Mawewe and Muzila were Zoshangana's sons who fought for the chieftainship after the death of their father in the late 1850s. Shinangana's chronology is a comprehensive and accurate history of the Tsonga people of South Africa. Bvesha is the land of the Venda people, which the Afrikaans voortrekkers called Spelonken (Valley). Kimberley, the diamond city of South Africa, was early known to the Tsonga people as Dayimani (written Daiman in the chronology). Today, because their brothers died there, many Tsonga women swear by saying, "E Dayimani!"—meaning, "I swear by my brother who died at Kimberley!" The practice of calling a year or any other period of time by the principal event that occurred in it is traditional among the Tsonga. For example, a child born during the First World War, 1914 to 1918, is said to have been born "hi Jarimani"—that is, during Germany. Shinangana, who was a friend of my great-grandfather, did not create this chronology. He recited it as it was handed down to him by older people [except for additions that he himself made to it—Ed.]."

THE ORIGIN OF THE VENDA PEOPLE

(ACCORDING TO VENDA TRADITION)

Kale, kale—long, long ago—before there were Venda people in the world, there was a large snake called Tharu (Python) living on the mountain slopes of the present land of the Vendas. That which came about happened during a year of prolonged drought. It was then that Tharu divided himself into two parts—Thoho, the Head, and Tshamutshila, the Tail. When Tharu had so divided himself, each part became a snake. They lived on, until one day Thoho said to Tshamutshila: "The

---

Set down by Daniel P. P. Marolen. Used by permission.

drought has brought great famine everywhere. I fear that we shall die of hunger unless we do something to avoid starvation. Therefore, let us separate. You go westward in search of food, and I shall search in the east."

Then Tshamutshila went westward searching, into the land that is now the country of the Vendas. When he arrived in that place he became a human being. He gathered herds of cattle, he married many wives, and these wives bore Tshamutshila numerous children. These numerous children married and begot more children, and in time all these people became a tribe. Tshamutshila became their chief, and he was called by the name Ramabulana. He built a Musanda, meaning Great Place, and from there he ruled.

The land of the Venda people was fertile and full of rivers and springs, and rain was plentiful. The people grew maize, millet, squash, pumpkins, peanuts, sweet potatoes, cassava, beans, sweet cane and many other kinds of crops. They had cattle, sheep, goats, fowls, dogs and cats. Food was plentiful and the people were prosperous. Tshamutshila, or Ramabulana as he was known, became a chief whose name was heard in far-off lands.

Now, Thoho went east to a place in what is now Mozambique, and there he founded the Ronga people. In time he also turned human, and he came to be known by the name Nyamusoro. But the lands he ruled were lands of drought and famine. The soil was not fertile, there were not many rivers, and little rain fell. In order to procure food for himself, Nyamusoro became a wandering singer and entertainer. He travelled from one village to another, from one country to another, and from one Great Place (dwelling of a chief) to another. He sang and danced in return for food to eat and beer to drink. And he arrived one day at the Great Place of Ramabulana, he who founded the Venda nation. He danced and sang at the outer gate of the Great Place, and the people gathered until there was a great crowd. His dancing stirred up a cloud of dust that rose into the sky and hung there over the town.

Many people went to Ramabulana to urge him to come and see the dancing, but he refused. Knowing that he and Nyamusoro were parts of Tharu, the Python, he feared that the two parts would again be joined. So he would not listen to those who urged him to come to the town gate. But Ramabulana's wives implored him even more strongly than others. They sang:

"Go out of your house, O Vhamusanda,
For Nyamusoro's singing and dancing, O Vhamusanda,
It is a spectacle too great to be missed by any living person,
A sight never before seen or heard,
Come out and go to the gate, O Vhamusanda!"

Importuned this way, at last Ramabulana could not resist. He agreed to go to the gate to hear Nyamusoro sing and see him dance. He arose. He went to the gate where the great crowd was watching, and where the dust was still rising from the ground into the air. He went forward, till he and Nyamusoro saw each other. And instantly they came together, the two parts of Tharu, and they joined and became Tharu the Python again. And even as the Venda people watched, Tharu coiled and uncoiled and then made his way out of the town into the forest.

Thus the Great Place of Ramabulana was a Great Place without a chief. Ramabulana's sons grew up, they married and had children; but they quarrelled among themselves and could not agree on anything. So they parted, each of the sons taking his family and his followers. Each chose a different direction. Wherever one of them settled with his people he became a chief. Thus the Venda people spread across the country, all of them the progeny of Ramabulana, who began as a part of Tharu, and who returned to Tharu.

How Phuti Became a Totem of the Tswana People

This legend, featuring an ancestral king named Khama, has as its setting the tribal wars set into motion by the conquests of the Zulu warrior-king, Chaka. The Zulu conquests resulted in a series of migrations, with one clan or tribe driving out another, and the second driving out a third. A Zulu chieftain named Mzilikazi went on a journey to escape the heavy rule of Chaka. He and his armies subdued all the settlements in their path as they migrated to Amandebele —a kingdom they would found in the region now known as Rhodesia. In the course of their movement they passed through Botswana, the country of the Tswana people. There they laid waste the land, burned the villages, and took much booty and many captives. The Tswana were no match for the Mandebele army. They scattered and hid and waited for the scourge to pass. Khama, chief of the Bangwato clan, was pursued by the invaders, who sought to kill him. His escape with the help of a buck (phuti) is recorded in the following story.

Set down by Daniel P. P. Marolen. Used by permission.

Long ago the land of Botswana was invaded by a powerful Zulu army from the south led by Mzilikazi. At that time the Tswana people were ruled by Khama, the grandfather of the present king Khama of Botswana. The fighters led by Mzilikazi were on their way to settle in a distant land to the north, and like locusts they ate whatever lay in their path. The Tswana warriors fought bravely against the invaders, but they lost many men on the battlefield and at last they fled in defeat. Khama also escaped death by fleeing into the wilderness. He looked for the remnants of his army, hoping to bring them together and again contest the ground with the invaders. But he was closely pursued by Mzilikazi's warriors. Khama went on, until exhaustion overcame him and he fell to the ground. Seeing this, his pursuers were heartened, and they raised a song of triumph. But Khama was not willing to be taken captive, for he intended to bring his people together and make them a nation again. He arose from where he lay and made another effort to escape his pursuers. He came to a dense thicket of thorn bushes, and disregarding the thorns that pierced him he plunged into it. And now, the strength gone from him, he threw himself down behind a rotting log.

As it happened, in the place where Khama lay in hiding, Phuti, the Buck, also was lying. But he did not move from the spot, he remained where he was, and the two of them, Khama and Phuti, lay side by side, touching each other. And as they lay there, after a while, Khama heard the Zulu warriors approaching the thorn bush thicket, shouting, "He entered here! Let us, also, enter, for we shall surely find him!" Again they shouted, "Here! He is among the thorn bushes! Let us take him!" The shouting of the Zulu warriors frightened the timid Phuti. He leaped to his feet and sprang from the thicket. He went running this way and that among the Zulu, dodging and veering through their ranks. The warriors were greatly surprised. They said to one another: "Now, how can it be said that Khama hides in the thicket among the thorn bushes? If Khama were there, would Phuti have shared the place with him? Will Phuti ever remain where a man has entered? No, Khama cannot be there among the thorns. Let us seek elsewhere." And so the Zulu warriors departed.

Thus it was that Khama was saved from death by Phuti, and that he was able to bring his people together again. And when the Tswana heard his story they were filled with a deep affection for Phuti. From that day to the present they have respected and venerated Phuti as a totem. This is the story of the first King Khama of the Tswana people.

Much Searching Disturbs Things That Were Lying Still

A TSWANA MORALIZING TALE

A man went out to cut wood; he tried the trees as he passed along, but they were all bad; so he climbed up a rock, and at last he saw a good tree. So then he took a rock, and rolled it down from under the tree; the rock rolled down, and went into a bush, and disturbed a duiker. The duiker ran, and got into a bush. A buffalo happened to be lying in the bush. The buffalo ran away, for it was afraid of the duiker. The buffalo met a man who was hunting, and it killed him. But when people saw the vultures, they ran, and found the man dead. They did not know what had killed him. So then they stood and asked one another, "What was this man killed by?"

Then they saw a hoofprint. "A fine hoofprint of a buffalo! When the buffalo went out to kill the man, where did it come from?" They followed it by the hoofprint; they found it came out of a bush. They said, "When the buffalo came out of the bush, what disturbed it?" They looked for what had disturbed it. They saw the hoofprint of the duiker. They asked one another, "When the duiker went to disturb the buffalo, where did it come from?" And they followed it also by the hoofprint; they said: "The duiker came out of this bush. But when the duiker went to come out of this bush, what disturbed it?"

They saw the rock; they said, "This rock when it went to disturb the duiker, where did it come from?" They said, "This rock came from those rocks." They followed it up, and said, "What pushed this rock?" They found the rock had come from under a tree. They said, "Oh! it was a man who moved the rock, in cutting down this tree." And so then they went, and said: "Whatever did that man want? There were plenty of trees; he went and disturbed things that were lying still."

So this is how the saying began; and people said: "The man went out to cut wood, and disturbed things that were lying still! Much searching disturbs things that were lying still!"

Thus the saying was made.

From From a Vanished German Colony, A Collection of Folklore, Folk Tales and Proverbs from South-West Africa, *by Odette St. Lys, London, 1916.*

Some Tswana Proverbs

The baboon is a climber, but he does not forget that he could fall.
In the dark, hold on to one another by the robe.
There are many dawns.
The thorn tree is climbed by its knobs [not its thorns].
To overfill the pot with meat is to break it.
The child of the saver is not saved.
The bitter heart eats its owner.
The well somewhere ahead is not to be depended on.
The breast [of man] is an intricate net [unfathomable].
The lion that kills is the one that does not roar.
The first one lamed is not the first to die.

A Xhosa Reproves a Missionary

Although many Africans must have listened uncritically to the European missionary who told them their ways were nothing but pure superstition, there clearly were those who resented the assertion that their traditional ways and beliefs were worthless. The Right Reverend Henry Callaway, M.D., D.D., Bishop of St. John's, was one of those who labored in the vineyards of the Xhosa people, and he recorded, most faithfully, it appears, the response of a man to whom it had been told that the Christians were bringing God to Africans.

"He came, the Renowned-one-from-across-the-sea came, one who
    spoke an unintelligible language,
He came without our seeing him, one who spoke an unintelligible
    language,
Concealed by the wood planks of the ship, one who spoke an
    unintelligible language,
By the planks of a yellow-wood tree, one who spoke an
    unintelligible language."

This song was sung before the missionaries came; when we of the present time hear it we call it a fiction; for the sayings of those who have been, we who live now regard as fictions. But they are not fictions, but the sayings of men who existed before us. The above song was sung by Gokozi. Gokozi was one of the women who lived in ancient times, and by Daus' and Nojiko and Nokika. So the song was sung by the people of that time.

We had this word before the missionaries came; we had God (Utikxo)

From St. Lys, ibid.

long ago; for a man when dying would utter his last words, saying, "I am going home, I am going up on high." For there is a word in a song which says:

> "Guide me, O Hawk!
> That I may go heavenward,
> To seek the one-hearted [sincere] man,
> Away from the double-hearted men
> Who deal in blessing [gifts] and cursing [witchcraft]."

We see, then, that those people used to speak of a matter of the present time which we clearly understand by the word which the missionaries teach us.

The God who is now, is the one who was from everlasting, before the missionaries came. Before they came we spoke of [God] Kamata, and we spoke of [God] Tiko; the word Kamata means Tiko. We trust that there were some of our people in heaven before the missionaries came. We had righteousness and evil; there were men-destroyers and there were good men; the men-destroyers were wicked men; we had life and death; and the graves which are now, were long ago.

So we say there is no God who has just come to us. Let no man say The God which is, is the God of the English. There are not many Gods. There is but one God. We err when we say, "He is the God of the English." He is not the God of certain nations; just as man is not English and Kosa; he is not Fingo and Hottentot; he is one man who came forth from one God.

How God Distributed Property: A Xhosa Account

Tiko, the Supreme Being, was the owner of all livestock. The nations that then existed in the world were three: the Whites, the Amaxhosa and the Hottentots. A day was set for all the nations to appear before Tiko to receive their shares of the things he was prepared to give them. The day came and the people began arriving. While they were assembling, a honey bird (honey guide) fluttered by, and all the Hottentots ran after it, whistling and making the sounds they usually do when the honey bird is guiding them to honey. Tiko remonstrated with them about their behavior, but they paid no attention to him. Exasperated, Tiko denounced them as a vagrant tribe that would thereafter have to exist on wild roots and honey beer and have no livestock whatsoever.

When Tiko's fine herds of cattle were at last brought before the Xhosa people they became excited, and they began to pick out cows for themselves. One exclaimed, "That black and white cow is mine!" Another called out, "That red cow and black bull are mine!" And so it went on until Tiko's patience was gone. He declared that the Xhosa were a

---

Rewritten from St. Lys, ibid.

restless people who would possess cattle but nothing else.

The Whites waited patiently, and Tiko gave them cattle, horses, sheep and all kinds of other property. Hence it is said by the Xhosa, "The Whites have everything, we Xhosa have only cattle, while the Hottentots have nothing."

> The collector of this tale, having seen Hotten-tots living far better than suggested here, says: "Apparently the Kafir who narrated [this story] can only have had impoverished specimens of the Hottentot race before his eyes."

The Story of Umkxakaza-wakogingqwayo

A ZULU EPIC

There was a certain king; he had a child; her name was Umkxakaza-wakogingqwayo (The-rattler-of-weapons-of-the-place-of-the-rolling-of-the-slain). That name was given because an army went out to battle rattling weapons, and so she was named Umkxakaza; and further, the name Wakogingqwayo was given because the army killed very many men, and when they were rolled altogether on the ground, she was named Wakogingqwayo. Again he had another child; she was named Ubalatusi, because she resembled brass [that is, her skin shone like polished brass].

From Nursery Tales, Traditions, and Histories of the Zulus, in Their Own Words, *by Henry Callaway, Natal, 1868. Three letters that appear in the Zulu words—*c, q *and* x—*indicate vocal clicks in the Zulu language for which there was no agreed-upon orthography at the time this book was published.*

When Umkxakaza was growing up, her father said: "Look you, on the day when you are of age there shall be collected many cattle for the purpose of bringing you home; for the cattle which shall be brought to you shall be taken at the point of the spear, and forays be made into distant nations, and when they come they will darken the sun."

At length she came to maturity. When she was with others in the open country she said to them, "I am of age." The young women rejoiced, and ran to all the villages, calling other young women; they came and remained with her; again they left her and went home, going to plunder the whole village. [When the daughter of a king comes of age she goes out into the wilds, and at the time she is brought back there is revelry in the form of permissible looting.]

But the town was immeasurably large; for the rows of its houses could not be counted, for if a man standing in the middle of the cattle enclosure shouted, people standing on one side could not hear that there was anyone shouting in the cattle enclosure; for a man standing on the top of a hill would say it was many villages, when in reality it was but one.

The young women returned to Umkxakaza. The people at home wondered when they saw the young women coming to plunder; they shouted, "The king's child is of age." The king selected twenty head of cattle to go and bring her back from the open country. But Umkxakaza said, "I do not see anything." They were taken home again. Then the father selected forty; they went with them to Umkxakaza; Umkxakaza said, "I do not see anything." They went home again. Her father selected a hundred, and said, "Go with them." They went with them to Umkxakaza. Umkxakaza said, "There is the globe of the sun." They returned home.

But all the men belonging to her father's tribe were running with cattle, shouting, "Umkxakaza-wakogingqwayo is of age." When those who had taken the cattle to Umkxakaza returned, they were given two hundred; they went with them; Umkxakaza said: "I still see the sun. Until the sun is darkened according to my father's saying I will not return." They returned to the king. Men ran to the whole nation, taking the cattle from her father's people, and the cattle of her father were collected and all brought to one place. Umkxakaza said, "I still see the sun." They returned home.

An army was levied; it went to spoil foreign nations of their cattle, and came back with them. They were brought to Umkxakaza. She said, "I still see the sun." Another army was levied, and returned with many thousand. But Umkxakaza said she still saw the sun.

Again an army was levied. They set out, and at length saw some cattle feeding in a very large valley. They did not count how many hundred they were. But there were both white and dun, and brown, and black, and red; the horns of some were directed downwards; the horns of others were moveable, others had only one horn. They were of various colors. And there was a very huge beast sitting on the hills overhanging that valley, where were the cattle. The name of the beast was Usilosimapundu. It was so called because there were hills, and elevations of little hills upon it; and so it was named Usilosimapundu. And there were on one part [of its back] many rivers; and on another side great forests; and on another side great precipices; and on another side it was open high land.

And amidst all the trees which were on the beast, there were two trees; they were very much higher than all the rest; they were both named Imidoni. It was they who were the officers of Usilosimapundu.

When Usilosimapundu saw the army driving away the cattle, he said, "Those—those cattle which you are driving away, to whom do they belong?" They replied, "Out on you; let the rugose beast get out of the way." He answered [threateningly] "Eh, eh! Go off with them then."

But as regards the beast there appeared only a mouth and eyes; his face was a rock; and his mouth was very large and broad, but it was red; in some countries which were on his body it was winter; and in others it was early harvest. But all these countries were on him.

They drove off the cattle of Usilosimapundu. As they were going with them near home, it was as if it was going to rain, for neither sun nor heaven appeared; they were concealed by the dust raised by the cattle. At length they said, "Hau! since the sky was clear, whence comes this mist through which we are no longer able to see?" Again they saw that it was occasioned by the dust; they came near home; and they saw it was dark, they could no longer see the cattle; they took them to Umkxakaza. She said, "Behold then the cattle which darken the sun."

So they went home again. On her arrival the umgonqo [a special chamber erected inside the house] was already completed, and the incapa spread on the ground. She entered the umgonqo with the young women and remained there.

And as for all the men who had gone out with the army, there was not one among them who had not killed a bullock; everyone in the town killed his own bullock. But many of the cattle were not skinned because they were so many. The crow skinned for itself; the vultures skinned for themselves; and the dogs skinned for themselves. There was no other smell but that of meat throughout the whole nation. But the cattle of Usilosimapundu were not slaughtered, only those belonging to her father.

She remained uncounted years in the umgonqo. The people no longer knew her; she was known only by the damsels, for they would not allow people to enter the umgonqo; and those who entered the house merely sat down without seeing her, she remaining inside the umgonqo. It happened after a long time all the people said, "Before Umkxakaza comes out, let all the people go to the royal garden." All the people agreed, for they had said, "It will be painful to harvest after she has come out, for beer will be made throughout the whole tribe." It happened when she was about to go out, all the people rose very early in the morning; but at her father's there was beer in the whole village; in one place it was strained; in another it was mixed with malt; in another it was soaking. In the morning all the people set out; there remained herself and her sister only at home. But the royal garden was very far off; when they arose they thought that by arising early they could return early in the evening.

Some time after their departure Umkxakaza and her sister heard the heaven thundering, and the earth moved even in the very house where they were sitting. Umkxakaza said, "Just go out and see, Ubalatusi, what this is, the heaven to thunder when it was so bright?" Ubalatusi went out, and saw a forest standing at the entrance of the village, and she could no longer see where the entrance was. She came into the house, and said, "You will see, child of the king, there is something huge at the gateway; the fence is broken down on one side, and is now just lying on the ground."

As they were speaking, two leaves broke off from the Imidoni, and entered the house where they were sitting. On their arrival they said, "Take a water-vessel, Ubalatusi, and go and fetch water from the river." She took the water-vessel and went to the river. They sat waiting for Ubalatusi. But at the river she dipped water into the water-vessel; when it was full she was unable to leave the place. At length the leaves said, "Go out, Umkxakaza, and look for water here at home." She said, "I am of age, and I do not yet quit the umgonqo." They replied: "We already knew that you were of age; but we say, Go and fetch water." She went and fetched water from another house, and came back with it. The leaves said, "Light a fire." She replied, "I cannot light a fire." They said, "We already knew that you could not light a fire; but we say, Light a fire." She lighted a fire. The leaves said, "Take a cooking-pot and place it on the hearth." Umkxakaza said, "I cannot cook." The leaves replied, "We already knew that you could not cook; but we say, Cook." She put the pot on the fire, and poured water into it. The leaves said, "Go and bring some corn from your corn-basket, and come and pour it into the pot." She went and fetched some corn, and put it on the fire. They sat; the corn was boiled. They said, "Turn up the millstone, and grind the boiled corn." She replied, "I cannot grind, I am the king's child. Look here."—showing them her hands, for her nails were very long. One of the leaves took a knife and said, "Hand hither your hand to me." It cut off the nails with the knife, and said, "Now grind." Umkxakaza said, "I cannot grind; I am the king's child." The leaves said, "We already knew that you could not grind, and that you were the king's child." One of the leaves arose and turned up the millstone, and took the upper stone, and put the boiled corn on it and ground it, and said, "See, that is called grinding." It quitted the stone, and said, "Grind." She ground a large mass of corn. They said, "Take your pot of amasi, and put it here." She took it. They said, "Take a large pot and place it here." She took it. The leaves said, "Wash it." She washed it. The leaves said, "Go and pick out the milk calabash from your calabashes, and bring it here." Umkxakaza said: "Our milk calabash is large; I cannot carry it alone. It is carried by three men." The leaves said, "Go, and we will go with you." They went and fetched the calabash, and came back with it. The leaves said, "Empty it." She brought the pot near, and they poured the amasi into it; they also poured it into the large pot. They took a basket, and placed in it some of the ground corn; they took another basket and placed it on the top of the ground corn. Again they took another basket, and covered the amasi which was in the pot. One of the leaves took a spoon, and put it on the top of the basket; and took the pot and the amasi to Usilosimapundu.

When the leaf came to him, he took the ground corn together with the basket, and together with the basket which covered the ground corn; he opened his mouth, and put it in his stomach, both the two baskets and the ground corn. Again he took the amasi which was covered with the basket, and put it all at once into his stomach, together with the spoon.

The leaf went up again and entered the house. It said, "Take down three spoons." It said, "Look here, here is a spoon; eat, and we will eat with you." Umkxakaza said, "For my part, I do not eat amasi, for I am still under the obligations of puberty." [That is to say, she could not eat amasi until she had completed the puberty rites.] The leaves said, "We already knew that you were of age, and that you did not yet eat amasi; but we say, Eat." Umkxakaza-wakogingqwayo cried, saying: "Hau! O! my mother! who would eat amasi before the ceremonies of puberty are completed?" She said this because when she should eat amasi many oxen would be slaughtered, because it would be given her properly by her father. The leaves said, "Eat immediately." She took a spoon; they ate all the amasi.

The leaves went down to the house which was near the gateway. As soon as they arrived, they took out the pots containing beer, and pots which contained the boiled meal, and mats and vessels; everything that was in the house they took to the gateway. And though the village was large, they took out the things from the whole village, and did not leave anything in a single house. When they were about to take the things from the house of Umkxakaza's mother, Umkxakaza said, "Just leave for me the little pot, it is in the upper part of the house, it is luted down with cowdung; you will see it, it is little." They went and took out the things; but they left the very large pots which contained beer which was strained [i.e., ready to drink], they left too the little pot. They went down to the gateway. Everything that was taken out of the village Usilosimapundu entirely ate up. But he did not chew it, he merely swallowed it.

At length all the things which were in that village were taken out, but Usilosimapundu was not satisfied. The leaves went up and entered the houses where they had left two pots of beer; one of the leaves threw itself into one of the pots, and the other cast itself into the other; and when the two leaves came out of the pots, both pots were empty. They took them and carried them to the gateway to Usilosimapundu. He took them both, and put them in his mouth, and swallowed them.

The mouth of Usilosimapundu moved with rapidity; he said, "Come down now then, Umkxakaza-wakogingqwayo." Umkxakaza went into the house, and took the little pot, and uncovered it; she took out the brazen ornaments for her body, and put them on; she took out her brass pillow; she took out her garment ornamented with brass; and her sleeping mat ornamented with brass; she took her walking stick of brass; she took out her petticoat ornamented with brass beads; she dressed herself and went outside; she stood holding her garment and pillow, resting on her sleeping mat and rod. Usilosimapundu said, "Just turn your back to me, Umkxakaza-wakogingqwayo." She turned her back to him. He said, "Now turn again, Umkxakaza-wakogingqwayo." She turned. Usilosimapundu said, "Just laugh now, Umkxakaza-wakogingqwayo." But Umkxakaza did not wish to laugh, for she was in trouble, because she was leaving her father and mother and her princely position. Usilosimapundu said, "Come down now, Umkxakaza-wakogingqwayo." She went down to Usilosimapundu.

But by her going down it was as if her little sister at the river felt her departure; she started up suddenly with her water-vessel, and went up to the village. And it was as if her mother felt it, for she left all the people behind which were walking with her.

Umkxakaza-wakogingqwayo mounted on Usilosimapundu. As soon as she had mounted, Usilosimapundu speedily ran off. When he was just becoming hidden behind a hill, the sister saw something which was disappearing, but did not know what it was. And the mother too, when it was becoming concealed, saw it; but did not know what it was.

They arrived home both together, the girl and her mother. The mother saw the fence broken down on one side; she said, "What has been here?" Ubalatusi said, "I say it was the beast whose cattle were taken away." The mother said, "Where had you gone?" She said: "I had been sent by the leaves to fetch water with a vessel from the river. On my arrival I was unable to get away again." Her mother said: "Alas! but do you say that my child is still here at home? What was that which became hidden yonder, as I reached that place yonder?" The mother ran, and entered the umgonqo; on her arrival she was not there. She went into another house; she did not find her there. She went into another; she did not find her there. She ran swiftly back again to the men, and said, "Make haste; my child is taken away by the beast who was plundered of his cattle." They said, "Have you seen him?" She replied: "There is something which disappeared behind the hill as I came near home. And my child is no longer there."

They went home, and all armed. They set out on the tracks of the beast; they saw it, they went to it, it having stood still and waited for them. They came to it; it laughed and said, "Do what you are going to do; do it quickly, that I may go; the sun has set." They hurled and hurled their spears. One spear was thrown into a pool; another on a rock; another fell in the grass; another fell in the forest; all were used, without stabbing anything. They had not a single spear left. The beast said, "Go and arm again." They went home to arm. Again they hurled their spears; it happened again as before; they did not stab anything. They said, "At length we are worsted." Usilosimapundu said, "Good-bye."

All the people cried, saying, "Let her come down." He assented, and she came down, on his saying, "Descend then." They kissed her, weeping, and she too weeping. The whole army of her people put Umkxakaza in the middle. But when the beast saw it, he said, "Forsooth they want to go off with her." He turned round, and passed through the midst of them; it was as though something threw Umkxakaza into the air; he turned back with her, and went away with her.

Her mother and sister, and father and brother, followed the beast. They went on, and where the beast rested, there they too rested. In the morning when he awoke, they too went with him. The mother went weeping. But the father and brother and sister were tired and turned back. Her mother accompanied the beast. They went some distance, and rested. Usilosimapundu plucked sugarcane and maize, and gave it to the mother of Umkxakaza. She ate.

In the morning, when Usilosimapundu set out, the mother of Umkxakaza set out. At length she was tired, and asked the beast to allow Umkxakaza to come down that she might see her. He replied, "Get down then, Umkxakaza-wakogingqwayo; get down, that your mother may see you." She got down. They both wept, both she and her mother. Her mother kissed her, saying, "Go in peace, my child."

Usilosimapundu said, "Get up, Umkxakaza." She got up. He went away with her, and put her afar off, where she did not know in what direction the country of her people was. He came to the site of an old village; there was a large tobacco garden in the midst of it; on the border of the garden there was a beautiful cave; its floor was smeared with fat, it was very bright inside; and there was a blanket and sleeping mat there, a pillow, and a vessel of water.

Usilosimapundu said: "Stay here, Umkxakaza-wakogingqwayo. I say, I have spoiled your father excessively; for when you married, he would have got many cattle for you. And I have spoiled him, for you will never see him again, and he will never see you. Stay here then. Your father spoiled me by taking away my many cattle; and now I have spoiled him."

So Usilosimapundu departed. And she remained there alone, with two sugarcanes and four ears of maize which Usilosimapundu had given her. She sat until she lay down to sleep there in the cave. In the morning she awoke and sat in the sun. She took a sugarcane, and broke off a joint, and threw it away. She broke off another, and threw it away; she left one joint only, she peeled it, and ate it. She took the ears of maize, and roasted them; she rubbed off the grain, she rubbed off the grain, and ate the portion which was in the middle, and threw the rest with the sugarcane. [Persons of prestige eat only the middle joints of the cane and the middle kernels of the maize as a sign of their importance, leaving the rest for others or throwing it away.]

At noon, the sun being now bright, she saw something coming in the distance; for it was on the high land; there was there one tree, one tree only. The thing went and sat under the tree. Again she saw it approaching by leaps. Umkxakaza went into the cave. The thing entered the tobacco garden; it went plucking the tobacco. When it saw footprints, it was frightened; it looked, and again plucked the tobacco, and went and put it outside the garden. It entered the cave. When Umkxakaza-wakogingqwayo saw it, she arose and thrust out her hand; it saw the hand, and fled, and left the tobacco. It went and disappeared over a hill. She remained till it was dark.

In the morning Umkxakaza went and sat outside; again she saw two things coming, proceeding by leaps; they went and sat in the shade of the tree. Again they arose and went to the tobacco garden. Umkxakaza went into the cave. On entering the garden they plucked the tobacco; the one which she saw the day before plucked starting and afraid; it said, "O footprints, footprints, whence did they come?" The other said, "Where did you see them?" It replied, "There." They went and put the tobacco outside. Again they entered the cave. Umkxakaza arose and thrust out both hands. When they saw the hands, they fled, and disappeared behind a hill. [As becomes apparent later, these strange creatures are one-sided, resembling half of an animal split lengthwise. Thus each of them has one forefoot and one hind foot. When the girl puts out two hands they assume that there are two individuals in the cave.] On reaching their chief, they told him, saying, "There is something in the chief's cave." The chief of the Amadhlungundhlebe said, "What is it like?" They said, "There are two."

Other Amadhlungundhlebe were summoned; and in the morning they went to the chief's cave. Umkxakaza saw very many coming, and said, "The day has now arrived in which I shall be killed." When they reached the tree they sat in the shade, there in the shade where they sat and took snuff; always when they went to pluck tobacco, they sat there in the shade. They arose and went into the tobacco garden, and plucked tobacco, and put it outside; for the chief of the country of the Amadhlungundhlebe had ordered that his cave should be regularly swept; and he had ordered that all people who went to sweep the cave should begin with plucking tobacco, and take and put it outside the garden. They inquired of the two Amadhlungundhlebe where they had seen it. They replied, "It appeared in the cave." They were told to go and look into the doorway, and see if it was there. They went stealthily, being afraid, and looked in; they were unable to see clearly, for her body glistened. They came back, and said, "It is one, it glistens; we cannot see it clearly." The chief of the Amadhlungundhlebe said, "Let us say all together, 'Is it a man or a beast?' " So all shouted, saying, "Are you a man or a beast?" Umkxakaza replied, "I am a human being." They said, "Come out, that we may see you." Umkxakaza said, "I do not like to come out, for I am a chief's child." The chief sent some Amadhlun-gundhlebe, telling them to run swiftly and fetch a bullock—a large ox —and run back with it. When the ox came it was slaughtered. Then Umkxakaza-wakogingqwayo came out, carrying her blanket and her sleeping mat, and pillow and rod, being girded with her petticoat which was ornamented with brass beads. She put down at the doorway the blanket and pillow, and rested on her rod, and on her sleeping mat she rested too. The chief of the Amadhlungundhlebe said, "Turn your back towards us." Umkxakaza turned her back to them. The chief of the Amadhlungundhlebe said, "Turn round." Umkxakaza turned. The Amadhlungundhlebe said: "Oh! The thing is pretty! But oh, the two legs!" Again they said, "It would be pretty but for the two legs." They told her to go into the cave; and they all went away.

Many Amadhlungundhlebe were called together. In the morning they went to Umkxakaza; they carried a veil through which, if anyone put it on, the body could be seen. They came and sat in the shade and took snuff. When Umkxakaza saw them, she said, "They are now coming to kill me." They came to the tobacco garden, they plucked tobacco, and put it outside the garden. They entered the cave, and told her to come out. She went out; they gave her the veil; she put it on, they looking at her and saying, "Oh, it would be a pretty thing,—but, oh, the two legs!" They said thus because she had two legs and two hands; for they are like,—if an ox of the white man is skinned and divided into two halves, the Amadhlungundhlebe were like one side, there not being another side. The Amadhlungundhlebe danced for Umkxakaza. When they had finished dancing, they went home with her.

When she saw the village of the chief of the Amadhlungundhlebe, she said, "Alas! oh this village; it is large like that of my father." For it was very great. She was placed in a house at the top of the village; many cattle were killed, and she ate meat. She was called the chief's child, for the chief of the Amadhlungundhlebe loved her very much, and called her his child. Umkxakaza lived in the private compound of the chief, there being a public royal compound at the lower part of the village.

At length Umkxakaza was very fat, and unable to walk. When she left the compound, on getting halfway between the two compounds she was tired, and returned to the house. When she rose up there remained a pool of fat. The chief of the Amadhlungundhlebe used to drink the pool of fat which came from Umkxakaza, for the nation of the Amadhlungundhlebe used to eat men. The people said, "O chief, let her be eaten, and the fat melted down, for the fat is being wasted on the ground." But the chief of the Amadhlungundhlebe loved Umkxakaza-wakogingqwayo very much, and said, "If she were eaten, where would I be?" The Amadhlungundhlebe said: "O chief, since she is a mere deformity? Of what use is a thing which can no longer walk, which is wasting the fat of the chief?"

At length the king assented, they having continued to beseech him for three months, saying, "Let the fat of the chief be melted down." So he assented. Many people of the Amadhlungundhlebe were summoned; they went and fetched much firewood; a great hole was dug; a large fire was kindled; a large sherd was taken and put on the fire which was kindled.

It was very bright; there was not a single cloud. At length the sherd was red. When it was very red, Umkxakaza was called; she went with them. When she was at the gateway, she looked; she saw that there were very many people; she sang, saying:

> "Listen, heaven. Attend; mayoya, listen.
> Listen, heaven. It does not thunder with loud thunder.
> It thunders in an undertone. What is it doing?
> It thunders to produce rain and change of season."

All the Amadhlungundhlebe saw a cloud gathering tumultuously. Umkxakaza again sang:

> "Listen, heaven. Attend; mayoya, listen.
> Listen, heaven. It does not thunder with loud thunder.
> It thunders in an undertone. What is it doing?
> It thunders to produce rain and change of season."

The whole heaven became covered with clouds; it thundered terribly; it rained a great rain. It quenched the red hot sherd, and took it and tossed it in the air; it was broken to pieces; the heaven killed the Amadhlungundhlebe who were walking with Umkxakaza, but left her uninjured; it killed some others also; but many remained with their chief.

Again the heaven became clear and bright. The Amadhlungundhlebe said: "Let a fire be kindled immediately, that the sherd may get hot at once; and let Umkxakaza be taken, and raised and placed on the sherd; then she will not be able to sing." The sherd was made hot; at length it was red. They went to fetch her; they lifted her up; when she was at the gateway, she looked up and said,

> "Listen, heaven. Attend; mayoya, listen.
> Listen, heaven. It does not thunder with loud thunder.
> It thunders in an undertone. What is it doing?
> It thunders to produce rain and change of season."

Again the clouds made their appearance. Again Umkxakaza said:

> "Listen, heaven. Attend; mayoya, listen.
> Listen, heaven. It does not thunder with loud thunder.
> It thunders in an undertone. What is it doing?
> It thunders to produce rain and change of season."

It rained and thundered terribly. It killed the chief of the Amadhlungundhlebe, and many other Amadhlungundhlebe; they died; there remained a small number only. The small remnant that remained were afraid, and said, "Let us not touch her again and again; but let us grudge her food, until she gets thin and dies."

Umkxakaza rejoiced because they now gave her but little food. She remained until she was thin; but she was not excessively thin, only much fat had disappeared. She took a basket, and placed in it the things which the king of the Amadhlungundhlebe had given her; she set out when she had put them in the basket; she carried it on her head, and went on her way burdened, for some of the garments were ornamented with brass beads. She journeyed sleeping in the open country, because she feared the Amadhlungundhlebe. She went a long time without eating, until she came among a nation of men. She travelled sleeping among them; sometimes at one village they gave her food; sometimes at another they refused her. She travelled until she was very thin.

It came to pass on a certain day she reached the top of a hill; she saw a very large town; she said, "Alas! O that town; it resembles the town of the Amadhlungundhlebe from which I come; and that was like my father's." She went down, seeing in the houses at the top of the town the smoke of fire; when she came to the gateway, she saw a man sitting in the shade; but his hair was as long as a cannibal's. She merely passed on; but she compared him, saying, "That man resembles my father."

She went to the upper end of the town, seeing that it was her father's. On her arrival her mother was making beer. She sat down under the wall, and said: "Eh! chieftainess! Give me of your beer-porridge." They said, "Good day." She saluted in return. She saw that her mother's head was disarranged, and asked: "But what is the matter at this kraal? And what is the matter with that man at the gateway?" The mother answered, saying, "You, whence do you come?" She replied, "I come from yonder." The mother said: "Oh, indeed, here, princess, death entered. The princess royal of my house went away. That is her father whom you saw at the gateway. Do you not see, too, in what condition I am?" She replied, "When she went away, whither did she go?" She said, "She went with the beast." She answered, "Where did he take her?" The mother said: "She was of age; the cattle of the beast were taken away; for her father had said, before she was of age, when she is of age, cattle should be taken with which to bring her home, which should darken the sun. But her father did not possess so many cattle; they went and took those of the beast." The girl said: "Oh, but, why do you cry then, since your child was treated badly by yourselves alone? Why did you take away the cattle of the beast? Forsooth, you killed her on purpose." The mother replied: "Oh, out upon the contemptible thing! it sees because I have given it my umhhikqo. It now laughs at me as regards my child which is dead. Does there exist a person who would be willing to give anything to the beast? From the day my child departed from the midst of her father's nation, has there been any longer any joy? do we not now just live?" She replied: "Here I am, I Umkxakaza-wakogingqwayo; although you left me, here I am again."

Her mother cried, and the others who were sitting by the door. The father came running, and saying, "Why are you crying?" They said, "Here is Umkxakaza come!" Her father said, "Well, since she has thus come, why do you cry?" Her father sent men, telling them to go to the whole nation, summoning the people and telling them to make beer throughout the land, for Umkxakaza-wakogingqwayo had arrived.

Beer was made throughout the land; the people collected, bringing cattle, and rejoicing because the princess had arrived. Cattle were killed, and her father and mother had a great festival; her father cut his hair, and put on a headring; her mother cut her hair, and put on a topknot. There was rejoicing throughout the land.

And it was rumored among all the nations that the princess had returned to her home, and that she was very beautiful. A chief came from another country to ask Umkxakaza of her father. He refused, saying: "She is just come home; she was carried off by the beast; therefore I do not wish that she should go away; I wish to live and be glad with her." Many chiefs came; but her father gave them all but one answer. At length the chiefs went away, without getting Umkxakaza for a wife.

But there was another chief of a distant country; he had heard that there was that damsel. He sent an old man; he said, "Let him go." The old man went. When he came to the entrance of the town, he turned into a beautiful and glistening frog. The frog entered leaping, and settled on the gatepost. Umkxakaza was playing with others near the gateway. They saw the frog. Umkxakaza said, "Come out and see this beautiful thing." All the people came out, looking at it, and saying, "What a beautiful frog!"

It leapt out of the gateway. When it had gone out Umkxakaza said, "Oh, give me my things; place them all in a basket, and set out with them." They cried and said, "Oh, you are just arrived; and where now are you going again?" She replied, "I am going to follow the frog, to see where it is going." The father selected twenty men, to carry food and her things. They set out, following the frog as it leapt, until they were tired.

Umkxakaza travelled alone with it; and when they were alone, the frog turned into a man. When it turned into a man, Umkxakaza wondered and said, "What was done to you, that you became a frog?" He said, "I just became a frog." She asked, "Where are you taking me?" He replied, "I am taking you home to our chief." They went together till they came to another nation. When they had gone a great distance, she saw a large forest, through which the path went. They reached the forest; but the old man knew that they were now near home. He said, "Make haste; the place to which we are going is afar off." She reached the forest. The old man took her, and quitted the path, and went into the midst of the forest. He said: "Nay! Shall I take so beautiful a thing as this just for another man?" He stood still with her in an open place. But Umkxakaza wondered to see a beautiful place in the forest, as if men dwelt there. The old man said, "Let all beasts come, which come of their own accord." Umkxakaza heard the whole forest in a ferment, and crashing; she was afraid. The old man departed, and went up the forest, and shouted, whistling, and saying: "Fiyo, fiyo! [whistling sound] let all beasts come which come of their own accord."

Umkxakaza stood still and said, "Open, my head, that I may place my things inside." Her head opened, and she put in all her things. Her head again closed, and it was as though it had not opened. But it was fearfully large; for when a man looked at it, it was fearful. She mounted a tree;

when she was on the top, the branches again came together; for she had mounted where the trees were thick and united; she turned aside the branches, and went up; they again closed behind her.

Umkxakaza saw a village in front of the forest. She remained on the tree. Wild beasts came, seeking for prey; they caught hold of the old man; he said: "No; do not eat me; she is no longer here for whom I called you; I no longer see her." They tore him. He scolded them and said, "Leave me alone, my children; I will give you something tomorrow." So they departed. The old man was left, and he set out and went home.

When Umkxakaza saw that he had gone outside the forest, she descended quickly, and ran out of the forest. When the old man was near the village, she saw him, and said, "Wait for me, for we travel together: why do you leave me?" He halted. But he wondered when he saw that her head was large, for Umkxakaza's head used to be small. But the old man was afraid to ask, "What has done this to you?" for he had called the beasts to her.

They entered the village; she stood at the doorway; the old man made obeisance to his chief, saying, "I have found a wife for you. But it is her head that is not right." They entered the house, and sat down. All the people wondered, saying, "Oh, she is beautiful; but the head is like that of an animal." They said, "Let her be sent away." But the chief's sister was there; she objected, saying, "Leave her alone: if she is deformed, what of that?"

But the bridegroom did not love her, and said, "Since I am taking my first wife, and I a king, should I begin with a deformed person?" His sister said: "It is no matter. Let her alone, that she may stay, even though you do not marry her." So she stayed, and the people called her Ukandakulu [Big-head]. There was a gathering of the people to a dance: the chief's sister asked her to go with her to look at the dance. But Ukandakulu said: "Since I am a deformed person, the people will laugh at me, when they drive me away, saying I came to spoil their dance; for if I make my appearance, the young women will leave off dancing, and run away when they see me." She said, "No, we will sit down at a distance if they laugh." Ukandakulu said, "Will not you yourself dance?" She replied, "No, I do not wish to dance, for I wish to remain with you." For the young woman loved her very much, and she loved her in return; therefore she did not like to go to dance, and leave her alone.

They put on their ornaments, and went both to the dance. Those who saw them fled, saying, "There is a deformed thing walking with the princess." They asked, "What is it like?" They said, "Oh, the head is very fearful." And immediately on their arrival at the dancing place, all the people fled; and some warned them off, saying, "Don't come here." They went away, and sat on a hill, until the dance was ended; then they returned and sat down at home. The whole nation exclaimed in wonder, "You should see the thing which the chief has married."

They remained at home many days. On a certain occasion they went to bathe. They bathed, they went out of the water, and stood on the sods of grass, that their body and feet might dry, for they had scraped their feet [with soft sandstone to make them smooth]. The young woman spoke, saying, "Oh, what caused you, Ukandakulu, to be as you are?" She replied, "It is natural to me merely." The young woman said, "Oh, you would be beautiful, child of my parents, Ukandakulu; you are spoilt by your head." Ukandakulu laughed and said, "Open, my head, that my things may come out." Her head opened immediately, her things came out, and she placed them on the ground. Her head closed and was small again. The young woman, on seeing this, threw herself on her, laying hold of her; they laughed immoderately, the saying: "Truly can it be she whom we call Ukandakulu?" They rolled each other in the mud, laughing, and unable to get up. At length they got up and bathed again. As they were standing, the young woman said, "What had you done?" She replied, "I had placed my things in my head." She then related all that was done by the old man. The young woman wondered; and Umkxakaza said, "That, then, was it that made me have a large head." Umkxakaza gave her one of her garments. She put on her own garment which was ornamented with brass beads, and told her, saying, "I am Umkxakaza-wakogingqwayo; that is my name."

They returned home; on their arrival they stood at the doorway. The people went out and said, "There is a young woman come to point out her husband." Others said, "Whose daughter is she?" Those who saw her said, "We do not know whence she comes." They asked, "Is she alone?" They replied, "There are two. But we say one accompanies the other." All the people went out and looked, asking, "Which of you two is come to point out a husband?" For they did not see them distinctly, for they had bent down their heads, looking on the ground. The young woman of the village raised her head, and said, "This is Ukandakulu." All the people wondered, and ran and told the chief, "You should see Ukandakulu when her head is as it is." The chief went out and saw her. He called for many cattle, and many were slaughtered. The whole nation was summoned; it was said, "Let the people assemble; they are going to dance for the queen." All wondered who saw Ukandakulu. Beer was made; the king danced; he loved Umkxakaza very much. His sister said, "How then is it now, since you gave directions that she should be sent away?"

The old man was killed because he was guilty of such practices. At length she returned to her father's with the cattle by which the bridegroom's people declared her his chosen bride. They arrived at her father's; they said, "Umkxakaza-wakogingqwayo is come." The bridegroom's people had many cattle killed for them; they paid her dowry immediately. She was married. The king loved her very much; she became his wife. She reigned prosperously with her husband.

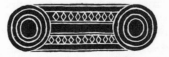

The King's Child and Ubongopa-kamagadhlela

A ZULU EPIC

In the times of long ago, a king took many wives. When one was with child, an ox was born. The king said, "When So-and-So gives birth, the child shall be placed on this ox." The name of the ox was Ubongopa-kamagadhlela. The child was born and put on the ox; he remained on it, and slept on it; he did not put on any blanket; food was taken there to him. When it was dark the gate of the village was closed, and the people went to sleep in the houses; the child slept on the ox.

In the morning the child said:

> "Ubongopa-kamagadhlela,
> Ubongopa-kamagadhlela,
> Awake now; it is time to awake;
> Awake now; it is time to awake."

Ubongopa stood up. He said:

> "Ubongopa-kamagadhlela,
> Ubongopa-kamagadhlela,
> Set out now; it is time to set out;
> Set out now; it is time to set out."

He went to graze; the cattle arrived at their pasture, and grazed. He said:

> "Ubongopa-kamagadhlela,
> Ubongopa-kamagadhlela,
> Return now; it is time to return;
> Return now; it is time to return."

So he returned; the cattle went home again. He said:

> "Ubongopa-kamagadhlela,
> Ubongopa-kamagadhlela,
> Enter the pen; it is time to enter;
> Enter the pen; it is time to enter."

So he entered, and all the cattle entered. His food was brought; he ate it on the top of his ox.

He lived thus until he grew up, being unacquainted with fire, not having worn any garment, and not having trodden on the ground. At length he was a young man.

There came some thieves from another tribe to steal the cattle. They

From Callaway, ibid.

opened the gate and went in, carrying sticks in their hands. The people, being asleep, heard nothing. They beat the cattle; they did not arise; the sticks which they carried were broken; and they went away again by night.

In the morning he said, "Awake, Ubongopa-kamagadhlela." He awoke. He said, "Go to graze." He went; and all the cattle went. He told them to graze; and all grazed; they went home again at noon. His food was brought, and he ate it on the ox. He told them to go, and they went; he told them to eat, and they ate; he told them to return, and they returned.

In the evening the gateway was closed; the people shut themselves up in their houses, and slept. The thieves came and opened the gateway, carrying sticks in their arms; they beat the cattle; they did not get up; the sticks broke. They went away again by night. They conversed as they were going, saying, "What is the matter with these cattle, that they do not get up?" They said, "Let us cut a great many sticks."

On the morning of the third day (they did not see a person on the ox), he told them to get up and go to graze. Ubongopa-kamagadhlela went; the cattle grazed. He told them to return on the third day. His food was brought; he ate it on the top of the ox, on Ubongopa. He told them to go and graze; they went: he told them to return home; they returned. It was dark; the thieves came by night; they beat the cattle; they did not awake; the sticks broke; the cattle did not get up. [The thieves] wrenched their tails; they did not get up. They went away in the night. They spoke passionately, saying, "Let us each cut two bundles of sticks, that when one bundle is broken, we may take the other." They said, "We never saw such a thing as this."

On the night of the fourth day, they brought the bundles by going and returning twice, and placed them outside the village. The gateway was shut, and the people slept. The thieves came by night; they opened the gate and went in; they beat the cattle; their sticks broke; the first bundles were used; they went and took the others, and went with them into the kraal; they beat the cattle; the sticks broke; and the thieves went away.

In the morning he told the cattle to go and graze on the fifth day. He did not tell the people that thieves came by night to steal the cattle; it was a matter known only to himself. They went; he told them to graze, and they grazed; he told them to return, and they returned home. His food was brought, and he ate. The people talked; his father said, "My child, you are passionate; you have beaten the cattle with many stripes." They saw that they were swollen, having been beaten by the thieves by night; and thought he had beaten them.

The next night the thieves came again; they opened the gateway and went in; they beat the cattle, they did not awake; their sticks broke, each man had but one left. One of the thieves saw him, and said, "There is the fellow who refuses to allow the cattle to move." They said to him, "Speak." He spoke and said:

> "Ubongopa-kamagadhlela,
> Ubongopa-kamagadhlela,
> Awake now; it is time to awake;
> Awake now; it is time to awake;
> Do you not see we are killed
> By thieves of another tribe?"

Ubongopa-kamagadhlela awoke and stood up. He said:

> "Ubongopa-kamagadhlela,
> Ubongopa-kamagadhlela,
> Go now; it is time to go;
> Go now; it is time to go;
> Do you not see we are killed
> By thieves of another tribe?"

Ubongopa went, and all the cattle. The calves came out of the house; they freed themselves from the cords by which they were tied; they opened the door, and followed their mothers. The people were asleep. They stood still at the gateway. The thieves said, "Speak, boy. You are [as good as] stabbed." He replied, "You cannot stab me," and said:

> "Ubongopa-kamagadhlela,
> Ubongopa-kamagadhlela,
> Go now; it is time to go;
> Go now; it is time to go;
> Do you not see we are killed
> By thieves of another tribe?"

Ubongopa-kamagadhlela went.

A man of the village from which the cattle had been driven went out of the house; he said, "The king [that is, the king's son] is of age, for he has aroused the cattle by night." He called his father; he said, "Let food be cooked; the king, the father of Ubongopa, is of age." The whole tribe of his father made beer. The sun declined, it set, it became dark. The people looked for him, and cried, saying: "What has devoured the child during the night? He set out with the cattle and the calves from the houses."

As they went the boy said:

> "Ubongopa-kamagadhlela,
> Ubongopa-kamagadhlela,
> Stand still now; it is time to stand still;
> Stand still now; it is time to stand still;
> Do you not see we are killed
> By thieves of another tribe?"

They stood still. They said, "Speak. You are stabbed." He said, "You cannot stab me." They said, "What are you?" He replied, "I am nothing." They said: "What do you boast of? Do you so speak because you would not let us take the chief's cattle, until we lost a whole month through you?" He said:

> "Ubongopa-kamagadhlela,
> Ubongopa-kamagadhlela,
> Go now; it is time to go;
> Go now; it is time to go;
> Do you not see we are killed
> By thieves of another tribe?"

So they went.

One thief was sent forward. When he came to the chief, he said: "We have lifted some cattle, they are under magical power; there is a man that lies on an ox, on Ubongopa-kamagadhlela." The chief told him to return and tell them to hasten with the cattle to him. They travelled rapidly; they appeared on a ridge; the thief said: "There they are; there is a boy on a white ox; he has magical power; he tells them to halt, and they halt." The chief said: "When he comes, the ox, by which he practices his magic, shall be killed. And although he does not rest on the ground, he shall be made to rest on it." They came to the open space in front of the village, and halted. The chief told them to go on. The men replied, "The boy will not permit them; they move at his word." He commanded him to speak. He said:

> "Ubongopa-kamagadhlela,
> Ubongopa-kamagadhlela,
> Go now; it is time to go;
> Go now; it is time to go;
> Do you not see we are killed
> By thieves of another tribe?"

Ubongopa went on, and the cattle too went on. He said:

> "Ubongopa-kamagadhlela,
> Ubongopa-kamagadhlela,
> Go into the pen now; it is time for going in;
> Go into the pen now; it is time for going in;
> Do you not see we are killed
> By thieves of another tribe?"

So he went into the pen.

They said, "Come down, boy." He replied: "I do not get off; I do not walk on the ground; I remain on the ox; from the time of my birth I have never felt the ground." The chief said, "Come down." He said, "I cannot." He said, "Speak, boy." He said:

"Ubongopa-kamagadhlela,
Ubongopa-kamagadhlela,
Let me get down; it is time for getting down;
Let me get down; it is time for getting down;
Do you not see we are killed
By thieves of another tribe?"

He got down. They told him to go into the house. He said, "I cannot live in a house." They said, "Go into the house." He said, "I do not go." They said, "What is the matter with you?" They took him to the house of a man who was dead, which was already falling into ruins, and the stars could be seen through its roof. They told him to go in. He went into the house. They gave him food. He said, "I do not understand food which is eaten on the ground." They said, "What are you?" The food was taken away.

He spat; the spittle boiled up and said, "Chief, thou child of the greatest, thou mysterious one who art as big as the mountains." It filled the house. It thundered and rained exceedingly; all the houses leaked, even those which had never leaked before. The people shouted, saying, "The chief is wet." The chief said, "The boy is already dead, since I am in this state, for I never saw a drop enter my house before." He said, "Since the boy was sitting outside, he no longer lives; he is dead." The heaven cleared. Some men were sent to go and see after him. When they arrived at his house, it was dry. They said: "How is it that it is dry in the boy's house? He is a boy possessed of magical powers. We saw that at the first. Let his ox be killed, that we may see if these tricks will then be done which we now witness."

All the people were summoned. A man took an assagai and entered the cattle pen. The boy was called; they said to him, "Let the ox be killed." He replied, "I shall die if that ox dies." They said, "What are you?" They gave one of the thieves the assagai; he stabbed at the ox with the assagai; but it pierced the thief. They said, "Speak, boy, that the ox may die." He said:

"Ubongopa-kamagadhlela,
Ubongopa-kamagadhlela,
Die now; it is time to die;
Die now; it is time to die;
Do you not see we are killed
By thieves of another tribe?"

The assagai pierced Ubongopa; he fell down. They took knives to skin him. A man divided the skin; he cut himself. They said, "Speak, boy. You are as good as stabbed." He said:

"Ubongopa-kamagadhlela,
Ubongopa-kamagadhlela,
Be skinned now; it is time to be skinned;

> Be skinned now; it is time to be skinned;
> Do you not see we are killed
> By thieves of another tribe?"

They accomplished the skinning.

The men said, "Light a large fire." The thieves said: "Let us just omit for a time to roast the ox; let us first wash our bodies to get rid of the bad omen. This bullock had magical properties; all matters connected with it differ from those of other cattle." At last they cut off the end of the tail; a man cut himself. They said, "Speak, boy. You are as good as stabbed." He said:

> "Ubongopa-kamagadhlela,
> Ubongopa-kamagadhlela,
> Let your tail be cut off; it is time to have it cut off;
> Let your tail be cut off; it is time to have it cut off;
> Do you not see we are killed
> By thieves of another tribe?"

They took the vessels for the blood, they dipped out from the carcass, and poured it into the vessels; they cut off the limbs, and hung up the bullock in the cattle kraal; the boys cut off slices, and went and set them aside for themselves. The chief called the people, and said, "Go and bathe, and eat it after you come back." All the people went.

When they were gone, the boy took the skin, and spread it on the ground; he placed the head on it; he took the ribs and put them in their place; he took one side, and placed it in its place; he took a shoulder, and put it in its place; he took a leg, and put it in its place; he took the intestines, and put them in their place; he took the liver, and put it in its place; he took the lungs, and put them in their place; he placed the paunch in its place; he took the contents of the paunch, and returned them to their place; he took the tail, and put it in its place; he took the blood, and poured it into its place; he wrapped all up with the skin, and said:

> "Ubongopa-kamagadhlela,
> Ubongopa-kamagadhlela,
> Arise now; it is time to arise;
> Arise now; it is time to arise;
> Do you not see we are killed
> By thieves of another tribe?"

His breath came back again and entered into him; he looked up. The boy said:

> "Ubongopa-kamagadhlela,
> Ubongopa-kamagadhlela,
> Stand up now; it is time to stand;

Stand up now; it is time to stand;
Do you not see we are killed
By thieves of another tribe?"

So he stood up. The boy said:

"Ubongopa-kamagadhlela,
Ubongopa-kamagadhlela,
Let me mount; it is time to mount;
Let me mount; it is time to mount;
Do you not see we are killed
By thieves of another tribe?"

He mounted the ox, and said:

"Ubongopa-kamagadhlela,
Ubongopa-kamagadhlela,
Go now; it is time to go;
Go now; it is time to go;
Do you not see we are killed
By thieves of another tribe?"

Ubongopa set out. And the houses and gardens, and cattle pen, and all the things of that village, followed him!

The men went up from the river. One exclaimed: "See, ye men, a prodigy! The whole country is going!" The chief summoned the whole tribe, and said, "Follow the boy, and let him be killed." He went rapidly; but when he heard that they were near him, he said:

"Ubongopa-kamagadhlela,
Ubongopa-kamagadhlela,
Stand still now; it is the time for standing still;
Stand still now; it is the time for standing still;
Do you not see we are killed
By thieves of another tribe?"

The cattle stood still. They shouted to him, saying: "Stand still in that very place, that we may kill you. For a long time you have practiced magic." They said, "Come down, that we may kill you." He descended to the ground. They told him to stand apart from the cattle, that the assagais might not pierce them. They hurled their assagais; they did not reach him, but struck the ground. He jeered them, saying, "Why what is this, you being men and so many too, the assagais do not reach me, but strike the ground?" One of the soldiers, laughing at them, said, "Why are you worsted by a boy, for the assagais strike the ground, and do not reach him?" Some gave in. He said, "Give me too an assagai, that I may make a stab at you." They refused, and said, "We are not yet worsted." They hurled their assagais at him; they struck the ground.

They picked them up, and hurled them at him; they did not strike him. They said, "We are worsted: do you try also."

They offered him many assagais; he refused them, and asked for one only. They gave him one. He said, "May I fling at you?" They laughed. He spat on the ground; the spittle fizzed, it said, "Chief, all hail, thou who art as big as the mountains." He said, "May I stab you?" They laughed and said, "Do so, that we may see." He hurled the assagai at their chief. They all fell down dead.

He took the haft of the assagai and smote their chief; he arose, and they all arose with him. They shouted to him, saying, "Stand where you are, that we may stab you." He laughed at them, and said, "Where have you already been?" They said, "We are just come." He said, "You were all dead." They said, "Bid the sun farewell." Others hurled many assagais at him; they struck the ground. They picked them up, and again hurled many of them at him; they struck the ground. The men laughed at them, and said, "Give us the assagais, that we may kill him." They hurled many assagais; they struck the ground. The men picked them up.

The chief said, "Get out of the way for me, that I may stab him." The chief hurled an assagai; it stuck in the ground. He said: "I am conquered, boy. Do you just try, that we may see." He said, "Give me an assagai, that I too may hurl it." They offered him many assagais. He refused them, and said, "I wish for one." They gave him one. He spat on the ground; the spittle said, "Chief, all hail! thou mysterious one, thou child of the greatest." He said, "May I stab you?" They laughed and said, "Do it, that we may see." He hurled the assagai; he struck their chief. He died, together with all his people.

He took an assagai and smote the people. The people arose, the chief remained still dead. They said: "We are now your people. We will now go with you."

They passed through another tribe. The people gave an alarm, and shouted: "Go and kill. There is a man going away with people." The chief called them, and ordered them to be killed. They went to them. They told him to come down from the ox. He replied, "I do not walk on the ground." The thieves told them, saying, "He killed us." They said, "But us he will not conquer." They hurled assagais at him; they struck the ground. One of the soldiers laughed at them, and said, "Make way for us, that we may stab him." They hurled their assagais; they struck the ground. They collected them. The chief said, "Hand them to me, that I may kill him." The people said, "We will praise you when you have killed him." He said, "I am very strong." He hurled the assagais; he was unable to kill him.

He said, "Do you try, boy, that I may see." He said, "Give me an assagai." He spat; the spittle remained on the ground and fizzed, and said, "Hail, chief, thou child of the greatest." They gave him assagais; he refused them, and took but one; he said, "May I hurl at you?" He threw the assagai at their chief. They all died. He took the assagai, and smote their chief; he arose, and all rose with him.

He said, "Will you yet again attack me?" They said, "For our part, we will still make another trial on you." They hurled the assagais; they struck the ground. They collected them, and threw them; they struck the ground. He asked for an assagai, and said, "Are you conquered?" They said, "We are." They gave him an assagai: he stabbed the chief; they all died. He took the assagai and struck one man; they all arose; the chief remained dead. They said, "We are now your people."

He sent some men to his father to tell him that Ubongopa-kamagadhlela was coming. His father cried, saying, "Where did you see him?" They said, "He has killed many people, and is coming with many cattle." His father told the men to go back again. On their arrival they told him his father refused to believe them. A few cattle were selected, and one bullock of a peculiar color was placed among them. For he said his father would see that he was still living by that bullock which belonged to his village.

His father summoned the nation, and commanded them to make beer. He said, "The chief is coming back." The people said it could not be true. He said, "Go and look at the bullock belonging to our village, which has come back." The people saw it, and said, "It is the truth." They said, "Let a young woman be found, that on his arrival he may find her already here." They sought for a daughter of Ubungani, the son of Umakulukulu.

Those who were sent by his father reached the top of a hill, and said, "Your father tells you to make haste." The men and the cattle went rapidly. They appeared on a hill near their home. They placed Ubongopa-kamagadhlela in front: the cattle went rapidly, and reached the gateway. The people went out to see. His father and mother rejoiced. He said:

> "Ubongopa-kamagadhlela,
> Ubongopa-kamagadhlela,
> Go in now; it is time to go in;
> Go in now; it is time to go in."

The cattle entered the enclosure.

Another village was built. He said, "I do not love the young woman, because she goes on the ground." The young woman departed. He said, "I will live on the back of Ubongopa-kamagadhlela till my death." So they said, "Stay then there on his back."

He herded the cattle of his people. And continued to practice the enchantments which he practiced from his childhood.

Uncama-ngamanzi-egudu's Journey to the Other World

A ZULU TALE

> The theme of the hunter or traveller who fol-
> lows a strange trail or who descends into an
> animal burrow and finds himself, in time, in the
> abode of spirit-animals or demons, or in the
> dwelling place of the dead ancestors is wide-
> spread in African tradition. Among some peo-
> ples the stories are told as spine-tingling adven-
> tures and are understood to be something that
> is *said* to have happened and which doesn't
> necessarily have to be believed. Among others
> such stories are considered to be accounts of
> events that really occurred, and to be consis-
> tent with the reality of a seen and an unseen
> world. The story of Uncama is presented as a
> true tale.

Uncama dug a mealie [millet] garden; when the mealies had begun
to get ripe, a porcupine entered it, and continually wasted it; and he
continually rose early, and arrived when the porcupine had devoured
his mealies. At length he waited for a day on which there was abundance of dew. On the day he saw much dew he arose and said, "Today
then I can follow it well, if it has eaten in the garden, for where it has
gone the dew will be brushed off. At length I may discover where it has
gone into its hole." Sure enough then he took his weapons, and went
out to the garden; it had eaten his mealies; he followed it by the trail,
it being evident where it had gone, the dew being brushed off. He went
on and on, until he saw where it had gone into a hole. And he too went
in, without inquiring a moment, saying, "Since it has gone in here, and
I have no dog, what can I do?" Because he was angry that the porcupine
had wasted his food, he went in, saying, "I will go till I reach it, and kill
it." He went in with his weapons. He went on and on, till he came to
a pool; he thought it was deep water; he looked carefully, until he saw
that it was only a pool. He went by the edge, and passed on. It was dark
in the hole, he not seeing clearly; at length his eyes became accustomed
to the hole, and he saw well. At length he lay down to sleep before he
had reached anywhere; and in the morning he awoke and set out again.
He went and slept until at length he came to a river; he crossed it and
went forward. He now no longer went forward because he still saw the
footprints of the porcupine; he now went because the hole was the same
as that by which he entered; he persevered, saying, "I shall at length
arrive at the end of the hole, whereupon I shall be satisfied."
    At length in front he saw it began to get light; he heard dogs baying,
and children crying; he passed on; he came upon a village; he saw

From Callaway, ibid.

smoke rising, and said: "Hau! what place is this? I said, 'I am following the porcupine'; I am come to a dwelling." Whereupon he returned, walking backwards, and returning on his path, and said: "Let me not go to these people, for I do not know them; perhaps they will kill me." He saw a great country. He fled, and went day and night, saying, "Perhaps they have seen me." At length he crossed that river which he crossed whilst he was pursuing the porcupine; he passed the pool which he passed at first; at length he went out of the hole.

He wondered on coming out; for at the place from which he came, he saw all things resembled those which are above, mountains, precipices, and rivers. So he went home, and came to his own house. He went in and asked his wife for a mat. His wife looked at him; she smote her hands and cried; the people started; they hurried in and asked, "What is it?" She said: "Behold Uncama is come!" The men wondered, and again shouted the funeral dirge. The woman said, "Your mat, and your blanket, and your kilt, and your pillow, and your vessels, everything I have buried, saying, you were dead; your blankets and mats I burnt."

So he told the tale, and said: "I am come from a distance; I am come from the men who live underground. I had followed a porcupine; I came to a village; I heard dogs baying, and children crying; I saw people moving backwards and forwards, and smoke rising. And so I came back again. I was afraid, thinking they would kill me. It is because I feared and returned that you see me this day."

That man was a very little whiskered man, who was hairy all over; his whole body was covered with hair; very ugly; he had many gaps in his mouth, his teeth being no longer complete. And I too know him. I saw him when I was a boy. It was continually said, "There is the man who went to the underground people." We were afraid to go into an antbear's hole from hearing that tale, to wit, "He went till he reached the underground people."

The Man Who Threw Away His Bread

A ZULU TALE

The tale of a man who was going on a journey carrying bread with him; he set out, having already eaten at home; and not knowing how to allowance himself by taking bread which was equal to his consumption, he took a large quantity of bread; he thought he should eat it all. But by the way he ate, until he could eat no more. He could not tell what to do with it. He did not say to himself: "Let me carry it; perhaps in front there is hunger, and I shall want food; perhaps I may meet a man who is hungry." There was no such thought as that. But through

From Callaway, ibid.

being satisfied, the thought of taking care of that bread was hidden; he did not wish to carry it, because he was then full; he saw one thing only which would enable him to go easily. He threw the bread on the lower side of the path, and so went on no longer burdened. He did not return by that path for many days. Mice took the bread, and ate it all up.

It came to pass when the land died, it being killed by famine, as he was going by that way, going and digging up roots (for there was no corn left; roots only were now eaten), the path made him remember the bread. He saw it still there; a year was as it were a day of yesterday. He was at once summoned by the place by merely seeing it, and said, "This is the very place where I threw away my bread." He arrived at the place; he saw where the bread had fallen; he said, "It fell yonder." He ran to find it. But he did not find it. He began to look earnestly in the long grass, for it was very thick; he searched thinking he should fall in with it, as he was feeling with his hands in the thick grass; until some time had elapsed. He rose up, and thought, saying: "Hau! What happened after I threw away the bread? For I say, I do not yet forget the place where I threw it. No, surely; there is no other; it is this very place." He stooped down and searched. For whilst he is thus seeking he has gained strength, and is now strong through knowing, to wit, "Though I am hungry, my hunger will end; I may find my bread." At length he was confused, he went up again to the path, he found the place where he first began to stand, he said, "I passed over all this place before I threw it away." For where he threw it away, there was an ant heap; he saw by that, and said, "Ah! when I was here, I did thus!" He said this, imitating with his arm; the arm goes in the direction in which he threw the bread. And now he runs quickly, following the direction of the arm. He came to the place, and at once felt about; he did not find the bread. He went back again, and said: "Hau! what has become of it? since I threw it exactly here; for no man saw me, I being quite alone." He ran. At length the time for digging roots had passed away; he went home without anything; he dug no roots. He now became faint again, because he had not found the bread.

And that man is still living, yonder by the sea. The man told the tale when the country was at peace, and the famine at an end. It was a cause of laughter that conduct of his, to all who heard it, and they said: "So-and-so, sure enough famine makes a man dark-eyed. Did you ever see bread, which was thrown away one year, found in another, still good to eat?" He said: "Sirs, famine does not make a man clever. I thought I was seeking wisely, and should find it. Famine takes away wisdom. And for my part, through my hunger, I believed in truth that I should find it; for I was alone, there being no man with me. But in fact that was the means of increasing my want, until I was nearly dead."

How the Zulu Experience Sympathy Through the Navel

AS DESCRIBED BY A ZULU, UMPENGULA MBANDA

The sympathy which men feel with each other through the navel is this: When a child, who is now grown, but is not yet called a boy or a girl, being too young for that, will not be taken by many people, but refuses to go to them, being sociable with its father and mother and the people of their household: but when there comes one who is a blood-relation, and calls the child, the parents say, "We shall now see, for he will not be taken by other people." When that blood-relation calls the child to kiss it, it jumps up, and goes to him without fear; so he kisses it, and places it in his lap. So the parents say, "Oh, truly! the child knows a blood-relation by the navel, that it must not object to him; he is one of us." This is what we mean by "to know by the navel."

Again, it happens with an elder person, when he has gone to a distant country, and has no acquaintance with any man there, he may be overtaken by night, and say, "Oh, since the sun has now set, let me not pass this village, for the sun has really set." He goes to it, being unacquainted with anyone, going there just to pass the night, and in the morning pass on to where he is going. When he comes to it he salutes the householder and enters and sits down; he is saluted in return, being like a stranger in the village; the eyes having no sympathy. They ask him whence he comes; he tells them. They give him food, if there is any; they treat him kindly, as if he belonged to them; they refuse him nothing. He eats and is satisfied; he loses all reserve; they ask each other of the news; they proceed with the news till they come to birth, and ask, "What is your father's name in such a nation?" mentioning the surname of the nation. He gives the name of his father. He who inquires says, "You are the son of So-and-So, the son of So-and-So," naming his grandfather. The man who is asked starts and asks, "Oh, how do you know my grandfather?" And he hears him say in reply, "Why do you say I ought not to know So-and-So, since I am the son of So-and-So, the son of So-and-So?" The grandfather of both of them is one. Then both begin to cry. So the people say: "A man knows one of his blood-relations by

From Callaway, ibid.

the navel. We have been wondering at the treatment of the man by So-and-So. We thought he knew him; yet he did not know him; he sympathized with him by the navel only."

Such, then, is the case of the navel. We do not hear from the old men that to sympathize by the navel is this or that, or how the navel acts that a man should know by it that such a man is his relation, because he feels his navel acting thus. We have not attained to such an understanding of what is said about it. But there is no doubt about it; it is confirmed constantly.

Further: among black men there is a desolation of the country; and parents separate from their children when quite young; one child is taken by a person who is going about objectless, not knowing whither he is going; but he knows his father's name and the family name also. They are scattered, and the children are provided for in different places; and each thinks that the child of his father is dead, saying thus because neither knows where the other is.

It happens because a man continually quits one place after another as he tires of them, he at length comes to a place where a child of his father is received into the household; if it is a girl, he may begin to court her, regarding her as any other girl, for her name which she received from her father has become lost; it is concealed because they suppose that then her people will be unable to find her; and the name of her father is no longer mentioned, by calling her the daughter of her own father; but it is now said, "She is the daughter of So-and-So," naming the person who has taken charge of her. But at length the woman says, calling him by the name he has received from those with whom he has lived, "So-and-So, I cannot associate with you; it is as though you were my brother; I do not think of it for a moment." The other perseveres, saying: "Not at all! you refuse me, that is all. I am of such a place. You merely refuse me. Don't hide your feelings by such an excuse." So they separate through the woman's refusal.

At length in the course of time when the man is getting accustomed to the place, and has a fellow feeling with the people of the village, they begin to ask each other respecting the news; and at length those with whom he is on good terms, not knowing that the man is one with the woman, thinking they are merely telling a matter of history to one whom they love, say: "That child is the daughter of So-and-So; he is her father. But the name of her father was lost, in order that we may get cattle by her." So, then, he hears that she is his sister; he does not start, but merely turns away their attention from himself; at length he communicates with the woman, and inquires thoroughly of her, saying, "As you are living here, are you acquainted with your own people?" If she knows them, she replies, "I know them." He asks her name, saying: "The name by which you are now called, do you understand it? Where did you receive it?" She says, "It is the name of the place where I have been taken care of." The other inquires the name she received from her father, saying, "What name did your father give you?" She says, "My name is So-and-So." He asks the names of all her people; she mentions those she knows; she is silent respecting those she does not know. He asks also as regards himself, saying, "Do you know So-and-So?" She replies, "I know him." He asks, "Could you point him out now, if you met with him?" She says: "I do not know; for growth changes a man." At the end of her words she hears the man rejoicing, and praising the Amatongo [the ancestral spirits] of their people; and at last he reveals himself, saying: "Behold, here I am, daughter of my father. I say the Itongo [spirit] of our house is still mighty. You see I was nearly committing uncleanness. All the time you are my father's child forsooth."

Both weep, and say: "It is the navel which has brought about such a thing as this. We had no knowledge of each other." At length the real facts of the case are related by those who have taken charge of her. When her brother first claims her, they endeavor to conceal her; but they are not able to do so through the knowledge the children have of each other, and by their knowledge of the names of their people, which they do not themselves know. They are unable to conceal her, and so they demand repayment for having brought her up; he gives it them, and his sister returns to him. That, too, is called a case of the navel.

Further, there is a matter which resembles this of the navel, but this is something which is really known, but it is indistinct through the desolation of the country.

It happened when our family was scattered when we lived with the Zulus, in consequence of Udingane having been unable to contend in battle with the Dutch, we had two uncles who were younger than our father; the youngest was called Umagushu. When the country was about to be desolated, he married the sister of the Manjanjas, the children of Unthlambela. When they had been married, and his wife Umanjonga had been with him now four months, we were scattered from that country, and came here into the country of the white man. But in the way she deserted, and returned to her own people; when she went away she was already beautiful [pregnant], but they were not yet sure about it. So she was lost; her husband continually looked for her, but saw no more of her; for at that time people were in confusion like maggots in the path, and did not know whither they were going.

So we came here into the country of the white man; and forsooth she too came, to a different place, with which we were not acquainted. We continually talked about her, saying, "Where could the wife of our uncle, who left us pregnant, have gone?" We asked about her whilst remaining at home. Until at length, when we too had grown up, we met with her, hearing her mentioned by the name by which we used to call her. We at once inquired, "Since you are really living, what became of the child with which you were pregnant when you went away?" She replied, "I miscarried." So we were satisfied, saying, "Well, then, since she miscarried, what have we to say to it?"

There was there a girl which when we saw we wondered, seeing that she resembled one of our own children; in fact, when we looked on her, we saw that she was one of our own. But we had no evidence, for it was said the child of our uncle died; but the navel felt her, and would not allow us to be satisfied; when we were not looking on her, we were satisfied; but when we looked on her, we fully believed that she was one of us. At length in time she married, being still concealed. When at her marriage she was asked the name of her father, she replied, "My father is Umagushu." So she was called Umamagushu at the kraal into which she married. We heard the name; and even now the matter is not settled; we know that she is our child by the navel, which causes us to have a sympathy with her.

Some Zulu Riddles

THE QUESTIONS

Guess you: a cow which never lies down. When it lies down it lies down forever; it will never rise up again. Its lying down is death. It is a very celebrated cow, and one which gives much milk; its children are preserved by it. The owner possesses only one; he does not want another; he only requires one.

Guess you: a pumpkin plant; it is single, and has many branches; it may be hundreds; it bears many thousand pumpkins on its branches; if you follow the branches, you will find a pumpkin everywhere; you will find pumpkins everywhere. You cannot count the pumpkins of one branch; you can never die of famine; you can go plucking and eat-

THE EXPLANATIONS

We mean a house by the cow which gives much milk; the milk is the joy a house affords those who live beneath it, for it remains a long time, the people being preserved, and not continually building. But when it falls it has fallen forever; it never rises up again.

A village and the paths which pass from it are the branches, which bear fruit; for there is no path without a village; all paths quit homesteads, and go to homesteads. There is no path which does not lead to a homestead. The pumpkins are villages from which the paths go out.

From Callaway, ibid.

ing; and you will not carry food for your journey through being afraid that you will find no food where you are going. No; you can eat and leave, knowing that by following the branches you will continually find another pumpkin in front; and so it comes to pass. Its branches spread out over the whole country, but the plant is one, from which springs many branches. And each man pursues his own branch, and all pluck pumpkins from the branches.

Guess you: a man who does not lie down; even when it is morning he is standing, he not having lain down.

A pillar does not lie down, for it stands constantly and watches the house. If the pillar lies down, the house may fall. But when one says "a man," he entangles the matter, that the thoughts of the men may not reach the things at once; but continually have their thoughts running on men in accordance with the word, man. When they cannot tell, one replies: "Why do you not say that the pillar is a man, since you see it upholding so great a house as this? But it does not fall."

Guess you: a man who does not move; although the wind blows furiously, he just stands erect; the wind throws down trees and houses, and much injury is done; but he is just as if the sky was perfectly calm, and does not move in the least.

The ear. One says to them when they cannot tell: "Whoever saw the ear of a man move, it being moved by the wind? We see trees and grass and houses move; but not the ear; the man only moves; if he is carried away by the wind, the ear is not carried away, it is he who is carried away; or if he falls, it still stands erect; or if he runs away, it still stands erect."

Guess you: some men who are many and form a row; they dance the wedding dance, adorned in white hip-dresses.

The teeth. We call them men who form a row, for the teeth stand like men who are made ready for a wedding-dance, that they may dance well. When we say, they are "adorned with white hip-dresses," we put that in, that people may not at once think of teeth, but be drawn away from them by thinking, "It is men who put on white hip-dresses," and continually have their thoughts fixed on men; for since white hip-dresses are put on by men when they are going to a wedding to dance, and to set men in order, they say continually, "The men of the riddle are men." And the man who is making them guess says, "But how can they dance if their bodies touch?" He continually draws them away by words from that which they say. He does not merely deny that they are right by saying: "No; it is not that. The riddle is not explained in that way." He draws them away by words, and they really believe that they see that they are not near the meaning of the riddle. At length he says: "Do you not see the teeth; their order like that of men; the white hip-dresses do you not see they mean the teeth?" They say, "You have beaten us."

Guess you: a man who lives in the midst of enemies every day, where raids are made without ceasing; and he is alarmed when the army sets out, knowing that he is then in the midst of death; he has no forest to which he can escape. He escapes only by the enemy retiring. He then eats food, saying: "Ah! escaped this time! I did not think that I could escape from the midst of the army." He has no children, because he lives in the midst of enemies, saying, "No; it is well that I should live by myself, and then when an alarm is given, I may be ready to escape."

The tongue is a man which is in affliction because it is in the midst of enemies; the teeth are the enemy; for when the teeth are eating, the tongue is often injured whilst they are fighting with the food, that they may grind it. The tongue, then, is not happy, for when the teeth are chewing food, the tongue continually moves from side to side between the teeth, and is on its guard when the food is killed; for the food is constantly killed by the teeth; but the tongue is not killed by them, for it is known, it is a man of that place; but it continually meets with an

Guess you: a man who does not lie down at night; he lies down in the morning until the sun sets; he then awakes, and works all night; he does not work by day; he is not seen when he works.

Guess you: some men who are walking, being ten in number; if there is one over the ten, these ten men do not go; they say, "We cannot go, for here is a prodigy." These men wonder exceedingly; they are slow in settling the dispute, saying, "How is it that our number is over ten, for formerly we did not exceed ten?" They have no love for the one over the ten.

Guess you: a man whom men do not like to laugh, for it is known that his laughter is a very great

accident, for there is fighting in the place where it dwells; it is happy before the food is eaten; but when the food is being eaten, it knows that it is in the midst of danger, and is about to be injured, without having had any charge made against it; it dies because the battle is fought in its presence. There, then, is the man who is in the midst of enemies, the tongue.

The closing poles of the cattle pen. Their work by night is to watch the cattle by closing the gateway; they are close together that the cattle may not find a place of escape; though one try to get out it may be unable to do so through the strength of the bars; and when it is morning the cattle have not got out; in the morning they go out because the gateway is opened for them, and so the closing poles lie on the ground.

The fingers. Their proper number is only ten; they are matched, going in pairs. [That is, the index and middle fingers go together, ring and little fingers go together, as do the thumbs.] Therefore, if there is a supernumerary finger, they are no longer fit either to go together in pairs or to count with; their counting is bad; there is no argument, but only difference. This is what we mean when we say they are slow in settling the dispute, that is, if it could be done without pain the supernumerary finger could be taken off with a word, truly it would be said, "Away with you; you are not fit for this place."

Fire. It is called a man that what is said may not be at once evident, it being concealed by the word, evil, and is followed by lamentation, and an end of rejoicing. Men weep, and trees and grass; and everything is heard weeping in the tribe where he laughs; and they say the man has laughed who does not usually laugh.

"man." A riddle is good when it is not discernible at once. We say "a man," because it is not liked that the fire, even indoors where it is kindled, should cause its sparks to start out and fall on the clothes. The owner of the clothes cries because it burns; and when he sees a hole in it, he cries again. Or if food is being cooked, if the fire is large the pot may be put on, and be burned by the fire, and the pot burn the food. So the man laughs, that is the fire. And the people cry. Again, if a spark is cast into the thatch of the hut, it is seen by the fire; all the men will come together when the flame of the fire appears, and burns the house with the things which are in it; and there is a great crying; and the goats are burnt, and the calves; and the children are burnt. The cows cry, crying for their calves which are dead; men cry, crying for their goats; the wife and husband cry, crying for their children which are burnt; and the children cry for their father who has been burnt, having died whilst fetching his precious things from the burning house, and the house fell in on him; and the husband cries, crying for his wife who has been burnt; she died when she was fetching her child which was in the house, and was burnt together with it; and the trees cry, crying for their beauty which is lost, being now destroyed by the fire, and the trees are shrivelled and withered, and their beauty gone; and the cattle cry, crying for the grass, because they no longer have anything to eat, but are dying of famine. This, then, is the laughing of fire.

Guess you: a man who makes himself a chief; who does not work, but just sits still; his people work alone, but he does nothing; he shows them what they wish, but he does nothing; his people do not see, he sees for them, they are blind, the whole of his nation; he alone can see. They know that though they cannot see, they see by him; for they do not go without anything they want; he takes them by the hand, and leads them to where there is food, and they return with it to their homes; but he touches nothing, for he makes himself a chief; he remains a chief forever, for his people are supported by him.

At first there was a dispute, and his people said: "You cannot be our king and do nothing; we cannot see the power of your majesty." He answered them, saying: "Since you say I am not a chief, I will just sit still, and look on the ground. Then you will see that I am truly a chief, for if I look on the ground the land will be desolate; you will fall over precipices and into pits; you will be eaten by wild beasts through not seeing them; and die through famine, being unable to find food; because you dispute with me, you are blind."

So they see that he is a chief, and say: "Let us acknowledge openly that he is our king, that we may live. If we die of famine, that majesty which we claim for ourselves will come to an end. We are kings by living." So he was acknowledged a chief, and reigned; and the country was peaceful.

And he is a man that never washes; he just sits still. And when

The eye.

he is ill even with a slight illness all his nation is troubled, and dies of famine; and the people are afraid to go out of their houses, because they would fall over precipices and be dashed to pieces. They long for him to get well at once; and the people rejoice when he is well.

Guess you: a bullock which has no flesh: no one can cut into it anywhere; it is a mere hard mass; it does not go unless it is forced, but always stands still, until it is pushed along by someone. It will not be pushed along if it is driven up a steep place; but it allows itself to be pushed down. It is a bullock which does not like to go uphill; it likes always to be made to go down, and then makes no opposition.

Further, it does not cross a river, it stands still on one side; if anyone wishes it to cross, he must push it with great strength; but if the water is very deep, it will not cross, but hides itself from him in the water; for it knows how to hide in deep water, and he can see it no more. One chooses for it a place where he can see the bottom, that he may see it and drive it forward by pushing it.

There is only one mode of eating it by paying a debt, if a man has a debt which can be paid by it. That, then, is the only work it can do.

And it is a very fierce bullock; if it is pushed uphill, the men who drive it are on their guard, and one says to the others: "Be on your guard; you know that this bullock does not like to go uphill; take care that it does not gore us; if it gores us it will be very bad indeed, for we are below, and it is above us, and we shall be unable to shield

A stone. When we say "paying a debt," we mean when it is wanted to stop up the gateway of an enclosed place with a stone; or to grind with it. That is to pay a debt; and therefore we say, "It is eaten," for it too has its work which can be done by it alone.

ourselves, for it is a bad place, and is not advantageous for us; and when we think we are shielding ourselves, we shall fall, and it come and make an end of us." It is driven with such care, that when it will not go up, and wishes to come back again, they may make way for it and it pass on; and perhaps they will not follow it anymore; for it will run away, and leave them behind, till it comes to a place which is good for it, but bad for the men. So they are beat.

News from Zululand

This description by a Bantu-speaking informant refers to an actual event that took place on January 22, 1879, in Zululand a few miles from Rorke's Drift, when a Zulu army of King Cetawayo attacked and annihilated an encampment of eight hundred British troops, one of three British columns invading the country. The actual site of the battle is called Isandhlwana, and for some years the event was referred to as the Isandhlwana Tragedy. Historical accounts say the British were outmaneuvered as well, seemingly, as caught by surprise. But as for the Zulu, they attributed their great victory not only to the courage and fighting talents of their warriors, but also to their powerful medicine, or magic.

At one of the camps of the white people in Zululand, as the white men were lying comfortably about, there came a decrepit old man, a Zulu. He was unarmed, and appeared broken down with age.

He said he had come to ask the white people for food and employment. They replied, "Where is your family?" The old man said, "I have left them behind." Then they said, "Go and fetch it, and we will receive you."

The old man then went off. When he was out of the camp, the white men saw that the old man was playing (dancing), having his shield and stabbing assagai. He now lost the decrepitude of old age, and danced with the vigor of youth, making feints towards the camp, singing the praises of his Chief Cetywayo [Cetawayo].

The Englishmen began to fire at him hotly; and the reports of the

From From a Vanished German Colony, A Collection of Folklore, Folk Tales and Proverbs from South-West Africa, *by Odette St. Lys, London, 1916.*

guns and whistling of the bullets were all that was heard at that place. Mother! The old man played with them! And not a bullet touched him!

After a time, the old man went away, and entered a forest nearby. A little time elapsed, not long, and a bluebuck [a small antelope] was seen coming out of the same bush, and running in the direction of the camp.

The bluebuck ran into the camp amongst the white people. They shouted "Game! Game!" and tried to kill it. It could not be done.

Some fired at it, some threw stones at it, and there were others who at last threw dishes at it, but no one hit it. In the confusion they suddenly saw that the bluebuck had become a young man, a Zulu, with a shield and stabbing assagai. This young man attacked them with his assagai, and stabbed them. While he was killing them, they not being able to do anything to him, Cetywayo's army came in sight. The white people did not know it; but this army was close by.

The white people begin to be on the alert; the army is amongst them, it killed them all! Not one escaped!

That is the news from Zululand.

I must tell you, the Zulus have medicines!

Fragments of the Zulu Past in Song

Countless fragments of Zulu experience, history, tradition and legend are preserved in songs, whether old or recently composed. Sometimes an event of long ago is alluded to in passing, other times the song bears directly on an old happening. The names of chiefs and other persons long dead are recalled. Wars between tribes and the brave men who died fighting are memorialized. Running through the songs dealing with the past are threads such as the heavy hand laid by Chaka, who once conquered a great part of the country, on the neighboring tribes and clans, and also the heavy burden that fell on Africans as a result of the European conquest.

Song texts from Lalela Zulu, 100 Zulu Lyrics, *by Hugh Tracey, Johannesburg, African Music Society, 1948 (?). By permission of Hugh Tracey.*

THE BAMBO PEOPLE

The Bambo people were one of the victims of
Chaka's scourge. They were driven out of their
country north of the Tugela River and fled
south into the Cape Colony. There, without
goods or food, they arrived amongst the Xhosa,
and asked for hospitality. As they came empty-
handed they were dubbed "Amamfengu," the
"Beggars." They intermarried with the Xhosa
who still despise them to this day on this account.

We Bambo come from far away,
From beyond the Tugela.
We were scattered by the plague
[i.e., Chaka's depredations],
We came to the Xhosa.
We said: "We are destitutes
Because we beg."
Now we yearn for our home
Beyond the Tugela
With but our hearts,
That country of our forefathers.

WAS IT ALL WORTHWHILE?

The land of the Baca is in the southern part of
Natal where they speak a dialect akin to Swazi.
The song refers to the time when the people
first began to wear clothes and lost their independence to the Europeans. It was composed,
it is said, by a Zulu in the Baca dialect.

Yiya wo! Was it all worthwhile?
This land of the Baca . . .
This land of ours . . .
We were nourished on it,
We were brought up on it.
We have grown old upon it, we and
our fathers.

Listen to a story of that time . . .
There came a European
Wearing trousers and fine clothes.
He said: "Take off
All this rubbish."
So we threw away our skins.
Yiya wo! Was it all worthwhile?

AN OLD BATTLEFIELD

An old song which refers to the field of battle at the Nkandhla Forest where the forces of Bambatha were finally destroyed, bringing to an end his ill-fated rebellion in 1906. Bambatha himself died as he was trying to effect his escape along the bed of the Mome stream.

You who know not come and see.
Here are white bones.
Do not make me weep.
The bones are white at Nkandhla.

THE S.S. MENDI

This song refers to the sinking of the troopship, the S.S. *Mendi*, by enemy action in 1917 during the First World War. It carried the African Labor Battalions on their way to France. Most of them were drowned. Ever since then Mendi Day (21st February or the nearest Sunday to it) has been observed by many Africans in South Africa with special gatherings, parades and singing.

The ship *Mendi* went down at sea
And sank there with the sons of Africa.
Can you picture the sea
Can you picture the ship with people
        in it?
Down went the *Mendi*,
Down into the sea.
Many were the orphans that were left,
With the sinking of the *Mendi*.
We fear you, waters of the sea.
Soften your hearts, you people.
What do you say, Africans?
Stay not asleep below!

MGIJIMI

A Zulu song which refers to the tribulations of one Mgijimi—an independent cult leader said to have been driven from his ancestral home by the Europeans, who accused him of combining religion with sedition. It appears that he encouraged his followers to die fighting rather than submit to the Whites. His resistance was fruitless, and he was driven away and effectively silenced.

Thus spoke the son of Mgijimi
As he began to speak he sobbed.
He said: "Here are the whites."
He said: "Here is a gun."
He said: "Here is greatness!"
They caught him.
They drove him to the Mgijimi Plain.
In confusion he snatched at this and
       that.

THE DURBAN RIOTS

The incidents referred to in this song were the
African riots in Durban in 1929. It was a popular rising against the Pass Laws. A crowd of
Zulus had collected at Cartwright's Flats
where they listened to speeches against the
Pass Laws and they burnt their passes in protest. When the police were called out to disperse the people they fired on them, killing
several, amongst whom was Makhalampongo,
one of the chief speakers that afternoon. The
Zulus claimed that, on their side, the whole
affair was badly organized, largely on account
of personal jealousies amongst their leaders.

Whatever shall we do?
Today we are troubled.
We are made to pay money that does
      not help us.
Our leaders strive for honors
While we do not know where to go.
Our precious Makhalampongo died.
He died with his men, son of Bulose!
They fought against the Special and
      Registration passes.
We don't know what to do with
      ourselves.
Where shall we go?

CHIEF NGQIKA

This old song refers to an event, they say, in the
early days when the 1820 settlers in the Eastern Cape first arrived in the country. What
concession it was the Englishman asked from
Chief Ngqika is not known. Bedford, Cape
Province, was named no doubt after the settlers' old home.

One bad day in the land of Bedford
A white man came to the Xhosa.
He came there looking for help
He came before Chief Ngqika.
He found great grief
Because of the chief's reply.
He went home disappointed,
Disappointed by Ngqika.
"I do not sit by the fire
Before first finding the direction of
    the wind,"
Said Chief Ngqika.
"I do not wish to be involved
In quarrels which do not concern the
    blacks.
There is no help for you, I regret,"
Said Chief Ngqika.
Thus spoke the chief,
Thus spoke Ngqika
Addressing the white man.
"There is no help for you, I regret."
The white man was grieved that
    there was no help.

THE BIRDS

Popular tradition says that Chief Chaka once
prophesied that white men would invade his
country, flying like birds and building their
houses with earth, as do the swallows. In Zulu
song literature, Whites are frequently referred
to as "the birds." This song consists of a single
line that is repeated over and over:

Our country is ruled by the birds.

The Hemp Smoker and the Hemp Grower

A SHONA TALE FROM RHODESIA

In a certain village there was a man who was a hemp smoker. One year there was a drought. The crops did not grow, and there was no hemp for the man to smoke. He longed greatly for it, but there was none to be had.

His eight sons said to their father, "If you wish it to be, we shall go to other places and search for hemp for you."

The father replied: "Yes, go to other places and seek hemp for me so that I may smoke. Take your three sisters with you. If you find a person who will provide me with hemp and if his house is a pleasant one, leave your sisters with him to marry his sons."

The eight young men went out of the village, taking their sisters with them. They searched everywhere for hemp, but there was none to be found. They were discouraged. Then one day they met strangers on the road and said to them: "We are searching for hemp. Our father is in need of it. Wherever will we find it?"

The strangers answered: "We know a man who grows hemp. Come with us." And they took the eight young men and their sisters to the house of a hemp grower.

The young men spoke to the grower, saying: "Our father said to us: 'Hemp, I have none. Go out in the world and find some for me, as I am in need.' Therefore, if you have hemp, will you not give us some?"

The hemp grower answered: "It is true that I have hemp. If I give you some to take to your father, what are you prepared to give me in return?"

They answered: "Our father has said to us, 'Take your three sisters with you. If you find a man who will give you hemp and if his house is pleasant, leave your three sisters with him as wives for his sons.' We have brought our sisters."

The hemp grower was glad. He killed a goat and fed his guests. He said, "We shall think about the matter."

When the next day came, he filled eight bags with hemp and gave them to the eight sons for their father. He called his own four sons together and said to them: "Return with these young men to their village. Take your two sisters with you. If you find it pleasant where these people live, leave your sisters there as wives for the smoker's sons."

The party then returned to the village of the hemp smoker. He was waiting. His sons said: "Here is the hemp. We left our sisters with the

From The King's Drum and Other African Stories, © *1962 by Harold Courlander. Reprinted by permission of Harcourt Brace Jovanovich, Inc. A rephrasing of a story in* Fables of the Veld, *by F. W. T. Posselt, Oxford, The Clarendon Press, 1929.*

man who provided it. He has sent his own sons with us to see if our house is pleasant."

"It is well," their father said.

In the morning the four sons of the grower said to him: "Indeed, it is pleasant in this place. According to the instructions our father gave us, we shall leave our two sisters with you as wives for two of your sons."

They went away.

Thus the smoker's daughters married sons of the grower, and the grower's daughters married sons of the smoker. The families became friends. The sons and daughters went back and forth between the villages to visit one another. But the grower and the smoker, they each stayed where they were; they never met face to face.

One day the smoker said: "I am old. I have never seen my friend the grower. Take me there to talk with him before I die."

His children agreed. They prepared for the trip and set out. The man's sons went ahead of him to announce his coming. When they arrived at the village, the children of the grower clapped their hands in greeting. The grower asked, "Who is it that is being greeted?"

His sons answered, "It is the father of the girls that were left with us long ago, the father of the young men who came searching for hemp."

The grower said: "I am ashamed to meet him. I accepted his daughters without discussing the matter with him. I sent my own daughters to his house without speaking to him about the affair. We should have met and discussed these questions. Now I am ashamed. Tell him that I am ill."

They went to the smoker and said, "Our father is sick."

The sons of the smoker said: "Our father also is sick. That is why he came, while he is still alive, so that he might meet with your father. Your father is ill, our father is ill. Therefore, they are both ill. Where is the difference?"

The sons of the grower said: "It is true. Enter this house and rest. Tomorrow we shall see how things are."

So the smoker and his sons entered the guesthouse, and the family of the grower prepared food for them. But just as the food was being brought, there arose a great wailing in the village. The children of the grower cried out: "Father is dead! Father is dead!"

Thereupon, the visitors in the guesthouse also began to wail. They cried out: "Our father is dead too! He died in a village far from his home!"

The sons of the two fathers discussed the funeral arrangements. When the next day came, the people of the village said to the visitors: "The day is here. Go choose a place where your father may be buried. We shall do the same for our father."

But the sons of the smoker said: "Let us not do it this way, a grave for your father and a grave for our father. They were friends; therefore let them be buried in the same grave."

The sons of the grower answered: "Can such a thing be done? Have people ever before been buried together in the same grave?"

To this the smoker's sons replied: "You say people are not buried together. This is usually true. But have you ever before heard of a man who went to visit his friend, and when he arrived, they both died in the same village at the same moment? When was this ever seen to happen? The two friends, they died at the same time. Let them be buried together."

They talked this way, back and forth. At last it was agreed that the two fathers should have one grave.

A grave was dug, deep enough for two men. They carried the bodies of the hemp grower and the smoker to the burial place. First they placed the grower in the grave, then, on top, the body of the smoker. They called out, "Bring stones now, so that we may fill up the grave."

But as they were about to put in the stones, the voice of the hemp grower was heard from the grave. He called out: "I am not dead! Do not cover me with stones! Take me out!"

And the voice of the smoker was heard calling out: "I am on top! I want to get out first!"

So the two men came out, and everyone went back to the village. There a feast was prepared, and everyone ate.

Then the hemp grower addressed his sons. He said: "I did not wish to see the man whose daughters came to us. I was ashamed because we accepted his daughters, yet I had not spoken with him. Therefore, I said I was sick, hoping that he would go away."

The smoker said: "It is so. Listen to what is true. When a girl is to be taken in marriage, the matter should be discussed with her father. This is the proper way."

In the old days this was not done, but now it is the custom.

Shona Walking Song

> Gumbukumbu, my mother's child,
> We are climbing a hill.
> We must keep strong and go on climbing.
> If you don't make the effort
> And continue climbing
> You will never get there,
> Or perhaps you will
> Though your children may never get there
> As you did.

THE BUSHMEN AND THE HOTTENTOTS

How long ago they came, or where they came from is not known, but the Bushmen, whose correct name is San, are probably the oldest surviving inhabitants of Africa. As physical types they are unique, and their language is a tongue apart. They are short in stature, and their yellowish skin is loose and wrinkled. They have peppercorn hair and small, lobeless ears. The true Bushman is steatopygic; his enlarged buttocks store fat, from which in former times he lived when food was scarce. His home today is the Kalahari Desert and its fringes, covering much of South West Africa, a part of Cape Colony in South Africa, and western Botswana.

The Bushmen were roving hunters in the old days, sole masters of their lands, unimpeded in their movements from one place to another in pursuit of game. But about a thousand or more years ago another people migrated slowly down the western side of the continent into southern Africa. These were the Hottentots, or Khoikhoi people. Like the Bushmen, the origins of the Hottentots are not known. They also had yellowish skins and were short in stature, though they were somewhat larger than the Bushmen. Offshoots of the southward migrations penetrated into Bushman country. The Bushmen resisted the Hottentot intrusion, but gradually they fell back. After the Portuguese arrived in the final years of the fifteenth century it was the Hottentots who had to give way, in particular when, in the seventeenth century, the Boer settlers moved inland. Many Hottentots became indentured servants on Boer farms. Others, still in conflict with the Bushmen, retreated beyond the Boer settlements. In time the expanding frontiers went past the lands claimed by the Hottentots, and the Bushmen, despised and harassed by Hottentot and Boer alike, moved back into the arid hills and desert country where they were relatively safe from the invaders.

Today the Bushmen are divided into three main tribes or groups—the Heikum, few in number, living in eastern Ovamboland in South West Africa; the Auen, in the southern Kalahari; and the !Kung, in the northern, central and western Kalahari. Collectively they number perhaps twenty-five thousand. Civilization, as it is called, is pressing them hard, and as a distinct racial and social entity they may soon cease to exist.

The Coming of the Sun in the Sky

A BUSHMAN TALE

> Explanation of the narrator: The Sun was a man, but not one of the early Bushmen. In the beginning he gave forth brightness only around his own dwelling. In those days before the children threw him upwards from the earth, the sky was dark. The light that shone from him came from one of his armpits as he lay with his arm lifted up. When he put his arm down darkness fell everywhere; when he lifted it up again it was as if day had come. When the Sun was thrown into the sky it became round, and after that it was never a man again.

The children who performed this deed did so because their mother had requested them to do it. It was another old woman who had told the mother about it, for she herself had no children. She told the mother of the children that they should approach the Sun gently and lift his arm, so that the Sun's armpit would make everything bright. The old woman also spoke to the children, saying: "O children! You must wait

From Specimens of Bushmen Folklore, *by W. H. I. Bleek and L. C. Lloyd, London, 1911. The text has been occasionally rephrased to make it more understandable.*

for the Sun to lie down to sleep, for we are cold. You shall gently approach to lift him up while he lies asleep. All together you shall lift him up and throw him into the sky." In this manner the old woman spoke to the mother of the children, and in this manner the mother also spoke to the children.

The children came, the children went away. The old woman had said, "You must go and sit down when you have found him, waiting to see if he sleeps." Therefore the children went out, they sat down while they waited. The Sun came, he lay down, he lifted up his elbow, his armpit shone on the ground. The old woman had instructed the children, saying: "O children who are going to that place! You must speak to him when you throw him up!" She had said to them: "O children! You must tell him that he must entirely become the Sun, and go forward through the sky as the Sun, which is hot, so that the Bushmen rice will dry while he is hotly passing along in the sky."

Thus the white-haired woman had spoken to them. And the children listened to her. And they listened to their mother, who repeated what the old woman had said. Therefore they knew what to do. They went out, an older child informing them what was to be done. They went out, they sat down while awaiting the old man who was the Sun. When he lay down and slept, they stealthily approached him. They stood still, they looked at him, they went forward. They stealthily reached him, they took hold of him, all of them together, they lifted him up, they raised him, feeling his hotness. Then, feeling his hotness, they threw him up, speaking to him, saying: "O Sun! You must entirely stand fast where we are throwing you. You must go along, standing fast, and remain hot."

The old woman who had instructed them said that they appeared to have thrown him into the sky and that he seemed to be standing fast. In this manner she spoke. And the father of the children said: "The Sun-armpit is standing fast in the sky over there, he whom the children have thrown up. He lay intending to sleep, but the children have thrown him upwards."

The children returned. They came and one of them said: "Our companion here, he took hold of him. I also took hold of him. My younger brother took hold of him. My other younger brother also took hold of him. Our companion who is here, his younger brother also took hold of him. I said, 'Grasp him firmly.' I spoke in this manner, saying, 'Throw him up!' I said, 'Throw the old man up!' Then the children threw up the old man, that old man, the Sun, doing as the old woman instructed us."

Another older child spoke, telling his grandmother: "O my grandmother! We threw him up, we told him that he must become entirely the Sun, which is hot, for we are cold. We said, 'O my grandfather, Sun-armpit! Remain at the place above. Become the Sun which is hot, so that the Bushmen rice may dry for us, that the whole earth may become light, that the whole earth may become warm in the summer, that you may provide heat. Therefore you must shine completely, taking away the darkness. You must come and the darkness go away.'"

Thus the Sun comes, the darkness goes away, the Sun comes, the Sun sets, the darkness comes, the Moon comes at night. The day breaks, the Sun comes out, the darkness goes away, the Sun comes. The Moon comes out, the Moon brightens the darkness, the darkness departs. The Moon comes out, the Moon shines, taking away the darkness. It goes along, it has made bright the darkness, it sets. The Sun comes out, the Sun follows the darkness. The Sun takes away the Moon, the Moon stands, the Sun pierces it with the Sun's knife as it stands. Therefore the Moon decays on account of it. Therefore it says, "O Sun! Leave for the children the backbone!" Therefore the Sun leaves the backbone for the children. The Sun does this. The Sun says that he will leave the backbone for the children, the Sun assents to the Moon's request. The Sun leaves the backbone for the children, the Moon goes painfully away, he painfully returns home. He goes to become another Moon, which is whole. He again lives. He lives again, knowing that he seemed to die. Therefore he becomes a new Moon, feeling that he has put on a stomach, he becomes large, feeling that he is a Moon which is whole. He is alive. He goes along at night, feeling that he is the Mantis's shoe walking in the night. [It is said that once the Mantis, inconvenienced by darkness, threw his shoe into the sky, where it became the Moon.]

The Sun is here, all the earth is bright. The people walk while the earth is light. The people perceive the bushes, they see other people; they see the meat which they are eating; they also see the springbok, they also head the springbok in summer; they also head the ostrich when they know that the Sun shines; they also steal up to the gemsbok; they also steal up to the kudu when they feel that the whole place is bright; they also visit each other when the Sun shines upon the path. They also travel in summer; they shoot in summer; they espy the springbok in summer; they go round to head the springbok; they lie down; they feel that they lie in a little house of bushes; they scratch up the earth in the little house of bushes; they lie down when the springbok come.

The Son of the Wind

A BUSHMAN TALE

The Wind [or the Young Wind, or the Son of the Wind] was formerly still. And he rolled a ball to !ná-ka-ti. [The mark ! indicates a palatal click.] He exclaimed, "Oh, !ná-ka-ti! There it goes!" And !ná-ka-ti exclaimed, "Oh, comrade! there it goes!" because !ná-ka-ti did not know the other one's name. Therefore, !ná-ka-ti said, "Oh, comrade! There it goes!" He who was the Wind, he was the one who said, "Oh, !ná-ka-ti! There it goes!"

From From a Vanished German Colony, A Collection of Folklore, Folk Tales and Proverbs from South-West Africa, *by Odette St. Lys, London, 1916. Edited for clarity of meaning.*

Therefore, !ná-ka-ti went to question his mother about the other one's name. He exclaimed: "Oh, our mother! Tell me yonder comrade's name; for comrade utters my name; I do not utter his name. I would also utter comrade's name when I am rolling a ball to him. For I do not utter comrade's name; I would also utter his name when I roll a ball to him." Therefore his mother exclaimed: "I will not utter to you comrade's name. For you shall wait; that father may first shelter for us the hut; that father may first strongly shelter the hut; and then I will utter for you comrade's name. And, when I have uttered for you comrade's name, you must scamper away, you must run home, that you may come into the hut, when you feel that the wind would blow you away."

Therefore the child went away; they [the boy and Young Wind] went to roll the ball there. Therefore, !ná-ka-ti again went to his mother, he again went to question his mother about the other one's name. And his mother exclaimed: "/érriten-!kuan-!kuan it is; !gau- !gaubu-ti it is. He is /érriten- !kuan-!kuan; he is !gua-!guabu-ti, he is /érriten-!kuan- !kuan."

Therefore, !ná-ka-ti went away. He went to roll the ball there, while he did not utter the other one's name, because he felt that his mother was not the one who had thus spoken to him. She said: "You must not at first utter comrade's name. You must, at first, be silent, even if comrade is uttering your name. Therefore, when you have uttered comrade's name, you must run home, when you feel that the wind would blow you away."

Therefore, !ná-ka-ti went away. They went to roll the ball there, while the other was the one who uttered !ná-ka-ti's name; while he felt that !ná-ka-ti intended that his father might first finish sheltering the hut, and when he beheld that his father sat down, then he would, afterwards, utter the other one's name, when he saw that his father had finished sheltering the hut.

Therefore, when he beheld that his father finished sheltering the hut, then he exclaimed: "There it goes! Oh, /érriten-!kuan-!kuan! There it goes! Oh, !gau-!gaubu-ti! There it goes!" And he scampered away, he ran home; while the other one leaned over, and fell down. He lay kicking violently upon the flat ground. Therefore the people's huts vanished away; the Wind blew away their sheltering bushes, together with the huts, while the people could not see for the dust. Therefore, the Wind's mother came out of the hut [i.e., out of the Wind's hut]; his mother came to raise him up; his mother, grasping him set him on his feet. Therefore the Wind became still; while the Wind had, at first, while it lay, made the dust rise. Therefore, we who are Bushmen, we are wont to say: "The Wind seems to have lain down, for it does not gently blow, it blows very strongly. For, when it stands upright, then it is wont to be still, if it stands; for it seems to have lain down when it feels like this. Its knee is that which makes a noise if it lies down, for its knee does make a noise. I had wished that it might be gently blowing for us, that we might go out; that we might ascend yonder hill, that we might look at yonder dry riverbed behind the hill. For we have driven away the springbok from this place. Therefore, the springbok have gone to yonder dry riverbed, behind the hill. For we have not a little shot springbok here; for we have shot, letting the sun set, at the springbok here."

The Wind in the Form of a Bird

A BUSHMAN TALE

The Wind [the Wind's Son] was formerly a person. He became a feathered thing (i.e., a bird). And he flew, while he no longer walked as formerly; for he flew, and he dwelt in a mountain hole. Therefore, he flew. He was formerly a person. He formerly rolled a ball; he shot; while he felt that he was a person. He became a feathered thing; and then, he flew, and he inhabited a mountain hole. And he comes out of it, he flies about, and he returns home to it. And he comes to sleep in it; and he early awakes and goes out of it; he flies away; again, he flies away. And he again returns home, after he has sought food. And he eats, about, about, about, about, he again returns home. And he again comes to sleep in his hole.

/ / góö ka !kui (i.e., "Smoke Man," brother to the narrator's wife) saw the Wind, when a child, at mountains at a place called by Europeans, "Haarfontein." Believing it to be only a certain kind of bird (the Bushman name for which is !kuerre- !kuerre) he threw a stone at it. And the Wind burst, blew very hard, and raised the dust, because he (/ / góö-ka-!kui) had intended to throw a stone at it. The wind had intended to fly away. It went into a mountain hole, and burst, blowing very hard. The boy, being afraid, and unable to see his master's sheep for the dust, went home, and sat under the hut's sheltering bushes, wishing that the dust might settle; and the sheep returned by themselves. [The narrator adds that "Africander" sheep will do this, but not the "Va'rland" sheep, which remain where they are left.]

The Lion's Dwelling Place

A BUSHMAN TALE

The girl who performed this deed, she lived with her people in a remote and distant place. Her father and mother went out from their dwelling, saying: "We are going in search for things. Remain this way, quietly, until we return." The girl remained quietly, they went out to search. She said, "My father, my mother, I am staying." The man and the woman went out. They did not return. The sun shone, the sun slept. There was light, there was darkness. Still the man and the woman did not return to the dwelling place. The moon became thin, it began to

From St. Lys, ibid. *Edited for clarity of meaning.*
Contributed by Daniel P. P. Marolen.

die. The man and woman who went out in search, they did not come back. When the girl beheld that her father and mother did not come back, she cried out, "O my father! O my mother!" But they did not return.

There was a being called Heyseb. It was he who found water for men in the dry desert. It was he who said to people, "Go this way" or "Go that way" when they were searching. Heyseb found the water, he sent people to it so that they could quench their thirst. He came one day to the dwelling place where she waited. He heard her crying out, "O my father! O my mother!" Therefore he went to the hut, saying, "Why do you call, 'O my father, O my mother?'" She answered, saying, "They went out in search, they do not return." Seeing her this way, Heyseb's heart went to her. He said: "Have they indeed been swallowed by the desert? Then, surely, you cannot remain here alone."

So Heyseb took the girl and placed her on his shoulders. And taking her this way on his shoulders, she sitting there and he walking, he continued on his way, searching for honey and water. And when he had walked far and the sun was dropping down from the sky Heyseb saw bees swarming in a certain direction. He followed them, coming at last to the place where they nested high in the rocks. Therefore he said, "Come down from my shoulders now, so that I may take honey from the nest." Yet the girl would not come down from his shoulders. Heyseb said to her, "Come down now, I will get honey." But she clung tightly there and would not come down. Then Heyseb went away from the place of the bees without eating and continued to walk.

The sun slept. Heyseb also slept, the girl still clinging to her place on his shoulders. The sun awoke. Heyseb went on, walking, walking, and again he saw bees swarming in a certain direction. He followed them, saying, "Now, surely, we shall have honey." But the girl would not descend, and so Heyseb could not climb for the honey. He went on. Thirst came upon him. And when he found a pool of water he wanted to drink. He said, "Come down now, let us drink water." Yet the girl would not come down. Heyseb could not drink. He called on her, saying: "How shall it be? Is it to be this way? I took you from your lonely dwelling place that you might not die there. And now, shall it be that I will never again satisfy my hunger or my thirst?" Still the girl clung strongly to Heyseb's shoulders.

He saw a large tree growing there among the rocks. He sought the shade of the tree. He sat there leaning against the large trunk. And in the branches above he saw a hut, and he smelled water and honey above him. He said to the girl: "In the hut that stands in the branches of the tree there is surely something to eat and drink. Climb, then, bring down food and water." The girl climbed into the branches of the tree where the hut stood. She entered the hut. And when she was no longer visible, Heyseb arose and departed. He left the tree behind, and the hut that was in it, and the girl that was in the hut, and he went on his journey alone.

Now, the hut that the girl had entered belonged to a lion, but he was not then at home. When he returned, he saw that someone was in his dwelling place. He said, "Whoever is there, come down." But the girl did not come down. Therefore the lion took up a long stick and thrust it at her, trying to make her descend. Yet she moved so rapidly from one side to the other that he could not dislodge her from the dwelling place. And so the lion called on his friend the hyena, saying: "Climb there, enter the dwelling place and bring down the child. I shall prepare a fire below. Bring down the girl who takes over my house, we shall have roast meat." The lion made a large fire, and the hyena went into the tree. The hyena sought to seize the girl, but she moved from one side to the other and he could not grasp her. And while they were struggling thus the hyena slipped and fell from the tree, landing in the fire below. He scrambled from the heat but his skin was scorched. The lion said, "Go up again." But the hyena declined, saying, "No, I will tend the fire and make it hotter, while you ascend and bring down our meal." The hyena brought more wood and made the fire hotter, and the lion went up for the girl. The lion tried to grasp the girl, but she moved rapidly from side to side. He leaped, then, with all his force, to make an end to the wrestling, and fell from the dwelling place into the fire that the hyena was tending. The hyena cried out to his friend the lion, thinking it was the girl who had fallen: "We have her in the fire. The smell of her flesh is sweet. Come down, now, lion, let us eat." And after the lion had roasted a while, the hyena looked into the tree and saw the girl there. He cried in astonishment, "Alas! I have roasted my friend!" And he went away in bitterness. But the girl remained, living on in the dwelling place of the lion.

The Cloud-Eaters

A HOTTENTOT TALE

> Thou who makest thy escape from the tumult!
> Thou wide, roomy tree!
> Thou who gettest thy share, though with trouble!
> Thou cow who art strained at the hocks!

This tale and the four immediately following are from Reynard the Fox in South Africa, *by W. H. I. Bleek, London, 1864.*

Thou who hast a plump round knee!
Thou the nape of whose neck is clothed with hair!
Thou with the skin dripping as if half-tanned!
Thou who hast a round, distended neck!
Thou eater of the Namaqua,
Thou big-toothed one!

—Praise poem to the Hyena

The Jackal and the Hyena were together, it is said, when a white cloud rose. The Jackal ascended upon it and ate of the cloud as if it were fat. When he wanted to come down, he said to the Hyena, "My sister, as I am going to divide with thee, catch me well." So she caught him, and broke his fall. Then she also went up and ate there, high up on the top of the cloud.

When she was satisfied, she said, "My greyish brother, now catch me well." The greyish rogue said to his friend: "My sister, I shall catch thee well. Come therefore down."

He held up his hands, and she came down from the cloud, and when she was near, the Jackal cried out, painfully jumping to one side: "My sister, do not take it ill. Oh, me! Oh, me! A thorn has pricked me, and sticks in me!" Thus the Hyena fell down from above and was sadly hurt.

Since that day, it is said, the Hyena's left hind foot is shorter and smaller than the right one.

[Both the poem and the tale allude to the fact
that when the hyena starts to walk it appears to
be lame in the back legs.]

The Fish-Stealers

A HOTTENTOT TALE

The fire threatens,
The stone threatens,
The assagais threaten,
The guns threaten,
Yet you seek food from me.
My children,
Do I get anything easily?

—The Hyena addresses her children

Once upon a time a Jackal, who lived on the borders of the colony, saw a wagon returning from the seaside laden with fish. He tried to get into the wagon from behind, but he could not; he then ran on before, and lay in the road as if dead. The wagon came up to him, and the leader cried to the driver, "Here is a fine kaross for your wife!"

"Throw it into the wagon," said the driver, and the Jackal was thrown in.

The wagon travelled on through a moonlight night, and all the while the Jackal was throwing the fish out into the road; he then jumped out himself, and secured a great prize. But a stupid old Hyena coming by, ate more than her share, for which the Jackal owed her a grudge; so he said to her, "You can get plenty of fish, too, if you lie in the way of a wagon as I did, and keep quite still whatever happens."

"So!" mumbled the Hyena.

Accordingly, when the next wagon came from the sea, the Hyena stretched herself out in the road.

"What ugly thing is this?" cried the leader, and kicked the Hyena. He then took a stick and thrashed her within an inch of her life. The Hyena, according to the directions of the Jackal, lay quiet as long as she could; she then got up and hobbled off to tell her misfortune to the Jackal, who pretended to comfort her.

"What a pity," said the Hyena, "that I have not such a handsome skin as you!"

A Nama Woman Married to an Elephant

A HOTTENTOT TALE

An Elephant, it is said, was married to a Nama Hottentot woman, whose two brothers came to her secretly, because they were afraid of her husband. Then she went out as if to fetch wood, and putting them within the wood, she laid them on the stage. Then she said, "Since I married into this kraal, has a wether been slaughtered also for me?" And her blind mother-in-law answered, "Umph! things are said by the wife of my eldest son, which she never said before."

Thereupon the Elephant, who had been in the field, arrived, and smelling something, rubbed against the house. "Ha," said his wife, "what I should not have done formerly, I do now. On what day did you slaughter a wether for me?" Then the mother-in-law said to him: "As she says things which she did not say before, do it now."

In this manner a wether was slaughtered for her, which she roasted whole, and then, in the same night after supper, asked her mother-in-law the following questions: "How do you breathe when you sleep the sleep of life? [light sleep, half-conscious]. And how when you sleep the sleep of death?" [deep sleep]

Then the mother-in-law said, "Umph, an evening full of conversation! When we sleep the sleep of death, we breathe thus: 'sũi sũi!' and when we sleep the sleep of life we breathe thus: 'Xou !áwaba! Xou !áwaba!' "

Thus the wife made everything right whilst they fell asleep. Then she listened to their snoring, and when they slept thus, sũi sũi, she rose and said to her two brothers, "The sleep of death is over them, let us make ready." They rose and went out, and she broke up the hut to carry away all that she could, and took the necessary things, and said, "That thing which makes any noise wills my death." So they kept altogether quiet.

When her two brothers had packed up, she went with them between the cattle, but she left at home one cow, one ewe, and one goat, and directed them, saying to the cow, "You must not low as if you were by yourself alone, if you do not wish for my death"; and she taught the ewe and the goat the same.

Then they departed with all the other cattle, and those who were left behind lowed during the night as if they were many, and as they lowed as if they were still all there, the Elephant thought, "They are all there." But when he rose in the morning, he saw that his wife and all the cattle were gone. Taking his stick into his hands, he said to his mother, "If I fall the earth will tremble." With these words he followed them. When they saw him approaching, they ran fast to the side, against a piece of rock at a narrow spot, and she said: "We are people behind whom a large party comes. Stone of my ancestors! divide thyself for us." Then the rock divided itself, and when they had passed through it, it closed again behind them.

Then came the Elephant, and said to the rock, "Stone of my ancestors! divide thyself also for me." The rock divided itself again, but when he had entered, it closed upon him. Thus died the Elephant, and the earth trembled. The mother at her hut said then: "As my eldest son said, it has happened. The earth shakes."

The Horse Cursed by the Sun

A HOTTENTOT TALE

It is said that once the Sun was on earth, and caught the Horse to ride it. But the Horse was unable to bear the Sun's weight, and therefore the Ox took the place of the Horse, and carried the Sun on its back. Since that time the Horse is cursed in these words, because it could not carry the Sun's weight:

"From today thou shalt have a certain time of dying.
This is thy curse, that thou hast a certain time of dying.
And day and night shalt thou eat,
But the desire of thy heart shall not be at rest,
Though thou grazest till morning and again until sunset.
Behold, this is the judgment which I pass upon thee," said the Sun.

Since that day the Horse's certain time of dying commenced.

The Origin of Death

A HOTTENTOT TALE

The Moon, it is said, sent once an Insect to Men, saying: "Go thou to Men, and tell them, 'As I die, and dying live, so ye shall also die, and dying live.'" The Insect started with the message, but whilst on his way was overtaken by the Hare, who asked: "On what errand art thou bound?" The Insect answered: "I am sent by the Moon to Men, to tell them that as she dies, and dying lives, they also shall die, and dying live." The Hare said, "As thou art an awkward runner, let me go." With these words he ran off, and when he reached Men, he said, "I am sent by the Moon to tell you: 'As I die, and dying perish, in the same manner ye shall also die and come wholly to an end.'" Then the Hare returned to the Moon, and told her what he had said to Men. The Moon reproached him angrily, saying, "Darest thou tell the people a thing which I have not said?" With these words she took up a piece of wood, and struck him on the nose. Since that day the Hare's nose is slit.

SOME EASTERN CATTLE PEOPLES:
MASAI, SHILLUK, NUER AND TUTSI

The Tutsi of Rwanda and Burundi

East of Lake Kivu and Lake Tanganyika are the countries of Rwanda
and Burundi, traditional homelands of the Nilotic Tutsi people, cattle
herders of Hima stock who migrated to this region some four or five
centuries ago. The Tutsi became the overlords of two other ethnic
groups with whom they shared the countryside, the Hutu—indigenous
agriculturalists, and the Twa—indigenous people of pygmoid stock. As
with certain other cattle people, the Tutsi valued cattle not as mere
wealth but as evidence of status and prestige. In theory, all cattle be-

Extracted from Songs of the Watutsi, *by Leo A. Verwilghen, booklet introduction to the record album by the same name, New York, Ethnic Folkways Library, 1952. By permission.*

longed to the Mwami, or king, expressing his authority and power. Before the independence of Rwanda and Burundi, the Mwamis of those countries were absolute rulers. With the coming of constitutional government the privileged position of the Tutsi in Rwanda was broken. Not only did the Hutu make their numbers felt politically, their pent-up hostility against their former masters resulted in violence that caused large groups of Tutsi to seek sanctuary in neighboring countries. Just prior to the period of great political change, and thus in the lifetime of many Tutsi still living in Rwanda, their customs and traditions were described in these terms:

The Tutsi believe in a single deity called Imana. He is the creating force of all things and is essentially good. The cult of the spirits of the dead is very widespread, and offerings must be made to these spirit beings. The casting of magic spells plays an important part in the life of the Tutsi.

Monogamy is the rule. The role of the woman is very important. Marriage is never imposed on a Tutsi woman against her will. Once a mother, she is deeply respected, and she is consulted in all affairs of the family. She is truly mistress of the house, and is responsible for the education of the boys up to the age of twelve and the girls until marriage.

True pastoral people, the Tutsi traditionally eat no meat but only milk, butter and honey, though at present they are adding certain other foods. Eating in public is regarded as unseemly. For this reason, the Hutu for many years believed the Tutsi lived without eating.

Tutsi dress has a national character. The men wear a piece of cloth around the hips and upper legs. Those Tutsi who wear European clothes continue, however, to wear the old-style cloth beneath. The women drape themselves very elegantly in long cloths; one arm is usually covered and the other is free.

Young men called to the court of the Mwami, or king, to learn the customs, manners and traditions of the Tutsi are known as Intore. In addition to learning dancing, the Intore receive an intense education in literature, history and self-control. They memorize the traditional national poetry and learn the art of poetic composition. They learn to speak in appropriate language, to act courteously, and to express their thoughts accurately.

Tutsi houses are usually extremely well cared for. The interior is divided into compartments by finely woven mats which are hung from the wooden understructure of the roof. The room of the parents is separated from that of the children by a curtain of otter skins.

Among the most prominent crafts are basketry for the women and ironwork for the men. Tutsi basketry is of a very high quality. Basket weaving is not practiced for commercial purposes, but is regarded as a "noble" art, requiring great patience. Basketry objects are not sold, but are sometimes given as presents. Ironwork is concerned primarily with the making of countless variations of swords and spears. There are four or five hundred different models of these weapons, each one having its own name and its own history.

Drums are usually very conspicuous in Tutsi music. The drum in Rwanda is the symbol of royalty. It is only by permission of the king that batteries of drums may be played together. Drums are not played with the hands among the Tutsi, but only with sticks. The rhythms are formal and standardized, and each one has its specific name, but this does not preclude the introduction of new rhythms. Drums are beaten on all important social and religious occasions.

But apart from this more conspicuous and intrusive form of music, the Tutsi have a precious repertoire of old legends, ballads, geneologies, love songs, hunting songs, war songs and epics which constitute a vital part of the musical culture and the history of the people. Many of these songs are of the type not performed publicly, but usually within the confines of the home or the court, or some other small gatherings.

The Hunting Ritual of Tutsi Kings

The royal rituals of ancient Rwanda are preserved in a group of texts, orally transmitted from one generation to another by court functionaries called Abiiru, who are the official custodians of these traditions. The Abiiru commit the rituals to memory, and pass them on, as circumstances warrant, to their successors. Revelation of these traditions to others outside the small circle of those entrusted with them is prohibited on pain of death. The rituals contain within them, it is believed, the means by which the Mwami, or king, deals with ancestral spirits and other supernatural forces to bring good to the kingdom, and to ward off misfortune. Eighteen separate rituals in all are involved, having to do with such things as floods, cattle sickness, war, fire and the enthronement of kings. The text given here is that of the royal hunt. It is a recitation of what must be done for the hunt to be carried out properly, beginning with the Mwami's decision to assemble a hunting party and ending with the return of the hunters from the bush.

I. Diviners ascertain for the king which of his royal ancestors will be favorable to and sponsor the hunt. Each of the former kings is identified with a particular capital that he built. Therefore, when the name of the sponsoring ancestor is known, it is also known which capital will serve as the headquarters of the Mwami and his party.

When the king wants to go hunting
Divination about the hunt takes place.
Through divination one chooses among former kings,
Either Mibambwe or Kigere,
He to whom the divination points.

Text extracted and freely translated from "The Sacred Royalty of Ancient Rwanda," by M. d'Hertefelt and A. Coupez, Annals of the Royal Museum of Central Africa, No. 52, Tervueren, 1964.

One divines to ascertain the capital where the Mwami will take up
    residence and command.
A house is built there in a single day.
When it is finished,
The king comes and indicates to the ancestral spirit his residence.
When the residence has been pointed out to the ancestral spirit
He is presented with the royal hammer (insignia of kingship).
The royal saluting drum salutes.
The [other] royal drums make their appearance.
They are presented to him, though not playing the igihubi rhythm.
Afterwards the drums go to the Cyirima House (a ritual hut
    dedicated to the spirits).

II. The king makes offerings to the designated ancestral spirit.

The next morning
The king places a drum before the shrine
And asks for help from the spirits, saying, "Be favorable.
Here is Rugiramusango's drum.
Here also, an animal trap."

III. The forthcoming hunt is announced to the public.

Rugiramusango (the king) goes to the village common.
The dweller in the Kabagari taps him with a stick,
Saying, "We have convened the hunting party.
After tomorrow the hunters will make their departure."
The next day the saluting drum is taken to the common.
The man strikes a signal and says, "We have gathered for the hunt,
    people, it is for tomorrow."

*IV. The king goes hunting, though without attempting to kill animals
that are difficult to bring down.*

The next morning
The king takes Nsinzumusazi and some large arrows.
He calls for the favor of the spirits and departs.
They build a lodging for the king in the bush.
He goes to pass the night there.
When he arises, a fire is built.
A fire is made of umukenya (a play on words, the name of the wood
    plus keny, the root whose name means "shorten the days").
They depart and go to the camp.
They break an umukenya
And the king says, "I make brief the days of a female,
I make short the days of a male."
The animal trap remains there.
In the king's dwelling, near the fire
The king may not draw the large arrows,

He may not strike with the ritual lance;
He uses other weapons for the hunt
So that the ritual arms will not end up lost in the bush
Or be carried away by animals in their flight.
When the king has killed game,
But not any elephant,
Leopard or lion,
An elephant tusk is sought
At the house of the keeper of royal effects,
The skin of one of the other animals
And the corpse of a hare.
It is these things
That are done in connection with the hunt.

V. The king returns from the bush, receives the hunters at his residence, and ritually celebrates the event.

Arriving at the village common,
The people assemble
Wearing on their heads the imihanda plant (to signal a successful
     hunt).
The king goes into his house,
While the hunters stop at the village common.
When the king enters his specially constructed residence
He is given the royal hammer (insignia of kingship).
The saluting drum salutes,
Then the royal drums are taken to the Cyirima House,
Followed by a designated woman (with whom the Mwami will have
     ritual intercourse).
The drums are on the threshold.
The designated woman approaches a sacrificial animal.
Karinga makes his entrance with the other drums.
The drummers beat the igihubi rhythm, as is the custom.
Then the drums are put in the storage place and tied down.
The designated woman follows and enters.
The king gets up
And goes to invite the hunters to come in.
The king ritually celebrates the hunt
With the spear and arrow.
The hunters proclaim their success.
The Vunangoma sing the chant of stirring up the game.
Those outside receive a bull
And a cow, which are killed and divided.
They pass the night without sleep in honor of the hunt.
The king ritually celebrates the end of the hunting.
The next morning
He distributes the parts of the meat, giving them to the children
     (i.e., the servitors).

When all is finished, the royal drums are carried in palanquins to
   the Cyirima House.
A bull is sacrificed,
And the next day the drums are smeared with its blood.

Royal Drums of the Tutsi

(AS PLAYED BY MWAMI RUDAHIGWA MUTARA AND HIS PROVINCIAL CHIEFS, 1936)

Ibabazabahizi

Fragment of a historical song-poem about a
Tutsi warrior group that was formed around
the year 1880. The song tells about wars in
Kigesi and Nkore, two provinces of Rwanda. It

Transcription by Rose Brandel, from Journal of the American Musicological
Society, *Spring 1952. By permission.*
From Songs of the Watutsi, *by Leo A. Verwilghen. By permission of Ethnic
Folkways Library.*

is in the form of a dialogue in which the
Mwami, or king, is asked for assistance.

Heroes are called to arms.
A man of Mulima comes to the house of King Musinga.
You hear of these heroes.
They go to battle.
And are you not equally courageous?
All have left, armed with their bows and spears.
You are brave in combat, that I know.
Heroes are attacking the fugitives.
They wildly attack the enemy.

Abagombozi Poetry of the Tutsi

The mugombozi (plural, abagombozi) is a herbalist-healer whose
function in the Tutsi society is to counteract the effects of snakebite and
to combat other body infections. His treatment of snakebite victims is
essentially medical. He prepares poultices and antidotes from roots and
leaves. Both the medical and ritual secrets of his profession are inherited, and he is considered to be a specialist whose particularized knowledge is not shared by generalists in herb medicine. He is not a "witch
doctor" as that term is understood outside of Africa, in that he does not
employ magic as one of his tools. His paraphernalia include only the
leaves, grasses and herbs out of which he makes his lotions and antidotes. It is apparent that the abagombozi possess herbal knowledge
that is generally effective in the treatment of snakebite, and in their
relationships with their patients they manifest an awareness of the
psychological needs of snakebite victims. Their knowledge of their
profession is believed to come from the dead ancestors of the tribe, who
hold that knowledge in trust from Imana, the Supreme Being.

Ritual accompanies the mugombozi's ministrations to afflicted persons. An important aspect of the ritual is the recitation of formalized,
though variable, poetry in which snakes are addressed, supplicated and
praised, reflecting religious conceptions of dealing with spirits, the
dead, and unknown forces. The snakes are addressed by their common
Tutsi names, by praise names, and by descriptive names involving
metaphors and similes. Woven into the recitatives are allusions that
would be understood readily by the Tutsi, but which elude the outsider.
Many of the statements are so enigmatic and esoteric as to challenge
translation. Yet the recitations as a whole have the sound and feel of
poetry. Imagery is piled on imagery, and one senses something of the
Tutsi world, man's relationship to it, and a spirit of humanity.

---

*Background information given by Leo A. Verwilghen. The ritual texts, given
here in free translation, were recited by Thomas Bazarusanga, a mugombozi of
Kigali, Rwanda. Author's collection.*

PRAISE RECITATIVES ADDRESSED TO THE SNAKE CALLED IMBARABARA

Imbarabara, the Cutter;
He-Who-Trips-People-Up;
Who-Makes-One-Fall-Heavily;
Who does not darken his nostrils
In the manner of a certain Hutu person of Gitare;
Who took the share rightly due to him.

* * *

Worthy Son-of-the-Killer
Who cuts down the brave man armed with a large club,
Worthy Son-of-Nkomo [a snake],
Inheritor of his line,
Sender of the deadly fever
That only experts recognize,
For he who does not recognize it
She urinates in your stomach.
And his name is Pincher,
And because of this he is the blood brother
To this same Nkomo, native of Gahombo,
None other than the one who accepted a quarrel
With Kajwiga
In the presence of Imfuha and Impfundura
With these words: Whom does it behoove to cut down a strong man?
And The Spitter replied in these words:
Let me cut, it belongs to the Hurting Snake.
My dear Winged Rapacious One,
You Bull of the Anthill.

PRAISE RECITATIVES ADDRESSED TO THE SNAKE CALLED INCIRA

It is he who launches the stinging streams,
He, himself, Great-One-with-Mouth-Behind,
He became the Crawling One.
In the corners of his jowls
He is armed with sharp swords
And stings the feet.
And I, I rise to give treatment.
The perfect Beautiful Brown One,
It is he whom I introduce to the king.
He is the Look-Full-of-Anger,
Worthy mother of Nkomyi (a snake).
Yet he does not kill, he only threatens,
He only defends himself.

He is the Brave-While-the-Others-Turn-Tail.
Here it is, the Lance-Attacks-While-the-Fugitives-Withdraw.

*   *   *

The Penetrator, the one that cuts,
He who holds hands with the courageous,
The Packet of Spears,
He becomes the Inimitable Knifer,
This brave bearded one,
Armed with streams of saliva,
Stinging the body sharply.

RECITATIVES OF THE EXORCISM RITUAL: FIRST PHASE, PRESENTING THE ACTORS

Listen, Great Gullet!
Listen, Tasted by Specialists!

Addressed to the patient:

I free you from Gahima,
I free you from Incarwatsi,
From the Accepter of Quarrels and the Liar,
I free you from Rainmaker,
I free you from Caterpillar,
I free you from the One Who Pierces,
I free you from the Nicked One,
I free you from the Little Butterfly,
I free you from the Usurper,
From the Euphoric Sleeper,
And Muhima, Senior-One-of-the-Anthill.

*   *   *

And now, Usurper,
If you have serious intentions,
Permit us each to live,
Accept your small fee.
As for mine, no place for it.
Kavubyi, Kamata, Gahoma,
Let us have a small conversation.

SECOND PHASE, QUESTIONS AND RESPONSES

Hé, Kamata, where do you live?
Hé, Winged One, where do you live?

Hé, One-Hurries, and you, Rewelder,
Where do you live?

I live on Murambi Hill,
I live on Kawangire Hill,
I live on Sakara Hill,
That is where I live.

THIRD PHASE, CHALLENGE AND HONORIFICS

I free you from Muhima and from the Tutsi person,
I free you from the Python,
I free you from Big Eye and Great Hyena,
I free you from the Stake, from Great Goat,
I free you from Scaley One, and the One Who Climbs the Grove,
    and the one who is equal to Great Goat.
Very well. You have chosen to challenge me
Before beating me in the contest?

Gihilihili: The Snake-Person

(TUTSI VERSION OF A WIDELY KNOWN TALE)

There was a certain woman. She was sterile. There were many years, she did not have a child. Then, at last, she conceived, and the child grew within her as with other women. Other women, when it was time, brought their children out into the world; but this woman, her child remained within her; it remained there for several years without her seeing it, without its seeing the light of day. And then, as it happened, the woman was taken with labor pains, and she gave birth to the child that was in her. But she did not give the light of day to an infant like other infants, but to a snake.

She called for her husband. He came. He looked attentively at the snake. He began to strike blows upon it. His wife said softly, "Treat it with gentleness, it is the fruit of my womb." The husband sent for respected men of the village. They came. They looked carefully at the snake. They said, "Take it into the forest, construct a house for it there. Abandon it in the forest, let it go and do what it will. Let it grow up and shed its skin."

They carried the snake into the forest. They built a house for it. They left it there. The snake lived in the forest. It grew up. It shed its skin, and now it was transformed into a young man. Seeing young people of his age gathering dead wood in the forest, he asked them to carry a message to his father. Tell him, the young man said, that the snake-person has now become a robust human being, and that he wants as a

---

Told by Thomas Bazarusanga of Kigali, Rwanda. Author's collection.

wife the daughter of Bwenge. The reason for the request is this: Each time Bwenge's daughter came into the forest to gather wood, my love went out to her. Each time she came to get water, my love went out to her. Each time she came to cut grass for the young cattle, my love went out to her.

The message was carried to his father. On hearing the news, the father, along with other members of the family, went out to the place in the forest. He found his son there. He had a fire made. Into the fire he threw the snakeskin in which his son had once been enveloped. As the skin burned it became transformed into objects of many kinds. It became transformed into drums, into cattle, into churns, into milk pots, and into other kinds of wealth.

Then the father took his son to find a wife for him. They went to the house of Bwenge. Things were arranged there, and they obtained Bwenge's daughter. The young man and his wife made a home. They were happy. In addition to all this good fortune, in time the young man became the ruler of the country.

The meanings of this story are these: Do not judge, do not condemn a person for his appearance. Never despair of yourself or of others. Do not allow yourself to be destroyed by unfortunate happenings.

SOME MASAI MYTHS AND TRADITIONS

How the Masai Got Their Cattle

In the beginning of things the Masai had no cattle. Only the Dorobo people had cattle.

Naiteru-kop, a lesser god, came down one time and spoke to a Dorobo, saying: "Meet me early tomorrow morning. I have something for you."

The Dorobo answered, "Very well." Then he went to his house and slept.

A Masai named Le-eyo overheard the conversation. He arose during the night and went to the place where Naiteru-kop had spoken. He waited. When the day dawned he approached Naiteru-kop.

From The Masai, Their Language and Folklore, *by A. C. Hollis, Oxford, The Clarendon Press, 1905. Edited from the original.*

Naiteru-kop said to him, "Who are you?"

The Masai said, "Le-eyo."

Naiteru-kop asked, "Where is the Dorobo?"

Le-eyo said, "I do not know."

Naiteru-kop then began lowering cattle down from the sky with a leather thong. One by one he let the cattle down until there were many, and the Masai told him to stop. In this way the Masai received their cattle from the demigod Naiteru-kop. The cattle wandered off, and as they did so the cattle of the Dorobo mingled with them. The Dorobo were unable to recognize which cattle were theirs, and so they lost them.

The Dorobo people were angry. They went to where the leather thong hung from the sky, and they shot it down with arrows. Seeing this, Naiteru-kop went away from there to a distant place.

After that it was the Masai who owned all the cattle. The Dorobo had to hunt wild beasts for their food.

Why Man Dies and Does Not Live Again

One day Naiteru-kop told Le-eyo that if a child were to die he was to say when he threw away the body: "Man, die, and come back again; moon, die, and remain away."

A child died soon afterwards, but it was not one of Le-eyo's, and when he was told to throw it away, he picked it up and said to himself: "This child is not mine; when I throw it away I shall say, 'Man, die, and remain away; moon, die, and return.' "

He threw it away and spoke these words, after which he returned home.

One of his own children died next, and when he threw it away, he said: "Man, die, and return; moon, die, and remain away."

Naiteru-kop said to him: "It is of no use now, for you spoilt matters with the other child."

This is how it came about that when a man dies he does not return, whilst when the moon is finished, it comes back again and is always visible to us.

How the Masai Split Off from Other People

When Le-eyo grew old, he called his children to him and said to them: "My children, I am now very old, I wish to bid you good-bye."

He then asked his elder son what he wanted out of all his wealth.

His son replied: "I wish something of everything upon the earth."

"Since you want something of everything," the old man said, "take a few head of cattle, a few goats and sheep, and some of the food of the earth, for there will be a large number of things."

The elder son replied: "Very well."

Le-eyo then called his younger son, and asked him what he wanted.

"I should like, Father," the younger one said, "the fan which you carry suspended from your arm."

His father replied: "My child, because you have chosen this fan, God will give you wealth, and you will be great amongst your brother's people."

The one who selected something of everything became a barbarian, and he who received the fan became the father of all the Masai.

The Sun and the Moon

We have been told that the sun once married the moon.

One day they fought, and the moon struck the sun on the head; the sun, too, damaged the moon.

When they had done fighting, the sun was ashamed that human beings should see that his face had been battered, so he became dazzlingly bright, and people are unable to regard him without first half closing their eyes.

The moon however is not ashamed, and human beings can look at her face, and see that her mouth is cut and that one of her eyes is missing.

Now the sun and the moon travel in the same direction for many days, the moon leading.

After a time the moon gets tired, and the sun catches her up and carries her.

She is carried thus for two days, and on the third day she is left at the sun's setting place.

At the expiration of these three days (i.e., on the fourth day), the donkeys see the moon reappear, and bray at her.

But it is not until the fifth day that men and cattle see her again.

When a Masai sees the new moon, he throws a twig or stone at it with his left hand, and says, "Give me long life," or "Give me strength"; and when a pregnant woman sees the new moon, she milks some milk into a small gourd which she covers with green grass, and then pours away in the direction of the moon. At the same time she says: "Moon, give me my child safely."

The Stars

The Masai know whether it will rain or not according to the appearance or nonappearance of the stars called 'n-Gokwa (the six visible stars of the Pleiades), which follow after one another like cattle.

When the month called Loo-'n-Gokwa (i.e., Of 'n-Gokwa) arrives and the six stars are no longer visible, the Masai know that the rains are over. For 'n-Gokwa sets in that month and is not seen again until the season of showers has come to an end. It is then that they reappear.

There are three other stars which follow one another like the cattle.

They are called The Old Men (Orion's sword). Three others which pursue them from the left are called The Widows. Now, the Masai say that as the widows have lost their husbands they are pursuing the old men to get married to them.

There is also Kileghen (Venus seen in the morning), and by this star the Masai know that it is near dawn. Women pray to Kileghen when warriors are late in returning from a raid. Then there is Leghen (Venus seen in the evening), which when visible is a sign that the moon will soon rise.

Sunrise and Sunset

If, when the sun rises, the heavens are red, the Masai say it will rain; and if, when the sun sets the sky is the color of blood, they say that there are some warriors out raiding who have been successful.

The Rainbow

If a rainbow is seen in the heavens whilst rain is falling, it is a sign that the rain will shortly cease.

Children call a rainbow "Father's garment" on account of its many colors, one part being red, another white, and a third variegated. They also say: "I will give it to father for he will like it."

Comets

When the Masai see a comet, they know that a great trouble will befall them, the cattle will die, there will be a famine, and their people will join the enemies.

It is said that a comet was once seen before the Europeans arrived, and as some Masai children were watering the cattle at a pond after herding them, a creature resembling an ox but green in color issued from the water. The children were frightened, and killed it. They then disembowelled it, and found that its body was full of caul-fat instead of blood. On returning to the kraal they related what had occurred.

When the medicine man heard the story, he said: "If we see another comet, people who are green in color will come out of the water and visit our country. Should they be killed, caul-fat instead of blood will be seen issuing from their bodies."

Shortly after the appearance of the next comet the Europeans arrived. It was formerly believed that they had no blood, and that their bodies were full of caul-fat.

Sheet Lightning

If during the months of hunger sheet lightning is seen in the west, the Masai say that there is a big bird of the heavens beating the water with its wings, and that what one sees flashing is the water.

The Story of the Flocks and the Rain and the Sun

When it rains, the goats say, "The enemy have beaten us," and they run away and hide themselves; but the sheep say: "Mother has oiled us," and they remain out in the rain.

When the sun burns fiercely, the sheep say, "The enemy have beaten us," and go hide themselves in the shade; but the goats say, "Mother has oiled us," and stay in the sun.

The Story of the Night and Day

According to tradition the night is a man and the day his wife. The origin of this is that men, who are strong, go and fight the enemy at nighttime, whilst women can only work by day.

Earthquakes

When the Masai feel a shock of earthquake, some say that a number of warriors are going on a raid, others, that a mountain is trembling.

Volcanoes and Steam Jets

If smoke or steam issues from the earth, as for instance at the active volcano Donyo Engai or at the steam jets near the Gilgil River, the Masai say that there is a large deposit of chalk lying beneath the surface and what one sees is dust.

Origin of the Lumbwa People

There is a cave near the River Athi, which river is called by the Swahili the Hippopotamus River. It is believed that when Naiteru-kop brought the Masai in olden days from the district round about Kenya, and they arrived at Donyo Sabuk, some of them saw this cave and entered it. They journeyed for ten days and eventually reached a salt lake, where they came out of the earth again and settled.

These people are the Lumbwa, who in appearance are like the Masai, but they till the earth.

The Giraffe Hunters

A MASAI TALE

A man named Kume once went hunting for game. He took his weapons and went out to the tall grass. He hunted a long while, and he found a giraffe eating the leaves of an acacia tree. This giraffe was a big one. Many hunters had pursued it but had not been able to catch it.

Kume wanted this giraffe. He went back to the village to get his friend Lumbwa. He told him: "The big giraffe that many men have hunted is out there in the grass. Come back with me. The two of us together will get it."

Lumbwa took his weapons, and the two of them went to the tall grass. But the giraffe was no longer standing under the tree. It had gone to the water hole to drink.

The two hunters made a plan. Kume would climb high into the branches of the tree. When the giraffe returned to eat there again, Kume would leap on its neck and kill it with his knife. Lumbwa would hide in the grass, and when the time came, he would shoot the animal with his bow.

Kume climbed into the tree. Lumbwa hid in the grass with his bow and arrows. They waited. When the sun grew hot, the giraffe came back to stand under the tree. Kume leaped on its neck, shouting at the same time for Lumbwa to shoot.

The giraffe began to run. Lumbwa jumped to his feet and put an arrow in his bow. He saw the giraffe running with Kume clinging to its neck. He began to laugh. When before had anyone ever seen a man riding on a giraffe's neck? He laughed so hard that he could not pull his bowstring. As the giraffe galloped past Lumbwa, Kume shouted, "Shoot! Shoot!" But Lumbwa could not shoot. He was laughing too hard. He laughed until he fell down. He could not stop laughing. He laughed until he became unconscious and lay silently on the ground.

Kume clung to the neck of the galloping giraffe. Then he remem-

Rephrased from Hollis, ibid.

bered his knife. He took it from his belt and stabbed the giraffe, so that it fell down and died. He skinned the animal and cut off a small portion of meat; then he walked back to where his friend lay on the ground as though he were dead.

Kume shook Lumbwa, but Lumbwa didn't wake up. So Kume built a fire and cooked a little of the meat, which he put under Lumbwa's nose for him to smell. When the odor of the cooked meat went into Lumbwa's nostrils, he woke up, shouting, "Do not finish the giraffe without me!"

The two hunters went back to the giraffe and cooked a little more of the meat and ate it. Then Kume said, "Now I shall cut up the giraffe, but I won't share it with you because you did not help me kill it. I said, 'Shoot! Shoot!' But you did not shoot. You only fainted. Therefore you don't deserve a share."

Hearing this, Lumbwa got up from where he sat and went back to the village. There he met Kume's wife. She asked him, "Have you seen my husband?"

Lumbwa answered, "Yes, I saw him. He is hunting. I hear he is very angry with you. He intends to beat you when he returns."

Kume's wife considered this. She thought it would be wise for her to stay with friends until Kume's anger had cooled. So she left her house and went away. As soon as she was gone, Lumbwa went into her house. He sat down and waited.

After a while, Kume came with a load of giraffe meat. He went to a small hole at the back of the house and called out to his wife, "Are you there?"

Lumbwa said in a voice like a woman's, "I am here."

"Take this meat," Kume said. "Then I will go back for another load." He passed the meat through the hole, and Lumbwa said, "I have it."

Kume then went back for more. When he was gone, Lumbwa took the meat and carried it to his own house. Then he returned to Kume's house and waited.

After a while Kume came again, saying, "Are you there?"

Lumbwa said in a voice like a woman's, "I am here."

Kume passed the meat through the hole, and Lumbwa said, "I have it." Kume went out for another load. When he was gone, Lumbwa carried the meat to his own house. Again he came back and waited.

Kume, he came back and forth carrying the meat. Lumbwa, he accepted it each time through the hole in the back of the house and then carried it to his place.

At last Kume said, "I am going for the last time, to get the skin."

This time when Lumbwa went home, he did not return again to Kume's house. He went instead to find Kume's wife, and when he met her, he said, "Your husband is not angry with you anymore." So she left her friends and returned to her own house.

Soon Kume came with the skin. He threw it on the ground and asked his wife to bring out his stool so that he might rest. She brought out his stool, and he sat on it. He asked for tobacco, and she brought it. Kume then asked her to go and invite all the neighbors to come at once.

When all the neighbors arrived, Kume asked his wife if the meat was ready.

"The meat?" she said. "What meat are you speaking of?"

"The giraffe meat, what else could I speak of? All the meat, the meat from the giraffe that I killed this morning. The meat that I carried piece by piece and gave you to take care of."

"There is no giraffe meat. There is no meat of any kind," the woman said.

Kume went in. He saw there was no meat. The neighbors saw there was no meat, and they went home.

So it happened. Kume was not willing to share his giraffe with his friend Lumbwa who went hunting with him. Because of that he lost it all.

THE NUER AND GOD

The Nuer people, closely related to the Dinka and the Shilluk, live in the southern part of Sudan. According to tradition they came to this region from somewhere west of the Nile. After migrations that carried them eastward into what is now Ethiopia, they returned and settled in the region in which they are now found.

Nuer stories say that an ancestral leader named Yul was travelling with his people when an enormous gourd, a spear and an animal skin fell from the sky. The people were much frightened by the gourd because it was so big, but Yul gave them the spear and the skin and sent them away to make a settlement somewhere. Yul himself took the gourd. He split it open and Kiir, a person with great magical powers, emerged. Yul tried to persuade Kiir to come and live with the others, but Kiir refused, so Yul went on and joined his people. In time

Story and prayer texts from Mitteilungen des Seminars für Orientalische Sprachen, Africanische Studien, *by D. Westermann, Berlin, 1912.*

they went again to Kiir and promised him a
wife if he would come and live with them.
Tired of being by himself, Kiir, the magician,
accepted. He entered the village, built a house
and took a girl to be his wife. The children who
were born to Kiir and his wife are said to have
been the first Nuer people, as distinguished
from other related or nearby tribes.

Early in the twentieth century numerous
missionaries appeared among the peoples of
this region. While they were primarily interested in making Christians out of pagans, they
made great efforts to learn the languages
spoken by the tribes and something about their
customs and traditions. It intrigued these missionaries greatly to discover religious attitudes
and concepts that seemed to have parallels
with Christian teachings. They even saw parallels that weren't there. And frequently, in recording their discoveries, they twisted things a
little to make it seem that some of these people,
despite their "superstitions," were essentially
naïve, unfinished Christians at heart. Sometimes the missionaries reconceived the myths
and traditions in such a way that the tribespeo-
ple detected in them a bridge to Christianity.

Early reports indicated that the Nuer had a
number of deities. The missionary-anthropolo-
gists gave particular attention to one named
Kot, which in Nuer signified rain, but which in
a particular context, they learned, meant God.
It may well be that the Nuer had a supreme
being called Kot. But it did not seem to occur
to these early recorders of Nuer tradition that
Kot might be a Nuer concession to the German
word for deity, Gott. Whether the name Kot
was ever heard among the Nuer before the German arrivals on the scene is far from certain.

Among many tales gathered by early twentieth century missionaries is the story of the
creation, in which Kot is the supreme being
and is called, in the missionary texts, God:

When God created the people, he created man, and he created the
cow, and dura for the people to eat, and goats to eat. He made a spear
and a fish-spear, and a dancing stick, such a one as is wrapped with gold.
He made the elephant, giraffe, buffalo, teang, waterbuck, reed-buck
and gazelle—the yellow and white one, the pig, the cattle-eating lion
and the man-eating lion, the hyena, the leopard, the civet-cat and the
fox, the rat, the crocodile and hippopotamus, the fish, turtle and snake,

the heglig, nabag and ardeb trees, the talh tree, the deleb palm, the kwar and lwal trees.

And God said to the men: "You are my children, whom I have created; you are four, this is the Dinka, this is the Shilluk, this is the Nubian, and this man shall rule over you; he has the gun, his name is Cwalcotke, he is also called the Turk. He has no cows, but you shall be caught by him, he shall govern."

> The prayers of the Nuer in content are essentially African, and there is no reason to doubt the integrity of the texts set down by the missionaries. But there was a compulsion, it seems, to give the Nuer prayer a more Christian feeling by making it sound Scriptural. Nevertheless, as in these texts recorded by Westermann, the Nuer substance prevails. This is a prayer for a sick person:

"Oh, God, let the man recover, let him become well, that he may get strength again. God, what is this? Leave the sick one with us, let him recover. Return to thine own body. Take thy cow, for she was ordered for the deliverance of souls. It is thee thyself who said thus. Take the cow that she may deliver the soul of the sick one. It is thou who created us, it is the cow that delivers souls. Here is the goat, and the wild cucumber. Let him recover! In what have we wronged? Give us the soul of the sick one. Thou art our father. Why shall we suffer from sickness all days? Give us the soul, we pray thee, our great-grandfather."

PRAYER BY THE CHIEF AT A BURIAL

"Oh, God, why dost thou pursue us? Return thyself, take this thy dead man and go; let him be sufficient, do not look at us again. In what have we failed?" Then a cow is speared, and the chief continues praying: "Oh, God, take thy cow. And you [dead man] turn away, do not look at us again. We will give you your own things, but then leave us alone." The wife of the deceased is now given to another male member of his family with these words: "Bear children by her, that their fire may be raised up [that their family may not be extinguished], and their family may be able to manage their own affairs."

PRAYER FOR A WOMAN IN LABOR

"God, what is it? why can the woman not bear? It is thou who has ordered the woman to bear children, that she may create descendents, that the man's family may be preserved."

PRAYER BEFORE TAKING THE CATTLE ACROSS THE RIVER TO NEW PASTURAGE

An important annual event is the bringing of the cattle across the river, where they find better pasturage. For this the help of the sorcerer is sought. He has to find a propitious day for the transaction and to perform the necessary magic rites. He spends the night before in making witchcraft, and the following morning he prays: "Oh, God, it is thou who said that I should be sorcerer, I should do witchcraft, I should bewitch the crocodile. The cattle has no more grass, let the cattle go across the river that they may graze on yonder shore. Oh, God, it is thou who created the cow, that man might be nourished by her, let them swim safely across." When the cows have been brought to the crossing-place, the sorcerer invokes the river or the spirit presiding over the river: "Thou river of a certain man, let the cattle go across safely, all of them, let them reach the shore safely, let no one be touched by the crocodile. We are making a bargain." As a ram is brought, he goes on saying: "Take it, O river!" The ram's mouth is tied, so he goes to the river with it, and drives it into the water. Now the cattle are driven into the boats and they begin rowing them.

DIALOGUES WITH EUROPEANS

Many stories are told revealing the gap in traditions between European administrators or missionaries, on one hand, and tribal peoples on the other. Such a tale is told about a British administrator dispensing justice among the Nuer, among whom cattle theft is regarded as a most serious offense. A man was accused of stealing several head of cattle from a fellow Nuer. While the British administrator listened thoughtfully, and with eagerness that right should prevail, a number of witnesses came forward to testify that the accused man had indeed stolen the cattle. Having heard everything, the British administrator ordered that the stolen cattle be returned to their rightful owner; and he ordered the guilty man, in addition, to pay to the rightful owner two more cows as a penalty. At this point there was much indignation among the

Paraphrased from anecdotes recounted in Gari-Gari, *by Hugo Adolf Bernatzik, New York, Holt, 1936.*

Nuer attending the hearing. They reproached the official, saying: "You are an Englishman and want to be just. Yet you condemn a man to two punishments for the same crime. It is enough that he return the stolen cattle, and that his effort in stealing them was in vain. But to take away his own cattle as well is the height of injustice."

A Catholic missionary found himself in similar difficulty with the Shilluk. He had painted a delightful word picture of the beautiful and bounteous life in Europe. A Shilluk warrior stood up and said: "It cannot be true. If it were, you white men would stay in Europe instead of bothering us here." "We don't want to disturb you," the missionary said, "we only want to teach you." "Well, then," the Shilluk answered, "what can you really do? Can you build a hut?" "No," the missionary said. "Or make a spear?" "No," the missionary replied, "I am unfamiliar with it." "Well, then, can you at least make pots?" The missionary acknowledged that he could not. The Shilluk warrior said, "Among us, even the women can make pots, yet you cannot do it." The harried missionary answered, "Oh, but those are very small things. Look at the steamers on the river—that's what we can do." "All right," the Shilluk said, "show us how to build a steamer."

ETHIOPIAN BEGINNINGS: THE AXUMITE EMPIRE

Modern Ethiopia is the heir to an ancient empire that arose around the city of Axum before the Christian era. It is believed that the city was founded by Sabaeans from South Arabia who migrated into the Tigre region of Ethiopia as early as the sixth or seventh century B.C. These Sabaeans, a Semitic people, brought with them elements of an old culture, including an alphabet related to the Phoenician. From the Sabaean language there developed, in time, Geez, the precursor of modern Amharic; and the Sabaean alphabet, transformed, became the alphabet known to Ethiopians today. Over the centuries the Sabaeans and their descendents mixed with darker-skinned peoples, producing a racial stock that is distinct from other African or Arabian groups. The modern Amhara are a blend of races. They themselves say they are Habisha, or "mixed people." Myth has intertwined with history, however, and it is commonly believed among the Amhara that the mixture began when young King Menelik the First returned from Jerusalem with a great host of Israelite warriors given to him by King Solomon.

The original country of the Sabaeans in South Arabia was called Saba, or Sheba, from which they derived their name. Saba meant the southern country. When the Sabaeans migrated to Tigre it was as if they had brought their original country with them; for in Ethiopian tradition, the land of which Axum became the capital was also called Saba, or Sheba. The Sabaeans apparently believed that the southland was wherever they lived; or it could be that the historical recollections and the legends that the Sabaeans brought to Axum as the record of their pre-African experience became garbled through the centuries, leaving later generations with the impression that the country over which the Axumite kings ruled was Sheba in fact.

No doubt because they possessed a written language, the Axumites had a sense of history, and their various kings left records of their achievements, at first inscribed in stone, later on parchment. The earliest of the stone inscriptions were probably in Sabaean. Later they were in the Geez language, and, in a few instances, in Greek.

Although the Axumite Empire declined in the eighth and ninth centuries A.D., the culture to which it had given such impetus continued to thrive. A new line of kings, then and now regarded as usurpers, emerged in country to the south of Axum in the tenth century and stayed in power for something like three hundred years. This new line was called the Zagwe dynasty. In the thirteenth century the Axumite or Solomonic line—which traced its descent from King Solomon through King Menelik the First—regained the throne.

Christianity—which made its appearance in Ethiopia in the fourth century A.D.—has been a powerful influence in the shaping of Ethiopian culture. The architectural achievements of the Amharic Ethiopians (for there are other Ethiopians as well) were strongly motivated by Christian beliefs, and by the Old and New Testaments in particular. Legends and history were infiltrated by angels, saints and story motifs echoing miraculous events described in the Bible. Whatever Axumite culture may have been in the beginning, it was surely something different, or perhaps merely additional, after Christian doctrine took hold.

The Queen of Sheba Legend: The Founding of the Solomonic Dynasty

The epic of epics of the Amhara of Ethiopia—the highland dwellers who have ruled for two millennia or more—is the legend of the founding of the Solomonic dynasty of Ethiopian kings. According to the legend, the first King, Menelik I, was the son of Solomon and the Queen of Sheba, or Saba. Emperor Haile Selassie was reckoned to be the one hundred tenth descendent of Menelik I. The tradition is woven from ancient myth-legends, Old Testament motifs and fragments, and elements of Christian and Islamic doctrines. The story appears in so many variants that it is impossible to designate any one of them as the central, true version. Variants heard among the more northerly Ethiopians speaking the Tigriña dialect of Amharic differ from those heard farther south. The cloth paintings that depict the events leading to the founding of the dynasty draw on diverse traditions. And the account that is written down in the *Kebra Negast,* the *Book of the Glory of Kings,* contains details that do not usually emerge in the versions that are recounted from memory. Yet all contain certain basic ingredients: Makeda, Queen of Sheba, travels from her capital city, Axum, to visit Solomon in Jerusalem. There she becomes pregnant by Solomon, and after she returns home she gives birth to a son, Menelik. When Menelik approaches manhood it becomes apparent to the people of Sheba that he is likely to succeed Makeda on the throne, but they reject him because he is regarded as fatherless—that is, a bastard. Menelik goes to Jerusalem where he is acknowledged to be Solomon's son. Eventually he returns to Axum with Solomon's blessings, an army, and the Ark of the Covenant which he has stolen from the Temple in Jerusalem. Impressed with Menelik and his accomplishments, the people accept him as their ruler.

The story that is given below is based on oral accounts of the circumstances surrounding Menelik's accession to the throne. It varies from the *Kebra Negast* in numerous details, but in particular it fails to explain how Menelik is counted as the first of the Ethiopian kings although his maternal grandfather ruled even before Makeda's time. Following this story is a portion of one of the variants strongly colored by Christian theology; and finally, an extract from the account given in the *Kebra Negast.*

How Makeda Visited Jerusalem, and How Menelik Became King

Where now stands Ethiopia, there was no such kingdom in ancient times, but only a land ruled by a great serpent, Arwe, and he was master over everything and was feared by all the people. If one sought to see Arwe and asked, "Where is he? Is he perhaps on the other side of the hill?" it was answered to him, "No, Arwe is not beyond the hill, for the hill you see *is* Arwe." The great serpent was the length of a river, and his flesh had the toughness of iron. His teeth were as long as a man's arm, and when his eyes were open they resembled fire. And Arwe consumed everything that the people grew, their sheep, their goats, and their cattle. He also demanded from them virgin girls whom he likewise ate in his endless hunger. If the people failed to provide these things, Arwe thrashed his tail in anger; the earth shook, and boulders fell from the mountains, and dust rose into the sky. The land lived in fear.

There came to this country a stranger. He saw that in a certain house

From oral accounts taken down by the author in northern Ethiopia in 1942.

a woman was crying. He asked her the cause of her misery, and she said that the next day she must give her daughter to the great serpent. The man asked her what serpent she spoke of, and she answered, "He who lies there on the horizon, whose name is Arwe, he who consumes our cattle, our goats, our daughters and every living thing." The stranger asked, "Why do you people diminish your lives by feeding him?" The woman answered, "Because he is our master and he rules here."

The stranger reflected upon things, and after a while he said: "If you bring me what is required I will destroy the serpent that devours the land. Find for me a white lamb without any faults or blemishes. And when that is done, bring me a bowl filled with the juice of a euphorbia tree." So the woman went out seeking what was required. She found a lamb without faults or blemishes and brought it. After that she went to where a euphorbia tree was growing. She pierced its outer skin with a sharp knife, and when the white fluid began to flow she caught it in her bowl. Returning to where the stranger waited she said, "Here is the other thing that you require."

The stranger took up the lamb and the bowl and went out to where Arwe rested like a hill on the horizon. He placed the lamb on the ground, saying, "Here is a token of our submission, a perfect lamb, one without faults of any kind." Arwe raised his head and looked fearsome. Then he snatched at the lamb with his teeth and swallowed it. The man said, "Here, now, is milk to quench your thirst." And Arwe instantly sucked up the euphorbia juice from the bowl. Instantly the poisonous fluid flowed into his veins. Arwe began to thrash about, causing the earth to shake. Mountains crumbled, making a noise like thunder, and living trees standing in the plains splintered and fell upon the earth. But soon the flames in Arwe's eyes faded and he became still. The stranger returned and said to the woman, "Arwe rules in this land no more, he is dead." The news was carried from one place to another. People came from all directions and went out to verify that the great serpent did not live anymore, and there was rejoicing in the land. There was a feast that lasted three days, and people danced to the sound of drums and bamboo pipes. At last, when the celebrating came to an end, the old men came in a group to the stranger and said: "We who were withering away, now we have life. Where you were going when you arrived in this country we do not ask. Whence you came, also, we do not ask. It is enough that you have killed the great serpent. Remain here, rule over us, and we shall look on you as our father."

So the man who had destroyed the serpent remained in the country and ruled. And when he began to grow old and feel the weight of his age he said to the people, "Soon I will go to join my fathers. Let my daughter Makeda take over my responsibilities. She is young, but she will rule you well." The people discussed the matter and agreed that Makeda would rule. Now the country of which Makeda became queen was called Saba, or Sheba, meaning the Land of the South, and the capital city of the country was Axum.

It happened one time that a prosperous trader came to Axum with a caravan of incense, silks and precious stones, and he displayed some of these things before Makeda in her palace. The trader spoke often of Solomon, the powerful king in the north whose capital was Jerusalem. The trader had been commissioned by Solomon to acquire for him rare materials for constructing the dwelling place of the Ark of the Covenant. He spoke of Solomon's wisdom, his prosperity and his fine appearance; and Makeda pressed for more descriptions of Solomon, and the trader described everything he could recall about Solomon and Jerusalem. Solomon had more than four hundred wives. His palace was made of timbers and stones brought from distant places. The pastures in which his cattle grazed spread as far as the eye could see. He ruled justly and the whole nation reflected his wise laws.

After the trader had departed from Axum, Makeda continued to think about Solomon. At last she was overcome by a desire to go to Jerusalem and see with her own eyes the things about which she had heard. A caravan was assembled, and a hundred camels were loaded with gold and silver gifts, with beautiful woven cloth and perfumes and incense, and with every other kind of thing that Makeda thought would please Solomon. She chose as her companion on the journey her lady-in-waiting, and the two of them travelled in sedan chairs mounted on the backs of camels. The caravan travelled by day and camped by night, and after many weeks it arrived at the edge of the sea. There a flotilla of vessels was gathered, and Makeda, along with her servants, her soldiers and her gifts for Solomon, was transported across the water. After that the journey was by land again until, in time, Makeda arrived in Jerusalem. There she was warmly greeted by Solomon. She presented him with the gifts she had brought from Axum, which pleased Solomon a great deal, but he was still more pleased by Makeda's youth and beauty.

Now, it was morning when Makeda and her party arrived, and Solomon had a feast prepared for the evening of that day. The feast was held in the great feasting hall of the palace, and those who were present numbered more than two thousand and included the most notable persons in Jerusalem. But Solomon arranged it so that he, Makeda and her lady-in-waiting should eat separately from the others because of their exalted rank. The table that was set for the three of them was in an adjoining room, elevated above the level of the feasting hall, from which they could look through a golden grill upon those others who were sharing the feast. Thus the three of them ate in private, and Solomon was much moved by the beauty of both of the women. The food that they ate was flavored with rare and very hot spices, and the women wondered at the wonders of Solomon's kitchen.

The night grew long and the time came for them to sleep. Solomon led his guests to their sleeping quarters. It was a large room with two beds on one side and one on the other, with a finely woven rug hanging between. Makeda asked Solomon who it was who would sleep in the third bed, and Solomon answered: "Why, it is my bed, for this is where I customarily sleep; and these two on the other side are yours. It would not be seemly for you to spend the night anywhere but in the royal quarters." Makeda said: "We know little about how things are done in this country, for we are strangers here. But is it fitting that we sleep in the same quarters with a man, even though he is Solomon himself?" Solomon assured Makeda, saying: "Fear nothing. I am a just and honorable king, as all of Jerusalem will testify. No person who respects the laws of my country needs to be concerned about his safety. As you honor my laws, my laws honor you. Take nothing that is not yours, and what is yours will not be taken from you." And so Makeda and her lady-in-waiting were reassured. They went to bed on their side of the rug, and Solomon went to bed on his. But Solomon, when he had lain down, closed only one eye and the other remained open.

In the middle of the night Makeda's lady-in-waiting felt a great thirst from the hotly spiced food she had eaten. She saw a small table near the hanging rug, and on the table was a carafe of water and a cup. She went to the table and drank. Solomon's open eye perceived her and what she was doing. He left his bed and took her wrist in his hand, saying: "Ah, you have broken a law of the land, which says that no person may take something belonging to another without first seeking permission. Therefore you are no longer entitled to protection." And he took the lady-in-waiting to his bed and lay with her. Afterwards she returned to her own sleeping place.

In time, Makeda also awoke. She also felt a great thirst from the hotly spiced food she had eaten. She also went to the carafe of water and drank. Seeing her with his single open eye, Solomon left his bed and took Makeda by the wrist, saying: "Alas! Have you not broken a just law by taking something belonging to another without being invited?" Makeda answered, "What I have taken is surely not of any importance. It is only a taste of water." Solomon said to her: "Why, water is the most valuable possession of my kingdom. Without it our grain would not grow, our grapes would shrivel on the vine, our throats would be parched, and we would surely perish. Of all things a person might take from another, water is the most cherished possession. As you have violated the law, so the law of the land no longer protects you." Having heard Solomon's wisdom, Makeda could say nothing in reply. Solomon took her to his bed and lay with her, and she did not complain anymore, but on the contrary she acknowledged that she had done him a wrong.

Makeda remained for some time in Jerusalem, witnessing Solomon's greatness in all its forms. But a day came when she prepared to return to Axum. Solomon lavished many gifts upon her. And because it was clear that both Makeda and her lady-in-waiting each carried a child of Solomon, Solomon said to them: "To each of you I am giving a gold ring and a silver staff. If your child is a boy, send him to me with the ring so that I may acknowledge him. If it is a girl, send her to me with the silver staff so that I may know her." After this, Makeda and her party started their long journey home, and in time they once again arrived in Axum.

When she had fulfilled the ninth month of her pregnancy, Makeda gave birth to a son, and she gave him the name Menelik. Makeda's lady-in-waiting also had a son. Because Solomon was their father, the two sons were half-brothers. They grew and approached manhood. The people began to perceive that Menelik might claim the throne.

But they despised him, saying, "He has no father. Who is a man without a father? We cannot accept such a person to rule over us." Even Menelik's friends spoke this way sometimes, until he went to Makeda and demanded to know the name of his father. Makeda said to him: "Indeed you have a father, and he is not a mere man. He is Solomon, the great king in Jerusalem. Now it is time for you to go there and be recognized. If you are to succeed to the throne in Axum, you surely will need Solomon's help. With his favor you will have the power to become negus of Saba. Therefore, prepare yourself for the journey." Menelik said, "Yes, I will go to Jerusalem and be recognized by Solomon." Makeda gave him the gold ring by which Solomon would know him, and Menelik made ready to depart.

Now, Makeda's lady-in-waiting overheard everything. She said to herself, "Is not Solomon the father of my son also? Does not my son therefore have a right to rule in Axum?" She gave her son the gold ring by which Solomon would know him, saying: "Go quickly to Jerusalem. Waste no time on the way. Heed nothing that is told to you by strangers. Make yourself known to the king in Jerusalem. With his favor it is you who shall become negus of Saba." So while Menelik was still making ready, his half-brother, the son of Makeda's lady-in-waiting, was already on his way. And when he had travelled several days he came to a certain cave, and his servant said to him: "In this cave resides a woman known for her reading of the future. Stop and consult with her, as do all other travellers on this trail." So the young man stopped and consulted with the oracle, and she said to him: "Where you are going, what appears high is low, and what appears low is high; the leader of the sheep trails behind, and he who leads is the follower." The young man departed from the cave of the oracle. He said: "The woman is merely old, her mind is gone. And did not my mother tell me, 'Heed nothing that is told to you by strangers'?" In time he reached the sea. He secured a vessel there and crossed, and from the other shore he continued his way until at last he arrived in Jerusalem.

The young man went directly to the gate of Solomon's palace and asked to enter. The guards said, "Who are you who demands to come in?" And he replied, "I am Solomon's son." But they only laughed and refused to allow him to enter. The next day he came again, saying: "I am Solomon's son. I wish to see my father." Again he was turned away. The next day and the next he came, until word reached Solomon that a young man was outside calling Solomon his father. At that moment the king was sitting on his throne and the hall was full of people. Solomon said: "Bring the young man in. We shall find out if he is a son of mine." He got up from his throne and placed another man there and gave him his rings to wear and his scepter to hold. Solomon himself mingled with the crowd and made himself inconspicuous. His servants brought the young man in, and he entered the room where Solomon held court. Seeing the man sitting on the throne, he went forward. He took the man's hand, saying, "Father, I am your son, and here is the gold ring by which you will know me." Solomon, where he stood, was greatly annoyed. He said, "Surely no one who is so easily misled can be my son." And he ordered that the young man be taken away.

Now, Menelik was many days behind the other young man in his journey. When he came to the cave where the oracle lived, his servant said, "Stop here and consult the old woman about the future." So Menelik stopped and asked her to give him wisdom. She said: "Where you are going, what appears high is low, and what appears low is high. The leader of the sheep trails behind, and he who leads is the follower." Having said this, the oracle gave Menelik a small mirror. "This mirror," she said, "contains the secret of the riddle." Menelik gave the old woman silver coins in exchange for her prophecy, then he continued his journey. A boatman took him across the sea, and after another land journey he came to Jerusalem. As his half-brother had done before him, Menelik went to Solomon's gate and asked to be admitted. The guards turned him away, saying, "Where do these young men come from, all claiming to be sons of Solomon?" But Menelik returned again and again. When word reached Solomon that another young man from Axum was claiming him as father, he said, "I cannot be disturbed with such nonsense." The month of Sene passed, the month of Hamle passed, and when the month of Nehasie was coming to a close, Solomon said: "This person at the gate is disturbing my peace of mind. Have him brought in."

As before, Solomon put another man on the throne. He gave the man his rings to wear and his scepter to hold. He himself put on clothing made of rags, and he went out and sat in the stables as though he were a low-born caretaker of the horses. When Menelik was brought to the chamber where Solomon held court, he approached the man who sat on the throne, but he did not reach out for his hand. He looked into the mirror that had been given to him by the oracle and examined his own features. To the man who sat on the throne he said: "No, you cannot be my father, nor can I be your son, for we do not resemble each other in any way, neither in our features nor in the color of our skins. And it has been said by the oracle that in this place what appears high is low, and what appears low is high; that the leader of the sheep trails behind, and he who leads is a follower." Menelik went through the assemblage looking into the faces of all who were present, consulting again and again with his mirror, but he found no one whom he was willing to acknowledge as his father. He went out of the court chamber and wandered through the palace grounds. He came at last to the stables, where he saw only a ragged man sitting in the straw. Menelik looked into the man's face and into his mirror. Then he went to Solomon and took his hand, saying, "I am your son, Menelik," and he gave him the gold ring that Solomon had given to Makeda. Solomon's surprise was great. He led Menelik back into the palace, telling the assemblage,

"This young man is truly my son. The resemblance of his face to mine is complete, he has the token I gave to his mother, and his wisdom is kin to my own."

Solomon was delighted with Menelik, and Menelik accompanied him wherever he went. When Solomon went out to inspect the public works in his kingdom, Menelik was with him. If Solomon received a dignitary from a foreign land, Menelik was there. Even when Solomon rendered legal judgments, Menelik was at his side. And it came to be that Solomon sometimes asked Menelik's opinions on matters of state, or on what was just or unjust. The people began to ask, "Is Solomon our king or is Menelik our king?" It happened one time that two litigants came to Solomon, one bitterly complaining about the other. He who complained said, "This man's cattle came into my fields and grazed there, eating and trampling on my grain, until everything was destroyed."And the other said, "I had no knowledge of it, I did not know that my cattle had strayed." After they had argued their cases, Solomon said: "It is the duty of one who owns cattle to watch over them. The one man, he planted and cared for his grainfields; the other man, he did not watch over his herds. Therefore the herds shall be given to the owner of the grainfields to compensate for the destruction of his crops."

But Menelik spoke, saying: "The judgment is too harsh. Shall a man lose everything because his cattle have strayed and eaten in another's fields? Let the cattle be merely placed in the care of the offended person, and he shall have full use of them for three years. The calves they produce shall be his, and the milk they produce shall be his. But after three years the cattle shall be returned to their rightful owner." Hearing this, Solomon assented, saying, "Yes, that is our judgment." The word of this judgment went through the city. People said: "Heretofore Solomon was our judge. Now Menelik judges his father's judgments. We do not want two kings. Therefore Menelik must be sent away." They made their feelings known to Solomon, saying, "Send Menelik back whence he came." And when Solomon told Menelik what the people were demanding, Menelik answered: "Yes, I will go. It is time that I return to Axum. But I am your son and they demand that you send me away. Therefore, let every family make an equal sacrifice. Let every father give up his firstborn son to accompany me." So Solomon made it known that Menelik would depart if every family gave its firstborn son to accompany him. And every family gave a son to go with Menelik to Axum. Solomon lavished precious gifts on Menelik, things made of gold or silver studded with rubies and garnets. He gave him rare woven cloths and incense and perfumes, and many other such things, and also carts in which to carry the gifts, and oxen to draw the carts.

But what Menelik wanted most was none of these things, but the Ark of the Covenant containing the two stone tablets that Moses had brought down from the mountain in Sinai with the Commandments inscribed on them. It was too grave a thing to speak about to Solomon. Instead, Menelik had a false Ark made, one that resembled the true Ark in every outward way, though it had no value whatever. And the night before his departure he went to the Tabernacle with the false Ark, and he removed the true Ark of the Covenant, replacing it with the false one. The false Ark he covered with the same cloth that had covered the true Ark. And the true one he placed in a cart that had been given to him by Solomon, hiding it among many other things. When daylight came, Menelik departed with a great company formed of the firstborn sons of every family in Jerusalem, every man armed with shield and weapons. They went toward Gaza, leaving Jerusalem behind.

Several days after Menelik and his armed company had departed, a violent storm came up and lashed the city of Jerusalem, persisting through a day and a night and continuing to destroy many buildings. Solomon slept, and he dreamed that something was amiss with the Ark of the Covenant. On awaking, he called his servants, saying: "The storm is a signal that the Ark is in danger. Go to the Tabernacle and see if something is wrong." The servants went to the Tabernacle, but they saw the shape of the Ark under its covering cloth, and they returned to Solomon with word that the Ark was still there. Yet the storm went on and Solomon's mind continued to be troubled. So he sent his servants to the Tabernacle again, and this time they removed the cloth and saw that what was underneath was only an imitation. When Solomon received the news he was in despair, for the Ark of the Covenant was the very heart of Zion. So he went out at once with an army in pursuit of Menelik. When Solomon and his army reached Gaza, Menelik and his company had already gone from there. The people of Gaza said that when Menelik passed that place his entire company and his carts and oxen were moving swiftly and above the ground, so that no man's foot and no beast's hoof touched the earth; and the cart that carried the Ark of the Covenant was surrounded by a blinding light. Hearing this, Solomon cried out and began to lament, and he turned back to Jerusalem knowing that the Ark of the Covenant was lost.

As for Menelik, he continued his way southward towards the city of Axum. And during the journey a man entrusted with transportation of the Ark died, and they stopped to bury him. When that had been done, they undertook to resume their way, but the cart carrying the Ark stood as if rooted in the earth and they could not make it move. So they hurriedly dug up the man they had buried and made a coffin for him; and when he had been placed in the coffin they buried him again. But still the cart carrying the Ark refused to move. Once more they dug up the body, and they found that one finger of the dead man protruded from the coffin. They rearranged the body so that the finger was contained inside the coffin, and they buried him for the third time. And now the cart moved and the Ark of the Covenant was transported to Axum.

Makeda welcomed Menelik with a great celebration. When the people saw the Ark and the host of soldiers that accompanied Menelik they ceased to speak of him as fatherless. Makeda made Menelik king of Saba. As for the Ark of the Covenant, it resided in Axum for all time, while the counterfeit Ark remained in Jerusalem.

Another Account of the Queen of Sheba

The following excerpt is from another account
of the Queen of Sheba legend. As this version
goes, Makeda is one of the firstborn (rather
than virgin) girls who are to be sacrificed to the
serpent-king, Arwe.The killers of the serpent
are seven saints, and their weapon is a cross. As
they battle with the monster a drop of its blood
falls on one of Makeda's feet, and it is changed
into an ass's hoof. She is made queen, and her
journey to see Solomon is motivated by her
belief that he is a great magician who can restore her foot to its normal form.

King Menelik's mother was a Tigre girl named Etiye-Azeb (Queen of
the South). And in her days the people were worshipping a dragon, and
the sacrifice which they brought to him was the following: each man
among them gave in turn his firstborn daughter and an entalam [about
300 liters] of mead and an entalam of milk to the dragon. Now when
the turn of Etiye-Azeb's parents came, they tied her to a tree for the
dragon. And to the place where she was tied to the tree came seven
saints [possibly angels] and seated themselves there in the shade. And
while they were sitting there in the shade, she began to weep, and one
of her tears fell upon them. And when this tear had fallen upon them,
they looked up and beheld her tied there, and they asked her, saying:
"What art thou? Art thou Mary [alternatively, an angel] or a human
being?" And she answered them, "I am a human being." They said to
her, "And why art thou bound here?" "They have bound me in order
that that dragon may devour me," said she. They asked her, "Is he on
the other side of the hill or on this side?" "He is the hill," was her
answer. And when they saw him, Abba-Cahama grasped his beard, and
Abba Garima said, "He has frightened me," and Abba Mentelit said,
"Let us seize him," and running he threw himself upon him and smote
him. Thereupon all of them attacked him and struck him with the cross
and killed him. And when they were killing him, blood trickled on her,
and it dropped on her heel, and her heel became an ass's heel. After
that they freed her and said unto her, "Go now to thy village." And
when she came to her village, the people of her village not knowing that
the dragon was dead, drove her away. Outside of the village she
climbed a tree and stayed there overnight. The next day she went back
to them, saying, "Come ye, and let me show you that he is dead." So
they followed her, and the dragon appeared lying dead before them.
And when they saw him lying dead, they said: "Let us make her our
chief! For if God had not given this to her, how could the dragon have

This excerpt comes from an account by Enno Littmann in his The Legend of
the Queen of Sheba in the Tradition of Axum, *Leyden and Princeton, 1904.*

met his death through her?" And they made her their chief. And after she had become chief, she made a girl like herself her minister.

Thereupon she heard that the following was reported: In Jerusalem there is a king named Solomon; whosoever goes to him, is cured of the disease which he has. "If thou shouldst go, as soon as thou shouldst enter his door, thy foot would become as it was before," was said to her. After she had heard this, she braided her hair so that she resembled a man; and her minister did the same. Then she and her minister girded themselves with sabers and went away. When she was approaching, King Solomon heard of her; it was said to him, "The king of Abyssinia is coming." "Bid him enter!" said he. And when she came, as soon as she entered the door, her foot became as it was before. And she entered to the king and grasped his hand. The king ordered, "Bring bread, meat and mead!" and they sat down to eat. And while they were eating, the women out of modesty ate and drank little. So the king suspected that they were women. When it grew evening he gave order, "Make their beds for them!" and in one and the same room with him they made them, one opposite the other. And he took a skin with honey and hung it up in the room, and he put a bowl under it; also he made a hole in the skin so it would trickle. Now it was his custom, when he was sleeping, to keep his eyes half open, and when he was awake, to close them. At night when they were resting, he fell asleep, and his eyes were half open. And the women said: "He does not sleep; he sees us. When will he sleep?" While they spoke thus, he awoke, and closed his eyes. "Now he has fallen asleep," they said, and began to lick from the bowl. So he knew for certain that they were women. And he approached them both and slept with them.

> (From this point on, the story line follows closely the narrative of the preceding version, though varying in a great many details.)

Menelik's Return to Axum, and How He Became King

ACCORDING TO KEBRA NEGAST, THE BOOK OF THE GLORY OF KINGS

> The *Kebra Negast* has much of the flavor of the Old Testament, and its imagery, its miracles and its accent on the divine have their roots in the ancient Jewish literature. One perceives in the *Kebra Negast* a reuse of biblical materials in new ways. Menelik's flight from Jerusalem

---

From The Queen of Sheba and Her Only Son Menyelik, *translated from* Kebra Negast *by Sir Ernest A. Wallis Budge. London, Oxford University Press, 1932. Reprinted here by the kind permission of the copyright holders, University College, Oxford and Christ's College, Cambridge.*

> with Solomon in pursuit, for example, has some
> of the flavor of the Israelites' flight from Egypt;
> and Solomon's lamentations when he hears the
> Ark of the Covenant has been stolen has some-
> thing of the quality of Job's lamentations. The
> brief portions of the *Kebra Negast* that follow
> describe the return of Menelik (referred to as
> David) to the chief city of his mother's king-
> dom, and how he was made king. His accession
> to the throne creates the dynasty that has ruled
> Ethiopia for most of its life.

And the king of Ethiopia returned to his country with great joy and gladness; and marching along with their songs, and their pipes, and their wagons, like an army of heavenly beings, the Ethiopians arrived from Jerusalem at the city of Wakerom in a single day. And they sent messengers in ships to announce their arrival to Makeda, the queen of Ethiopia, and to report to her how they had found every good thing and how her son had become king, and how they had brought the heavenly Zion. And she caused all this glorious news to be spread abroad, and she made a herald to go round about in all the country that was subject unto her, ordering the people to meet her son and more particularly the heavenly Zion, the Tabernacle of the God of Israel. And they blew horns before her, and all the people of Ethiopia rejoiced, from the least to the greatest, men as well as women; and the soldiers rose up with her to meet their king. And she came to the city of the government, which is the chief city of the kingdom of Ethiopia; now in later times this city became the chief city of the Christians of Ethiopia. And in it she caused to be prepared perfumes innumerable from India, and from Balte to Galtet, and from Alsafu to Azazat, and had them brought together there. And her son came by the Azyaba road to Wakerom, and he came forth to Masas, and ascended to Bur, and arrived at the city of the government, the capital of Ethiopia, which the queen herself had built and called "Dabra Makeda," after her own name.

And David the king came with great pomp unto his mother's city, and then he saw in the height the heavenly Zion sending forth light like the sun. And when the queen saw this she gave thanks unto the God of Israel, and praised Him. And she bowed low, and smote her breast, and then threw up her head and gazed into the heavens, and thanked her Creator; and she clapped her hands together, and sent forth shouts of laughter from her mouth, and danced on the ground with her feet; and she adorned her whole body with joy and gladness with the fullest will of her inward mind. And what shall I say of the rejoicing which took place then in the country of Ethiopia, and of the joy of the people, both of man and beast, from the least to the greatest, and of both women and men? And pavilions and tents were placed at the foot of Dabra Makeda on the flat plain by the side of good water, and they slaughtered thirty-two thousand stalled oxen and bulls. And they set Zion upon the fortress

of Dabra Makeda, and made ready for her three hundred guards who
wielded swords to watch over the pavilion of Zion, together with her
own men and her nobles, the mighty men of Israel. And her own guards
were three hundred men who bore swords, and in addition to these her
son David had seven hundred guards. And they rejoiced exceedingly
with great glory and pleasure being arrayed in fine apparel, for the
kingdom was directed by her from the Sea of Aleba to the Sea of Oseka,
and everyone obeyed her command. And she had exceedingly great
honor and riches; none before her ever had the like, and none after her
shall ever have the like. In those days Solomon was king in Jerusalem,
and Makeda was queen in Ethiopia. Unto both of them were given
wisdom, and glory, and riches, and graciousness, and understanding,
and beauty of voice (or, eloquence of speech) and intelligence. And gold
and silver were held as cheaply as brass, and rich stuffs wherein gold
was woven were as common as linen garments, and the cattle and the
horses were innumerable.

And on the third day Makeda delivered over to her son seventeen
thousand and seven hundred chosen horses, which were to watch the
army of the enemy, and would again plunder the cities of the enemy,
and seven thousand and seven hundred mares that had borne foals, and
one thousand female mules, and seven hundred chosen mules, and
apparel of honor, gold and silver measured by the gomor, and measured
by the kor, some six and some seven, and she delivered over to her son
everything that was his by law, and all the throne of her kingdom.

And the queen said unto her nobles: "Speak ye now, and swear ye by
the heavenly Zion that ye will not make women queens or set them
upon the throne of the kingdom of Ethiopia, and that no one except the
male seed of David [i.e., Menelik], the son of Solomon the king, shall
ever reign over Ethiopia, and that ye will never make women queens."
And all the nobles of the king's house swore, and the governors, and the
councillors, and the administrators.

And she made Elmeyas and Azaryas (Azariah) the chief of the priests
and the chief of the deacons, and they made the kingdom anew, and
the sons of the mighty men of Israel performed the Law, together with
their King David, in the Tabernacle of Witness, and the kingdom was
made anew. And the hearts of the people shone at the sight of Zion, the
Tabernacle of the Law of God, and the people of Ethiopia cast aside
their idols, and they worshipped their Creator, the God who had made
them. And the men of Ethiopia forsook their works, and loved the
righteousness and justice that God loveth. They forsook their former
fornications, and chose purity in the camp that was in the sight of the
heavenly Zion. They forsook divination and magic, and chose repen-
tance and tears for God's sake. They forsook augury by means of birds
and the use of omens, and they returned to hearken unto God and to
make sacrifice unto Him. They forsook the pleasures of the gods who
were devils, and chose the service and praise of God. The daughters of
Jerusalem suffered disgrace, and the daughters of Ethiopia were held

in honor; the daughter of Judah was sad, whilst the daughter of Ethiopia rejoiced; the mountains of Ethiopia rejoiced, and the mountains of Lebanon mourned. The people of Ethiopia were chosen from among idols and graven images, and the people of Israel were rejected. The daughters of Zion were rejected, and the daughters of Ethiopia were honored; the old men of Israel became objects of contempt, and the old men of Ethiopia were honored. For God accepted the peoples who had been cast away and rejected Israel, for Zion was taken away from them and she came into the country of Ethiopia. For wheresoever God is pleased for her to dwell, there is her habitation, and where He is not pleased that she should dwell she dwelleth not; He is her founder, and Maker, and Builder, the Good God in the temple of His holiness, the habitation of His glory, with His Son and the Holy Spirit, forever and ever. Amen.

And Makeda, the queen of Ethiopia, gave the kingdom to her son David [i.e., Menelik], the son of Solomon, the king of Israel, and she said unto him: "Take the kingdom. I have given it unto thee. I have made king him whom God hath made king, and I have chosen him whom God hath chosen as the keeper of His Pavilion. I am well pleased with him whom God hath been pleased to make the envoy of the Tabernacle of His Covenant and His law. I have magnified him whom God hath magnified as the director of His widows, and I have honored him whom God hath honored as the giver of food to orphans."

And the king rose up and girded up his apparel, and he bowed low before his mother, and said unto her: "Thou art the queen, O my Lady, and I will serve thee in every thing which thou commandest me, whether it be to death or whether it be to life. Wheresoever thou sendest me I will be sent, and wheresoever thou orderest me to be there will I be, and whatsoever thou commandest me to do that will I do. For thou art the head and I am the foot, and thou art the lady and I am thy slave; everything shall be performed according to thy order, and none shall transgress thy commandment, and I will do everything that thou wishest. But pray for me that the God of Israel may deliver me from His wrath. For He will be wroth—according to what they tell us—if we do not make our hearts right to do His will, and if we do not readily observe all His commands in respect to Zion, the habitation of the glory of God. For the Angel of His host is with us, who directed us and brought us hither, and he shall neither depart from us nor forsake us.

"And now, hearken unto me, O my lady. If I and those who are after me behave rightly and do His will, God shall dwell with us, and shall preserve us from all evil and from the hand of our enemy. But if we do not keep our hearts right with Him He will be wroth with us, and will turn away His face from us, and will punish us, and our enemies will plunder us, and fear and trembling shall come to us from the place whence we expect them not, and they will rise up against us, and will overcome us in war, and will destroy us. On the other hand, if we do the will of God, and do what is right in respect of Zion, we shall become chosen men, and no one shall have the power to treat us evilly in the mountain of His holiness whilst His habitation is with us.

"And behold, we have brought with us the whole law of the kingdom and the commandment of God, which Zadok the high priest declared unto us when he anointed me with the oil of sovereignty in the house of the sanctuary of God, the horn of oil, which is the unguent of priesthood and royalty, being in his hand. And he did unto us that which was written in the law, and we were anointed; Azariah to the priesthood and I to the kingdom, and Almeyas, the mouth of God, keeper of the law, that is to say, keeper of Zion, and the ear of the king in every path of righteousness. And they commanded me that I should do nothing except under their advice, and they set us before the king and before the elders of Israel, and all the people heard whilst Zadok the priest was giving us the commands. And the horns and the organs were blown, and the sounds of their harps and musical instruments, and the noise of their outcries which were made at that time were in the gates of Jerusalem. But what shall I tell unto you, O ye who were present there? It seemed to us that the earth quaked from her very foundations, and that the heavens above our heads thundered, and the heart trembled with the knees."

The Ten Churches of Lalibela

One of the great monuments of Ethiopian history is a group of ten churches hewn out of living rock in the thirteenth century at a place called Lalibela. They are called, variously, House of Mary, Mount Sinai, Golgotha, House of the Cross, House of the Virgins, House of Gabriel, House of Abba Matae, House of Mercury, House of Emmanuel and the House of George. The architecture of these buildings is remarkable, and the dedication and labor that went into their construction have aroused awe and created myths. To produce such structures required not only master architectural planners but great numbers of stonecutters. To carve the church of St. George, for example, a deep circular trench was cut in the rock, leaving a monolithic core, and from this core was shaped a building in the form of a cross. The inner portion was hollowed out, and windows and decorative motifs were carved in the walls. The roof of the church is level with the ground, and beneath the main structure are subterranean passages and rooms. Other buildings have similar wonders. Deep within the Church of Golgotha are two tombs, one of which is said to contain the remains of King Lalibela, the other the remains of Adam, the first man. The architecture of the structures is notable, among other reasons, for the variety of cultural influences apparent in the decorative motifs. The mural paintings on the inner walls, depicting biblical scenes, are in pure Ethiopian style. But some of the windows are of Moorish design, Romanesque arches decorate the exterior walls, Greek crosses form windows, and Indian swastikas reveal influences from the East. Whether these various motifs are to be explained as the work of foreign artisans, or merely as influences filtering into the Ethiopian heartland, is not known.

According to historical accounts, the complex of churches was built by King Lalibela in his capital city, then known as Roha, to gain the favor of the country's priesthood. For Lalibela belonged to the Zagwe dynasty, which traced its lineage to Moses, while the priesthood recognized only the kings descended from Solomon and Menelik the First. The Zagwe kings came into power sometime around the tenth century, and though they retained control until about 1270, they were widely regarded as usurpers. To this day they are remembered with disfavor; all, that is, except Lalibela, whose name and works—primarily the ten churches hewn from solid rock—are honored.

While history is matter-of-fact about King Lalibela's motives, legend is not. Nor are the *Royal Chronicles,* according to which Lalibela was guided by divine revelation and assisted by heavenly intervention. The *Chronicles* say that when Lalibela was yet a young man, the king of the country was Harbay, and that Harbay was suspicious that Lalibela aspired to the throne. For it was said that at the time of Lalibela's birth a cloud of bees surrounded him, causing his mother to exclaim, "The bees know that this child is king!" And he was named, therefore, Lalibela, meaning "The bee recognizes his kingship." Because of Harbay's suspicions about Lalibela, the story says, he attempted to poison the young man, though in vain.

Then followed the major miracles. Some angels came to Lalibela and carried him to the first, second and third heavens, where God revealed to him ten churches carved out of living rock. And God declared to Lalibela that he would make him king, but that Lalibela would construct on earth ten churches exactly like those he had seen in the three heavens. After this, God appeared to Harbay and commanded him to abdicate so that Lalibela could take the throne. And when Harbay had left the throne and Lalibela had been crowned, God came again to Lalibela and instructed him to begin at once the building of the churches. And so the construction began, with God's promise that his angels would assist in the great work. According to the *Chronicles*:

Lalibela ordered the manufacture of a large number of iron tools of all kinds, some to cut out the stone, others to hew it, as well as many others for the construction of a temple in the rock. From that moment Lalibela no longer thought of his own needs or those of his wife, but fortified in everything by the Holy Spirit, dreamt each day of constructing the churches on the model of those which he had seen in Heaven. After having made the tools necessary for this work he ordered everyone to assemble and spoke to them, saying: "You who are all gathered together here, tell me what wages you want to help build these churches which God has ordered me to erect; let every man, stonemason and excavator of the soil alike, inform me as to the wage which he requires. Speak up, all of you, and what you ask of me I will give you so that you will not say that I made you work against your will, for I do not want your labor to be without recompense nor that you should murmur."

Each person thereupon made known what he wanted, and the king paid what he had promised. He did this without fail from the day the construction of the churches began till the day when it was finished. He gave wages to everyone, to those who cut the stone, to those who fashioned it, and to those who carried away the debris resulting from the cutting. . . .

The angels who were with the king made the measurements, indicating the required dimensions for all the churches, large and small. The land where the churches were to be built he purchased with gold, which was a great kindness on his part, for if he had wished to take it without payment who could have prevented him since he was king?

He first built a church resembling the one which God had shown him, an admirable work of art which a man could not create without divine wisdom; he embellished the inside and outside and gave it beautiful latticed windows. In front of this church he made two others, each with its own exit and separated inside by a partition provided with a door. Behind this he erected another large church which he adorned not with gold or silver, but with sculptures cut in stone; this latter church had seventy-two pillars. To the left and right of this first church he dug out two others.

He named the first church Beta Maryam (House of Mary), the two in front Dabra Sina (Mount of Sinai) and Golgotha, that on the right Beta Masqal (House of the Cross), and that on the left Beta Danagel (House of the Virgins); he thus grouped together five beautiful churches cut from the same rock.

Near to these five churches he built two others which were very beautiful, but of a different construction; they were separated from each other by a partition wall; he called one Beta Gabriel (House of Gabriel) and the other Beta Abba Matae. He thus united these two churches, surrounding them with a single wall, and separated them within by a partition. He also built two other very beautiful churches, again of a different design; he called one of them Beta Marqorewos (House of Mercury) and the other Beta Amanuel (House of Emmanuel). Having grouped these two latter churches together, he built another, isolated church; it was constructed in a different way in the form of the cross, as the angels had indicated to him when they were making their measurements on the land; he gave it the name of Beta Giyorgis (House of George). He thus completed the construction of ten churches, each with different architecture and appearance. . . .[1]

As for the manner in which the angels joined in the labor of the construction of the ten earthly replicas of the churches Lalibela had seen in heaven, the *Chronicles* state:

When he began to construct these churches angels came to help him in each of the operations; there were thus a company of angels at work as well as a company of men, for angels joined the workers, the quarrymen, the stonecutters and the laborers. The angels worked with them by day and by themselves by night. The men would do a cubit's work during the day, but would find a further three cubits completed on the morrow for the angels worked throughout the night. Seeing this the workers exclaimed, 'How wonderful! We did a cubit yesterday and today we have four!' They doubted whether angels were doing this work because they could not see them, but Lalibela knew, because the angels, who understood his virtue, did not hide from him; the angels were his companions and for that reason did not hide from his sight.[2]

Thus it was, the *Royal Chronicles* conclude, that these ten churches were built out of a single stone.

A Proclamation of Menelik II

(EMPEROR OF ETHIOPIA FROM 1889 TO 1913)

Menelik the Second is regarded as the ruler who brought Ethiopia into the modern age. During his rule as king of Shoa (1865–1889) the city of Addis Ababa was founded, and it became the capital of the nation. As emperor he initiated various technological advances that previously had been unknown in Ethiopia. He had fresh water piped to the capital city from the mountains. He introduced the eucalyptus tree to Addis Ababa and its environs to provide wood, which had been

---

[1] *Richard K. P. Pankhurst,* The Ethiopian Royal Chronicles, *Oxford University Press, Eastern Africa, 1967. Quoted by permission of the publishers.*
[2] *Pankhurst, ibid.*

very scarce in this region. He initiated a national currency and established a mint, built the Jibuti railway, set up schools, and instituted, at least formally, cabinet government. The *Chronicles* say that in 1899–1900 "they began in Ethiopia to speak through a wire." Menelik II was acutely aware of the need to transform ancient patterns and prejudices, and in the year 1908 he issued this proclamation:

"Let those who insult the worker on account of his labor cease to do so! Until this time you called blacksmiths teyib; those who wove the shamma you called shammane; those who wrote you called tankway; those who worked for the church you called debtera. The farmer, who produced all our food and is known to be better even than the king, you called gabare; the merchant, who brought gold, you called negade, and insulted him on account of his trade. The lazy man whose son is ignorant causes trouble by insulting the clever man. All mankind is descended from Adam and Eve; there was no other ancestor. Discrimination is the result of ignorance. God said to Adam, 'In the sweat of thy face shalt thou eat bread.'

"If we do not carry out this injunction, if everyone is idle, there will be neither government nor country. In European countries when people undertake new kinds of work and make cannons, guns, trains and other things revealed by God, the people concerned are called engineers; they are praised and given more assistants, not insulted on account of their craft. But you, by your insults, are going to leave my country without people who can make the plow; the land will thus become barren and destitute.

"Hereafter anyone who insults these people is insulting me. From this time forth anyone found insulting another on account of his work will be punished by a year's imprisonment. If officials find it difficult to imprison such persons for a year, let the latter be arrested and sent before me!"[1]

---

[1] *Pankhurst*, ibid.

THE SENSE OF WHAT IS JUST

FIVE ETHIOPIAN TALES

The Donkey Who Sinned

A lion, a leopard, a hyena and a donkey came together to talk about how bad conditions were. There was no rain, and food of all kinds was scarce.

"How can this thing have happened?" they said over and over.

"Some one of us must have sinned, else God would not have done this to us," one of them said.

"Perhaps we should confess our sins and repent," another said.

To this all of them agreed, and the lion began: "Oh, I have committed an awful sin. Once I found a young bull near the village, and I trapped him and ate him."

The other animals looked at the lion, whom they all feared for his strength, and shook their heads.

"No, no," they protested, "that is no sin!"

Then the leopard said: "Ah, I have committed a dreadful sin. When I was in the valley I found a goat that had wandered from the herd, and I caught him and ate him."

The other animals looked at the leopard, whose hunting talents they all greatly admired, and protested: "No, no, that is no sin!"

The hyena then spoke: "Oh, I have committed a terrible sin. Once I stole into the village and caught a chicken, which I carried away and ate."

"No, no!" the animals said. "That is no sin!"

Then the donkey spoke: "Once when my master was driving me along the road he met a friend, and he stopped to talk. While he talked I went to the edge of the road and nibbled a few blades of grass."

The other animals looked at the donkey, whom no one feared or admired. There was silence for a moment. Then they all shook their heads sadly, and said: "*That* is a sin! Yes, indeed, a terrible sin! You are the cause of all our misery!"

And so the lion, the leopard, and the hyena turned upon the donkey and devoured him.

This tale and the four that follow—"The Goats Who Killed the Leopard," "The Judgment of the Wind," "Fire and Water, Truth and Falsehood," and "Justice" —are from The Fire on the Mountain and Other Ethiopian Stories, *by Harold Courlander and Wolf Leslau,* ©1950 by Holt, Rinehart and Winston, Inc. By *permission of the publishers.*

The Goats Who Killed the Leopard

Once a leopard cub wandered away from his home into the grass-lands where the elephant herds grazed. He was too young to know his danger. While the elephants grazed one of them stepped upon the leopard cub by accident, and killed him. Other leopards found the body of the cub soon after, and they rushed to his father to tell him of the tragedy.

"Your son is dead!" they told him. "We found him in the valley!"

The father leopard was overcome with grief.

"Ah, who has killed him? Tell me, so that I can avenge his death!"

"The elephants have killed him," the other leopards said.

"What? The elephants?" the father leopard said with surprise in his voice.

"Yes, the elephants," they repeated.

He thought for a minute.

"No, it is not the elephants. It is the goats who have killed him. Yes, the goats, it is they who have done this awful thing to me!"

So the father leopard went out in a fit of terrible rage and found a herd of goats grazing in the hills, and he slaughtered many of them in revenge.

And even now, when a man is wronged by someone stronger than himself, he often avenges himself upon someone who is weaker than himself.

The Judgment of the Wind

A great snake hid in the forest and preyed upon many living creatures who happened to pass his way. He sometimes went out of the forest and ate goats and cattle of villagers who lived nearby. At last a party of hunters went out to destroy him so that their cattle would be safe. With their spears and shields and hunting knives in their hands they looked for the snake where they found signs of him. Hearing them approach, he fled into a cotton field where a farmer was working.

The farmer was about to drop his tools and run away, but the snake said: "Brother, enemies are following me to kill me. Hide me so that I shan't die."

The farmer thought for a moment and then said: "Though you have a bad reputation, one must have sympathy for the hunted."

And he hid the snake in a large pile of cotton standing in his field. When the hunters came along they asked: "Have you seen the serpent that kills our cattle?"

"I have not seen him," the farmer replied, and the hunters went on.

The snake came out from under the cotton.

"They are gone," the farmer said. "You are safe."

But the snake did not go away. He took hold of the farmer.

"What are you doing?" the farmer asked.

"I am hungry," the snake said. "I shall have to eat you."

"What? I save your life and then you wish to destroy mine?"

"I am hungry," the snake replied. "I have no choice."

"You are ungrateful," the farmer said.

"I am hungry," the snake said.

"Since it is like this, let us have our case judged," the farmer said.

"Very well. Let the tree judge us."

So they went before the huge sycamore tree which grew at the side of the road. Each of them stated his case, while the tree listened.

Then the tree said to the farmer: "I stand here at the edge of the road and give shade. Tired travelers come and sit in my shade to rest. And then when they are through they cut off my branches to make axe handles and plows. Man is ungrateful for the good I do him. Therefore, since it is this way, I cannot judge in your favor. The snake is entitled to eat you."

The snake and the man went then to the river, and again they told their story. The river listened, and then it said to the farmer: "I flow here between my banks and provide man with water. Without me, man would suffer; he would not have enough to drink. In the dry season when there are no rains, man comes and digs holes in my bed to find water for himself and his cattle. But when the heavy rains come I am filled to the brink. I cannot hold so much water, and I overflow onto man's fields. Then man becomes angry. He comes to me and curses me and throws stones at me. He forgets the good I do him. I have no use for man. Therefore, since this is man's nature, I cannot judge in your favor. The snake may eat you."

The snake and the man went to the grass, and once more they told their story. The grass listened, and then it said to the farmer: "I grow here in the valley and provide food for man's cattle. I give myself to man to make roofs for his houses, and to make baskets for his kitchen. But then man puts the torch to me when I am old, and burns me. And after that he plows me under and plants grain in my place, and wherever I grow among the grain he digs me out and kills me. Man is not good. Therefore, I cannot judge in your favor. The snake may eat you."

The snake took hold of the farmer and they went away from the grass.

"The judgment is very cruel," the farmer said.

But on the road they met the wind. And though he had no hope, the farmer once more told his story. The wind listened, and then it said: "All things live according to their nature. The grass grows to live and man burns it to live. The river flows to live, and overflows its banks because that is its nature; it cannot help it. And man grieves when his planted fields are flooded, for they are his life. The tree cherishes its branches because they are its beauty. And the snake eats whatever it finds, for that, too, is his nature. So you see one cannot blame the tree, the grass, and the river for their judgment, nor can one blame the snake for his hunger."

The farmer became even more sad, for he saw no way out for him. But the wind went on: "So this is not a matter for judgment at all, but for all things acting according to their nature. Therefore, let us dance and sing in thanks because all things are as they are."

And the wind gave the farmer a drum to play, and he gave the snake a drum to play also. In order to hold his drum the snake had to let go of the farmer.

"As your nature is to eat man, eat man," the wind sang to the snake.

The wind turned to the farmer, "As your nature is not to be eaten, do not be eaten!" it sang.

"Amen!" the farmer replied with feeling. And as the snake was no longer holding him, he threw down his drum and fled safely to his village.

Fire and Water, Truth and Falsehood

Truth, Falsehood, Fire and Water lived together. They went out one day to hunt, and they found many cattle. Afterwards they decided to divide the cattle so that each of them received his share. But Falsehood wanted more for himself. So he went secretly to Water and said:

"You have the power to destroy Fire. If you do this, we can take his part of the cattle."

Water believed what Falsehood said, and he threw himself upon Fire and destroyed him.

Then Falsehood went to Truth.

"Fire is dead. Water has killed him, and he does not deserve to share with us. Let us take the cattle into the mountains for ourselves."

So Truth and Falsehood drove the cattle into the mountains. Water saw them go, and he tried to pursue them, but he found he couldn't run uphill, but only down, and so they escaped.

When they arrived at a resting-place in the mountains, Falsehood turned to Truth and said: "Foolish one, I am strong and you are weak; I am the master and you are the servant. Therefore, all the cattle shall belong to me."

"No," Truth said, "I am not your servant. It is I who am strong, and therefore, I am the master." And he went forward and fought with Falsehood. They struggled back and forth across the mountain, without either one destroying the other.

So at last they went to the Wind and asked him to judge which was right. He listened to their arguments, and then he said: "It is this way: Truth is destined to struggle with Falsehood. Truth will win, but Falsehood will return, and again Truth must fight. As long as time, Truth must fight with Falsehood, because if he does not do so he is lost forever."

Justice

A woman one day went out to look for her goats that had wandered away from the herd. She walked back and forth over the fields for a long time without finding them. She came at last to a place by the side of the road where a deaf man sat before a fire brewing himself a cup of coffee. Not realizing he was deaf, the woman asked: "Have you seen my herd of goats come this way?"

The deaf man thought she was asking for the water hole, so he pointed vaguely towards the river.

The woman thanked him and went to the river. And there, by coincidence, she found the goats. But a young kid had fallen among the rocks and broken its foot.

She picked it up to carry it home. As she passed the place where the deaf man sat drinking his coffee, she stopped to thank him for his help. And in gratitude she offered him the kid.

But the deaf man didn't understand a word she was saying. When she held the kid towards him he thought she was accusing him of the animal's misfortune, and he became very angry.

"I had nothing to do with it!" he shouted.

"But you pointed the way," the woman said.

"It happens all the time with goats!" the man shouted.

"I found them right where you said they would be," the woman replied.

"Go away and leave me alone, I never saw him before in my life!" the man shouted.

People who came along the road stopped to hear the argument.

The woman explained to them: "I was looking for the goats and he pointed towards the river. Now I wish to give him this kid."

"Do not insult me this way!" the man shouted loudly. "I am not a leg breaker!" And in his anger he struck the woman with his hand.

"Ah, did you see? He struck me with his hand!" the woman said to the people. "I will take him before the judge!"

So the woman with the kid in her arms, the deaf man and the spectators went to the house of the judge. The judge came out before his house to listen to their complaint. First, the woman talked, then the man talked, then people in the crowd talked. The judge sat nodding his head. But that meant very little, for the judge, like the man before him, was very deaf. Moreover, he was also very nearsighted.

At last, he put up his hand and the talking stopped. He gave them his judgment.

"Such family rows are a disgrace to the Emperor and an affront to the Church," he said solemnly. He turned to the man.

"From this time forward, stop mistreating your wife," he said.

He turned to the woman with the young goat in her arms.

"As for you, do not be so lazy. Hereafter do not be late with your husband's meals."

He looked at the baby goat tenderly.

"And as for the beautiful infant, may she have a long life and grow to be a joy to you both!"

The crowd broke up and the people went their various ways.

"Ah, how good it is!" they said to one another. "How did we ever get along before justice was given to us?"

Four Poems from the Amharic

EXTRACTED FROM SONGS SUNG TO THE ACCOMPANIMENT OF THE BEGENNA, THE ETHIOPIAN HARP.

INVOCATION TO WARRIORS

> Strike them! Strike them!
> If we flee, the road is long.
> If we want the road to be short,
> Let us attack the enemy.
> Even though they are many,
> We are not less courageous than dogs.

AFTERMATH

> When one looks ahead,
> The valley grass is high.
> When one looks towards the mountains,
> The rocks are numerous.
> Who then will carry home
> The bodies of our companions?

O MY COUNTRY

> Listen, O my country!
> Does not a man say, "O my country"

From the author's ms. notes, and from the text accompanying the record album, Folk Music of Ethiopia, *by Harold Courlander. New York, Ethnic Folkways Library, 1951.*

When things go badly for him?
They say that death came.
Oh, misery, oh, misfortune!
Even if death devours men,
What should I do?
Listen my country! Listen my country!
The land lies neglected,
There is no durra to be harvested.
There is no threshing in the fields,
Which are overgrown with wild brush.
Yet even though the times are bad,
Does not a man go on living?
Does he not hold the mountain passes
And guard the wells against the enemy?
A man goes on living
Even when his companions have died in battle.
Listen, O my country!

I BEG YOU, HEART

I beg you, heart,
Accept it.
I have no family.
I beg you, heart,
I have no family,
So be you my family.
I beg you, heart,
I have no refuge,
So be you my cavern to live in.

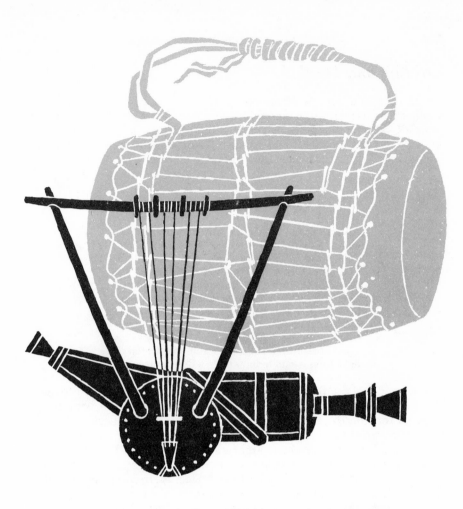

MYTHS AND LEGENDS OF THE MENSA
BET-ABREHE

The Mensa are a Cushitic people of northern
Ethiopia descended from ancient immigrants
from Arabia. There are two separate groups of
these people—the Mensa Bet-Abrehe (House
of Abrehe) and the Mensa Bet-Esc'haqan
(House of Esc'haqan). The stories and traditions given here are those of the House of
Abrehe tribe, and all of them come from *Publications of the Princeton Expedition to Abyssinia,* by Enno Littmann, Leyden, E. J. Brill,
1910.

Creation and Death

God said to men: "Multiply on earth and bring forth and become families!" And the human race multiplied very much. But they revolted against God. Then God said to men again, "Well then, man, bring forth and bury, that thou be ill and grieved!" And by this curse the human race brings forth and buries until this day. This is what they say.

The Rom, a Race of Giants

> According to the Mensa, the Habab and various other Cushitic peoples of northern Ethiopia, a race of giants, called Rom, once inhabited their country. According to tradition, the Rom were nomadic herdsmen. Old tombs made of stone slabs are believed to have been built by the Rom, as explained in one of the following stories. People of this region sometimes point out peculiar rock formations as other creations of the giants, and one stretch of flat stones is said to have been a Rom causeway.

The people of the Rom were living with their cattle everywhere. And the wells from which the Rom watered their cows were very deep, about of the length of a packing-rope [for mules]. And every Rom man when watering his cows used to draw the water putting his one foot in the well and the other in the trough; and his water-vessel was the entire hide of a bull. When he ate he was never satisfied; and he milked his cattle into a vessel made of an elephant's skin and drank it; and he killed one cow for every meal, and without cutting her into pieces, he roasted her on a wood fire and glutted her down. And when he gathered wood for his fire, he tore the aqba tree out with its roots and shoved it into the fire. And at a certain place there was living a man with his wife, both of the now-living mankind. Now, the wife abused the man and said to him: "What power have you? You cannot raid the cattle of the Rom!" The man replied: "Now, if I do not take some of them and come back with them, I shall be a weakling according to your word!" And the man went to the Rom, and came to a Rom man, a cattle-owner. And he sat down near his cattle. When the giant saw him, he went straightway to him and greeted him and asked him: "From where do you come?" The human answered: "I am from such and such a place." Thereupon the giant tore out the aqba trees and put them together for a fire. Then taking the elephant skin vessel he milked all his cows. When the visitor saw his doings he was frightened and said to himself: "Who can raid this man's cattle?" The giant, having milked, said to the man: "Take and drink!" But the man was not able to receive and hold the skin and the milk. Thereupon the giant seized it and gave him to drink. But when the man had drunk a little, he said: "I am satisfied now!" The giant said:

"Drink! How can you be satisfied, not having begun?" The man said: "I am satisfied; this is my limit." And the giant went away with his milk saying: "What sort of a manikin are you? You have no belly!" And he drank it himself. Thereupon he killed a cow and roasted her; and for his visitor he tore off a hindquarter and gave it to him. And after the man had eaten a little of it, he said to him: "I am satisfied." But the giant glutted all the meat of the cow. Thereupon, belching, he said: "Praise be to God! This little locust has made us belch." And when the man saw all this he said all night: "Thy wonder, O God!" The next morning the giant asked him, saying: "Why have you come and what do you wish?" The man replied: "I have become poor, and I am come to tend your cattle." But the other said: "What power have you to tend my cattle? You cannot water them nor carry the skin into which they are milked. But live from these cows!" And he gave him a few cows. The man returned with the cows to his wife and said to her, "I have taken away the giant's cows." And when they were living together, the wife said to her husband, "Now since you are courageous, take again the giant's cattle away!" And the man went to the giant. Said the giant to him, "Why have you come? Have I not given you cows to live from?" The man answered: "Those cows have perished. Now make me your herds-man; I can tend your cattle." The giant said: "Very well then! We shall see whether you can." Then he said, "Drive the cattle!" and giving him the bullskin he added: "Take it down and water them from my well! But this, my daughter, shall go down with you to hold back the cattle while they are not drinking. Do not let her draw the water of the well: descend into the well yourself and water them!" The man, with the giant's daughter driving the cattle, went down to the riverbed. There-upon when he saw the depth of the well, he did not know what to do: if he went down he would find nobody to take the water from him; and if he went up, he could not reach the water. Then he let down the bucket of the bullskin into the water, but when it was wetted and he wanted to lift it, he could not do so. And the cattle grew very thirsty. Thereupon the girl said to him: "I shall water the cattle the way my father waters them. Then wipe the sand of the well thoroughly off from me, lest my father see it and kill you!" The man said to her: "I shall thoroughly wipe it off from you." Now the girl descended into the well, and she put her one foot into the water and the other into the trough, and drawing the bucket she watered the cattle. After she had come up from the well, the man wiped the sand off from her. When they came home towards evening the giant asked, "Have the cattle drunk?" The man replied, "Yes, I have watered them myself." But the giant said to him: "How could you by yourself? Probably you have made my daugh-ter draw the water." The man: "I have watered them myself; she has only kept back the cattle for me." Now the giant looked for sand on the body of his daughter, and searching her, he found some grains of sand in her ear. And he said to the man: "You have made my daughter draw; is this not sand?" and he sprang upon him to kill him. The man fled and came to another giant and asked for his protection; that giant was plowing. The other giant running after him came to kill him. But the giant who was plowing said, "He is my client, I shall not give him to you!" And when he refused him to the other, the giant tore up a baobab tree to kill his brother, and came towards him. But the other put his client into the fold of his cloak at his waist and went straightway against the other with his plowing instruments. And they struck each other and wounded each other. Thereupon their friends came and reconciled them. The other returned home, and the plowman stayed with his client. Then, in his anger he prepared his pipe and smoked; he opened his belt and took the man out of the fold. But he had been crushed and was dead now. Then the giant was frightened, but afterwards he said: "Be like fencic [a small bitter herb], you manikin! For thy sake I have been fighting in vain, since your soul is as weak as this!"

How the Giants Disappeared

While the giants were living on and on, the time of their end was ripe. And God gave the tribe of the giants the choice of one of these two ways: "Shall I now make you perish by a blessing or by a curse? Which do you wish?" And the tribe of the giants said to God: "Now then, since you are to destroy us, let us perish by a blessing!" And God said to them: "Perish by a blessing then. Your wives shall bring forth male children unto you; your cows, however, shall all bring forth female calves unto you!" And all came to pass as God had spoken. Their wives brought forth only male children; and when they grew up they found no wives to marry, for their whole tribe had begotten male children only. And all their cows brought forth female calves; and when they grew up they found no bull to cover them, and they died, weak from old age. Then the tribe of the giants assembled to hold a council: "What shall we do now? Our sons have found no wives to marry and they shrivel up in old age, and our offspring has diminished. Our cows have found no bull to cover them; they have had no milk nor covering." Thereupon they decided thus: "Let everyone dig his grave and put the stones of his tomb together like a hut over it, but let him leave a door in it. Then let him enter through the door with all his property and close the door!" And everyone went to his place to do thus. And they did thus. Every one of them dug his grave and built up the stones of his tomb like a hut over it, and left a door to enter by it; and taking whatever he owned and his cows he entered his grave and closed it. And in this way they all perished at the same time. And their tombs are to be found until this day everywhere, those that have heavy and large stones. But they have left no known village or settlement, because they were uncivilized and roaming herdsmen only. And now people say as a proverb when the rain grows plentiful beyond measure, "O Lord, do not let us perish by a blessing like the giants!" And again as a proverb they say: "Does a man dig his tomb like the giants? On the contrary, his people bury him."

Certain Years as They Are Remembered in Mensa Bet-Abrehe Tradition

In the country of the Mensa Bet-Abrehe they know the years and the periods in which some great wonders and signs have happened. Or rather they tell about the times at which those happened, and they reckon the birth of their children according to them. Also they reckon the birth of their children from the death of a well-known man or from the times of their raiding or their being raided. Now the great years that are very well known and about which they tell much are the following:

THE YEAR OF STAGNATIONS

In the Year of Stagnations rain disappeared from the earth, and famine came over men and over beasts. And they fed the animals with leaves, stripping the trees. And when the leaves were burned they went with all their animals to the lowlands near the sea; and there they found locusts for them and fed them on them. And the milk of the animals resembled the color of the locusts. And those that were born in this year have died as old people long ago, they say.

THE YEAR OF THE FIRST OBE [1844]

When Dagac Obe had begun to reign he made a raiding excursion against the country of the Bet-Abrehe and the Bogos [Dagac Ubie, who ruled in northern Abyssinia about the middle of the nineteenth century, and who was vanquished by King Theodoros in 1885]. At first Dagac Obe had said to the Bet-Abrehe, "Give me tribute." But the Bet-Abrehe had not known of tribute up to that time; thus, they refused it to him. And for this reason he made a raid upon them. The flocks fled from him, he found little, but he killed many people. Those that were born in this year have died as old people not long ago.

THE YEAR OF DEGGE-TASASA OR OF THE SECOND OBE [1849]

Dagac Obe made a second time a raid upon the Bet-Abrehe, when their village was in Tasasa. And he took many animals from them. And those that were born in this year are living yet, approaching old age.

THE TIME OF EMPEROR THEODOROS [1855–1868]
THE YEAR OF THE SMALLPOX

Even before that year they had known the smallpox, but up to that year it had not come in all its strength. And in that year there died of the Bet-Abrehe about seven hundred people, old and young. And they vaccinated the people from the matter of each other. Those that were born in this year, are living in the prime of life.

THE YEAR OF THE DENIAL

In this year there was a great denial. At that time there was the malaria in the country of the Bet-Abrehe, and many people died of it. And the denial was about death: for the old people buried the youths. [That is, the young did not bury the old.] Those that were born in it are living as young men.

THE YEAR OF THE PULMONARY DISEASE

The Bet-Abrehe had not known cattle diseases up to that time. And in that year a pulmonary disease came over their cattle: every cow began to cough and died after a short sickness. And when they skinned her they found that her lung was swollen and that there was in her abdominal cavity something spun like a spider-web. And they called the disease *sambu* [lung]. They vaccinated the cattle from the blood of each other. And this year of the pulmonary disease is known in all the Tigre country. And only one or the other cow escaped from the disease. Those that were born in this year are also living as young men.

THE TIME OF EMPEROR JOHN AND OF RAS ALULA [1870–1890]
THE YEAR OF THE EARTHQUAKE

In this year there was an earthquake in the whole Tigre country. About noontime the earth was torn asunder and trembled much; and on the mountains fires [volcanos?] were kindled. And many large boulders that are now in the plain fell down from the mountains at that time, they say. And by the stones that fell down some people were wounded in the country of the Mensa Bet-Abrehe. And in the clefts of the earth also fire was seen, they say. And there are persons who have seen a cow swallowed by the earth. And the earthquake stopped after a short while. And also the fires were soon extinguished. Even those that were born in that year are living as young men. And this time is very well known.

THE YEAR OF WAD-QEDRAS

In this year the Bet-Abrehe quarrelled among themselves, and they were divided into three factions. Now Wad-Qedras was a follower of the party of Kantebay Be'emnat. And he insulted a man, calling him "sorcerer" without any reason. And the man that had been insulted had Wad-Qedras killed for this word. But afterwards he paid the weregelt and gave also "house and cattle" to the son of the dead [i.e., he married his daughter to him without bride payment and gave her a dowry].

THE YEAR OF GERDEFAN

Gerdefan was a man of the Ad Takles. And the Bet-Abrehe made a raid upon his flocks and killed him there. And they came with his cattle and divided it.

THE YEAR OF AZZAZI

The Bet-Abrehe were once split into parties. And Azzazi, the son of Hebtes, sided with the one party. And when the two parties fought, Azzazi killed a prominent man of the other party, and afterwards he died there also. Those that were born in this year are living as youths.

THE TIME OF EGYPTIAN RULE OR THE TIME OF MESTENGER-BASA [1870–1880]
THE YEAR OF THE TURKS AND THE AMHARA [1876]

In this year the Turks fought with Emperor John at Gera [Gura] and at Kesad-Eqqa, and Emperor John was victorious.

THE YEAR OF THE MURRAIN

In this year a disease came over the cattle. And it made them sick: it made their hair look singed, their ears hang down, their eyes water and their mouths drivel. Finally they died of it. And that was the end of their abundance of cattle. And because it did not leave anything, they called it *gelhay*, i.e., the shaved [bald] one.

THE YEAR OF ENTI-CEWU [THE BATTLE OF ADUA, 1896]

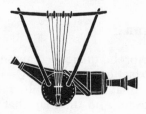

PHILOSOPHICAL AND PROVERBIAL SAYINGS OF THE MENSA, AND THE TALES FROM WHICH THEY DERIVED

The Two Donkey Owners

"EVERY CREATURE LONGS FOR LIBERTY."

Two men met each other on the road; and each of them had a donkey. Then the men greeted each other: the donkeys also, putting their mouths together, sniffed at each other. And the one man asked his fellow, saying: "We have greeted each other. Why have the donkeys also put their heads together?" The other man answered him: "Do you not know this? The donkeys have sent a strong donkey to the Lord to enter their plaint before him, that is to say, that the Lord should free them from the tyranny of men. Now they ask each other, saying: 'Has the messenger-donkey returned or not?' " And it is said that all donkeys ask each other about this matter putting their mouths together. By this tale it is seen that every creature longs for liberty.

The Prophet and the Hyena

"YOUR VOW HAS BECOME LIKE THAT OF THE HYENA."

A Moslem prophet said to the hyena: "Pronounce the creed and make a vow to eat only what you yourself have killed." And the hyena made a vow to refrain from all carrion. And the prophet set out to go away and mounted his camel, and he let the hyena ride behind him on the camel. And while they were travelling, everybody that saw him with the prophet was very much astonished that he had taken the vow and become a pupil of the prophet. And while they were thus travelling with each other, they met a carcass on the road. And the hyena sniffed the smell of the carcass. Said the prophet to him: "Daughter of Moses [a name of the hyena], do not sniff at this now after you have taken the vow to refrain from it!" But he sniffed again at the carcass and said to the prophet, "May we not even sniff at it?" He replied, "No!" And after a little while the hyena got off from his place behind the prophet, saying, "This is the food of my mother and my father!" He jumped at the carcass. And the prophet was sorry because the hyena had broken his vow, and he went his way. And now they say as a proverb to people who do not keep their oath or their vow: "Your vow has become like that of the hyena."

The Proverb of Adeg wad Fedel

"IS NOT THE JOURNEY ON WHICH I AM GOING LONGER?"

Adeg wad Fedel fell sick; and in his sickness he grew very thin. Being weak he had no desire for food, but, with difficulty, he managed to swallow milk. And one day he wished to drink milk and asked for it. But his attendants said to him: "Today your son drank it; there is no milk. He went to the Barka country; and thinking that he had a long journey before him we gave it to him." Said Adeg, "Is not the journey on which I am starting longer?" And this has become a proverb until the present day: " 'Is not the journey on which I am starting longer,' said Adeg wad Fedel." This is what they say.

God's Gift to Children

"HE WHO BEGETS, LOSES."

When God created the little children he gave them the choice between two gifts: "Shall I sew every morning a new cloth and give it to you, or shall I make you to rule over your fathers and mothers?" And the little children chose to rule over their parents. And for this reason the children when they are little rule their parents and cry to them and try to get their will whatever it be. And the parents are under their rule; and they obey them and whenever anything happens to them they are grieved about them. And they say as a proverb: "He who begets, loses."

A Proverb Made by the Ad Takles People

"AND DOES NOT THE DISEASE OF ANIMALS ATTACK THE DONKEY?"

Once some people of Ad Takles came as strangers into the Belen country. And Adeg wad Fedel received them and entertained them well. Afterwards when they were joking with each other, the people of Ad Takles said to Adeg wad Fedel: "O son of Fedel, how is it that you, being a prominent and honored man, have been called by this name Adeg (i.e., Donkey)?" And he answered and said to them: "My mother was losing her children by sickness and death; thereupon when I was born she called me Adeg lest I should die also. Said they: "And does not the disease of animals attack the donkey?" And they all laughed together. And now they say as a proverb: " 'And does not the disease of animals attack the donkey?' said the Ad Takles."

The Leopard in His Old Age

"WHEN THE LEOPARD GROWS OLD, THE GOATS MOCK AT HIM."

When the leopard grew old he became gap-toothed; and he had no means of killing the wild animals or the goats. So he shrivelled up with hunger; and while he was cowering, shrunk up in this way, he saw goats roaming about near him. But he had no teeth to kill them with, since old age had come upon him; and he remembered the meat which formerly, when young, he used to eat after killing the goats; and in his sadness he sang this song:

> "Woe is me! O dark Nali [name of a goat]!
> I am too old for the meat of the goat:
> The two kidneys, the two arm muscles;
> The heart and the dark liver;
> A bunch of entrails spread on the rock!"

And the goats were mocking at him. And when he had sung this, his soul left him. Now they say as a proverb: "When the leopard grows old, the goats mock at him."

The Debbi

"HE PROBABLY HAS A HAIR OF THE DEBBI WITH HIM."

The debbi is a wild animal; its height is less than that of a dog. They say that it frightens all the wild animals. Once a man went down to a lonely river to fetch water. But at the river he found all the eatable and uneatable animals drinking. So the man hid himself in a certain place until all the animals had drunk and gone away. But while the man was hiding thus he observed all the animals. And after all had drunk, each went to its place. And the elephants were romping together, and the lions together, and the hyenas together. And they all were scuffling, each with its kind. Now while they were in this state, the debbi came down to the river. And when it came, all the animals became wildly excited and fled instantly; and all left the riverbed. The man was very much astonished and exclaimed: "Thy wonder, God! What is this?"

Thereupon the debbi came down to the well, and after it had drunk it went up, then it wallowed at a certain spot, and went out by the way in which it had come down. Now, when all had gone away from the riverbed, the man rose from his hiding place wondering that all the eatable and uneatable animals had fled from the little one. He drew water from the well and started on his way. But then he thought, "I had better try to find out exactly of what sort that is which has put them all to flight." And he came to the place where it had weltered, and there he found a hair. Then the man took the hair and tied it up with a knot in the corner of his cloak. Afterwards when he entered a village, all the people of the village fled from him. But the man did not know for what reason they fled from him. And he went to another village; but that village also fled from him. And the man was frightened and said to himself, "What have I become that all flee from me as from a madman?" But of the people of the village a brave and courageous man stood before him and shouted at him, saying: "You man, what have you by which you put us to flight?" The other replied: "I have no weapons; on the contrary you flee from me by yourselves!" Again the man said to him: "No! Have you perhaps some root with you?" Then he thought of the hair and answered him: "I have no root; but I went down to a riverbed, and because I found there all the wild animals I hid myself until they made room for me. And from my hiding place I observed this: a little hairy one smaller than a dog came down to the river; and when the animals saw it, they all fled from it, even the elephants. And after it had drunk from the well and gone up, it wallowed at a certain spot. Thereupon, wondering very much, I took a hair from its wallowing place, and it has been in the end of my cloak until now." And the other man bought the hair from him with money. Then he sewed it up in a leather case, and it became his talisman, and he hung it around his neck. And the people of every village and tribe were afraid of him. Whatever he took raiding he brought in; and when his village was raided he made the raiders give up their booty. And there was nobody who could stand before him in a fight. But afterwards when he lost the talisman with the hair, warriors killed him, they say. And now men say of a man who has something frightful about him, "He has probably a hair of the debbi with him." This debbi is only seen at times; and then everybody, be it man or animal, flees from it. But he who finds some of its hair fallen on the ground and carries it on his body is feared by all men. And the abiding place of the debbi is generally the region of the Barka; but it is not often seen.

The Descent of Mount Gadam

"DO NOT MAKE A MISTAKE, LET EACH ONE STAND IN ITS PLACE."

Once all the mountains held a council, saying: "Let us go down to the lowlands!" And when they rose to go down, Mount Gadam was the first to set out, and going onward his one end was planted in the sea without his knowing it. Now the sea was upon him so that he could not march on; and his one end was firm in the ground so that he could not return. [Mt. Gadam stands near the city of Massawa.] So he shouted and said to his company, "Let every one of you stand still at his place!" And all the mountains back of Mount Gadam stood each in its place, and they are there until this day. And for this reason Mount Gadam is ahead of all the other mountains on the seashore. And they say as a proverb: "'Do not make a mistake, let each one stand in its place,' said Mount Gadam." And as another proverb they say: "We have been mistaken like Mount Gadam."

Dannas and His Slave

"BECAUSE MY MASTER HAS DRAWN, I HAVE DRAWN."

Dannas was with his slave at a place called Ayde. And while he was travelling with his slave, he drew his sword. When the slave saw that his master had drawn, he too drew his sword. Dannas asked his slave, "Why have you drawn?" And the slave replied, "Because my master has drawn, I have drawn." Now Dannas thought he would frighten him, and he lifted up his sword against him without striking. But the slave said to himself: "He is going to kill me, but I shall anticipate him." So he cut his master's throat. In this way Dannas, intending to try his slave, brought death upon himself. And now they say as a proverb: "'Because my master has drawn, I have drawn,' said the slave."

The Heway Snake

"DRINK FROM THE WELL OF HEWAY."

Among the serpents there is a large snake called heway. His color is white, and his eyes are big. Now this heway kills by his leer, be it a man or an animal. But if men, before heway looks at them, notice him first and run away closing their eyes tight, they are saved from him. If, on the other hand, heway sees them first, be it a man or an animal, they die suddenly on the spot. But he is not seen very often. They say that in the days of old some people died of his glance. Once heway drank water from a well. And after him cowherds came down there and drew water for their cattle out of the well into the trough. And when the first division of the cattle had tasted the water, they fell dead. The herdsmen went with the rest of their cattle to another well and watered them from it. And the first well they called the Well of Heway, as it is told; but they did not see heway, it may have been merely something imagined. And men say, cursing: "Drink from the Well of Heway!" And again, of a man with the evil eye they say: "His face is like that of heway; it is disagreeable."

The Poison of the Chameleon

"THEY ATE CHAMELEONS, SO THEY DIED."

Of the chameleon some medicine is obtained. This animal changes its color all the time. And a man who is smitten with headache sits down and wraps himself up in his cloth; then others catch a chameleon and put it on his head. And when, creeping on him, it has changed its color, it has taken away the disease of his head, they say. Thereupon they take it from him and throw it away. And in this way the headache leaves him, they say. But the chameleon is poisonous, and camels that eat it with the foliage die; and then men say: "They ate chameleons, so they died."

The Tail of the Wolf

"MY BLOOD IS THE BLOOD OF A WOLF."

There are wolves in the Tigre country. And sometimes a wolf kills a goat, or when they are many, they kill a cow. And men make them give up what they kill; but they do not throw a weapon or a stick or a stone at them, but they throw only pebbles. If the wolves do not heed them, but refuse to give up what they have killed and eat it, men do not wound them with iron or wood or stones for this reason: when the wolf is wounded he sheds blood, and then he dips his tail in the blood and flicks it at him who wounded him. And that man dies if the blood touches him. For this reason they do not throw at the wolves anything but pebbles, because they are afraid of their blood. And so far nobody has ever killed a wolf. And the wolves do not kill men either; but they threaten to kill them. The wolves live in packs, or sometimes they go singly. They are of all colors, and their height is like that of a dog. Men say as a proverb: "My blood is the blood of a wolf," that is to say, it kills him who sheds it.

HISTORICAL RECOLLECTIONS OF THE MENSA

The Fight at Balqat

Once the Ad Takles were enemies with the Habab. The head of the Habab party was Kantebay Gaweg wad Fekak; and the head of the Ad Takles party was Fekak wad Nauraddin. At first, the Ad Takles had killed a man of the Habab. And the Habab, mourning for their man, had ceased to shave until they should destroy each other. Now the armor-bearer of Fekak wad Nauraddin was in the country of the Habab; and Kantebay Gaweg was asking him every day about the ways of Fekak wad Nauraddin. And the armor-bearer of Fekak said: "The ways of the son of Nauraddin are hard, who can resist him? When he fights he is valiant; when he jumps, he is a falcon." And Kantebay Gaweg said to him, "How do you think that he can be reached?" The armor-bearer of Fekak replied: "There is no way to reach him, unless he be reached in one single way: He has two wives, and they sometimes quarrel with the words: 'Make you his meal for him.' Now he is an obstinate man, and he then refuses the meal and does not take it for three days. At that time when he, after having fasted, jumps, the strap of his sandal being long may make him stumble." When Fekak wad Nauraddin was playing fersit[1] at Balqat near the frontier of the Ad Takles country, the Habab party invaded it. And one of the players seeing the army of the Habab said to Fekak: "We are robbed! An army has come." But Fekak said: "It is they who are robbed; what are they but an army of men with pubes!" Then he planted his staff in the midst of the pebbles of the game, so that they should not be mixed up with each other; for he said when he had driven the army back, he was to continue the game. He swung his sword high up so that its scabbard flew off; and a hawk, thinking the scabbard was a piece of meat, plunged down upon it. And Fekak struck three men of the Habab army, and when he jumped up intending to strike others the strap of his sandal made him stumble because he had been fasting, and he fell. The Habab army killed him; and at this place the Ad Takles and the Habab destroyed each other. And until the present day their tombs are seen there; and the place has been called "The Fight of Balqat."

The Battle of Sangera

Another time again the Ad Takles and the Habab were at enmity with each other. That Mahammad, the son of Kantebay Gaweg, after his father's death, was to take vengeance for the death of his father, this it was which for a second time caused enmity between the Habab and the Ad Takles. And with the Ad Takles there were the sons of Nauraddin, the brothers of Fekak: Eshaq, Hebtes-Sangab, Hadambas and Sawes;

---

[1] See page 566.

the head of the Ad Takles party was Eshaq wad Nauraddin. And the head of the Habab party was Mahammad, the son of Kantebay Gaweg. And these two parties met at a place between the Ad Takles country and the Habab country, called Sangera: there they fought and wrought havoc with each other. And Eshaq wad Nauraddin said to a slave named Hamad-Nor, son of Gamilay, of the Ad Amdoy branch, but a slave of the Habab, "Come here, slave!" But Hamad-Nor replied: "Do not call me slave, Armasis, but call me mountain [brave]. Formerly their slave, today their mountain!" Then he and Eshaq broke through the lines making for each other. Eshaq struck him with the sword and cut his side open. But Hamad-Nor with his lungs hanging out of his body cut off both legs of Eshaq, and Eshaq died on the spot. And even after that Hamad-Nor killed Hadambas wad Nauraddin. And again, the warriors of the Ad Takles pierced Hamad-Nor with the spear. But even pierced as he was he killed many people; for he was brave and a clever fighter. And finally he died on the spot. For this reason do many of the bards in their songs say, "like Hamad-Nor of Sangera." Even until the present day they speak of a brave and strong man "like Hamad-Nor of Sangera." And these two parties destroyed each other: there were more dead on the Habab side, but the Ad Takles had lost their leaders. And until the present time their tombs are in this place. Thereupon when the two parties had returned home, the Habab said, "It is the Ad Takles who have wronged us, and therefore we have become enemies." Temaryam wad Gerub, a man of Ad Takles, sang when he heard of the talk of the Habab, the following song:

"Are they of guilt afraid or not afraid, the Bet-Asgade [the Habab],
    of their guilt?
Upon us have they put the blame for all the bloodshed of Sangera.
Since they have killed our brothers, since we have seen their
    blood,
There is no one now to give us milk when we enter their village.
The noble ones are no more our brothers, nor are the bondmen
    our bondmen.
Our beast of burden is our shoulder, we carry a small measure
    journey after journey.
Of all the camels no camel is ours, of all the donkeys no donkey.
We and the Bet Asgade have become like a cleft rock."

Besides this, the Ad Takles used always to split up into parties among themselves and to ruin each other with sword and spear. Once they split and were divided into two parties: the party of Geme wad Derar was the one; and the other was the party of Galaydos wad Ezaz. And these two parties met at a place of their country called Laba; and there they wrought havoc with each other. And at another time they destroyed each other's cattle at Caamur. And again at another time two parties of them destroyed each other at Ede-Atba. And again at Habaro two parties of them destroyed each other. Therefore they were always food for the sword and the spear, and everywhere they slaughtered each other. Since the establishment of the rule of Egypt, however, they have become people that are safe from each other and have also made peace with all others.

Kantebay Sallim and Ali Wad Mao

A man named Kantebay Sallim with his family had built his village on the top of a mountain. And another man named Ali wad Mao was abiding with his village in Daset. And Kantebay Sallim betrothed his son to the daughter of Ali wad Mao. Thereupon when the "constellation" was near, Kantebay Sallim requested the wedding. And Ali wad Mao replied, "I have granted your request, come to me!" But in his village he sent a message about speaking thus: "Now the nuptial cortege of Kantebay Sallim is on the way towards us. Give them no wood, and even when the people of the cortege wish to gather wood themselves tell them: 'It is forbidden; the wood of Daset is not to be burned; do not break any of it.'" And all of them accepted his plan. Thereupon the nuptial cortege of Kantebay Sallim arrived in the evening and halted at the nuptial bower. And the people of the village greeted the cortege and gave them mats. Ali wad Mao brought barren cows for the cortege and said to them, "These are your dinner." So the people of the cortege accepted the cows from him, killed them, skinned them and prepared them for the meal. Thereupon they asked water and wood and fire from the people of the village, who said to them: "Water and wood and fire, all of this we shall not give. You yourselves may take water and fire only! For wood is forbidden; the wood of Daset is not to be burned." And even when the people of the cortege wished to gather it themselves, they were told: "It is forbidden; the wood of Daset is not to be burned. Do not break a piece of its wood!" Then the people of the cortege said to Kantebay Sallim: "What shall we do? They have refused us wood. We have found nothing with which to cook the meat." He said to all the people of the cortege: "Take off the points of your spears and cook the meat with the shafts, then eat your meal. And he who has a saddle, let him break it, then cook his meal with it!" And after they had done thus, they ate their meal. And the next morning they took their bride and went to their village. And when they had entered the village, they found at once that the bride was pregnant with a bastard. Kantebay Sallim heard that his son's wife was with child; and he returned the dowry that had come with the bride, and the bride also, mounting her on a beast, to her father. And after this Kantebay Sallim rose in a storm with all those of his men that were good for work, to overrun and plunder Daset, the village of Ali wad Mao. But at that time Ali wad Mao was not at home; for he used to pass little time at home, being a restless wanderer. Then Kantebay Sallim attacked the village of Daset with his army swarming on all sides, and destroyed its people and its cattle. And his men pierced the bride, the daughter of Ali wad Mao, with a broad pointed lance, so that her embryo and her kidneys became visible. And Kantebay Sallim, having destroyed what he destroyed and having taken what he had gathered, returned to his village. When Ali wad Mao, after his walking about, came to his village he found his village totally destroyed and forsaken, and his daughter only met him with her embryo almost outside of her body. Then she told him that Kantebay Sallim had annihilated them; thereupon her soul left her. When Ali was looking at his daughter's body he sang thus:

"Fatna, your father's plan has wronged you,
That he would not have a piece of wood broken of all Daset.
Now the embryo is moving out of the open side.
Between me and you is only the afternoon of this day."

When Ali saw the destruction of his village and the cruel death of his daughter, fire began to burn within him. For all this had come to pass through his own decision; first he had ordered that the wood be refused to the people of the cortege; then he had married his daughter knowing that she was with child; therefore he felt a most poignant grief. He had left his weapons in his house, and the robbers had taken them; now as he sought some weapon he did not find any. But afterwards he found an Arabian razor. That he took, made a cut in his calf and hid the razor in it. Then he went to the village of Kantebay Sallim. When he arrived there, he went straightway to the council-place. The men of the council said to each other by themselves, "This newcomer resembles Ali wad Mao." But some of them said, "Is Ali wad Mao not dead and his village destroyed?" However, when they saw that he was without arms, they said: "Even if it is he, what are we to fear? This one here is a man without arms." And when Ali came to them he greeted them, "Peace be upon you!" And they answered him, "Welcome!" And Ali said to Kantebay Sallim: "Kantebay, rise and come to me; we have some business apart." And Kantebay Sallim rose and came towards him, but the people of the council said to him, "Do not go to him!" But Kantebay Sallim replied to them: "What weapons has he wherewith to kill me? And if he bites me, you will help me." And he went to him, and after they had gone a little beyond the council-place, they sat down. Ali said to Kantebay Sallim: "What is there that you have done and I have not done? I am the guilty one. And now allow me to live in this your country under your rule!" He spoke this way, deceitfully. Kantebay Sallim was very fat and his beard was long. Now Ali seized him by his beard and taking his razor out of his calf he cut him with it and made his entrails to come out. And when the people of the council saw their wrestling, they stood up and sprang upon them. But they found that Kantebay Sallim had given up the ghost. Saying, "With what has he cut him?" they looked closely, and afterwards they saw the razor. Then they said, "Since he has killed the Kantebay, with what and in what way shall we kill him?" And they took council about him. Thereupon they decided, in the same way as he had done to the Kantebay, to cut his belly and to make his entrails come out. And then when they had cut him open, fire came out of his inside, and it burnt those that had cut him; and afterwards it spread all over the village and burnt down everything. And in this way, at first Kantebay Sallim destroyed the village of Ali wad Mao; and then, on the other hand, the fire that came out from Ali wad Mao ruined the village of Kantebay Sallim, and they both died in each other's presence. And the mountain on which the village of Kantebay Sallim had been is called "Kantebay Sallim" or "Mount Kantebay Sallim"; and on the top of the mountain there are, as they tell, until the present day the ruins of the walls of the village. And in the village of Ali wad Mao, in Daset, there are the tombs of those who died. And those who left the village fleeing, are called Dagdage, and they are now to be found everywhere.

How the Game of Fersit Is Played

IN THE WORDS OF A MENSA INFORMANT

Fersit is a gambling game. It is played in the following way: Each player has a die of bone; the side where the marrow has been, and which is dark, is called "front"; the other, white side is called "back." Besides this a larger die is needed, which also has front and back; the larger, common die is called "mother," the smaller are called "children." Each player knows his die by its somewhat different shape. If the stake is money or property, pebbles are used while playing. If the stake is grain, piles of grain are taken and won during the play. Thus, each player has an equal number of pebbles or a pile of grain before him. The stakes are put up, and someone takes all the dice in his hand and shakes them a little; then he drops them on the ground. If the "mother" die falls on its back, all the other dice that fall in the same way have lost. Those which fall the other way have won, and vice versa. Those who have won receive a stake each. If all the dice fall differently from the "mother" die, nobody wins. The first stage of the game lasts until all stakes are won; those who have won nothing are out of the game. The rest play on; each one puts about five pebbles up as a stake. When there are only two winners left, they play for the whole. He who has all the pebbles wins what is played for; the others pay in equal parts. Now the Mensa do not gamble so much as they used to do. Formerly they gambled a great deal and often lost their houses, their cattle and much other property.

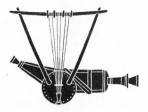

THREE LAMENTS OF THE MENSA BET-ABREHE

For a Distinguished Man

> A dead person of high rank is compared to a
> boulder for his firmness and strength, and is
> described as a rope that holds the land to-
> gether. The proper nouns are names of regions
> of the country. Strictly speaking, Amhara refers
> to the Amharic-speaking people of the high-
> lands, but it is used here in the sense of "the
> country."

From the top of Haygat
    Came down a heavy thunder.
Segli and Sabara
    And Karer were settled.
He is a boulder, he leads Amhara,
    He, having laid many traps.
The sword-hilt shone brightly,
    Set with its jewels.
The sky from one end to the other,
    He was the rope that held the land together.

For a Brave Man

> This song draws the picture of a warrior living
> the hard life when circumstances require it—
> wearing armored clothing and sandals of hard
> leather, eating uncooked meat, and fighting the
> enemy.

His sword is not fastidious.
    It eats three kinds of meat.
Fresh-cut meat and dried portions.
    And human flesh it eats.

A shirt of armor is his dress.
Thus he makes an attack.
Hurriedly putting on sandals of untanned leather.
He brings down much booty from the highlands.

For One Who Died Young

The song recalls the activities of the half-grown
boy, who is likened to a camel of dancing age,
comments on his good character, and inter-
sperses momentary images of his life.

Truly, you mourners, say something for him.
About the breaking of the young camel, you mourners.
The young, the young one, the young.
The young, young camel, the young.
The young, and young one, the young.
The young, young camel of the dancing age.
The boy of the resting places in the field.
And of dancing and of music.
He whose scarf hung down to the ground.
He whose sense of honor was high.
His ball and his stick.
He at the age of the wooden spear.
Say to him *aulele*, you mourners.
Be it a rescue for him, mourners.
And a bridegroom of sorrow.
A shrouder draws a cover over him.
We saw N____, son of N____, being broken.
May his foe be broken. But he himself, broken we saw him

THE SOMALI AND THE SWAHILI

Ojje Ben Onogh

A SOMALI STORY

> In this story we have an Islamic development
> of events described in the Old Testament. It
> recalls the encounter between David and
> Goliath, but more specifically it refers to ex-
> periences of the Israelites while they are still in
> the desert following their escape from Egypt.

This tale and the one that follows, "The Battle of Eghal Shillet," are from The
Fire on the Mountain and Other Ethiopian Stories, *by Harold Courlander and
Wolf Leslau,* © 1950 by Holt, Rinehart and Winston. Reprinted by permission
of the publishers.

> Moses sends out scouts to see what kind of peo-
> ple occupy the land through which the Israel-
> ites wish to pass. The scouts return with the
> report that the sons of Anak (Ben Onogh), a
> race of giants, live in that place (Numbers, 13).
> The Israelites avoid a confrontation with the
> giants, but a little later there is a fight with the
> people of Bashan (Numbers, 21), whose king is
> called Og. The Israelites win the contest and
> King Og is slain. In the Islamic tradition, as
> recorded here, the two events are merged into
> one in a tale of colossal exaggeration.

Once there was a man named Ojje Ben Onogh. He was four thousand
five hundred years old. He was so large that wherever his shadow fell
it was like night. When he went for a walk his footprints filled with
water and became lakes. When he sneezed there were sandstorms, and
where his clothes dragged on the ground they swept away the trees and
grass, and the earth became desert. He stood in the middle of the sea
to catch fish, and to cook them he held them up against the face of the
sun.

He planted a field of corn, and the corn grew so fast and so tall it took
all the water from the earth and dried up the rivers. The people became
angry, because there wasn't enough water left to grow their grain.

Moses gathered an army to fight Ojje Ben Onogh. The army stretched
from Hargeisa to Dahmal. It covered a valley six miles wide and six
miles long. When Ojje Ben Onogh saw the army coming he picked up
a mountain to throw at them. Just at this moment, a small bird flew over
the mountain and dropped a tiny straw on it. That made the mountain
too heavy, and Ojje Ben Onogh put it down.

Moses came forward with his staff. It was thirty yards high. When he
was close to Ojje Ben Onogh, Moses leaped thirty yards into the air and
struck him with the end of his staff. The blow landed on Ojje's ankle,
and he fell dead.

Moses and his army went away. The wolves came to gnaw Ojje's
bones. It took them forty years to eat the marrow, and they had to walk
from Burao to Berbera to do it.

The Battle of Eghal Shillet

A SOMALI STORY

In Somalia, near the old town of Hargeisa, there was once a man of
the Essa tribe named Eghal Shillet.

It is said that one day warriors of the Haweia tribe came to fight with
the Essa people. The men of the Essa tribe prepared for battle. They
took their spears and knives, saddled their horses, and rode off to meet
the enemy.

Eghal Shillet cried loudly to his wife, "Bring my shoes!" And his wife brought his shoes so he could go into battle.

Eghal Shillet watched the other Essa men riding away. He shouted to his wife, "Saddle my horse!" And she saddled his horse.

Eghal Shillet sang:

> Eya, I go to fight!
> Eya, I go to fight!
> I will scatter my enemies!
> May they have terror!
> May they have death!

He looked again. The Essa men were still going out to battle. He said to his wife, "Help me on my horse!"

She helped him on his horse. The Essa men were meeting the enemy on the hill. He said, "Give me my knife!"

She gave him his knife.

He said, "Give me my shield of elephant hide!"

She gave him his shield.

He said, "Give me my spear!"

She gave him his spear. The men were still fighting. He sat in his saddle. Then he said, "Give me another spear!"

She gave him another spear and said, "Are you ready?"

Eghal Shillet said, "Yes, I am ready."

Then he sang:

> Eya, I go to fight!
> Eya, I go to fight!
> I will scatter them!
> May they have death!
> May they have terror!

He looked. The battle on the hill was furious.

"Give me another spear!" he said.

His wife gave him another spear. He said: "I am ready. If I do not return from the hill, remember only how I scatter the Haweia dogs to the wind!"

He sat in his saddle and scowled. "Give me another spear!" he said.

"There are no more spears," his wife replied.

He closed his eyes.

"I leave you," he said. Then he opened his eyes and asked: "Has my horse been fed?"

"Your horse has been fed," his wife said.

"Has he had water?"

"Yes, he has had water."

"Well, I am ready. Let them take care!"

And Eghal Shillet rode away. The battle was straight ahead, but Eghal Shillet's horse turned into the valley.

"Not to the valley, to the hill!" he shouted.

But the horse kept going into the valley.

"Ah, you! I wish to scatter my enemies and you go to market!" Eghal Shillet shouted.

The horse continued his way.

"Turn, you devil, so that they may feel the sharpness of my weapons!"

But the horse did not turn, and Eghal rode on. An Essa man came riding down the hill.

"What is the matter?" he asked.

"My worthless horse will not respond. I cannot steer him!" Eghal said dismally.

"You do it this way," the man said. He took hold of the bridle and pulled gently. The horse turned and headed for the hill.

"Ah, now you are willing!" Eghal said. "Run like the evil one you are, so that their bodies grow numb with fear!"

The horse plodded along. And Eghal sang:

> Eya, I go to fight!
> Eya, I go to fight!
> I will make them fly!
> I will make their blood turn cold!
> They will run before the wind!

Soon he was close enough to hear the clash of weapons.

"I will strike them from down under!" he said, and he crawled around to the underside of his horse, clutching his knife, his three spears, and his shield. He clung tightly to the lines, and the horse, feeling the violent tugging, turned and walked back towards the village. As they approached the door of Eghal's house, Eghal rattled his weapons and sang hoarsely:

> Eya, let them run, I am here!
> Eya, let them run, I am here!
> I will strike them from down under!

"What are you doing under the horse?" his wife asked.

"Ah, this devil betrays me!" Eghal Shillet said, peering from underneath. "Must I then fight like an animal, with my feet on the ground?" He dismounted.

"The fighting is over," his wife said.

He looked out across the fields. He saw a party of horsemen riding towards the village.

"We have lost! The Haweia are upon us!" Eghal cried. He ran into his house and lay on his back on his sleeping mat. "When they arrive, tell them I've been dead since yesterday!" he said, and he closed his eyes.

The horsemen came into the village. Eghal Shillet's wife moaned loudly and wrung her hands. The horsemen dismounted and entered the house. They were Essa warriors.

"What is it?" one of them asked.

"Alas, he has been dead since yesterday," she said.

"The Haweia have fled," the Essa warriors said.

Eghal Shillet sat up.

"Give me my spear and my shield!" he shouted to his wife. "Saddle my horse and help me to mount!"

"The war is over," the men said.

"Ah! I am cheated!" Eghal cried. And he sang:

> Eya, the Haweia have died!
> Fortunate they are in death!
> They haven't seen the flash of my spear!
> They haven't felt terror!
> How lucky for them!

The Lion's Share

A SOMALI STORY

The lion, the jackal, the wolf and the hyena had a meeting and agreed that they would hunt together in one party and share equally among them whatever game they caught.

They went out and killed a camel. The four animals then discussed which one of them would divide the meat. The lion said, "Whoever divides the meat must know how to count."

Immediately the wolf volunteered, saying, "Indeed, I know how to count."

He began to divide the meat. He cut off four pieces of equal size and placed one before each of the hunters.

The lion was angered. He said, "Is this the way to count?" And he struck the wolf across the eyes, so that his eyes swelled up and he could not see.

The jackal said: "The wolf does not know how to count. I will divide the meat."

He cut three portions that were small and a fourth portion that was very large. The three small portions he placed before the hyena, the wolf and himself. The large portion he put in front of the lion, who took his meat and went away.

"Why was it necessary to give the lion such a large piece?" the hyena said. "Our agreement was to divide and share equally. Where did you ever learn how to divide?"

"I learned from the wolf," the jackal answered.

"Wolf? How can anyone learn from the wolf? He is stupid," the hyena said.

From The King's Drum and Other African Stories, © *1962 by Harold Courlander, by permission of Harcourt Brace Jovanovich.*

"The jackal was right," the wolf said. "He knows how to count. Before, when my eyes were open, I did not see it. Now, though my eyes are wounded, I see it clearly."

Adventures of Abunuwas, Trickster Hero

Abunuwas (also called Kibunwasi) is a folk-lore trickster-hero known in East Africa and such offshore islands as Zanzibar, Madagascar and Mauritius, where Arabic cultural influences have been felt. The original, real-life Abu Nuwas was a celebrated eighth-century Arab poet born in Persia and a long-time resident of Baghdad. According to tradition he was a favorite of Harun el-Rashid and the caliph el-Amin. In literature he is portrayed as genial, clever, cynical and a flouter of morals. All of these personal attributes are reflected in the purely folkloric Abunuwas, about whom have clustered hundreds, perhaps thousands, of apocryphal tales, many of them non-Arabic in origin, and some obviously borrowed from a general reservoir of African folklore. Abunuwas as a trickster-hero is a human equivalent of the spider, tortoise and hare which play this role in other regions of the African continent.

One day Abunuwas took a hundred of his dinars and went to the market where he bought a fine donkey and rode it away home. One day a man came to borrow his donkey. Abunuwas said the donkey was out. At that moment the donkey brayed. The man said, "Isn't that the donkey braying? You said it was out." Abunuwas said, "Now look here: have you come to borrow a donkey or have you come to borrow a bray? If you have come to borrow a bray I will bray for you." So he brayed, "Ee-ore, Ee-ore, Ee-ore," and said to him, "There, get on it and go away."

From Abu Nuwas in Life and Legend, *by W. H. Ingrams, Port Louis, Mauritius, 1933.*

One day Abunuwas's donkey was thirsty and he had nothing to put water in to give it to drink. He went to a neighbor and said, "Lend me a saucepan that I may give my donkey water to drink." He was given a saucepan and went away. He kept it three days. On the fourth day he took the saucepan and put inside it a little saucepan and took it back to the owner. When the owner saw the little saucepan he said, "This is not mine." Abunuwas said: "I am not a thief. I cannot steal people's property. Your saucepan gave birth while it was with me and this is its child."

The owner of the saucepan was very pleased and said, "The house of Abunuwas is blessed indeed, even the saucepans bring forth there."

Three days afterwards Abunuwas sent to borrow the saucepan again and was given it, and this time Abunuwas kept it and did not return it. The owner of the saucepan went to ask Abunuwas for it. Abunuwas said to him, "Your saucepan is dead." The owner said, "Can copper die?" Abunuwas said, "Did it not bring forth?" He answered, "It did." Then Abunuwas said to him, "Everything that bringeth forth, its fate is to die." And he could not answer him.

He went away and asked the learned men and they replied to him in the same way, "Certainly, that which brings forth must also die."

Abunuwas kept the saucepan.

It came to pass that Abunuwas was unpopular in the town of Baghdad. One day the great men made mischief about him to the sultan and wanted to destroy him by guile. So the sultan said to him, "Abunuwas, I want you to build me a house up in the air, and if you cannot build it you will be killed." Abunuwas replied, "I hear and I obey." And he was told that the time he could have in which to build the house was three days.

He went forth into the town and he got paper and wood. He joined them together with paste and he made a big kite. He tied on to it bells and fastened it with a long string. He waited until the wind rose and then he made it fly. It flew very high and he fastened it to a tree.

The people in the town saw something in the air, and they heard the bells, and they were astonished, because they had not yet seen anything like this. Abunuwas went to the sultan and said to him, "I have finished building your house. Open the window and look." The sultan looked and Abunuwas said to him, "Do you hear the noise?" The sultan said, "Yes." And he said: "That is the workmen making the roof and what you hear are the hammers and nails. But I am a bit short of timber. I want you to give me some and the men to take it." The sultan said, "Which way will the men go?" Abunuwas said, "The same way as I went."

The sultan gave him the timber and the men. Abunuwas led them to the place where he had fastened the string and said, "This is the way, pass along it." They said, "We cannot pass along a string." Abunuwas said, "You must." They declared they were unable to and returned to the sultan and told him. The sultan said: "It is true. There is no man who can walk up a string." Abunuwas said: "Oh! you know that. Why then did you tell me to build a house in the air?" The sultan could not reply. Abunuwas went out and loosened the string and the kite flew away.

There was an old man with his wife and son and they were very poor. A merchant came and said to the youth, "If you can spend the night in a frozen lake I will give you ten thousand dinars." As the youth was very poor he thought he would try. His mother was afraid for him so she sat and held a light for him. In the morning the youth went to the merchant and said, "Give me the money." The merchant refused because he said his mother had given him warmth all night. The youth went and accused him before Abunuwas and he agreed to take up his case if he were given three thousand dinars. He told the youth to accuse the merchant before the sultan, but the sultan told him that he had no case.

So Abunuwas bought a goat and some rice and all the accessories of a feast. He put the meat into a saucepan and the rice into another. He lit a fire and kept the food and the fire apart. He invited people to come to a feast and included the sultan and his wazirs.

They came and sat round Abunuwas's door, and waited until the evening without even getting coffee. They were very cross. They went into the kitchen and saw that the fire and the food were apart. The sultan said to Abunuwas: "You are quite mad. Since morning we have sat here and we've put nothing in our bellies"; and Abunuwas said, "People are cooking, Master, but the meat is not yet done." The sultan went into the kitchen and saw that the meat and the rice and the fire were all apart. He said, "This food won't get done in ten years." Abunuwas said, "It will." The sultan said: "I know it won't. I'm going home and I shall tell everybody else to go home." Abunuwas said: "Don't get angry, my lord. Do you remember that youth who lay all night in a frozen pool and came with his case to you, and you said that the merchant's words were true, and that the boy had got warmth by being given a light by his mother? How should he get warmth? Please give that youth his right, because if he got warmth this food will get cooked." The sultan said, "It is true," and told the merchant to give the youth what was right. He gave it to him.

When he had done so Abunuwas ordered the food to be cooked and the people had their feast and Abunuwas got his share of the money.

One day Abunuwas said, "Should God offer me nine hundred and ninety-nine dollars I would not take them until they were a thousand complete." People said, "Is he mad that he should get nine hundred and ninety-nine dollars and not receive them?" These words spread about in the city until a merchant heard them and said he would test Abunuwas. He put nine hundred and ninety-nine dollars in a purse and left them on Abunuwas's verandah. When Abunuwas went out he saw the money and took it inside and counted it, and he gave thanks and said: "Thanks be to God who has heard my petition for a thousand dollars, and now he has given me nine hundred and ninety-nine. Never mind, I will lend the other one to God and I am sure he will give it me some other day to make the account complete."

The merchant went to Abunuwas and asked him if he had found the purse, and if so, how many dollars were in it. Abunuwas said, "A thousand less one." He said, "Well, give it to me, because you said that should God give you a thousand less one you would not take them and that they must be a thousand complete." Abunuwas said: "No. This is my sustenance from God, I prayed to Him for it and He gave it me. If He has given me nine hundred and ninety-nine dollars will He be defeated in giving me one dollar?" The merchant saw that Abunuwas was making trouble, so he said, "Let us go to Harun Rashid." Abunuwas said: "If it's like this I cannot go in this way. Give me a cloak and a turban and a donkey like yours. Then we will go to the Diwan." The merchant agreed and they went.

When they got there the merchant spoke his complaint against Abunuwas and Harun Rashid asked Abunuwas for his answer. Abunuwas said: "These people give me a lot of trouble. If he can tell a tale like this over the money he can easily say that this donkey is his, and the cloak is his and the turban is his." The merchant said, "What is this? Aren't they mine?" Abunuwas said, "You see." So Harun Rashid thought that it was true that they were slandering him and he decreed that Abunuwas should have everything.

One day Abunuwas was cutting a tree and he was sitting on the end of the branch and cutting at the trunk. A man passed by and said to him: "You are sitting in a bad position. When the branch falls you will fall with it because you are sitting on the end of it and are cutting at the trunk." Abunuwas said: "I shan't fall. This is the way to cut trees. I haven't started doing it today." The man went on his way.

Abunuwas went on cutting and when the tree fell, he fell with it. He got up quickly and ran after the man and said to him: "Tell me the day on which I shall die. You were able to tell me I should fall down and I have fallen down, and now I want to know when I shall die." The man said he could not tell him but as Abunuwas pressed him he said: "On the day on which you are riding your donkey and it throws you three times before you arrive at your destination. On that day you will die."

Some time afterwards Abunuwas was riding his donkey to his plantation. Long before he got there he hit the donkey and it went very fast, and because it was going at such a speed it threw him. He got on again and was thrown a second time. He said, "My death is near." He went ahead and was thrown a third time. He lay down and covered himself with his cloth and stayed quiet like a man who is dead. He lay like that for three days and the people of the town looked for him.

On the third day a man passed by and he saw Abunuwas and asked him, "Where is the road to Harun Rashid's place?" Abunuwas woke up and said, "I remember that when I was alive it passed by that mango tree until you get to the town." The man said to him, "Why do you say, 'When you were alive'?" He said, "Yes, I am dead now," and he lay down again. Then there passed some Beduins on camels. When they saw Abunuwas the camels shied. The Beduins were annoyed. They saw that it was Abunuwas who had made the camels shy and they beat him hard with a stick, but Abunuwas lay quiet because he was dead.

When the man who had asked the way reached Harun Rashid he was asked about Abunuwas. He said: "He is over there asleep. He says he is dead." Harun Rashid said: "I know Abunuwas. If you only go and call him he won't come. Take a horn and when you get near him blow it and then say to him, 'Get up, the Resurrection has come.' " They went and did it. Abunuwas got up and brushed himself and put on his clothes and followed them to the town.

When he got there men made fun of him, "Abunuwas has risen again." Some people asked him about the next world. He said, "There's nothing in it. People only frighten you by saying "the next world is thus and thus" but it's nothing at all. There's only one thing about it, there's no eating." And this was true, for he had not eaten for three days. And then he said: "There's another thing that I saw which was very bad, and it was this, there are Beduins there who are mounted on camels and if you fall foul of them they beat you very hard."

Harun Rashid asked him about his death. He told him everything. Harun said to him, "This man has caused you a lot of annoyance." He said: "No, he has not annoyed me at all. He has done me a lot of good. Now I know everything about the next world."

Abunuwas built a two-story house. When it was finished he looked for someone to buy it, but could not find anyone. But luckily he got a merchant who agreed to buy. However, Abunuwas sold him the top story only and put him a ladder outside. Matters remained like this for a long time. At last Abunuwas wanted to conclude the business and make the merchant buy the bottom half from him. The merchant refused to buy.

Abunuwas looked for another client but could not find one. So he made another plan. He collected a large number of laborers and came with them to his house. He called out to the merchant who was above and said to him, "I want to break up my house below, so you look after your house above, and don't come and say I didn't tell you."

The merchant was defeated by the guile of Abunuwas and he bought the house at Abunuwas's price.

One day Abunuwas was going along the road with his goat and he met three thieves, who, when they saw him coming, agreed that one of them should pretend to have a stomachache and lie down on the ground. Abunuwas came up, and seeing the man on the ground, asked what was the matter, and he said, "I am in great pain." So Abunuwas said, "Are you able to hold a goat's string?" and he replied, "Yes." So he took the man up and carried him, and gave him the goat's rope to hold.

On the way the thief let the goat go, unknown to Abunuwas, who, on reaching his house, asked the thief what had happened to it. And the man said, "I was in great pain, and the string slipped out of my hand."

Meanwhile the other two thieves had caught the goat and killed it, and divided it into three parts, and their companion, who had pretended to be ill, managed to escape from Abunuwas's house while he was away, and soon rejoined them. When Abunuwas found out he had gone, he told his wife that he must go and find them, but before doing so he got two gazelles, which he fastened in the yard, and a bladder which he filled with blood. He said to his wife, "I will follow the thieves with one gazelle, and you must fasten the bladder of blood to your throat." And she did so.

He then went and found the thieves, and after talking to them for some time, told them he wanted to join them, and they agreed to let him. Whilst they were going back to his house he hit the gazelle with a stick and said, "Go to my wife and tell her to cook food for three." The gazelle ran away into the bush. When they arrived home at Abunuwas's house, he called out, "Wife, have you cooked the food?" and she said, "No. Why?" And he said, "Didn't the gazelle tell you to?" She replied, "The gazelle came back and went into the hut and told me nothing." Then Abunuwas fetched the second gazelle and asked why it hadn't told her, and the gazelle cried, "I told her a long time ago to do it." Abunuwas then went and knocked his wife down, cutting the bladder at her throat, and she pretended to be dead. The thieves were very frightened, and said, "He has killed his wife." But Abunuwas said, "She has no sense, so I punished her," and he took a bottle of medicine and let her smell it, then touched her with a stick. When she got up he told her to wash herself and then cook some food, then they all sat down and ate.

After they had finished, the thieves, who had been greatly struck with what they had seen, asked if he would let them have the gazelle, the stick and the medicine, and after some discussion he sold them to them for a thousand rupees, and they took the things and went away. After they had gone Abunuwas ran away from that place and went and lived in another country.

One day when the thieves were out with the gazelle, one of them hit it with the stick and told it to go home and tell his wife to cook some food, and it ran away into the bush. When they got home they found nothing ready, and the man asked his wife why she had not done as the gazelle had told her. She said, "No gazelle has come here." And he, thinking she was lying, knocked her down and cut her throat, and she kicked out in her death struggles and expired. He then gave her the medicine to smell and hit her with the stick, but they saw she did not revive and was really dead.

Abunuwas was much disliked by the people of Baghdad because he annoyed people and they accused him to Harun Rashid. Harun ordered him to be thrown into a pit in which there was a lion. When he was in the pit he made it his business to scratch the lion until it was tame, and he lived on the meat that was thrown to the lion every day.

He stayed there for a long time until he was forgotten in the town. One day a great marvel came forth in the town. When the people woke in the morning they saw that a hand had come out of the sea with three fingers extended. They told the king and all the wise men were sent for, but nobody could interpret it and nobody could remove the hand. At last some people remembered Abunuwas and they sent for him from the pit. But before he consented to come out they had to give him clothes, a turban, a loincloth, a vest, a shirt, and a cloak; and then they threw him a rope and he came out.

They told him what they wanted and he said, "Give me food first." Then Abunuwas went to the shore, and the king and crowds of people followed. He stood near the hand and he put out his own hand in the same way as if denying something. The hand in the sea closed one finger, Abunuwas put out his hand again and the hand closed a second finger, so that there was one left, Abunuwas answered and the hand went. The people were astonished and asked the interpretation. Abunuwas said: "The hand came to ask if there was a secret in the world among three people. I replied 'No.' There were left two fingers and the meaning is, 'Is there a secret between two people?' There was left one and I said, 'Yes, a secret is only for one man,' and the hand disappeared."

The people praised Abunuwas for his intelligence and Harun Rashid gave him a house and many gifts.

After some time the king dreamed that there were jars of silver buried on the left side of the house he had given Abunuwas. He sent men to dig without giving information to Abunuwas. They dug and got nothing. When Abunuwas knew he was angry and said, "Never mind, I will have my revenge." He told his wife to cook rice and chicken and then told her to go for a walk. He took a plate and a basin for the gravy and put them on a tray under the table and covered them with a white cloth. Then he locked up the house and put the key over the door and went away.

On the road he met three youths and said to them: "I know you young men are very troublesome these days. When you go by my house do not go and take the key over the door and open the house and look under the table and see a plate of rice and chicken, or eat and cover the plate and the basin with the tray without washing them." The young men thought that the words of Abunuwas were remarkable, but they went to the house and did all the things that he had told them not to and went away.

Abunuwas gave them sufficient time to eat, and when they had finished he went home and saw what they had done. He took the tray and the plate covered in the same way to Harun Rashid and he said, "There are people I accuse of eating my rice," and Harun asked, "Where are they?" and Abunuwas replied, "I have covered them in the plate." He uncovered it and there came out three flies which flew away. He said, "These are they that I accuse." The king said: "Abunuwas, do you accuse even flies?" He replied: "It is even they that have done me wrong. If they did not do me wrong I could not accuse them and I wish you to give me justice according to law."

The king replied, "I give you permission that everywhere you see a fly has settled you may strike it," and he gave him a writing under his hand.

Abunuwas made a heavy stick with a big knob on the end. As he went round the shops, if he saw flies settled on dates, he would strike them and scatter the dates everywhere. If he saw them on dried shark he would strike the shark and flatten it, and when people raised a commotion because he damaged their goods Abunuwas used to say, "I do not hit the goods, I hit the flies." And he went on like this for a long time.

At last one day Abunuwas said to his wife, "Today I will take my revenge for my house being dug up." He went to the king's diwan with his stick and sat down near the king. When the conversation was in full swing there came a fly which settled on the king's thigh. Abunuwas took his stick and he hit the king with it on his thigh—vengeance for having his house dug up. The people seized Abunuwas and wanted to imprison him, but he said: "If you imprison me you only do it to annoy me, because I didn't strike the king, I struck the fly which settled on him, and he himself has given me permission in this writing under his hand to strike every fly wherever I see one settle." They examined Abunuwas's writing and saw it was true so they let him go. He went home to his house.

There was a man who went on a journey and he had a cow, and before he left he took his cow to a big man in the town, and that man had a bull. While the man was on the journey his cow calved seven times. When he came back he went to fetch his cow and he had heard that his cow had calved. When he got there he said, "I want my cow and its calves." The old man replied, "Go to the pen and take that cow of yours which you left behind." The man said, "And how can that be when my cow has calved?" The old man replied: "It is my bull which has calved. When yours came it had no calf, and now take it itself."

The man was grieved and went to Abunuwas who agreed to help him. Abunuwas dressed himself up as a poor man and went to the old man with much weeping and said, "Lend me three rupees so that I may help my father who has just given birth." The old man said: "Don't make fun of me. If your mother has given birth I will give them to you." Abunuwas said, "No, master, it's my father who has given birth." The old man replied, "I have never yet heard of a man giving birth." Abunuwas said, "Well, you hear it today," but the old man wouldn't agree. So Abunuwas said: "If a man doesn't give birth how is it that you have cheated this poor fellow of his oxen? You say that it is your ox that has given birth and it is a bull. It would have been better if you had said that you had wanted a fee for looking after the cow." The man could make no answer to Abunuwas and he gave him all seven calves.

One day a merchant killed a goat. At the time of cooking there came a beggar and by way of feeding he sat down to the leeward of the food so that he got the smell. In the morning the beggar met the merchant and said to him, "Master, you were very good to me yesterday. I was nourished on the smell of your goat until I was well fed." The merchant said, "That's it. That's why my goat was tasteless, because you took all the flavor," and he went and accused him before Harun Rashid, who was very fond of merchants and ordered the beggar to pay twelve rupees.

The beggar went and cried, for he had no money. He met Abunuwas who said he would help him and gave him twelve rupees telling him not to pay it until he himself should come. In the morning they met before the sultan. When the beggar stood forth to pay, Abunuwas said, "You have your twelve rupees?" He answered, "I have them." Abunuwas took them and called the merchant to fetch them. When the merchant wanted to receive them Abunuwas said "Wait," and flung them on the floor, saying, "There you are, take the chink of these rupees because the beggar didn't eat the meat but only had the smell." The merchant was astonished at the wisdom of Abunuwas and was defeated.

Abunuwas left the twelve rupees for the beggar and went home.

A certain king was very fond of Abunuwas because of his jests, until one day when they were at the diwan the king called, "O wazir." The wazir answered, "Here am I," and went and stooped over the king who whispered in his ear, and Abunuwas wanted very much to be treated like that, and said, "O king, I dreamed that every day you ought to call me and whisper to me, even if you have nothing to say." The king said, "Certainly, Abunuwas."

The next morning when he got to the diwan the king called for him. He went to the king and the king whispered nothing but a joke in his ear. Abunuwas, however, said aloud, "God willing, I will do all that you have told me." The people were troubled and the wazir said, "Well, I told the king a long time ago that Abunuwas was a man of no account, and now everything in the town will go wrong." And the king said, "Well what shall I do to get rid of Abunuwas?" The youngest there said to him, "Arrange that every man who comes here tomorrow has an egg wrapped in his girdle, and when the diwan is over you must say, 'Everybody who is present must lay an egg, and if anyone doesn't lay it, I will kill him.' Abunuwas doesn't know of this so he will be defeated and he will die."

The king did as he suggested, and when he made his edict the next morning everybody except Abunuwas produced an egg. The king said to Abunuwas: "This is no joke. If you don't produce an egg you shall die." Abunuwas replied, "The reason I haven't laid an egg is that all these people are hens and I am the cock." The king was defeated and told him he could go.

The Story of Liongo

A TALE OF THE SWAHILI PEOPLE

The Swahili are an east coast people of Bantu and Arab ancestry. Their culture reflects considerable Islamic influence, and the Swahili language contains considerable Arabic vocabulary. The story of Liongo given here was translated from Swahili by Edward Steere, well known for his collection of traditional tales from the offshore island of Zanzibar.

In his book, *Swahili Tales*, published in the latter half of the nineteenth century, Steere said of this story: "The Story of Liongo is the nearest approach to a bit of real history I was able to meet with. It is said that a sister of Liongo came to Zanzibar, and that her descendents are still living there. Sheikh Mohammed bin Ali told me that in his young days he had seen Liongo's spear and some other relics then preserved by his family; there seem, however, to be none such now remaining. No one has any clear notion how long it is since Liongo died, but his memory is warmly cherished, and it is wonderful how the mere mention of his name rouses the interest of almost any true Swahili. There is a long poem, of which the tale [given here] is an abridgement, which used often to be sung at feasts; and then all would get much excited, and cry like children when his death was related, and particularly at the point where his mother touches him and finds him dead."

In the times when Shanga was a flourishing city, there was a man whose name was Liongo, and he had great strength, and was a very

From Swahili Tales as Told by Natives of Zanzibar, *by Edward Steere, London, 1870.*

great man in the city. And he oppressed the people exceedingly, till one day they made a plan to go to him to his house and bind him. And a great number of people went and came upon him suddenly in his house, and seized him and bound him, and went with him to the prison, and put him into it.

And he stayed many days, and made a plot to get loose. And he went outside the town and harassed the people in the same way for many days. People could not go into the country, neither to cut wood nor to draw water. And they were in much trouble.

And the people said, "What stratagem can we resort to, to get him and kill him?" And one said, "Let us go against him while he is sleeping, and kill him out of the way." Others said, "If you get him, bind him and bring him." And they went and made a stratagem so as to take him, and they bound him, and took him to the town. And they went and bound him with chains and fetters and a post between his legs.

And they left him many days, and his mother used to send him food every day. And before the door where he was bound soldiers were set, who watched him; they never went away except by turns.

Many days and many months had passed. Every day, night by night, he used to sing beautiful songs; everyone who heard them used to be delighted with those songs. Everyone used to say to his friend, "Let us go and listen to Liongo's songs, which he sings in his room." And they used to go and listen. Every day when night came people used to go and say to him, "We have come to sing your songs, let us hear them." And he used to sing, he could not refuse, and the people in the town were delighted with them. And every day he composed different ones, through his grief at being bound. Till the people knew those songs little by little, but he and his mother and her slave knew them well. And his mother knew the meaning of those songs, and the people in the town did not.

At last one day their slave girl had brought some food, and the soldiers took it from her and ate it, and some scraps were left, and those they gave her. The slave girl told her master, "I brought food, and these soldiers have taken it from me and eaten it; there remain these scraps." And he said to her, "Give me them." And he received them and ate, and thanked God for what he had got.

And he said to the slave girl (and he was inside and the slave girl outside the door)—

> "Ewe kijakazi nakutuma uwatumika,
> Kamwambia mama, ni mwinga siyalimka,
> Afanye mkate, pale kati tupa kaweka,
> Nikeze pingu na minyoo ikinyoka,
> Ningie ondoni ninyinyirike ja mana nyoka,
> Tatange madari na makuta kuno kimeta."

And its meaning was: "You, slave girl, shall be sent to tell my mother I am a simpleton. I have not yet learnt the ways of the world. Let her make a cake, in the middle let be put files, that I may cut my fetters, and the chains may be opened, that I may enter the road, that I may glide like a snake, that I may mount the roofs and walls, that I may look this way and that."

And he said, "Greet my mother well, tell her what I have told you." And she went and told his mother, and said, "Your son greets you well, he has told me a message to come and tell you." And she said, "What message?" And she told her what she had been told.

And his mother understood it, and went away to a shop and exchanged for grain, and gave it her slave to clean. And she went and bought many files, and brought them. And she took the flour, and made many fine cakes. And she took the bran and made a large cake, and took the files and put them into it, and gave to her slave to take to him.

And she went with them, and arrived at the door, and the soldiers robbed her, and chose out the fine cakes, and ate them themselves. And as for the bran one, they told her to take that to her master. And she took it, and he broke it, and took out the files, and laid them away, and ate that cake and drank water, and was comforted.

And the people of the town wished that he should be killed. And he heard himself that it was said, "You shall be killed." And he said to the soldiers, "When shall I be killed?" And they told him, "Tomorrow." And he said, "Call me my mother, and the chief man in the town, and all the townspeople, that I may take leave of them."

And they went and called them, and many people came together, and his mother and her slave.

And he asked them, "Are you all assembled?" And they answered, "We are assembled." And he said, "I want a horn, and cymbals, and an upato." And they went and took them. And he said, "I have an entertainment today, I want to take leave of you." And they said to him, "Very well, go on, play." And he said, "Let one take the horn, and one take the cymbals, and one take the upato." And they said, "How shall we play them?" And he taught them to play, and they played.

And he himself there, where he was inside, sang, till when the music was in full swing, he took a file and cut his fetters. When the music dropped, he too left off and sang, and when they played he cut his fetters.

And the people knew nothing of what was going on inside till the fetters were divided, and he cut the chains till they were divided. And the people knew nothing of it through their delight in the music. When they looked up, he had broken the door and come out to them outside. And they threw their instruments away to run, without being quick enough; and he caught them and knocked their heads together and killed them. And he went outside the town, and took leave of his mother, "to see one another again."

And he went away into the forest, and stayed many days, harassing people as before, and killing people.

And they sent crafty men, and told them, "Go and make him your friend, so as to kill him." And they went fearingly. And when they arrived they made a friendship with him. Till one day they said to him, "Sultan, let us entertain one another." And Liongo answered them—

"Hila kikoa halipani mkatamno?"

Which means, "If I eat of an entertainment, what shall I give in return, I who am excessively poor?" And they said to him, "Let us entertain one another with koma fruit." And he asked them, "How shall we eat them?" And they said: "One shall climb into the koma tree, and throw them down for us to eat. When we have done, let another climb up, till we have finished." And he said to them, "Very well."

And the first climbed up, and they ate. And the second climbed up, and they ate. And the third climbed up, and they ate. And they had plotted that when Liongo should climb up, "Let us shoot him with arrows there, up above."

But Liongo saw through it by his intelligence. So when all had finished they said to him, "Come, it is your turn." And he said, "Very well." And he took his bow in his hand, and his arrows, and said—

"Tafuma wivu la angania, tule cha yayi."

Which means, "I will strike the ripe above, that we may eat in the midst." And he shot, and a bough was broken off; and he shot again, and a second was broken off; and he gave them a whole koma tree, and the ground was covered with fruit. And they ate. And when they had done, the men said among themselves, "He has seen through it; now what are we to do?" And they said, "Let us go away." And they took leave of him, and said—

"Kukuingia hadaani Liongo fumo si mtu,
Yunga jini Liongo okoka."

Which means, "Liongo the chief, you have not been taken in, you are not a man, you have got out of it like a devil."

And they went away and gave their answer to their headman there in the town, and said, "We could do nothing."

And they advised together, "Who will be able to kill him?" And they said, "Perhaps his nephew will." And they went and called him. And he came. And they said to him: "Go and ask your father what it is that will kill him. When you know, come and tell us, and when he is dead we will give you the kingdom." And he answered them, "Very well."

And he went. When he arrived he welcomed him and said, "What have you come to do?" And he said, "I have come to see you." And he said, "I know that you have come to kill me, and they have deceived you."

And he asked him, "Father, what is it that can kill you?" And he said, "A copper needle. If anyone stabs me in the navel, I die."

And he went away into the town, and answered them, and said, "It is a copper needle that will kill him." And they gave him a needle, and he went back to his father. And when he saw him, his father sang, and said—

> "Mimi muyi ndimi mwe mao, situe
> Si mbwenge mimi muyi ndimi mwe mao."

Which means: "I, who am bad, am he that is good to you: do me no evil. I that am bad, am he that is good to you." And he welcomed him, and he knew, "He is come to kill me."

And he stayed two days, till one day he was asleep in the evening, and he stabbed him with the needle in the navel. And he awoke through the pain, and took his bow and arrows and went to a place near the wells. And he knelt down, and put himself ready with his bow. And there he died.

So in the morning the people who came to draw water saw him, and they thought him alive, and went back running. And they gave out the news in the town, "No water is to be had today." Everyone that went came back running. And many people set out and went, and as they arrived, when they saw him they came back, without being able to get near. For three days the people were in distress for water, not getting any.

And they called his mother, and said to her, "Go and speak to your son, that he may go away and we get water, or we will kill you."

And she went till she reached him. And his mother took hold of him to soothe him with songs, and he fell down. And his mother wept: she knew her son was dead.

And she went to tell the townspeople that he was dead, and they went to look at him, and saw that he was dead, and buried him, and his grave is to be seen at Ozi to this day.

And they seized that young man and killed him, and did not give him the kingdom.

Poem of Liongo

> This poem is not the epic from which the preceding prose tale was condensed, but a later composition, though rendered in what was apparently an archaic Swahili. Edward Steere, to whom we are indebted for this English translation, noted that although the composer of the poem described it as made up of five-line stanzas, the fourth and fifth lines were written as one. His informants told him that the combined fourth and fifth lines were supposed to

From Steere, ibid.

have been Liongo's own words, prefaced by
three lines of commentary by the poet Sheikh
Abdallah Muyuweni. Thus, Steere observed,
the combined fourth and fifth lines of each
stanza may be read consecutively, skipping the
three introductory lines.

I begin a poem in stanzas of five lines passing quickly,
That I may make it clear, and it may give light like a lamp,
In order to follow Liongo, the lion of cities.
Oh! much, much, I begin with many, as well as go forward and
    finish, the child of good things.

Then if you see a wrongdoer, a man your equal,
Turn your heart and put on vigor and bitterness,
Be like a leopard, a she-leopard, among the flock.
Child, how see you your goat in the pathway; its horns held and a
    milker milking it?

My brother, oh, my friend, let us say words to profit you,
The gentleman must take away shameful things,
I fear dying for you, such things are not before the man of
    position.
My child, how see you his vileness standing; without his consenting
    to die, and regrets follow after.

I swear by the Gospel and the Psalms a firm oath,
I turn not my back if evil is before me,
And his heart faces it and seeks evil wherever it is.
He who strives for his rank, having rank, striving against wrong and
    wrong, till his soul meets its fate.

I make myself a slave to my equals to get honor,
Nor is there anything I do not obey them in,
But I refuse a vile person and an evil speaker.
I melt like wax when I am held, I melt exceedingly; I am bad like
    war when I hear evil speaking.

I go not into war if I have not something which makes me beat
    my breast,
But what is praised when it has evil praise,
I make great war to make it insignificant.
I am bold, and love the acceptance of death; for fear of disgrace and
    of the enemy's speaking of me.

If I see war, though I am sick, I find health,
I rejoice as a bridegroom when he goes to his bride,
I fix my heart before God without turning.

I am a young lion who loves the acceptance of death; for fear of
    disgrace and of the enemies seeing me backward.

I swear by God, and God is indeed an oath,
I love anyone so long as he loves me,
But when my brother puts upon me a little disgrace.
I am a young falcon, I am not seen when I pounce; the evil bird
    that preys upon the flock.

By Allah, though I am bound, my greatness is not false,
When I strive for my rank, being black, I am white,
When I am before the face of the enemy he must shrivel up.
I am like a young vulture, who shares with the wild beasts, and they
    that eat grass in the valleys and hills.

Would that a creature when circumstances stop him,
There in the desert when he sees his enemies,
He breaks their crowns and their collarbones.
Would that I were an eagle flying in the air, eating small animals,
    even to the lion, chief of the beasts.

I would have cut them to pieces with sword and knife,
Sending a sharp falchion up and down,
Blowing like a rock, where there is no place for anger and
    bitterness to enter.
But both my feet are in fetters, and on my neck I wear a chain of
    iron.

I should have called the Koran as a witness to my words,
But God the bountiful has refused to be made a song;
"He has not been a singer of songs in any way."
The boiling of the water roars in the deep sea; you cannot stand
    where the wave dashes over Ungama.

Leave plans and intentions which you intend,
Hold not your hand to do to him as he does to you,
To pay a man the debt in measure as he gave in advance to you.
Let not your heart hesitate to surprise your victim; and if you kill
    not your enemies they will eat flesh.

I fear not to deal with him who does me malicious evil,
As he declares to us in His own book who is the Highest,
"O thou who doest, do as thou hast been done by."
Then when you perceive the fire of war roaring, la Allah! it is I who
    light as well as extinguish it.

Who turns back my heart when it has taken strength?
When I strive for my rank I recognize no one,

I am as though those people were like outcasts.
I draw myself together and cast myself among the bad; and I
    slaughter a-slaughtering and satiate my heart.

O my friend, let us say as we think,
How can a creature like yourself harm you?
Strive for your right and put yourself among injuries.
Fear not their arrow nor their shining spears; there are many who
    strike down, and turn and come back again.

Who that fears has been saved by his fear?
Or what bold man's life has been shortened?
Friend, give up fear, and go not with the fearful.
How many that feared in war have fallen; and those that stood firm
    have got through safely.

Woe to the coward who fears and considers not,
Death is not a thing of choice but of necessity to the finite,
Woe to the coward, he who fears death gets no honor.
He meets with destitution and confusion and vileness by fearing for
    his life, and his end comes to remove him.

If I see a disgraceful thing, the world disgusts me,
My heart is nauseated till it is dark within,
And outside the eyelid the tear of vileness drops.
The lion cries with a cry, blowing out a great cry which brings pity
    home to a man.

What makes the lion cry is every vileness and iniquity,
The lion cries from remembering, and I tell you,
Think him not a lion with four feet that tracks a scent.
The great male lion strives for his object and his rank; he strives for
    his object till his eyes are closed.

I am valiant, a lion with claws, taker away of disgrace,
Breaker of prisons and forts by stratagems,
I beat my breast and cast myself among evils.
I fear not their bows and spears that shine; many are they who are
    cast down, and who flee and go backward.

I am a lion that is of use to gain an object or a rank,
I cast myself into the midst and humble those who praise
    themselves;
Fear not your enemies when they are gathered, because of their
    numbers.
I fear not their thousands, I alone it is who am myself a thousand by
    being brave.

I am the great one that strives for my honor,
I accept not the vileness of a creature that had a maker,
I draw my dagger where a thousand are and rush among them,
I make my breast my shield; where they are pressed together I
    divide them, without fearing the thorns or prickles to prick
    me.

Friend, leave fear, and go not with the fearful,
And leave your life to God who saves,
Fear not creaturely things, nor dreads which affright you.
Dying is of God, and the snare that takes him, not of the men of
    this world, though a thousand arrows should pierce you.

They who strive for their rank, their hearts are right, they fear no
    curses,
They take the bodies and feed their falchions and swords,
Who take away vileness, where reproach is, and set it aside.
They are not lions with tails, and hair growing on the neck and
    back; but lions are heroes, who have nothing to do with skins
    and beasts.

It is done, I have finished the stanzas of five lines which I
    composed
Of Liongo the chief, I have finished completing them.
He who sees a bad expression if he takes it away is not to blame;
He will get a reward, which the bountiful Lord will pay him when
    the days are accomplished for repaying bad and good.

And the author, I will tell you his name,
It is Abdallah Muyuweni, remember him,
Son of Ali, son of Nasr the glorious,
A branch of Mecca, sprouting from Farimu [in Hathramaut], a
    descendent of Muthar, Mutalib, and Hashim.

Listen to me, that I may tell you his tribe,
It was of Sheikh Ali our lord Abubakr,
Son of Salim, a choice rank,
Working many wonders, his signs are manifest; in his time was no
    likeness to be found like his.

A Swahili Poet of Mombasa

There was an early nineteenth-century poet of Mombas (Mombasa),
whose name is not given, who was famous for his verses, epigrams and
poetic compositions. It is said that he went with his king to fight against

From Steere, ibid.

the people of Lamoo, and in the course of the battle he was struck by an arrow. He asked the king to remove the arrow for him, but the king refused to do it until the poet composed some verses on the event. So the poet, the arrow still in him, recited the following four-line poem, which in the original Swahili both scans and rhymes:

Nalishika gurumza kwa mkono kushoto,
Na mato hiyang'ariza yakawaka kana moto,
Waamu hiwafukuza kama mbuzi na ufito;
Nikatupwa majini, hapigwa chombo kizito.

I held a musket in my left hand,
And glared with my eyes, they blazed like fire,
Driving the people of Lamoo like goats with a switch,
And I was cast into the water, and struck by a heavy weapon.

Presumably the king then removed the arrow.

Swahili Dance Song

Give me a chair, that I may sit down,
    And soothe my Mananazi,
That I may soothe my wife,
    Who takes away my grief and heaviness.
She stands under the door,
    When I go out to walk,
When I go out on business,
    She tells her servants,
And says to them, "Sada and Rehema,
    "Cook, and do not delay,
"Cook, and make haste,
    "Cook rice and curry."
If she finds I stay long,
    She sends her slave girl,
"Look for him in the sultan's way:
    "Or there with the sovereign prince,
"Look for him on the seats at his brother's,
    "Or at his mother's, his aunt's,
"And take him, come with him quickly,
    "(What are you doing till this time?)
"And tell him, 'Master, you are called,
    " 'Let us go quickly, do not be slow,
" 'Your delay makes her weary of standing,
    " ' And tears come from her eyes.'

From Steere, ibid.

"And tell him, 'Let us go, go before, I am coming,
"'And comfort her that she may leave grieving.'
"And follow him behind, walking elegantly,
"As he smells of musk and ambergris."
When he goes and salutes her,
The child of Hejaz replies to him,
At once she rises and stands,
And puts her hand on his shoulder.
And he prays for her to God the Lord of all,
"O mother, may God supply your needs."
And the mistress lifts up her hand,
And puts it up to the bamboo,
And takes down a large cloth of ancient work
With a beautiful border woven into it.
And he puts a handkerchief to her eyes,
The child of his father and child of his aunt.
And she says to him: "Master, let us sit down
"Do not stand overmuch, and make yourself tired.
"Call that Timé, let her come
"Quickly, and leave off sleeping,
"Let her dish up an Indian pillaw,
"With raisins without curry.
"Bring a fine European chair,
"And a good Persian tray
"Engraved with engravings,
"And a dish shining like the moon."
And she says, "Let the slaves come too,
"Why are you not singing?"
Immediately it is laid for him,
And Timé has taken the water bottle,
In it has been put the juice of raisins,
And she makes him drink it like a drinker of wine.
And she feeds him, putting morsels in his mouth,
And shows him a good place for lying down,
Giving him to chew betel leaf from Siwi,
Soft and smooth from Ozi.
She folds it and puts it into his mouth,
With cardamoms and almonds.
I have finished praising the girl,
My choice one, Mananazi.

APPENDIX

EXCERPT FROM A UNITED NATIONS REPORT ON BRIDE-PRICE

A number of African stories included in this anthology refer to lobola, payment for wives, or bride-price. The nature and function of bride-price has been much misunderstood by non-Africans, and for this reason the following excerpt from a report made by the U.N. Secretary-General to the Economic and Social Council (document E/CN.6/295, dated 24 January, 1957) is given here.

BRIDE-PRICE

General

Bride-price, for the purpose of this report, is defined as the payment made on behalf of the bridegroom to the bride's family. It has been described as the "quid pro quo" given by the husband or by his senior relatives on his behalf to the parents or other senior relatives of the wife. A Committee on Bride-Price appointed by the Eastern Regional Government of Nigeria defined it as "those things, whether cash, gifts in kind or labor services, which a man gives when he marries a woman and which are regarded in a case of divorce as refundable." In the United Kingdom report on the administration of Tanganyika, bride-price is defined as "the payment of livestock, grain, or other food stuff, clothing or money (in some tribes partly paid in labour) made by the bridegroom to the parents of his bride in order to seal the marriage contract."

The use of the term "bride-price" has been often criticized as misleading. In Nigeria, the Committee on Bride-Price stated that "many complaints have been received against the use of the objectionable and derogatory term 'bride-price.' " Many anthropologists prefer the more literal translation of "marriage payment" or sometimes "bride wealth," or, less usual, "marriage consideration." Occasionally, the marriage payments by the man to the woman's family are called "dowry" or "dower" but these terms as understood in continental European and in English common-law systems describe totally different legal institutions. The term "bride-price" while subject to criticism, appears to be the most familiar and therefore useful, provided that it is not interpreted as necessarily implying a mercenary element of purchase and sale.

Bride-price was once a prevalent marriage custom in many parts of the world. It is still practiced in several areas including certain parts of India, the Malay Archipelago (including Indonesia), New Guinea and the Persian Gulf states. It is, however, in Africa that the bride-price presently holds a most important place among marriage customs of the indigenous populations including many Moslems and Christians.

Since throughout Africa there are many types of societies with differing social and kinship strictures and differing economies, it is only to be expected that there be wide differences in the form and function of the bride-price.

Payment of Bride-Price

Among pastoral peoples, marriage payments are usually made in cattle. This is the case among most of the indigenous peoples of the Union of South Africa, Southern Rhodesia, many peoples in East Africa, the Southern Sudan, in West Africa, among cattle-keeping people who inhabit the northern Gold Coast and the adjacent French territory. In areas where cattle payments are the rule under customary law, they are made by Moslems as well although Moslem law itself does not require it.

Among nonpastoral peoples marriage payments are made in such goods as hoes, clothes, spears, cowry, shells, iron bars, beer, gin and money. Where there is marriage payment by service, the bridegroom, aided in some cases by his father or by members of his age group, works for his wife's family before the marriage and in some cases also makes a payment when the bride leaves her family's home. In some matrilinear societies, the groom lives and works in the home of the wife's family both before and after the marriage.

Marriage payment traditionally is made by the bridegroom's kin, the entire marriage being an alliance between two family groups rather than solely a personal association between the man and the woman. Bride-price is received by the girl's family and there are many different patterns for distributing it among her mother's family and her father's family.

Often the relative, father, uncle or other senior family member who is, according to the mores, primarily responsible for paying the bride-price on behalf of a male kinsman, receives the bulk of the payment for the girl.

The amount to be given is among some peoples fixed and among others a matter for negotiations. A tribe in West Africa recognizes a fixed bride-price composed of three cows and a bull. Another tribe has an established rate of forty hoes in addition to a period of service.

But it appears to be more typical to settle the bride-price by negotiations, taking into consideration the "current rate." It has been observed that the amount then tends to be fixed at what the wealthiest can pay because of each father's fear that what is received for a daughter will not be enough to obtain a wife for the son next in line to be married. "We see that all the other fathers are asking so much for their daughters so we also demand the same" is the explanation of bride-price fixing offered by members of the cattle-raising Gusii tribe of Kenya. The bargaining process usually works out, it is said, so that only one marriage can be made from any given herd at one time; the bridegroom's brother then, for example, would have to wait until the family's herd was replenished by the marriage payment for a sister before he could obtain a wife.

Among some peoples the bride-price is not, traditionally, fixed nor is there any "current rate." According to the description of the traditional bride-price system in Nigeria, it was never fixed and "the number of years during which labor services were rendered varied with the age of the girl when the marriage was first agreed on, and where cows and goats were also given, their number varied with the wealth of the young man and his family."

The economic value of bride-price varies greatly among the African peoples. Among many it represents a substantial outlay by the groom's family and a substantial gain to the bride's; and this is true of the pastoral peoples as well as of some of those whose payments are in goods or other media of exchange. On the other hand, among some groups, the bride-price may be insignificant as compared with gifts to the couple from both sides and might be less than the cost of festivities or the total outlay by the girl's family.

It appears that high bride-price is generally characteristic of patrilinear societies, where children belong to the father's family, and low bride-price is more usual in matrilinear societies where children are affiliated to the mother's kinship group.

According to custom, in some areas the amount of the marriage payment determines to which side the children belong. Thus two types of bride-price coexist in some groups. Among certain tribes in Nigeria, the marriage is typically sealed by payment of a "big bride-price"; this is called a "father-right" marriage signifying that the children are affiliated to the father's family as distinguished from a "small bride-price" or "mother-right" marriage in which the children belong to the mother's family. Similar practices are reported elsewhere; for example, among the Verre in the Cameroons forty hoes and labor service is the usual bride-price, but socially recognized marriages may be based on a payment of about ten hoes, the husband then having no legal right to the children of the marriage.

There is also great variation in custom with respect to the time for completion of payment. The payment of a bride-price may be a long-term transaction sometimes beginning with betrothal and terminating either before the marriage is consummated or at the time the girl leaves her family, which is among certain peoples considerably after consummation. Among peoples of the Upper Nile, it is reported that theoretically the wife will not take up residence with her husband until the marriage payments have been completed and in any case not permanently until her first child is born; but elopement after partial payment is frequent, particularly in periods when epidemics have depleted herds and the traditionally invariable cattle payment of ten head becomes excessively burdensome. It has been observed that although full payment of the bride-price is not always made, the marriage is unlikely to last unless the marriage payments are sufficient to satisfy the wife's kinsmen. When conditions make full payment difficult, the amount owing remains a debt which may continue to the next generation.

According to the customs of the Gusii people in Kenya, partial payment of the bride-price cattle is followed by a honeymoon away from the girl's home. After the honeymoon she comes back to her family for a time during which either party may, if dissatisfied, arrange for the return of the cattle. If both wish to continue with the marriage, final arrangement is made and the girl joins her husband in his home. Children born before the final payment belong to the wife's family. This type of trial period before final payment is observed among several other African tribes including those where bride-price is paid in goods or money.

If a girl of the Gusii tribe runs off with a man (a breach of duty to her family, putting them at grave disadvantage in negotiation with his family) and eludes recapture or keeps returning to him, the father may waive part of the normal bride-price; it is usual in such case for the man's kin to help raise the necessary amount even if it is not his turn to marry since "it would be a pity if her children were lost to our lineage for lack of cattle." If an adequate payment cannot be assembled the father might accept a promise before witnesses specifying the number and source of cattle. This may amount to a pledge of the bride-price received for the marriage of the first daughter of the union; but even with that lapse of time, it is reported that "there is not the slightest likelihood that the creditor family will forget."

Among the Ashanti, a very numerous tribe in the Gold Coast whose society is matrilinear (children attached to mother's family), the bride-price due before the husband acquires the right to cohabit is comparatively small. But in addition, he may be obligated to make a "loan" to his wife's family intended to help pay off their debts, and this loan, the size of which depends on the debts of the family, is never claimed or repaid unless the marriage is dissolved; before he makes this loan the husband has no right to claim damages for adultery and no formalities are necessary if the couple decides to separate.

Refund of Bride-Price

A basic characteristic of the bride-price is that it is refundable to the husband on divorce, and that marriage continues until it is refunded. When marriage payment is rendered in services, these are not of course refundable, but such additional payments as were made in fulfillment of the man's obligations to his wife's family are repayable to him on divorce. A wife can generally under customary law secure a divorce by repaying the bride-price.

The members of the wife's family who have received or have used the payment are expected to give her refuge if she leaves her husband and to attempt reconciliation; they are responsible for knowing where she is if her husband comes to look for her and, if she does not resume her wifely duties, they must repay the appropriate amount. If she refuses to return, the husband is entitled to the refund.

If, instead of returning to her family, the wife abandons her husband for another man, there are variant rules. For examples, under Somali customary law, the bride-price should in such a case be refunded as a "gentlemanly" act and there is usually some compromise reached between the families. But the claim is not actually considered legally enforceable unless the wife is living with her family. Elsewhere, the family has the obligation, regardless of where the wife has gone, to refund the bride-price if she has failed to perform her wifely duties. And sometimes the man for whom she has left her husband pays the bride-price to her family, who repays it to the husband, the husband then having no further claim on her or on the children born to the other man.

The conditions under which a refund of bride-price may be claimed depend of course on what duties the society places on the wife or widow. For example, where the wife has the recognized right to enter into "secondary marriages" such cohabitation with another man is no violation of her duty, and the husband may not claim refund of the bride-price solely because of it. Among many peoples the wife is free to remarry or return to her home after the husband's death. But in areas where levirate marriage (marriage of man to his deceased brother's widow) or inheritance of widows is customary, the husband's family may claim refund if a widow refuses to marry a kinsman of her deceased husband. It has been reported in this connection that among many peoples who do not consider marriage to be dissolved by the husband's death, a widow may cohabit with anyone of her choice but the children of such unions are counted as belonging to the deceased husband and thus (since most such groups are patrilinear) to his family. The widow may enter into a valid new marriage only after repayment of the bride-price.

Custom varies between those groups where grounds for repudiation or divorce of the wife by the husband are very restricted and those where such grounds as her quarrelsome disposition or barrenness or laziness may give rise to divorce and refund of bride-price; in all cases it is traditional for kinsmen and elders to attempt reconciliation. Among some peoples a man who drives his wife away and will not take her back even though he has inadequate justification according to the custom, loses his right to the children as well as to his wife but receives full refund of the original bride-price.

It is reported that in the great majority of cases it is the woman and not the man who seeks divorce. In this connection it is interesting to note that under customary law the wife may secure a divorce by refunding the bride-price. Refund is necessary for divorce according to customary law in most of Africa; in few groups does customary law consider that the husband by his conduct may forfeit his right to refund. Among many African Moslems even if a woman has grounds for divorce under Moslem law, the bride-price must still be refunded, although deductions may be made in respect of the husband's maltreatment of her.

The amount refundable is computed according to different and often complex rules among the various peoples. Generally, in patrilinear societies, very substantial deductions are made for each child of the marriage and in many cases this completely offsets the original bride-price. These deductions are made even if the children are young and stay with the mother; for the children still belong to the father's family and usually return to that family. The acceptance by the husband of the refund of the full amount of the original bride-price may deprive him and his family of any claims or rights with respect to the children.

The duration of the marriage is also an important factor, and in many areas no refund at all is claimed with respect to a woman past child-bearing age even if she has no children.

In some instances, the obligation of having to refund the bride-price is considered so onerous and serious an obligation that it outweighs the benefit of receiving it. Among the Yako tribe of Nigeria, it is traditionally the wife's mother's family (matrilinear relations) who are held responsible for her upbringing and who receive the bulk of the marriage payments; it is consequently to them, particularly the mother's brother, that claim for refund is made. The father receives only a small portion of the marriage payment, which is viewed primarily as compensation for loss of his paternal authority. However, this custom is not followed if the father is a very rich man as compared with the mother's family. In such case, he will, as an act of generosity and pride, retain the whole of his daughter's bride-price, thus indicating his ability to assume the burden of having to repay it—a responsibility which the mother's family will be loath to assume if without means. And among another people, one of the several deterrents to a woman's breaking away from her husband is that after repayment her father may not be willing to risk again accepting bride-price for her remarriage.

Traditional Role of Bride-Price

The bride-price payment, large or small, in cattle, goods or money, establishes, according to customary law in most of Africa, the legality of marriage.

No attempt will be made here to describe all the legal effects of the payment which would involve description of the different legal consequences of marriage according to the diverse African family systems. It may, however, be said that under African customary laws, bride-price is a necessary condition of legitimate marriage with whatever consequences the group assigns thereto. This aspect is emphasized by the frequent recognition in customary law that partial payment may result in the husband's acquisition of some but not all the rights implicit in legal marriage. For example, in some patrilocal societies (where wife and children typically live in husband's home) a man may cohabit with his bride but not have her reside with him after partial payment; there are patrilinear societies (children typically attached to father's family) in which the woman may take up residence with the man before full bride-price is paid but the children will be affiliated to her family; there are matrilinear societies when partial bride-price gives the man the right to cohabit with the bride but not the exclusive right.

In addition to marking the legal union of the man and woman, the bride-price among many African peoples establishes kinship particularly with respect to persons whose marriages have involved the payment of the same bride-price. For example, when bride-price is in cattle and the particular animals and their offspring are used for successive marriages, families are accordingly "linked." Most generally—regardless of what the bride-price is composed of—the brother whose wife has been obtained with the bride-price received for a sister, has a special relationship with that sister and this relationship, involving various rights and duties, extends to their children as well.

The tradition of some peoples is that the bride-price expresses an exchange between families and establishes a continuing alliance marked by successive marriages between the two groups concerned. Bride-price marriage is reported to have replaced, among some peoples, marriage by actual exchange of girls between families.

Particular stress has been laid on the significance of the bride-price for stability of marriage where, as is generally the case, it is refundable on divorce. This, it is considered, makes the success of the marriage of direct concern to the family of the girl who serve as mediators and counsellors and encourage reconciliation where possible. Some writers however feel that this aspect of the custom has been exaggerated and that refund of bride-price is not so important a factor in frequency of divorce. It has been suggested that it is a kinship structure in which divorce is difficult and rare which allows high bride-price rather than the high price which prevents divorce.

While "compensation" to the girl's family for the loss of a member or for the loss of paternal authority is often cited as one of the roles of bride-price, anthropologists and many missionaries have generally agreed that the idea of "purchase and sale" was not traditionally a significant element of the custom, nor was commercial profit typically an important motive for the girl's family. Bride-price is recognized, even traditionally, as an influence tending to the earlier marriage of girls and delayed marriage of men, particularly among patrilinear cattle-raising people.

A SELECTIVE BIBLIOGRAPHY OF WORKS CONSULTED IN THE PREPARATION OF THIS COLLECTION

African Arts (quarterly). Los Angeles: African Studies Center, University of California, Autumn 1967 (date of first issue) to Winter 1974.

Antubam, K. *Ghana's Heritage of Culture*. Leipzig: Kohler and Amelang, 1963.

Barker, W. H., and Sinclair, C. *West African Folk Tales*. London: George Harrap and Co. and Sheldon Press, 1917.

Beier, Ulli. *The Origin of Life and Death*. London: Heinemann, 1966.

Benton, P. A. *The Languages and Peoples of Bornu, Being a Collection of the Writings of P. A. Benton* (2 vols.). London: Frank Cass and Co., 1968.

Bérenger-Féraud, Laurent Jean-Baptiste. *Les Peuplades de la Sénégambie*. Paris, 1879.

———. *Recueil de Contes Populaires de la Sénégambie*. Paris, 1885.

Bernatzik, Hugo Adolf. *Gari-Gari*. Translated by Vivian Ogilvie. New York: Holt, Rinehart and Winston, 1936.

Bianco, F. M. *The African Saga*. Translated by Margery Bianco from *Anthologie Nègre*, by Blaise Cendrars. New York: Payson and Clark, 1927.

Biebuyck, Daniel. *Lega Culture—Art, Initiation, and Moral Philosophy Among a Central African People*. Berkeley: University of California Press, 1973.

———, and Mateene, Kahombo C. *The Mwindo Epic*. Berkeley: University of California Press, 1969.

Bleek, W. H. I. *Reynard the Fox in South Africa*. London: Trubner and Co., 1864.

———, and Loyd, L. C. *Specimens of Bushmen Folklore*. London: George Allen and Co., 1911.

Bowdich, T. Edward. *Mission from Cape Coast Castle to Ashantee*. London, 1819.

Brownlee, Frank. *Lion and Jackal, with Other Native Folk Tales of South Africa*. London: George Allen and Unwin, 1938.

Budge, Sir Ernest A. Wallis. *The Queen of Sheba and Her Only Son Menyelik*. Translated from *Kebra Negast*, or *Book of the Glory of Kings*. London: Oxford University Press, 1932.

Busia, K. A. *The Position of the Chief in the Modern Political System in Ashanti*. London: Oxford University Press, 1951.

Callaway, Henry. *Nursery Tales, Traditions and Histories of the Zulus, in Their Own Words*. Natal, 1868.

———. *The Religious System of the Amazulu.* Publications of the Folk-lore Society, XV, London, 1884.

Cardinall, A. W. *Tales Told in Togoland.* Oxford: Oxford University Press, 1931.

Cendrars, Blaise. *The African Saga.* Translated from *L'Anthologie Negre,* by Margery Bianco. New York: Payson and Clarke, 1927.

Chatelain, Heli. *Folk-Tales of Angola: Fifty Tales, with Ki-Mbundu Text, Literal English Translation, Introduction, and Notes.* Vol. I of the *Memoirs of the American Folklore Society,* Boston and New York: G. E. Stechert and Co., 1894.

Christaller, J. G. *Twi Mmebusem Mpensa-Ahansia Mmoaano (A Collection of Three Thousand and Six Hundred Tshi Proverbs In Use Among the Negroes of the Gold Coast Speaking the Asante and Fante, i.e., the Akan, Language).* Basel, 1879.

Christensen, James Boyd. *Double Descent Among the Fanti.* New Haven: Human Relations Area Files, 1954.

Cobham, Henry. "Animal Stories from Calabar," *Journal of the African Society,* Vol. IV, 1904–5 (pp. 307–9).

Courlander, Harold. *Tales of Yoruba Gods and Heroes.* New York: Crown Publishers, Inc., 1973.

———. *The King's Drum and Other African Stories.* New York: Harcourt Brace Jovanovich, 1962.

———. "The Ethiopian Game of Gobeta," *Negro History Bulletin,* October 1943.

———. "Notes from an Abyssinian Diary," *The Musical Quarterly,* Vol. XXX, No. 3, July 1944.

———, with Ezekiel A. Eshugbayi. *Olode the Hunter and Other Tales from Nigeria.* New York: Harcourt Brace Jovanovich, 1968.

———, and Herzog, George. *The Cow-Tail Switch and Other West African Stories.* New York: Holt, Rinehart and Winston, 1947.

———, and Leslau, Wolf. *The Fire on the Mountain and Other Ethiopian Stories.* New York: Holt, Rinehart, and Winston, 1950.

———, with Albert Kofi Prempeh. *The Hat-Shaking Dance and Other Ashanti Tales from Ghana.* New York: Harcourt Brace Jovanovich, 1957.

Cronise, Florence M., and Ward, Henry W. *Cunnie Rabbit, Mr. Spider and Other Beef.* London, 1903.

Danquah, J. B. *The Akan Doctrine of God.* London, 1944.

———. *Gold Coast: Akan Laws and Customs and the Akan Abuakwa Constitution.* London: George Routledge and Sons, 1928.

Davidson, Basil, and the editors of Time-Life Books, *African Kingdoms.* New York: Time Inc., 1966.

———, with F. K. Buah and the advice of J. F. Ade Ajaye. *A History of West Africa to the Nineteenth Century.* Garden City, New York: Doubleday, 1966.

Dayrell, Elphinstone. *Folk Stories from Southern Nigeria.* London, 1910.

Debrunner, H. *Witchcraft in Ghana.* Accra: Presbyterian Book Depot, 1959.

de Kolb, Eric. *Ashanti Goldweights.* New York: Gallery d'Hautbarr, 1968.

Dennett, R. E. "Notes on the Folklore of the Fjort," *Publications of the Folklore Society,* XLI. London, 1898.

Doke, C. M. "Lamba Folk-Lore," *Memoirs of the American Folk-Lore Society,* Vol. 20, 1927.

Egharevba, Jacob Uwadiae. *Some Stories of Ancient Benin.* Benin, 1951 (2d ed.).

Ellis, A. B. *The Ewe-Speaking Peoples of the Slave Coast of West Africa.* London, 1890.

_____. *The Tshi-Speaking Peoples of the Gold Coast of West Africa.* London, 1887.

_____. *The Yoruba-Speaking Peoples of the Slave Coast of West Africa.* London, 1894.

Finnigan, Ruth. *Oral Literature in Africa.* Oxford Library of African Literature. Oxford: The Clarendon Press, 1970.

Frobenius, Leo. *Atlantis, Volksmärchen und Volksdichtungen Africas,* Jena, 1926.

_____, and Douglas C. Fox, *African Genesis.* New York: Stackpole, 1937.

Gutmann, B. *Die Stammeslehren der Dschagga.* Munich: C. H. Beck, 1932–38.

Henries, Doris Banks. *Liberian Folklore.* New York: The Macmillan Company, 1966.

Herskovits, Melville J., *Dahomey, an Ancient West African Kingdom* (2 vols.). New York: J. J. Augustin, 1938.

_____, and Herskovits, Frances S. *Dahomean Narrative, a Cross-Cultural Analysis.* Evanston: Northwestern University Press, 1958.

Herzog, George. "Drum Signalling in a West African Tribe." *Word.* December 1945.

_____, and Blooah, Charles. *Jabo Proverbs from Eastern Liberia.* Oxford: Oxford University Press, 1936.

Holiday, Finola, and Holiday, Geoffrey. *Tuareg Music of the Southern Sahara,* booklet introducing record album of same name. New York: Ethnic Folkways Library, 1960.

Hollis, A. C. *The Masai, Their Language and Folklore.* Oxford: The Clarendon Press, 1905.

Huffman, R. *Nuer Customs and Folklore.* London: Frank Cass and Co., 1931.

Hughes, Langston. *An African Treasury.* New York: Crown Publishers, Inc. 1960.

Italian Tourist Bureau. *Africa Orientale Italiana.* Milan, 1938.

Jacottet, E. *The Treasury of Ba-Sutu Lore.* London, 1908.

Johnston, H. A. S. *A Selection of Hausa Stories.* Oxford: The Clarendon Press, 1966.

Junod, Henri A. *The Life of a South African Tribe* (2 vols.). London, 1927 (second edition).

Kyerematen, A. A. Y. *Panoply of Ghana.* London: Longmans, 1964.

Le Herissé, A. *L'Ancien Royaume du Dahomey.* Paris, 1911.

Leslau, Charlotte and Wolf. *African Folk Tales.* Mt. Vernon, New York: Peter Pauper Press, N.D.

Librarian Information Service, *Proverbs of Liberia.* Monrovia, 1963.

Lips, Julius E. *The Savage Hits Back.* New Haven: Yale University Press, 1937.

Littmann, Enno. *Publications of the Princeton Expedition to Abyssinia,* Vol. 2. Leyden: E. J. Brill, 1910.

_____. *The Legend of the Queen of Sheba in the Tradition of Axum,* in the series *Bibliotheca Abessinica, Studies Concerning the Languages, Literature and History of Abyssinia.* Leyden and Princeton, 1904.

Marolen, Daniel P. P. *Mitlangu Ya Vafana Va Vatsonga.* Johannesburg: Central Mission Press, 1954.

_____. *Garingani-Wa-Garingani.* Pretoria, 1966.

Mbiti, John S. *Akamba Stories.* Oxford: The Clarendon Press, 1966.

Meek, C. K. *Law and Authority in a Nigerian Tribe.* London: Oxford University Press, 1937.

Merriam, Alan P. *Africa South of the Sahara,* booklet accompanying record album by the same title. New York: Ethnic Folkways Library, 1957.

Meyerowitz, Eva L. R. *Akan Traditions of Origin.* London: Faber and Faber, 1952.

_____. *The Sacred State of the Akan.* London: Faber and Faber, 1951.

_____. "The Concept of the Soul Among the Akan of the Gold Coast." *Africa,* XXI. 1951.

Mofolo, Thomas. *Chaka.* London: Oxford University Press, 1931.

Morris, Donald R. *The Washing of the Spears, the Rise and Fall of the Zulu Nation.* New York: Simon and Schuster, 1965.

Murgatroyd, Madeline. *Tales from the Kraals.* [South Africa] Central News Agency, 1944.

Nassau, Robert H. *Where Animals Talk.* London: Duckworth and Company, 1914.

Norris, Robert. *Memoirs of the Reign of Bossa Ahadee, King of Dahomy, an Inland Country of Guiney.* London, 1789.

Palmer, Sir Herbert Richmond. *Sudanese Memoirs.* London: Frank Cass and Company, 1967 (1st edition published in Lagos, Nigeria, 1928).

_____. *The Bornu Sahara and Sudan.* London: John Murray, 1936.

Pankhurst, Richard K. P. *The Ethiopian Royal Chronicles.* Addis Ababa: Oxford University Press, 1967.

Patterson, J. R., trans. *The Stories of Abu Zeid the Hilali.* London: Routledge and Kegan Paul, 1930.

Plass, Margaret Webster. *African Miniatures, Goldweights of the Ashanti.* New York: Praeger, 1967.

Posselt, F. W. T. *Fables of the Veld.* Oxford: The Clarendon Press, 1929.

Radin, Paul, with Elinore Marvel and James J. Sweeney, *African Folktales and Sculpture.* New York: Bollingen Foundation, 1964.

Rattray, R. S. *Hausa Folk-Lore, Customs, Proverbs.* Oxford: The Clarendon Press, 1913.

———. *Ashanti.* London: Oxford University Press, 1923.

———. *Akan-Ashanti Folk-Tales.* Oxford: The Clarendon Press, 1931.

———. *Ashanti Law and Constitution.* London: Oxford University Press and the International African Institute, 1956.

Ritter, E. A. *Shaka Zulu, the Rise of the Zulu Empire.* New York: Putnam, 1955.

Rodén, K. G. *Storia dei Mensa.* Place of publication unknown, 1912.

Roscoe, J. *The Baganda, an Account of Their Customs and Beliefs.* London: Frank Cass and Company, 1911.

Routledge, W. S. and K. *With a Prehistoric People: the Akikuyu of British East Africa.* London: Edward Arnold, 1910.

St. Lys, Odette. *From a Vanished German Colony, a Collection of Folklore, Folk Tales and Proverbs from South-West Africa.* London, 1916.

Schlenker, C. F. *A Collection of Temne Traditions, Fables and Proverbs.* London, 1861.

Schneider, G. D. *Cameroons Creole Dictionary* (alternately called *Pidgin-English Vocabulary*). Mimeographed manuscript of thesis submitted to the Council for Advanced Studies of Hartford Seminary Foundation. Bamenda, 1960.

Schon, Jacob. *Magana Hausa.* London, 1885.

Schwab, George. "Bulu Tales," *Journal of American Folk-Lore,* Vol. XXXII, 1922.

Schweinfurth, Georg. *The Heart of Africa* (2 vols.). Trans. by Ellen E. Frewer. New York: Harpers, 1874.

Shinnie, Margaret. *Ancient African Kingdoms.* New York: St. Martin's Press, 1966.

Stayt, H. A. *The Bavenda.* London: Oxford University Press, 1931.

Steere, Edward. *Swahili Tales, as Told by the Natives of Zanzibar.* London, 1870.

Talbot, P. Amaury. *In the Shadow of the Bush.* London: William Heinemann, 1912.

———. *The Peoples of Southern Nigeria* (4 vols.). London, 1926.

Theal, G. McCall. *Kaffir Folk Lore.* London: George Allen and Unwin, 1886.

Thomas, Northcote W. "Thirty-two Folk-Tales of the Edo-Speaking Peoples of Nigeria," *Folk-Lore,* Vol. XXXI, 1920.

Torrend, J. *Specimens of Bantu Folklore from Northern Rhodesia.* London: Kegan Paul, Trench, Trubner and Company, 1921.

Tracy, Hugh. *Lalela Zulu, 100 Zulu Lyrics.* Johannesburg: African Music Society, 1948.

Tremearne, A. J. N. *Hausa Superstitions and Customs.* London: John Bale Sons and Danielson, 1913.

Turnbull, Colin M., and Chapman, Francis S. *The Pygmies of the Ituri Forest,* introductory booklet to record album by same title. New York: Ethnic Folkways Library, 1958.

Vansina, Jan. "Inner Africa," *The Horizon History of Africa.* New York: American Heritage, 1971.

Van Vorst, Bessie, translator from the French of Hugues Le Roux. *Kebra Negast, Magda, Queen of Sheba. London* (?), 1907.

Vernon-Jackson, Hugh. *West African Folk Tales.* London: University of London Press, 1958.

Weeks, J. H. *Among the Congo Cannibals.* Philadelphia: Lippincott, 1913.

Werner, A. "African Mythology," *Mythology of All Races,* Vol. 7, Boston, 1925.

Westermann, D. *Mitteilungen des Seminars für Orientalishe Sprachen, Afrikanishe Studien.* Berlin, 1912.

Whitting, C. E. J. *Hausa and Fulani Proverbs.* Farnborough (England): Gregg, 1940.

INDEX